The Insanity Defense

The Insanity Defense

Multidisciplinary Views on Its History, Trends, and Controversies

Mark D. White, Editor

An Imprint of ABC-CLIO, LLC
Santa Barbara, California • Denver, Colorado

Copyright © 2017 by Mark D. White

All rights reserved. No part of this publication may be reproduced, stored in a retrieval system, or transmitted, in any form or by any means, electronic, mechanical, photocopying, recording, or otherwise, except for the inclusion of brief quotations in a review, without prior permission in writing from the publisher.

Library of Congress Cataloging-in-Publication Data

Names: White, Mark D., 1971– editor.
Title: The insanity defense : multidisciplinary views on its history, trends, and controversies / Mark D. White, editor.
Description: Santa Barbara, California : Praeger, 2017.
Identifiers: LCCN 2016036080 (print) | LCCN 2016036453 (ebook) | ISBN 9781440831805 (hardback) | ISBN 9781440831812 (ebook)
Subjects: LCSH: Insanity defense—History. | Insanity (Law) | Law—Psychological aspects. | Criminal intent.
Classification: LCC K5077 .I49 2017 (print) | LCC K5077 (ebook) | DDC 345/.04—dc23
LC record available at https://lccn.loc.gov/2016036080

ISBN: 978-1-4408-3180-5
EISBN: 978-1-4408-3181-2

21 20 19 18 17   1 2 3 4 5

This book is also available as an eBook.

Praeger
An Imprint of ABC-CLIO, LLC

ABC-CLIO, LLC
130 Cremona Drive, P.O. Box 1911
Santa Barbara, California 93116-1911
www.abc-clio.com

This book is printed on acid-free paper ∞

Manufactured in the United States of America

Contents

Acknowledgments vii

Introduction ix

Part I   Essentials of the Law 1

Chapter 1   The Insanity Defense: Nine Myths That Will Not Go Away   3
Michael L. Perlin

Chapter 2   The Temporary Insanity Defense   23
Russell D. Covey

Chapter 3   Mens Rea and Mental Disorder   61
Craig A. Stern

Part II   Psychiatry and the Law 95

Chapter 4   The Shadows of Normality: Legal Insanity under Modern Criminal Law   97
Gabriel Hallevy

Chapter 5   Insanity Constructs   133
Meron Wondemaghen

Chapter 6   Insanity: Neurolaw and Forensic Psychiatry   153
Maartje Katzenbauer and Gerben Meynen

Part III   Philosophy and the Law 183

Chapter 7   The Mistaken Quest for a Control Test: For a Rationality Standard of Sanity   185
Paul Litton

Chapter 8	Legal Insanity and Executive Function *Katrina Sifferd, William Hirstein, and Tyler Fagan*	215
Chapter 9	Insanity and Free Will: The Humanitarian Argument for Abolition *Michael Louis Corrado*	243

Part IV Law, Policy, and Reform 271

Chapter 10	Abolishing Insanity: Proposals from England and Wales *Paul Catley*	273
Chapter 11	Mental Insanity at the International Criminal Court: Proposal for a New Regulation *Natalia Silva*	307
Chapter 12	Andrea Yates: A Continuing Story about Insanity *Deborah W. Denno*	367

About the Contributors and Editor 417

Index 425

Acknowledgments

I would like to thank Alicia Merritt for inviting me—"enticing" might be a better word—to begin this project, and Debbie Carvalko at Praeger/ABC-CLIO for patiently shepherding it through the development and publication process (with added emphasis on the word "patiently").

One of the reasons I like to edit collected volumes is to learn more about a subject, and I probably learned more from the chapters in this volume than I have from any other. In that spirit, I would like to thank every one of the contributors to this volume: Paul Catley, Michael Corrado, Russell Covey, Deborah Denno, Tyler Fagan, Gabriel Hallevy, William Hirstein, Maartje Katzenbauer, Paul Litton, Gerben Meynen, Michael L. Perlin, Katrina Sifferd, Natalia Silva, Craig A. Stern, and Meron Wondemaghen.

Finally, I would like to thank Christopher Slobogin, whose work first prompted me to think about the purpose and role of the insanity defense, and without whom I would not be writing this note.

Acknowledgments

Introduction

Insanity is a legal concept with a long history and jurisprudence, and its definition, elucidation, and application depend critically on basic concepts of psychiatry and philosophy. Philosophers of criminal law who take widely disparate views of the purpose of punishment—whether that be deterrence, retributivism, or rehabilitation—all agree that people who commit crimes while unaware they were doing wrong, or who were unable to resist doing wrong, should be excused from punishment due to a lack of moral responsibility, often rooted in some mental disorder or illness. This is a basic demand of justice, yet the insanity defense strikes many people outside the realms of law, philosophy, or psychiatry as profoundly unjust, which suggests that there is still work to be done in explaining and justifying the basic concepts of legal insanity.

The present volume is an attempt to explore the intricacies and controversies regarding the insanity defense from the perspectives of these three fields. The 15 scholars collected here represent legal scholars and practitioners, philosophers, and psychiatrists—several of them fitting into more than one of these categories—and their chapters provide a wide range of perspectives on an issue that demands such a multidisciplinary approach.

The first part of the book offers three pre-eminent scholars of the insanity defense providing essential background while also offering new thoughts about the doctrine and its application. First, in "The Insanity Defense: Nine Myths That Will Not Go Away," **Michael Perlin** offers a brisk overview of widespread misunderstandings among the public regarding the insanity defense, many of them due to erroneous news reports and depictions in television and movies. Perlin concludes with a call for *therapeutic jurisprudence*, a way of thinking about the law that takes into the account its effects on people's well-being, and one that supports the insanity defense in principle while at the same time urging critical reflection on its implementation.

Next, **Russell Covey** continues the theme of countering popular mythology in "The Temporary Insanity Defense," in which he offers a detailed examination of the various uses and understandings of the temporary insanity defense throughout history and its relationship to other legal defenses, including insanity itself (the distinction from which has diminished in practice), as well as the traditional doctrines of excuse and justification. Covey argues that, in practice, the temporary insanity defense often fills gaps where traditional legal excuses fail to address behavior that is morally excusable for intuitive reasons, which he finds to be useful and equitable, serving general principles of justice at the risk of making the insanity defense resemble a type of nullification.

Finally, in "*Mens Rea* and Mental Disorder," **Craig Stern** emphasizes the importance of *mens rea*, a criminal or "bad" state of mind, as the link between the purposes of the criminal law and the role that considerations of mental disorder play in the administration of the criminal law. After concisely surveying the history of *mens rea*, Stern uses hypothetical cases to show that different approaches to *mens rea* in the law correspond to different approaches to using the concept of mental disorder in the law, and argues that these connections deserve much more attention and reflection by legal professionals and scholars working in the area.

The second part of the book looks at psychological and psychiatric perspectives on the insanity defense and the law incorporating it. **Gabriel Hallevy** provides an excellent transition between the two parts of the book by considering the history of the insanity defense and several bases for its definition in "The Shadows of Normality: Legal Insanity under Modern Criminal Law." He considers the intersections between legal, medical, and social understandings of insanity, outlines the details of its use at trial, and argues that insanity is best understood functionally through its effect of offenders' behavior through their cognition or volition, rather than as an ideal concept divorced from practical application.

In the next chapter, "Insanity Constructs," **Meron Wondemaghen** examines and illuminates the impact of legal and psychiatric constructs such as "disease of mind," "nature and quality," and "wrongness" within insanity defense jurisprudence (building on the previous chapter's focus on the social nature of insanity and the role played by contingent judgments of normality). She explains that such constructs are, to some extent, necessarily arbitrary, but at the same time they are very influential in crafting legal and popular impressions about insanity and the insanity defense. These effects include excluding non-psychotic mental illnesses such as depression from the insanity defense as well as exaggerating the incidence of violence of the part of the mentally ill.

In the final chapter of this part, "Insanity: Neurolaw and Forensic Psychiatry," **Maartje Katzenbauer** and **Gerben Meynen** survey the relatively new field of *neurolaw*, detailing its contributions and limitations, with particular attention to its interaction with forensic psychiatry in terms of neuroimaging. For instance, they ask if neuroimaging can detect the type of mental disorder traditionally associated with the insanity defense (discussed in the previous two chapters), or if this is a matter best left to psychiatry. They conclude with recommendations for the practice of neurolaw, including increased involvement and cooperation between legal professionals, psychiatrists, neurologists, and neuropsychologists.

The third part of the book deals with philosophical issues relevant to the insanity defense, in particular those of moral responsibility, rationality, and free will. In "The Mistaken Quest for a Control Test: For a Rationality Standard of Sanity," **Paul Litton** investigates the relationship between the two traditional prongs of the insanity defense: cognition and volition. He discusses the views of prominent scholar (and contributor to this volume) Michael Corrado, who argues that a volition test is both necessary and sufficient to establish legal insanity. Litton analyzes the volition prong in terms of several senses of control that branch philosophy of mind, action theory, and moral philosophy, and concludes that a volition test is neither necessary nor sufficient for a just insanity standard.

Katrina Sifferd, **William Hirstein**, and **Tyler Fagan** give a different perspective on the two prongs of cognition and volition in their chapter "Legal Insanity and Executive Function." They identify *executive functions*, general and practical capacities in the brain, as essential to both prongs and to some extent unifying them. Similar to Stern's chapter, they ground the legal relevance of particular executive functions in the goals of the criminal law itself, which they survey and use to motivate their concept of the appropriate executive functions that will further these goals. Their emphasis on executive functions also bridges the gap between mental illness and legal insanity while weakening the direct link between them, thereby making room for a broader range of mental phenomena to affect legal responsibility (such as depression, as identified by Wondemaghen in her chapter).

Finally, in "Insanity and Free Will: The Humanitarian Argument for Abolition," **Michael Corrado** discusses an argument for the abolition of punishment altogether based on the standard argument for the insanity defense—that people are not responsible for their actions—but expanded to all offenders due to the absence of free will in a metaphysical sense. As mentioned by Litton in his chapter, Corrado supports a deterministic worldview, as opposed to a libertarian or compatibilist one, and draws out the implications of this for criminal justice. He argues for a shift in legal thinking toward correction over punishment, but also suggests a rationale for retaining the insanity defense even in a world in which no one is held morally responsible for their actions.

The three contributors to the last part of the book offer valuable insight and perspective on reform, expansion, and application of insanity defense doctrine. In "Abolishing Insanity: Proposals from England and Wales," **Paul Catley** provides a detailed review of the history of insanity defense jurisprudence in England and Wales, including the famous case of Daniel M'Naghten and the resulting M'Naghten Rules. Following this, he considers a recent proposal for reform that would make significant changes to the concepts and language used in reference to the insanity defense, addressing—while not necessarily satisfying—some of the concerns raised in other chapter in this book (such as those by Wondemaghen and Siffered, Hirsten, and Fagan).

In "Mental Insanity at the International Criminal Court: Proposal for a New Regulation," **Natalia Silva** investigates the relative neglect of diminished responsibility in international criminal law. She surveys approaches to insanity law in other jurisdictions and considers how the goals of those criminal justice systems differ from that of the International Criminal Court (ICC). She focuses on the lack of consideration given to rehabilitation in the ICC in favor of retribution for those accused of the most heinous crimes against humanity. Finally, she investigates the possibility of implementing an insanity defense standard at the ICC, taking into account the unique nature and goals of the forum.

In the last chapter of this part and the volume, "Andrea Yates: A Continuing Story about Insanity," **Deborah W. Denno** provides valuable detail behind a recent but famous case mentioned by several other contributors, that of Andrea Yates. Not only does Denno's chapter contribute actual accounts of courtroom debates concerning a vivid, heartbreaking, and controversial legal case dealing with post-partum depression and psychosis, but she also highlights the different roles that the members of the court, expert witnesses, and the media play in the adjudication of insanity defense cases.

As the editor of this volume, I hope the chapters contained herein will not only answer readers' questions about the insanity defense, but will also pique their interest (as mine was long ago), and lead to further discussion and investigation into an area of law that will only grow more fascinating as we continue to learn about the human brain, psychology, and behavior.

PART 1

Essentials of the Law

CHAPTER ONE

The Insanity Defense: Nine Myths That Will Not Go Away

Michael L. Perlin

Writing about the insanity defense over a quarter of a century ago, I stated: "Until we 'unpack' the empirical and social myths that underlie our misconceptions about the insane and the insanity defense and hold us in a paralytic thrall, we cannot begin to move forward."[1] Some five years later, I began a full-length book on the insanity defense by alleging that "our insanity defense jurisprudence is incoherent."[2] Five years after that, I concluded that "we as a society remain fixated on the insanity defense as a symbol of all that is wrong with the criminal justice system and as a source of social and political anger."[3] Returning to this issue two years ago, I concluded that "nothing has happened in the intervening decade to lead me to change my mind."[4] The myths have stayed with us, and we willfully blind ourselves to the empirical and behavioral realities.

At the roots of this incoherence and fixation is our nation's irrational belief system in a series of myths about the defense, each of which has been discredited, yet each of which continues to dominate political and social discourse. Multiple scholars have identified these myths, but their power still controls the debate.[5] There is no disputing that Cynthia G. Hawkins-León was correct when she characterized the insanity defense literature and case law as based upon "epic myths."[6] Simply put, the valid and reliable research on the insanity defense contradicts most of the "commonly-held beliefs" about the defense's usage.[7]

There are multiple reasons for this disconnect between myth and reality. We cannot understand the insanity defense unless we look at it through the cognitive psychology construct of *heuristics*—that is, the way that we seek to simplify information-processing tasks by privileging the vivid, negative, accessible anecdote, and by subordinating the factual, the logical, the statistical, the rational.[8] For these purposes, the most pernicious of the heuristics is the *vividness heuristic*: a cognitive simplifying device that teaches us that "when decisionmakers are in the thrall of a highly salient event, that event will so dominate their thinking that they will make aggregate decisions that are overdependent on the particular event and that overestimate the representativeness of that event within some larger array of events."[9] One single vivid, memorable case overwhelms mountains of abstract, colorless data upon which rational choices should be made.[10] Empirical studies reveal jurors' susceptibility to the use of these devices.[11] Furthermore, we cannot understand the insanity defense unless we come to grips with the meretricious allure of a false "ordinary common sense"[12] that has long pervaded, and poisoned, our jurisprudence in this area.[13] Ordinary common sense is self-referential and non-reflective: "I see it that way, therefore everyone sees it that way; I see it that way, therefore that's the way it is."[14] We must also understand that there are socio-political myths "at play" in addition to empirical myths adding to this miasma of misinformation: by way of example, the (utterly unsupported) "fear that the soft, exculpatory sciences of psychiatry and psychology, claiming expertise in almost all areas of behavior, will somehow overwhelm the criminal justice system by thwarting the system's crime control component."[15]

This chapter will consider the political/social myths that continue to dominate the insanity defense conversation; present the empirical realities that refute each and every one of these myths; briefly consider these issues through the lens of therapeutic jurisprudence; and offer some conclusions as to why these myths continue to so hold us in thrall.

1 Empirical Data and Myths[16]

Soon after John Hinckley was found not guilty by reason of insanity in the attempted murder of President Ronald Reagan,[17] commentators began to examine carefully the "myths"[18] that had developed about the insanity defense and insanity defense pleaders in an effort to determine the extent "to which this issue has been distorted in the public eye."[19] The empirical research[20] revealed that at least nine myths[21] had arisen and been perpetuated, but that all were "unequivocally disproven by the facts."[22] Valid and reliable research unanimously agrees that juror attitudes in insanity defense cases reflect bias,[23] and research has both validated the mythic nature of each of these erroneous beliefs[24] and has supported the findings of distortion and infection.[25] Valid and reliable research further demonstrates that jurors also often act quite independently from court instructions, based on their *a priori* "intuitive understanding of mental disease, responsibility, culpability, punishment, and treatment."[26]

Myth #1: *The insanity defense is overused.*[27]

All empirical analyses have been consistent:[28] the public at large[29] and the legal profession in particular[30]—especially legislators[31]—"dramatically"[32] and "grossly"[33] overestimate both the frequency and the success rate of the insanity plea,[34] an error that is "undoubtedly . . . abetted"[35] by the media's "bizarre depictions,"[36] "distortion[s],"[37] and inaccuracies[38] in portraying mentally ill individuals charged with crimes.[39] Not even expert witnesses are immune from these myths.[40]

Myth #2: *Use of the insanity defense is limited to murder cases.*[41]

In one jurisdiction where the data has been closely studied,[42] contrary to expectations,[43] slightly less than one-third of the successful insanity pleas entered over an eight year period were reached in cases involving a victim's death.[44] Further, individuals who plead insanity in murder cases are no more successful in being found not guilty by reason of insanity (NGRI) than persons charged with other crimes.[45] Remarkably, in at least one state (Oregon), the insanity defense is used strategically as a *diversion* mechanism in the cases of defendants charged with misdemeanors.[46]

Myth #3: *There is no risk to the defendant who pleads insanity.*[47]

It has been found that defendants who asserted an insanity defense at trial, and who were ultimately found guilty of their charges, served significantly longer sentences than defendants tried on similar charges who did not assert the insanity defense.[48] The same ratio is found when only homicide cases are considered.[49]

Myth #4: *NGRI acquittees are quickly released from custody.*[50]

One of the prevailing insanity defense myths is that insanity acquittees "spend much less time in custody than do defendants convicted of the same offenses."[51] Contrary to this myth, NGRI acquittees actually spend almost double the amount of time that defendants convicted of similar charges spend in prison settings and often face a lifetime of post-release judicial oversight.[52] Most important for the perspectives of this presentation, the less serious the offense, the longer the gap is between the amount of time that an insanity acquittee serves and the amount of time that a convicted defendant serves. A California study, by way of example, has revealed that those found NGRI of non-violent crimes were confined for periods over nine times as long.[53] Thus, it makes progressively less sense for a defendant to raise the insanity defense.[54] Remarkably, a National Mental Health Association report has found that as many as 86 percent of insanity pleas occur in nonviolent felonies and misdemeanors.[55]

Of the entire universe of individuals found NGRI over an eight year period in one jurisdiction, only 15 percent had been released from all restraints;[56] 35 percent remained in full custody, and 47 percent were under partial court restraint following conditional release.[57]

Myth #5: *NGRI acquittees spend much less time in custody than do defendants convicted of the same offenses.*[58]

Contrarily, NGRI acquittees spend almost *double* the amount of time that defendants convicted of similar charges spend in prison settings,[59] and often face a lifetime of post-release judicial oversight.[60] Importantly, insanity acquittees' rearrest rate has been found to be statistically significantly lower than rates of convicted felons or of mentally disordered prisoners transferred for hospital treatment.[61]

Myth #6: *Most insanity defense trials feature "battles of the experts."*[62]

Dramatic, televised cases lead the public to assume that *all* insanity defense cases involve a "battle of the experts" who "will say whatever they are being paid to say," especially if they are experts testifying on behalf of the defense.[63] The empirical reality is quite different. In a Hawaii survey, there was congruence on the question of insanity in over 90 percent of all cases, and in Oregon, the prosecutor's expert agreed with the defense expert in 80 percent of such cases.[64] These findings have been consistent since the 1950s.[65] In short, the common perception here is another myth.

Myth #7: *Criminal defense attorneys overuse the insanity defense as a means of "beating the rap."*[66]

This in no way comports with reality. First, the level of representation made available in many jurisdictions to the population in question is significantly substandard, and the case law is replete with examples of lawyers who have totally "missed" the evidence that an insanity defense would be the appropriate defense strategy; this has been clear for decades.[67] Second, there is significant empirical that *some* attorneys proffer an insanity defense for independent strategic reasons: as a plea-bargaining chip, as a vehicle by which they can obtain mental health treatment for their clients, and even as a pre-emptive maneuver to avoid feared malpractice litigation.[68] Third, the best evidence tells us that juror bias exists independently of what defense lawyers do, and is "not induced by attorneys."[69]

Myth #8: *The insanity defense is a "rich man's" defense.*

At the Congressional hearings that led to the adoption of the Insanity Defense Reform Act of 1984—sharply limiting the substantive scope of the defense and tightening procedures employed when the defense is pled[70]—prominent U.S. senators characterized the defense saw it as a "rich man's defense."[71] This allegation has always been a "textbook parody of empirical and behavioral reality."[72] The defense is, rather, disproportionately used in cases involving indigent defendants.[73] But this myth persists, in significant part, because of the vividness heuristic: most high-profile cases involving the insanity defense are cases that are the focus of exaggerated media attention, thus creating the illusion that these cases are reflective of the entire universe of insanity cases, or even the entire universe of all cases.[74]

Myth #9: *Criminal defendants who plead insanity are usually faking.*[75]

This is perhaps the oldest of the insanity defense myths, and is one that has bedeviled American jurisprudence since the mid-19th century.[76] It continues to be reflected contemporaneously on a regular basis in prosecutorial summations,[77] especially in cases in which the defendant's appearance does not comport with "ordinary common sense" characterizations of insanity.[78] Courts profess their inability to determine whether pleas of insanity are real or feigned.[79]

The empirical data is radically different. Of the 141 individuals found NGRI in one jurisdiction over an eight-year period, there was no dispute that 115 were schizophrenic (including 38 of the 46 cases involving a victim's death),[80] and in only three cases was the diagnostician unwilling or unable to specify the nature of the patient's mental illness.[81] The most comprehensive multi-state survey reveals that 84 percent of those acquitted by reason of insanity carried a diagnosis either of schizophrenia or other major mental disorder.[82]

2 From the Perspective of Therapeutic Jurisprudence[83]

Therapeutic jurisprudence "asks us to look at law as it actually impacts people's lives"[84] and focuses on the law's influence on emotional life and psychological well-being.[85] The ultimate aim of therapeutic jurisprudence is to determine whether legal rules, procedures, and lawyer roles can or should be reshaped to enhance their therapeutic potential *while not subordinating due process principles.*[86] There is an inherent tension in this inquiry, but David Wexler clearly identifies how it must be resolved: The law's use of "mental health information to improve therapeutic functioning [cannot] impinge upon justice concerns."[87] Again, it is vital to keep in mind that

"An inquiry into therapeutic outcomes does not mean that therapeutic concerns 'trump' civil rights and civil liberties."[88] In its aim to use the law to empower individuals, enhance rights, and promote well-being, therapeutic jurisprudence has been described as "a sea-change in ethical thinking about the role of law . . . a movement towards a more distinctly relational approach to the practice of law . . . which emphasizes psychological wellness over adversarial triumphalism."[89]

In a series of earlier writings, I have concluded that, in the context of therapeutic jurisprudence, the insanity defense is therapeutic,[90] that the substantive standard and procedural rules actually do matter,[91] that current post-acquittal rules that follow the U.S. Supreme Court's dictates in *Jones v. United States* are anti-therapeutic,[92] and that therapeutic jurisprudence principles must be more rigorously applied to issues involving post-acquittal institutionalization and community monitoring.[93] I believe that it is only through the use of therapeutic jurisprudence that we can seek to eradicate the "irrational prejudice based predominantly upon stereotype, myth, superstition and deindividualization" that is at the core of our insanity defense policies.[94]

Some 20 years ago, in a book-length examination of the insanity defense, I concluded:

> [W]e must rigorously apply therapeutic jurisprudence principles to each aspect of the insanity defense. We need to take what we learn from therapeutic jurisprudence to strip away sanist behavior,[95] pretextual reasoning[96] and teleological decision making[97] from the insanity defense process. This would enable us to confront the pretextual use of social science data in an open and meaningful way.[98]

The myths discussed in this chapter are textbook examples of sanism, pretextuality and teleological thinking. It is only through the use of therapeutic jurisprudence that we can hope to "expose pretextuality and strip bare the law's sanist facade"[99] by rebutting the myths that continue to dominate insanity defense jurisprudence.

3 Conclusion

Some years ago, in reviewing the evidence surrounding these myths, two colleagues and I suggested that:

> Clearly, this data reflects the extent to which myths have permeated the debate [on] the insanity defense, and the extent to which much of the new

legislation represents "an unnecessary and extreme reaction to a group of serious misconceptions." . . . What is clear is that "each and every one of the false premises" raised in support of abolition or evisceration of the defense is disproved by the evidence.[100]

Nothing that has transpired in the intervening three decades has caused him to reconsider this conclusion.

Notes

1. Perlin, "Unpacking the Myths," 603.
2. Perlin, *The Jurisprudence of the Insanity Defense*.
3. Perlin, *The Hidden Prejudice*, 224.
4. Perlin, "'Wisdom Is Thrown into Jail,'" 357.
5. See, e.g., Shannon, "The Time Is Right to Revise the Texas Insanity Defense," 81n119 (discussing how social science research has dispelled myths about the insanity defense); Ewing and McCann, *Minds on Trial*, 239 (same); Harris, "Rotten Social Background and the Temper of the Times," 144 (discussing research reported in Perlin, "Unpacking the Myths," and Perlin, "'The Borderline Which Separated You from Me'").
6. Hawkins-León, "'Literature as Law,'" 405.
7. Borum and Fulero, "Empirical Research on the Insanity Defense and Attempted Reforms."
8. "Heuristics" is a cognitive psychology construct that refers to the implicit thinking devices that individuals use to simplify complex, information-processing tasks. See, e.g., Perlin, "Psychodynamics and the Insanity Defense"; see generally Saks and Kidd, "Human Information Processing and Adjudication." The use of heuristics frequently leads to distorted and systematically erroneous decisions and causes decision makers to "ignore or misuse items of rationally useful information" (Perlin, "Are Courts Competent to Decide Questions of Competency?," 966n46, quoting Carroll and Payne, "The Psychology of the Parole Decision Process," 21. For the most recent reconsideration of insanity defense myths through the heuristics filter, see Maryns, "The Interdiscursive Construction of Irresponsibility as a Defence Strategy in the Belgian Assize Court."
9. Schauer, "Do Cases Make Bad Law?," 895, as discussed in Perlin, "'Everybody Is Making Love/Or Else Expecting Rain,'" 492.
10. Rosenhan, "Psychological Realities and Judicial Policy," 13.
11. See, e.g., Koehler and Shaviro, *Veridical Verdicts*, 264–65; Perlin, "Psychodynamics and the Insanity Defense," 39–53; Lieberman and Krauss, "The Effects of Labeling, Expert Testimony, and Information Processing Mode on Juror Decisions in SVP Civil Commitment Trials." See also Roberts and Golding, "The Social Construction of Criminal Responsibility and Insanity," 372 (jurors' pre-existing attitudes toward insanity defense strongest predictor of individual verdicts).

12. Ordinary common sense regularly pervades the judiciary in deciding cases involving individuals with mental disabilities. See Perlin, "'The Borderline Which Separated You from Me,'" 1417.

13. Ibid., 1377.

14. Perlin, "'And I See Through Your Brain,'" 8n84.

15. Perlin, "'The Borderline Which Separated You from Me,'" 1408.

16. See generally Perlin and Cucolo, *Mental Disability Law*, §14–3.2.

17. See generally Caplan, *The Insanity Defense and the Trial of John W. Hinckley, Jr.*

18. For an excellent consideration of all myths, see Bredemeier, "Hollow Verdict," 730–45.

19. Rodriguez, LeWinn, and Perlin, "The Insanity Defense Under Siege," 400. Among the most important empirical studies are Callahan et al., "The Volume and Characteristics of Insanity Defense Pleas," and Steadman, "Before and After Hinckley." For more recent studies, see e.g. Cirincione, Steadman, and McGreevy, "Rates of Insanity Acquittals and the Factors Associated with Successful Insanity Pleas"; Linhorst, "The Impact of System Design on the Characteristics of Missouri's Insanity Acquittees"; Studebaker, "Evaluating the Insanity Defense"; Skeem and Golding, "Describing Jurors' Personal Conceptions of Insanity and Their Relationship to Case Judgment."

20. For early comprehensive overviews, see Steadman, "Empirical Research on the Insanity Defense"; Keilitz, "Researching and Reforming the Insanity Defense"; Steadman, "Mental Health Law and the Criminal Offender."

21. See Morse, "Excusing the Crazy," 795–801 (characterizing the arguments based on some of these myths as "insubstantial objections to the insanity defense").

22. Perlin, "Whose Plea Is It Anyway?", 6. See Faigman et al., *Modern Scientific Evidence*, § 9:1 n.8, citing Perlin, *Jurisprudence*, 108–14.

23. See, for example, Bloechl et al., "An Empirical Investigation of Insanity Defense Attitudes"; Tygart, "Public Acceptance/Rejection of Insanity"; Skeem et al, "Venirepersons's Attitudes Toward the Insanity Defense"; Louden and Skeem, "Constructing Insanity."

24. See Daftary-Kapur et al., "Measuring Knowledge of the Insanity Defense."

25. See e.g., *State v. Moore*, 525 So. 2d 870 (Fla. 1988) (reversible error where trial judge failed to excuse juror who said his beliefs about insanity defense would probably prevent him from following court's instructions on issue); compare *Boblett v. Commonwealth*, 396 S.E.2d 131 (Va. Ct. App. 1990) (no abuse of discretion where trial court failed to strike for cause juror whose statements indicated he would "have difficulty" acquitting defendant in insanity defense case); *State v. Pierce*, 109 N.M. 596, 788 P.2d 352 (1990) (juror's misrepresentations as to his own mental illness did not require new trial), but see at 365 (Montgomery, J., dissenting) (charging that juror bias tainted trial where he "displayed a willingness to translate [his] feelings [about mental illness] into a premature judgment about defendant's guilt"); see also *People v. Seuffer*, 582 N.E.2d 71, 77–79 (Ill. 1991) (prospective jurors' views that insanity defense was "overused" did not warrant

removal for cause); compare *Noe v. State*, 586 So. 2d 371, 374–79 (Fla. Dist. Ct. 1991) (reversible error where trial judge refused to grant defendant's "for cause" challenge to jurors who indicated that they had "philosophical problems" with the insanity defense).

26. See Finkel et al., "Insanity Defenses," 80, 92. See also, e.g., Finkel and Slobogin, "Insanity, Justification and Culpability"; Finkel, "Culpability and Commonsense Justice."

27. Perlin and Cucolo, *Mental Disability Law*, §14–2.1; see also Perlin, *Jurisprudence*, 108–09.

28. For the most comprehensive studies, see Hans, "An Analysis of Public Attitudes Toward the Insanity Defense," and Cirincione and Jacob, "Identifying Insanity Acquittals." See also Cirincione et al., "Rates of Insanity Acquittals and the Factors Associated with Successful Insanity Pleas," and Breheney et al., "Gender Matters in the Insanity Defense," 97.

29. Pasewark et al, "The Insanity Plea in New York State, 1965–1976." See also Jeffrey and Pasewark, "Altering Opinions about the Insanity Plea"; Pasewark and Seidenzahl, "Opinions Concerning the Insanity Plea and Criminality Among Mental Patients."

30. Pasewark and Craig, "Insanity Plea," 415, 436–40. See also McGinley and Blau, "The Success of the Insanity Plea."

31. Pasewark and Pantle, "Insanity Plea" (1979) (in response to survey, one state's legislators estimated that 4400 defendants pled insanity and that 1800 were found NGRI in a sample time period; in reality, 102 defendants asserted the defense, and only one was successful).

32. Pasewark et al, "The Insanity Plea in New York State," 186.

33. Pasewark and Pantle, "Insanity Plea," 223.

34. In New Jersey, for instance, in fiscal 1982, of the more than 32,500 cases handled by the state office of the public defender, NGRI pleas were entered only in 50 cases, and were successful 15 times (or about 1⁄20 of 1 percent of all cases). See Rodriguez, LeWinn, and Perlin, "The Insanity Defense Under Siege," 401. A later study has suggested that, while plea incidence is fairly uniform in all jurisdictions, the plea's success rate is "quite variable." See Pasewark and McGinley, "Insanity Plea." A comprehensive multi-state survey reveals a plea incidence of slightly less than one percent, and a success rate of 26 percent. See Callahan et al., "The Volume and Characteristics of Insanity Defense Pleas," 336.

35. Rodriguez, LeWinn, and Perlin, "The Insanity Defense Under Siege," 401.

36. Steadman and Cocozza, "Selective Reporting and the Public's Misconceptions of the Criminally Insane," 532. See also Nairn, Coverdale, and Claasen, "What Is the Role of Intertextuality in Media Depictions of Mental Illness?"

37. Steadman and Cocozza, "Selective Reporting and the Public's Misconceptions of the Criminally Insane," at 523.

38. Ibid., 532.

39. On the significance of public misperceptions in this area generally, see Cavanaugh and Rogers, "Convergence of Mental Illness and Violence." See generally

Perlin, "Unpacking the Myths," 18–20, 108–14; Perlin, "After Hinckley"; Steadman, "Before and After Hinckley"; Silver, Cirincione, and Steadman, "Demythologizing Inaccurate Perceptions of the Insanity Defense"; Nevins-Saunders, "Not Guilty As Charged," 1423n15 (citing statistics). For an important case that carefully examines the roots of the empirical and behavioral myths, see *United States v. Denny-Shaffer*, 2 F.3d 999 (10th Cir. 1993), discussed in this context in Perlin, "'Half-Wracked Prejudice Leaped Forth.'"

40. On the ways that expert witnesses misunderstand the relevant principles, see R. Rogers et al., "Forensic Psychiatrists' and Psychologists' Understanding of Insanity." On the varying attitudes of public defenders and prosecutors, see Jordan and Myers, "Attorneys, Psychiatrists, and Psychologists."

41. Perlin and Cucolo, *Mental Disability Law*, § 14–3.2.2; see also Perlin, *Jurisprudence*, 109.

42. For a survey of those jurisdictions where significant empirical data has been developed, see Boehnert, "Psychological and Demographic Factors Associated with Individuals Using the Insanity Defense," 30n3. See also Petrila, "The Insanity Defense and Other Mental Health Dispositions in Missouri"; J. Rogers et al., "Women in Oregon's Insanity Defense System."

43. See generally *State v. Lucas*, 152 A.2d 50, 77 (N.J. 1959) (Weintraub, C.J., concurring).

44. Rodriguez, LeWinn, and Perlin, "The Insanity Defense Under Siege," 402. Among the other underlying charges were writing false checks, carrying an unloaded starter's pistol, and drug use (ibid.). See also *Jones v. United States*, 463 U.S. 354, 359 (1983) (attempted petit larceny).

For an earlier survey of the same jurisdiction, see Singer, "Insanity Acquittal in the Seventies." A comprehensive multi-state survey reveals that 13.6 percent of those pleading insanity were charged with murder, while another 36 percent were charged with assault or other crimes of violence. See Callahan et al, "The Volume and Characteristics of Insanity Defense Pleas," 336.

A more recent Missouri study found that only 13.3 percent of all NGRIs in that state had been charged with homicide. See Dirks-Linhorst and Kondrat, "Tough on Crime or Beating the System," 134.

45. Steadman et al., "Factors Associated with a Successful Insanity Plea," 402–03. See also Boehnert, "Psychological and Demographic Factors" (NGRI acquittees found to commit less heinous offenses than similar samples consisting of defendants who were unsuccessful in their reliance on defense and those who were evaluated for defense and ultimately chose to enter into plea bargain agreements). Cf. Packer, "Insanity Acquittals in Michigan 1969–1983" (since Michigan amended its insanity defense statutes to create a "guilty but mentally ill" verdict, while there has been little change in the total number of insanity acquittals, the number of such verdicts in homicide cases has decreased while the number in cases involving less serious offenses has increased).

46. Schaefer and Bloom, "The Use of the Insanity Defense as a Jail Diversion Mechanism for Mentally Ill Persons Charged with Misdemeanors."

47. Perlin and Cucolo, *Mental Disability Law*, §14–3.2.3; see also Perlin, *Jurisprudence*, 109.

48. Rodriguez, LeWinn, and Perlin, "The Insanity Defense Under Siege," 401–02. A possible explanation for this is discussed in Perlin, "The Supreme Court, the Mentally Disabled Criminal Defendant, and Symbolic Values"; see also Steadman, "Predicting Dangerousness among the Mentally Ill."

49. Rodriguez, LeWinn, and Perlin, "The Insanity Defense Under Siege," 402n32.

50. Perlin and Cucolo, *Mental Disability Law*, §14–3.2.4; see also Perlin, *Jurisprudence*, 109–10.

51. See generally Perlin, "'The Borderline Which Separated You from Me.'"

52. Perlin, "Unpacking the Myths," 651 (citing empirical results reported in Rodriguez, LeWinn & Perlin, "The Insanity Defense Under Siege," 403–04, and Pogrebin et al., "Not Guilty By Reason of Insanity," 240).

53. Perlin, "'The Borderline Which Separated You from Me,'" 1405 (discussing research reported in Steadman et al., *Before and After Hinckley*, 94).

54. See, e.g., Vitro, "Promoting Therapeutic Objectives Through LB 518," 844 (1993) ("[A]n individual in need of treatment may fail to assert the insanity defense because a criminal sentence would be of definite and frequently shorter duration.").

55. See Nevins-Saunders, "Not Guilty As Charged," at 1454n72 (discussing National Commission on the Insanity Defense, "Myths & Realities").

56. Rodriguez, LeWinn, and Perlin, "The Insanity Defense Under Siege," 403

57. Ibid.

58. See Perlin and Cucolo, *Mental Disability Law*, §14–3.2.5; see also Perlin, *Jurisprudence*, 110–11.

59. Rodriguez, LeWinn, and Perlin, "The Insanity Defense Under Siege," 403–04. See also Harris et al., "Length of Detention in Matched Groups of Insanity Acquittees and Convicted Offenders"; Breheny et al., "Gender Matters in the Insanity Defense," 97; *Archuleta v. Hedrick*, 365 F.3d 344 (8th Cir. Mo. 2004), cert. denied, 543 U.S. 999 (2004) (prisoner was not entitled to habeas relief on grounds that his detention was longer than if he had been found guilty and completed his sentence).

60. Rodriguez, LeWinn, and Perlin, "The Insanity Defense Under Siege," 403–04.

61. Silver et al., "Follow-Up after Release of Insanity Acquittees, Mentally Disordered Offenders, and Convicted Felons." Compare Bieber et al., "Predicting Criminal Recidivism of Insanity Acquittees" (NGRI escapees have lower rearrest rate than NGRI acquittees who are released from hospitalization); see also Rice et al., "Recidivism Among Male Insanity Acquittees."

62. See Perlin, *Jurisprudence*, 112–13.

63. Moore, "Learning about Forensics."

64. J. Rogers et al., "Insanity Defense"; Fukunaga et al., "Insanity Plea," 326.

65. Acheson, "McDonald v. United States," 589.

66. See Perlin, *Jurisprudence*, 113–14.

67. See Perlin, "Fatal Assumption"; Perlin, *Mental Disability and the Death Penalty*, 123–34.

68. Pasewark and Craig, "Insanity Plea."

69. Tanford and Tanford, "Better Trials Through Science," 748–49.

70. See Perlin, *Jurisprudence*, 95–100.

71. Ibid., 18 (citing Senate hearings).

72. Ibid., 19.

73. See Hearings on Bills to Amend Title 18 to Limit the Insanity Defense Before the S. Judiciary Comm., 97th Cong., 2d Sess. 80 (testimony of Dr. Henry Steadman); see also National Commission on the Insanity Defense, "Myths & Realities," at 14, 22–23 (criticizing as unfounded the proposition that the insanity defense is a "rich-man's defense").

74. Perlin, "'His Brain Has Been Mismanaged with Great Skill,'" 903. But see ibid., speculating "that there may be some truth to this myth in the case of insanity pleaders who seek to use neuroimaging evidence in support of their plea, in large part because of the extra expenses that would be incurred in such cases." There is no empirically reliable database on this cohort of cases at this time.

75. Perlin and Cucolo, *Mental Disability Law*, §14–3.2.6; see also Perlin, *Jurisprudence*, 111–12.

76. See Isaac Ray, *A Treatise on the Medical Jurisprudence of Insanity*, 243; Clinton, *Defense of Insanity in Criminal Cases*; and generally Perlin, "The Supreme Court, the Mentally Disabled Criminal Defendant, and Symbolic Values." For a stark case example, see *State v. Inglis*, 698 A.2d 1296, 1298 (N.J. Law Div. 1997) ("the insanity defense has a high potential for serving as an instrument of pretext") (citing to no authority).

77. For a case example, see *People v. Lundell*, 538 N.E.2d 186, appeal denied, 545 N.E.2d 122 (Ill. 1989) (prosecutor's closing statement that defendant had fabricated insanity defense with aid of his counsel was reversible error); see also *Commonwealth v. Goulet*, 522 N.E.2d 417 (Mass. 1988); *Winiarz v. State*, 752 P.2d 761 (Nev. 1988), appeal after remand, 820 P.2d 1317 (Nevv. 1991); *Fulghum v. Ford*, 850 F.2d 1529 (11th Cir.), cert. denied, 488 U.S. 1014 (1989); *People v. Christopher*, 566 N.Y.S.2d 167 (A.D. 1991), appeal denied, 573 N.Y.S. 2d 473 (1991).

78. On the question of whether or not defendant's insanity comports with "ordinary common sense," see *People v. Tylkowski*, 524 N.E.2d 1112, appeal denied, 530 N.E.2d 260 (Ill. 1988); see generally Perlin, "Psychodynamics and the Insanity Defense"; Perlin, "'The Borderline Which Separated You from Me.'"

79. See, e.g., *People v. Marshall*, 61 Cal.Rptr.2d 84, 100 (1997) ("[a]n appellate court is in no position to appraise a defendant's conduct in the trial court as indicating insanity, a calculated attempt to feign insanity and delay the proceedings, or sheer temper").

80. Rodriguez, LeWinn, and Perlin, "The Insanity Defense Under Siege," 404; see also Steadman, supra note 21.

81. Rodriguez, LeWinn, and Perlin, "The Insanity Defense Under Siege," 404. For a relevant empirical inquiry, see Warren et al., "Criminal Offense, Psychiatric Diagnosis, and Psycholegal Opinion." On the question of reliability of forensic evaluations, see Gowensmith, Murrie, and Boccaccini, "How Reliable Are Forensic Evaluations of Legal Sanity?" (reliability may be poorer than the field has tended to assume; when judges disagreed with the prevailing forensic opinion, it was more often to find defendants legally sane, rather than insane).

82. Callahan et al, "The Volume and Characteristics of Insanity Defense Pleas," 336

83. This section is largely adapted from Perlin and Lynch, "'Had to be Held Down by Big Police.'"

84. Winick, "Foreword," 535.

85. See Wexler, "Practicing Therapeutic Jurisprudence."

86. See Perlin, "'And My Best Friend, My Doctor, Won't Even Say What It Is I've Got,'" 751; Perlin, "'Everybody Is Making Love/Or Else Expecting Rain,'" 510n139.

87. See Wexler, "Therapeutic Jurisprudence and Changing Concepts of Legal Scholarship," 21; see also Wexler, "Applying the Law Therapeutically."

88. Perlin, "A Law of Healing," 412; Perlin, "'Where the Winds Hit Heavy on the Borderline,'" 782.

89. Brookbanks, "Therapeutic Jurisprudence," 329–30; see also Winick, "Overcoming Psychological Barriers to Settlement," and Winick and Wexler, "The Use of Therapeutic Jurisprudence in Law School Clinical Education," 605–06.

90. Perlin, *Jurisprudence*, 289–95.

91. Ibid., 295–97.

92. Ibid., 297–99.

93. Ibid., 299–300. See generally Perlin, "'God Said to Abraham/Kill Me a Son,'" 6–62.

94. Perlin, "'The Borderline Which Separated You from Me,'" 1378.

95. Sanism is an irrational prejudice based predominantly upon stereotype, myth, superstition, and deindividualization. See e.g., ibid.

96. This refers to the ways that courts often accept testimonial dishonesty and engage in dishonest decision making in cases involving criminal defendants with mental disabilities. See Perlin, *Jurisprudence*, 395–96.

97. On teleology and the insanity defense, see e.g. Perlin, "'The Borderline Which Separated You from Me,'" 1414. See also Perlin, "'Half-Wracked Prejudice Leaped Forth,'" 30: "Researchers must carefully examine case law and statutes to determine the extent to which social science is being teleologically used for sanist ends in insanity defense decisionmaking."

98. Perlin, *Jurisprudence*, 443.

99. Perlin, "'And My Best Friend, My Doctor, Won't Even Say What It Is I've Got,'" 751.

100. Rodriguez, LeWinn, and Perlin, "The Insanity Defense Under Siege," 425.

Resources

Acheson, David C., "*McDonald v. United States*: The Durham Rule Redefined." *Georgetown Law Review* 51(1962): 580–91.

Bieber, Stephen L., Richard A. Pasemark, Katherine Bosten, and Henry J. Steadman, "Predicting Criminal Recidivism of Insanity Acquittees." *International Journal of Law and Psychiatry* 11(1988): 105–12.

Bloechl, Angela L., Michael J. Vitacco, Craig S. Neumann, and Steven E. Erikson, "An Empirical Investigation of Insanity Defense Attitudes: Exploring Factors Related to Bias." *International Journal of Law and Psychiatry* 30(2007): 153–61.

Boehnert, Caryl E., "Psychological and Demographic Factors Associated with Individuals Using the Insanity Defense." *Journal of Psychiatry and Law* 13(1985): 9–31.

Borum, Randy, and Solomon M. Fulero, "Empirical Research on the Insanity Defense and Attempted Reforms: Evidence toward Informed Policy." *Law and Human Behavior* 23(1999): 117–35.

Bredemeier, Sarah J., "Hollow Verdict: Not Guilty by Reason of Insanity Provokes Animus-Based Discrimination in the Social Security Act." *St. Mary's Law Journal* 31(2000): 697–750.

Breheney, Christian, Jennifer Groscup, and Michele Galietta, "Gender Matters in the Insanity Defense." *Law and Psychology Review* 31(2007): 93–123.

Brookbanks, Warren, "Therapeutic Jurisprudence: Conceiving an Ethical Framework." *Journal of Law and Medicine* 8(2001): 328–41.

Callahan, Lisa A., Henry J. Steadman, Margaret A. McGreevy, and Pamela C. Robbins, "The Volume and Characteristics of Insanity Defense Pleas: An Eight State Study." *Bulletin of the American Academy of Psychiatry and Law* 19(1991): 331–38.

Caplan, Lincoln, *The Insanity Defense and the Trial of John W. Hinckley, Jr.* Hopkins, MN: Olympic, 1984.

Carroll, John S., and John W. Payne, "The Psychology of the Parole Decision Process: A Joint Application of Attribution Theory and Information-Processing Psychology." In *Cognition and Social Behavior*, ed. John S. Carroll and John W. Payne (New York: Psychology Press, 1976), 13–32.

Cavanaugh, James, and Richard Rogers, "Convergence of Mental Illness and Violence: Effects on Public Policy." *Psychiatric Annals* 12(1982): 537–41.

Cirincione, Carmen, Henry J. Steadman, and Margaret A. McGreevy, "Rates of Insanity Acquittals and the Factors Associated with Successful Insanity Pleas." *Bulletin of the American Academy of Psychiatry and Law* 23(1995): 399–409.

Cirincione, Carmen, and Charles Jacob, "Identifying Insanity Acquittals: Is it Any Easier?" 23 *Law and Human Behavior* 23(1999): 487–97.

Clinton, Henry L., *Defense Of Insanity in Criminal Cases: Argument of Henry L. Clinton*. New York: Unknown, 1873.

Daftary-Kapur, Tarika, et al., "Measuring Knowledge of the Insanity Defense: Scale Construction and Validation." *Behavioral Sciences and the Law* 29(2011): 40–63.

Dirks-Linhorst, P. Ann, and David Kondrat, "Tough on Crime or Beating the System: An Evaluation of Missouri Department of Mental Health's Not Guilty by Reason of Insanity Murder Acquittees." *Homicide Studies* 16(2012): 129–50.

Ewing, Charles P., and Joseph T. McCann, *Minds on Trial: Great Cases in Law and Psychology*. Oxford: Oxford University Press, 2006.

Faigman, David et al., *Modern Scientific Evidence: The Law and Science of Expert Testimony*, vol. 2. Eagen, MN: Thomson West, 2012–2013.

Finkel, Norman, "Culpability and Commonsense Justice: Lessons Learned Betwixt Murder and Madness." *Notre Dame Journal of Law, Ethics & Public Policy* 10(1996): 11–64.

Finkel, Norman, Ray Shaw, Susan Bercaw, and Juilann Koch, "Insanity Defenses: From the Jurors' Perspective." *Law and Psychology Review* 9(1985): 77–92.

Finkel, Norman, and Christopher Slobogin, "Insanity, Justification and Culpability Toward a Unifying Schema." *Law and Human Behavior* 19(1995): 447–64.

Fukunaga, Kenneth K., Richard A. Pasewark, Michael Hawkins, and Howard Gudeman, "Insanity Plea: Interexaminer Agreement and Concordance of Psychiatric Opinion and Court Verdict." *Law and Human Behavior* 5(1981): 325–28.

Gowensmith, W. Neil, Daniel C. Murrie, and Marcus T. Boccaccini, "How Reliable Are Forensic Evaluations of Legal Sanity?" *Law and Human Behavior* 37(2013): 98–106.

Hans, Valerie, "An Analysis of Public Attitudes Toward the Insanity Defense." *Criminology* 24(1986): 393–414.

Harris, Angela, "Rotten Social Background and the Temper of the Times." *Alabama Civil Rights and Civil Liberties Review* 2(2011): 131–46.

Harris, Grant T., Marnie E. Rice, and Catherine A. Cormier, "Length of Detention in Matched Groups of Insanity Acquittees and Convicted Offenders." *International Journal of Law and Psychiatry* 14(1991): 223–36.

Hawkins-León, Cynthia G., "'Literature as Law': The History of the Insanity Plea and a Fictional Application within the Law & Literature Canon." *Temple Law Review* 72(1999): 381–449.

Jeffrey, Richard W., and Richard A. Pasewark, "Altering Opinions about the Insanity Plea." *Journal of Psychiatry and Law* 11(1983): 29–40.

Jordan, Kareem L., and David L. Myers, "Attorneys, Psychiatrists, and Psychologists: Predictors of Attitudes toward the Insanity Defense." *Criminal Justice Studies* 16(2003): 77–86.

Keilitz, Ingo, "Researching and Reforming the Insanity Defense." *Rutgers Law Review* 39(1987): 289–322.

Koehler, Jonathan, and Daniel N. Shaviro, "Veridical Verdicts: Increasing Verdict Accuracy Through the Use of Overtly Probabilistic Evidence and Methods." *Cornell Law Review* 75(1990): 247–79.

Lieberman, Joel D., and Daniel A. Krauss, "The Effects of Labeling, Expert Testimony, and Information Processing Mode on Juror Decisions in SVP Civil Commitment Trials." *Journal of Investigative Psychology and Offender Profiling* 6(2009): 25–41.

Linhorst, D.M., "The Impact of System Design on the Characteristics of Missouri's Insanity Acquittees." *Journal of the American Academy of Psychiatry and Law* 25(1997): 509–29.

Louden, Jennifer E., and Jennifer L. Skeem, "Constructing Insanity: Jurors' Prototypes, Attitudes, and Legal Decision-Making." *Behavioral Sciences and Law* 25(2007): 449–70.

Maryns, Katrijn, "The Interdiscursive Construction of Irresponsibility as a Defence Strategy In The Belgian Assize Court." *Language & Communication* 36(2014): 25–36.

McGinley, Hugh, and George Blau, "The Success of the Insanity Plea: A Survey of Attorneys." Presented at the biannual meeting of the American Psychology-Law Society, March 1986.

Moore, Ronald L., "Learning about Forensics: What You Don't Know Can Hurt You, and Your Client." In *Utilizing Forensic Science in Criminal Cases* (Eagen, MN: Thompson Reuters/Aspatore, 2012), 49–70.

Morse, Stephen, "Excusing the Crazy: The Insanity Defense Reconsidered." *Southern California Law Review* 58(1985): 777–836.

Nairn, Raymond, John H. Coverdale, and Donna Claasen, "What Is the Role of Intertextuality in Media Depictions of Mental Illness? Implications for Forensic Psychiatry." *Psychiatry, Psychology and Law* 13(2006): 243–50.

National Commission on the Insanity Defense, *Myths & Realities: A Report of the National Commission on the Insanity Defense.* Arlington, VA: National Mental Health Association, 1983.

Nevins-Saunders, Elizabeth, "Not Guilty As Charged: The Myth of Mens Rea for Defendants with Mental Retardation." *University of California Davis Law Review* 45(2012): 1419–86.

Packer, Ira K., "Insanity Acquittals in Michigan 1969–1983: The Effects of Legislative and Judicial Changes." *Journal of Psychiatry and Law* 13(1985): 419–34.

Pasewark, Richard A., and Paul L. Craig, "Insanity Plea: Defense Attorneys' Views." *Journal of Psychiatry and Law* 8(1980): 413–42.

Pasewark, Richard A., and Hugh McGinley, "Insanity Plea: National Survey of Frequency and Success." *Journal of Psychiatry and Law* 13(1985): 101–08.

Pasewark, Richard A., and Mark L. Pantle, "Insanity Plea: Legislators' View." *American Journal of Psychiatry* 136(1979): 222–23.

Pasewark, Richard A., Mark L. Pantle, and Henry J. Steadman, "The Insanity Plea in New York State, 1965–1976." *New York State Bar Journal* 51(1979): 186–225.

Pasewark, Richard A., and Deborah Seidenzahl, "Opinions Concerning the Insanity Plea and Criminality among Mental Patients." *Bulletin of the American Academy of Psychiatry and Law* 7(1979): 199–202.

Perlin, Michael L., "After Hinckley: Old Myths, New Realities, and the Future of the Insanity Defense." *Directions in Psychiatry* (Watherleigh Co.), vol. 5 (1985), Lesson 22.

Perlin, Michael L., "'And I See Through Your Brain': Access to Experts, Competency to Consent, and the Impact of Antipsychotic Medications in Neuroimaging Cases in the Criminal Trial Process." *Stanford Technology Law Review* (2009): 4–*48. Available at journals.law.stanford.edu/sites/default/files/stanford-technology-law-review/online/perlin-and-i-see.pdf.

Perlin, Michael L., "'And My Best Friend, My Doctor, Won't Even Say What It Is I've Got': The Role and Significance of Counsel in Right to Refuse Treatment Cases." *San Diego Law Review* 42(2005): 735–55.

Perlin, Michael L., "Are Courts Competent to Decide Questions of Competency? Stripping the Facade from *United States v. Charters*." *University of Kansas Law Review* 38(1990): 957–1001.

Perlin, Michael L., "'The Borderline Which Separated You from Me': The Insanity Defense, the Authoritarian Spirit, the Fear of Faking, and the Culture of Punishment." *Iowa Law Review* 82(1997): 1375–1426.

Perlin, Michael L., "'Everybody Is Making Love/Or Else Expecting Rain': Considering the Sexual Autonomy Rights of Persons Institutionalized Because of Mental Disability in Forensic Hospitals and in Asia." *Washington Law Review* 83(2008): 481–512.

Perlin, Michael L., "Fatal Assumption: A Critical Evaluation of the Role of Counsel in Mental Disability Cases." *Law and Human Behavior* 16(1992): 39–59.

Perlin, Michael L., "'God Said to Abraham/Kill Me a Son': Why the Insanity Defense and the Incompetency Status Are Compatible with and Required by the Convention on the Rights of Persons with Disabilities and Basic Principles of Therapeutic Jurisprudence." Working paper (2015), available at http://papers.ssrn.com/sol3/papers.cfm?abstract_id=2683480.

Perlin, Michael L., "'Half-Wracked Prejudice Leaped Forth': Sanism, Pretextuality, and Why and How Mental Disability Law Developed As It Did." *Journal of Contemporary Legal Issues* 10(1999): 3–36.

Perlin, Michael L., *The Hidden Prejudice: Mental Disability on Trial*. Washington, DC: American Psychological Association, 2000.

Perlin, Michael L., "'His Brain Has Been Mismanaged with Great Skill': How Will Jurors Respond to Neuroimaging Testimony in Insanity Defense Cases?" *Akron Law Review* 42(2009): 885–916.

Perlin, Michael L., *The Jurisprudence of the Insanity Defense*. Durham, NC: Carolina Academic Press, 1993.

Perlin, Michael L., "A Law of Healing." *University of Cincinnati Law Review* 68(2000): 407–33.

Perlin, Michael L., *Mental Disability and the Death Penalty: The Shame of the States*. Lanham, MD: Rowman & Littlefield, 2013.

Perlin, Michael L., "Psychodynamics and the Insanity Defense: Ordinary Common Sense and Heuristic Reasoning." *Nebraska Law Review* 69(1990): 3–70.

Perlin, Michael L., "The Supreme Court, the Mentally Disabled Criminal Defendant, and Symbolic Values: Random Decisions, Hidden Rationales, or "Doctrinal Abyss"?" *Arizona Law Review* 29(1987): 1–98.

Perlin, Michael L., "Unpacking the Myths: The Symbolism Mythology of Insanity Defense Jurisprudence." *Case Western Reserve Law Review* 40(1989–90): 599–731.

Perlin, Michael L., "'Where the Winds Hit Heavy on the Borderline': Mental Disability Law, Theory and Practice, 'Us' and 'Them.'" *Loyola of Los Angeles Law Review* 31(1998): 775–93.

Perlin, Michael L., "Whose Plea Is It Anyway? Insanity Defense Myths and Realities." *Philadelphia Medicine* 79(1983): 5–10.

Perlin, Michael L., "'Wisdom Is Thrown into Jail': Using Therapeutic Jurisprudence to Remediate the Criminalization of Persons with Mental Illness." *Michigan State University Journal of Medicine and Law* 17(2013): 343–71.

Perlin, Michael L., and Heather Ellis Cucolo, *Mental Disability Law: Civil and Criminal*, 3rd ed. Lexis Law Publishing, 2016.

Perlin, Michael L., and Alison J. Lynch, "'Had to be Held down by Big Police': A Therapeutic Jurisprudence Perspective on Interactions between Police and Persons with Mental Disabilities." *Fordham Urban Law Journal* 42(2016), in press.

Petrila, John, "The Insanity Defense and Other Mental Health Dispositions in Missouri." *International Journal of Law and Psychiatry* 5(1982): 81–101.

Pogrebin, Mark, Robert Regoli, and Ken Perry, "Not Guilty By Reason of Insanity: A Research Note." *International Journal of Law and Psychiatry* 8(1986): 237–41.

Ray, Isaac, *A Treatise on the Medical Jurisprudence of Insanity.* Ed. Winfred Overholser. Cambridge, MA: Belknap Press, 1962.

Rice, Marnie E., Grant T. Harris, Carol Lang, and Valerie Bell, "Recidivism among Male Insanity Acquittees." *Journal of Psychiatry and Law* 18(1990): 379–403.

Roberts, Caton F., and Stephen J. Golding, "The Social Construction of Criminal Responsibility and Insanity." *Law and Human Behavior* 15(1991): 349–76.

Rodriguez, Joseph, Laura LeWinn, and Michael L. Perlin, "The Insanity Defense Under Siege: Legislative Assaults and Legal Rejoinders." *Rutgers Law Journal* 14(1983): 397–430.

Rogers, Jeffrey L., Joseph D. Bloom, and Spero M. Manson, "Insanity Defense: Contested or Conceded?" *American Journal of Psychiatry* 141(1984): 885–88.

Rogers, Jeffrey L., William H. Sack, Joseph D. Bloom, and Spero M. Manson, "Women in Oregon's Insanity Defense System." *Journal of Psychiatry and Law* 11(1983): 515–32.

Rogers, Richard, R. Edward Turner, Randa Helfield, and Susan E. Dickens, "Forensic Psychiatrists' and Psychologists' Understanding of Insanity: Misguided Expertise?" *Canadian Journal of Psychiatry* 33(1988): 691–95.

Rosenhan, David L., "Psychological Realities and Judicial Policy." *Stanford Lawyer* 19(1984): 10–15, 57.

Saks, Michael J., and Robert F. Kidd, "Human Information Processing and Adjudication: Trial by Heuristics." *Law and Society Review* 15(1980–81): 123–60.

Schaefer, Michele N., and Joseph D. Bloom, "The Use of the Insanity Defense as a Jail Diversion Mechanism for Mentally Ill Persons Charged with Misdemeanors." *Journal of the American Academy of Psychiatry and Law* 33(2005): 79–84.

Schauer, Frederick, "Do Cases Make Bad Law?" *University of Chicago Law Review* 73(2006): 883–918.

Shannon, Brian D., "The Time Is Right to Revise the Texas Insanity Defense: An Essay." *Texas Tech Law Review* (2006): 67–100.

Silver, Eric, Carmen Cirincione, and Henry J. Steadman, "Demythologizing Inaccurate Perceptions of the Insanity Defense." *Law and Human Behavior* 18(1994): 63–70.

Silver, Stuart B., Marcia I. Cohen, and Michael K. Spodak, "Follow-Up after Release of Insanity Acquittees, Mentally Disordered Offenders, and Convicted Felons." *Bulletin of the American Academy of Psychiatry and Law* 17(1989): 387–400.

Singer, Anne C., "Insanity Acquittal in the Seventies: Observations and Empirical Analysis of One Jurisdiction." *Mental Disability Law Reporter* 2(1977): 406–17.

Skeem, Jennifer L., and Stephen Golding, "Describing Jurors' Personal Conceptions of Insanity and Their Relationship to Case Judgment." *Psychology, Public Policy, and Law* 7(2001): 561–621.

Skeem, Jennifer L., Jennifer Eno Louden, and Jennee Evans, "Venirepersons's Attitudes toward the Insanity Defense: Developing, Refining, and Validating a Scale." *Law and Human Behavior* 28(2004): 623–48.

Steadman, Henry J., "Empirical Research on the Insanity Defense." *Annals of the American Academy of Political and Social Science* 477(1985): 58–71.

Steadman, Henry J., "Mental Health Law and the Criminal Offender: Research Directions for the 1990's." *Rutgers Law Review* 39(1987): 323–37.

Steadman, Henry J., et al., *Before and After Hinckley: Evaluating Insanity Defense Reform*. New York: Guilford, 1993.

Steadman, Henry J., "Predicting Dangerousness among the Mentally Ill: Art, Magic and Science." *International Journal and Law and Psychiatry* 6(1983): 381–90.

Steadman, Henry J., and Joseph J. Cocozza, "Selective Reporting and the Public's Misconceptions of the Criminally Insane." *Public Opinion Quarterly* 41(1977): 523–33.

Steadman, Henry J., L. Keitner, J. Braff, and T.M. Arvantes, "Factors Associated with a Successful Insanity Plea." *American Journal of Psychiatry* 140(1983): 401–05.

Studebaker, Christina A., "Book Review: Evaluating the Insanity Defense: Identifying Empirical and Moral Questions." *University of Chicago Law School Roundtable* 5(1998): 345–51.

Tanford, J. Alexander, and Sarah Tanford, "Better Trials through Science: A Defense of Psychologist-Lawyer Collaboration." *North Carolina Law Review* 66(1988): 741–80.

Tygart, Clarence E., "Public Acceptance/Rejection of Insanity—Mental Illness Legal Defenses for Defendants in Criminal Homicide Cases." *Journal of Psychiatry and Law* 20(1992): 375–89.

Vitro, Sherin S., "Promoting Therapeutic Objectives Through LB 518: A Sane Amendment to Nebraska Law Governing the Disposition of Insanity Acquittees." *Nebraska Law Review* 72(1993): 837–59.

Warren, Janet I., W. Lawrence Fitch, Park E. Dietz, and Barry D. Rosenfeld, "Criminal Offense, Psychiatric Diagnosis, and Psycholegal Opinion: An Analysis of 894 Pretrial Referrals." *Bulletin of the American Academy of Psychiatry and Law* 19(1991): 63–69.

Wexler, David B., "Practicing Therapeutic Jurisprudence: Psycholegal Soft Spots and Strategies." In *Practicing Therapeutic Jurisprudence: Law as a Helping Profession*, ed. Dennis P. Stolle, David B. Wexler, and Bruce J. Winick (Durham, NC: Carolina Academic Press, 2000).

Wexler, David B., "Therapeutic Jurisprudence and Changing Conceptions of Legal Scholarship." *Behavioral Sciences and the Law* 11(2006): 17–29.

Wexler, David, "Applying the Law Therapeutically." *Applied and Preventive Psychology* 5(1996): 179–86.

Winick, Bruce J., "Foreword: Therapeutic Jurisprudence Perspectives on Dealing with Victims of Crime." *Nova Law Review* 33(2009): 535–43.

Winick, Bruce J., "Overcoming Psychological Barriers to Settlement: Challenges for the TJ Lawyer." In *The Affective Assistance of Counsel: Practicing Law as a Healing Profession*, ed. Marjorie A. Silver (Durham, NC: Carolina Academic Press, 2007).

Winick, Bruce J., and David B. Wexler, "The Use of Therapeutic Jurisprudence in Law School Clinical Education: Transforming the Criminal Law Clinic." *Clinical Law Review* 13(2006): 605–32.

CHAPTER TWO

The Temporary Insanity Defense

Russell D. Covey

The temporary insanity defense has a prominent place in the mythology of criminal law.[1] Because it seems to permit factually guilty defendants to escape both punishment and institutionalization, some imagine it as the "perfect defense." In fact, the defense has been invoked in a dizzying variety of contexts and, at times, has proven highly successful. Successful or not, the temporary insanity defense has always been accompanied by a storm of controversy, in part because it is often most successful in cases where the defendant's basic claim is that honor, revenge, or tragic circumstance—not mental illness in its more prosaic forms—compelled the criminal act.

Although the temporary insanity defense continues to be regularly invoked, it is far less robust than it once was, largely because the law governing the insanity defense has coalesced around a psycho-medical model of insanity predicated upon the existence of a clinical, diagnosable mental disease or defect.[2] Temporary insanity claims, like insanity claims in general that lack this psycho-medical foundation, rarely reach the jury. While courts have struggled to draw reliable parameters around this concept, by holding temporary insanity claims to the same psycho-medical threshold as conventional insanity claims, courts have largely rejected attempts to establish temporary insanity as a distinct type of affirmative defense arising from causes or conditions that would not otherwise suffice.

Moreover, in a sense, all insanity claims are a species of temporary insanity. Because only legally competent defendants may stand trial (or enter valid pleas), the only type of insanity claim a defendant logically can assert is that he or she was legally insane at the time the crime was committed but not insane at present.[3] Of course, the legal standards defining competence to stand trial and those defining legal insanity are not identical. One might be presently insane and yet competent to stand trial although common sense suggests that such defendants will be atypical. Still, given the requirement of legal competence, the conceptual distinction between insanity and temporary insanity is quite thin. The principal difference lies in the consequences of success. A verdict of not guilty by reason of (conventional) insanity invariably leads to institutionalization. A finding of temporary insanity does not. Even here, however, the distinction between the two defenses has tended to shrink as jurisdictions mandate minimum observational periods for persons acquitted on all mental capacity grounds.

Still, the strange history and popular fascination of the temporary insanity defense shows how deeply the defense resonates with popular ideas about criminal justice. That resonance is strengthened by those rare—and usually highly publicized—cases in which a temporary insanity defense seems to provide the complete exoneration of an "obviously guilty" defendant. Indeed, a sampling of the temporary insanity defense's history provides a virtual zoology of exotic and controversial criminal law cases. Defendants have asserted successful temporary insanity defenses involving infanticide, battered spouses, homosexual panic killings, black rage, pre-menstrual syndrome and menstruation-related dysfunctions such as "congestive dysmenorrhoea," post-partum psychosis, the cultural defense, mercy killings, war atrocities, deific decrees, so-called honor killings, junk-food overdoses, and adverse reactions to psychotropic medications, to name only some. Many more exotic defenses predicated on temporary insanity have been tried unsuccessfully.

Because the temporary insanity defense permits juries to resolve difficult cases in a manner consistent with the deep purposes of the criminal law, it is misleading to conceptualize that defense as a nullification doctrine, as have many of its critics. Temporary insanity rather should be viewed as an equitable defense that provides relief where the traditional legal doctrines exclude or are inadequate to the defendant's particular circumstances.

1 The Myth and the Reality of the Perfect Defense

Currently, the temporary insanity defense is a recognized, viable defense in some 44 states.[4] Two states—Colorado and Arizona—bar defendants from asserting temporary insanity as a defense. Colorado courts have interpreted their state statutes to preclude insanity claims based on "mental disease or defect" that are "temporary in nature."[5] Arizona similarly modified its insanity defense to exclude any "momentary, temporary conditions arising under the pressure of the circumstances" as well as "depravity or passion growing out of anger" in a person who "does not suffer from a mental disease or defect."[6] Four more states—Idaho, Kansas, Montana, and Utah—do not recognize insanity as a defense at all. The defense appears to be cognizable in the other states, as well as in the District of Columbia, although some states have placed across-the-board limits on the insanity defense, making temporary insanity claims harder to raise. For instance, California has narrowed access to the temporary insanity defense by requiring that it result from "an organic mental disease or defect" in order to constitute an excuse.[7]

Films and television shows—indeed, productions in a variety of media—have helped construct the myth of temporary insanity as the perfect defense by depicting criminal defendants "getting off" despite their clear factual guilt.[8] After all, if successful, a temporary insanity defense frees the defendant not only from criminal punishment for wrongdoing but also—because the excusing conditions causing irresponsibility were temporary—from any mandatory civil institutionalization. Typically, popular media productions construct an image of temporary insanity as a kind of wild-card defense or an outright sham. Hollywood has also invoked this image in more sinister ways to show dangerous, clearly guilty defendants escaping justice through temporary insanity pleas.

Contrary to popular belief, however, juries rarely acquit based on temporary insanity. Studies suggest that the insanity defense is raised in only a small number of cases, and that when it is raised, in about three out of four cases it fails.[9] In addition, defendants acquitted on grounds of temporary insanity do not always walk out of the courtroom free. Some defendants are institutionalized for extended periods of time.[10] Some states require that temporary insanity acquittees spend a minimum period of time in a mental institution for observation and treatment. Arizona, for example, now mandates a minimum observational period of four months.[11] If some courts treated temporary insanity as a special plea during prior periods,[12] the claim no longer possesses much of a distinct character. Like conventional insanity claims, virtually every jurisdiction that permits the defense requires temporary insanity claims to comport with the jurisdiction's general test for criminal responsibility. In jurisdictions that follow the *M'Naghten* test, for example, a defendant pleading temporary insanity must, like any insanity pleader, establish that, at the time of the crime, she was unable to understand the nature and quality of her acts or their wrongfulness.[13] In addition, she must establish that the disabling condition was caused by a "disease of the mind."[14] Occasionally, legal implications do flow from the decision to plead temporary rather than permanent insanity. In Florida, for instance, evidence that a defendant was insane prior to committing a crime creates a presumption that the defendant was insane at the time of the crime, which the state has the burden to overcome.[15] A defendant who pleads temporary insanity, however, is not entitled to such presumption and must carry his burden to establish insanity at the time of the crime. Normally, however, a temporary insanity plea is treated indistinguishably from a general plea of insanity. Even more so than with the general insanity defense, the criteria for determining whether an individual's alleged cognitive or volitional dysfunction was the product of a "diseased mind"—and indeed, what such a thing is—lies at the heart of the controversy and confusion surrounding the temporary insanity defense.

Every formulation of the legal test for the insanity defense, temporary or otherwise, requires evidence that the defendant's mental dysfunction was caused by a diseased mind.[16] Typically, an insanity defense will not succeed unless the defendant can proffer convincing evidence that the defendant suffered from a psychosis or mental retardation.[17] More broadly, many jurisdictions preclude assertion of the defense unless there is evidence of a "known diagnosable mental disorder."[18] Although the legal test of insanity requires proof of mental disease or defect, few jurisdictions have defined the term. Substantial confusion thus remains as to how to identify an impairment of the mind or even whether such an impairment refers to a neurological, psychological, or cognitive characteristic of the individual. As one writer long ago stated, outside of the "central core of the concept," what constitutes mental disease depends wholly on the "philosophy" of the expert.[19] As a result, a diseased mind is often simply inferred from the cognitive or volitional incapacities of the individual, leading courts to conclude that a diseased mind is any condition that prevents a defendant from knowing or appreciating the nature of his or her circumstances or from distinguishing right from wrong. As criminal law Professor Wayne LaFave has complained, "[I]t would seem that any mental abnormality, be it psychosis, neurosis, organic brain disorder, or congenital intellectual deficiency . . . will suffice *if* it has caused the consequences described in the second part of the test."[20] Temporary insanity cases are especially problematic in this sense, given that almost by definition, a temporary insanity pleader is usually not claiming to suffer from a major or well-recognized cognitive disorder. As a result, temporary insanity cases frequently give rise to hard philosophical questions about the nature of criminal responsibility, an individual's responsibility for his or her emotions, and the nature of mind itself.

Largely to limit overuse of the insanity defense, courts and lawmakers began at the start of the 20th century to demand medical evidence as a prerequisite to any insanity defense. This movement to "medicalize" the insanity defense has been met by efforts to expand or creatively redefine the scope of mental disease. Not only do major mental illnesses such as psychosis and schizophrenia satisfy the diseased mind requirement, but so also do a vast array of syndromes, conditions, and hazily defined diagnoses of disassociation, trauma, and emotional crisis that are difficult, if not impossible, for lay jurors to evaluate. Such diagnoses may include well-recognized trauma syndromes, such as post-traumatic-stress-disorder (PTSD) and battered women's syndrome (BWS), as well as more exotic syndromes such as "postconcussion syndrome," "low serotonin syndrome," organic personality syndrome, psychological decompensation, and a variety of controversial psycho-medical claims, such as hypoglycemia-induced insanity resulting from sugar overdose.

The diseased mind requirement has made the proffer of expert testimony in temporary insanity cases essential, even (and perhaps especially) where the primary claim is that external stimuli triggered or caused the defendant's temporary breakdown. This fact prompted some critics of the defense to complain that "what differentiates a crime due to temporary insanity from the so-called crimes of passion is chiefly the financial standing of the defendant" and the persuasiveness and creativity of the expert.[21] In sum, the requirement continues to shape the form in which the temporary insanity defense is proffered, but because of the lack of consensus regarding what constitutes a mental disease, and because of the relative ease with which situational stressors can be characterized as mere catalysts of mental dysfunction, it arguably does little to bar criminal defendants with the means to hire expert witnesses from presenting a temporary insanity defense to a jury.

2 Conceptions of Temporary Insanity

There is little consensus about what it means to be "temporarily insane." Sometimes, temporary insanity has been understood to signify little more than a momentary lapse of sanity at the time of a crime. At other times, temporary insanity means that the cause of a defendant's inability to understand or conform her conduct to the law was something other than mental disease or defect, the traditional requirements to establish insanity.[22] Frequently, a case is styled as temporary insanity where the alleged cause of the defendant's loss of control is extreme anger, rage, or jealousy.[23] This understanding of temporary insanity has also been frequently borrowed by Hollywood and frequently criticized as a corruption or misapplication of the traditional heat of passion defense. Courts have used strong language to condemn the defense so understood, describing it, as one California court did, as "always used as a pretext by weak-minded jurors, unmindful of their oaths, to render a verdict of acquittal in cases where guilt has been incurred."[24]

At still other times, temporary insanity has been understood as a synonym for irresistible impulse (or "insane impulse"),[25] particularly where the allegedly irresistible impulse was the product of strong emotion.[26] Such a theory was illustrated in the 1959 film *Anatomy of a Murder*. Fyodor Dostoevsky, author of *Crime and Punishment*, also had this understanding when he described temporary insanity as a "darkening" or "clouding" of the mind.[27] In such instances, courts' receptivity to the defense has usually turned on whether the jurisdiction's insanity defense permits claims of irresistible impulse. Because many jurisdictions continue to permit an insanity defense based on a claim of impaired volitional control, temporary insanity continues to be understood in some jurisdictions at least in part as a volitional defect.[28]

Although what it means to be temporarily insane has varied considerably among courts, the temporary insanity defense itself is a venerable one, readily found in the writings of the classic common law authorities. According to Edward Coke, the *non compos mentis* fell into four camps: 1) idiots, i.e., those born with mental defect; 2) those who "by sicknesse, griefe, or other accident wholly loseth [their] memorie and understanding"; 3) lunatics, i.e, those whose understanding comes and goes; and 4) persons who are intoxicated.[29] Of these categories, only the first is incompatible with a claim that the mental affliction was temporary in kind, while irresponsibility due to intoxication directly contemplates it. While Coke rejected temporary insanity as a defense in cases of voluntary intoxication, his understanding of "lunacy" quite clearly accommodates an insanity claim in cases where the dysfunction is temporary, while nothing in his description of the *non compos mentis* precludes the defense from being raised based on durational concerns. Still, he was quite clear that only where the particular dementia causes "a total alienation of the mind or perfect madness," should it provide a valid defense.[30] Where such total alienation of mind accompanies the commission of a crime, however, no matter how brief its duration, Coke asserted that a defense should be available, for "the person that is absolutely mad for a day, killing a man in that distemper, is equally not guilty, as if he were mad without intermission."[31] "On the other hand, a lunatic who commits crimes during lucid intervals is subject to liability as if he had no such insanity."[32] Like the other classic common law writers, including Henry de Bracton and Sir Matthew Hale, Coke strongly insisted that for a lunatic to prevail on an insanity defense, "he must prove that at the time of the act he was *furiosus*—totally insane."[33]

Like Coke, Hale distinguished idiocy—that is, congenital mental defect—from what he referred to as *dementia accidentalis vel adventitia*—that is, dementia arising from causes varying from "distemper of the humours of the body, as deep melancholy or adjust choler; sometimes from the violence of a disease, as a fever or palsy; sometimes from a concussion or hurt of the brain."[34] Such conditions, Hale noted, frequently disrupt rationality by causing, for instance, "excessive fears and griefs," and should not excuse crime in most cases because "doubtless most persons, that are felons of themselves, and others are under a degree of partial insanity."[35] Notwithstanding the advances of psychiatry, neurology, and medicine in the intervening years, thinking about the legal status of temporary insanity in the centuries since has brought only relatively minor changes, and the categories identified by Coke and Hale—hereditary or acquired mental illness (madness) or mental retardation (idiocy), emotional upset (melancholy and choler), recurrent or cycling mental conditions (lunacy), and intoxication—continue to substantially exhaust the main types of temporary insanity claims that tend to be brought.

2.1 Episodic Insanity

To the classic common law writers, "lunacy was a form of temporary insanity, which derived its name from the popular belief that it was caused by the phases of the moon."[36] Lunatics were thought to have a valid basis to assert an irresponsibility defense as long as their claims met certain criteria. Although today it is more common to speak of mental illnesses that "cycle," such as bipolar disorder, or that manifest periods of "remission," such episodic or transitory dementia described by Coke and Hale continues to provide a valid basis for an insanity defense.

After surveying the cases, leading 20th-century insanity defense authority Abraham Goldstein concluded that temporary insanity was a defense only where it resulted, as with the classic notion of lunacy, from a permanent condition marked by lucid intervals and where the defendant could carry his burden of proof that the crime was not committed during a period of lucidity.[37] Goldstein cited epilepsy as a paradigmatic example of a recurrent mental disease that rendered persons legally insane during an episode but perfectly lucid, and hence criminally responsible, otherwise.[38] Assuming that the defendant can establish the authenticity of the diagnosis, such conditions provide a relatively uncontroversial basis for an insanity claim.[39] Indeed, insanity caused by such a condition is arguably not even truly "temporary" in that even during lucid periods the underlying condition still exists in a latent state.[40]

Episodic mental dysfunction caused by more ephemeral conditions, however, can be more problematic. The common law writers accepted that physical hardships might trigger a bout of temporary insanity. Hale, for instance, approvingly cited the acquittal of a married woman of good reputation who shortly after childbirth, killed her newborn baby in a "phrenzy" apparently brought about by an extended labor and lack of sleep. The jury was instructed that "if they found her under a phrenzy, tho by reason of her late delivery and want of sleep, they should acquit her," which, finding no evidence that she had feigned her condition, it did.[41] Female lunacy has frequently been attributed to childbearing and more controversially to the hormonal fluctuations caused by female biology. "Suppression of the menses" or "congestive dysmenorrhoea" was commonly thought to cause women to become temporarily insane and was successfully utilized as the basis of a temporary insanity defense in numerous cases.[42] In addition, temporary insanity defenses have succeeded based on such scientifically questionable diagnoses as "puerperal mania," "lactational insanity," "transitoria mania," "ephemeral mania," and "morbid impulse."[43] Such theories, which generally reflected lay assumptions about human psychology more than proven psychiatric knowledge, have attempted to identify a biologically identifiable dysfunction in order to excuse female aggression or criminality under sympathetic circumstances.[44]

Courts routinely permit juries to consider temporary insanity that arises from such transitory causes as a blow to the head or body or a lightning strike.[45] Even major mental psychoses can "wax and wane," such that they render a defendant insane for only a short duration.[46]

2.2 Irresistible Impulse

Courts, commentators, and screenwriters occasionally have treated temporary insanity as a synonym for "irresistible impulse," generally defined as the "impairment of the power of volition, resulting from mental disease."[47] In *Anatomy of a Murder*, the defendant's temporary insanity defense was alleged to consist of an "irresistible impulse" springing from a "dissociative reaction." Lorena Bobbitt's defense likewise was predicated on the notion that "she cut off her husband's penis because of an 'irresistible impulse' born of temporary insanity."[48] In such cases the temporary insanity defense has absorbed the skepticism that surrounds the controversial irresistible impulse doctrine.

The irresistible impulse doctrine was formulated as a supplement to the *M'Naghten* test by those critical of its exclusive focus on cognitive understanding of the wrongfulness of one's criminal conduct. Although a significant minority of jurisdictions has adopted it at one time or another, it has never won support in the majority of U.S. courts.[49] The concept of irresistible impulse came under heavy criticism by the middle of the 20th century. In its influential report released in 1954, the British Royal Commission described it as "largely discredited" and "inherently inadequate and unsatisfactory."[50] Although few states continue to recognize irresistible impulse expressly as a defense, the American Law Institute (ALI) insanity test includes a volitional component and is currently utilized by a significant minority of the states.[51]

Ultimately, whether lack of volitional control should render criminal conduct irresponsible is a matter of the breadth of a jurisdiction's insanity defense. In theory, just as a person might be temporarily unable to distinguish between right and wrong, a person might be temporarily unable to exercise volitional control, making clear that the occasional tendency to treat irresistible impulse and temporary insanity as synonymous is in error.

2.3 Emotional Insanity

Authorities like Coke and Hale did not believe that strong passions provided an appropriate basis for a temporary insanity defense.[52] Despite that fact, emotional insanity claims flourished for a time during the 19th century. Temporary insanity cases involving female defendants nicely illustrate the strong ties between extreme passion and temporary insanity. Pasqualina Robertiello, for example, was charged with first-degree murder after she shot and killed her betrothed, Nicolo Pierro, in front of two eyewitnesses.[53] Trial testimony established that after seducing, ravishing, and impregnating Pasqualina, Nicolo "grew weary of the girl" and abandoned her. Pasqualina argued that she "suffered from temporary insanity precipitated by her agonizing circumstances."[54] Popular sentiment throughout the trial was strongly in favor of Pasqualina. One contemporary commentator opined that Pasqualina "*should* have killed the man" as the killing, though technically murder, was sanctioned "according to the broad tenets of that high law by which communities are guided and nations governed."[55]

As a basis for a temporary insanity defense, emotional insanity eventually fell out of favor. An increasing number of courts began to reject insanity pleas absent evidence—typically expert testimony—of a diagnosable mental disease or defect. An 1895 case from the District of Columbia Court of Appeals illustrated, albeit with some degree of overstatement, the growing consensus that "the theory of emotional insanity . . . has sometimes been resorted to as a defence of crime, but . . . has always and uniformly been reprobated and repudiated by the courts" and that "[t]he theory of emotional insanity is untenable under any circumstances."[56]

Although a simple claim of emotional insanity would undoubtedly fail today, defendants continue to proffer a wide variety of relatively exotic defenses that locate the cause of the defendant's insanity in an emotionally-charged situational stressor. These exotic defenses can be understood as variations on the emotional insanity theme. Women who kill abusive husbands sometimes prevail on a temporary insanity defense through reliance on evidence of battered spouse syndrome. A similar dynamic underlies the "homosexual panic defense," which is predicated on the claim that the sexual advance toward a person of the same sex with latent homosexual tendencies "precipitated the homosexual panic that triggered the acute psychotic reaction."[57] Although "the de-medicalization of homosexuality by the APA in 1973 and the declassifying of [homosexual panic] in 1980 have rendered the latency argument specious from a psychological point of view," the defense continues periodically to be raised.[58]

These various manias and panic defenses are ultimately predicated on the existence of an allegedly extreme situational stressor that triggers a strong emotional reaction as the cause of temporary insanity. In all such cases, the defendant attempts to identify extreme "agonizing circumstances" that can be blamed for causing her to become temporarily insane, thus relieving her of responsibility for her criminal acts.[59] As courts continue to permit such claims, the flat assertion that emotional insanity is not a valid basis for a temporary insanity defense would seem to be incorrect. Indeed, the continuing viability of the abuse excuse illustrates the extent to which emotion or passion remains a legally plausible basis of a temporary insanity defense.

2.4 Intoxication

Nothing is more likely to render a person temporarily out of his senses than an excess of intoxicants. According to Hale, drunkenness is a type of dementia that "doth deprive men of the use of reason, and puts many men into a perfect, but temporary phrenzy."[60] It is thus no surprise that temporary insanity cases frequently involve intoxication claims. Precisely because intoxication is such a common partner of crime, however, the criminal law has long—and virtually without exception—barred defendants from asserting an insanity excuse under circumstances in which the defendant voluntarily consumed the intoxicants. Since Hale's time the argument that those who commit crimes while drunk should not be punished for the crime but rather merely for the drunkenness that was its cause has fallen on deaf ears.[61]

Still, temporary insanity claims involving intoxication are common. The oldest reported case in the United States mentioning the temporary insanity defense, in fact, concerned a defendant who suffered from "mania a potu."[62] As Delaware's Court of Oyer and Terminer recognized in that case, where the use of intoxicants triggers, but is not the cause of, some other underlying physiological or psychological condition, an insanity defense is available notwithstanding the general bar in cases of voluntary intoxication.[63] A withdrawal reaction—such as delirium tremens—provides one example. Similarly, where the intoxicants trigger a pre-existing mental illness, a temporary insanity defense will usually be permitted notwithstanding that the resulting mental state was caused by the use of intoxicants.

In addition, under the "settled insanity" doctrine, insanity that results from habitual or extended use of intoxicants, even if the use of the intoxicants was voluntary, can be a defense if the effects of the extended use of the intoxicants have caused either temporary or permanent mental or physical damage to the defendant.[64] In such cases, "[t]he *plea of insanity avails* the party," just as with any other reason-inhibiting disease or condition, as long as the defendant can establish the necessary elements of the insanity defense—that is, that he did "not know at the time he committed the act, that he was doing an immoral and unlawful act."[65] To assert a settled insanity claim, the defendant must establish that the triggering cause was the underlying condition brought about by extended use of intoxicants, and not the effects of the intoxicant, when the crime was committed.[66] Such a triggering effect was claimed in *People v. Gross*, where the defendant's experts attributed his psychotic disorder in whole or part to amphetamine or cocaine abuse.[67] The California Supreme Court reached a similar finding in overturning the conviction of Valerie Kelly, who, after taking mescaline and LSD some 50 to 100 times over a two-month period, stabbed her mother with an assortment of kitchen knives.[68] Trial testimony established that Kelly was not acting simply as a person who, after ingesting drugs or alcohol, was unable to perceive reality and reason properly. Rather, the drug abuse was deemed the indirect cause of a legitimate, temporary psychosis that would remain even when the defendant was temporarily off drugs.

Temporary insanity claims predicated on intoxication succeed more frequently where the intoxication was involuntary or pathological. For example, defendants have found some success in cases in which the temporary insanity allegedly resulted from the use of Prozac, Halcion, or other selective serotonin reuptake inhibitors (SSRIs).[69] Such claims have been permitted, notwithstanding that the drugs were consumed voluntarily, on grounds that the resulting psychological reaction was unanticipated and thus "pathological" in nature.[70] In these cases, courts quite readily concede that the effects of intoxication are often indistinguishable from other disabling causes of cognitive dysfunction.

Inadvertent consumption of or exposure to other types of chemicals has also been recognized as a valid basis for a temporary insanity defense. In one case, a defendant contended that "an acetylcholinesterase inhibitor, which was concentrated in the lawn care product, acted upon his nervous system to profoundly affect his ability to control his temper," causing him to kill the victim.[71] Thus, although intoxication is not generally a defense, the line between intoxication and a valid temporary insanity defense is not always clear.

3 Square Pegs and Round Holes

A review of the historical uses to which the temporary insanity defense has been put suggests that the defense tends to find favor in a particular set of circumstances. Temporary insanity pleas recur in contexts in which the law applied literally or formalistically leads to results that diverge from jurors' intuitive, or commonsense, assessments of culpability. The most notable cases where this happens are those in which the law's own contradictions are starkly displayed.

This section makes three main claims about the defense. First, I argue that temporary insanity is a gap-filling doctrine that is usually invoked to supplement another criminal defense that on its own falls short. Second, I argue that the defense tends to succeed only where there is a perceived divergence between the legal and equitable application of those defenses. Third, the temporary insanity defense is used where one or more of the basic presuppositions of the criminal law, given the particular facts of the case, is subject to challenge. What is distinctive about temporary insanity is its versatility: it can and does permit defendants in a wide variety of seemingly disparate circumstances to invoke what is, ultimately, a type of equitable defense where the criminal law's formal categories fail to fit the moral and social facts.

3.1 Temporary Insanity As an Excuse Doctrine

Criminal law theorists have long distinguished between two types of affirmative defenses: justifications and excuses. Justification defenses are claims that the defendant's acts, though apparently in conflict with the law, are in fact consonant with it. Excuses concern the blameworthiness of the actor rather than the desirability of the act. A valid excuse defense exists where circumstances establish that the defendant was not ultimately to blame for the harm or transgression at issue. In other words, justifications concern acts, and excuses concern actors.

Like the conventional insanity defense, the temporary insanity defense is most typically thought of as an excuse doctrine, and it undoubtedly functions, like the conventional insanity defense, as an excuse in the majority of cases in which it is raised. Insanity, after all, is usually cited as the paradigmatic excuse defense, and as noted previously, modern insanity law usually makes no formal distinction between temporary and non-temporary insanity claims.

3.1.1 Insanity

In its simplest form, temporary insanity is a straightforward incapacity claim, indistinguishable from insanity claims writ large. In such cases, the cause of a defendant's alleged irresponsibility stems from mental disease or defect as those terms are conventionally understood. Be it chronic mental illness characterized by periods of latency or acute mental illnesses that, for whatever reason, are not lasting in effect, some cases in which temporary insanity claims are made are entirely in conformity with the legal doctrine of insanity. These cases raise no special issues or concerns apart from those that generally bedevil the insanity defense.

As the prior discussion suggests, the classic common law writers would have treated such cases as instances of lunacy or transitory dementia. Recent examples include the case of Peter Bradley, who committed an apparently inexplicable attack on the passengers and crew of an airplane as a result of encephalitis.[72] Other examples include cases where the defendant engaged in criminal acts after failing to take prescribed antipsychotic medication, or during some forms of epileptic seizure, or while experiencing a psychotic state brought on by bipolar disorder. Because the underlying mental disease or defect seems safely "psycho-medical" in origin, the use of the temporary insanity defense in such cases raises no red flags. This is not so, however, where the claimed mental disease or defect lacks a widely-accepted psycho-medical status.

In some cases, a fit of temporary insanity appears to have been triggered by some cause other than mental disease or defect. One of the most controversial of such claims arises where the temporary insanity was allegedly caused by mistreatment or abuse.[73] Take, for example, a recent case involving a Filipino domestic helper named May Vecina who killed her

7-year-old Kuwaiti ward and wounded his siblings. According to Vecina, the attack occurred during "a fit of temporary insanity caused by the anger and depression she was feeling" after "her male employer had tried to rape her, she was starved, made to sleep on the floor, and was not paid her wages."[74] A case such as this, where the abused defendant lashes out at an innocent victim rather than her abuser, lacks any element of self-defense or provocation. Her claim is, in effect, that the abuse itself sufficiently unhinged her mind that it created, or perhaps even constituted, the mental disease or defect that the insanity defense requires. Where abuse is the supposed cause of a person's loss of control, rather than mental disease, temporary insanity diverges functionally from the conventional version of the defense. In the vast majority of cases, as will be discussed later, the temporary insanity defense's main function is to provide a doctrinal framework for claimed excuses under circumstances where the cause of the defendant's supposed lack of control can be traced to external, situational pressures rather than to some organic disease.

3.1.2 *Infanticide and Situational Pressures*

As the infamous lifeboat cannibalism cases illustrate, a wide variety of situational pressures can induce normally sane people to commit terrible crimes.[75] When those pressures are sufficiently powerful and apparent, the case for moral (and hence legal) condemnation diminishes.[76] A classic example of such situational pressures, and their complex role in assessing a defendant's blameworthiness, arises in the context of infanticide, where the temporary insanity plea has a long history. As far back as the 18th century, acquittals in infanticide cases based on temporary insanity were common.[77] The reasons women kill their infants are quite obviously varied, but some recurrent patterns appear. Those patterns—some of which echo justificatory concerns, others which sound more firmly in excuse—demonstrate the complex nature of the moral issues confronting juries in such cases.[78]

According to Lawrence Friedman, a "positive epidemic" of infanticide swept England in the 19th century.[79] The mothers were often domestic servants, extremely poor, unmarried, and as a result quite economically vulnerable. Loss of a job meant economic disaster to these women, and the prospects of surviving on the streets with a child were at best negligible. Moreover, powerful social norms regarding extramarital sex marked such women as social outcasts and deeply stigmatized their illegitimate children. Women who committed infanticide to avoid social stigmatization received mixed messages from society regarding appropriate choices. "[S]ince women who killed their illegitimate babies were conforming to society's moral standards, they were viewed as acting both 'irrationally' and 'properly.'"[80] The temporary insanity defense provided a means to reconcile those mixed messages. It provided an excuse for criminal conduct triggered by an extreme social and moral predicament, and motivated by "proper" moral sentiments.

The sense that women in these cases were as much victims as wrongdoers was and continues undoubtedly to be exaggerated by other deeply-rooted gender stereotypes. Certainly, powerful social expectations surround the mother–child bond. To most, there are few ties stronger than this bond; a mother's love for her children is assumed, taken for granted, accepted as a "natural fact."[81] So powerful is the bond assumed to be that people may, in fact, fail to perceive a clear distinction in interest between the child and its mother. While modern abortion law recognizes that a child in the womb is both part of its mother and a distinct entity, people may widely perceive that unity beyond the moment of birth even when the law does not. Thus, when a woman kills her own child, she seems in some ways to be attacking or wounding herself.[82] She is perpetrator and victim at the same time. As such, punishment may appear to be simply redundant. Where one victimizes oneself, punishment only compounds the victimization.

It may be that juries are reluctant to convict in infanticide cases where they cannot perceive a sufficient social harm, or at least one that is sufficiently distinct from the mother's own interests, to view her as the perpetrator rather than the victim. The overlap of the homicidal mother's status as both victim and wrongdoer puts her in a position similar to that of one who attempts or commits suicide, where the act almost by definition can only be committed by one not in one's right mind.[83] Idealization of motherhood also helps explain the readiness of experts to link female aggression toward offspring with mental illness, as well as the readiness of juries to find those experts credible, at least as long as the female defendant otherwise conforms to "stereotypical gender norms."[84]

In many cases where biological explanations appear dubious, childbirth has nonetheless been successfully claimed to cause a propensity to temporary derangement. As Sir James Fitzjames Stephens wrote in the 19th century, "women in that condition [having recently undergone childbirth] do get the strongest symptoms of what amounts almost to temporary madness, and . . . often hardly know what they are about, and will do things which they have no settled or deliberate intention whatever of doing."[85]

At the turn of the century, medical experts favored such diagnoses as "puerperal insanity"[86] and "lactational insanity"[87] to describe the seemingly obvious female abnormality. After all, "[i]f there is any condition of mind which can rightly be described as insane, it is that in which a mother loses all maternal instinct."[88] Experts thus reasoned backwards from the infanticidal act to infer the existence of a mental "disease" that may or may not have had any basis in biology.

Modern psychiatric science continues to recognize the potentially disruptive effects of childbirth on women's mental health. Conditions such as postpartum psychosis frequently are blamed for infanticidal conduct. In other cases, infanticidal acts are attributed to vaguer forms of mental dysfunction, as in the case of Claire Moritt, who was charged with first-degree murder after drowning her newborn son in a dormitory toilet. The jury acquitted Moritt by reason of temporary insanity, leading to Moritt's immediate release. According to newspaper accounts, at trial, "[t]en psychologists and psychiatrists testified that Ms. Moritt suffered from a rare dissociative disorder in which she detached herself from her pregnancy and was out of touch with reality when she gave birth."[89] Likewise, in many cases women with chronic mental disabilities are pushed past the breaking point by the stresses of childbirth and child rearing in the absence of adequate assistance or supervision.

The use of the temporary insanity plea in infanticide cases sometimes fits well within the long-recognized parameters of the defense. Post-partum psychosis provides an almost paradigmatic case in point, as the condition is characteristically "brief in duration and, even if untreated, symptoms virtually always disappear within several months of onset."[90] The temporary insanity plea, moreover, provides a means to seamlessly stitch together these various facts to produce a verdict that accords with the jury's sense of justice. In some cases, an infanticidal mother's break with reality will be so complete as to clearly require a verdict of not guilty because of insanity. Juries will readily perceive that such women need treatment rather than punishment. In other cases, the infanticidal conduct may appear to be the product of a complex of pressures, some situational, some psychological, some biological, and some moral. Where rational choice is clouded by such factors, juries might well find that punishment is an inappropriate, unnecessary, and cruel response. Here, the classic and often vilified image of temporary insanity is clearly at work because the defendant's "insanity" often will turn out to have been extinguished at the precise moment the criminal deed was completed—not because of any wondrous serendipity but because the act removed the situational pressures that prompted the deed.

The temporary insanity plea has been invoked in other circumstances where the pressures that caused the criminal act were allegedly situational in origin. The homosexual panic defense is one example. "Black rage," "urban psychosis," and "urban survival syndrome" are others. In all these cases, defendants attempt to convince juries that situational pressures—homosexual advances, desperation born of dire social and economic conditions in inner-cities, or the realities of life on the streets—are to blame for the defendants' criminal acts. While such claims find no traction in traditional criminal law defenses, the defendants rely on temporary insanity to provide a bridge to a viable legal claim. In each case, the theory is that some aspect of the defendant's mind—be it a latent homosexuality or a brain disfigured by urban conditioning—interacted with a specific situational pressure to cause the criminal conduct. The alleged insanity is temporary because the situation that triggered it is allegedly abnormal.

3.2 Temporary Insanity As a Justification Doctrine

In some ways, insanity and justification are directly at odds. A defendant who asserts a justification defense alleges that she was confronted with a choice of evils, and she purposely, and correctly, chose the lesser evil. Generally, a defendant who asserts an insanity defense alleges that, at the time of his criminal act, he either did not know what he was doing or he did not know what he was doing was wrong. What motivated an actor to engage in otherwise unlawful conduct matters because the defense is only available where benefiting society "is not incidental to some self-interested goal of the actor" but rather "is the underlying motivation" for the conduct.[91] Justification thus suggests praise for persons who are able to see situations clearly and exercise sound judgment under difficult circumstances. Insanity suggests tolerance or empathy for those who cannot see clearly at all.

3.2.1 Extreme Provocation and the Unwritten Law

It might seem all the more puzzling, therefore, that some of the most prominent cases in which the temporary insanity defense has succeeded involve justification-type claims. These cases tend to involve various elements of provocation, self-defense, and necessity. A good example are cases involving the so-called "unwritten law," the first, and one of the most prominent of which, was the 1859 prosecution of New York congressman Daniel Sickles for the murder of Philip Barton Key (the son of Francis Scott Key).[92] The younger Key had been carrying on a notorious affair with Sickles' wife. Ultimately, Sickles discovered the infidelity and forced his wife to confess. The following day, upon spotting Key strolling near Lafayette Square, Sickles pulled a gun from his coat and cried out, "Key, you scoundrel . . . you have dishonored my house—you must die."[93] Sickles then shot and killed Key. At trial, Sickles contended that the killing was the product of "an uncontrollable 'irresistible impulse.'"[94] Often cited (incorrectly, it appears) as the first use of the defense in the United States, Sickles did not deny killing his wife's lover in a duel, but claimed that his wife's infidelity caused him to become temporarily insane. The jury acquitted, largely, it appears, because it concluded that Sickles' actions were justified under the unwritten law.[95]

Under the "unwritten law"—the subject of numerous high-profile murder trials in the 19th century—a husband who discovered that his wife was involved in an adulterous affair was thought justified in killing the "libertine" and, perhaps, the adulterous wife.[96] The unwritten law was also invoked to justify killings of male seducers by fathers and brothers of their once-virtuous daughters and sisters, and in a smaller number of cases, killings by women seduced and abandoned by men promising marriage. In discussing the prominent unwritten law cases of the 19th century, legal historian Lawrence Friedman described the defense as a blend of provocation and temporary insanity, with the latter element functioning to elevate the defense from one that mitigated a murder to one that provided a complete excuse.[97]

Unwritten law cases followed logic similar to the common law heat of passion doctrine, which mitigates murder to manslaughter. To establish a provocation defense, the defendant must demonstrate that the killing occurred while the defendant was acting in the heat of passion; the passion must have been caused by a legally adequate provocation; the killing must have occurred before a reasonable cooling off period had elapsed; and there must have been a causal link between the provocation, the passion, and the killing. Discovering one's wife engaged in an adulterous act was considered the quintessential adequate provocation. Defendants in the unwritten law cases, however, confronted two major obstacles to proffering a provocation defense. First, as a formal doctrinal matter, "the reasonable man, however greatly provoked he may be, does not kill."[98] Even where a provocation is legally cognizable, therefore, a successful provocation defense is merely a partial excuse that results in mitigation, not exoneration. Second, in the unwritten law cases, the defendants were almost uniformly unable to establish a provocation defense given the circumstances of the killings. In none of the cases discussed in Robert Ireland's history of the defense, for example, did the defendant actually catch his wife *in flagrante delicto*, as the provocation doctrine traditionally required.[99] In many cases, a significant time elapsed between the defendant's discovery of the adulterous affair and his killing of the paramour, which, because of the extent of the cooling period, would bar a heat of passion defense as a matter of well-established law.

Nonetheless, defendants typically presented unwritten law cases to the jury functionally as provocation cases. Trial defenses invariably dwelt upon the libertine's defilement of the marital bed to establish the moral enormity of the provocation. Defendants also invariably adduced evidence that the defendant killed in a state of extreme passion. As one scholar has noted, at trial, "[m]ost of the witnesses, lay and expert, recounted observing the defendants in highly agitated conditions; wild-eyed, tearful, sometimes screaming in agony."[100] Given the circumstances of these killings, the causal nexus between the adulterous provocation, the defendants' embroiled passions, and the killings was in little doubt. In cases where a substantial period of cooling time separated the discovery of the infidelity from the homicidal act, defendants implicitly questioned the premises of the cooling doctrine. For example, when Sickles killed Key a day after learning of Key's affair with his wife, Sickles' counsel contended that "there is no cooling off after such an offence. Talk about the cooling of the provocation of defiling a man's wife! A mere personal indignity can be cooled over; but if Mr. Sickles is cool now he is more than human."[101]

Juries were, in other words, asked to understand these killings through the lens of provocation, even though provocation was technically unavailable. Temporary insanity effectively permitted them to make an "end-run around the cooling-time doctrine."[102] The frequent success of this strategy is apparent in the jury charge given in Cole's case. Immediately after informing the jury that heat of passion was legally barred as a defense because of the extent of the cooling period, the judge charged the jury that "if, notwithstanding this lapse of time, the crushing weight of this domestic tragedy had driven the prisoner's mind to absolute distraction, and dethroned the reason of the husband, he is permitted to find immunity from punishment in the mental alienation with which he was thus overwhelmed."[103]

It might also be argued that the rigidity of the cooling doctrine virtually necessitated some other defense for sympathetic defendants. This necessity is well-illustrated in *Ragland v. State*, where the defendant waited four hours before killing the victim after discovering a letter revealing that his daughter had been seduced and impregnated by a local shopkeeper.[104] According to the court, defendant "had cooling time" enough to bar a heat of passion defense as a matter of law. As a result, the jury was necessarily forced to choose between conviction for murder or acquittal on grounds of temporary insanity.

The provocation defense contains elements of both excuse and justification.[105] Temporary insanity in some cases seems to share this hybrid quality. As with provocation, there is nothing conceptually incoherent in claiming that a criminal act was both partially justified (because reasonably provoked) and grounds for excuse (because it was the product of insanity). Certainly, one could be grievously wronged by another and be so emotionally disturbed as a result that she does not know what she is doing, or even affirmatively believe that retribution is the morally appropriate response.

If the extreme provocation claim implicit in unwritten law cases mixed justification and excuse, defendants also frequently bolstered the provocation account with pure justificatory strategies based on analogies to other justification doctrines, such as self-defense and defense-of-others. The defense-of-others analogy was frequently invoked by defendants who killed the corruptors and debauchers of the women they loved in order "to protect the weaker sex."[106] Sickles did this rather creatively by likening his wife's adulterous affair to a kind of continuing rape and arguing that in killing Key, Sickles had in effect acted to prevent an imminent—indeed ongoing—felony:

> The wife's consent cannot shield the adulterer, she being incapable by law of consenting to any infraction of her husband's marital rights, and that in the absence of consent and connivance on his part every violation of the wife's chastity is, in the contemplation of law, forcible and against his will, and may be treated by him as an act of violence and force on his wife's person. . . . The husband beholds him in the very act of withdrawing his wife from his roof, from his presence, from his arm, from his wing, from his nest, meets him in that act and slays him, and we say that the right to slay him stands on the firmest principles of self-defence.[107]

And indeed, Sickles' theory was accepted as the law at least in Georgia, where the courts repeatedly held, based on a Georgia statute that permitted defendants to argue that a killing was justifiable homicide in circumstances analogous to statutorily-enumerated defenses like self-defense and defense of others, that killing to prevent an imminent act of adultery was justifiable homicide.[108]

In addition to provocation and self-defense, defendants in unwritten law cases played upon yet a third line of justification by arguing that the victims deserved to die. Of all the themes developed by defendants in the unwritten law cases, the theme of revenge was one of the most prominent and consistently pursued. Defendants pointed to the relatively lenient penalties applicable to the crimes of adultery and seduction in order to justify private vengeance, arguing that "libertines would escape punishment unless loved ones were allowed to avenge the dishonor of their fallen women."[109] Accordingly, "a husband who killed his wife's seducer committed an honorable act of 'revenge for . . . attacks upon [his] proprietary rights as a married man.' "[110] In some sense, the act of vengeance was portrayed both as necessary to prevent further harm and as the lesser evil, in that the killing of the libertine was preferable to the continued humiliation of the cuckolded husband or fallen woman. Dressler labels this justification theory "moral forfeiture," by which one whose conduct crosses some threshold of acceptability "forfeits" his or her moral claim to social concern.[111] The wrongdoer, it might be said, "no longer merits our consideration, any more than an insect or a stone does."[112] Regardless of label, the basic claim is that because the victim deserved what was coming to him, the defendant was justified in delivering it. Although it finds no footing in the formal criminal law, the notion that private vengeance is a morally acceptable response to bad acts and bad people is deeply embedded in the popular conscience. This theory, too, is reflected in Sickles argument to the jury that the libertine Key got precisely what he deserved: "It may be tragical to shed human blood; but I will always maintain that there is no tragedy about slaying the adulterer; his crime takes away the character of the occurrence."[113]

These justificatory arguments, in varying combinations, were presented frankly in the unwritten law cases and commonly understood to be the primary substantive basis of the defense. Yet they were necessarily accompanied by temporary insanity pleas, which in some cases were the sole *legal* defense actually presented to juries. To some, this made the insanity claim a legal fiction, a "pretext for an acquittal according to the forms of law."[114] Critics lambasted the temporary insanity defense as providing an easy out to juries in such cases. Regarding a case in which the defendant claimed to have killed while suffering from "transitory homicidal mania," one critic derided the defense as "invented by ingenious lawyers to afford the jury a safe bridge upon which to pass from the disagreeable technical duty to the accomplishment of their desire to acquit a murderer whose victim, according to the consensus of opinion, ought to have been killed."[115] Or, as Paul Biegler advised his client in *Anatomy of a Murder*, where the defendant acts to avenge a serious wrong to a loved one, he will have the jury's sympathy, in which case, all the defendant will "need is a legal peg which will let the jury hang up their sympathy in the defendant's behalf." Temporary insanity provides that legal peg. Time and again juries have accepted the defense in the wake of evidence of the victim's transgressions against the defendant.

3.2.2 Self-Defense and the Battered Spouse

As in the unwritten law cases, elements of at least three types of justification defenses—provocation, self-defense, and necessity—are in play when a battered woman kills her abuser. Of these, self-defense plays a particularly prominent role. The iconic case in this genre is that of Francine Hughes, whose killing of her sleeping, abusive husband was dramatized in the book and made-for-TV movie, *The Burning Bed*.[116]

Hughes endured years of wretched abuse at her husband's hands. She testified at trial to countless humiliations, beatings, and physical and psychological torture and recounted incidents in which Mickey, her husband, had come close to killing her. Thus atmospherically, at least, Francine relied heavily on a claim of self-defense. Her defense focused largely on two arguments: (1) that she reasonably believed Mickey would either kill or seriously injure her, and (2) that she, in fact, had little practical ability to escape the threat. The defense put on testimony from deputy police officers detailing past domestic incidents at the Hughes' home in which Mickey choked and beat Francine and, in the officers' presence, threatened to kill her as soon as the officers left. It also showed that, given her inability to support her family in a new location, the fact that neither police nor the legal system was effective in protecting her or her children from Mickey after past attacks, and Mickey's credible threats that he would kill her if she ever tried to leave, "retreat" was not a viable option.

The problem for Francine, as well as for other battered women who kill their sleeping spouses, is that traditional law permits lethal force to be used in self-defense only in response to imminent threats. At the least, as the Model Penal Code provides, lethal force must be "immediately necessary" to ward off a threat of death or serious bodily injury "on the present occasion."[117] For her self-defense claim to prevail, Francine was required to show that she acted in response to such an imminent threat, and that killing Mickey was necessary "then and there to fend off death or serious injury and that [she] could not have left or stepped away."[118] With Mickey asleep in the bedroom, this element of self-defense, though Francine quite plausibly might have believed it to be true, was objectively implausible. Though battered women may well reasonably fear that a violent or lethal attack is just around the corner, it is not, strictly speaking, actually imminent. As a result, battered women like Francine Hughes find their self-defense claims difficult to sustain. After all, as long as the victim is asleep he poses no immediate threat; retreat seems like a viable option, and the killing seems like a choice rather than a necessity. Francine's use of force on this particular occasion, under these circumstances, was a preemptive strike, which the law of self-defense simply does not permit.

As a general proposition, the moral argument for formally permitting the preemptive use of lethal force would seem rather thin. It seems right that the law discourages killing where less drastic measures are available to potential victims to avoid harm. But data on gender violence suggests that there might be some reason to treat battered women cases differently. Most important, the documented frequency of so-called "separation attacks" severely limits the options available to female abuse victims to safely extricate themselves from abusive relationships.[119] Indeed, data suggest that women are most at risk when they attempt to separate from an abuser.[120]

But because self-defense law makes no provision for the preemptive use of force, Francine's self-defense claim would likely have failed, notwithstanding that her conduct was easily understood in light of self-defense principles. Thus, on trial for murder, Francine declined to argue self-defense.[121] Instead, she argued that the years of violence, abuse, and terror rendered her temporarily insane when she poured gasoline around the bed in which her husband slept and lit a match. While self-defense typically requires an objective inquiry into the circumstances of the killing, pleading temporary insanity permitted Francine to tell her story in much finer detail, including historical events that might be deemed irrelevant and therefore inadmissible to a claim of self-defense. Her testimony about the events immediately preceding the killing suggests, even more than a rational immediate fear for her life, that she killed Mickey in response to circumstances that can only be characterized as "extreme provocation." According to Francine, on the day of the killing Mickey had beaten her, destroyed her school books, and took a sledgehammer to her car so she could not attend school. At dinner, he dumped all the food on the dinner table and forced her to clean it up, and after she complied, he dumped it out of the garbage and made her do it again. He then smeared food on her back and in her hair, and later raped her before finally falling asleep. Once he was asleep, Francine decided to flee with her children, but before leaving, she "decided that there wouldn't be anything to come back to. [She] was going to burn everything."[122]

In fact, at the moment she apparently decided to kill Mickey, Francine did not testify that she was especially fearful for her immediate safety. Rather, she seemed to have been pushed past the tipping point by an unrelenting series of outrageous personal provocations. The assaults, the smeared food, Mickey's domineering commands and calculated assault on her sense of personhood, topped off with what was, in effect, a rape, are more than merely reasonable provocations. A jury might well have been convinced that Mickey simply deserved to die.[123] At the least, Francine's acquittal is consistent with the observation that juries will sometimes depart from the formal rule of law and "recognize an insult as sufficient aggression to privilege violence."[124]

The Lorena Bobbitt case provides another example of a battered spouse case in which the battered spouse was acquitted on grounds of temporary insanity in circumstances that suggest her loss of self-control arose from extreme provocation rather than fear.[125] Like Hughes, Bobbitt was a battered spouse who had suffered numerous beatings and rapes by her husband. After one such incident, Bobbitt used a kitchen knife to sever her sleeping husband's penis.[126] She threw the dismembered organ into a field as she drove away from their home.[127] Bobbitt's conduct is hard to characterize as an act of self-defense. Indeed, a comment she made to the police after the crime suggested that sexual frustration was as much a motive for the attack as fear.[128] Certainly, her highly symbolic wounding of her husband—the likely consequence of which would be to provoke, rather than prevent, a homicidal attack—seems explicable only if Bobbitt at the time was unafraid of reprisal.

For all its titillating details, and the explosion of popular concern in the 1990s about the supposed outbreak of jury nullifications in "abuse excuse" cases following Bobbitt's acquittal (to use lawyer Alan Dershowitz's term), the storyline of the case was nothing new. Indeed, in 1906, New York was captivated by the case of another victim of abuse, a young girl named Josephine Terranova.[129] Josephine was sent from Sicily to live with her aunt and uncle in New York at the age of nine. She soon became the victim of terrible abuse: she was starved and forced to work 20-hour days scrubbing, cleaning, and ironing. Beginning at the age of 11, she was sexually abused by her uncle. At the age of 17, her uncle arranged for her marriage to a Brooklyn contractor, but upon learning of her past degradation and that she was now pregnant with her uncle's child, her new husband renounced the marriage. Shortly thereafter, Josephine purchased a "revolver and a long potato knife" and with them murdered her aunt and uncle.[130] At trial, Josephine proffered a temporary insanity defense, and the jury, moved by the pathetic state of the victim and the vile conduct of her victimizers, acquitted her for the murders.

Imminence aside, it is not hard in some cases for battered spouses to establish that the killings were necessary in the sense that the battered woman sometimes may have had no practical or reasonable alternative. Where police or courts cannot promise effective protection and where exit is not a realistic option because of an abusive spouse's credible threats, economic necessity, or a combination of both, the array of alternatives open to a battered spouse greatly diminishes. Under these conditions, preemptive force may be both reasonable and necessary to prevent death or further felonious abuse.

The battered woman who kills preemptively may well believe that preemptive force is necessary to avert an otherwise unavoidable threat by an aggressor, and that what she has chosen to do is therefore entirely consistent with the moral structure of the law of self-defense. To the extent that the law says she is mistaken in those judgments, the killing was not justifiable self-defense. But to the extent she honestly believed in them, she did not know that her act was unlawful. At least with respect to the required degree of cognitive dysfunction, she is like an insane person under the M'Naghten Rules because she is honestly incapable of understanding that her act was either morally or legally wrong. And if the jury agrees with the substance of her judgments—that she really had no practical alternative, that sooner or later she would be the victim of lethal abuse, that waiting for her victim to strike first was not a reasonable strategy, and that the victim was fundamentally the aggressor—then she really was mistaken only about how the law would technically apply to her self-defense claim rather than about the principles that underlie the defense. At a deeper level, she is not culpable. Permitting a jury to come back with a temporary insanity verdict under such circumstances thus vindicates, rather than subverts, the moral structure of self-defense law.

3.2.3 Imperfect Necessity and Mercy Killing

Mercy killings provide a final class of cases in which the temporary insanity defense appears grounded in justification. There are numerous examples of mercy-killing cases in which defendants have been acquitted, or in which grand juries have refused to indict, on grounds of temporary insanity. Take, for instance, the case of 72-year-old Justina Rivero.[131] Rivero's husband, who was 84 years old, was afflicted with Alzheimer's disease. Ms. Rivero, who tried to kill herself and her husband with rat poison, claimed at trial that she had grown despondent over her and her husband's living situation and feared that her husband would be subject to abuse if she was unable to care for him. The judge acquitted Rivero on grounds of temporary insanity.[132] Juries similarly acquitted defendants Carol Paight and Eugene Braunsdorf in cases involving mercy killings.[133] Paight, a college student, killed her father, who was hospitalized and dying of cancer. Braunsdorf, a symphony musician, shot and killed his 29-year-old daughter, who had been crippled and hospitalized her entire life. Both successfully asserted temporary insanity defenses at trial. In a more recent case, Dan McKay killed his newborn infant shortly after his wife gave birth after discovering that the child suffered severe deformities that likely would have resulted in the baby's death within three months.[134] McKay argued temporary insanity at the trial, which ended in a mistrial after jurors could not reach a verdict.

As in the unwritten law and battered spouse cases, widespread popular sympathy exists for defendants in mercy killing cases but for somewhat different reasons. In mercy killing cases, judges and jurors are frequently persuaded that, in choosing to kill a suffering loved one, the defendants chose the lesser evil. Defendants contend that their acts were motivated by good reasons and resulted in a reduction of harm. The arguments against punishment in mercy killing cases thus parallel the necessity defense. But as in the unwritten law and battered woman syndrome (BWS) cases, although the types of arguments presented by the defendants are clearly justificatory, traditional criminal law precludes assertion of a justification defense (here, necessity) in circumstances involving mercy killing. A necessity or lesser-evil defense requires proof that the chosen course was necessary to avoid an imminent or immediate harm, and that no alternative course of action involving a lesser harm was available. This showing is difficult to make in mercy killing cases. After all, objectively speaking, there are almost always alternatives to killing. To prevail, the mercy killer must convince the jury that killing the suffering victim was the only reasonable way to minimize the victim's pain. In some circumstances, such a claim might well be compelling, but despite popular sympathy for defendants caught in such circumstances, killing to relieve suffering is flatly foreclosed as a matter of law. The common law, at least, has never recognized the necessity defense as viable in homicide cases, and no jurisdiction in the United States recognizes euthanasia as a viable defense to homicide.[135]

In mercy killing cases, the temporary insanity defense functions as a kind of rogue or "imperfect necessity defense," albeit one that is consistent with the moral principles underlying the defense. As in the other contexts in which temporary insanity factors recurrently, the temporary insanity defense supplies a cognizable legal claim in circumstances in which some other defense—here, necessity—has moral appeal but lacks fit due to its doctrinal structure.

4 A Legitimate Legal Fiction?

More than any other recognized criminal law defense, temporary insanity creates space for what one court described as "common sense and the feeling for substantial justice possessed and applied by the average jury."[136] Cases involving the unwritten law in the 19th century, like battered spouse cases today, intuitively imply such defenses as "extreme provocation" and "preemptive deadly force"—neither of which, of course, exists under the law. Infanticide cases put factfinders in the uncomfortable position of being asked to punish the victim, either because the law requires them to treat the infant and mother as legally distinct entities while social conventions suggest a fuzzier boundary or because the law does not permit them to take into account the social circumstances surrounding the act. Mercy killing cases, where the defendant is almost always a spouse or loved one of the victim, evoke similar conflicts between simple legal rules and nuanced factual contexts and similar practical uncertainties about victim and perpetrator that are obvious to factfinders but ignored by the law. Indeed, such cases illustrate a persistent failure of the criminal law in general: its wholesale tendency to ignore important social and moral facts when they lack direct relevance to pre-established legal categories. In all these cases, temporary insanity seems to serve as a way to correct a failure of the law to address some moral or social complexity that eludes redress through simple rulemaking.

5 Conclusion

In short, a temporary insanity defense is most likely to succeed where enforcement of the criminal law seems unwarranted but where a conventional defense falls short due to some doctrinal rule that forecloses it under the circumstances, or because the asserted defense—while coherent and perhaps even intuitive—is not recognized by law. So used, the defense is fundamentally equitable in nature in that it is grounded not in the formal doctrinal rules of the criminal law but rather in the values and principles that shape it.

Such use of the defense is arguably a form of jury nullification. By anchoring acquittals in these cases on a formally permissible legal defense, juries are not simply refusing to bring back a guilty verdict against the evidence. They are, however, shifting the terms of the inquiry to an issue that might fairly be described as a legal fiction that serves as a "surrogate[s] for the jury's true discomfort with the propriety of the conviction."[137]

While that characterization of jury conduct is probably accurate, dismissing the temporary insanity defense as "mere nullification" doctrine misrepresents the nature of the moral inquiry at the heart of these cases because it implies that the decision makers disregarded the law and, for reasons extraneous to it, refused to reach the appropriate result. That dynamic does not appear to be at work in most temporary insanity cases.

More often than not, juries who accept the defense seem to be attempting to conform their verdicts to a set of principles that underlies, or is at least consistent with, the formal doctrinal rules.

No violence to the legal imagination results from characterizing the actions of defendants in these cases as the product of "temporary insanity." These defendants face a dilemma that can be framed in the language of the traditional standards that govern criminal responsibility: In some cases, the pressure of circumstances may well have rendered the defendant momentarily ignorant of right and wrong or engendered an "irresistible impulse" to commit a crime. In other cases, the defendant may not have chosen to do wrong simply because he or she, in fact, reasonably believed that killing was the right thing to do under the circumstances.

Notes

1. This chapter is an adaptation of a previously published article (Covey, "Temporary Insanity: The Strange Life and Times of the Perfect Defense").

2. I use the term "psycho-medical model" to refer to the view that some diagnosable mental disease or defect must cause insanity, but that the disease or defect may have a biological, psychological, or neurological etiology; others describe this view as the "medical model" (see Melton et al., *Psychological Evaluations for the Courts*, 195).

3. Tiffany and Tiffany, *The Legal Defense of Pathological Intoxication*, 230.

4. See 41 Am. Jur. 2d American Jurisprudence *Proof of Facts* 615 § 10 (1985).

5. *People v. Sommers*, 200 P.3d 1089, 1093 (Colo. App. 2008) (quoting *People v. Garcia*, 113 P.3d 775, 782 (Colo. 2005)); *People v. Low*, 732 P.2d 622, 632 (Colo. 1987).

6. Ariz. Rev. Stat. Ann. § 13-502(A) (2015). The Arizona law, the principal purpose of which was to eliminate the temporary insanity defense, was largely a reaction to the 1994 acquittal of Mark Austin, who stabbed to death his estranged wife and injured her lover, and who was released from the mental institution to which he had been placed approximately six months after his acquittal (see Melançon, "Arizona's Insane Response to Insanity").

7. See Lashbrook, "The Insanity Defense," 1604.

8. Novelist Frances Trollope utilized this theme in her novel about infanticide, *Jessie Phillips*. In the novel, notwithstanding that "[t]he jury believes that Jessie killed her child," it nonetheless acquits on grounds of temporary insanity (Ledwon, "Melodrama and Law," 159).

9. See Melton et al., *Psychological Evaluations for the Courts*, 187–88; Finkel, Burke and Chavez, "Commonsense Judgments of Infanticide," 1120.

10. Indeed, because terms of institutionalization in an asylum can often exceed those of imprisonment when a defendant wins an acquittal on insanity grounds, and the conditions of detention are often worse in the asylum than the

prison, it may often be true, as one writer stated, that "only a lunatic would allow himself to be acquitted by reason of insanity" (Bishop, "Book Review: Law, Liberty and Psychiatry," 1516).

11. See Ariz. Rev. Stat. Ann. § 13-3994C-F (2001); *Blake v. Schwartz*, 42 P.3d 6, 11 (Ariz. Ct. App. 2002) (upholding constitutionality of 120 day mandatory evaluation period).

12. At one point, a Washington statute required defendants pleading not guilty by reason of insanity to also specify if "the condition still exists, or [if] the defendant has since become sane" (Weihofen, *Mental Disorder as a Criminal Defense*, 358). Some states still permit, at least as a practice if not a legal requirement, defendants to enter separate pleas of "temporary insanity" and "insanity" (See, e.g., *Jones v. State*, 43 So. 3d 1258, 1279 (Ala. Crim. App. 2007)).

13. *State v. Lynch*, 32 A.2d 183, 185 (N.J. 1943).

14. Ibid.

15. See *Yohn v. State*, 476 So. 2d 123, 124–25 (Fla. 1985).

16. Melton et al., *Psychological Evaluations for the Courts*, 195; Redding, "The Brain-Disordered Defendant," 87n225.

17. Melton et al., *Psychological Evaluations for the Courts*, 196.

18. Howell, "The Temporary Insanity Defense," 85.

19. Waelder, "Psychiatry and the Problem of Criminal Responsibility," 384.

20. LaFave, *Criminal Law*, 377.

21. Floch, "The Concept of Temporary Insanity Viewed by a Criminologist," 687.

22. Pustilnik, "Prisons of the Mind," 251–52.

23. See, e.g., Wiehofen, *Mental Disorder as a Criminal Defense*, 122.

24. *People v. Kernaghan*, 14 P. 566, 574 (Cal. 1887); see also *Barnett v. State*, 39 So. 778, 780 (Ala. 1905) (stating that one who is "insanely jealous" may have temporarily lost one's moral compass, but cannot claim a legal excuse on that basis).

25. See, e.g., *State v. Buck*, 219 N.W. 17, 20 (Iowa 1928).

26. *Collins v. State*, 102 So. 880, 882 (Fla. 1925) (affirming conviction for killing wife's alleged rapist where there was no intermittent insanity or mental disorder, instead only "a moment of uncontrollable impulse, or . . . a condition of mental irresponsibility equivalent to temporary insanity").

27. Dostoyevsky, *Crime and Punishment*; see also Batey, "In Defense of Porfiry Petrovich," 2297.

28. See, e.g., *Robey v. State*, 456 A.2d 953, 959 (Md. Ct. Spec. App. 1983) (finding that a woman diagnosed with "atypical impulse disorder" was temporarily insane during beatings of her baby, and that insanity was triggered by, and coextensive with, the baby's cries, so that when the baby stopped crying, her insanity ceased as well).

29. Coke, *The Third Part of the Institutes of the Laws of England*. The fourth category is actually somewhat wider than the merely intoxicated. In Coke's words, it includes "hee that by his owne vitious act for a time depriveth himself of his memorie and understanding, as he that is drunken."

30. Hale, *Historia placitorum coronae*, 29–30.
31. Ibid., 31.
32. Milhizer, "Justification and Excuse," 782.
33. Finkel, *Insanity on Trial*, 9.
34. Hale, *Historia placitorum coronae*, 30.
35. Ibid.
36. Milhizer, "Justification and Excuse," 782.
37. Goldstein, *The Insanity Defense*.
38. That was precisely the theory asserted by the defendant in *State v. Cortez*, 218 N.W.2d 217 (Neb. 1974), where evidence that the defendant had been subject to blackouts for decades and that he had a convulsive disorder equivalent to epilepsy was enough to put a temporary insanity charge to the jury.
39. An example of such a diagnosis whose authenticity is subject to challenge can be seen in *Phillips v. State*, 863 S.W.2d 309, 312 (Ark. 1993), in which defendant's psychiatrist attributed his temporary insanity to "intermittent explosive disorder," while admitting that the disorder was not widely accepted and was perhaps better classified as a mere "personality disorder."
40. As a result, courts have supported continued institutionalization of persons acquitted by reason of temporary insanity on the grounds that a person may have a mental disease, even though presently free of symptoms, if the disease is judged to be in "remission" (see *Revels v. Sanders*, 531 F.3d 724 (8th Cir. 2008) (Colloton, J., dissenting from denial of rehearing en banc); *United States v. Weed*, 389 F.3d 1060 (10th Cir. 2004)).
41. Hale, *Historia placitorum coronae*, 36.
42. Severe congestive dysmenorrhoea was diagnosed by Dr. Calvin M. Fitch at the trial of Mary Harris for killing her seducer Adoniram J. Burroughs (see Ireland, "Insanity and the Unwritten Law," 161). Menstruation problems are still acknowledged as a potential basis for mental illness (see Grose, "Premenstrual Dysphoric Disorder as a Mitigating Factor in Sentencing," 226).
43. Jones, *Women Who Kill* (as quoted in Stark, "Re-Presenting Woman Battering," 993).
44. Kramar and Watson, "Canadian Infanticide Legislation," 239.
45. See *Ragland v. State*, 27 So. 983, 985 (Ala. 1900) (describing defendant's argument that a blow to the head was the cause of "recurrent manifestations" of insanity); *Hankins v. State*, 201 S.W. 832, 833 (Ark. 1917) (reporting witness testimony that after being struck by lightning, defendant "did not seem like the same boy"); *Mitra v. Commonwealth*, 5 S.W.2d 275, 276–77 (Ky. 1928) (allowing jury to consider temporary insanity defense on the basis that the defendant had been struck by a meat cleaver right before murdering victim, even though it was rejected by jury, undoubtedly in part because defendant was at that time attempting to rob a grocery store); *Crum v. Commonwealth*, 259 S.W. 708, 709 (Ky. 1924) (holding that it was a reversible error to refuse to permit a doctor's testimony that if defendant had been struck in the head by a big enough rock it could have made him temporarily insane).
46. *People v. Gross*, No. D041448, 2004 WL 792093, at *9 (Cal. Ct. App. Apr. 14, 2004).

47. Kuh, "The Insanity Defense," 786; Weihofen, *Mental Disorder as a Criminal Defense*, 94.

48. Odum, "A Difficult Defense in Bobbitt Trial." Bert Stacy presented a similar defense while on trial in Vermont for the murder of his wife. At trial, Stacy contended that "he did not shoot his wife, but that if he did he was temporarily insane at the time and governed by an irresistible impulse, caused by information he had received concerning her improper relations with other men, and certain incidents which he had observed which corroborated that information" (*State v. Stacy*, 160 A. 257, 263 [Vt. 1932]).

49. See LaFave *Criminal Law*, 389n1.

50. Hall, "Psychiatry and Criminal Responsibility," 776, quoting *Royal Commission on Capital Punishment* 1949–1953, Report 109 (1953).

51. See LaFave *Criminal Law*, 399–400.

52. See Hale, *Historia placitorum coronae*, 36.

53. Ramsey, "Intimate Homicide," 118–20.

54. Ibid., 119.

55. Ibid., 120.

56. *Taylor v. United States*, 7 App. D.C. 27, 41, 44 (1895); see also *State v. Lynch*, 32 A.2d 183, 185 (N.J. 1943).

57. Chen, "Provocation's Privileged Desire," 203.

58. Charles, "Panic in *The Project*," 234.

59. Ramsey, "Intimate Homicide," 119–20.

60. Hale, *Historia placitorum coronae*, 32.

61. Hale, however, summarily rejected this position, explaining that "by the laws of *England* such a person shall have no privilege by this voluntary contracted madness, but shall have the same judgment as if he were in his right senses" (*Historia placitorum coronae*, 32, 36).

62. *State v. Dillahunt*, 3 Del. (3 Harr.) 551, 552 (1842) ("Doctor L. P. Bush, of Wilmington, testified that the prisoner was at the time laboring under confirmed mania a potu, brought on by abstaining from liquor, after free indulgence."). The condition resulting from alcohol withdrawal is today more commonly referred to as "delirium tremens."

63. Ibid., 553 ("The frenzy of *drunkenness* is no *excuse*, but there is a disease of *insanity* called *mania a potu*, which may be the result of a condition of the system produced by habitual *intoxication*, and yet is not the frenzy of drunkenness.").

64. Hale, *Historia placitorum coronae*, 32.

65. *State v. Dillahunt*, 3 Del. (3 Harr.) 553 (1842).

66. See *People v. Travers*, 26 P. 88, 91 (Cal. 1891).

67. *People v. Gross*, No. D041448, 2004 WL 792093, at *9 (Cal. Ct. App. Apr. 14, 2004).

68. *People v. Kelly*, 516 P.2d 875, 883 (Cal. 1973) (holding that defendant may have been insane at the time she stabbed her mother even if the insanity resulted from "repeated voluntary intoxication").

69. Cohan, "Psychiatric Ethics and Emerging Issues of Psychopharmacology," 151; Myers, "Halcion Made Me Do It," 643–45.

70. Myers, "Halcion Made Me Do It," 640–43.

71. See Brewer, "Violent Behavior Associated with Acetylcholinesterase Inhibitors," 121–22.

72. See Denno, "Crime and Consciousness," 381–84.

73. The so-called "abuse excuse" differs from other instances of violence against "deserving victims" discussed further on, where the resort to violence is neither necessary nor morally justifiable.

74. Aning and Balana, "Grateful for Miracle, Doomed Maid Returns."

75. See, e.g., *Regina v. Dudley & Stephens*, [1884] 14 Q.B.D. 273.

76. After their justification defense for killing and eating the cabin boy failed, the Crown commuted Dudley's and Stephens's death sentences to a term of six months imprisonment (ibid., 288n2).

77. Hoffer and Hull, *Murdering Mothers*, 146.

78. Ibid., 100–01, 108–09.

79. Friedman, *Crime and Punishment in American History*, 231.

80. Kramar and Watson, "Canadian Infanticide Legislation," 239.

81. See, e.g., *Gonzales v. Carhart*, 550 U.S. 124, 128 (2007).

82. Indeed, many cases of infanticide documented by Hoffer and Hull appeared to be, in essence, "delayed abortions" (*Murdering Mothers*, 155–56). Abortion, even where illegal, was not homicide (ibid., 155).

83. Coroners in the 18th century deemed "every one who kills himself . . . *non compos* . . . ; for it is said to be impossible that a man in his senses should do a thing so contrary to nature and all sense and reason" (Hawkins, *A Treatise of the Pleas of the Crown*, ch. 9, sect. 2).

84. See March, "The Conflicted Treatment of Postpartum Psychosis under Criminal Law," 250–51.

85. Finkel, *Insanity on Trial*, 57.

86. Puerperal insanity was thought to affect "women at childbirth as a result of septicaemia, [and] was the closest medical-psychiatric analogue of the lay theory of women's propensity to temporary derangement during childbirth" (Kramar and Watson "Canadian Infanticide Legislation," 244).

87. Lactational insanity was a diagnosis often given to "poor nursing mothers, often with many children," and was "conceived as an 'exhaustion psychosis'" (ibid.).

88. Heath, *Some Notes on the Punishment of Death*.

89. Cavanaugh, "Dead Baby's Mother Wins Her Gamble."

90. Oberman, "Mothers Who Kill," 35.

91. Dressler, *Understanding Criminal Law*, 209.

92. Brandt, *The Congressman Who Got Away with Murder*.

93. Ibid., 121.

94. Ibid., 172.

95. LaCroix, "To Gain the Whole World and Lose His Own Soul," 561.

96. Ireland, "Insanity and the Unwritten Law," 157; "The Libertine Must Die," 27.

97. Freidman, *Crime and Punishment in American History*, 146–47.
98. LaFave, *Criminal Law*, 777.
99. Ireland, "Insanity and the Unwritten Law," 159; Lee, *Murder and the Reasonable Man*, 25.
100. Ireland, "Insanity and the Unwritten Law," 161.
101. Brandt, *The Congressman Who Got Away with Murder*, 173.
102. Ramsey, "Intimate Homicide," 154.
103. *Cole's Trial*, 7 Abb. Pr. (n.s.) 321, 338.
104. *Ragland v. State*, 27 So. 983 (Ala. 1900).
105. Scholars heatedly debate whether provocation is a partial justification or partial excuse. For an excellent recent overview of the debate, see Garvey, "Passion's Puzzle."
106. Phillips and Gartner, *Murdering Holiness*, 122.
107. Brandt, *The Congressman Who Got Away with Murder*, 179–80.
108. See *Cloud v. State*, 7 S.E. 641, 641 (Ga. 1888). *Cloud* distinguished killing in revenge of adultery, which is murder, from killing when necessary to prevent adultery, which might be justifiable. Said the judge, "Speaking for myself, I think that gunpowder and ball are great preservers of human virtue; and, if I were on a jury, I do not hesitate to say that I would acquit a man who would kill another under such circumstances." Ibid., 642; see also *Brown v. State*, 184 S.E.2d 655, 657–58 (Ga. 1971).
109. Ireland, "The Libertine Must Die," 30.
110. Ganz, "Wicked Women and Veiled Ladies," 265, quoting "The Lessons of the MacFarland Trial," 478.
111. Dressler, *Understanding Criminal Law*, 209.
112. Bedau, "The Right to Life," 570.
113. Brandt, *The Congressman Who Got Away with Murder*, 173. Harry Thaw's lawyer made precisely the same argument to Thaw's jury (see Umphrey, "The Dialogics of Legal Meaning," 397–98).
114. "The Lessons of the McFarland Case," 386.
115. Appel, "The Girl-Wife and the Alienists," 229.
116. McNulty, *The Burning Bed*.
117. Model Penal Code § 3.04(1) (1985).
118. *People v. Vronko*, No. 279857, 2009 WL 348830, at *1 (Mich. Ct. App. Feb. 12 2009).
119. Mahoney, "Legal Images of Battered Women," 65.
120. Angel, "Susan Glaspell's *Trifles* and *A Jury of Her Peers*," 810nn236–266.
121. McNulty, *The Burning Bed*, 220.
122. Ibid., 271.
123. Like the libertines in the unwritten law cases, the abusers in BWS cases readily fit the "moral theory of forfeiture" argument and "had it coming" (Dressler, "Battered Women and Sleeping Abusers," 465). Alan Dershowitz locates the "he had it coming" defense within a broader class of "abuse excuse" cases. According to Dershowitz, juries' sympathy for such defendants can be traced to a

pro-vigilante ethic that became popular in late-20th-century American culture (*The Abuse Excuse*, 3–4). Jurors acted on similar sentiments in a case documented by Kalven and Zeisel in which a wife killed her husband during a "drunken brawl"; according to the judge presiding in the case, the jury likely acquitted because it "thought itself well rid of decedent" (*The American Jury*, 282–833).

124. Kalven and Zeisel, *The American Jury*, 229.
125. Angel, "Susan Glaspell's *Trifles* and *A Jury of Her Peers*," 813.
126. Posner, "Lorena Bobbitt Describes Knife Attack."
127. Angel, "Susan Glaspell's *Trifles* and *A Jury of Her Peers*," 813.
128. Posner, "Lorena Bobbitt Describes Knife Attack."
129. Appel, "The Girl-Wife and the Alienists," 203–04.
130. Ibid., 209–10.
131. Sterghos and Lade, "Judge Rules Wife Insane."
132. Ibid.
133. Sherman, "Mercy Killing and the Right to Inherit," 824n106.
134. Shipp, "Mistrial in Killing of Malformed Baby Leaves Town Uncertain about Law."
135. Some foreign jurisdictions expressly treat mercy killings differently, and more leniently, than other homicides. According to David Meyers, "[t]he German Penal Code makes provision for 'homicide upon the request of the person killed,'" and Norway and Sweden make "special provision for mercy-motivated or requested killing of hopelessly ill persons" (*The Human Body and the Law*, 152–53).
136. *United States v. Fielding*, 148 F. Supp. 46, 55 (D.D.C.), *rev'd*, 251 F.2d 878 (D.C. Cir. 1957).
137. Dorfman and Iijima, "Fictions, Fault, and Forgiveness," 864.

Resources

Angel, Marina, "Susan Glaspell's *Trifles* and *A Jury of Her Peers*: Woman Abuse in a Literary and Legal Context." *Buffalo Law Review* 45(1997): 779–844.

Aning, Jerome, and Cynthia D. Balana, "Grateful for Miracle, Doomed Maid Returns." *Philippine Daily Inquirer*, July 1, 2009.

Appel, Jacob M., "The Girl-Wife and the Alienists: The Forgotten Murder Trial of Josephine Terranova." *Western New England Law Review* 26(2004): 203–32.

Batey, Robert, "In Defense of Porfiry Petrovich." *Cardozo Law Review* 26(2005): 2283–2302.

Bedau, Hugo, "The Right to Life." *The Monist* 52(1968): 550–72.

Bishop, Jr., Joseph W., "Book Review: Law, Liberty and Psychiatry." *Harvard Law Review* 78(1965): 1510–18.

Brandt, Nat, *The Congressman Who Got Away with Murder*. Syracuse, NY: Syracuse University Press, 1991.

Brewer, Janet K., "Violent Behavior Associated with Acetylcholinesterase Inhibitors and Liability of Prescribers of Donepezil." *Widener Law Journal* 16(2006): 111–30.

Cavanaugh, Joanne, "Dead Baby's Mother Wins Her Gamble, Verdict of Insanity Means Her Freedom." *Buffalo News*, April 18, 1990.

Charles, Casey, "Panic in *The Project*: Critical Queer Studies and the Matthew Shepard Murder." *Law and Literature* 18(2006): 225–52.

Chen, Christina P.-L., "Provocation's Privileged Desire: The Provocation Doctrine, 'Homosexual Panic,' and the Non-Violent Unwanted Sexual Advance Defense." *Cornell Journal of Law and Public Policy* 10(2000): 195–235.

Cohan, John A., "Psychiatric Ethics and Emerging Issues of Psychopharmacology in the Treatment of Depression." *Journal of Contemporary Health Law and Policy* 20(2003): 115–72.

Coke, Edward, *The Third Part of the Institutes of the Laws of England: Concerning High Treason, and Other Pleas of the Crown, and Criminal Causes*. London: A. Crooke, 1681.

Covey, Russell D. "Temporary Insanity: The Strange Life and Times of the Perfect Defense." *Boston University Law Review* 91(2011): 1597–1668.

Denno, Deborah W., "Crime and Consciousness: Science and Involuntary Acts." *Minnesota Law Review* 87(2002): 269–400.

Dershowitz, Alan M., *The Abuse Excuse and Other Cop-Outs, Sob Stories, and Evasions of Responsibility*. Boston: Little, Brown, and Company, 1994.

Dorfman, David N., and Chris K. Iijima, "Fictions, Fault, and Forgiveness: Jury Nullification in a New Context." *University of Michigan Journal of Law Reform* 28(1995): 861–929.

Dostoyevsky, Fyodor, *Crime and Punishment: A Novel in Six Parts with Epilogue*. Translated by R. Pevear and L. Volokhonsky. (New York: Vintage Books, 1866 [1993 ed.]).

Dressler, Joshua, "Battered Women and Sleeping Abusers: Some Reflections." *Ohio State Journal of Criminal Law* 3(2008): 457–71.

Dressler, Joshua, *Understanding Criminal Law*, 5th ed. New Providence, NJ: LexisNexis, 2009.

Finkel, N. J., *Insanity on Trial*. New York: Plenum Press, 1988.

Finkel, N.J., J.E. Burke, and L.J. Chavez, "Commonsense Judgments of Infanticide: Murder, Manslaughter, Madness, or Miscellaneous?" *Psychology, Public Policy, and Law* 6(2000): 1113–37.

Floch, Maurice, "The Concept of Temporary Insanity Viewed by a Criminologist." *Journal of Criminal Law, Criminology, and Police Science* 45(1955): 685–89.

Friedman, Lawrence M., *Crime and Punishment in American History*. New York: Basic Books, 1993.

Ganz, Melissa J., "Wicked Women and Veiled Ladies: Gendered Narratives of the McFarland-Richardson Tragedy." *Yale Journal of Law and Feminism* 9(1997): 255–303.

Garvey, Stephen P. "Passion's Puzzle." *Iowa Law Review* 90(2005): 1677–1746.

Goldstein, Abraham S., *The Insanity Defense*. New Haven: Yale University Press, 1967.

Grose, N. R., "Premenstrual Dysphoric Disorder as a Mitigating Factor in Sentencing: Following the Lead of English Criminal Courts." *Valparaiso University Law Review* 33(1998): 201–30.

Hale, Matthew, *Historia placitorum coronae: The History of the Pleas of the Crown*, vol. 1. edited by P. R. Glazebrook. (London: Professional Books Limited, 1847 [1971 ed.]).

Hall, Jerome, "Psychiatry and Criminal Responsibility." *Yale Law Journal* 65(1956): 761–85.

Hawkins, Williams, *A Treatise of the Pleas of the Crown*, 7th ed. Dublin: E. Lynch, 1795.

Heath, Carl, *Some Notes on the Punishment of Death*. London: Society for the Abolition of Capital Punishment, 1908.

Hoffer, Peter C., and N.E.H. Hull, *Murdering Mothers: Infanticide in England and New England, 1558–1803*. New York: New York University Press, 1981.

Howell, Robert J., "The Temporary Insanity Defense." *American Journal of Forensic Psychology* 2(1984): 83–9.

Ireland, Robert M., "Insanity and the Unwritten Law." *American Journal of Legal History* 32(1988): 157–72.

Ireland, Robert M., "The Libertine Must Die: Sexual Dishonor and the Unwritten Law in the Nineteenth-Century United States." *Journal of Social History* 23(1989): 27–44.

Jones, Ann, *Women Who Kill*. New York: Holt, Rinehart, and Winston, 1980.

Kalven, Jr., Harry, and Hans Zeisel, *The American Jury*. Boston: Little Brown & Company, 1966.

Kramar, Kirsten J., and William D. Watson, "Canadian Infanticide Legislation, 1948 and 1955: Reflections on the Medicalization/Autopoiesis Debate." *Canadian Journal of Sociology* 33(2008): 237–64.

Kuh, Richard H., "The Insanity Defense: An Effort to Combine Law and Reason." *University of Pennsylvania Law Review* 110(1962): 771–815.

LaCroix, Alison L., "To Gain the Whole World and Lose His Own Soul: Nineteenth-Century American Dueling as Public Law and Private Code." *Hofstra Law Review* 33(2004): 501–70.

LaFave, Wayne R., *Criminal Law*, 4th ed. St. Paul, MN: Thomson/West, 2003.

Lashbrook, Stephanie K., "The Insanity Defense." *Loyola of Los Angeles Law Review* 36(2003): 1596–1626.

Ledwon, Lenora, "Melodrama and Law: Feminizing the Juridical Gaze." *Harvard Women's Law Journal* 21(1998): 141–78.

Lee, Cynthia, *Murder and the Reasonable Man: Passion and Fear in the Criminal Courtroom*. New York: New York University Press, 2003.

"The Lessons of the MacFarland Trial." *Old and New* 2(1870): 476–86.

"The Lessons of the McFarland Case." *Albany Law Journal* 1(1870): 385–87.

Mahoney, Martha R., "Legal Images of Battered Women: Redefining the Issue of Separation." *Michigan Law Review* 90(1991): 1–94.

March, Cristie L., "The Conflicted Treatment of Postpartum Psychosis under Criminal Law." *William Mitchell Law Review* 32(2005): 243–63.

McNulty, Faith, *The Burning Bed*. New York: Harcourt Brace Jovanovich, 1980.

Melançon, Renée, "Arizona's Insane Response to Insanity." *Arizona Law Review* 40(1988):287–318.

Melton, Gary B., John Petrila, Norman G. Poythress, and Christopher Slobogin, 1997. *Psychological Evaluations for the Courts: A Handbook for Mental Health Professionals and Lawyers*, 2nd ed. New York: Guilford Press, 1997.

Meyers, David W., *The Human Body and the Law: A Medico-Legal Study*. Chicago: Aldine, 1970.

Milhizer, Eugene R., "Justification and Excuse: What They Were, What They Are, and What They Ought to Be." *St. John's Law Review* 78(2004): 725–895.

Myers, Todd P., "Halcion Made Me Do It: New Liability and a New Defense—Fear and Loathing in the Halcion Paper Chase." *University of Cincinnati Law Review* 62(1993): 603–53.

Oberman, Michelle, "Mothers Who Kill: Coming to Terms with Modern American Infanticide." *American Criminal Law Review* 34(1997): 1–110.

Odum, Maria E., "A Difficult Defense in Bobbitt Trial." *Washington Post*, January 16, 1994, available at http://wpo.st/N5IX1.

Phillips, Jim, and Rosemary Gartner, *Murdering Holiness: The Trials of Franz Creffield and George Mitchell*. Vancouver: University of British Columbia Press, 2003.

Posner, Michael, "Lorena Bobbitt Describes Knife Attack." *Denver Rocky Mountain News*, January 12, 1994.

Pustilnik, Amanda C., "Prisons of the Mind: Social Value and Economic Inefficiency in the Criminal Justice Response to Mental Illness." *Journal of Criminal Law and Criminology* 96(2005): 217–66.

Ramsey, Carolyn B., "Intimate Homicide: Gender and Crime Control, 1880–1920." *University of Colorado Law Review* 77(2006): 101–92.

Redding, Richard E., "The Brain-Disordered Defendant: Neuroscience and Legal Insanity in the Twenty-First Century." *American University Law Review* 56(2006): 51–128.

Sherman, Jeffrey G., "Mercy Killing and the Right to Inherit." *University of Cincinnati Law Review* 61(1993): 803–76.

Shipp, E. R., "Mistrial in Killing of Malformed Baby Leaves Town Uncertain about Law." *New York Times*, February 18, 1985.

Stark, Evan, "Re-Presenting Woman Battering: From Battered Woman Syndrome to Coercive Control. *Albany Law Review* 58(1995): 973–1026.

Sterghos, Nicole, and Diane Lade, "Judge Rules Wife Insane." *South Florida Sun-Sentinel*, February 24, 1999.

Tiffany, Lawrence P., and Mary Tiffany, *The Legal Defense of Pathological Intoxication: With Related Issues of Temporary and Self-Inflicted Insanity*. New York: Quorum Books, 1990.

Umphrey, Martha M., "The Dialogics of Legal Meaning: Spectacular Trials, the Unwritten Law, and Narratives of Criminal Responsibility." *Law and Society Review* 33(1999): 393–423.

Waelder, Robert, "Psychiatry and the Problem of Criminal Responsibility." *University of Pennsylvania Law Review* 101(1952): 378–90.

Weihofen, Henry, *Mental Disorder as a Criminal Defense*. Buffalo, NY: Dennis, 1954.

CHAPTER THREE

Mens Rea and Mental Disorder

Craig A. Stern

1 Introduction

1.1 A Case

Annie is on trial in criminal proceedings for the killing of Bertha. What facts should figure in the judgment? Certainly we should like to know whether Annie caused Bertha's death. We should like to know whether Annie is a police officer, and whether Bertha was an armed attacker. These external facts, and others like them, should figure in the judgment. But what of internal facts, facts to do with Annie's state of mind to the extent such facts can be known? Should it matter that Annie intended to kill Bertha, or acted carelessly, or really had no way of knowing that she was causing Bertha's death? Should it matter that a mental disorder led Annie to be distracted in her behavior towards Bertha, or led her to hear God's voice commanding her to kill Bertha? How is the court to decide what internal facts should figure in its judgment?

1.2 Mind Over the Matter

The answers to these questions depend on the law of *mens rea*, or criminal mind. For every offense, the law establishes what state of mind the prosecution must prove that the defendant harbored concurrently with performing the criminal act, the *actus reus*. If the prosecution fails to prove both *mens rea* and *actus reus*, the defendant is not guilty.

The term *"mens rea"* sometimes is rendered "criminal intent," a good translation of the Latin. *"Mens"* in context means intention, as in the English sentences, "I have a mind to set him straight," or "I've changed my mind about going to the game tonight." But *"mens rea"* often embraces states of mind other than intention strictly speaking. It may denote such elements of offenses as "knowingly," "recklessly," or "negligently," for example. Say a statute declares, "It shall be a crime purposely to make a report to the police, knowing that it is false, and with recklessness as to whether the report causes the police to treat the falsely reported information as true." This statute requires the proof beyond a reasonable doubt of the *mens rea* of purpose, knowledge, and recklessness as to their respective elements for a defendant to be found guilty of this offense. Nevertheless, without explicitly requiring that the prosecution prove the defendant intended to mislead the police, the purpose, knowledge, and recklessness that the statute explicitly requires the prosecutor to prove do demonstrate the quality of the will, the intention, of the defendant. More on this later. For the time being, it suffices to note that *mens rea* embraces any mental element of an offense, any state of mind the prosecution must prove.

Sometimes the criminal law establishes that the defendant is *not* to be found guilty if he harbored a certain state of mind. In the situation of self-defense for example, one is not guilty of an assaultive offense if he honestly and reasonably believed countervailing force was necessary to prevent unlawful bodily harm immediately threatened by his victim. If the defendant was reasonable, he is not guilty, if unreasonable, he is guilty.[1] In this context, "reasonable" might be called a term of *"mens bona,"* but the law has not bothered to do so. Instead, it is easier to assimilate this good state of mind to *mens rea*. If a defendant acted in self-defense without reasonable belief in the need to act, it is as if he harbored *mens rea*. In some sense he did harbor *mens rea*: he acted unreasonably, negligently. Accordingly, throughout this chapter the consideration of *mens rea* encompasses situations like a defendant's lack of a mental state the law requires for a successful assertion of self-defense.

So the law defining the *mens rea* for offenses will tell our judge whether it makes a difference in Annie's case whether she intended to kill Bertha, or acted carelessly, or had no way of knowing that she was causing Bertha's death. Annie's *mens rea* will determine whether she is criminally liable at all for the killing, and if liable, for what grade of homicide. What then of the influence of mental disorder on Annie's behavior? Does the law of *mens rea* tell the judge whether distraction or delusion caused by mental disorder should matter in Annie's case?

No, not directly. But it is the thesis of this chapter that the law of *mens rea* should go a long way in answering it indirectly. This chapter suggests that the law on *mens rea* entails law on the relevance of the defendant's mental disorder. For example, whether there should exist an insanity defense, and of what type, follows at least in part from how the law treats *mens rea*. Beyond the question whether evidence of the defendant's psychological condition may be used to suggest that the defendant lacked the *mens rea* required to commit the offense charged, the whole range of questions on the relevance of the defendant's mental health should find answers flowing from how the law resolves questions on *mens rea*.

How the law resolves questions on *mens rea*, in turn, flows from the purpose the law pursues in its doctrine of *mens rea*, and this purpose flows from the purpose the law pursues in its doctrine of the criminal law itself. The links between the criminal law on mental disorder, the law on *mens rea*, and the whole of the criminal law mean that the questions posed in Annie's case find ultimate answers, at least in part, from the purpose of the criminal law itself.

1.3 Criminal Law and Criminal Minds

This chapter will demonstrate this linkage from the purpose and doctrine of the criminal law, through the purpose and doctrine of *mens rea*, to the purpose and doctrine for evidence regarding mental disorder in the criminal law. Four major approaches to *mens rea* stand for the range of available options. The chapter hopes to show that these four approaches suggest corresponding approaches to the relevance of mental disorder. To be sure, there is more variety and nuance to the purposes and doctrines of the criminal law and of *mens rea* than this analysis captures in its four approaches. Furthermore, there are determinants for the rules on the relevance of mental disorder beyond these four approaches. Nevertheless it is hoped that this chapter, simplifying matters as it does, will show important connections between the criminal law as a whole, *mens rea*, and the criminal law on mental disorder.

The first of the four approaches to the criminal law and *mens rea* has the criminal law not requiring proof of *mens rea* at all. Offenses comprise simply the criminal act. Perhaps the criminal law exists simply to prevent feuds, so the focus on dealing peaceably with offensive harm crowds out attention to the state of mind of the offender. Perhaps the criminal law exists to subject to corrective treatment all those failing to meet the established standard of behavior, whatever their state of mind. Perhaps the criminal law—or the relevant subset of it—exists simply to secure by general deterrence obedience to the law, so actors act at their own peril if they chose to act at all. Without *mens rea* playing a role in the criminal law, what role is to be played by mental disorder? If Annie's state of mind has nothing to do with her criminal liability for killing Bertha, what about a psychotic delusion that God commanded her to kill?

The second approach to the criminal law and *mens rea* sees the criminal law as punishing offenders' moral fault, with *mens rea* signaling that moral fault. Perhaps civil government is seen as a ministry ordained by God to apply a measure of retributive justice, "to execute wrath upon him that doeth evil."[2] If moral fault is what the criminal law is about, very likely the criminal law will treat a mad defendant differently from a bad defendant. Annie's psychotic delusion now should demand the attention of the judge, else he will mistake a mad Annie for a bad Annie and adjudge her guilt in a way inconsistent with the purpose of the criminal law and *mens rea*.

If we label the second approach "immoral *mens rea*," let us label the third, "elemental *mens rea*." In this approach, *mens rea* does not measure "general moral blameworthiness" as in the second approach.[3] Instead, *mens rea* measures the defendant's state of mind with respect to specific elements of the offense. Not enough that the defendant harbored "malice," for example. The defendant must have "known" the defaulted payments were due, or "recklessly" misled by speaking an untruth to someone he "believed" to be a federal officer, for example. Two underlying purposes for the criminal law might lead to this elemental approach for *mens rea*. On the one hand, the criminal law might no longer exist to administer deserved punishments for moral faults. It might exist for social control—to deter, to incapacitate, to rehabilitate. Elemental *mens rea* allows the civil government to set with precision the bounds of social control. On the other hand, the criminal law might still exist to render just deserts, but adopt the elemental approach to *mens rea* so that it might render these just deserts with more certainty, precision, and uniformity than under the immoral *mens rea* approach. Each of these two purposes could lead to the elemental approach to *mens rea*, as could some (uneasy) combination of the two, as in the mixed regime that now dominates American criminal law.[4] Evidence of a defendant's mental disorder could play a role in an elemental regime that varies according to the purpose(s) served by the doctrine of *mens rea* as it serves the purpose(s) of the criminal law. If Annie, misled by her mental disorder, thought Bertha a vicious Martian needing instant extermination, perhaps the judge should take that into account, focusing on how Annie's mental disorder affected Annie's *mens rea* for the element "human being" in the applicable definition of homicide.

The fourth approach to the criminal law and *mens rea* is unlike the other three. Those three seem to flow more or less deductively from the underlying purpose of the criminal law. The criminal law is to reduce the recourse to feuding, so it does not bother with *mens rea*. The criminal law is to punish immorality, so it uses *mens rea* as a test of immorality. The criminal law is to control society or to mete out punishment for specific wrongs, so it uses *mens rea* to identify clearly the offenses and offenders to target for these ends. The fourth approach, however, flows uphill, as it were, shaping the doctrine of *mens rea* as the consequence of adopting a policy on the use and significance of evidence of mental disorder in criminal trials. Settling upon the liberal use and significance of such evidence, proponents of this approach, in effect, advocate an expansive—one might say, "enriched"—version of *mens rea* that is present only if the defendant's state of mind is free from untoward psychological influence. Only defendants harboring such free, enriched *mens rea* should suffer criminal convictions. From this doctrine on *mens rea* one could suppose that the criminal law exists to apply its special force for social control to those who need that force rather than some milder and more therapeutic treatment. If Annie did not actually *think* Bertha a vicious Martian to be exterminated, but Annie's psychological make-up caused her to need to *treat* Bertha as if she were a vicious Martian to be exterminated, perhaps the judge should take that into account.

Taking each of these four approaches to *mens rea* in turn, this chapter explores the link between *mens rea* and evidence of mental disorder. If more than one purpose animates a given approach to *mens rea*, more than one approach to evidence on mental disorder may follow. Nevertheless, the links between all three elements—the whole body of criminal law, the doctrine on *mens rea*, and the doctrine on mental disorder—remain.

1.4 Insanity beyond *Mens Rea*

This chapter traces the links between these three elements to suggest that these links supply a useful way to understand the criminal law regarding evidence of a defendant's mental disorder. The tracing of these links, however, is not to suggest that they alone determine the contours of this evidence. At least three considerations apart from the *mens rea* link may also come into play.

First, whatever the purposes and shape of the criminal law and its doctrine on *mens rea*, the law might permit evidence of mental disorder to show that the defendant is not a fit subject of the criminal law at all. Perhaps "[v]ery crazy human beings are not enough like us in one of our essential attributes, rationality, to be considered persons to whom moral and legal norms are addressed."[5] Perhaps such folks are to be viewed as outside the realm of the criminal law altogether, even if the criminal law includes no element of *mens rea* (no feud if no "offending man," and no "man" if "very crazy" actor). A universal principle such as this would transcend the differences between the four approaches that occupy this chapter and so, in that sense, transcend the focus on *mens rea*.[6]

Second, the use and range of evidence on mental disorder reflect not only the substantive criminal law but also principles of criminal procedure and of the law of evidence. Beyond the general rules regarding expert evidence and burden of proof, for example, special rules may control the admission of certain psychological evidence. Where such special rules have to do with the doctrine of *mens rea*, they receive consideration further on. But, again, where they transcend the distinctions between the four major approaches to *mens rea* that occupy this chapter, their impact, though real, will go unaddressed.

Third, the use of psychological evidence in the sentencing of offenders convicted under the criminal law—or in the alternative dispositions of those not convicted—depends upon considerations that may differ significantly from those regarding whether offenders should be convicted in the first place. Consequently, this chapter generally prescinds from questions on mental disorder other than the test of criminal guilt.

It bears repeating that this chapter pretends to no comprehensive treatment of the role of evidence on mental disorder in the criminal law. It does not argue that the role of such evidence is fully determined by the doctrine of *mens rea*. It hopes to escape charges of reductionism. What it does attempt is an exploration of the great extent to which the role of *mens rea* affects the role of this evidence in the criminal law.

2 No *Mens Rea* Required for Offense

2.1 A Case (or Two)

Suppose Bill is on trial for the killing of Andy. Suppose further that the law cares not at all that Bill simply intended to wound Andy, or even that the killing was wholly accidental. In such a regime, should the judge admit evidence that Bill acted under the influence of mental disorder when he killed Andy?

Now suppose instead that William is on trial for polluting Andrew's lake. Suppose further that the law cares not at all that William could reasonably have thought the material he dumped on his own land would never reach Andrew's lake, or was not listed by law as a pollutant. In such a regime, should the judge admit evidence that William was insane when he dumped the material?

2.2 Insanity Escapes the Hatfields and McCoys

Long ago, it is said, in primitive times, crimes largely required proof of no mental element, no *mens rea* at all.[7] Several reasons for this regime suggest themselves. First, the means of finding facts and generating judgments were too crude to embrace the question of a defendant's state of mind. Trial by battle, by ordeal, or by wager of law seems ordained to resolve the ultimate liability of a defendant without much attention to the niceties. (Of course, the question of liability possibly could be posed to embrace such niceties, and if important enough, form might follow substance in such matters. But, as the next two paragraphs explain, the nicety of the defendant's state of mind was not important enough.)

Second, primitive crimes could be viewed as torts also. Before the papal revolution of 1075, civil justice in Europe was to restore direct victims and their families rather than (also) to vindicate the king's peace or satisfy the demands of abstract justice.[8] Like some areas of modern tort law, a delictual system combining tort with crime could follow a rule of strict liability, thereby rendering the mental state of the defendant irrelevant.

Third, and likely the most important reason, these provisions were adopted to establish an alternative to the feud.[9] Instead of feuding, offended parties (or their families) were to be paid off. Typically, the pay-off was negotiated, with the law helping to settle what was the appropriate composition for various offenses. In such a regime, though an offense (especially to the honor so valued in such times) might be graver the more it approached the intentional, the physical harm to the victim, the lasting and generally public result of the offense, predominated in the calculation of what would suffice to buy off the feud. *Mens rea* was not worth the complication.

It would scarcely seem likely that the mental disorder of the offender would matter in such a system. The procedures were no more adept at determining mental disorder than mental state. If the strict liability—liability without proof of *mens rea*—were by virtue of the delictual nature of crime, an insanity defense would be as out of place as it is in tort today.[10] The harm to be made good by the defendant (or rather his family, under these circumstances?) is no less for having been done by a mentally disordered actor. Likewise if the law is to prevent feuds by substituting peaceful resolution, and if preventing feuds between families and between tribes was the chief aim, the familial and tribal context of the settlement would reinforce the irrelevance of any mental disorder of the offender. The family or tribe would stand accountable for the offense of its member. If it failed to keep its mentally disordered member secure from harming others, so much the worse for it. In a primitive system of criminal law without concern for *mens rea*, Bill's mental disorder also would be of no concern.

2.3 For Prevention, Never Mind

It is not only a primitive system of criminal law that leaves *mens rea* out of account. Recent proposals for reform do likewise.[11] As with the primitive criminal law, practical problems regarding proof of *mens rea* may argue against its admission. Similarly, the criminal law may be cast in a role other than rendering deserved punishment to the offender. As avoiding feuds or restoring victims places the offender's state of mind to the side and focuses instead on the offensive act, so does a system of criminal law designed to advance the prevention of crime, or so it is said. The matter of *mens rea* distracts from the all-important harm that is to be deterred, or that signals the appropriate treatment of the offender who caused it.

The general deterrence that prevents offenses in the first place and the treatment that prevents repeat offenses by former offenders, again as it is said, leaves as little room for evidence of mental disorder as it does for evidence of *mens rea*.[12] The act alone matters for assessing criminal liability. As to deterrence, the possibility of a defense based upon mental disorder can only dilute it. As to treating offenders, there is no need in assessing criminal liability to distinguish between those who should receive ministrations to improve mental health and those who should undergo some other technique to modify their behavior in favor of obeying the law. "Both [prison and hospital] will be simply 'places of safety' in which offenders receive the treatment which experience suggests is most likely to evoke the desired response."[13] To prevent future Bills from killing future Andys, future Bills must not imagine mental disorder will offer them cover. To prevent our own Bill from killing again, the criminal law must entrust him to the civil government for whatever treatment best secures this result. A regime of preventive criminal law is therapeutic not penal, and conviction is simply the rite of entry into institutions that help law breakers become law keepers.

2.4 The Offense to Public Welfare

Strict liability in the criminal law need not come only full-bore. Instead, pockets of strict liability can exist within a system of criminal law that usually does attend to *mens rea*. Contemporary American law presents such pockets. Many violations of traffic laws, infractions against regulatory standards, and such misdeeds are defined—in whole or in part—without regard to *mens rea*. Typically, these misdeeds are classified as public welfare offenses. They present within the law an island that resembles the protective regime of criminal law just discussed, the major distinction being the island's emphasis on deterrence and not so much the treatment of offenders. The notion is to secure compliance with regulations for those who choose to act within the realm governed by those regulations. Within this realm, actors act at their peril, their state of mind being irrelevant to criminal liability.

To the extent public welfare offenses ignore *mens rea* in the defendant they should ignore mental disorder.[14] Perhaps a mental disorder that influenced the defendant's choice to enter the realm governed by strict liability should have some exculpatory effect.[15] Generally, however, if requiring *mens rea* is thought to compromise social control by public welfare offenses, so should allowing a defense based upon mental disorder. And so William has no such defense to liability for polluting Andrew's lake. To deter others from polluting, the criminal law takes no notice of the innocence of his mistake. That a mental disorder might render his mistake innocent is therefore of no concern.

2.5 Upshot

Bill and William have no defense that they acted by mistake. Preventing the feud after the fact or preventing future violations of the law takes no benefit from allowing such a defense. To the contrary, the defense would render the criminal law less effective a tool for achieving these ends. The question of *mens rea* is beside the point, an unwelcome complication.

The question of mental disorder falls to the same analysis. A mentally ill attacker may be no less a provocation to a feud. A mentally ill offender needs preventive treatment of some sort, and to allow a defense on the grounds of the illness would dilute the deterrent effect of the criminal law. As far as it depends upon the approach to *mens rea*, a criminal law regime of strict liability is unlikely to countenance a defense resting upon a defendant's mental disorder.

3 Immoral *Mens Rea* Required for Offense

3.1 A Case

Another killing. This time Adam kills Betty and thereafter stands trial for murder. To be guilty of murder, Adam must have killed Betty with malice—ill will. Not enough for liability that Adam caused Betty's death.

He must have manifested wickedness deserving the condemnation of the criminal law. In Adam's trial, what role is to be played by evidence of his mental disorder?

3.2 Room for Desert

The purpose of the criminal law might be wholly preventive. It might be to prevent feuds by supplying some alternative satisfaction for the affront of causing harm. It might be to prevent offenses by deterring the offense or treating the offender. As we have seen, the defendant's state of mind may be of little concern in such regimes. But if instead of for prevention, the criminal law is for rendering justice to immorality, the defendant's state of mind should occupy center stage.[16] The ill will behind the defendant's offense becomes fundamentally more important than the criminal act the defendant performed.[17]

A turn in the criminal law towards punishing immorality occurred in the West in the early middle ages. In the wake of the Papal Revolution of 1075, civil government became an agent of justice and not just an agent to keep the peace.[18] Criminal law became an instrument of justice to render deserved punishment, with *mens rea* as a measure of desert. In this transformation of the criminal law, the specifically Christian appreciation of the role of the will in assessing the moral quality of human action—enough here to mention the Sermon on the Mount—pointed the way.[19] "By [the 12th century] . . . the influence of the church law was becoming dominant. The canonists had long insisted that the mental element was the real criterion of guilt and under this influence the conception of subjective blameworthiness as the foundation of legal guilt was making itself strongly felt."[20] *Mens rea* in the sense of "general moral blameworthiness"[21] became an essential element of crime.

To some degree, this understanding of *mens rea* and of its centrality to the definition of crimes persists. "Malice" as immoral state of mind is an element of offenses in some American jurisdictions. Sometimes this fact is most evident when considering the effect of mental disorder on criminal liability, and to this effect we now turn.

3.3 With Malice towards None

"It is clear that the recognition of the insanity defense follows from the requirement of moral blameworthiness as a precondition for punishment."[22] If malice, for example, stands for the *mens rea* of general moral blameworthiness, evidence of a defendant's mental disorder might establish that the malice suggested by the defendant's act was actually no malice at all.[23] *Mens rea* as ill will gives rise to the need to examine the operation of the will itself:

> The consent of the will is that, which renders human actions either commendable or culpable. . . . And because the liberty or choice of the will presupposeth an act of the understanding to know the thing or action chosen by the will, it follows that, where there is a total defect of understanding, there is no free act of the will in the choice of things or actions.[24]

It may look for all the world as if Adam viciously intended to kill Betty. But if Adam's mental disorder made him think Betty a robot, or a human being God had told Adam to kill, the moral quality of his act appears in a wholly different light.

What kind of mental disorder in a defendant disproves the *mens rea* of general moral blameworthiness? The three major types of American tests for the insanity defense provide a convenient range of options. The first type is the cognitive test, the classic statement of which comes from *M'Naghten's Case*:

> [T]o establish a defence on the ground of insanity, it must be clearly proved that, at the time of the committing of the act, the party accused was labouring under such a defect of reason, from disease of the mind, as not to know the nature and quality of the act he was doing; or, if he did know it, that he did not know he was doing what was wrong.[25]

This test follows closely the rationale given here for admitting evidence of mental disorder to dispel the suggestion of *mens rea* arising from the facts of a criminal case. An earlier court had explained in its charge to the jury:

> That [the defendant] shot [at the victim], and that willfully [is proved]: but whether maliciously, that is the thing: that is the question; whether this man hath the use of his reason and sense? If he was under the visitation of God [i.e., mentally deranged], and could not distinguish between good and evil, and did not know what he did, though he committed the greatest offence, yet he could not be guilty of any offence against any law whatsoever; for guilt arises from the mind, and the wicked will and intention of man. If a man be deprived of his reason, and consequently of his intention, he cannot be guilty. . . .[26]

The moral quality of an act depends upon the orientation of the actor's will, and that in turn depends upon what the actor knows, or, rather, thinks he knows. Recall Adam and Betty: if Adam thinks he knows that Betty is a robot, or that God has commanded him to kill Betty, the moral evaluation of his act varies significantly from what it otherwise would be.

The second of the three tests for insanity is the volitional. This test exists as an addition to the cognitive test in some American jurisdictions. It asks whether "a psychological defect of the defendant, whatever his understanding, rendered him unable to control his conduct. This added volitional component of the insanity defense thereby extend[s] it beyond defects of reason, such as schizophrenia, to include compulsions like kleptomania and pyromania."[27] This second test, unlike the first, assesses more the cause of an evil will than whether the will is evil.[28] Many are the influences that may lead a defendant to harbor an evil will bringing forth a criminal act. Nature and nurture both may play a role. But unless the criminal law seeks to go behind the evil will to plumb its sources, and to find some sources—presumably not all if the criminal law is to endure—exculpatory, mental disorder that explains volition offers no exculpation.[29] If it is an irresistible impulse that impels Adam to kill Betty, he harbors no less malice. We may simply have some insight into why he harbors the malice.

The third test of insanity is today to be found in New Hampshire alone.[30] Under it, "an accused [is] not criminally responsible if his unlawful act was the product of mental disease or mental defect."[31] Though hard to parse and to apply, it seems clear enough that the product test would extend a defense to defendants who would meet the volitional test. It likely departs still further from the cognitive test, excusing defendants whose evidence somehow attributes their actions to mental disorder. Like the volitional test, the product test (when it does more than replicate the operation of the cognitive test) does not serve to negate a defendant's malice but only to explain it. Adam's ill will may have an explanation, but explaining ill will does not counter it.

If the criminal law requires the *mens rea* of general moral blameworthiness for a defendant to be guilty of an offense, the criminal law should allow a defendant to answer a suggestion of *mens rea* by showing that what appears to be *mens rea* is something else instead. A cognitive, but not a volitional, mental disorder could supply such a showing. Making *mens rea* an element of crime makes the issue of mental disorder negating *mens rea* an important element of the criminal law.

3.4 *Mens Rea* for the Soft-Headed

The requirement of *mens rea* as general moral blameworthiness developed in Anglo-American law to measure guilt worthy of criminal punishment in a system of criminal law designed to punish criminals according to moral desert. Christian thinking on sin and guilt emphasized the will, and through canon law this emphasis found its way into the criminal law. But there are other paths by which general moral blameworthiness may find its way into the criminal law.

One of these other paths is marked by Oliver Wendell Holmes, Jr., for whom the criminal law is not meant to punish wickedness but rather to shape behavior. "For the most part, the purpose of the criminal law is only to induce external conformity to rule."[32] In principle, then, Holmes should support a regime of strict criminal liability, liability without regard *to mens rea*. But Holmes, taking the criminal law as he found it—a system requiring at least some low level of *mens rea* as a requisite for liability—explained why a criminal law dedicated to social control would include some *mens rea* in its definitions of offenses. Although "we should expect . . . more [in the criminal law] than elsewhere to find that the tests of liability are external, and independent of the degree of evil in the particular person's motives or intentions," "to deny that criminal liability . . . is founded on blameworthiness . . . would shock the moral sense of any civilized community. . . ."[33] Because that moral sense governs prosecutors, judges, and juries, the criminal law cannot take the form that strict social control would lead it to assume. At least some *mens rea* to signal moral blameworthiness must be an element of crimes because "a law [that] punished conduct [that] would not be blameworthy in the average member of the community would be too severe for that community to bear."[34]

What then of mental disorder? Community cooperation in the enforcement of the criminal law requires that liability be limited to the blameworthy, with basic *mens rea* signaling that blameworthiness. Perhaps evidence of mental disorder would negate the blameworthiness, much as the *mens rea* of malice is negated (as discussed previously). Perhaps the social control that is the very purpose of the criminal law would prevail, with the community satisfied enough with the finding of *mens rea* and paying no mind to mental disorder. It comes down to sociology and public opinion, not logic, for one like Holmes. As far as logic goes, however, it would seem that the criminal law constructed on Holmes's plan should take mental disorder into account if it draws in question the link between *mens rea* and blameworthiness. How it may draw that link in question occupies later pages of this chapter.

3.5 Upshot

Adam's criminal liability for the killing of Betty depends in part upon his *mens rea*, understood as an indicator of his wickedness in the killing.

The criminal law might include this *mens rea* requirement for liability because the object of the criminal law is to render deserved punishment to offenders. Or the criminal law might include this *mens rea* requirement because the object of social control must be pursued through human beings unwilling to inflict necessary criminal penalties on those it finds unblameworthy in the criminal conduct. Whichever purpose exists for the *mens rea* requirement, Adam's liability for killing Betty hinges in part on moral blame.

When moral blameworthiness itself actually is the *mens rea*—as in some versions of the *mens rea* "malice"—mental disorder has been taken simply to negate the mens rea. A mentally ill Adam has no malice, whatever otherwise might appear from the facts of the killing. When *mens rea*, instead of constituting moral blameworthiness itself, indirectly indicates moral blameworthiness, mental disorder may suggest that the defendant lacks moral blameworthiness despite his *mens rea*. A mentally ill Adam may have had *mens rea* in the killing of Betty, but his illness may prevent the implication of blameworthiness from his *mens rea*, as explained in pages to follow. Once *mens rea* plays a role in assessing criminal liability, mental disorder also plays a role.

4 Elemental *Mens Rea* Required for Offense

4.1 A Case

Barbara killed Alex, a police officer on duty. She is charged with the offense of knowingly killing a police officer on duty, an offense requiring that she knew her victim was a police officer on duty. Should evidence of Barbara's mental illness be considered in her trial? If so, as to what question—as to whether she had the *mens rea* (the knowledge that she was killing a police officer on duty), or as to something else?

4.2 Precision Control

Mens rea developed in Anglo-American criminal law originally because the criminal law was to accord wrongdoers their just deserts, and just deserts depended upon the moral quality of the intention of defendants. Holmes rationalized the continued use of the *mens rea* of basic criminal intent as a means to accommodate the social instrument of criminal law to the moral sense of those necessary to its administration. In both regimes, *mens rea* connected the criminal law to the moral blameworthiness of offenders.

The dominant purpose for criminal law these days tends to be social control—the general deterrence of wrongdoing and the incapacitation, rehabilitation, and specific deterrence of past wrongdoers to prevent their doing wrong again. Under this system of criminal law, *mens rea* comes to serve a new purpose.

> The conception of *mens rea* has varied with the changing underlying conceptions and objectives of criminal justice. . . . Under the dominating influence of the canon law and the penitential books the underlying objective of criminal justice gradually came to be the punishment of evil-doing; as a result the mental factors necessary for criminality were based upon a mind bent on evil-doing in the sense of moral wrong. Our modern objective tends more and more in the direction, not of awarding adequate punishment for moral wrong-doing, but of protecting social and public interest. To the extent that this objective prevails, the mental element requisite for criminality . . . is coming to mean, not so much a mind bent on evil-doing as an intent to do that which unduly endangers social or public interest.[35]

The *mens rea* of offenses is to fine-tune their focus, specifying with some precision what ought not to be done in the context of what is, for example, intended or known by the actor. Such precision permits the application of social control to achieve the desired effect, both concentrating control on shaping behavior as desired and also reducing the chill on other behavior. It also permits the rationing and application of the appropriate degree of force given the nature and degree of the danger to social interests.

Again, Holmes offers a helpful discussion. Holmes explained why, to his mind, the definition of larceny requires that the defendant intend permanently to deprive the owner of his property. It is not because a defendant harbors a will more evil by virtue of so intending and therefore deserves more punishment than one who merely takes another's property without permission. For Holmes, the specific intent of larceny is a placeholder for social harm beyond that mere taking.

> In larceny the consequences immediately flowing from the act are generally exhausted with little or no harm to the owner. Goods are removed from his possession by trespass and that is all, when the crime is complete. But they must be permanently kept from him before the harm is done which the law seeks to prevent. A momentary loss of possession is not what has been guarded against with such severe penalties. . . .
>
> There must be an intent to deprive [the owner of his property]. . . . [T]he intent is an index to the external event which probably would have happened, and if the law is to punish at all, it must, in this case, go on probabilities,

not on accomplished facts. . . . In theft the intent to deprive the owner of his property establishes that the thief would have retained, or would not have taken steps to restore, the stolen goods.[36]

According to Holmes, *mens rea* can augment or supply information regarding the circumstances of an offense, thereby fitting it to the penal consequence. Efficient social control is the purpose of the criminal law and of its mental component, *mens rea*.

This approach to criminal law and *mens rea* invites precision in the assignment of *mens rea* requirements to offenses. The ultimate in this precision is an elemental version of *mens rea*. In this version, a stated *mens rea* applies to each *actus reus* element of an offense. The Model Penal Code presents a pinnacle of the elemental version of *mens rea*: "a person is not guilty of an offense unless he acted purposely, knowingly, recklessly or negligently, as the law may require, with respect to each material element of the offense."[37] In Barbara's case, the *mens rea* term "knowing" applies to the circumstance element that her victim be a "police officer on duty." The presumably heightened penal consequences for someone knowingly killing a police officer on duty are thought to advance efficient social control. One that knows an on-duty police officer is endangered by his conduct may be expected to take extra care, or one especially tempted to kill an on-duty police officer for the very reason that he is such might be dissuaded by the aggravated penalty. So much for general deterrence. As to dealing with one guilty of committing this offense, a heightened penal consequence (apart from making good on the threatened penalty for the sake of general deterrence) ensures that the one who knowingly committed so grave (and perhaps so tempting) an offense will be subject to enhanced preventive treatments suited to so dangerous an offender.

In a regime of elemental *mens rea* calibrated for efficient social control, what role is to be played by evidence of a defendant's mental disorder? The role will differ from that it played in the regime of *mens rea* as general moral blameworthiness. There, the evidence suggested that the defendant was not morally blameworthy, either by negating the *mens rea* or by offering an explanation other than wickedness for the apparent *mens rea*. In the modern elemental approach dedicated wholly to social control, moral blameworthiness has no bearing on criminal liability. It is the *mens rea* itself and its significance for setting general deterrence and individual prevention that are determinative, not some moral assessment of the defendant's acts for the purpose of meting out just deserts.

So, if Barbara knows that Alex is a police officer on duty and kills him, the statute that has made that knowledge an element of the offense has prescribed (in the context of sentencing provisions and such) penal consequences for Barbara calculated most efficiently to deter others and to prevent Barbara from committing this (and perhaps other) crime in the future. Barbara's knowledge is itself significant for this calculation. Whether she wanted to kill Alex to resist arrest or because a psychotic delusion led her to believe she was commanded to kill Alex should not matter. The general deterrence from the statute will be less effective if folks contemplating the killing of police officers on duty think a (feigned) mental disorder might lessen penal consequences. Individual prevention—incapacitation, rehabilitation, special deterrence—might be compromised. If Barbara is the sort of person knowingly to kill on-duty police officers, she might be inclined to repeat her offense if the next command were to come from a source other than a psychotic delusion. In this regard she differs not at all from another convicted of the same offense without any evidence of mental disorder.

Two further considerations support the view that evidence of mental disorder in a defendant that harbored the requisite *mens rea* should play no role in a system of criminal law dedicated to social control and for that reason embracing a regime of elemental *mens rea*. First, the preventive ends that animate social control distinguish moral condemnation from criminal liability. Criminal liability is a matter separate from moral desert. It exists solely to shape behavior. This is not to say that criminal law has no connection whatever to morality. Morality may supply a strong impetus for wanting to prevent certain behaviors. But the criminal law itself and its instrument of criminal conviction import no necessary moral conclusion of their own beyond any moral conclusion to be drawn directly from the facts of the case. Therefore, there is no need to permit evidence of mental disorder to deflect the criminal law in the direction of just deserts. Second, and similarly, the criminal conviction of defendants such as Barbara need not bar them from the appropriate treatment of their mental disorder. Prevention can include the therapeutic. Criminal conviction simply certifies that a person is to be subjected to enhanced state control to prevent his offending again. (In this respect, what major difference in disposition exists if the person instead were found not guilty by reason of insanity and committed to an asylum?) In the presence of *mens rea*, evidence of mental disorder adds nothing significant to the defendant's case.

So far we have considered whether a system of elemental *mens rea* to secure social control has room for evidence of mental disorder when the defendant has harbored the requisite *mens rea*. It seems there is no such room. But evidence of a defendant's mental disorder may have a more direct bearing upon *mens rea* than explaining how it was that the defendant harbored the *mens rea*. Such evidence may go to disproving (or raising a reasonable doubt) that the defendant harbored that *mens rea* at all. It may show what is sometimes called "diminished capacity," the inability or simple failure of the defendant to have had the *mens rea* sufficient to support conviction for the offense.

Again, back to Barbara. If Barbara's psychotic delusion somehow leads her to kill Alex, knowing that he is a police officer on duty, her delusion will not prevent her conviction under the statute against killing a police officer on duty with knowledge that he is such. Very different is the case, however, if her psychotic delusion interferes with her knowing that Alex is a police officer on duty. In such circumstances, she lacks the very *mens rea* that the statute requires she possess before she can be convicted. If the elemental *mens rea* within a criminal law regime built upon social control signals the penal response appropriate for a particular offense, that penal response is not called for in the absence of that *mens rea*. A Barbara without the requisite knowledge ought not to be treated as a Barbara with the requisite knowledge (though some other treatment there may be for a Barbara subject to dangerous psychotic delusions).

Far from being irrelevant, evidence of mental disorder that suggests a defendant lacked the *mens rea* requisite for conviction may be especially important in a system of elemental *mens rea*. In the prosecution of Barbara, for example, the state's evidence likely will show circumstances calling for the jury to infer that Barbara knew that Alex was a police officer on duty when she killed him. The evidence will show that Alex was in uniform, identified himself as a police officer, was performing the duties of a police officer, and that Barbara was in a position to observe these facts. Because a normal person in Barbara's position was sure to know that Alex was a police officer on duty, the jury will be led to find that Barbara herself knew the same. For this very reason, Barbara should be able to show that she is not a normal person if her abnormality undercuts the minor premise necessary to the jury's conclusion that she knew Alex was a police officer on duty. Expert testimony explaining how her mental disorder blocked her knowledge of Alex's situation could be essential to the case.

In strict logic and in theory, evidence—including qualified expert medical or psychological evidence—that may suggest the absence of requisite *mens rea* in the defendant should be welcome in an elemental-*mens-rea*, social-control regime of criminal law. Here again, the Model Penal Code points the way: "Evidence that the defendant suffered from a mental disease or defect is admissible whenever it is relevant to prove that the defendant did or did not have a state of mind which is an element of the offense"[38] (Sometimes American jurisdictions disallow such evidence entirely, or limit it to questions of the higher level of *mens rea*—so called "specific intent" of the sort involved, for instance, in Barbara's case. The reasons tend to be practical. One important practical reason comes to the fore soon in this discussion, another in the next subpart.) The relevance of evidence of mental disorder under a rule like that of the Model Penal Code depends upon the nature of the particular *mens rea* involved. Regarding the four levels of *mens rea* used by the Code, the relevance to purpose and knowledge seems clear enough. Think of Barbara's case. Furthermore, although the discussion of section 4.02 in the official comment seems to limit itself to questions involving these two levels of *mens rea*,[39] presumably this sort of evidence would be admissible to prove lack of yet another level of *mens rea*, recklessness. The Code defines recklessly:

> A person acts recklessly with respect to a material element of an offense when he consciously disregards a substantial and unjustifiable risk that the material element exists or will result from his conduct. The risk must be of such a nature and degree that, considering the nature and purpose of the actor's conduct and the circumstances known to him, its disregard involves a gross deviation from the standard of conduct that a law-abiding person would observe in the actor's situation.[40]

It would seem that evidence of a defendant's mental disorder could disprove conscious disregard as easily as knowledge or purpose. If Barbara were held to answer under a statute that punished the killing of an on-duty police officer if the defendant were reckless as to that circumstance, she should be able to adduce evidence that her mental disorder induced a distraction that prevented her from being conscious of a risk of which the other evidence suggests she was aware.

Section 4.02(1) likely goes no further. Though language in section 2.02(2)(c) speaks regarding the defendant of "circumstances known to him" and "the actor's situation," these subjectivizing provisions (and the same to be found in the definition of "negligently"[41]) apparently invite no inquiry into the mental health of the defendant.[42] The objective component of recklessness and the objective nature of negligence are not to be adjusted for a defendant's mental disorder. It stands to reason that the standard of care for these levels of *mens rea* would not be that of a mentally ill person.

The inherent limitation of evidence of mental disorder to the negation only of subjective components of *mens rea* serves a practical purpose well suited to a criminal law regime established for social control. Usually, offenses that require proof of higher levels of *mens rea* stand alongside other offenses that punish similar conduct accompanied by some lesser level of *mens rea*. If Barbara is not guilty of killing Alex under the statute that requires proof she knew Alex was a police officer on duty, she may be guilty of murder plain and simple. Offenses of recklessness or negligence, or of the lower general intent instead of the higher specific intent, stand as a backup to the type of offenses more susceptible to a defense based upon the defendant's mental disorder. The social control secured by these lesser offenses remains intact, providing the appropriate deterrent and individual prevention for the offense the defendant actually did commit, *mens rea* and *actus reus*.

Another factor minimizing the deleterious effect of diminished capacity evidence on social control is that such evidence is very rare:

> The fear for public safety [inspired by the admission of evidence of diminished capacity] is genuine but overwrought.... [T]he effect of mental disorder, including severe mental disorder, is seldom to negate the "subjective" *mens reas*, such as purpose, knowledge, and recklessness, that are part of the definitions of crimes. Mental disorder may give people irrational reasons to form the *mens rea*, but it almost never interferes with formation of that mental state. There are instances in which subjective *mens rea* is entirely negated, but they are few, indeed.[43]

When evidence of mental disorder does speak to a lack of *mens rea*, a social control regime with elemental *mens rea* should entertain it. To do so is no great threat to social control, but rather helps refine it.

To be sure, some diminished capacity defenses threaten the social control supposedly put into place by the criminal law. Experts may give opinions ill-supported by science or that otherwise mislead juries as to the facts of the case. They may give evidence from perspectives inconsistent with the presuppositions of the criminal law. In fact, they may encourage juries, functionally at least, to redefine *mens rea* itself. These matters merit discussion later in this chapter.

A system of elemental *mens rea* complements a criminal law regime designed for social control. If Barbara has the *mens rea* sufficient for conviction, no evidence of her mental disorder should be permitted to bar her conviction. Even if the mental disorder somehow led her to have the *mens rea*, the purpose of social control allows her no such defense. If, on the other hand, evidence of her mental disorder militates against her having the *mens rea* required by the definition of the offense, the matter stands on wholly different ground. If Barbara lacks the necessary *mens rea*, she is not guilty of the offense. The need to prove *mens rea* makes such a mental disorder a very important matter.

4.3 The Morality of Elemental *Mens Rea*

The previous section of this chapter explained the move to elemental *mens rea* as an advance in social control. Leaving the retributivism of general moral blameworthiness behind, the matter becomes one of precision in directing the force of criminal law toward efficient general deterrence and individual prevention. Elemental *mens rea* is a major tool for that purpose. Permitting the introduction of evidence of mental disorder that raises a reasonable doubt that the defendant harbored the requisite *mens rea* would seem an integral part of such a regime.

But there is a purpose elemental *mens rea* may serve other than social control, the purpose of retribution. Retributivism in the criminal law need not conceive of *mens rea* as general moral blameworthiness. Instead, *mens rea* may signal the precise moral blameworthiness pertaining to specific elements of the particular offense involved.

Under the system of *mens rea* as general moral blameworthiness, "malice," for example, could embrace any wickedness that was involved with, or led to, the *actus reus* of an offense. Old formulations of the felony murder rule that classified as murder any death that occurred in the course of a felony are an example.[44] The evil of unlawfully hunting the king's game made murder out of a fluke human death in the hunt, perhaps by the heart attack of a hunting partner overjoyed by a good shot. Though not manifesting an evil state of mind regarding the taking of human life, the defendant was manifesting *general* moral blameworthiness in the unlawful hunting that eventuated in the death. That sufficed for malice. Criminal law was to render to offenders the punishment their wickedness deserved, and even a chance death supplied the occasion for retribution according to the offender's evil, perhaps in the sense of his evil character.

A retributivism that understands the purpose of criminal law differently leads to a different understanding of *mens rea*. The criminal law still punishes evil. That evil, though, is more the evil of the offense than that of the offender. Offenses mark particular evil acts performed with particular states of mind regarding those very acts. Unlawful hunting should not supply a predicate for murder unless the defendant harbored a blameworthy mental state regarding the human death involved. *Mens rea* is not general moral blameworthiness, but rather a gauge of the precise blameworthiness directed toward the forbidden *actus reus*. The criminal law is to punish certain evil deeds done with a certain state of mind attendant upon those very deeds. Elemental *mens rea* serves this purpose. Beyond this change in the purpose of the criminal law, other considerations favor elemental *mens rea* over *mens rea* as general moral blameworthiness. To punish as murder both a death incidental to unlawful hunting and a death deliberately caused for spite seems unjust. Elemental *mens rea* allows precision and clarity in the definition of offenses, but it also allows a more just proportionality and equality before the law in the rendering of deserved punishment for wrongs.

A regime of elemental *mens rea* may find support from two different conceptions of the purpose of the criminal law, social control and retributivism. This chapter will suggest that these two different conceptions lead to two different approaches to linking the structure and operation of *mens rea* with evidence of mental disorder. These two different conceptions also lead to divergent interpretations and practice within the criminal law in other respects. Nevertheless, the dominant approach to the criminal law in contemporary America melds these two conceptions. Probably the typical approach is "limiting retributivism," or a "mixed" approach. This approach takes the purpose of the criminal as social control. Offenders are to be punished to deter others and to prevent offenders themselves from offending again. To pursue these ends single-mindedly, however, would produce a system of draconian punishment, and even the infliction of "punishment" on those yet to offend. So double-mindedness suggests itself: punish for social control, but not to exceed what the defender deserves. Because social control and retributivism spawn divergent doctrine and practice, combining them yields more a mixture than a compound. Nevertheless, the following discussion of elemental *mens rea* and evidence of mental disorder focuses on what the retributive approach brings to these matters to the extent the criminal law embraces that approach, whether in whole or in part.

The social control use of elemental *mens rea* was straightforward. The definitions of criminal offenses establish various states of mind as sufficient for conviction. Those states of mind themselves indicate what is to be deterred in others and what severity of penal response offenders need for prevention. Because *mens rea* itself serves these purposes directly, evidence of mental disorder pertains to the question of *mens rea* only inasmuch as it shows that the defendant lacked *mens rea* at all. If Barbara killed Alex, knowing that Alex was a police officer on duty, both the example to the public and the magnitude of the consequences she needs should follow, whatever her mental health. Not so, if her mental disorder interferes with her acquiring the *mens rea*.

The role elemental *mens rea* plays in a retributive system of criminal law is more subtle. The importance of the will to the moral quality of human acts has already received attention in this chapter. If the elemental *mens rea* is "purpose," or "intentionally," or the like, the link between *mens rea* and evil will may be clear. But if the elemental *mens rea* is "knowingly," or "recklessly," or "negligently," how do these states of mind indicate an evil will? Degrees of dangerousness they may signal well enough for social control. Retributivism demands more.

The more comes from understanding how various levels of *mens rea* actually reveal the quality of the will of the defendant. Take Barbara and her killing of Alex, the on-duty police officer. Barbara faces prosecution under a statute that punishes knowingly killing a police officer on duty. Barbara must have willed to act, knowing that she causes the death of an on-duty police officer.[45] If so, her will appears evil with respect to Alex's status. Compare the situation if the statute instead required recklessness or negligence regarding the victim's being an on-duty police officer. Again, the defendant must have willed to act, but now in the face of awareness of an unreasonable risk that the victim is such, or in the face of circumstances that the defendant should have understood as indicating this unreasonable risk.[46] A defendant that wills to act aware of this risk but disregarding it still manifests ill will regarding the victim's status as on-duty police officer, but less than if he is purposed the death for that very reason, or acted knowing his victim was such. He should have taken care not to cause this death once aware that the aggravating factor could be present. Likewise, if only negligence was required to be proved, the defendant must have willed to act without bothering to assure himself that the life of an on-duty police officer would not be put at unreasonable risk by his action. His will, still blameworthy with respect to the victim's status, is less so than that of a defendant with purpose, knowledge, or recklessness instead. The more markedly the victim's status plays an actuating role—or fails to play a cautionary role—in the defendant's willing, the more blameworthy the defendant regarding that element.

Note how even an objective standard of *mens rea*—negligence—indicates an evil will in one willing to act negligently. H.L.A. Hart illustrated: "'I didn't *mean* to do it. I just didn't think.' 'But you should have thought.' . . . [M]ost people would think that . . . such a rejection of 'I didn't think' as an excuse is quite justified."[47] Later, he explained:

> Only a theory that mental operations like attending to, or thinking about, or examining a situation are somehow "either there or not there," and so utterly outside our control, can lead to the theory that we are *never* responsible if . . . we fail to think or remember. And this theory of the uncontrollable character of mental operations would, of course, be fatal to responsibility for even the most cold-blooded, deliberate action performed by an agent with the maximum "foresight."[48]

Acting negligently is an act of the will. And that choice (in most, at least) is wrong, as Morse and Hoffman explain:

> The culpably careless have the capacity to pay attention and to be as careful as we expect them to be, yet they have not exercised that capacity. They have failed to respect the rights and interests of their victims. Such a failure is the essence of blameworthiness in our system of morality and law.[49]

Again, it is not that being unaware of things is in itself a moral wrong. Rather, it is that negligence signals a moral fault in one who decides to act when circumstances counsel that inaction is the proper course.

Elemental *mens rea* in a retributive system of criminal law works as a measure of the ill will the defendant harbors with respect to other elements of the offense. But this measure presupposes a sound working between state of mind and will, between head and heart. If the evidence shows simply that Barbara knew Alex was a police officer on duty when she killed him, the evidence shows she willed evil with respect to this status of Alex. She killed despite knowing her victim was worthy of special regard, so to speak. But if the evidence shows, further, that she killed Alex because a psychotic delusion led her to believe that on-duty police officers are all brainwashed operatives that need violent removal, or crazed terrorists conspiring to destroy the earth any minute, an evaluation of her will no longer makes the usual move from knowledge to evil will. The *mens rea* remains: Barbara knows Alex is an on-duty police officer. But her mental disorder makes her think she knows more about Alex. It is her psychosis that prompts her action on her knowledge that Alex is an on-duty police officer. Consequently, evidence of mental disorder prevents a mistaken inference of ill will, an inference justified only by the presupposition that Barbara's mind and will work together after the usual fashion.

Note that the analysis here is not that mental disorder negates *mens rea*. That analysis was offered regarding *mens rea* as general moral blameworthiness, or as an elemental tool for social control. Rather, the analysis here is that mental disorder requires an adjustment in the usual step from level of *mens rea* to level of evil will. An affirmative insanity defense is what is needed to perform this adjustment.

As to what type of insanity defense follows from a retributive system of elemental *mens rea*, much of what has been said above about mental disorder in the older system of *mens rea* as general moral blameworthiness remains pertinent. A volitional or product test that goes toward explaining *why* a defendant willed evil is beside the point, if willing evil suffices (tautologically?) to establish an evil will. A cognitive test, on the other hand, seems precisely to fit the bill. This test invites an inquiry into the defendant's understanding of the circumstances of his actions to see whether his *mens rea* stood for some crucial misunderstanding instead of ill will. To ensure that the intellect and will truly were engaged without a significant distortion from mental disorder, perhaps an "affective" version of the cognitive is best. Take, for example, the federal statute:

> It is an affirmative defense to a prosecution under any [f]ederal statute that, at the time of the commission of the acts constituting the offense, the defendant, as a result of severe mental disease or defect, was unable to appreciate the nature and quality or the wrongfulness of his acts. Mental disease or defect does not otherwise constitute a defense.[50]

If a defendant cannot "appreciate the nature and quality or the wrongfulness of his acts," the presence of *mens rea* will mislead the factfinder into finding an evil will where there is none.

One obvious question remains in discussing evidence of mental disorder within a system of retributive elemental *mens rea*. What if this evidence goes not towards adjusting the usual link between *mens rea* and evil will but instead towards the absence of *mens rea* altogether? The regime of elemental *mens rea* for social control seems to invite such evidence. One would think the same would obtain here as well.

So say some, and the options discussed here previously have found their way into the mixed social-control-with-limiting-retributivism regimes in America today. The same cautions discussed here and to be discussed further later on may give some pause. An additional complication comes from the interplay between the affirmative insanity defense that a retributive elemental system of *mens rea* involves and the derivative defense (so called because deriving from the definition of the offense itself) of lack of *mens rea* as supported by evidence of mental disorder. If the affirmative defense places the burden of proof on a defendant to show an excusing mental disorder, a problem may arise if the defendant's mental disorder could negate *mens rea*:

> [I]f a State is to have this authority [to impose upon a defendant the burden of proof to establish an insanity defense] in practice as well as in theory, it must be able to deny a defendant the opportunity to displace the presumption of sanity more easily when addressing a different issue in the course of the criminal trial. Yet . . . just such an opportunity would be available if expert testimony of mental disease and incapacity could be considered for whatever a factfinder might think it was worth on the issue of *mens rea*. . . . [T]he presumption of

sanity would then be only as strong as the evidence a factfinder would accept as enough to raise a reasonable doubt about *mens rea* for the crime charged; once reasonable doubt was found, acquittal would be required, and the standards established for the defense of insanity would go by the boards.[51]

While this argument has not gone unanswered,[52] it may serve to distinguish a system of criminal law with elemental *mens rea* for retribution from a system of criminal law with elemental *mens rea* solely for social control. The affirmative insanity defense of the former may give rise to limits on evidence of mental disorder to challenge a finding of *mens rea*. Not without irony, then, might Barbara be allowed to show that her mental disorder led her to think that Alex, though a police officer on duty, was also a bloodthirsty demoniac, but not be allowed to show that her mental disorder kept her from knowing that Alex was a police officer on duty at all.

4.4 Upshot

If the criminal law under which Barbara is prosecuted for the killing of Alex includes a system of elemental *mens rea*, that system should allow her to adduce evidence of her mental disorder. If for social control alone, it should allow her to show she lacked *mens rea*. If for retributivism—or partly for retributivism—it should allow her to show (perhaps in addition) that the *mens rea* she harbored does not indicate that her will was evil. It is the purpose served by the system of elemental *mens rea* that entails the relevance of evidence of mental disorder. Barbara's case would vary accordingly.

Again, it bears repeating that reasons other than the system of *mens rea* may support the admission of evidence of a defendant's mental disorder. Possibly, limiting retributivism may inspire an insanity defense that is not tightly linked to the system of elemental *mens rea*.[53] Nevertheless, that system itself gives rise to a corresponding use of evidence of mental disorder, and that correspondence is the subject of this chapter.

5 Enriched *Mens Rea* Required for Offense

5.1 A (Final) Case

Yvonne killed her lover, Zed. The evidence shows that she intended to kill him, and that she had carefully planned the killing over the course of weeks. She faces a charge of first-degree murder, a charge that requires the state to prove malice, deliberation, and premeditation. Though malice typically includes intentional killing, and deliberation and premeditation typically would be demonstrated by weeks of planning, Yvonne seeks to introduce evidence of a mental disorder to raise a reasonable doubt as to malice, deliberation, and premeditation in her case. She would show that her disorder caused her to believe absolutely and without hesitation that killing Zed was the loving and right thing to do, and that this belief prevented her from soundly reflecting upon the enormity of her act. Does the state's need to prove the *mens rea* of malice, deliberation, and premeditation entail the admissibility of Yvonne's evidence?

5.2 Disordered *Mens Rea*

This chapter so far has observed how rules on evidence of mental disorder follow from rules on *mens rea*. Now, it observes how rules on mens rea may follow from rules on evidence of mental disorder. Instead of the law on *mens rea* implying the law on mental disorder, the law on mental disorder implies for courts inclined to this approach the law on *mens rea*.

The most likely scenario for this "reverse implication" takes place within a system of criminal law that uses elemental *mens rea* for retributive purposes, at least in part. The system includes an insanity defense perhaps, but not as broad a defense as the courts think appropriate. The system also permits the introduction of evidence of mental disorder to suggest the absence of *mens rea* in the defendant. The path to enlarge the defensive effect of this evidence lies in adjusting the definition of *mens rea*. If the court thinks the evidence should exculpate a defendant, it need only make sure that the required *mens rea* be defeated by the evidence. It can accomplish this end by enriching the definition of *mens rea* so the disordered defendant will have lacked this newly enriched *mens rea*. For example, if a cognitive insanity defense is thought too narrow, something that functions as a volitional test of insanity can be created by requiring that *mens rea* be present in the defendant in some rich form free of the effects of mental disorder. This move converts a diminished capacity defense into what is in effect a defense of diminished (or partial) responsibility:

> Courts are often faced . . . with defendants whose conduct meets the technical *mens rea* requirements, yet whose mental abnormality seems to require mitigation of culpability by providing a form of excuse in addition to a reduction of sentence. Some activist and "creative" courts have solved the quandary by interpreting the *mens rea* elements in a way that adopts the partial responsibility variant. These courts have often tortured the ordinary meanings of *mens rea* terms in order to achieve a result they perceive is just.[54]

So, for example, in a series of cases like Yvonne's, the California Supreme Court, until overturned by the legislature, enlarged the concept of *mens rea* in homicide to provide defendants with derivative defenses from evidence of mental disorder.[55] Malice, deliberation, and premeditation then require thoughts unaffected by mental disorder; evidence of mental disorder therefore supplies a defense.

Though the upshot of such a move may be clear enough as to the admission of evidence of the mental disorder of the defendant, it may be difficult for a court to explain precisely the newly enriched concept of *mens rea* itself. "The diminished capacity rationale of [the California] cases reflected a broader and more amorphous view of *mens rea* which allows the fact-finder to consider any evidence which may negate, excuse, or mitigate the actor's culpability."[56] "Not surprisingly, the expert testimony admitted under this broader view of *mens rea* does not correlate with any specific statutory state of mind requirement,"[57] and as to the "something more" beyond the formerly sufficient *mens rea*, "[a]rticulation of what that 'something more' is has proven to be an extremely difficult task."[58]

The alteration of *mens rea* to provide a broader derivative defense based upon mental disorder may take another turn when supported by psychodynamic psychology, "the theory of human behavior that posits unconscious variables and processes, especially psychological instincts, conflicts, anxieties, and defenses, as the primary cause of behavior."[59] If Yvonne intended in some superficial sense to kill Zed, and in mechanical fashion planned the killing, but her psychological makeup both drove her to the act and at the same time prevented her from fully understanding what she was up to, a court could rule that she lacked the sort of intention necessary for malice. Her mental disorder impelled her to the killing, but that differs from the cold-blooded "pure" intention contemplated by that standard of *mens rea*. She suppressed from her consciousness a full understanding of what she was about. Perhaps a scenario like this could give rise to evidence a court could consider as negating *mens rea*.[60] Doing so, a court likely elevates the *mens rea* required by the criminal law to heightened levels of consciousness. As ordinarily construed, even "specific intent crimes [i.e., crimes typically requiring proof of the defendant's ulterior purpose or of the defendant's knowledge of a circumstance element] can be committed by stupid, unstable and quite peculiar people and . . . intent or conscious purpose does not require a cool head, clear thinking, or indeed, very much in the way of mental activity. . . ."[61] To require that *mens rea* be fully formed and pure, unclouded and unconstrained by disordered psychology, requires more than *mens rea* is accustomed to reflect. Rather than taking form from the need to graduate degrees of ill will, this form of *mens rea* takes form from notions of excuse that for some reason must find an outlet other than the affirmative insanity defense. Extended to its extreme, an extreme toward which a full embrace of psychodynamic psychology might lead, *mens rea* could become an elusive quality very hard to find in any defendant.

5.3 Upshot

Were *mens rea* to take the form described in this part, it would restore, in a sense, a version of *mens rea* like that of general moral blameworthiness. Only a *mens rea* that itself indicates moral fault and not some psychological quirk would be inculpatory. Of course, by the standard of psychodynamic psychology, that *mens rea* would be very rare. In reaction, perhaps the criminal law would adopt a system like that of strict liability, dispensing with the need to prove *mens rea* at all. Or, rejecting either move, the criminal law could retain the system of *mens rea* common in America these days. Without demanding that *mens rea* sometimes assume the level of dispassionate philosophical reflection, the law of *mens rea* satisfies well enough and for the most part the need to graduate social control and, especially, retribution when accompanied by the appropriate insanity defense. If Yvonne had the malice of intending to kill Zed, and she deliberated and premeditated upon the killing, it may be best not to indulge nice psychological theories uninvited by the insanity defense. Her evidence of mental disorder may suggest she had no thorough, self-conscious intention, no careful, reflective deliberation, or no focused, single-minded premeditation. Nevertheless, what *mens rea* she did have would suffice if the criminal law is to use a system of *mens rea* without undermining its purpose and presuppositions.

6 Conclusion

It has been the aim of this chapter to trace the links between approaches to *mens rea* in the criminal law and approaches to evidence of mental disorder in the criminal defendant. Certain regimes regarding *mens rea* seem to correspond to certain regimes regarding such evidence. Usually, but not always, the correspondence flows logically from the former to the latter. Regimes without *mens rea* seem to have little room for evidence of mental disorder. Regimes with *mens rea* as general moral blameworthiness seem to entail admitting such evidence that negates this type of *mens rea*. Elemental *mens rea* likewise invites evidence that negates *mens rea*, and a regime of elemental *mens rea* designed to assess ill will invites a cognitive affirmative insanity defense also. A fourth sort of *mens rea* regime seems to follow from notions of the relevance that evidence of mental disorder should have for criminal liability, rather than the other way around. Regardless, this chapter suggests the need to reflect upon the relations between *mens rea* and mental disorder in assessing the role that evidence of mental disorder should play in determining criminal liability. Other factors there surely are, but this factor is important and should not escape the attention of those who would understand the significance of mental disorder in the criminal law.

Notes

1. Of course, this statement simplifies the matter. The law may actually provide that if the prosecutor fails to prove beyond a reasonable doubt that the defendant lacked the reasonable belief as to the victim's threat, the defendant is to be found not guilty.
2. *Romans* 13:4.
3. Sayre, "Mens Rea," 988.
4. See Bonnie et al., *Criminal Law*, 2.
5. Moore, *Law and Psychiatry*, 65.
6. Of course, it is possible that theories on the role of psychological evidence very similar to the ones mentioned in this paragraph could be linked to the theory of *mens rea*. Such theories receive consideration further on in the chapter.
7. Sayre, "Mens Rea," 975–82.
8. See generally Berman, *Law and Revolution*.
9. Coquillette, *The Anglo-American Legal Heritage*, 38–39.
10. Stern, "The Heart of Mens Rea and the Insanity of Psychopaths," 649n191.
11. For example, Wootton, *Crime and the Criminal Law*, 32–57.
12. Ibid., 58–84.
13. Ibid., 80.
14. Sayre, "Public Welfare Offenses," 78, 83.
15. Recall also the general proviso explained above in the section of this chapter entitled "Insanity Beyond *Mens Rea*."
16. Kant, *Foundations of the Metaphysics of Morals*, 9–13.
17. Stern, "Crime, Moral Luck, and the Sermon on the Mount."
18. Berman, *Law and Revolution*, 181–94.
19. *Matthew* 5, especially.
20. Sayre, "Mens Rea," 980.
21. Ibid., 988.
22. Hermann, *The Insanity Defense*, 75.
23. Lewin, "Psychiatric Evidence in Criminal Cases for Purposes Other Than the Defense of Insanity," 1066–67.

24. Hale, *Historia Placitorum Coronae*, vol. 1, 14–15.
25. *M'Naghten's Case*, (1843) 8 Eng. Rep. 718, 722 (H.L.); 10 Cl. & Fin. 200, 210.
26. *R v. Donald*, Y.B. 10 Geo. 1 (1724), reprinted in Howell, *A Complete Collection of State Trials*, vol. 16, 764 (third alteration in original).
27. Stern, "The Heart of Mens Rea and the Insanity of Psychopaths," 646 (footnotes omitted).
28. Hawkins-León, "'Literature as Law,'" 397.
29. Stern, "The Heart of Mens Rea and the Insanity of Psychopaths," 655.
30. LaFave, *Criminal Law*, 414–20.
31. Ibid., 414.
32. Holmes, *The Common Law*, 49.
33. Ibid., 50.
34. Ibid.
35. Sayre, "Mens Rea," 1016–17 (footnote omitted).
36. Holmes, *The Common Law*, 70–72.
37. *Model Penal Code* (1962), § 2.02(1).
38. Ibid., § 4.02(1).
39. Ibid., part 1, vol. 2, 216–20.
40. Ibid., § 2.02(2)(c).
41. Ibid., § 2.02(2)(d).
42. Ibid., part 1, vol. 1, 241–42.
43. Morse, "Mental Disorder and Criminal Law," 924–25.
44. Stern, "Torah and Murder," 487–91.
45. This discussion speaks of the willing to act, but a like analysis governs the culpable failure to act.
46. This discussion takes its definition of the levels of *mens rea* from section 2.02 of the Model Penal Code.
47. Hart, *Punishment and Responsibility*, 136.
48. Ibid., 151.
49. Morse and Hoffman, "The Uneasy Entente Between Legal Insanity and Mens Rea," 1128.
50. 18 United States Code § 17(a) (2012).
51. *Clark v. Arizona*, 548 U.S. 735, 771–72 (2006).
52. Morse and Hoffman, "The Uneasy Entente Between Legal Insanity and Mens Rea," 1105–11.
53. The section of this chapter entitled "Insanity Beyond *Mens Rea*" explains.
54. Morse, "Undiminished Confusion in Diminished Capacity," 24.
55. Peter Arenella, "The Diminished Capacity and Diminished Responsibility Defenses," 839–49; Morse, "Undiminished Confusion in Diminished Capacity," 25–26.
56. Arenella, "The Diminished Capacity and Diminished Responsibility Defenses," 846.
57. Ibid., 847.

58. Ibid., 844.

59. Morse, "Failed Explanations and Criminal Responsibility," 985.

60. See generally Bonnie and Slobogin, "The Role of Mental Health Professionals in the Criminal Process," 478–81; Morse, "Failed Explanations and Criminal Responsibility," 1073–76.

61. Murphy, "The Intoxication Defense," 13.

Resources

Arenella, Peter, "The Diminished Capacity and Diminished Responsibility Defenses: Two Children of a Doomed Marriage." *Columbia Law Review* 77(1977): 827–65.

Berman, Harold J., *Law and Revolution*. Cambridge, MA: Harvard University Press, 1984.

Bonnie, Richard J., Anne M. Coughlin, John C. Jeffries, Jr., and Peter W. Low, *Criminal Law*. St. Paul, MN: LEG, 2015.

Bonnie, Richard J., and Christopher Slobogin, "The Role of Mental Health Professionals in the Criminal Process: The Case for Informal Speculation." *Virginia Law Review* 66(1980): 427–522.

Coquillette, Daniel R., *The Anglo-American Legal Heritage*, 2nd ed. Durham, NC: Carolina Academic Press, 2004.

Hale, Matthew, *Historia Placitorium Coronae*. Philadelphia: R.H. Small, 1847.

Hart, H.L.A., *Punishment and Responsibility*. New York: Oxford University Press, 1968.

Hawkins-León, Cynthia G., "'Literature as Law': The History of the Insanity Plea and a Fictional Application Within the Law & Literature Canon." *Temple Law Review* 72 (1999): 381–450.

Hermann, Donald H.J., *The Insanity Defense: Philosophical, Historical, and Legal Perspectives*. Springfield, IL: Charles C. Thomas, 1983.

Holmes, Jr., Oliver W., *The Common Law*. Boston: Little Brown, 1881.

Howell, Thomas B. (ed.), *A Complete Collection of State Trials* (London: Longman, Hurst, Rees, Ome and Brown, 1816).

Kant, Immanuel. *Foundations of the Metaphysics of Morals*. Trans. Lewis White Beck. Indianapolis: Liberal Arts Press, 1959.

LaFave, Wayne R., *Criminal Law*. St. Paul, MN: West, 2010.

Lewin, Travis H.D., "Psychiatric Evidence in Criminal Cases for Purposes Other Than the Defense of Insanity." *Syracuse Law Review* 26(1975): 1051–1116.

Moore, Michael S., *Law and Psychiatry: Rethinking the Relationship*. Cambridge: Cambridge University Press, 1984.

Morse, Stephen J., "Failed Explanations and Criminal Responsibility: Experts and the Unconscious." *Virginia Law Review* 68(1982): 971–1084.

Morse, Stephen J., "Mental Disorder and Criminal Law." *Journal of Criminal Law & Criminology* 101(2011): 885–968.

Morse, Stephen J., "Undiminished Confusion in Diminished Capacity." *Journal of Criminal Law & Criminology* 75(1984): 1–55.

Morse, Stephen J., and Morris B. Hoffman, "The Uneasy Entente Between Legal Insanity and Mens Rea: Beyond *Clark v. Arizona*." *Journal of Criminal Law & Criminology* 97(2007): 1071–1149.

Murphy, Arthur A., "The Intoxication Defense: An Introduction to Mr. Smith's Article." *Dickinson Law Review* 76(1971): 1–14.

Sayre, Francis B., "Mens Rea." *Harvard Law Review* 45(1932): 974–1026.

Sayre, Francis B., "Public Welfare Offenses." *Columbia Law Review* 33(1933): 55–88.

Stern, Craig A., "Crime, Moral Luck, and the Sermon on the Mount." *Catholic University Law Review* 48(1999): 801–42.

Stern, Craig A., "The Heart of Mens Rea and the Insanity of Psychopaths." *Capital University Law Review* 42(2014): 619–62.

Stern, Craig A., "Torah and Murder: The Cities of Refuge and Anglo-American Law." *Valparaiso University Law Review* 35(2001): 461–98.

Wootton, Barbara, *Crime and the Criminal Law*. London: Stevens & Sons, 1963.

PART 2

Psychiatry and the Law

PART 3

CHAPTER FOUR

The Shadows of Normality: Legal Insanity under Modern Criminal Law*

Gabriel Hallevy

A judge must decide whether the arrested person who has been brought before her is insane. The person occasionally hears voices that tell him to perform various acts. As long as these acts caused no damage, no one paid much attention. But recently the voices told him to kill his son, a helpless child. He therefore tied up the child and pulled out a knife, intending to kill him. Suddenly, the voices told him to stop, at which point he was arrested for abusing a helpless child. Is this person insane and a public danger? The case, naturally, recasts the biblical story of Abraham and Isaac:

> And Abraham said unto his young men, Abide ye here with the ass; and I and the lad will go yonder and worship, and come again to you. And Abraham took the wood of the burnt offering, and laid it upon Isaac his son; and he took the fire in his hand, and a knife; and they went both of them together.... And they came to the place which God had told him of; and

---

*Portions of this chapter have been adapted from G. Hallevy, *The Matrix of Insanity in Modern Criminal Law*. Heidelberg: Springer, 2015. Used with permission.

Abraham built an altar there, and laid the wood in order, and bound Isaac his son, and laid him on the altar upon the wood. And Abraham stretched forth his hand, and took the knife to slay his son. And the angel of the LORD called unto him out of heaven, and said, Abraham, Abraham: and he said, Here am I. And he said, Lay not thine hand upon the lad, neither do thou any thing unto him: for now I know that thou fearest God, seeing thou hast not withheld thy son, thine only son from me.[1]

In most legal systems this is a case of an attempted murder. Nevertheless, Abraham is considered a cultural hero. Millions of people worldwide accept him as the father of their nation. Today he would probably be excluded from society for being dangerous, and separated from his son. This makes us wonder whether insanity is a cultural rather than a psychiatric matter, whether medical definitions of insanity are relevant to law and society, and whether insanity may be dependent on time, place, and social environment rather than a medical diagnosis. In this chapter, we try to answer these questions.

1 The Legal Evolution of Insanity in Modern Criminal Law: A Duet between the M'Naghten Rules and the Irresistible Impulse Test

The legal evolution of insanity, especially as a general defense in criminal law, was not isolated from its medical evolution. Some crucial points in the legal evolution were influenced and encouraged by the medical evolution.[2] Under Roman law, it was not acceptable to impose criminal liability upon the mentally ill, and in certain circumstances of public danger, mentally ill persons were held in public custody, not in order to cure them or treat their illness, but to keep them away from the public and prevent potential harm to society.[3] The custody was not considered punishment, but a cautionary measure to protect society.

By the 12th century, courts in Europe pointed out the need for a general and accurate theory that accounts for the essence of insanity in order to exempt insane offenders from criminal liability.[4] This approach was probably the consequence of the academic legal studies in the new European institutions called "universities." Legal academic studies required a general scientific methodology, which had to address the issue of insanity as well. The legal examination of insanity did not require an understanding of the reasons for insanity, only the identification of its overt symptoms, in order to determine the extent of the criminal liability of the offender.

Theories of criminal law have spawned various legal indicators and tests used to identify insane offenders in order to determine their criminal liability.

These indicators reflect the social, religious, theological, and medical developments in the area of insanity. By the mid-19th century, three main tests were developed to legally diagnose the insane offender, to be replaced in 1843 in England by the M'Naghten Rules. The three tests were the good and evil test, the wild beast test, and the right and wrong test.

1.1 Early Modern Developments

The good and evil test appeared for the first time in 1313 in English common law.[5] The offender in that case was under the age of seven, which was the minimal age for imposing criminal liability under English common law. The test reflected medieval theological concepts regarding mental illness. Mentally ill persons, like infants, were considered incapable of committing sins because they were not capable of free will in their condition. Consequently, these offenders lacked the capability to distinguish between good and evil, and could not choose between the two of their own free will.[6]

The terminology of the good and evil test is theological, derived primarily from the biblical story of the original sin and the expulsion from Eden.[7] The exemption from criminal liability of the insane offender was based on the concept that insanity was in itself a punishment and satisfied the necessity to punish offender. Additional punishment was considered double punishment, and therefore it was not acceptable.[8] This was the prevailing test in the English common law between the 14th and the 18th centuries.[9] During that time, English courts needed a concrete way to examine the capability of the offender to distinguish between good and evil.

Therefore, in 1616 the test was redefined to refer to persons who were not capable of counting from one to 20, who did not understand the quantity implied by the number 20, who did not recognize their parents, or did not distinguish between useful and harmful matters. Such persons were considered "idiots," unless they were able to read and write.[10] An offender who has been identified as an idiot was not considered to have legal personhood, and therefore was not subject to the imposition of criminal liability.

Without a basic understanding of the moral value of the conduct it was not possible to impose criminal liability, but in practice only extreme cases of insanity passed the test. Most cases, as understood at the time, were not accepted as insanity.[11] The good and evil test was modified from time to time by the courts in order to fit the factual reality and developments in the understanding insanity, and in 1724 it was replaced by the wild beast test.

To apply the wild beast test, the judge instructed the jury to exonerate the offender for reason of insanity if it was found that he did not understand his conduct and behaved no better than a wild beast. Such a person did not deserve punishment under criminal law.[12] This test was a combination of 17th-century doctrines regarding criminal liability and religious attitudes towards insanity, which prevailed in England in those days. Indeed, the term "wild beast" was a mistranslation of the original Latin term "*brutis*" (brutes), from the 13th century, when the concept was enunciated by the English jurist, Bracton.[13]

This term did not appear before in any description of insanity. At the beginning of the 18th century, "wild beast" referred mostly to livestock and to animals of the meadow such as badgers, foxes, dear, and rabbits.[14] The wild beast test raised the criteria for being considered insane, reducing the rate of acceptance of the insanity defense in criminal cases. The test emphasized the cognitive capabilities of the offender rather than his impulses, as its name might imply.[15]

The test prevailed in English common law until 1812, when it was replaced by the right and wrong test, which was the most significant step toward the M'Naghten Rules, adopted in 1843. According to the right and wrong test, the insanity defense could not be accepted, if the offender had adequate understanding to distinguish between right and wrong or good and evil.[16] Because the terms good and evil were too vague to be interpreted, the courts preferred right and wrong as sole criterion for the test.[17] The principal difference between the wild beast and the right and wrong tests was that the latter abandoned all moral standards affected by religion in favor of the legal standards of right and wrong.

These standards were not based on moral understanding but on broad definitions of criminal offenses. "Wrong" parallels "forbidden" by the law, and "right" parallels "allowed." Criminal offenses define the borderline between what is legally right and wrong, so that the function of the court is to determine whether the offender understood the prohibition. This test opened wider opportunities for an insanity defense, and it was criticized for not embracing the medical developments of insanity.[18] The test prevailed in English courts until 1843.

1.2 The M'Naghten Rules

On January 20, 1843, Daniel M'Naghten (or McNaughton) shot Edward Drummond, the private secretary of the British Prime Minister Robert Peel, while intending to assassinate the Prime Minister. Drummond was wounded and died five days later. M'Naghten suffered from symptoms of paranoia and believed that he was persecuted by the Tory party. The court of first instance heard testimonies of experts in mental illnesses in order to understand the mental capabilities of the offender.[19] The court understood that acquitting the offender would result in his being placed in a psychiatric hospital because he was dangerous to the public.

At the end of the trial, the court acquitted M'Naghten for reason of insanity based on the right and wrong test, provoking a sharp debate in Britain. With the encouragement of Queen Victoria, a special session of the House of Lords was convened. The House of Lords presented to the Court five questions to determine the effect of insanity on the imposition of criminal liability. The answers of the Court amount to the M'Naghten Rules, which are considered to be the modern legal basis for the insanity defense in criminal law.[20]

Under the M'Naghten Rules, criminal liability is imposed on the offender even if he committed the offense in a state of insanity as long as he was aware of the criminal prohibition while he was committing the offense. The court presumes the offender sane unless otherwise is proven. The insanity must relate to the time when the offense was committed, and it refers to the cognitive capability of the offender to distinguish between right and wrong. The criminal liability is imposed only based on the subjective understanding of the factual situation by the offender, including a factual mistake. Medical reports may be relevant only if the question before the court is medical.

The M'Naghten Rules formed the legal basis for the insanity defense in the Anglo-American legal systems,[21] but the terms used in these rules were not clear enough to be interpreted by the lawyers. After the M'Naghten Rules were adopted, mental illness was interpreted narrowly, and it referred mostly to specific types of psychosis.[22] Later it was interpreted more broadly, to include other mental disorders, among them other types of psychosis, neurosis, and even very low IQ, as long as it could be identified as the cause for the offender's inability to understand the difference between right and wrong.[23]

This legal situation does not reduce the definition of insanity to certain types of mental disorders or mental phenomena, but it examines the effect of given mental disorder on the understanding of individual persons of the difference between what is legally right and wrong. Thus, when the functional effect of the mental disorder is emphasized, significant types of mental disorder would not be classified as insanity under criminal law because the M'Naghten Rules require a causal relation between the mental disorder and the inability to distinguish between right and wrong.[24]

The factual causal relation is at the heart of the M'Naghten Rules and the basis for accepting insanity as a defense in a given criminal trial. The ability to distinguish between right and wrong was interpreted to relate to the cognitive abilities of the offender to understand properly the legal social control system in a given society. These abilities may be summed up as awareness of the general meaning of a criminal prohibition.[25] In most Anglo-American courts, these cognitive abilities were interpreted as the offender's ability to understand the nature of his conduct and its quality in light of the criminal prohibition.[26]

The general understanding of the offender that his conduct represents the commission of an offense is the key term in determining insanity under the M'Naghten Rules. If the offender lacks these cognitive abilities he is considered insane under the substantive criminal law, and incompetent to stand trial (*non compos mentis*) under procedural criminal law.

The key term "wrong," which refers to the criminal prohibition, was not easily interpreted after M'Naghten. It was asked whether it refers to the legal or to the moral meaning of the prohibition.[27] For example, the offender who sets fire to a brothel under the delusion that he is commanded by God to do so in order to advance his redemption, he is fully aware of the criminal prohibition against setting the fire. The offender understands that his conduct is legally prohibited, but he considers it to be morally commendable. The M'Naghten Rules did not explicitly interpret which type of "wrong" the court must address: the legal or the moral one. English common law preferred the legal meaning over the moral one,[28] and American courts have left the decision to the jury,[29] so that at times the wrong is legal and at others it is moral.[30]

The M'Naghten Rules also address the factual mistake doctrine. Factual mistake functions as independent defense in criminal law, irrespective of what caused it. Naturally, the cause may be insanity, but not necessarily. Insanity may make it easier to prove factual mistake, but it is not necessary for such a proof. The reference the M'Naghten Rules make to medical reports is not only for cases of insanity, but applies to any expert report. According to the rules of evidentiary law, such a report is admissible only if it refers to the one of the factual issues raised in the trial.

The M'Naghten Rules were criticized primarily for three reasons. The first was that the rules are based on archaic insights and perspectives, no longer in use. Mental disorder is not considered to affect only the cognitive capabilities of the person but all aspects of human personality, including volition and feelings, which in most cases are also involved in delinquency.[31] The second reason was that the rules are not sufficiently accurate to identify the individuals on whom no criminal liability should be imposed. The general distinction between right and wrong does not satisfy this purpose.[32] The third reason was that the questions presented in M'Naghten Rules were not answerable by psychiatrists or expert physicians.

The distinction between right and wrong is not a medical matter, at least not only a medical matter, and it involves deep understanding of social sciences, philosophy, and more.[33] In light of this criticism of the M'Naghten Rules, various changes were suggested, some slight, others quite comprehensive.

To answer the first critique, it has been suggested to expand the legal definition of insanity beyond the cognitive elements, as understood based on the M'Naghten Rules. The suggestion was to add a parallel test to the M'Naghten Rules, which is not restricted to the cognitive aspects of insanity; it has come to be known as the irresistible impulse test, focused on the volitional aspects of the human mind. Thus, if mental disorder produced uncontrollable conduct, it should be legally valid as an insanity defense.[34]

1.3 The Irresistible Impulse Test

The irresistible impulse test was not based on the cognitive understanding of the criminal prohibition. Insanity based on the irresistible impulse test was accepted by the courts as a defense against the imposition of criminal liability even if the offender understood the factual reality, distinguished between right and wrong, and was fully aware of the wrongfulness of his conduct. Therefore, in various legal systems the irresistible impulse test has led courts to accept the insanity defense in cases of uncontrollable will or feelings even if the alleged mental disorder did not affect directly the cognitive aspects of the offender's mind. The irresistible impulse test was considered to supplement the M'Naghten Rules with regard to the principle of fault in criminal law. Whereas the M'Naghten Rules related to the cognitive aspects of the human mind, the irresistible impulse test related to volition, resembling the structure of the principle of fault in criminal law.

The irresistible impulse test, however, is based on earlier rulings than the M'Naghten Rules,[35] and some courts have used it before the M'Naghten Rules were formulated. Three years before M'Naghten, an English court in Oxford handed down a ruling based on insane volition.[36] The Oxford case was not mentioned in M'Naghten probably because delusions were considered to affect human cognition rather than volition, and Daniel M'Naghten suffered from delusions. The court in M'Naghten seems to have considered the irresistible impulse test to be irrelevant to its case. But because of the wide acceptance of the M'Naghten Rules, the irresistible impulse test was rejected in the English common law, and considered "most dangerous."[37]

The reappearance of the irresistible impulse test was due only to the criticism of the M'Naghten Rules for abandoning the volition aspects of the human mind. Embracing the irresistible impulse test together with the M'Naghten Rules was possible because of some adjustments in the original test for the M'Naghten Rules. Thus, it was required that the irresistible impulse be derived from a mental illness, and that the impulse be of sufficiently high degree to nullify the free choice of the offender to decide whether or not to commit the offense, even if the impulse was not accidental or temporary, but permanent and foreseeable by the offender.[38]

In practice, this "adjustment" deviates from the literal meaning of the term "impulse." Most impulses are neither permanent nor foreseeable, but this interpretation fits many of the symptoms of mental illness that affect the volition of the human mind.[39] A general criticism of the adjusted irresistible impulse test and of its legal combination with the M'Naghten Rules focuses on the uncontrollable character of the conduct, which is the consequence of mental illness. In general, complete loss of control over the volition of the offender was required to pass the test. When the loss of control is not complete, the irresistible impulse test does not qualify the offender as insane.[40]

Thus, the criticism of the M'Naghten Rules was that the test restricts insanity to a minority of the cases, and to the rarest ones.[41] By contrast, it was argued that the irresistible impulse test widens excessively the boundaries of the insanity defense. Therefore, it was regarded to be more suitable as a consideration in sentencing the offender rather than in determining his criminal liability, because it includes some indirect ingredients of the distinction between right and wrong.[42] This argument was too robust to be ignored, and therefore some courts preferred not to apply the test as a basis for accepting the insanity defense.[43] Application of the irresistible impulse test was not considered to reduce the level of deterrence in criminal law.[44]

1.4 The Worldwide Duet between the M'Naghten Rules and the Irresistible Impulse Test

Because of the general criticism of the M'Naghten Rules and of the irresistible impulse test, various legal systems adopted different attitudes toward these tests and their combination. American law accepted the criticism of the M'Naghten Rules and of the irresistible impulse entirely. In 1871, the M'Naghten Rules were fully rejected, together with the irresistible impulse test, in a New Hampshire ruling owing to the above criticism. A new indicator for insanity was established, according to which, if commission of the offense was the product of mental illness, the offender was exempt from criminal liability.[45] This general indicator was not accepted outside New Hampshire,[46] but in the meantime, until 1954, American courts did not consider themselves as bound by the M'Naghten Rules of by the irresistible impulse test.

In 1954, the New Hampshire indicator was used to fill the vacuum resulting from the rejection of the M'Naghten Rules and of the irresistible impulse test.[47] The ruling was that no criminal liability is imposed on any offender if commission of the offense was the product of any "mental disease or defect." This indicator, destined to replace the much criticized combination of the M'Naghten Rules and the irresistible impulse test, offers an adequate theoretical alternative. But the courts did not interpret the relevant terms included in the alternative, which consequently became vague and too flexible.

The alternative indicator determined no guidelines for recognizing mental diseases or defects. Therefore, it is possible to infer that any slight mental defect can become the basis for an exemption from criminal liability for reason of insanity. Furthermore, the term "product" was not interpreted either, leading to the question whether any product may be considered a "product" in this context. If, for example, the commission of the offense is a by-product of various phenomena, only one of which, even a secondary one, is a mental defect, is it considered to be an adequate basis for the insanity defense?

As a result, this alternative was criticized by both lawyers and psychiatrists.[48] The main criticism focused on the fact that the terms "mental disease or defect" and "product" were not defined. In individual cases, the courts attempted to interpret these terms,[49] but eventually, the alternative was rejected entirely in 1972 because of this criticism.[50] The American Law Institute Model Penal Code proposed using the M'Naghten Rules together with the irresistible impulse test, with a slight rephrasing concerning the substantial capacity of the offender.[51]

The principal elements of the M'Naghten Rules were incorporated into the Model Penal Code under the test for evaluating the criminality of the offender's conduct using the terms of the right and wrong test. The significant elements of the irresistible impulse test were also accepted under the alternative for determining whether the offender's conduct conforms to the requirements of law. The Model Penal Code proposal, designed to provide an adequate answer to both the cognitive and volitive aspects of the mental defect, was embraced by various courts across the United States.[52]

The U.S. Congress accepted a test based on the M'Naghten Rules in 1984 as part of its legislation.[53] Thus, both the M'Naghten Rules and the irresistible impulse test, with the slight rephrasing, are now the conclusive test for the acceptability of the insanity defense in American criminal law.[54]

In Britain, the M'Naghten Rules remain the legal basis for the acceptance of the insanity defense in criminal law. Although in Britain mentally deficient offenders plea diminished responsibility rather than insanity, the defense is still widely used in British courts. The irresistible impulse test has been rejected in Britain as "most dangerous,"[55] therefore insanity is examined only in relation to its cognitive aspects. The volition aspects of insanity are not considered legitimate criteria for the acceptance of the insanity defense.

The legal debate in Britain over the insanity defense parallels the discussion about the mental element requirement.[56] This attitude is consistent with the legal understanding that the mental element is the positive aspect of the principle of fault, and insanity is part of its negative aspect. A favorable court ruling on an insanity defense is considered a legal rather than a medical ruling.[57] In general, English law any mental deficiency may be considered insanity for purposes of the application of the M'Naghten Rules, if it interferes with the offender's ability to make the distinction between right and wrong.[58]

In France, the insanity defense applies to any mental or neurologic deficiency, if it denies the offender the capability to distinguish between right and wrong or prevents physical control over his conduct.[59] There is no restriction to specific types of mental deficiency. Thus, factual causation is required between the mental or neurologic deficiency and the commission of the offense. The French law emphasizes the free choice of the offender with regard to the commission of the offense. An offender who commits an offense in a state of insanity is considered to be coerced and not having a free choice as to whether or not to commit the offense, therefore it is not legal to impose criminal liability on him. The coercion, in this case, is internal and its cause is mental.[60] The insanity test references the time of the commission of the offense, not to the time of the trial.

In Germany, insanity is an integral part of the offender's fault. The presumption of insanity is explicitly stated in the German Penal Code.[61] This presumption negates the offender's fault if all conditions are met, leaving two possible options: that no criminal liability is imposed or that diminished responsibility is attributed to the offender.[62] The conclusive test for insanity in German criminal law is whether the offender is mentally capable of understanding the prohibition breached by his conduct. The relevant prohibition is legal, not moral or other. Inability to understand the prohibition is the result of a pathologic mental or cognitive deficiency, of mental illness, or of volitive deficiency.⁶³ Thus, German criminal law is open to all plausible causes for insanity, which is examined dynamically and subjectively for the individual offender.⁶⁴

In sum, the legal evolution of insanity as a general defense in criminal law may be described as an interplay between the M'Naghten Rules and the irresistible impulse test. This interplay delineates an approach toward insanity that combines both the cognitive and volitive aspects of the human mind. Deviation from this combination is rare, and generally both aspects play a role in the legal definition of insanity.

2 The Legal Spectrum of Normality and Insanity

2.1 The Relativity of Social Normality

To understand what insanity is, we must make a detour into the social understanding of normality. Most people consider a person insane relatively to themselves or to other so-called normal people. If a standard normal person could be described accurately, this could form the basis for a comparison between any individual person and normality. But inevitably questions arise: Who is a normal person? How is normality defined? Or more radically, are there any normal people? Can normality be defined at all?

People use the expression "normal" when referring to human behavior that is not considered exceptional from their point of view. Certain groups of people may share a common view of what is exceptional behavior. But there is no generally accepted definition for exceptionality. Various societies and cultures, at different times, may develop different points of view in this regard. For example, talking to invisible spirits may be considered normal in some religious societies, but abnormal in others.

Nevertheless, that which is exceptional is not necessarily banned or oppressed. It would be inaccurate and simplistic to divide all possible types of human behavior into normal and abnormal. A more accurate division includes at least three categories: normal, above-normal, and sub-normal.⁶⁵ Both above-normality and sub-normality are infinite and may include infinite types of human behavior, even exceeding the "normal" imagination. The key difference between above-normality and sub-normality is not necessarily intrinsic, but a function of the way the society treats the two: the abnormality of above-normality is generally encouraged, whereas that of sub-normality is generally deprecated.

Two mothers meet with their children's elementary school teacher. One is told that her child is a mathematical genius, far ahead of her biological age. The other is told that her child is exceedingly nervous and violent, much beyond his age. Both children are outside the range of normality, but in most modern societies the first mother would be advised how to encourage her daughter's abnormality, whereas the other would be advised how to repress that of her boy. These recommendations are entirely dependent on the prevalent views of society and the given time. The exceptionally aggressive boy may have been categorized as above-normal in ancient Sparta and encouraged to develop his tendencies into a professional skill, whereas the mathematical skills of the young girl may have resulted in her being declared a witch in some medieval societies. The skills are the same, but the societies in which they manifest are different. Therefore, normality is a social matter, dependent on time and culture rather than on the chemistry of the brain.

Similarly, there is no assurance that what is currently considered subnormal behavior will not be categorized normal or even above-normal in the future. Various normal and above-normal behaviors in the past would definitely be categorized sub-normal today, and some would even require exclusion from society on grounds of dangerousness. It would be instructive to reexamine some model behaviors of past cultural heroes based on the current understanding of normality in most Western societies.

People, who claim to hear voices that others cannot hear, and that these voices command them to take certain actions, are generally referred to psychiatric evaluation. In most cases, they would be classified as abnormal, and therefore insane. These people match the profiles of most of the ancient prophets, whom modern Western society tends to admire, teach their prophecies, and even learn about their ways. Nevertheless, some of their acts would be classified as criminal offenses under modern criminal law, and people committing these acts today would be excluded from society. The Biblical character of Abraham is a good example.

Abraham heard voices that others couldn't hear, commanding him to kill his son. He obeyed these voices, committing what in modern criminal law would be called attempted murder.[66] Under modern criminal law, the courts would have to protect society from such persons. What made Abraham into a cultural hero was the combination of the time and society in which his acts were committed. The Bible supplies many such examples, as well as examples of the opposite nature. In biblical times, people who favored the voice of logic were not necessarily considered heroes.[67]

It is puzzling that although times and cultures have changed, people worldwide still consider some of the past heroes as cultural models to this day, despite the fact that today many would have been referred to psychiatric evaluation and separated from society. The answer to this puzzle may have to do with the collective memory of society, in which past understandings, attitudes, and insights passed from one generation to the next are accumulated.

Even when the general attitude of society toward such cases has changed entirely, the interpretation of the past may still remain unchanged, not unlike the way children remember adults. The child usually remembers an adult as a giant. After many years of not seeing that adult, the grown-up child of yore is surprised that the adult is in reality much shorter than imagined, but even after discovering the true height of the adult, the image of the adult as a giant is still difficult to supplant. It is interesting, however, that it is much easier to cross from sub-normality to beyond-normality and from beyond-normality to sub-normality rather than to cross from each of them to normality. That may reflect that most societies make small changes in their understandings of normality in comparison to dramatic changes through time in their understandings towards abnormality.

The ambivalent attitude of modern society toward the abnormal heroes of the past may be one of the reasons for the complicated present approaches to abnormality. In some cases, the analogy with heroes of the past would be expected to raise doubts in the judges' minds regarding the insanity of the offender. The more attached society is to its past culture, the easier it should be for its judges to recall the past heroes. In traditional cultures, this can be a crucial factor in the assessment of insanity.

The key question is how abnormality is reflected in insanity. Clearly, not all cases of abnormality are automatically classified as insanity. Moreover, abnormality and normality are not inclusive or total. A person's behavior may be classified as normal in one aspect and abnormal in another, and similarly, it may be classified sub-normal at one respect and above-normal in another. For example, some autistic persons have extremely high powers of concentration and analysis of detailed information. At the same time, they experience difficulties in creating social connections. Both characteristics are considered abnormal, but one is above-normal and the other sub-normal.

It is not accurate, therefore, to classify the person in general as normal, above-normal, or sub-normal, but rather particular behaviors should be classified as such. Thus, a person who hears voices may behave normally in every other respect, so that the terms normal and abnormal would not be sufficiently accurate to describe the person, but would be accurate enough to describe his behavior. Naturally, the accuracy must be considered within the range of social norms, that is, society would consider the behavior to be normal or abnormal based on the concrete circumstances surrounding the matter at hand.

The social meaning of insanity is not some monovalent abnormality or sub-normality. First, not all abnormality or sub-normality is automatically considered insanity. Second, the reason of abnormality is inherent in the classification. Neither a mathematical genius nor an extremely aggressive person is necessarily insane. Nevertheless, because normality is not part of insanity, the connection between normality and insanity is essential but not sufficient.

If a person behaves "normally" based on how society defines normality, he is not within the spectrum of insanity. Even if he suffers from a mental deficiency, as long as it does not affect his behavior to the extent that it exceeds the boundaries of normality, he cannot be considered insane. This classification is purely social, regardless of any medical diagnosis. For example, a person who hears voices but has trained himself to ignore them would not be considered abnormal because his behavior is not affected by the mental deficiency. The public interest is raised only when behavior exceeds the range of normality.

Is any deviation from normality a form of insanity? If the exceptional behavior is encouraged by society, the public interest is not aroused and no criminal liability is contemplated. Thus, only when the deviation is within the sub-normality range may the abnormality be relevant to insanity. And only when the abnormality is the result of problematic behavior, based on the perspective of society, is it considered an object for social intervention by means of criminal law. Otherwise, there is no public interest in initiating such a process.

Every society defines its own range of sub-normal behavior that requires intervention. That range is relative to the fundamental social values in effect in a given society. For example, cheating may be deemed sub-normal behavior in certain societies, but only some types of cheating may be considered subject to social intervention. In most Western societies, cheating the tax system is considered to justify intervention, but not cheating on one's spouse.

The sub-normality used to assess insanity is not measured by the degree that the behavior exhibits, lest any commission of a severe offense is classified as insanity. Sub-normality refers to the routine mental processes of a person. Murdering a business competitor is not necessarily the result of insanity, but murdering that competitor because the murderer thinks he has the divine right to kill anyone interfering with his activities may be considered insanity in its social meaning. Raping a woman because of sexual lust is generally not considered insanity, but doing so because the rapist thinks that this is the proper way to treat a woman may be considered insanity.

Exceeding normality is an essential condition for insanity, but not a sufficient one. The cause for the abnormality must be mental or internal. If the manner in which the person understands factual reality because of mental deficiency affects his behavior and brings it into the abnormal range, the conditions for social insanity are met. Otherwise, the behavior may be the result of a simple factual error. A mental deficiency affects the way in which the person understands factual reality in general, which may constitute the main difference between factual mistake and insanity as general defenses.

Consider a person charged with rape. The defense claims that the offender had thought the intercourse was consensual. If this error is circumstantial, owing to particular facts, it may be considered a factual mistake but not insanity. But if the offender in general does not accept the possibility of anyone refusing to have sexual relations with him, insanity may be considered. First, it is necessary to examine whether the behavior is within the range of abnormality. If in the given society men are wooed extensively, and sexual offers by men are seldom refused, such behavior may not necessarily be abnormal.

Next, if the behavior is classified as abnormal, its cause is examined. If the cause is mental, insanity may be relevant. Different societies may have different definitions for what is considered to be a mental cause or mental deficiency. The mental cause may have to do with both cognition and volition, and the different balance of the two in the definitions of the mental cause in different societies reflects the significant social aspect of insanity.

Therefore, the range of normality is relative. This relativity is measured in social terms, and any society may have different ranges of normality, bounded by different borderlines. As a result, abnormality is also relative. Different societies may consider the same types of behavior as normal, above-normal, or sub-normal. Given that abnormality is the social trigger for insanity, insanity is also socially relative, defined differently in different societies. This raises two additional questions about the meaning of insanity: is insanity a social phenomenon or medical one, and what classification is relevant for legal purposes?

2.2 Medical, Functional, and Legal Insanity

The medical understanding of insanity has begun relatively late. When insanity became a subject for research, medical scholars began to categorize the various symptoms of different types of insanity. This classification served as the basis for psychiatry as a branch of medicine. Today, when a psychiatrist treats a patient, diagnosis of the symptoms is the initial step.

Then symptoms are assembled into a wider diagnosis of the mental deficiency or illness of the patient, which in turn makes it possible to apply the right treatment.

By categorizing the symptoms and the mental deficiency, the psychiatrist can benefit from the experience of other psychiatrists, who have already treated patients with the same symptoms. It is the assumption of the medical understanding of insanity that mental deficiency is a medical problem, and that medical problems can be solved by medical means. Thus, at the focus of medical insanity are the chemistry of the brain and other physical descriptions of the patient's body. In its methodology, this treatment is not substantially different than the medical treatment of influenza.

It is therefore not uncommon to find a solution for insanity based on medications. Although the medications are not intended to cure the mental deficiency, they can be used to balance the mental state of the patient. From the point of view of social insanity, as discussed previously, medications contain chemicals intended to suppress those characteristics of the patient that are considered to be sub-normal. The chemical suppression is intended to reduce to a minimum all types of behaviors that society or the psychiatrist consider sub-normal. Naturally, psychiatrists from different cultures with different behavioral habits may recommend different medical treatments.

The medical diagnosis is affected by the social understanding of insanity. In general, when behavior falls within the normal range, no psychiatric treatment or medication are considered, regardless of whether or not a person suffers from mental deficiency. The argument applies to all types of mental deficiency, so that if the mental deficiency has some external behavioral symptoms, it is subject to psychiatric treatment. Unrelated to any of the above, people who are aware of mental deficiency that involves no behavioral symptoms can initiate treatment voluntarily, but this is of no concern to criminal law.

Medical insanity is therefore governed by the categorization of symptoms relating to the person's external behavior. But insanity may have a wider meaning, and we must take into account that the medical understanding of insanity is most likely not complete yet. If psychiatry cannot explain every type of insanity and all mental deficiencies, medical insanity is too narrow a tool for evaluating insanity for legal purposes. If there is even one mental phenomenon that is not properly explained from the medical point of view, medical insanity cannot be the ultimate way of understanding insanity, and psychiatry cannot define insanity for criminal law purposes.

If not psychiatry, what is there to help us define insanity unequivocally? The answer to this question represents the most significant step toward defining legal insanity. If criminal law is concerned with anti-social behavior, legal insanity must be determined based on a person's behavior. The relevant connection that must be taken into account is the effect of mental deficiency on a person's behavior as it relates to the criminal sphere. Thus, the determination of insanity for legal purposes is functional and not medical or merely social. The question, therefore, is whether mental deficiency had any effect on the functionality of the person in the commission of the anti-social behavior.

Medical or social analysis may support the understanding of the mental situation of the offender and the severity of the deviation from normality, but the ultimate determination of legal insanity can be achieved only through functional analysis. It is the task of the court to analyze the connection between mental deficiency, if alleged, and the commission of the offense. Every society may choose the relevant aspects of functionality that it is willing to accept under given circumstances for the purpose of determining legal insanity. Therefore, if mental deficiency is shown to have affected a person's cognition or volition, in most legal systems it can become the basis for legal insanity.

How can the court determine whether mental deficiency has affected the offender functionally? In other words, how can the court be convinced that mental deficiency is the reason for the anti-social behavior? Moreover, how can the court be sure that the offender suffers from mental deficiency at all? These questions are still within the legal sphere, and therefore psychiatry is not required to provide the ultimate answers. Functionally, as long as the reason is internal, the medical categorization into mental deficiencies and illnesses is immaterial. Thus, functional insanity is dynamic and informed by its concrete effect on the person, even if the medical categorization does not support that conclusion.

Consequently, legal insanity can be broader or narrower than medical insanity, as the case may be. If the court is persuaded that the offender's behavior is deeply affected functionally by internal reasons, the fact that these internal reasons are not categorized medically as insanity would not prevent it from accepting the insanity defense in a given case. Furthermore, when psychiatry categorizes the offender's symptoms as clear indications of mental illness, but this does not functionally affect the offender, the court is not bound to accept the insanity defense.

The ultimate test for legal insanity is therefore functional. The legal elements of insanity are concerned with its functional meaning. Medical measures may assist in painting a clearer image of the offender's mental deficiency from the evidentiary point of view. If the offender claims that he suffers from certain symptoms that impair the clarity of his mind, and if psychiatric evaluation supports this claim based on the categorization of these symptoms into certain mental deficiencies that affect the human mind in a way described by the offender, this may provide helpful evidence for the court to reach the factual conclusion that the offender indeed suffers from a mental deficiency that affects his mind.

At the same time, ascribing excessive importance to the medical analysis in determining legal insanity is wrong and can be dangerous. It is wrong because legal insanity can be determined only by functional analysis; and it can be dangerous because the offender may manipulate the medical analysis to benefit from the insanity defense. Thus, when the offender knows the medical manifestation of a given mental deficiency, he may be able to fake the symptoms in order to obtain the required medical diagnosis, although functionally he may not have been affected by any internal reasons in the commission of the offense. The only way to prevent such manipulation is to avoid a situation in which the court automatically embraces the psychiatric report.

Psychiatric reports, therefore, have no more than evidentiary value that either supports or undermines claims of insanity. These reports bring evidence, but should not replace judicial discretion with respect to the functional analysis of the offender's state of mind at the time of the commission of the offense. The separation of legal insanity from medical or social insanity forms the basis of the discussion of the legal elements of insanity.

3 The Legal Elements of Insanity as General Defense in Modern Criminal Law

The legal basis for the acceptance of the insanity defense in criminal law is the presumption of insanity. The legal evolution of insanity within the various legal systems has produced different contents for this presumption. The presumption of insanity is an absolute presumption (*praesumptio juris et de jure*), or, in other words, an irrefutable one. Thus, when the elements of the presumption are consolidated, the conclusion cannot be legally rebutted. Despite differences between various legal systems, the legal basis for the acceptance of insanity in criminal law appears to be the same.

The presumption may be generally formulated this way: A person, who as a result of uncontrollable mental deficiency, subjectively lacks cognitive or volitive capabilities to assess a certain conduct that was factually caused by his mental deficiency, is presumed to be incapable of consolidating the required fault for the imposition of criminal liability. Based on this presumption, the offender's fault is nullified when the uncontrollable mental deficiency disabled his cognitive or volitive capabilities to evaluate a certain conduct. The general defense of insanity is defined based on this presumption as part of the principle of fault in criminal law. Insanity becomes part of the negative fault element of criminal liability, similarly to all other general defenses in criminal law.

Analytically, the presumption of insanity includes five elements, which function as cumulative conditions for the application of the presumption by the court:

1. The identity of the offender (a legal personhood);
2. The mental deficiency;
3. The inability to control the mental deficiency, from the offender's point of view;
4. The nullification of:
   (i) the cognitive abilities of the offender with respect to the commission of the given offense, or
   (ii) the volitive capabilities of the offender with respect to the commission of the given offense;
5. The factual causal link between the mental deficiency and the commission of the given offense.

These conditions are discussed here.

The burden of proof for all five elements is on the party that wishes to rely on it during the trial. In most cases, this means that the burden of proof is on the offender, who seeks to prevent the imposition of criminal liability on the ground of insanity. It is not always the offender, however, who claims insanity. In some legal systems, in order to begin psychiatric procedures for the treatment of a person, it is necessary to initiate criminal proceedings, in which case the prosecution makes a claim of insanity. In such cases, the court stops the criminal proceedings, and after being persuaded of the offender's insanity, psychiatric procedures are initiated accordingly.

The party that bears the burden of proof, whether it is the prosecution or the offender, needs to raise no more than a reasonable doubt regarding the sanity of the offender. In some legal systems, general defenses must be proven by a preponderance of evidence. If the presumption is properly proven, the conclusion of the presumption is absolute, and therefore the offender is presumed to be incapable of consolidating the required fault for the imposition of criminal liability. Such a person would not be convicted under the given charge, and no criminal liability would be imposed on him.

The presumption relates to the time of the commission of the offense, and not the time of the trial. The time of the trial is relevant for procedural purposes. For the imposition of criminal liability, the time of the commission of the offense is the only relevant time, exactly as it is the relevant time for checking all the other requirements for criminal liability, including the factual and mental elements. Thus, to use the insanity defense, a reasonable doubt must be raised regarding the sanity of the offender when committing the offense.

For the insanity defense to apply, an offender must be considered insane at the time of the commission of the offense. If by the time he stands the trial, his mental deficiency abates or is completely cured, it does not affect the status of the criminal liability of the offender because the relevant time is that of the commission of the offense. The change may affect his competence to stand trial, but not the imposition of criminal liability. This is because the presumption refers to the substantive law and to criminal liability, and it is therefore examined in relation to the commission of the offense. When the offender undergoes psychiatric evaluation at the beginning of the criminal trial to assess his present mental condition, the result is irrelevant for the purposes of the imposition of criminal liability.

Because the presumption of insanity is an absolute presumption, the conclusion cannot be refuted as long as all its five elements are proven. In this situation, no criminal liability is imposed on the offender if the offense has been committed while the offender was considered insane. Even if it is proven beyond a reasonable doubt that, although he was insane at the time of the commission of the offense, the offender has consolidated the required fault for the imposition of criminal liability, no criminal liability is imposed. Consequently, as an absolute presumption, it can be voided in two principal ways: negating the elements of the presumption or imposing legal restrictions on applying the presumption.

To negate the elements of the presumption, it is necessary to prove the inexistence of at least one of them in the supplementary burden of proof. For example, if the offender must prove all five elements by raising a reasonable doubt regarding their existence, the prosecution needs to prove beyond reasonable doubt that at least one of them did not exist at the time of the commission of the offense. It is not necessary to prove the nonexistence of all elements, but only of one, because the elements are cumulative conditions, and if even one of these conditions is not proven, the entire presumption is not proven. When the relevant party fails to prove the existence of the elements of the presumption, the court cannot apply the presumption and the insanity defense is rejected.

The imposition of legal restrictions on the application of the presumption is part of the *ex ante* considerations of the legislator or the court. The legislator can exclude certain situations from the applicability of insanity. For example, certain offenses may not be subject to the insanity defense, certain mental deficiencies may not be considered insanity, etc. Using this alternative may result in unjust outcomes for the offender, who may be quite insane and incapable of consolidating the required fault, therefore this alternative is rarely used. The elements of the presumption are discussed below.

3.1 Legal Personhood

The first element of the presumption of insanity is the identity of the offender (a legal personhood). The reference of the presumption to human beings is obvious, because humans are subject to mental deficiencies since time immemorial. Nevertheless, the question remains whether the insanity defense is exclusive to humans. Humans are not the only legal entities that can commit offenses; so are corporations. The key question here is whether a physical body is required for insanity. However, this question exceeds from the boundaries of this article, and has been discussed elsewhere as to corporations and artificial intelligence entities.[68]

3.2 Temporary and Permanent Mental Disorders

The second element of the presumption of insanity is the mental deficiency. The main purpose of this element is to distinguish between different reasons for nullifying the offender's fault. This element is also significant for the offender's therapy and rehabilitation, if he were to be found incompetent to stand a trial. In general, there can be two main options for identifying the mental deficiency as such, but only one of these is relevant to the presumption of insanity. One is categorical and the other is functional.

Based on the categorical option, mental deficiency is identified as such according to a determined list of accepted mental deficiencies, regardless of the effect the deficiency had on the individual offender in any given case. There are two main difficulties with this option. First, it is over-inclusive. Lists of this type may include mental deficiencies that may affect most of the population in ways that would justify the insanity defense. Second, it is under-inclusive. Lists of this type may fail to include various mental deficiencies that might justify applying the insanity defense for the individual offender, although most of the population may not be affected by the given mental deficiency in the same way. Furthermore, for such a list to be complete, it would be necessary to predict mental deficiencies that have not yet been discovered or categorized.

Based on the functional option, a given mental deficiency must be examined for its *de facto* effect on the individual offender, with respect to both his cognitive and volitive capabilities. The question whether this mental deficiency is categorized as such or not is irrelevant for the functional option. The same mental deficiency may be considered to justify the insanity defense for one offender but not for another, depending on the particular symptoms of the mental deficiency of each offender. If these symptoms include, for the individual offender, the negation of cognition or volition, the insanity defense may be justified regardless its medical categorization.

The functional option includes a de facto examination of the cognitive and volitive capabilities of the offender. No assumptions are made based on general medical or psychiatric research that does not relate specifically to the particular offender. Because the person's fault is personal and subjective, this is the most relevant option for examining mental deficiencies for the purpose of applying the insanity defense. The term "mental deficiency" can have different interpretations in different contexts, but in the specific context of the presumption of insanity in criminal law the functional option appears to be the most appropriate way of implementing the basic rationales of the insanity defense.[69]

The functional examination of mental deficiency is traditionally regarded as requiring "mental deficiency" and not any other kind. This traditional requirement is reexamined below. If the traditional requirement is valid, when the cause of a given deficiency in the offender's brain is the presence of certain chemicals, it may be classified as being more relevant to intoxication than to insanity.[70] But if the chemicals are part of the natural secretion of the offender's endocrine system, is their presence considered relevant to insanity or to intoxication?

The functional examination does not require a permanent mental deficiency, spanning the offender's entire life. The mental deficiency must be functional, that is, affecting the cognition or volition of the offender only at the time when the offense was committed. The consequences of the mental deficiency relate only to the commission of the offense. For the purpose of the applicability of the insanity defense, the relevant time of the mental deficiency is the time of the commission of the offense, that is, the exact time when the offender committed the conduct component of the offense. Whether the mental deficiency existed at any other time is not relevant for the applicability of the insanity defense. For example, if the mental deficiency worsened after the commission of the offense, this does not affect the criminal liability of the offender, but it may affect the question of his competence to stand trial. Thus, use of the functional examination of mental deficiency raises the question of temporary insanity.

The term "temporary insanity" generally refers to a mental deficiency that occurs in response to certain stimuli. The outburst affects the offender's cognition or volition and places it within the realm of insanity. As long as the stimulus is absent, the offender displays full cognition and control over his volition. After he experiences an outburst, when the stimulus subsides, its effect over cognition and volition subsides as well. Indeed, temporary insanity refers to a permanent mental deficiency of a low intensity, which under a certain stimulus escalates to a degree where the mental deficiency affects functionally the offender's cognition or volition.

Under the functional examination of mental deficiency there is no legal reason to prevent the acceptance of temporary insanity as part of the insanity defense in criminal law. If at the time when the offense was committed the mental deficiency functionally affected the offender's cognition or volition, the behavior is covered by the insanity defense. The temporary character of the mental deficiency is immaterial as long as it was fully functional at the time when the offense was committed. The fact that in his daily life the offender is generally unaffected by the mental deficiency makes no difference for the insanity defense as long as it was in effect at the time of the commission of the offense.

The attitude toward other *in personam* defenses is analogous. For example, the fact that an offender is often intoxicated does not affect the applicability of the intoxication defense as long as he is affected by intoxication at the time the offense is committed. In the same way, if the offender acts under automatism when the offense is committed he may be covered by the automatism defense, even if he never experienced automatism at any other time in his life. Similarly, various legal systems have accepted the fact that temporary insanity is covered by insanity defense in criminal law.[71]

3.3 Uncontrollable Mental Disorder

The third element of the presumption of insanity is the inability to control the manifestations of the mental deficiency, specifically, his awareness and the means available to respond adequately. The element of control is examined from the offender's subjective point of view, not objectively. For example, if the mental deficiency can be balanced by medication but the offender is not aware of it (or of the mental deficiency itself), subjectively the mental deficiency is not considered controllable.

When the offender suffers from mental deficiency that affects his cognition or volition, but he is being treated medically and his mental state is therefore balanced, the mental deficiency is considered to be controllable. If the offender continues medical treatment, and the deficiency is under his mental control, the presumption of insanity does not apply. It is necessary to distinguish between the ability to control the mental deficiency and de facto control over it. To control the mental deficiency, by medications or by any other means, it must be controllable from the offender's point of view.

The ability to control the mental deficiency is indeed a preliminary condition for controlling it. Nevertheless, control *de facto* over the mental deficiency may not be achieved for various reasons, some of which may be related, directly or indirectly, to the offender, and others, which may not be related to him. The third element of the presumption of insanity does not require *de facto* control over the mental deficiency, only the capability to control it. In other words, only the preliminary condition is required. If the offender has no capability to control the mental deficiency, he could probably not have controlled it.

The ability to control the mental deficiency is examined subjectively, through the eyes of the offender. The offender may not be aware of the existence of the mental deficiency or of the medical treatment needed to alleviate its symptoms. Consequently, the presumption of insanity is not applicable to an offender who is undergoing medical or other treatment to control his mental deficiency (which is therefore controllable). For example, if the offender deliberately avoids taking his medication in order to experience a violent outburst of his mental illness, and during this outburst he commits a criminal offense, the insanity defense is not applicable.

If the deliberate avoidance is specifically intended to facilitate the commission of the offense, the insanity defense does not apply, as noted. This type of situations is covered by the concept of the transformation of fault, when the offender who has the ability to control his mental deficiency chooses not to do so. The fault of not controlling the mental deficiency may be transferred to the point when the offense was committed. Naturally, if the mental deficiency is controllable and the offender has in practice brought it under control, the insanity defense does not apply because the offender did not act under the influence of insanity.

3.4 Negation of Cognition or Volition and Partial Insanity

The forth element of the presumption of insanity involves the negation of either the cognitive or of the volitive capabilities of the offender with respect to the commission of the offense. Both alternatives of this element are supplementary to the functional examination of the mental deficiency, as discussed previously. The functional examination concerns both the cognitive and the volitive aspects of the mental deficiency, therefore incorporation of the two alternatives into the fourth element reflects this functional examination.

The combination of cognitive and volitive elements has been accepted in Anglo-American legal systems that embraced the M'Naghten Rules with the irresistible impulse test, as well as in European-Continental legal systems. The negation of the offender's cognitive capabilities may refer to his understanding of his conduct or of the legal prohibition against it. Naturally, only the legal prohibition is subject to this understanding, not the morality of the conduct. For instance, an offender who is under the delusion that God commanded him to set fire to a brothel executes the command based on the understanding that his conduct brings redemption to all mankind. He fully understands that this conduct is prohibited by human law, but from his point of view the conduct is morally correct.

Because the offender understood that setting on fire to the brothel is legally prohibited, his cognitive capabilities concerning the existence of the legal prohibition and his duty to observe it were not negated by his mental deficiency. He therefore set the fire while fully aware that his conduct represented a criminal offense, even if he found some moral, religious, or other justification for his conduct. Consequently, in this case the fourth element has not been consolidated, and the presumption of insanity does not apply.

The negation of the offender's volitive capabilities refers to his inability to control his will or the conduct that serves that will. When the will becomes irresistible, the offender has no internal powers to oppose it. This deficiency may be manifest both as acts and as omissions. When the mental deficiency creates an impulse to act in a certain manner or creates a feeling of paralysis that prevents acting in a certain manner, both are manifestations of the negation of the offender's volition with respect to a certain conduct. In these situations the offender is internally coerced to engage in a certain conduct (act or omission).

The internal coercion negates the offender's free will to choose between permitted and prohibited conduct. For example, a person sees another person in danger and need of immediate help, but does not provide the required assistance. In some legal systems this is considered a criminal offense.[72] In this case, however, the reason for the conduct is that the offender's memory of a similar event from the past causes an internal spasm that paralyzes him. The spasm coerces the offender's conduct. Similarly, a father yelling aggressively at his son causes a psychotic spasm that makes the son assault his father to stop the yelling. Again, it is the spasm that coerces the offender's conduct.

In both examples here, the offender's will is negated as far as the conduct in question is concerned, irrespective of the cognitive capabilities of the offender. The negation of the will does not assume or require a simultaneous negation of cognitive abilities. The negations of cognition or of volition are alternatives and not independent preliminary conditions. These alternatives are part of the functional examination of mental deficiency for the applicability of the insanity defense. Consequently, for the consolidation of the forth element, it is sufficient to negate either the cognition or the volition of the offender, and it is not necessary to negate both.

The availability of two alternatives may raise a question regarding partial insanity. Partial insanity refers to the full negation of the offender's cognition with regard to some of the components of the factual element of the offense. Partial insanity does not involve the negation of the will or of any volitive aspects of insanity, only to the cognitive aspects. Under partial insanity, cognition is fully negated, as the partiality does not refer to the degree of negation (that is, the degree of cognition) but to its objects. Thus, partial insanity refers to full cognition with regard to a portion of the objects (components of the factual elements).

Complete insanity manifests as the full negation of all components of the factual element. For example, in the case of rape the offender is required to be aware of the conduct (having sexual intercourse) and of the circumstances (human victim and absence of consent). If the offender experiences full insanity with regard to cognition, it manifests as lack of awareness of both conduct and circumstances. The offender is required not to be aware of conduct (he is not aware of having sexual intercourse) or of circumstances (he is not aware that the victim is human and that no consent has been given for the conduct). Such situations are very rare.

In most cases, the offender is aware of some of the components of the factual elements, although not of all of them. In the example just mentioned, the offender might be aware of the conduct and of the human victim, but not of the absence of consent. Such situations are much more common. Therefore, partial insanity is much more common than full insanity. Because criminal liability requires meeting cumulative conditions, partial insanity is legally equal to full insanity. This means that the negation of even one component of the mental element, required for the full imposition of criminal liability, nullifies the possibility of imposing criminal liability.

If follows that for the presumption of insanity, it is not necessary to experience the symptoms of full insanity at the time of the commission of the offense with regard to all components of the factual element. If the mental deficiency caused the offender not to be aware of one of the components of the factual element, this completely negates the offender's fault as far as the imposition of criminal liability is concerned. In the example mentioned previously, if the offender was not aware of the absence of the victim's consent because of mental deficiency, an adequate basis exists for the applicability of the presumption of insanity, and subject to the other elements of the presumption, no criminal liability is imposed on the offender.

At the same time, partial insanity does not necessarily prevent imposition of all criminal liability. Certain types of criminal liability may be imposed on an offender experiencing partial insanity if his personal fault satisfies another criminal offense, although not the original one. Only if the partial insanity negates the fault required by all criminal offenses with respect to the same factual element, is no criminal liability imposed in any case. In the above example, if the partial insanity negates the awareness of the absence of consent, the offender is not criminally liable for rape, because consensual sexual relations with an adult are not considered rape.

But the legal result is different if the victim is a minor. If the partial insanity negated the awareness of the absence of consent but did not negate the awareness of the victim's biological age, criminal liability may still be imposed. In this case, the partial insanity negated one of the components of fault required for the imposition of criminal liability, but it did not negate the fault required for statutory rape. Having consensual sexual relations with a minor is statutory rape, and in this case the partial insanity did not negate any of the fault components required to impose criminal liability for the offense.

Thus, practically, the court must examine the fault components present in each case after the components affected by the partial insanity have been eliminated. The remaining fault components must then be matched with the factual element components present in the case. If the combination of fault and factual element components meets the requirements of certain criminal offense, the court may impose criminal liability for that offense. Only if that combination does not match the requirements of any criminal offense is the offender free from criminal liability.

3.5 Factual Causation

The fifth element of the presumption of insanity is factual causal relation between the mental deficiency and the commission of the particular offense. This element refers only to factual causation, because legal causation is already incorporated in the mental element requirement of the offense.[73] The definition of factual causation for the presumption of insanity is similar to the requirement of factual causal relation between the conduct and the results within the general requirements of the factual element, mutatis mutandis. Thus, the mental deficiency must function as a causa sine qua non for the commission of the offense.

The mental deficiency must be considered as the ultimate cause for the commission of the offense in the way in which it was committed. The commission of the offense must be a direct result of the mental deficiency. It is immaterial whether this factual cause is supplementary to other causes, as long as without the certain mental deficiency the criminal offense at hand could not have been committed in the way that is was. The general rules of factual causation accepted in criminal law are relevant for the fifth element of the presumption, with a slight change: conduct is replaced with mental deficiency, and result with the commission of the offense.

Naturally, this factual causation requirement is not a substitute for the factual causation requirement that is part of the factual element, if required. For example, if the offender is charged with murder, the prosecution must still prove beyond reasonable doubt the factual causation between the offender's conduct and the result (the victim's death). Additionally, if the offender wishes to use the presumption of insanity, he must raise at least a reasonable doubt regarding the factual causal relation between his mental deficiency and the commission of the offense. The two factual causal relations represent two separate requirements, and one does not replace the other.

Nevertheless, the general rules of factual causation are applicable to both requirements. These rules include the legal definition of the ultimate reason (*causa sine qua non*), raising the probability of the occurrence of the factual event, situations with multiple reasons (alternative, supplementary, cumulative, and parallel reasons), the continuity of causation, and the intervening cause (*novus actus interveniens*).[74] Consequently, if the offender suffers from a certain mental deficiency that was not the ultimate cause for committing the offense in the way in which it was committed, no factual causation exists between them.

In this case, it turns out that the offense would have been committed anyway, regardless the offender's mental deficiency. Therefore, the mental deficiency was not involved in the internal process of the offender and it did not cause him to commit the offense in the exact way in which it was committed. The presumption of insanity, therefore, is inapplicable. In this case, the mental deficiency is nothing more than part of the external background circumstances that do not affect the commission of the offense. If all five elements of the presumption of insanity are consolidated, the presumption is applicable and the insanity defense can be used.

4 Legal Consequences

The legal consequences of insanity are relevant when the offender is legally recognized as insane. Insanity has two main legal aspects: substantive and procedural. The substantive aspect relates to criminal liability (rejecting it), whereas the procedural aspect has to do with the offender's competence to stand trial (rejecting it as well). Nevertheless, the two represent different legal aspects of insanity, and their consequences are not identical. The offender may be criminally liable, as far as the substantive law is concerned, but incompetent to stand trial, or conversely, the offender competent to stand trial but not liable criminally.

The basic distinction between the two legal aspects derives from the distinction between substantive and procedural law. The insanity defense grants the offender personal substantive immunity from criminal liability. This immunity is not formed at the time of prosecution or of the trial, only at the time when the offense was committed. If the offender's mental condition has changed since then, this has no bearing on the criminal liability. The offender is criminally liable only if at the time when the offense has been committed the presumption of insanity did not exist.

Incompetence to stand trial grants the offender immunity from prosecution. Under this immunity, the offender is not charged with any offense, whether or not he is criminally liable. Similarly to all procedural immunities, the relevant time is the time of the trial, not the time when the offense was committed. Consequently, two relevant time points must be examined with respect to the offender's insanity: the time of the commission of the offense and the time of the trial. The two points in time are distinct, and generally the time of the trial is later than the time of the commission of the offense.

In some situations, insanity at one point in time may reflect insanity at the other point, but still the two points in time are distinct and must be examined separately. Based on this distinction, we can identify four possible situations of insanity that may have different consequences:

1. Insanity at the time of the commission of the offense, but not at the time of standing trial;
2. Insanity at the time of standing trial, but not at the time of the commission of the offense;
3. Insanity at both points in time;
4. Insanity at none of these points.

In the first situation, the offender is competent to stand the trial and can be prosecuted for the offense, but when the court comes to decide on the issue of criminal liability, the substantive immunity (that is, the insanity defense) becomes relevant and no criminal liability is imposed on the offender. Indeed, this is the only situation in which the insanity defense can be claimed. Only if the offender is competent to stand trial, is there a trial at which the issue of criminal liability is decided. If the offender is incompetent to stand trial, the opportunity for resorting to the insanity defense never arises.

The second situation is one in which, for example, the offender suffers from mental deficiency that did not affect his cognition at the time he committed the offense. After the offense is committed, the offender experiences a worsening in his mental deficiency, which passes the threshold at which cognition is affected to the point of insanity, and by the time of the trial the offender is incompetent to stand trial. The relevant point of time for examining the offender's incompetence is any point of time in the course of the trial. Thus, if the insanity sets in after the offender has been charged, no further actions are taken. If the insanity occurs later, after the trial has started, the trial is stopped and no further action is taken.

In the third situation, insanity is claimed at both points in time: the offender was insane both at the time of the commission of the offense and at the time of the trial. Thus it appears that no criminal liability may be imposed on the offender, and he is incompetent to stand trial. In this case, however, the procedural insanity takes precedence. If the offender is incompetent to stand trial, whether or not he was insane at the time of the commission of the offense, no criminal proceedings are initiated against him and therefore the opportunity to claim substantive insanity does not arise. Thus, when the offender is incompetent to stand trial, the procedural immunity obviates the need for claiming the insanity defense.

In the fourth situation, the offender may have experienced insanity at some point in his life, but none of the episodes occurred at the time when the offense has been committed or at the time of the trial. Under these circumstances, the offender is considered perfectly sane both for the purpose of standing trial and for the imposition of criminal liability. At most, his mental background may serve as mitigating considerations when the appropriate punishment is considered.

5 Conclusion

Our investigation of the insanity defense began with an exploration of the evolution of defense in criminal law. As a general defense in criminal law, insanity is defined socially rather than medically, and functionally rather than categorically. Insanity defense has the legal structure of absolute legal presumption, and has both legal and social consequences. The legal consequences are both substantial and procedural. However, insanity is defined socially rather than medically, and it is a cultural rather than a psychiatric matter. Medical definitions of insanity are not necessarily relevant to law and society. Insanity may be dependent on time, place, and social environment, rather than a medical diagnosis.[75]

Notes

1. Genesis 22.
2. For the medical evolution of insanity see Hallevy, *The Matrix of Insanity in Modern Criminal Law*.
3. *Digesta*, 21.1.23.2 and 1.18.13.1; see Robinson, *The Criminal Law of Ancient Rome*, 16.
4. Sendor, "Crime as Communication," 1380; Rodriguez, LeWinn and Perlin, "The Insanity Defense Under Siege," 406–07; Crotty, "The History of Insanity as a Defense to Crime in English Common Law," 105.
5. Y.B., 6 & 7 Edw. II (1313).
6. Platt and Diamond, "The Origins of the 'Right and Wrong' Test of Criminal Responsibility," 1231–1233; Michel, *Ayenbit of Inwyt*, 86.
7. Genesis 2:9, 16, 3:1–21.
8. Golding, "Mental Health Professionals and the Courts," 287.
9. Platt and Diamond, "The Origins of the 'Right and Wrong' Test of Criminal Responsibility," 1233–34.
10. Crotty, "The History of Insanity as a Defense to Crime," 107–08, quotes the definition of the term "idiot" from the 1616 edition of *Novel Natura Brevium*.
11. Hans and Vidmar, *Judging the Jury*, 187–88.
12. Arnold, (1724) 16 How. St. Tr. 695.
13. Platt and Diamond, "The Origins and Development of the 'Wild Beast' Concept of Mental Illness," 360; Bracton, *De Legibus et Consuetudinibus Angliae*.
14. Quen, "Isaac Ray and Charles Doe," 237.
15. Perlin, *The Jurisprudence of the Insanity Defense*, 76.
16. Collinson, *Idiots, Lunatics, and Other Persons Non Compos Mentis*, 477, 636, 671.
17. Oxford, (1840) 9 Car. & P. 525, 173 Eng. Rep. 941.
18. Hovenkamp, "Insanity and Responsibility in Progressive America," 552.
19. M'Naghten, (1843) 10 Cl. & Fin. 200, 8 Eng. Rep. 718.
20. For the questions and their legal interpretation see Hallevy, *Matrix of Insanity*.
21. English, "The Light Between Twilight and Dusk"; *State v. Holder*, 15 S.W.3d 905 (Tenn.Crim.App.1999); *State v. Smith*, 256 Neb. 705, 592 N.W.2d 143 (1999);

Finger v. State, 117 Nev. 548, 27 P.3d 66 (2001); *Vann v. Commonwealth*, 35 Va.App. 304, 544 S.E.2d 879 (2001).

22. Goldstein, *The Insanity Defense*, 48.

23. *State v. Elsea*, 251 S.W.2d 650 (Mo.1952); *State v. Johnson*, 233 Wis. 668, 290 N.W. 159 (1940); *State v. Hadley*, 65 Utah 109, 234 P. 940 (1925); Weihofen, *Mental Disorder as a Criminal Defense*, 119.

24. See the Model Penal Code—Official Draft and Explanatory Notes (1962, 1985), article 4.01, Appendix A.

25. LaFave, *Criminal Law*, 382–83.

26. *Montgomery v. State*, 68 Tex.Crim.App. 78, 151 S.W. 813 (1912); *Jessner v. State*, 202 Wis. 184, 231 N.W. 634 (1930); *Cochran v. State*, 65 Fla. 91, 61 So. 187 (1913); *State v. McGee*, 631 Mo. 309, 234 S.W.2d 587 (1950).

27. Stephen, *A History of the Criminal Law of England*, 149.

28. Windle, [1952] 2 Q.B. 826, [1952] 2 All E.R. 1, 36 Cr. App. Rep. 85, [1952] W.N. 283.

29. *State v. Hamann*, 285 N.W.2d 180 (Iowa 1979); *State v. Andrews*, 187 Kan. 458, 357 P.2d 739 (1960).

30. *People v. Schmidt*, 216 N.Y. 324, 110 N.E. 945 (1915).

31. Royal Commission on Capital Punishment, 1949–53 Report 80 (1953).

32. Brakel and Rock, *The Mentally Disabled and the Law*, 386; Guttmacher and Weihofen, *Psychiatry and the Law*, 420.

33. Model Penal Code, article 4.01, Appendix A; Allen, "The Rule of the American Law Institute's Model Penal Code," 498.

34. Dix, "Criminal Responsibility and Mental Impairment in American Criminal Law," 7; *State v. Hartley*, 90 N.M. 488, 565 P.2d 658 (1977); *Vann v. Commonwealth*, 35 Va.App. 304, 544 S.E.2d 879 (2001); *State v. Carney*, 347 N.W.2d 668 (Iowa 1984).

35. Ray, *Treatise on the Medical Jurisprudence of Insanity* (1st ed.), 263; Winslow, *The Plea of Insanity in Criminal Cases*, 74; Glueck, *Mental Disorders and the Criminal Law*, 153, 236–237.

36. Keedy, "Irresistible Impulse as a Defense in the Criminal Law," 961; Oxford, (1840) 9 Car. & P. 525, 173 Eng. Rep. 941.

37. Burton, (1863) 3 F. & F. 772, 176 Eng. Rep. 354.

38. *State v. Thompson*, Wright's Ohio Rep. 617 (1834); *Clark v. State*, 12 Ohio Rep. 483 (1843); *Commonwealth v. Rogers*, 48 Mass. 500 (1844); *Parsons v. State*, 81 Ala. 577, 2 So. 854 (1887).

39. *State v. Davies*, 146 Conn. 137, 148 A.2d 251 (1959); *Commonwealth v. Harrison*, 342 Mass. 279, 173 N.E.2d 87 (1961).

40. Wechsler, "The Criteria of Criminal Responsibility," 375.

41. Model Penal Code, article 4.01, Appendix A; *United States v. Kunack*, 17 C.M.R. 346 (1954).

42. Waite, "Irresistible Impulse and Criminal Liability," 454.

43. *People v. Hubert*, 119 Cal. 216, 51 P. 329 (1897).

44. Hoedemaker, "'Irresistible Impulse' as a Defense in Criminal Law," 7. For the deterrence considerations in criminal law, see Hallevy, *The Right to Be Punished*, 25–36.

45. *State v. Jones*, 50 N.H. 369 (1871); *State v. Pike*, 49 N.H. 399 (1870); *State v. Cegelis*, 138 N.H. 249, 638 A.2d 783 (1994); Ray, *Treatise on the Medical Jurisprudence of Insanity* (1st ed.), 39.

46. *State v. Peel*, 23 Mont. 358, 59 P. 169 (1899); *State v. Keerl*, 29 Mont. 508, 75 P. 362 (1904); *State v. Narich*, 92 Mont. 17, 9 P.2d 477 (1932).

47. *Durham v. United States*, 214 F.2d 862 (D.C.Cir.1954).

48. Grazia, "The Distinction of Being Mad"; Hill, "The Psychological Realism of Thurman Arnold"; Guttmacher, "The Psychiatrist as an Expert Witness"; Katz, "Law, Psychiatry, and Free Will"; Hall, "Psychiatry and Criminal Responsibility."

49. For the term "product," see *Carter v. United States*, 252 F.2d 608 (D.C.Cir.1957); *Blocker v. United States*, 288 F.2d 853 (D.C.Cir.1961); *Wright v. United States*, 250 F.2d 4 (D.C.Cir.1957); *Washington v. United States*, 390 F.2d 444 (D.C.Cir.1967); For the term "mental disease or defect," see *Blocker v. United States*, 274 F.2d 572 (D.C.Cir.1959); *McDonald v. United States*, 312 F.2d 847 (D.C.Cir.1962).

50. *United States v. Brawner*, 471 F.2d 969 (D.C.Cir.1972).

51. Model Penal Code, 61–62.

52. *United States v. Freeman*, 357 F.2d 606 (2nd Cir.1966); *United States v. Currens*, 290 F.2d 751 (3rd Cir.1961); *United States v. Chandler*, 393 F.2d 920 (4th Cir.1968); *Blake v. United States*, 407 F.2d 908 (5th Cir.1969); *United States v. Smith*, 404 F.2d 720 (6th Cir.1968).

53. 18 U.S.C.A. §17.

54. *Commonwealth v. Herd*, 413 Mass. 834, 604 N.E.2d 1294 (1992); *State v. Curry*, 45 Ohio St.3d 109, 543 N.E.2d 1228 (1989); *State v. Barrett*, 768 A.2d 929 (R.I.2001); *State v. Lockhart*, 208 W.Va. 622, 542 S.E.2d 443 (2000).

55. Burton, (1863) 3 F. & F. 772, 176 Eng. Rep. 354; Kopsch, (1925) 19 Cr. App. Rep. 50; True, (1922) 16 Cr. App. Rep. 164; Sodeman, [1936] 2 All E.R. 1138; *Attorney-General for the State of South Australia v. Brown*, [1960] A.C. 432, [1960] 1 All E.R. 734, [1960] 2 W.L.R. 588, 44 Cr. App. Rep. 100. In Canada see Creighton, (1909) 14 C.C.C. 349.

56. Roach, [2001] E.W.C.A. Crim. 2698; Attorney-General's Reference (No. 3 of 1998), [2000] Q.B. 401, [1999] 3 All E.R. 40, [1999] 3 W.L.R. 1194, 49 B.M.L.R. 124, [1999] 2 Cr. App. Rep. 214, [1999] Crim. L.R. 986.

57. Sullivan, [1984] 1 A.C. 156, [1983] 2 All E.R. 673, [1983] 3 W.L.R. 123, 77 Cr. App. Rep. 176, 148 J.P. 207.

58. Kemp, [1957] 1 Q.B. 399, [1956] 3 All E.R. 249, [1956] 3 W.L.R. 724; *Bratty v. Attorney-General for Northern Ireland*, [1963] A.C. 386, [1961] 3 All E.R. 523, [1961] 3 W.L.R. 965, 46 Cr. App. Rep. 1.

59. See the first part of article 122-1 of the French Penal Code.

60. Elliott, *French Criminal Law*, 120.

61. See article 20 of the German Penal Code.

62. Due to article 21 of the German Penal Code.

63. RG 21, 131; RG 73, 121; BGH 3, 194; BGH 7, 238; BGH 7, 325; BGH 8, 113; BGH 11, 20; BGH 14, 30; BGH 19, 201; BGH 23, 133; BGH 23, 176; BGH 23.

64. Jescheck and Weigend, *Lehrbuch des Strafrechts*, 437–43.

65. We prefer these terms to "infra-normality" and "ultra-normality," particularly because "ultra-normality" seems to mean "very normal," which is simply "normal."

66. Genesis 22:3–13.

67. See e.g. 2 Kings 16:2, 5–9.

68. For the applicability of insanity defense in criminal law to corporations see Hallevy, *Matrix of Insanity*. For the applicability of insanity defense in criminal law to artificial intelligence entities see Hallevy, *When Robots Kill*, 128–30.

69. *State v. Elsea*, 251 S.W.2d 650 (Mo.1952); *State v. Johnson*, 233 Wis. 668, 290 N.W. 159 (1940); *State v. Hadley*, 65 Utah 109, 234 P. 940 (1925); Weihofen, *Mental Disorder as a Criminal Defense*, 119; Fulford, "Value, Action, Mental Illness, and the Law."

70. *State v. White*, 27 N.J. 158, 142 A.2d 65 (1958); *Barbour v. State*, 262 Ala. 297, 78 So.2d 328 (1954).

71. Kemp, [1957] 1 Q.B. 399, [1956] 3 All E.R. 249, [1956] 3 W.L.R. 724; Kingston, [1995] 2 A.C. 355, [1994] 3 All E.R. 353, [1994] 3 W.L.R. 519, [1994] Crim. L.R. 846, 99 Cr. App. Rep. 286, 158 J.P. 717; *People v. Sommers*, 200 P.3d 1089 (2008); *McNeil v. United States*, 933 A.2d 354 (2007); *Rangel v. State*, 2009 Tex. App. 1555 (2009); *Commonwealth v. Shumway*, 72 Va.Cir. 481 (2007).

72. In most European-Continental legal systems, it is considered a criminal offense, whereas in the Anglo-American legal tradition, it is not in general.

73. For the elements of legal causation see Hallevy, *Theory of Criminal Law*, Vol. II, 103–119 (*mens rea*), 314–331 (negligence), and 366–373 (strict liability).

74. Ibid.

75. I thank Mark D. White for the invitation to participate in this project.

Resources

Allen, Francis A., "The Rule of the American Law Institute's Model Penal Code." *Marquette Law Review* 45(1962): 494–505.

[De] Bracton, Henry, *De Legibus et Consuetudinibus Angliae*. Edited by G. E. Woodbine, translated by S. E. Thorne. 1260, available at http://bracton.law.harvard.edu/.

Brakel, Samuel J., and Ronald S. Rock (eds.), *The Mentally Disabled and the Law*. Rev. ed. Chicago: University of Chicago Press, 1971.

Collinson, George D., *Idiots, Lunatics, and Other Persons Non Compos Mentis*. London: W. Read, 1812.

Crotty, Homer D., "The History of Insanity as a Defense to Crime in English Common Law." *California Law Review* 12(1924): 105–23.

Dix, George E., "Criminal Responsibility and Mental Impairment in American Criminal Law: Responses to the Hinckley Acquittal in Historical Perspective." In *Law and Mental Health: International Perspectives*, vol. 1, edited by D.N. Weisstub (New York: Pergamon Press, 1984), 1–44.
Elliott, Catherine, *French Criminal Law*. Cullompton, UK: Willan, 2001.
English, Jodie, "The Light Between Twilight and Dusk: Federal Criminal Law and the Volitional Insanity Defense." *Hastings Law Journal* 40(1988): 1–52.
Fulford, K. W. M., "Value, Action, Mental Illness, and the Law." In *Action and Value in Criminal Law*, edited by Stephen Shute, John Gardner, and Jeremy Horder (Oxford: Calrendon Press, 1993), 279–310.
Glueck, S. Sheldon, *Mental Disorders and the Criminal Law: A Study in Medico-Sociological Jurisprudence*. Boston: Little, Brown, and Co., 1927.
Golding, Stephen L., "Mental Health Professionals and the Courts: The Ethics of Expertise." *International Journal of Law and Psychiatry* 13(1990): 281–307.
Goldstein, Abraham S., *The Insanity Defense*. New Haven: Yale University Press, 1967.
Grazia, Edward de, "The Distinction of Being Mad." *University of Chicago Law Review* 22(1955): 339–55.
Guttmacher, Manfred S., "The Psychiatrist as an Expert Witness." *University of Chicago Law Review* 22(1955): 325–30.
Guttmacher, Manfred S., and Henry Weihofen, *Psychiatry and the Law*. New York: W.W. Norton and Co., 1952.
Hall, Jerome, "Psychiatry and Criminal Responsibility." *Yale Law Journal* 65(1956): 761–85.
Hallevy, Gabriel, *The Matrix of Insanity in Modern Criminal Law*. Heidelberg: Springer, 2015.
Hallevy, Gabriel, *The Right to Be Punished: Modern Doctrinal Sentencing*. Heidelberg: Springer, 2013.
Hallevy, Gabriel, *Theory of Criminal Law*, vol. II. Bnei Brak, Israel: Bursi, 2009.
Hallevy, Gabriel, *When Robots Kill: Artificial Intelligence under Criminal Law*. Lebanon, NH: Northeastern University Press, 2013.
Hans, Valerie P., and Nigel Vidmar, *Judging the Jury*. New York: Plenum Press, 1986.
Hill, Warren P., "The Psychological Realism of Thurman Arnold." *University of Chicago Law Review* 22(1955): 377–96.
Hoedemaker, Edward D., "'Irresistible Impulse' as a Defense in Criminal Law," *Washington Law Review* 23(1948): 1–7.
Hovenkamp, Herbert, "Insanity and Responsibility in Progressive America." *North Dakota Law Review* 57(1981): 541–76.
Jescheck, Hans-Heinrich, and Thomas Weigend, *Lehrbuch des Strafrechts: Allgemeiner Teil*. Berlin: Duncker & Humblot, 1996.
Katz, Wilber G., "Law, Psychiatry, and Free Will." *University of Chicago Law Review* 22(1955): 397–404.
Keedy, Edwin R., "Irresistible Impulse as a Defense in the Criminal Law." *University of Pennsylvania Law Review* 100(1952): 956–93.

LaFave, Wayne R., *Criminal Law*. 4th ed. Eagen, MN: Thomson/West, 2003.

Michel, Dan, *Ayenbit of Inwyt: Or, Remorse of Conscience*. Edited by Richard Morris. London: N. Trübner and Co., 1866 (orig. 1340).

Perlin, Michael L., *The Jurisprudence of the Insanity Defense*. Durham, NC: Carolina Academic Press, 1993.

Platt, Anthony M., and Bernard L. Diamond, "The Origins and Development of the 'Wild Beast' Concept of Mental Illness and Its Relation to Theories of Criminal Responsibility." *Journal of the History of the Behavioral Sciences* 1(1965): 355–67.

Platt, Anthony M., and Bernard L. Diamond, "The Origins of the 'Right and Wrong' Test of Criminal Responsibility and Its Subsequent Development in the United States: An Historical Survey." *California Law Review* 54 (1966) 1227–60.

Quen, Jacques M., "Isaac Ray and Charles Doe: Responsibility and Justice, Law and the Mental Health Professions: Friction at the Interface." In *Law and the Mental Health Professions: Friction at the Interface*, edited by Walter E. Barton and Charlotte J. Sanborn (New York: International Universities Press, 1978), 235–50.

Ray, Isaac, *Treatise on the Medical Jurisprudence of Insanity*. 1st ed. Boston: Little and Brown, 1838.

Ray, Isaac, *Treatise on the Medical Jurisprudence of Insanity*. 5th ed. Boston: Little and Brown, 1871.

Robinson, Olivia F., *The Criminal Law of Ancient Rome*. Baltimore, MD: Johns Hopkins University Press, 1995.

Rodriguez, Joseph H., Laura M. LeWinn, and Michael L. Perlin, "The Insanity Defense Under Siege: Legislative Assaults and Legal Rejoinders." *Rutgers Law Journal* 14(1983): 397–430.

Sendor, Benjamin B., "Crime as Communication: An Interpretive Theory of the Insanity Defense and the Mental Elements of Crime." *Georgetown Law Journal* 74(1986): 1371–1434.

Stephen, James Fitzjames, *A History of the Criminal Law of England*. New York: Burt Franklin, 1964 (orig. 1883).

Waite, John Barker, "Irresistible Impulse and Criminal Liability." *Michigan Law Review* 23(1925): 443–74.

Wechsler, Herbert, "The Criteria of Criminal Responsibility." *University of Chicago Law Review* 22(1955): 367–76.

Weihofen, Henry, *Mental Disorder as a Criminal Defense*. Buffalo, NY: Dennis, 1954.

Winslow, Forbes, *The Plea of Insanity in Criminal Cases*. London: H. Renshaw, 1843.

CHAPTER FIVE

Insanity Constructs

Meron Wondemaghen

If mental illness is an issue in the context of violent crimes such as homicide, it may affect all stages of the legal process. Before trial, mental illness may be raised to address questions about an offender's fitness to stand trial. During trial, it serves to determine whether the accused was of sound mind at the time of the crime; in which case, the legal criteria of insanity are tested. And after trial, it may be considered during sentencing so that appropriate dispositions can be made depending on the severity of the illness at the time of sentencing regardless of culpability. Of these, the trial stage of the legal process presents difficulties in establishing which mental disorders ought to receive special treatment from the criminal law to exculpate criminal responsibility because what constitutes insanity is legally and psychiatrically constructed. In addition to these constructs—often in conflict with one another—also exist popular perception about madness and legal insanity.

Using insanity as a defense to negate criminal responsibility has been established since the early 18th century in *Arnold* (1724) and further developed in *Hadfield* (1800) and *Oxford* (1840). In *Arnold*, the "wild beast test" emerged: the judge ruled that a defendant is insane and criminally irresponsible if he did not know what he was doing and was doing no more than a "wild beast" would do. In *Oxford*, the criteria were further refined in that insanity was established if the defendant suffered from a "diseased mind" and was "quite unaware of the nature, character, and consequences of the act he was committing." But it was the British case of Daniel M'Naghten in 1843 that formed the basis for the common law defense of insanity. The M'Naghten test sets out the criteria that must be satisfied to establish insanity and is the basis for the statutory defense of insanity in Australia (Criminal Code Act 1995), Canada (Criminal Code of Canada), England and Wales (Criminal Procedure (Insanity) Act 1991), New Zealand (Crimes Act, 1961), and several states in the United States that use the M'Naghten test alone or in conjunction with the "irresistible impulse" test. In the M'Naghten case, the House of Lords established that if an accused did not know the nature and quality or wrongness of the conduct, he or she is legally insane and not criminally responsible. The defense thus operates outside the *mens rea/actus reus* elements and is concerned with defects of reason that must arise from a "disease of mind." That is, though mental illness can be used to negate *mens rea*, it is rarely used for this purpose than it is for the defense. Drawing from the medico-legal debate about what constitutes insanity, this chapter examines the practical implications of legal constructs such as "disease of mind," "nature and quality" and "wrongness" for mentally ill offenders with various diagnostic labels.

1 Psychiatric Constructs

There are two main systems for defining and classifying mental disorders: the *Diagnostic and Statistical Manual of Mental Disorders*, 4th edition (DSM-IV), which discusses 17 mental disorders, and *The ICD-10 Classification of Mental and Behavioural Disorders*, with a classification of nine mental disorders. The ICD-10, published by the World Health Organization in 1992, defines the term "mental disorder" as "the existence of a clinically recognizable set of symptoms or behaviors associated in most cases with distress and with interference of personal functions."[1] The DSM-IV, published by the American Psychiatric Association in 1994, defines "mental disorder" as a "clinically significant behavioral or psychological syndrome or pattern in an individual, associated with present distress or disability" that exhibits patterns that cannot be "an expectable response to a particular event, such as death of a loved one" and must be considered a "manifestation of a behavioural, psychological or biological dysfunction in the person."[2] A "text revision" of the DSM-IV was published in 2000 in order to maintain consistency with the ICD-10 and the latest revision, the DSM-V, was published in 2013 with 15 new mental disorders to its list.

Mental illnesses can further be classified into psychotic and non-psychotic based on patients' ability to make sense of reality. Characteristic to psychotic illnesses—such as schizophrenia or delusional paranoia—is the loss of touch with reality. Psychotic disorders are mainly characterized by delusions and prominent hallucinations; patients lose touch with reality and are unable to make sense of their thoughts, feelings, or their environment.[3] What sufferers perceive as real is not experienced by others around them because delusions and hallucinations cause patients to see, hear, or feel sensations that are not present. Patients also have false beliefs of persecution, guilt, or grandeur. On the other hand, non-psychotic illnesses are characterized by overwhelming feelings of depression, sadness, anxiety, tension, or fear, and can impair affected individuals from coping with day-to-day activities.[4] These include phobias, some forms of depression, and obsessive-compulsive disorder.

The aforementioned clinical definitions, in both the DSM-IV and ICD-10, are broad because the aim is to accommodate a range of diagnoses for treatment purposes. In contrast, because courts seek to answer questions of justice by establishing whether an individual is criminally responsible or not, legal definitions are narrow. Issues arise when one seeks to examine which mental disorders ought to be treated specially in matters of criminal responsibility because clinical diagnosis is not only heterogeneous but also based on behavioral indicators. That is, diagnosis of mental disorders is based on the subjective observation of abnormal behaviors by a mental health practitioner rather than scientific methods outlining specific neuro-physiological pathways of causation. Indeed, mental disorders are, unlike physical illnesses, also socially constructed because sufferers' symptoms are often viewed as "offenses against implicit social understandings."[5] Psychiatrist Thomas Szasz, a well-known critic of the lack of objective methods in psychiatry, argues that "mental illnesses are for the most part communications expressing unacceptable ideas" by psychiatrists who are "participant observers" and who judge behavior based on what they or society consider reality.[6] Even with the use of the same diagnostic manual, psychiatrists often make different diagnoses about the same patient. Szasz insists that psycho-social manifestations that are labelled as "mental illness" and pathologized are actually "expressions of man's struggle with the problem of how he should live" in light of interactions with the environment, self-awareness, and self-reflectiveness.[7]

So given the subjective nature of psychiatric constructs and the great heterogeneity amongst disorder classifications, how does the law deal with mental disorders in matters of criminal responsibility? Who is criminally irresponsible because of a mental disorder that sufficiently impairs one's ability to reason about his or her conduct? Though in theory one does not require a specific type of mental disorder to raise the insanity defense successfully, in practice, diagnostic labels matter. As will be explored in more detail in the next section, the defense is successfully employed by those who are diagnosed with psychotic mental illnesses and were suffering from delusions or hallucinations at the time of the offense. In some of the cases I examined, such as R v. Xiang (2004) and R v. Konidaris (2012), there was consensus amongst expert psychiatric witnesses called by the defense and prosecution that one of the legal criteria for insanity was met because the offenders suffered from a psychotic mental illness that impaired their perception of reality at the time of the killings. Disputes arose amongst psychiatrists if the accused—such as in R v. Fitchett (2010), R v. Freeman (2011), and R v. Fitchett (2012)—made claims of insanity on the basis of depression.

2 Legal Constructs

Criminal responsibility is established upon satisfying two elements of a crime. The onus is on the prosecution to prove beyond reasonable doubt that the act is committed voluntarily and intentionally; that is, the required *mens rea* (intent to harm) and *actus reus* (volition to harm) must be satisfied to prove guilt. If one of these elements is not, the accused is fully acquitted. The defense can challenge *mens rea* if the defendant is suffering from a mental illness because the required intent for culpability may be absent. The volitional component can also be challenged in cases of an accident or a reflex action.

Outside this framework, the law can exculpate mentally ill offenders if they were legally insane at the time of the offense due to a defect of reason as a result of a "disease of mind." Insanity is only explored during trial if the defendant is found to be fit to plead or to stand trial in the pretrial process. This is necessary because the accused must understand the procedures of the trial with sound intellectual function, is able to communicate to their counsel about the legal process, and must remain fit for the duration of the trial in order to be tried.

Section 20(1) of Australia's Criminal Code states that the defense of a mental impairment can be successfully raised if, at the time of the crime, the person was suffering from a mental impairment so that "he or she did not know the nature and quality of the conduct or, he or she did not know that the conduct was wrong or, the person was unable to control his or her conduct." Similarly, section 16(1) of the Criminal Code of Canada outlines that the mental disorder defense is satisfied "for an act committed or an omission made while suffering from a mental disorder that rendered the person incapable of appreciating the nature and quality of the act or omission or of knowing that it was wrong." Both are essentially based on the two criteria formulated in the M'Naghten case. In the United States Model Penal Code, s4.10(1), "a person is not responsible for criminal conduct if at the time of such conduct as a result of mental disease or defect he lacks substantial capacity either to appreciate the criminality (or wrongfulness) of his conduct or to conform his conduct to the requirements of the law." In addition, several states in the United States also use the M'Naghten test alone or in conjunction with the "irresistible impulse" test.[8]

Such legal characterizations reflect the law's focus on the psychiatric aspect of the issue—with terms such as "mental disease," "mental defect," "mental disorder," and "disease of mind"—rather than socio-cultural underpinnings of criminal offending. Indeed, when the issue of mental illness arises in the context of serious violence, courts rely on psychiatrists' opinions and their professional judgments about an offender's legal insanity at the time of the crime despite the lack of consensus amongst mental health experts in relation to specific diagnoses, violence, and culpability. But more importantly, medico-legal issues arise when considering how to deal with violent mentally ill offenders because the legal definition in relation to the inability to reason about right and wrong is not relevant to the diagnosis of mental illnesses or psychiatric definitions of abnormality and disease severity. This conflict between psychiatric and legal constructs is reflected in the restrictive way the M'Naghten-based insanity defense operates in practice. Whatever the link between some mental illnesses and violent offending, the law is concerned not with the clinical severity of the illness, but with whether it impaired one's capacity to reason about their conduct such that it mitigates or excuses criminal responsibility. The following section examines these legal constructs.

2.1 The M'Naghten Test

The M'Naghten test was formulated following the 19th-century case of Daniel M'Naghten who, having suffered from delusional paranoia, killed the private secretary of then Prime Minister of England, Robert Peel, believing he was actually shooting Peel.[9] The House of Lords considered the existing defense of insanity in the case of offenders such as M'Naghten who suffered from delusions, making the formulation cognitive-based, concerned with knowledge and appreciation of the act at the time of a crime, and with a focus on a defendant's inability to reason about the conduct:

> To establish a defense on the grounds of insanity, it must be clearly proved that, at the time of committing the act, the party accused was labouring under such a defect of reason, from a disease of mind, as not to know the

nature and quality of the act he was doing; or, if he did know it, that he did not know he was doing what was wrong.[10]

Though some jurisdictions also have a volitional component to broaden the scope of the defense, the criteria that must be satisfied in order to establish insanity in the traditional defense are lack of 1) knowledge of the nature and quality of the act, and 2) knowledge of the wrongness of the act.

2.1.1 Nature and Quality

Knowledge of the nature and quality here refers to the physical element of the act and its significance—for example, appreciating the literal meaning of stabbing someone as well as understanding that its consequence may be death. Bronitt and McSherry argue that knowledge may be understood in the "verbalistic" sense "to know," but it can also refer to the appreciation of the act in terms of its consequences.[11] Both meanings are necessary when considering the scope of the defense because if only the latter was required, then psychopathy or antisocial personality disorder may satisfy this limb of the defense. There is some guidance in case law as to what is meant by "nature and quality." In *Willgoss v. The Queen* (1960) the criterion "refers to the physical character of the act, in this case, a capacity to know or understand the significance of the act of killing."[12] Further, in *Cooper v. The Queen* (1970), it is the "estimation and understanding of the consequences of the act."[13] In practice, this limb of the defense is rarely employed to satisfy legal insanity. Its formulation and requirements would only allow those with the most severe of the psychoses to employ it successfully. The more commonly used limb is the second: not knowing the conduct was wrong.

2.1.2 Wrongness

In Australia, s7.3 (1) b of the 1995 *Criminal Code Act* defines "not knowing the conduct was wrong" to mean that the defendant "could not reason with a moderate degree of sense and composure about whether the conduct, as perceived by reasonable people, was wrong." This "reasonable man" test suggests that the concern is not with whether the defendant knew the conduct was legally or morally wrong; the issue is whether the defendant could reason about the conduct, as reasonable people would, that it was wrong. But in the Canadian case of *R v. Chaulck* (1990), the expression was determined to satisfy both the lack of knowing the conduct was legally or morally wrong. More recently, the Law Reform Commission in the Australian State of Victoria proposed a reform of the statutory insanity defense in the state. One of the recommendations is to change the legal meaning of the second limb of the defense—not knowing the conduct was wrong—so that the focus is on the accused's capacity to think rationally rather than their ability to "reason with a moderate degree of sense and composure."[14]

So under which circumstances is this limb satisfied to establish legal insanity? In practice, lack of knowledge or appreciation about whether the conduct was wrong tends to be satisfied if the accused was suffering from psychotic symptoms at the time of the offense: delusions or hallucinations. In 2004, the Victorian Law Reform Commission found that in all the cases in which the defense was employed successfully, the defendant was suffering from a psychotic mental illness at the time of the offense. The defense is narrow and restrictive in this sense because it is problematic for those who suffer from non-psychotic illnesses such as depression.[15] I argue that this is because of the intact reality testing in depressive illnesses; conflicting psychiatric opinions about depression and legal insanity; and public perception and familiarity with depressive illnesses.

Many have argued that people affected by mental disorders of the psychotic type are more prone to violence than those who are not,[16] even when socio-demographic variables such as substance abuse are controlled.[17] Psychotic symptoms with delusions, obsessive thoughts, paranoid notions, and hallucinations are believed to strengthen the link between violence and mental illnesses[18] although others dispute this relationship.[19] It is argued that people with psychotic illnesses are significantly more likely to engage in violent crime than those without because these illnesses disconnect sufferers from reality.[20] Often, homicides and unprovoked assaults by those with psychotic illnesses arise from the belief that they are in danger because of their hallucinations or persecutory beliefs.[21] Sufferers of psychotic mental illnesses engage in violence because it is the reasonable response to the distorted perception of their reality. The symptoms that produce feelings of personal threat or intrusion of thoughts that override self-control can lead to violence as a coping mechanism.[22] The authors describe "control-override" as the lack of inhibition in "internal controls that might otherwise block the expression of violence."[23] Whether or not these beliefs are based on reality, they influence the individual's definition of the situation so that lethal violence is highly likely. Experiences of active delusions or hallucinations lead to perceptions of personal threat resulting in acts of violence for "self-defense."[24] There is a "twisted" logic to the insanity.

But even within psychotic symptoms, it is only those that result in control-override that express in violence rather than all psychotic illnesses.[25] Similarly, studies that looked at psychiatric case registers in

Australia found that the psychoses are a modest risk factor for violent offending compared to the general population group.[26] Australian psychiatrist Paul Mullen argues that the general literature on the link between severe mental illness and violence appears to suggest that the illness, of itself, does not reliably predict violence,[27] although symptoms such as hallucinations and delusions can be related to risk particularly without treatment.[28]

On the other hand, non-psychotic conditions such as depression are perceived to be caused by psychosocial stresses rather than biological abnormalities leading to the presumption that sufferers can control their behavior and distinguish between right and wrong. Major depressive disorder, more commonly known as depression, is defined in the DSM-IV as "a clinical course characterized by a period of at least two consecutive weeks during which there is depressed mood or loss of interest and pleasure in nearly all activities."[29] The individual experiences changes in appetite, weight, decreased energy levels, reduced concentration, indecisiveness, feelings of worthlessness, guilt, or suicidal ideations.[30] The disorder can be classified as mild, moderate, or severe, with or without psychotic features based on the number of symptoms, their severity, and the degree of functional disability and distress they cause the patient.[31] Because non-psychotic illnesses are, generally, exaggerated feelings of sadness or fear and they do not impair perceptions of reality, they are not readily accepted as impairing knowledge or appreciation of the nature and quality or wrongness of an act. Depressive illnesses tend to be viewed as illnesses that can "affect anyone"[32] and an aspect of the human condition.[33]

Further to these popular perceptions, there are also disagreements among mental health practitioners about whether an illness like depression can render someone legally insane such that they cannot distinguish right from wrong. There is only consensus if the offender in question suffered from psychotic symptoms at the time of the offense. In *R v. Freeman* (2011), one of the expert psychiatrists called by the prosecution argued that in terms of knowing the wrongfulness of an act, for people with depression, the capacity for moral reasoning and the knowledge of right from wrong is intact and "preserved"[34] unless suffering from the severe form with psychotic features. In fact, he argued, as people get more depressed but falling short of having psychotic features, their "moral sensibility becomes heightened . . . rather than losing an ability to think about the difference between right and wrong through that self-blaming mindset that the person acquires; there is a sharpened sense of wrongfulness and rightness and their own place in that."[35] This was echoed by another expert witness called by the prosecution in *R v. Fitchett* (2008) and *R v. Freeman* (2011): depression without psychotic features cannot render sufferers mentally impaired such that they cannot understand the difference between right and wrong. But psychiatrists called by the defense team in R v. Fitchett (2008) disagreed with the view that depression cannot satisfy legal criteria of insanity. Fitchett had killed her sons following marital difficulties and claimed to have killed the children because they would be better off dead than in her care (because she was suicidal) or the care of their father and other family members. She claimed to have been insane at the time of the killings due to severe depression. One of the defense psychiatrists gave evidence that although the mental impairment defense is frequently raised for "significant brain injuries or intellectual disability or psychotic illnesses, the test is not specifically defined that there must be a psychotic illness present"[36] and it can also extend to "disorders of thinking." So even if the offender may not have overt psychotic symptoms, the rationalizations given about the crime can give insight into a "grossly irrational" state of mind at the time of the offense that indicates an "inability to reason at the time."[37]

Despite conflicting psychiatric opinions on the matter of depression and insanity, the arguments of expert witnesses called by the prosecution in such matters seem to be endorsed by jurors. Because of the restrictive legal criteria, non-psychotic mentally ill offenders whose perception of reality and, therefore, right and wrong are intact are not considered to potentially be legally insane at the time of a violent crime. Indeed, one may argue that the reasons Fitchett gave about why she killed her children are not short of delusional and grossly irrational. But the diagnostic label of "depression" seems to have had implications on how her claims of legal insanity were viewed. Depressive illnesses cannot excuse criminal responsibility. Furthermore, the medico-legal discrepancy in how "mental illness" is conceptualized contributes to the small number of cases in which the defense is employed successfully because what is considered to be a severe mental illness that impairs reasoning from a psychiatric perspective may not necessarily satisfy the legal criteria that must be satisfied as a consequence of a "defect of reason." Crucially, this defect of reason that fits either one of the M'Naghten criteria must be the result of a "disease of mind." This means that one may not know the nature and quality or wrongness of a criminal conduct due to mental states or conditions that may not satisfy a "disease of mind" test. So how does the law test this matter and make the distinction? What constitutes a "disease of mind"?

2.2 Disease of Mind

The term "disease of mind" is a legal construct reflecting a state that impairs the ability to reason about a criminal conduct. As such, it is not restricted to disorders of the brain and mental illnesses but also includes physical diseases such as hyperglycemia (*R v. Hennessy*, 1989, 1 WLR 287), arteriosclerosis (*R v. Kemp*, 1957, 1 QB 399), or epilepsy (*R v. Sullivan*, 1984, 1 AC 156) because these conditions can impair the capacity to reason within the scope of the criteria set out in the defense. Whether a condition linked to violence amounts to a "disease of mind" is determined by the following three tests:

i. Recurring/Continuing Danger Test
ii. Internal/External Test
iii. Unsound/Sound Mind Test

The first test holds that a disease of mind test is satisfied if a mental illness is permanent or is likely to recur, in which case the disposition ought to take into account the issue of continuing danger. But if it is a temporary or transient mental state, then the case is one of sane automatism: involuntary criminal conduct without a mental disorder. This distinction is explained in *Bratty* by Lord Denning:

> Any mental disorder which has manifested itself in violence and is prone to recur is a disease of the mind. At any rate it is the sort of disease for which a person should be detained in a hospital rather than be given an unqualified acquittal.[38]

But the recurrent condition must be so because it has an internal cause. This is the aim of the second test: to distinguish between a mental state that is internal to the accused and one that is externally caused. As noted in *R v. Rabey*, the impairment must arise from a cause internal to the accused having its source in the "psychological or emotional make-up, or in some organic pathology" and not the "transient effect" caused by external factors such as a concussion.[39] This is further elaborated by the third test, in *R v. Radford*, which separates "the reaction of an unsound mind to its own delusions or the external stimuli" (thus a disease of mind), from "the reaction of a sound mind to external stimuli including stress producing factors."[40]

What does this mean for the operation of the insanity defense? What is the purpose of the "disease of mind" construct? Given my earlier discussion about the distinct ways in which psychotic and non-psychotic mental illnesses are dealt with when the defense is employed, I shall focus the following discussion on the test that is more relevant for this distinction: the internal/external test. In the previous section, I argued that psychotic mental illnesses are more persuasive to the courts and jurors when it comes to negating criminal responsibility under the insanity defense. But if psychotic illnesses such as schizophrenia are the type of disorders that fit the narrow and restrictive M'Naghten criteria, how do courts deal with drug-induced psychoses that arise as the direct result of the voluntary action of the accused?

Voluntary ingestion of psychoactive substances that produce mental states that lead to insanity and serious violence pose some legal challenges. Historically, courts could never accept voluntary intoxication as a sufficient basis to excuse criminal responsibility. Even if these mental states satisfy the legal criteria of insanity, courts have generally been reluctant to negate criminal responsibility because at the time of substance use, the defendant ought to know or does know the effects of the substance. The cause of insanity here is externally caused by the voluntary action of the subject rather than having causes internal to the accused. As noted in the United States Insanity Defense Reform Act, "the voluntary use of alcohol or drugs, even if they render the defendant unable to appreciate the nature and quality of his acts, does not constitute insanity."[41] But one must distinguish between voluntary intoxication that leads to drunkenness from one that leads to the development of psychotic symptoms. The former cannot excuse culpability even if the mental state at the time of the offense satisfies the criteria of legal insanity[42] although it can diminish culpability if the intoxication impaired *mens rea* and the accused, therefore, lacked "specific" intent. However, because the *actus reus* was present, only a partial defense is available. So long as (specific) intent to harm did not precede voluntary intoxication, it may be used to reduce a charge of murder to manslaughter in Australia,[43] United Kingdom,[44] and United States.[45] Contrarily, involuntary intoxication can meet the threshold for legal insanity because such a defendant does not (or have reason to) know the effects of the substance nor their susceptibility to the substance.[46]

Unlike voluntary drunkenness, acute psychosis following voluntary ingestion of psychoactive drugs cannot mitigate or excuse criminal responsibility. According to the Victorian Law Reform Commission however, it is the defect of reason, not its cause, that should matter. Although one can argue that a defendant "should not be allowed to benefit as a result of a condition which they have been responsible for producing,"[47] the law does allow intoxication to mitigate a criminal act if specific intent is lacking and not making similar allowances for cases in which insanity results from drug induced psychoses is inconsistent and unjust. But why should one who creates the state that mitigates or excuses his culpability benefit by employing an exculpatory defense successfully? Is doing so not "tantamount to an intention to commit or risk committing such an offense" given the widespread knowledge of the risks associated with psychoactive drugs?[48] Surely, negligence or recklessness ought to be considered in such circumstances. So while the psychoses are more persuasive in meeting the threshold of what constitutes legal insanity, psychoses with external causes, such as those drug-induced, will not suffice.

However, voluntary use of psychoactive drugs and its interaction with an existing mental disorder is another matter. If it either exacerbates an existing psychotic illness or triggers psychotic symptoms that were fixed and permanent due to chronic intoxication but are distinct and independent of the acute intoxication ("settled insanity"), it is no longer a case of an externally caused disease of mind.[49] Settled insanity, is when a mental condition is "fixed and stable" lasting for a "reasonable duration of time" and is independent of the consumption or duration of the effects of the substance,[50] when voluntary intoxication "creates a state of mind that negates culpability"[51] diminishing the aggravating factors of voluntary substance use.[52] If voluntary substance abuse is going to satisfy the criteria of the defense, it must trigger or exacerbate an "independent syndrome . . . which pre-dates and continues beyond the incident of intoxication that was linked to the crime."[53]—that is, a permanent and diagnosable disorder. Permanency can be established by testing if the disorder, whether it resolves or not, is present before and after the acute intoxication.[54] This is thus the aim of the internal/external test: it allows distinctions between mental impairments with internal and external causes. An internal cause is determined if the disorder persists long after the effects of acute intoxication but, also, if it predates the intoxication. Making these distinctions was not, however, an issue in *People v. Skinner*; a fixed disorder independent of voluntary drug use sufficed in satisfying legal insanity. One is compelled to ask how psychotic symptoms following consumption of psychoactive substances such as amphetamines can be identified as existing independently of psychotic symptoms from a comorbidly occurring mental disorder.

As a potential solution, Meloy's proposal is that "settled insanity" should be limited to cases with a predisposition to psychosis where "but for the presence of a vulnerability to psychosis, settled insanity would not apply."[55] So in the absence of a history or diagnosis of mental illness, voluntary drug abuse resulting in legal insanity at the time of the offense would not suffice. This approach would allow examination of variables other than "ingestion and duration" of intoxication, not least because "fixed" and "reasonable duration" do not provide a useful guidance.[56] If, on the other hand, one is biologically prone to psychosis and abused psychoactive drugs, the defense should be available to such a defendant because the proneness beyond his volitional control, is "the most salient factor in his exculpation."[57] Proneness to psychosis can be established, Meloy argues, by examining the premorbid or familial history of mental illness, psychological testing, or any psychiatric history before intoxication.[58] This proposition assumes psychoactive substances such as methamphetamine do not induce psychotic symptoms in most consumers, meaning that those who do develop psychotic symptoms do so because they were prone to them. The evidence suggests, however, that psychosis following methamphetamine consumption is significantly high, ranging between 23 percent to approximately 50 percent.[59] Another method of testing proneness to psychosis may be by distinguishing between chronic and infrequent use although chronic symptoms can develop in users without apparent predispositions or family history.[60] The likelihood is that proneness to a particular psychoactive substance depends on many variables and evaluators ought to take considerations on a case-by-case basis , such as the characteristics of the drug, and the mental health history of the offender.

The internal/external test of insanity is concerned with the cause of the disease mind that led to insanity. When the causes are combined, from both an internal illness but also an external psychoactive substance, one cannot make definitive conclusions about which symptoms led to insanity. What can be argued is that, in these cases, the ensuing insanity did arise due to the voluntary action of the defendant[61] who chose to engage in an act that negates criminal liability because, given the various degrees of intoxication, one cannot establish if this defendant's capacity to reason would be impaired if intoxication was excluded[62] to the extent that one can definitively conclude the internal disorder alone was the cause of the violence.[63]

3 Conclusion

Constructs of what constitutes insanity have implications for those suffering from a specific type of mental illness because diagnostic labels matter. Familiar and common mental illnesses like depression pose difficulties in employing the insanity defense successfully. The psychoses, on the other hand, seem to satisfy what are narrow and restrictive criteria developed in 1843 and not in line with the progression of our psychiatric and neuro-scientific knowledge about mental disorders. This is precisely why the United Kingdom Law Reform Commission has recently proposed reforming a defense that is based on a 19th-century common law defense of insanity. Yet, the lack of compatibility between legal and psychiatric knowledge is not only a matter of using dated criteria of the defense but, more important, it is also an issue of construction. Psychiatric constructs about disorder, abnormality, and severity do not necessarily meet legal criteria of "severity" in terms of defect of reason or disease of mind.

Furthermore, the restrictions around the operations of the defense reflect the policy considerations and implications of its broadening to defects of reason that arise from non-psychotic illnesses and those that have external causes. With mental health services that are already understaffed and underfunded (globally), lowering the threshold of meeting the criteria of the defense through various reforms would overwhelm already strained services. The reality of this issue and the state of the general mental health care following deinstitutionalization affects the way the defense will operate in practice. Indeed, Yannoulidis argues that "it is a public policy consideration, and not scientific research, which is determinative of an accused's criminal responsibility."[64]

Popular perception of this matter is also a significant component of the way criminal responsibility and insanity are constructed. The public's perception of the risk of violence by people with a diagnosis of mental illness is that it is individually determined and higher than those without a mental disorder.[65] Further, individuals with psychotic mental illnesses are perceived to be more dangerous and unpredictable because of the nature of their illness.[66] Phelan et al. argue that, although extreme beliefs about mental illness and what it constitutes have decreased since the 1950s in the United States, associations of dangerousness and violence have more than doubled since then in relation to psychotic illnesses, often seen as "alien" and "something" to be feared.[67] In contrast, such negative views have decreased for those affected by non-psychotic disorders such as anxiety and depression, now seen as part of everyday life. Similarly in Australia, Jorm and colleagues show that the public underestimates the seriousness of depressive illnesses and are skeptical about medical treatment, preferring instead to be with family, friends, or in relaxation courses.[68] Although these are perceptions that may alleviate some of the social stigma that may have been faced by this particular group of people with mental illness, they also explain why familiar and recognizable illnesses like depression are not easily associated with dangerousness, serious violence towards others, and legal insanity. These popular constructs in turn do affect who is considered to be of sound mind and who is mentally impaired and criminally irresponsible.

Notes

1. World Health Organization, *ICD-10 Classification of Mental and Behavioural Disorders*, 11.
2. American Psychiatric Association, *Diagnostic and Statistical Manual of Mental Disorders*, xxi.
3. Ibid., 273 and 275.
4. Mouzous, "Mental Disorder and Homicide in Australia."
5. Scheff, "Labeling Madness," 8.
6. Szasz, "The Myth of Mental Illness."
7. Ibid, 117.
8. Grachek, "Insanity Defense in the Twenty-First Century"; Robinson, "The Effect of Mental Illness Under U.S. Criminal Law."
9. *R v. M'Naghten* (1843), 8 ER 718, UKHL J16.
10. Ibid.
11. Bronitt and McSherry, *Principles of Criminal Law*.
12. *Willgoss v. The Queen* (1960), 300.
13. *Cooper v. The Queen* (1970), 145.
14. Victorian Law Reform Commission, "Defences to Homicide."
15. Wondemaghen, "Depressed but not Legally Mentally Impaired."
16. Wisdet et al., "Pharmacotherapy for Aggressive and Violent Behaviour"; Link et al., "Psychotic Symptoms and Violent Behaviours"; Link et al., "Real in their Consequences."
17. Stueve and Link, "Violence and Psychiatric Disorders."
18. Link and Stueve, "Psychotic Symptoms and the Violent/Illegal Behavior of Mental Patients Compared to Community Controls"; Swanson et al., "Psychotic Symptoms and Disorders and the Risk of Violent Behaviour in the Community"; Link et al., "Psychotic Symptoms and Violent Behaviours."
19. Appelbaum et al., "Violence and Delusions"; Monahan et al., *Rethinking Risk Assessment*.
20. Link et al., "Real in their Consequences"; Arseneault et al., "Mental Disorder and Violence in a Total Birth Cohort"; Douglas et al., "Psychosis as a Risk Factor for Violence to Others."
21. Nielssen et al., "Homicide during Psychotic Illness in New South Wales between 1993 and 2002."
22. Link et al., "Real in Their Consequences," 318.
23. Ibid.
24. Link et al., "Real in Their Consequences"; Taylor, "Mental Disorder and Crime."
25. Link et al., "Real in Their Consequences."
26. Mullen, "Dangerousness, Risk and the Prediction of Probability."
27. Mullen, "The Dangerousness of the Mentally Ill and the Clinical Assessment of Risk."
28. Mullen, "Dangerousness, Risk and the Prediction of Probability."

29. American Psychiatric Association, *Diagnostic and Statistical Manual of Mental Disorders*, 320.
30. Ibid.
31. Ibid., 376.
32. Phelan et al., "Public Conceptions of Mental Illness in 1950 and 1996."
33. Hogg, "'Your Good Days and Your Bad Days.'"
34. *R v. Freeman* [2011] VSC 139, 828.
35. Ibid., 828–29.
36. *R v. Fitchett* (2008), 327.
37. Ibid.
38. *Bratty v. A-G for Northern Ireland* (1963), AC 386, 412.
39. *R v. Rabey* (1977), 37CCC (2d) 461, 477.
40. *R v. Radford* (1985), 42 SASR 266, 276.
41. Insanity Defense Reform Act (2000) 18 U.S.C. x 17, 229.
42. *Downing v. Commonwealth* (1998) 496 S.E.2d 164, 5.
43. *R v. O'Connor* (1980), 146 CLR 64.
44. *DPP v. Beard* (1920) AC 479.
45. *State of WV v. Bush* (1994).
46. Marlowe et al., "Voluntary Intoxication and Criminal Responsibility."
47. Victorian Law Reform Commission, "Defences to Homicide," 215.
48. Yannoulidis, "Drug Use and the Defence of Mental Impairment."
49. *People v. Skinner* (1986) 228 Cal. Rptr. 652; *State v. Wicks* (1983), 98 Wn.2d 620; *Gills v. Commonwealth* (1925), 141 Va. 445.
50. *People v. Skinner*, 12.
51. Meloy, "Voluntary Intoxication and the Insanity Defense."
52. Feix and Wolber, "Intoxication and Settled Insanity."
53. Marlowe et al., "Voluntary Intoxication and Criminal Responsibility," 201.
54. Ibid.
55. Meloy, "Voluntary Intoxication and the Insanity Defense," 451.
56. Ibid.
57. Ibid., 452.
58. Ibid., 451.
59. The lower figure is from McKetin et al., "The Prevalence of Psychotic Symptoms among Methamphetamine Users"; the higher figure is from Hall et al., "Psychological Morbidity and Route of Administration among Amphetamine Users in Sydney, Australia."
60. Dore and Sweeting, "Drug-Induced Psychosis Associated with Crystalline Methamphetamine"; Schuckit, *Drug and Alcohol Abuse*.
61. *United States v. Burnim*, 576 F.2d 236 (1978).
62. *State of Hawaii v. Freitas*, 608 P.2d 408 (1980).
63. *United States v. Knott*, 894 F.2d 1119 (1990).
64. Yannoulidis, "Drug Use and the Defence of Mental Impairment."
65. Hiday, "Understanding the Connection between Mental Illness and Violence"; Silver, "Understanding the Relationship Between Mental Disorder and Violence."

66. Angermeyer and Matschinger, "Public Beliefs about Schizophrenia and Depression: Similarities and Differences"; Van Dorn et al., "A Comparison of Stigmatizing Attitudes Toward Persons with Schizophrenia in Four Stakeholder Groups"; Nordt et al., "Attitudes of Mental Health Professionals Toward People With Schizophrenia and Major Depression."

67. Phelan et al., "Public Conceptions of Mental Illness in 1950 and 1996."

68. Jorm et al., "Belief in the Harmfulness of Antidepressants"; Jorm et al., "Mental Health First Aid Training for Members of the Public."

Resources

American Psychiatric Association, *Diagnostic and Statistical Manual of Mental Disorders*, 4th ed. Washington, DC: American Psychiatric Publishing, 2000.

Angermeyer, Matthias C., and Herbert Matschinger, "Public Beliefs about Schizophrenia and Depression: Similarities and Differences." *Social Psychiatry and Psychiatric Epidemiology* 38(2003): 526–34.

Appelbaum, Paul S., Pamela C. Robbins, and John Monahan, "Violence and Delusions: Data from the MacArthur Violence Risk Assessment Study." *American Journal of Psychiatry* 157(2000): 566–72.

Arseneault, Louise, et al., "Mental Disorder and Violence in a Total Birth Cohort." *Archives of General Psychiatry* 57(2000): 979–86.

Bronitt, Simon, and Bernadette McSherry, *Principles of Criminal Law*, 3rd ed. Pyrmont, N.S.W.: Thomson Reuters, 2010.

Dore, Glenys, and Melinda Sweeting, "Drug-Induced Psychosis Associated with Crystalline Methamphetamine." *Australasian Psychiatry* 14(2006): 86–89.

Douglas, Kevin S., Laura S. Guy, and Stephen D. Hart, "Psychosis as a Risk Factor for Violence to Others: A Meta-Analysis." *Psychological Bulletin* 135(2009): 679–706.

Feix, Jeff, and Greg Wolber, "Intoxication and Settled Insanity: A Finding of Not Guilty by Reason of Insanity." *Journal of the American Academy of Psychiatry and the Law* 35(2007): 172–82.

Grachek, Julie E., "Insanity Defense in the Twenty-First Century: How Recent United States Supreme Court Case Law Can Improve the System." *Indiana Law Journal* 81(2006): 1479–1502.

Hall, Wayne, Julie Hando, Shane Darke, and Joanne Ross, "Psychological Morbidity and Route of Administration among Amphetamine Users in Sydney, Australia." *Addiction* 91(1996): 81–87.

Hiday, Virginia A., "Understanding the Connection between Mental Illness and Violence." *International Journal of Law and Psychiatry* 20(1997): 399–417.

Hogg, Christine, "'Your Good Days and Your Bad Days': An Exploration and Consideration of How Lay People Conceptualize Depression." *Journal of Psychiatric and Mental Health Nursing* 18(2011): 851–61.

Jorm, Anthony F., Helen Christensen, and Kathleen M. Griffiths, "Belief in the Harmfulness of Antidepressants: Results from a National Survey of the Australian Public." *Journal of Affective Disorders* 88(2005): 47–53.

Jorm, Anthony F., Betty A. Kitchener, Leonard G. Kanowski, and Claire M. Kelly, "Mental Health First Aid Training for Members of the Public." *International Journal of Clinical and Health Psychology* 7(2007): 141–51.

Link, Bruce G., and Ann Stueve, "Psychotic Symptoms and the Violent/Illegal Behavior of Mental Patients Compared to Community Controls." In *Violence and Mental Disorder: Developments in Risk Assessment*, edited by John Monahan and Henry J. Steadman (Chicago: University of Chicago Press, 1994), 137–60.

Link, Bruce G., Ann Stueve, and Phelan, Jo, "Psychotic Symptoms and Violent Behaviours: Probing the Components of 'Threat/Control-Override' Symptoms." *Social Psychiatry and Psychiatric Epidemiology* 33(1998): S55–S60.

Link, Bruce G., John Monahan, Ann Stueve, and Francis T. Cullen, "Real in Their Consequences: A Sociological Approach to Understanding the Association between Psychotic Symptoms and Violence." *American Sociological Review* 64(1999): 316–32.

Marlowe, Douglas B., Jennifer B. Lambert, and Robert G. Thompson, "Voluntary Intoxication and Criminal Responsibility." *Behavioral Sciences and the Law* 17(1999): 195–217.

McKetin, Rebecca, Jennifer McLaren, Dan I. Lubman, and Leanne Hides, "The Prevalence of Psychotic Symptoms among Methamphetamine Users." *Addiction* 101(2006): 1473–78.

Meloy, J. Reid, "Voluntary Intoxication and the Insanity Defense." *Journal of Psychiatry and Law* 20(1992): 439–52.

Monahan, John, et al., *Rethinking Risk Assessment: The MacArthur Study of Mental Disorder and Violence*. Oxford: Oxford University Press, 2001.

Mouzos, Jenny, "Mental Disorder and Homicide in Australia." *Research and Public Policy* series no. 133. Canberra: Australian Institute of Criminology, 1999.

Mullen, Paul E., "The Dangerousness of the Mentally Ill and the Clinical Assessment of Risk." In *Psychiatry and the Law*, edited by Warren Brookbanks (Wellington, NZ: Brooker's, 1996), 93–116.

Mullen, Paul E., "Dangerousness, Risk and the Prediction of Probability." In *New Oxford Textbook of Psychiatry*, edited by Michael G. Geldner, Nancy Andreasen, Juan J. López-Ibor, Jr., and John R. Geddes (Oxford: Oxford University Press, 2000), 2066–78.

Nielssen, Olav B., et al., "Homicide during Psychotic Illness in New South Wales between 1993 and 2002." *Medical Journal of Australia* 186(2007): 301–04.

Nordt, Carlos, Wulf Rössler, and Christophe Lauber, "Attitudes of Mental Health Professionals Toward People With Schizophrenia and Major Depression." *Schizophrenia Bulletin* 32(2006): 709–14.

Phelan, Jo C., Bruce G. Link, Ann Stueve, and Bernice A. Pescosolido, "Public Conceptions of Mental Illness in 1950 and 1996: What Is Mental Illness and Is It to Be Feared?" *Journal of Health and Social Behavior* 41(2000): 188–207.

Robinson, Paul H., "The Effect of Mental Illness Under U.S. Criminal Law." *Northern Ireland Legal Quarterly* 65(2014): 229–42.

Scheff, Thomas J., *Labeling Madness*. Englewood Cliffs, NJ: Prentice-Hall, 1975.

Schuckit, Marc A., *Drug and Alcohol Abuse: A Clinical Guide to Diagnosis and Treatment*, 5th ed. New York: Kluwer Academic/Plenum Publishers, 2000.

Silver, Eric, "Understanding the Relationship Between Mental Disorder and Violence: The Need for a Criminological Perspective." *Law and Human Behavior* 30(2006): 685–706.

Stueve, Ann, and Bruce C. Link, "Violence and Psychiatric Disorders: Results from an Epidemiological Study of Young Adults in Israel." *Psychiatric Quarterly* 68(1997): 327–42.

Swanson, Jeffrey W., Randy Borum, Marvin S. Swartz, and John Monahan, "Psychotic Symptoms and Disorders and the Risk of Violent Behaviour in the Community." *Criminal Behaviour and Mental Health* 6(1996): 309–29.

Szasz, Thomas S., "The Myth of Mental Illness." *American Psychologist* 15(1960): 113–18.

Taylor, Pamela J., "Mental Disorder and Crime." *Criminal Behaviour and Mental Health* 14(2004): S31–S36.

Van Dorn, Richard, Jeffrey W. Swanson, Eric B. Elbogen, and Marvin S. Swartz, "A Comparison of Stigmatizing Attitudes Toward Persons with Schizophrenia in Four Stakeholder Groups: Perceived Likelihood of Violence and Desire for Social Distance." *Psychiatry* 68(2005): 152–63.

Victorian Law Reform Commission, *Defences to Homicide: Final Report*. Victoria: Victorian Law Reform Commission, 2004.

Wistedt, Börje, Lars Helldin, Majda Omerov, and Tom Palmstierna, "Pharmacotherapy for Aggressive and Violent Behaviour: A View of Practical Management from Clinicians." *Criminal Behaviour and Mental Health Education* 4(1994): 328–40.

Wondemaghen, Meron, "Depressed but not Legally Mentally Impaired." *International Journal of Law and Psychiatry* 37(2014): 160–67.

World Health Organization, *The ICD-10 Classification of Mental and Behavioural Disorders: Clinical Descriptions and Diagnostic Guidelines*. Geneva: World Health Organization, 1992.

Yannoulidis, Steven, "Drug Use and the Defence of Mental Impairment: Some Conceptual and Explanatory Issues." *Bond Law Review* 18(2006): 165–91.

CHAPTER SIX

Insanity: Neurolaw and Forensic Psychiatry

Maartje Katzenbauer and Gerben Meynen

Neurolaw is a rapidly growing, interdisciplinary field of research, studying the influence of neuroscience on the law and legal practices.[1] The past decade has seen an almost exponential increase in the number of publications on neuroscience and the law.[2] The topics covered are diverse. For example, some of these publications concern general issues and developments, such as "neuroimaging in the courtroom," others focus on specific techniques, and yet another subset relates to landmark legal cases such as *Roper v. Simmons* (2005). In *Roper,* neuroscience findings were considered by the U.S. Supreme Court to reach a decision about abolishing capital punishment for juvenile offenders. Several professional organizations[3] argued in amicus briefs that the brain of adolescents, and in particular the prefrontal cortex, is immature, and that juveniles, for example, "are less likely to consider properly the consequences of their actions." Although the Supreme Court clearly took other information into account as well, neuroscientific information appears to have played a role in the Supreme Court's decision about the death penalty for juveniles, showing the relevance of neuroscience for criminal law.[4] Inevitably, with the growing number and increasing accuracy of neuroscience techniques, the field of neurolaw will continue to expand, and the introduction of new neuroscientific techniques to the courtroom is bound to give rise to further complex (neuro)ethical, technical, medical, political, and philosophical questions.[5]

Even though neurolaw is a profoundly interdisciplinary endeavor, in this chapter, we will take a forensic psychiatric perspective on the developments and debates, with an emphasis on assessments of legal insanity. Forensic psychiatry provides a unique perspective on neurolaw developments.[6] For instance, from the perspective of forensic psychiatry, neuroscientific contributions to understanding psychopathology are highly relevant, while those pertaining to the detection of pain—also potentially relevant to (civil) law[7]—are less important from such a point of view. In addition, the topic of legal insanity is clearly a central issue from the perspective of forensic psychiatry. Notably, according to Michael S. Pardo and Dennis Patterson, "proof of insanity and related issues constitutes . . . one of the more plausible avenues by which neuroscience may contribute to the law."[8]

The outline of this chapter is as follows. First, we will continue to introduce the field of neurolaw by distinguishing and discussing three domains of research: revision, assessment, and intervention. Then we consider the relationship between forensic psychiatry and neuroscience, and in the following section we discuss some observations of brain imaging techniques[9] and forensic psychiatry, based on a literature search. Next, we consider the role neuroscience can play in forensic psychiatry, draw a number of conclusions, and offer a few recommendations regarding the role of forensic psychiatrists in the assessment of criminal defendants. We will conclude with three points. First, psychiatrists should be actively involved in neurolaw developments. Second, apart from psychiatrists and neurologists, neuropsychologists should more often participate in the evaluations of defendants. Third, the combined field of forensic psychiatry and criminal law can benefit from standardization regarding the use of neuroscience techniques.[10]

1 Neurolaw: Three Domains of Research

Neurolaw examines the possible impact of neuroscience on the law, but in what ways can neuroscience influence (criminal) law? For reasons of clarity, we divide the field of neurolaw into three main domains: revision, assessment, and intervention.[11]

1.1 Revision of Laws and Legal Procedures

This domain of research concerns the question how neuroscience might affect the law and legal procedures. An example of a research topic in this domain is the case of *Roper v. Simmons* as discussed in the introduction. The U.S. Supreme Court based its decision, as it appears, partly on information derived from neuroscience showing that the adolescent brain is not fully mature.[12] Note, meanwhile, that this finding was in line with psychological and other behavior data that were already available. Still, neuroimaging confirmed this view. Steinberg writes about several U.S. Supreme Court cases and neuroscience, among which *Roper* and *Graham*:

> Because the Supreme Court justices' deliberations are never made public, it is impossible to know just how much neuroscience findings influenced the Court's decisionmaking above and beyond the impact of the behavioural evidence. Nevertheless, a close reading of the transcripts of the oral arguments and opinions makes it clear that the attorneys and justices involved in these cases certainly paid attention to the neuroscience. At times they even insinuated that it was somehow more compelling than the behavioral evidence (as one attorney stated during oral arguments in *Roper*, "I'm not just talking about social science here, but the important neurobiological science").[13]

This passage illustrates the particular weight neuroscience may have in revision of the law and legal practices, including when compared to other areas of science.

Another topic in the revision domain concerns free will, one of the most abstract and philosophical issues in neurolaw. In brief, some argue that neuroscience shows that free will is an illusion, and that, therefore, nobody is truly responsible for his actions. Consequently, all elements in the law related to responsibility and especially retribution would have to be omitted, which would mean a profound revision of criminal law, as described by Greene and Cohen.[14] The famous Libet experiment is sometimes referred to as a study that would show that free will is illusory.[15] Libet concluded that the conscious intention to act was preceded by the so-called readiness potential by about half a second, sometimes even longer. Some authors have argued that this finding provides (strong) evidence that free will is an illusion.[16] Clearly, interpretations of Libet's results and which conclusions to draw from them strongly diverge. Meanwhile, Libet's research paradigm (with some modifications) has been used to replicate the findings.[17]

If, based on neuroscience findings like these, it were accepted that we do not have free will, this radical view could lead to drastic changes in the foundational thinking behind criminal law and punishment that rely on legal and moral responsibility. However, Greene and Cohen state that even if we accept this view, much of criminal law could remain intact because there are other reasons, consequentialist ones, to keep it in place. Because we need to protect our society certain "punishments" are required, not because certain people "deserve" to be punished in a moral sense, but to prevent the occurrence of illegal and harmful actions by some people. In fact, in the future, neuroscientific techniques may reveal that a particular individual poses a threat to society and it could be necessary to remove someone from society to prevent harm. Such an intervention, however, would not be based on concepts like free will, responsibility, or retribution. In other words, an intervention is still possible, but the rationale behind the intervention has changed: it would become utilitarian and consequentialist rather than retributivist. As it appears, most authors in the field of neurolaw do not feel that such a drastic revision is justified, at least not based on current neuroscience.[18]

1.2 Assessment of Individuals (Defendants, Prisoners, and Prospective Jurors)

While researchers in the first domain—law revision—investigate how general neuroscientific knowledge (for example, that regarding free will or about adolescent brains) may lead to modification of the law or legal practice, the second domain concerns research on the *assessment of an individual person* using neuroscientific techniques. The type of assessment as well as the group in which it is performed may vary considerably. Examples include risk assessment regarding future violence in prisoners, assessment of mental illness, criminal responsibility as well as brain-based lie-detection in defendants, and evaluating biases in prospective jurors.[19] Because psychiatrists are often involved in assessments of individuals, in particular of defendants, this domain is of special interest to forensic psychiatry. Although there is ongoing discussion about the value of neuroimaging techniques regarding detecting psychiatric diseases (including forms of dementia), it does not appear improbable that such techniques could be helpful in this respect in the near future.

One topic in this domain concerns evaluating pain. Salmanowitz introduces the subject of brain-based pain detection as follows:

> Why are bruises so perversely satisfying? Despite the aesthetically unpleasant discoloring of the skin that accompanies them, bruises serve as an externally visible signal that effectively communicates and legitimizes pain. Unfortunately, the majority of pain that people endure does not manifest itself through bruising, and subjective measures are frequently used to rate and quantify levels of discomfort. Consequently, there is often a disconnect between an individual's perception of pain and an observer's understanding of its degree or intensity.[20]

In other words, pain is a subjective phenomenon and therefore it may be hard to objectify or to prove. Greely emphasizes how helpful it could be if a neuroscientific technique would become available that could help to assess pain and its intensity.[21] The reason is that in many civil cases—for example, those related to compensation after accidents—a person's level of pain plays a central role.

At this moment, neuroscience already provides some promising leads regarding neuroscience techniques (fMRI) for pain detection, possibly for legal purposes. Yet, as Salmanowitz writes, much effort is still needed "to improve accuracy rates, test the techniques across various population groups, establish the efficacy in real-world settings, and determine safeguards against countermeasures." Countermeasures are actions the subject can perform to influence the outcome of the test through distortion or manipulation.[22] Possibly, this can be done just by imagining pain, and perhaps a more reliable option is to hurt oneself (in an invisible way) in order to experience real pain.[23] Such pain will then be from another source than the alleged pain that is central in the legal case. But the brain scan may not be able to reveal the difference between various sources of pain, or whether it is chronic pain or not. In any case, if the person would be successful taking such countermeasures, the brain imaging will show that the claimant is in pain, even though he was only imagining pain or only in pain for the duration of the neuroimaging (because he hurt himself), and not every day and night, as he may have claimed in the legal case.

Risk assessment using neurotechniques—"neuroprediction"—is an important area of research as well. An example is the finding by Aharoni et al. that the odds that offenders with low activity in the anterior cingulate cortex would be rearrested were approximately twice as high compared to offenders with high activity in this region, which suggests a "potential neurocognitive biomarker for persistent antisocial behavior."[24] Brain-based predictions of violence and reoffending could be of great value. One reason is that the current risk assessment tools for the assessment of recidivism risk as used in forensic psychiatry are far from perfect.[25] A study by Coid et al. showed that recidivism in psychopaths is particularly hard to predict using current tools, yet psychopaths are a group for whom we have good reason to predict risk very accurately.[26] Notably, also regarding brain imaging for prediction, in principle we have to be aware of the risk of countermeasures a subject might take.[27] Yet, the nature of such countermeasures may be less clear than in the pain case, where imagining pain or inflicting pain to oneself could be a straightforward way to distort or manipulate the measurements.

Another topic in the assessment domain is the admissibility of specific neuroimaging techniques in the courtroom.[28] In the United States, admission of scientific evidence in court is, depending on the jurisdiction, based on *Daubert* and *Frye*. As Jones et al. put it, *Frye* requires that the (neuro) scientific technique "is generally accepted by the field," while *Daubert* requires "that judges themselves assess whether the expert's testimony is grounded in valid science."[29] Clearly these requirements may lead to different outcomes for the admissibility of a specific technique such as fMRI. In addition, certain techniques may be admissible for a well-defined purpose, but not for other purposes. For instance, a technique may be admissible to diagnose the presence of a brain tumor, but not as a technique for lie-detection. Notably, in other jurisdictions a standard like *Frye* or *Daubert* may not be available, such as in the Netherlands. What is the criterion for admissibility of neuroscience data and techniques in these legal systems? Which techniques should or should not be allowed in the courtroom in order to assess the defendant? Is fMRI lie detection sufficiently advanced to be used in court? In practice, it may be up to the court-appointed expert either to use or not to use a specific neuroscientific technique in the evaluation of the defendant. In addition, an important question regarding assessment is whether such assessment techniques could, in principle, be used against a defendant's or prisoner's will—a matter that is also likely to depend, at least in part, on the legal system.[30]

Recently, a group of experts at a multidisciplinary consensus conference on the "use and abuse of neuroimaging in the courtroom" proposed guidelines on expert testimony: "the purpose of the conference was to inform the development of guidelines on expert testimony for the American Society of Neuroradiology and to provide principles for courts on the ethical use of neuroimaging data as evidence."[31] Among other things, it is recommended that drawing conclusions about specific behaviors merely based on neuroimaging is to be avoided and that guidelines are used to determine whether the neuroimaging technique used is appropriate to answer the question at hand. In our view these are important recommendations, and, in general, holding such conferences and developing guidelines like these is helpful to improve the quality of forensic neuro-testimony.

1.3 Intervention in an Individual's Brain

The third domain of neurolaw research concerns brain-based treatment and more generally neuroscientific intervention techniques.[32] There are cases described in which deep brain stimulation (DBS) apparently triggered mania.[33] As Müller and Walter state, "several cases of mania, loss of normal social inhibitions, and hypersexuality have been described."[34] The behavior of some patients treated with DBS drastically changed: "they planned hazardous business investments, wrote books or religious poems (without being religious), drove their cars in a reckless manner, showed deviant sexual behavior (e.g., seductive behavior against female medical staff, exhibitionism, pedophilia, and leisure tourism), resumed or abandoned studies, bought excessive amounts of clothing, or stole unnecessary items because of kleptomania."[35] We may ask to what extent is a person responsible for his criminal actions if the action was "induced" by DBS-treatment?[36] For instance, does it matter whether or not the DBS-patient complied with his doctor's advice for regular checks? Or should, in certain circumstances at least, the doctor be held responsible, or rather the company that produces these DBS devices? Suppose that the DBS device was hacked by criminals[37] and that the patient was manipulated to commit a crime: who is responsible then? Should the patient be considered "legally insane" or should another term or category be used or invented to cover such a situation?[38]

Other possibilities that may be opened up by DBS are therapeutic brain interventions aimed at risk reduction. Possibly, in the future, DBS may help prevent pursuit of criminal behavior by reducing certain pathological urges. Recently, a paper was published by Fuss et al. on the use of DBS to reduce sexual drive.[39] One of the reasons such an intervention could be valuable is that, as they explain, current interventions to reduce testosterone levels have serious side effects. They suggest that, at this moment in time, the most likely candidate brain area for such an intervention would be the ventromedial hypothalamus. They base this hypothesis among others on reports of lesions that have been made in this area. Obviously, Fuss et al. also pay attention to ethical and legal considerations. Those who are candidates for this type of intervention, should "have to be capable of understanding risks and giving informed consent without any form of legal pressure. Mandatory DBS (as well as mandatory antiandrogen medication) should absolutely not be an option."[40] In addition, they argue, consent to the intervention "should not be connected to any hopes/promises of prematurely leaving prison or a forensic treatment facility."[41] If DBS for sexual drive would become available for use in an offender population, the ethical dimension of the intervention will most probably lead to intensive debates in medicine, law, and in society.

Perhaps, DBS devices may also become sensitive and responsive to certain environments in which the person is more likely to commit a crime. In principle, we can even imagine types of DBS-stimulation that become "active" only in circumstances where, for example, increased sexual drive is registered. There is already discussion about predictive brain implants that may have certain programmed responses to identified parameters and how this would affect a person's autonomy.[42] Clearly many neurolaw questions are to be asked regarding possible future applications of neuroscience techniques aimed at influencing people's (criminal) behavior.

2 Neuroscience and Forensic Psychiatry

The developments in neuroscience have had major impacts on medicine. Diagnostic procedures in clinical medicine—in particular in neurology—are to a considerable extent based on neuroimaging. Neuroimaging techniques in medicine are relatively new; the first developments in MRI and CT date from the 1970s and 1980s.[43] In general, structural brain imaging techniques (which show brain structure, anatomy) have been in use slightly longer than functional neuroimaging techniques (which show brain functioning).[44] Clinical medicine could not exist in the way we know it today without neuroimaging techniques, such as CT-scan, MRI, EEG, and PET (positron emission tomography). In psychiatry, neuroimaging techniques play a much more modest role. In fact, they have a special position: generally they are used to exclude a somatic illness rather than to confirm a psychiatric disorder. Relating psychopathology to neuroimaging findings is still a challenge.

Notably, forensic psychiatrists may well face challenges that are, in part, different from those encountered in general psychiatric practice. General psychiatry often operates at the level of symptoms, focusing for example on anxiety, apathy, weight loss, and loss of appetite, which may lead to a diagnosis such as depression. Forensic psychiatry is not just interested in symptoms and diagnosis, but especially in their impact on (criminal) *behavior*. The emphasis of the evaluation of an individual within the context of forensic psychiatry may thus differ significantly from an evaluation in general psychiatry. Therefore, it is not unthinkable that, in the future, certain neuroimaging techniques will be developed especially for forensic psychiatric evaluations of defendants, focusing on the impact of a mental disorder on criminal behavior, in particular regarding questions about legal insanity and risk of recidivism.[45]

The specific standard or test for legal insanity in a particular jurisdiction may be relevant here as well. For instance, some jurisdictions use M'Naghten, which determines a defendant to be legally insane if "at the time of committing the act the party accused was laboring under such a defect of reason, from disease of the mind, as not to know the nature and quality of the act he was doing, or if he did know it, that he did not know what he was doing was wrong."[46] Because this standard focuses exclusively on a person's knowledge and not on behavioral control, it is considered a "cognitive" standard. This means that neurotechniques that may shed light on a defendant's knowledge are valuable for jurisdictions that use the M'Naghten Rules. Meanwhile, brain imaging techniques that shed light on a defendant's capacity for behavioral control do not appear to be relevant regarding insanity in such legal systems. Yet, many jurisdictions use insanity standards that do include a control prong. An example is the Model Penal Code, according to which a mental illness can lead to insanity if the defendant was unable to "conform his conduct to the requirements of the law."[47] This means that future neurotechniques that are able to detect control problems may be relevant for assessments of insanity in these jurisdictions, even though they may not be used in M'Naghten jurisdictions. As such, whether or not a neurotechnique will be helpful in the evaluation of a defendant's sanity is likely to depend, at least in part, on the specific legal standard for insanity used in that legal system.

In general, forensic psychiatrists assessing a defendant rely to a considerable extent on the defendant's own story (anamnesis) about his experiences and behavior at the moment of the crime as well as in the preceding period of time. Relying on the defendant's own account is also a weakness of the evaluation: the defendant may have problems remembering what happened or communicating his feelings, or the defendant may lie or otherwise deceive the psychiatrist.[48] Usually, neuroimaging techniques—and possibly other neuroscience techniques—do not rely on the defendant's own account of what happened. Adding such techniques to the forensic evaluation repertoire may be very valuable.

3 Neurolaw Literature Search: Some Observations

We performed a literature search to gain additional insight in the use of neuroimaging techniques to evaluate defendants. The question was: What neuroimaging techniques, in the domains of revision, assessment, and intervention are used or discussed in literature, in particular regarding the evaluation of a defendant's insanity in criminal law?

Because our perspective is primarily psychiatric, our search strategy consisted of a search of Pubmed, a life sciences and biomedical sciences database, for relevant articles on neuroimaging techniques[49] and criminal law.[50] Clearly, adding other databases, such as legal databases in individual jurisdictions, would have yielded more cases and results. Within the scope of this chapter, however, it was not our purpose to perform a comprehensive review of *all* documented neurolaw cases in the literature. Rather, our aim was to get some more insight into the main characteristics of the scholarly and scientific debate on neurolaw pertaining to forensic psychiatry and legal insanity.

We searched English-language articles and, in addition, found some Dutch-language articles through an independent search. We included articles published through June 2015 that reported cases of criminal law in which neuroimaging techniques were used, as well as those in which the (potential) use and position of neurotechniques in criminal law, especially in terms of forensic psychiatry, was discussed. Titles and abstracts were screened to identify potentially relevant articles. The reference lists were screened for additional relevant articles. Because many neurolaw articles did not mention or specify the neuroimaging technique used when discussing a criminal case, we could not perform a qualitative-comparative assessment of types of neurotechniques in criminal law cases. The results provide a sketch of characteristics of the neurolaw debate, rather than an exhaustive overview of legal cases and specific neuroscientific techniques.[51] The literature, it turns out, tends to focus on the revision and assessment domains; publications on interventions are scarce.

Neuro-evaluation of defendants is not a standard procedure in any of the jurisdictions covered in our literature search. There are several ways in which neuroimaging techniques can be introduced into the courtroom: they may be introduced by the defense lawyer, the prosecution, or the court. It need not be introduced directly by any of these, however. It may well be that the court orders a psychiatric evaluation and that the forensic psychiatrist decides that brain imaging and perhaps neurological or neuropsychological evaluation are required: for instance, because the psychiatrist suspects a neurodegenerative disease. In the literature, no standardized guideline was found specifying under what conditions a psychiatrist should involve a neurologist or should have brain imaging performed during an evaluation of a defendant. In one article, a multidisciplinary proposal was made on the ethical use of neuroimages in medical testimony.[52] An alternative way for introducing neuroscience in a legal case is by submitting *amicus curiae* briefs to the Supreme Court.

Many articles generated by our search did not mention specific techniques but instead dealt with general topics like neuroethics, criminal responsibility, violent behavior, and the future of neuroscience in forensic psychiatry. Often, neurolaw articles contained a combination of topics, sometimes illustrated by criminal law cases or focused on prevention, prediction and risk assessment.[53] Articles with a specific scope were often about antisocial personality disorder/traits or psychopathy in relation to neuroimaging.[54] Other major topics included brain-based lie detection and brain immaturity in relation to juvenile justice (as discussed previously).

Interestingly, although our search focused especially on neurotechniques, few articles dealt with a specific neuroscience technique such as invasive brain stimulation (deep brain stimulation) and non-invasive brain stimulation (transcranial magnetic stimulation), fMRI, and PET. Some articles considered brain injury and trauma and sleep-related violence and evaluation. More conceptual and general issues include free will and impulse control.[55]

It appears from the literature search that the value of neuroimaging in criminal cases is frequently related to the defendant's impulse control, rather than on "cognitive" (knowledge) factors. Often, go/no-go tasks are performed to examine self-control.[56] Motor decision tasks relate more directly to actual impulse control compared to traditional tools such as personality tests and history taking, and could perhaps be useful for the prediction of future behavior.[57]

Furthermore, it appears from the literature that neuroimaging techniques are more often used and accepted with regard to diagnosing *neurological* diseases (such as dementia, brain tumors, mental retardation, or traumatic brain injury), than with regard to psychiatric illnesses (depression, bipolar disorder, schizophrenia)—even though the latter, in particular psychosis, are more common in legal insanity pleas.

Perhaps unsurprisingly, neuroscience techniques appear to be introduced more often in severe crime cases: murder, manslaughter, and sexual offense and capital punishment cases. Widely-cited cases seem to have specific traits: (severe) violence and sexual abuse and/or landmark decisions (*Roper v. Simmons*, *People v. Weinstein*, *Graham v. Florida*).

As said, psychiatrists often rely on the defendant's story (although not exclusively) and the criminal court is an environment in which people may be tempted to lie and deceive. Therefore it may be helpful, at least in principle, to make use of some form or "lie detection" or other type of access to a defendant's mind/brain as part of psychiatric evaluations.[58] Neuroscience-based assessments in this area basically consist of two types: brain-based lie detection (such as using fMRI), in which the person has to make a statement or other utterance of which the truthfulness can then be established, and brain-based mind reading (such as P300 or a controversial technique like BEOS), in which case the person does not have to make a statement because the brain can be "read" directly.[59] Although brain-based lie detection is widely discussed, it is generally rejected in court. An often-cited criminal law case in this respect is the case of *Harrington v. State*, in which a defendant underwent a Brain Fingerprinting test (P300 ERP).[60] The court rejected the P300 method because of the lack of general acceptance.[61] Major problems regarding mind reading and lie detection remain, including the discrepancy between the laboratory and the field, the problem of testing "lying," and the group to individual problem. As Greely warns in the *New York Times*, "We keep looking for a magic, technological solution to lie detection. Maybe we'll have it someday, but we need to demand the highest standards of proof before we ruin people's lives based on its application."[62]

A special topic in the literature is "sleepwalking." *R. v. Parks* (1992) is a landmark case of violent behavior during sleep in which the defendant was acquitted of murder. In a state of sleepwalking Parks, who was under financial stress of his gambling addiction, drove 23 kilometers to his parents-in-law's house, killed his mother-in-law, and inflicted life-threatening injuries on his father-in-law. Parks was acquitted of murder because he was not conscious (asleep) and therefore not responsible. A systematic review of medical-legal case reports by Ingravallo et al. shows that "sleep disorder" has been used as a defense during several criminal trials.[63] The defendants in the nine sleep-related violence cases surveyed were accused of murder or attempted murder (or both). The forensic evaluation consisted, depending on the case, of psychiatric and/or neurological assessment and the following techniques: EEG, CT brain, PSG (polysomnography) and MRI.[64] Meanwhile, according to Bordenave and Kelly, "most courts that have considered the question have held that the insanity defense is an improper fit for what is best classified as a defense of unconsciousness."[65]

Clearly, it is highly relevant to know whether a person was actually asleep when committing a crime, which may resemble a crime committed during an epileptic seizure. Yet, there is also controversy about the reliability of the evidence. It may be very hard to establish what actually happened at the time of the crime and to estimate the likelihood that a defendant was asleep while performing (complicated) legally relevant acts. Ingravallo et al. conclude their paper stating: "An international expert consensus among sleep experts, medical-legal experts, and psychiatrists for the forensic evaluation of SRV [sleep-related violence] and SBS [sexual behavior in sleep] cases should be developed, which we consider to be an urgent priority."[66] Others believe that the current evidence is not powerful enough to develop a set of international guidelines and that more research needs to be done on the behaviors of people with parasomnias and violent behavior during sleep.[67] From a forensic psychiatric perspective, sleepwalking and related disorders may be less relevant because, in practice, they may be evaluated by neurologists rather than psychiatrists. Yet, parasomnias are part of the DSM-5 and it is necessary that forensic psychiatrists know about these disorders and their potential legal relevance, and in particular about the signs and symptoms that warrant further neurological evaluation.

4 Neuroimaging and Forensic Psychiatry: Limitations and Opportunities

Psychiatry and criminal law have different responsibilities, aims, and interests. Nonetheless, there are some shared interests between psychiatry and criminal law, including human behavior and mental states. Our brains appear to be relevant for both our behavior and our mental states.[68] So, even though it is true, as Steinberg states, that "the law is concerned with how we behave and not with how our brains function,"[69] an interest in behavior is not in conflict with an interest in our brains. Neuroscience, in particular brain imaging techniques, may be valuable in answering questions concerning behavior, mental states, and particularly mental illness in the courtroom.

Ideally, brain imaging techniques in court are used together with other assessment tools. The fact that brain imaging should not be used in isolation is not a reason to disregard neuroscience, nor a reason to be overly skeptical about it. It implies that we have to be careful when and how to use neuroscience and how to interpret the findings in view of other types of information. This challenge is complicated further by the fact that, in the standard case, the final interpretation will not be conducted by a neuroscientific expert, but by judges and jury members—who, most likely, are not neuroscientists. As our analysis so far suggests, neuroscientific information will have to be integrated in a bigger picture. In fact, neuroimaging data may help to put other findings into perspective.

To illustrate this point, let us consider a unique case, reported by Burns and Swerdlow.[70] A 40-year-old school teacher "developed an increasing interest in pornography, including child pornography" and "acquired an expanding collection of pornographic magazines and increasingly frequented Internet pornography sites." As Burns and Swerdlow write: "The patient went to great lengths to conceal his activities because he felt that they were unacceptable. However, he continued to act on his sexual impulses, stating that 'the pleasure principle overrode' his urge restraint. He began making subtle sexual advances toward his prepubescent stepdaughter, which he was able to conceal from his wife for several weeks." The schoolteacher was "legally removed from the home, diagnosed as having pedophilia, and prescribed medroxyprogesterone. He was found guilty of child molestation (. . .)."[71] The judge allowed him to follow a rehabilitation program to avoid prison. However, even during this program he solicited sexual favors from staff and other clients and consequently, he was sent to prison.

The evening before he was to leave for prison, he went to a hospital emergency department complaining of a headache. As Greely emphasizes, "they thought he was faking it."[72] Neurological examination showed some abnormalities, and neuropsychological examination showed grave abnormalities. Yet, poor results on a neuropsychological test can, in principle, be faked. Finally, an MRI was performed and a huge orbitofrontal tumor was clearly visible. Even though such a finding does not answer all questions one might have concerning the schoolteacher's behavior and, especially, his criminal responsibility, it cannot be faked. This is an interesting and valuable property of brain imaging techniques in general (although there may be exceptions in which imaging findings can be influenced or manipulated by subjects, as noted above). After the tumor was resected, the legally relevant behavior disappeared. Then it returned, and, as it turned out on examination, the tumor had grown again. It was resected for the second time, and has stayed away (as far as is known).

What can we learn from a case like this?[73] Firstly, we see that imaging data are hard to fake, which may be important in a court of law where the stakes are high and people may be tempted to lie and deceive. Secondly, imaging data may add another piece to the already available information, and in fact help to put the other pieces together. The imaging results made it possible to understand and put into perspective the already available neurological and neuropsychological findings, as well as to understand more about the sudden change of behavior in a 40-year-old man.

There is another lesson to be learnt from this case: even though medically relevant information was uncovered after the MRI (and neuropathological assessment), this does not imply that all relevant legal questions are answered. Although all of us can agree that this schoolteacher suffered from a serious brain tumor, the exact implications of the medical condition for his criminal responsibility are less clear. Note that although an intervention took place and even though we know that the return of the behavior was accompanied by regrowth of the tumor, we may still disagree about the schoolteacher's criminal responsibility (or degree thereof). For instance, we may ask if he shouldn't have seen a doctor when he first noticed his "unacceptable" behavior. Nevertheless, we may feel that this case is unique because it strongly suggests a direct (causal) link between neuroscience and behavior, especially in view of the intervention that took place.[74]

In criminal law cases, several neuroimaging techniques are being used which have different characteristics, advantages and disadvantages, and pitfalls, and some of which are more suitable for answering specific questions than others. What should be the threshold or criterion for admission of a neuroimaging technique? We may answer this question referring to common psychiatric or neurological practice: If a technique is good enough to be used in psychiatric practice, it is good enough to be used in court. At first sight, this may seem a reasonable criterion. Suppose a civil case where one of the parties claims to be suffering from a neurological disorder. In order to provide evidence of such a disorder it is reasonable that the party provides the type of evidence that is used in common neurological practice. But is it always reasonable to use common clinical practice as a standard or the point of reference?

As already emphasized, legal questions in the courtroom may be different from medical interests in clinical practice. The questions asked to forensic psychiatrists evaluating a defendant are to some extent identical to those asked in a clinical context, but in some regards they are different, for example, as far as they concern the specific criteria for a defendant's legal insanity such as knowledge about the wrongfulness of the act. As neuroscience and neurolaw develop, might certain techniques be developed for specific use in the court of law context? Particular techniques may not be relevant or helpful in clinical practice but still they could serve to answer questions: for example, those related to the legal insanity standard in a particular jurisdiction.[75] In principle, a neurotechnique that is not really helpful or suitable for clinical practice could still be valuable in a court of law. We feel that this possibility should be taken seriously. It means that forensic psychiatrists cannot just rely on and refer to techniques used in clinical practice, but that they should be open to the possibility of the development of new techniques for the courtroom setting. If forensic psychiatrists accept this possibility, then it seems reasonable to develop criteria for the suitability of techniques in the courtroom context.

Note that neuroimaging techniques are deployed *after* the crime has happened, not during the commission of the act. This is the case for the other examination tools in the forensic psychiatric assessment also, but it must be taken into consideration as far as the issue of insanity is concerned. Another problem is that (current) neuroimaging in principle takes place in a context that is different from the context of the crime. A crime is often stimulus-related, and high stress levels may play a role, as well as alcohol and drugs. It may be that a defendant's mental problems (or aspects thereof) become evident only in a certain environment or when a certain constellation of factors is present, such as being insulted, being tired, and feeling stressed.

The view shared by most authors in the neurolaw literature appears to be that, at present, the usefulness of neurotechniques in court is very limited.[76] They refer to group level correlations that are hard to use in individual cases, difficulties interpreting data, and the unsuitability of neuroscience techniques to answer legal questions. Still, there are several cases in which neuroscience techniques did not merely show correlations; in the case described by Burns and Swerdlow, for example, there was an intervention (tumor resection), and later a recurrence of the symptoms and the tumor. In our view, this points to the challenge for forensic psychiatrists (as well as for defense lawyers, prosecutors, and judges) to be alert regarding those cases in which neurotechniques may generate valuable information. Those techniques that enable us to measure functionality rather than anatomy appear to be the most promising tools for forensic psychiatry. These techniques come closest to questions about cognitive (in)capacities and abnormal behavior—precisely the types of questions that are of legal relevance. However, functional techniques may also be more susceptible to manipulation than those techniques that merely show anatomical or pathological brain structures.

In fact, it may be wise to combine neuroimaging with a neuropsychological evaluation. Brain imaging as such may not provide much information about mental capacities and behavioral abnormalities. Yet, in combination with a state of the art neuropsychological assessment it may be possible to somehow bridge the gap between brain image on the one hand and criminal behavior on the other. If various imaging techniques and neuropsychological assessment all point in the same direction, this can be very valuable information for the court. Perhaps, the recommendation is justified that, in principle, neuroimaging techniques should not be used in isolation, but rather in combination not just with psychiatric evaluation, but also with neuropsychological assessment.

Although the use of neuroscience in the courtroom is on the rise, the percentage of criminal cases in which it is used is still very small. In theory, it may be that, in all the cases in which neuroscience did *not* play a role, it was irrelevant. It could also be that potentially legally relevant brain lesions were missed, possibly in many cases, but it can never be known. It is not impossible that, in coming years when neuroscience will play an increasing role in more and more cases, psychiatrists and others will realize they missed many potentially relevant brain problems in the past. We may be missing a lot of neurological lesions in defendants just because we currently do not look for such brain injuries, especially in less severe cases (because, as we noted, neuro-evidence usually features in severe cases, such as those involving capital crimes). In less serious crimes, defendants may also have suffered traumatic brain injury that can be equally or even more relevant to their criminal behavior than for defendants in murder cases.

According to Jones et al., "the legal system needs neuroscientists who are willing to serve as experts, so that countervailing views of the evidence can be aired."[77] Also, it would be good if there are professionals who are not only able to interpret but also to *integrate* neuroscience findings into other pieces of information about a defendant's medical history, psychiatric diagnoses, (neuro)psychological evaluations, and social situation. In other words, it would be helpful if neuroscientific findings can be put into some perspective by clinicians, who are used to interpreting (brain) findings with respect to an individual. Perhaps psychiatrists can play the role of those who integrate various pieces of evidence regarding a defendant's brain, mental functioning, and behavior.[78] One reason is the "natural" role forensic psychiatrists currently have in the court of law. Another reason is that, as doctors, they have basic knowledge about the brain and psychopathology, and regarding the translation of laboratory findings to an individual. In addition, the professional and ethical codes and standards developed in forensic psychiatry are likely to be an advantage compared to some other non-clinical disciplines. Still, this would be a challenge for psychiatrists, including because the field of neuroscience and the number of techniques used is expanding so rapidly. In any case, in our view, availability of an expert who would be able to integrate the variety of findings regarding brain, mind, and behavior in a criminal case would be very valuable.

Although, as emphasized, neuroscience cannot directly answer the legal question concerning a defendant's responsibility, it can provide important insights for the court's decision on such matters.[79] In the coming years, neuroscience may even try to develop tools and techniques that are of specific relevance to the questions of central interest in a court of law. In the past, technical developments such as fingerprinting and DNA-evidence have "revolutionized" criminal law. Neither of them replaces the legal judgments, however, and neither of them is flawless; both need to be interpreted with caution. Neuroscientific techniques may also improve the quality of legal decision making, especially by improving the quality of forensic psychiatric evaluations of defendants.

5 Conclusion

The field of neurolaw is fascinating, multifaceted, and rapidly expanding, and one of its most obvious applications is regarding legal insanity. In the near future, forensic psychiatrists evaluating defendants will increasingly be confronted with questions about brain abnormalities and neuroimaging techniques to detect them—and with questions about the right interpretation of neuroscientific findings. Some neuro-skepticism is certainly warranted: the contribution of neuroscience to forensic psychiatric assessments and assessments of defendants in general is still very limited. Yet, we see already that neuroimaging techniques have added value to the assessment of defendants in some cases, and neuroscience appears to have contributed to legal decisions that led to revision of the law or legal practices.

Interpreting neuroimaging in the courtroom is challenging, and in our view, neuroimaging techniques should not be used in isolation, but rather in combination not just with psychiatric evaluation, but preferably also with (neuro)psychological assessment and, if available, other types of evaluation. Note that the introduction of yet another type of assessment may further complicate the matter as well. The reason is that experts with different types of expertise have to be involved: psychiatrists, (neuro)psychologists, possibly neurologists, neuroradiologists, and so forth. If experts with different backgrounds provide information, it would be valuable if one of them would be able to integrate the information derived from the various sources. We suggest that psychiatrists could take on this role, but this is not an easy task. The speed of the expansion of the neurolaw research area will require much effort from psychiatrists to stay up to date.[80] In any case, assessments of legal insanity involving brain data should in principle be multidisciplinary in nature, as should be neurolaw research on legal insanity. Only then can excessive skepticism and optimism be balanced and legal decision making in criminal cases be improved.[81]

Notes

1. On the field of neurolaw as discussed in this section and the next, see also Meynen, "Neurolaw: Neuroscience, Ethics, and Law," *Legal Insanity: Explorations in Psychiatry, Law, & Ethics*, and "Neurolaw: Recognizing Opportunities and Challenges for Psychiatry." Aggarwal and Ford define neurolaw as "the application of neuroscience findings to legal topics such as criminal, tort, and administrative litigation and justice, agency, responsibility, intent, adjudication, and policy" ("The Neuroethics and Neurolaw of Brain Injury," 790). On neurolaw, see also Schleim, "Brains in Context in the Neurolaw Debate."

2. Between 1984 and 2012, the cumulative growth of published articles on neurolaw went from 0 to over 1000 in 2012, see Jones et al., "Neuroscientists in Court."

3. *Roper v. Simmons*, 543 U.S. 551 (2005). The amicus briefs were not only from the American Medical Association and the American Psychiatric Association, but also from the American Society for Adolescent Psychiatry, American Academy of Child and Adolescent Psychiatry, and the American Academy of Psychiatry and the Law (among others).

4. Cohen and Casey, "Rewiring Juvenile Justice," and Steinberg "The Influence of Neuroscience on U.S. Supreme Court Decisions about Adolescents' Criminal Culpability."

5. Neuroethics is a field of research that partially overlaps with neurolaw; see Meynen, "Neurolaw: Neuroscience, Ethics, and Law." On neuroethics, see also Moreno, "Neuroethics," and on neuroethics and psychiatry, see Ford and Aggarwal, "Neuroethics of Functional Neuroimaging in the Courtroom."

6. See Casartelli and Chiamulera, "Opportunities, Threats, and Limitations of Neuroscience Data in Forensic Psychiatric Evaluation" and "Which Future for Neuroscience in Forensic Psychiatry," as well as Silva, "The Relevance of Neuroscience to Forensic Psychiatry" and "Forensic Psychiatry, Neuroscience, and the Law."

7. Greely, "Mind Reading, Neuroscience, and the Law."

8. Pardo and Patterson, *Minds, Brains, and Law*, 140. On neurolaw and psychiatric evaluations of insanity, see also Meynen, "A Neurolaw Perspective on Psychiatric Assessments of Criminal Responsibility" and "Neurolaw: Recognizing Opportunities and Challenges for Psychiatry," and, with specific reference to the Dutch context, see Meynen, "Neurolaw: de Relevantie voor de Forensische Psychiatrie."

9. Neuroscientific techniques are not limited to brain imaging ("pictures of the brain"). Other types of neurobiological assessment or research that may also be used in court include neuroendocrine assessments (hormones, neurotransmitters) and genetic assessment. Here, we focus on brain imaging techniques like MRI, fMRI, CT, SPECT, PET, EEG.

10. Van der Gronde et al., "Neurobiological Correlates in Forensic Assessment."

11. See Meynen, "Neurolaw: Neuroscience, Ethics, and Law," *Legal Insanity*, and "Neurolaw: Recognizing Opportunities and Challenges for Psychiatry."

12. Steinberg, "The Influence of Neuroscience."

13. Ibid., 516, based on the transcript of oral argument in *Roper v. Simmons*, S. Ct. (2004) (No. 03–633). See also *Graham v. Florida* 130 S. Ct. 2011 (2010).

14. Greene and Cohen, "For the Law, Neuroscience Changes Nothing and Everything."

15. Libet et al., "Time of Conscious Intention to Act in Relation to Onset of Cerebral Activity." For a critical discussion, see Radder and Meynen, "Does the Brain 'Initiate' Freely Willed Processes?"

16. Wegner, *The Illusion of Conscious Will*, and Spence, "Free Will in the Light of Neuropsychiatry."

17. See Soon et al., "Unconscious Determinants of Free Decisions in the Human Brain," and Fried, Mukamel, and Kreiman, "Internally Generated Preactivation of Single Neurons."

18. For example, Morse and Roskies, *A Primer on Criminal Law and Neuroscience*, and Pardo and Patterson, *Minds, Brains, and Law*.

19. See Greely, "Mind Reading, Neuroscience, and the Law"; Greely and Illes, "Neuroscience-Based Lie Detection"; Brown and Murphy, "Through a Scanner Darkly"; and Meynen, "Toerekeningsvatbaarheid. Over Zekerheid en Neurowetenschap."

20. Salmanowitz, "The Case for Pain Neuroimaging in the Courtroom," 2.
21. Greely, "Mind Reading, Neuroscience, and the Law."
22. Morse and Roskies, *A Primer on Criminal Law and Neuroscience*.
23. Salmanowitz, "The Case for Pain Neuroimaging in the Courtroom."
24. Aharoni et al., "Neuroprediction of Future Rearrest," 6223.
25. Meynen, "Neurolaw: Recognizing Opportunities and Challenges for Psychiatry."
26. Coid, Ullrich, and Kallis, "Predicting Future Violence among Individuals with Psychopathy."
27. Morse and Roskies, *A Primer on Criminal Law and Neuroscience*.
28. See, e.g., *People v. Jones*, 210 A.D.2d 904 (N.Y. App. Div. 1994).
29. Jones et al. write about these standards (references omitted): "Since 1993, all US federal courts have been required to apply a different test to determine admissibility, and many state courts have chosen to adopt this test as well. That test is reflected in Rule 702 of the Federal Rules of Evidence, which instantiates the so-called 'Daubert standard' (named after the 1993 US Supreme Court case *Daubert v. Merrell Dow Pharmaceutical* and further articulated in several subsequent cases.). Under the Daubert standard, which is sometimes described as the 'gate- keeping standard', the opinions of scientific expert witnesses are admissible only if a judge is satisfied that they are helpful and appropriately scientific and that they have been correctly applied to the case at hand. Unlike the Frye test, which calls upon judges to inquire whether the science is generally accepted by the field, the Daubert standard requires that judges themselves assess whether the expert's testimony is grounded in valid science. Relevant (but emphatically non-exclusive) factors in making this assessment include: first, whether the theory or technique can be tested and has been tested; second, whether the theory or technique has been subjected to peer review and publication; third, the known or potential rate of error of the method used; fourth, the existence and maintenance of standards controlling the technique's operation; and fifth, whether the theory or method has been generally accepted by the relevant scientific community" ("Neuroscientists in Court," 732). On admissibility, see also Moriarty, "Flickering Admissibility."
30. Pardo and Patterson, *Minds, Brains, and Law*.
31. Meltzer et al., "Guidelines for the Ethical Use of Neuroimages in Medical Testimony," 635. Proposed guidelines for neuroradiology imaging testimony:

1. "Experts should present all relevant facts available in their testimony, ensure truthfulness and balance, and consider opposing points of view.
2. Experts should specify known deviations from standard practice.
3. Experts should have substantive knowledge and experience in the area in which they are testifying.
4. Experts should use standard terminology and describe standardization methods and the cohort characteristic from which claims are determined, when applicable.
5. Nonvalidated findings that are used to inform clinical pathology should be approached with great caution.

6. Recognized appropriateness guidelines should be used to assess whether the imaging technique used is appropriate for the particular question.
7. Experts should avoid drawing conclusions about specific behaviors based on the imaging data alone.
8. Experts should be willing to submit their testimony for peer review.
9. Experts should be prepared to provide a description of the nature of the neuroimages (e.g., representational/statistical maps when derived from computational postprocessing of several images) and how they were acquired.
10. Raw images and raw data should be made available for replication if requested.
11. Experts should be able to explain the reasoning behind their conclusions.
12. False-positive rates should be known and considered if the expert's testimony includes quantitative imaging.
13. Experts should be prepared to discuss limitations of the technology and provide both confirming research and disconfirming studies" (ibid.).

32. Cited from Pereira et al., "Deep Brain Stimulation" (591): "Deep brain stimulation is a minimally invasive targeted neurosurgical intervention that enables structures deep in the brain to be stimulated electrically by an implanted pacemaker. It has become the treatment of choice for Parkinson's disease, refractory to, or complicated by, drug therapy." Furthermore: "Multifarious clinical indications for deep brain stimulation now exist, including dystonia and tremor in movement disorders; depression, obsessive-compulsive disorder and Tourette's syndrome in psychiatry; epilepsy, cluster headache and chronic pain, including pain from stroke, amputation, trigeminal neuralgia and multiple sclerosis."

33. Kulisevsky et al., "Mania Following Deep Brain Stimulation for Parkinson's Disease."

34. Müller and Walter, "Reviewing Autonomy," 210.

35. Ibid.

36. Denys and van de Beek, "Enkele Juridische Aandachtspunten bij Diepe Hersenstimulatie."

37. See Gasson and Koops, "Attacking Human Implants."

38. See Bublitz and Merkel, "Guilty Minds in Washed Brains?"

39. Fuss et al., "Deep Brain Stimulation to Reduce Sexual Drive."

40. Ibid., 430.

41. Ibid.

42. Gilbert, "A Threat to Autonomy?," and, in response to this paper, Widdershoven, Meynen, and Denys, "Autonomy in Predictive Brain Implants."

43. Filler, "MR Neurography and Diffusion Tensor Imaging."

44. Roskies, "Brain Imaging Techniques."

45. On these issues, see also Meynen, "Neurolaw Perspective on Psychiatric Assessments of Criminal Responsibility" and *Mad or Bad?*

46. *M'Naghten's Case*, 10 Cl. & Fin. 200. 8 Eng. Rep 718 (H.L. 1843). See also Simon and Ahn-Redding, *The Insanity Defense, the World Over*, and Packer, *Evaluation of Criminal Responsibility*.

47. More completely, §4.01 states that "a person is not responsible for criminal conduct if at the time of such conduct as a result of mental disease or defect he lacks substantial capacity either to appreciate the criminality of his conduct or to conform his conduct to the requirements of the law."

48. Meynen, "Neurolaw: de Relevantie voor de Forensische Psychiatrie" and "Toerekeningsvatbaarheid. Over Zekerheid en Neurowetenschap."

49. We only studied neuroimaging techniques, and did not search for other types of neurobiological techniques such as neuroendocrinological evaluation (hormones, neurotransmitters) and genetic assessment.

50. The following search strategy was used. The search included terms indexed in MeSH vocabularies and in free text (and word variations): (Neuroscience, neuroimaging, EEG, MRI, PET, DBS, CT, TMS, SPECT, DTI, fNIRS, BEOS, brain mapping, neurolaw, neuroprediction) AND (forensic psychiatry, psychiatric jurisprudence, insanity defense, legal insanity, criminal law, criminal justice, mental (in)competency, pretrial evaluation, criminal responsibility, not-guilty by reason of insanity). In addition, the following free terms were used: fMRI lie detection, neurolaw.

51. In all, 324 publications were found, abstracts were screened and 101 articles were excluded because the abstract revealed that the papers were not relevant for our research question. From the 223 remaining articles, 177 articles were further considered. Fourteen articles were excluded based on irrelevance, 21 on language, and 11 articles were not available. We added nine additional articles from cross references and hand-searching: Bordenave and Kelly, "Not Guilty by Reason of Somnambulism"; Casey et al., "Behavioral and Neural Correlates of Delay of Gratification 40 Years Later"; Grubin, "The Polygraph and Forensic Psychiatry"; Ingravallo et al., "Sleep-related Violence and Sexual Behavior in Sleep"; Ingravallo et al., "An International Consensus on the Forensic Assessment of Sleep-Related Violence and Sexual Behavior in Sleep"; Liu et al., "Changes in Low-Frequency Fluctuations in Patients with Antisocial Personality Disorder"; Moriarty, "Flickering Admissibility"; Rumbold, Morrison, and Riha, "Calls for an International Consensus"; and Sinnott-Armstrong et al., "Brain Images as Legal Evidence."

52. Meltzer et al., "Guidelines for the Ethical Use of Neuroimages in Medical Testimony."

53. Examples are Aharoni et al. "Predictive Accuracy in the Neuroprediction of Rearrest," and Nadelhoffer et al., "Neuroprediction, Violence, and the Law."

54. For example, Liu et al., "Changes in Low-Frequency Fluctuations"; Calzada-Reyes et al., "EEG Abnormalities in Psychopath and Non-Psychopath Violent Offenders" and "Electroencephalographic Abnormalities in Antisocial Personality Disorder."

55. On deep brain stimulation, see Klaming and Haselager, "Did My Brain Implant Make Me Do It?"; on transcranial magnetic stimulation, see Heinrichs, "The Promises and Perils of Non-Invasive Brain Stimulation"; on fMRI, see Dressing, Sartorius, and Meyer-Lindenberg, "Implications of fMRI and Genetics"; on

PET, see Moriarty, Langleben, and Provenzale, "Brain Trauma, Pet Scans and Forensic Complexity"; on brain injury and trauma, see McBride et al., "It's Not All in Your Head (or at Least Your Brain)"; on sleep-related violence and evaluation, see Ingravallo et al., "Sleep-Related Violence and Sexual Behavior in Sleep"; on free will, see Greene and Cohen, "For the Law, Neuroscience Changes Nothing and Everything"; and on impulse-control, see Penney, "Impulse Control and Criminal Responsibility."

56. Casey et al., "Behavioral and Neural Correlates of Delay of Gratification," and Aharoni et al., "Neuroprediction of Future Rearrest."

57. Aharoni et al., "Neuroprediction of Future Rearrest."

58. See also Meynen, "Neurolaw: de Relevantie voor de Forensische Psychiatrie" and "Toerekeningsvatbaarheid. Over Zekerheid en Neurowetenschap," and Grubin, "The Polygraph and Forensic Psychiatry."

59. Aggarwal writes about a 2008 case from India that shows the risk of misinterpretation of poorly understood techniques in which two suspects were convicted of murder ("Neuroimaging, Culture, and Forensic Psychiatry," 239). In this case the court largely based their conclusions on Brain Electrical Oscillations Signature (BEOS), allegedly a type of brain fingerprinting with EEG. According to Puranik et al., the technique is used "to identify the presence of Experiential Knowledge in the perpetrator of the crime" ("Brain Signature Profiling," 816). The case received a lot of media attention. Aggarwal writes: "Within three months, a committee of experts from the Indian National Institute of Mental Health and Neuro Sciences (NIMHANS) recommended discontinuing BEOS in investigative and evidentiary procedures, since the studies had not accounted for constitutional variations such as body temperature, heart rate, sex, endurance, and age. American experts also expressed alarm that Indian BEOS experiments had not undergone peer review in academic journals or replication in other laboratories" ("Neuroimaging, Culture, and Forensic Psychiatry," 239).

60. *Harrington v. State of Iowa*, No. 96-1232 1997.

61. Meixner, "Applications of Neuroscience in Criminal Law."

62. As cited by Giridharadas, "India's Novel Use of Brain Scans in Courts Is Debated."

63. Ingravallo et al., "Sleep-Related Violence and Sexual Behavior in Sleep."

64. Apart from EEG, polysomnography (PSG) could have a role to gain insight in precipitating and modulating factors, see Ebrahim and Fenwick, "Sleep-Related Automatism and the Law."

65. Bordenave and Kelly write about the U.S. legal context, in particular discussing a ruling by the Supreme Court of Georgia ("Not Guilty by Reason of Somnambulism"). The classification of sleep disorders also depends on the jurisdiction, in some jurisdictions it is considered automatism rather than insanity.

66. Ingravallo et al., "Sleep-Related Violence and Sexual Behavior in Sleep," 934. See also Ingravallo et al., "An International Consensus," 1255: "in our view the consensus should focus on the standards for the sleep expert workup, and not on legal questions, which are necessarily related to the various domestic laws."

67. Rumbold et al., "Calls for an International Consensus."

68. On issues discussed in this section, see also Meynen, "Neurolaw: de Relevantie voor de Forensische Psychiatrie" and *Legal Insanity*.

69. Steinberg, "Influence of Neuroscience on US Supreme Court Decisions," 517.

70. Burns and Swerdlow, "Right Orbitofrontal Tumor with Pedophilia Symptom and Constructional Apraxia Sign." On this case see also Meynen, "Neuroethics of Criminal Responsibility," "Neurolaw: Recognizing Opportunities and Challenges for Psychiatry," and "Neurolaw: de Relevantie voor de Forensische Psychiatrie."

71. Burns and Swerdlow, "Right Orbitofrontal Tumor," 437.

72. Greely, "Brain Research at Stanford."

73. On what follows, see also Meynen, "Neurolaw: de Relevantie voor de Forensische Psychiatrie," *Legal Insanity*, and "Neuroethics of Criminal Responsibility."

74. Glenn and Raine, "Neurocriminology."

75. According to Harman, "some commentators, among them Steinberg, argue that present research is a step towards a future of neuroscience capable of giving to courts the power of distinguishing between those who couldn't stop themselves from committing a crime and those who could stop themselves but chose to commit it anyway—a rather important distinction when it comes to culpability before the law" ("Unformed Minds," 457).

76. See also Casartelli and Chiamulera, "Which Future for Neuroscience in Forensic Psychiatry," 2 (references omitted): "We have stressed the idea that empirical data cannot directly assess criminal responsibility. Neuroscience data may be useful—in specific and limited circumstances—to give aid to traditional forensic assessment for mental capabilities. Clearly, not all neuroscience data may assume the same explanatory value, and not all data may be useful in FPE [forensic psychiatric examination]. The renowned debate on fMRI data is illustrative. On one side, researches both in biological psychiatry and neuropsychology have been considerably improved by fMRI studies; on the other side, the effective implications of such studies are still controversial in clinical practice and also in different research fields (e.g., economic behaviors, forensic settings, moral development, etc.). Nevertheless, the debate on the probative value of specific neuroscientific techniques overcomes the aim of this work."

77. Jones et al., "Neuroscientists in Court," 733.

78. See Meynen, "Neurolaw: de Relevantie voor de Forensische Psychiatrie," and also Aggarwal, "Neuroimaging, Culture, and Forensic Psychiatry," 240: "Forensic psychiatrists can contribute valuable observations given their roles within patient care and their familiarity with medicine and the law."

79. Cf. Aharoni et al., "Can Neurological Evidence Help Courts Assess Criminal Responsibility?," 157: "Chemists perhaps cannot determine if a cake was baked with love, but they can determine if it was baked with cyanide, which in turn provides circumstantial evidence against the love hypothesis. Likewise, although neuroscience cannot locate responsibility in the brain, perhaps it can identify maladies that provide at least circumstantial evidence against guilt or liability."

80. See also Silva, "The Relevance of Neuroscience to Forensic Psychiatry" and "Forensic Psychiatry, Neuroscience, and the Law," and on what follows see Meynen, "Neurolaw: Recognizing Opportunities and Challenges for Psychiatry."

81. The authors thank Caroline Planting and Jopie van der Spek, GGZ InGeest, for their advice regarding the literature search.

Resources

Aggarwal, Neil K., "Neuroimaging, Culture, and Forensic Psychiatry." *Journal of the American Academy of Psychiatry and the Law* 37(2009): 239–44.

Aggarwal, Neil K., and Elizabeth Ford., "The Neuroethics and Neurolaw of Brain Injury." *Behavioral Sciences and the Law* 31(2013): 789–802.

Aharoni, Eyal, et al., "Neuroprediction of Future Rearrest." *Proceedings of the National Academy of Sciences* 110(2013): 6223–28.

Aharoni, Eyal, et al., "Predictive Accuracy in the Neuroprediction of Rearrest." *Social Neuroscience* 9(2014): 332–36.

Aharoni, Eyal, Chadd Funk, Walter Sinnott-Armstrong, and Michael Gazzaniga, "Can Neurological Evidence Help Courts Assess Criminal Responsibility? Lessons from Law and Neuroscience." *Annuals New York Academy of Sciences* 1124(2008): 145–60.

Bordenave, Franklin J., and D. Clay Kelly, "Not Guilty by Reason of Somnambulism." *Journal of the American Academy of Psychiatry and the Law* 37(2009): 571–73.

Brown, Teneille, and Emily R. Murphy, "Through a Scanner Darkly: Functional Neuro-imaging as Evidence of a Criminal Defendant's Past Mental States." *Stanford Law Review* 62(2009): 1119–1208.

Bublitz, Christoph, and Reinhard Merkel, "Guilty Minds in Washed Brains? Manipulation Cases and the Limits of Neuroscientific Excuses in Liberal Legal Orders." In *Neuroscience and Legal Responsibility*, edited by Nicole A. Vincent (New York: Oxford University Press, 2013), 333–72.

Burns, Jeffrey M., and Russell H. Swerdlow, "Right Orbitofrontal Tumor with Pedophilia Symptom and Constructional Apraxia Sign." *Archives of Neurology* 60(2003): 437–40.

Calzada-Reyes, Ana, Alfredo Alvarez-Amador, Lidice Galán-García, and Mitchell Valdés-Sosa, "EEG Abnormalities in Psychopath and Non-Psychopath Violent Offenders." *Journal of Forensic and Legal Medicine* 20(2013): 19–26.

Calzada-Reyes, Ana, Alfredo Alvarez-Amador, Lidice Galán-García, and Mitchell Valdés-Sosa, "Electroencephalographic Abnormalities in Antisocial Personality Disorder." *Journal of Forensic and Legal Medicine* 19(2012): 29–34.

Casartelli, Luca, and Cristiano Chiamulera, "Opportunities, Threats, and Limitations of Neuroscience Data in Forensic Psychiatric Evaluation." *Current Opinion in Psychiatry* 26(2013): 468–73.

Casartelli, Luca, and Cristiano Chiamulera, "Which Future for Neuroscience in Forensic Psychiatry: Theoretical Hurdles and Empirical Chances." *Frontiers in Psychiatry* 4(2013): 74.

Casey, B.J., et al., "Behavioral and Neural Correlates of Delay of Gratification 40 Years Later." *Proceedings of the National Academy of Sciences* 108(2011): 14998–15003.

Cohen, Alexandra O., and B.J. Casey, "Rewiring Juvenile Justice: The Intersection of Developmental Neuroscience and Legal Policy." *Trends in Cognitive Sciences* 18(2014): 63–65.

Coid, Jeremy W., Simone Ullrich, and Constantinos Kallis, "Predicting Future Violence among Individuals with Psychopathy." *British Journal of Psychiatry* 203(2013): 387–88.

Denys, Damiaan, and Paul van de Beek, "Enkele Juridische Aandachtspunten bij Diepe Hersenstimulatie." *Nederlands Juristenblad* 45(2013): 3143–47.

Dressing, Harald, Alexander Sartorius, and Andreas Meyer-Lindenberg, "Implications of fMRI and Genetics for the Law and the Routine Practice of Forensic Psychiatry." *Neurocase: Case Studies in Neuropsychology, Neuropsychiatry, and Behavioural Neurology* 14(2008): 7–14.

Ebrahim, Irshaad O., and Peter B. Fenwick, "Sleep-related Automatism and the Law." *Medicine, Science and the Law* 48(2008): 124–36.

Filler, Aaron, "MR Neurography and Diffusion Tensor Imaging: Origins, History and Clinical Impact of the first 50,000 cases with an Assessment of Efficacy and Utility in a Prospective 5,000 Patient Study Group." *Neurosurgery* 65(2009): A29–A43.

Ford, Elizabeth, and Neil Aggarwal, "Neuroethics of Functional Neuroimaging in the Courtroom." In *Neuroimaging in Forensic Psychiatry: From the Clinic to the Courtroom*, edited by Joseph R. Simpson (Chichester, UK: John Wiley & Sons, 2012), 325–40.

Fried, Itzhak, Roy Mukamel, and Gabriel Kreiman, "Internally Generated Preactivation of Single Neurons in Human Medial Frontal Cortex Predicts Volition." *Neuron* 69(2011): 548–62.

Fuss, Johannes, et al., "Deep Brain Stimulation to Reduce Sexual Drive." *Journal of Psychiatry and Neuroscience* 40(2015): 429–31.

Gasson, Mark N., and Bert-Jaap Koops, "Attacking Human Implants: A New Generation of Cybercrime." *Law, Innovation and Technology* 5(2013): 248–77.

Gilbert, Frederic, "A Threat to Autonomy? The Intrusion of Predictive Brain Implants." *AJOB Neuroscience* 6(2015): 4–11.

Giridharadas, Anand, "India's Novel Use of Brain Scans in Courts Is Debated." *The New York Times*, September 15, 2008, A10.

Glenn, Andrea L., and Adrian Raine, "Neurocriminology: Implications for the Punishment, Prediction and Prevention of Criminal Behaviour." *Nature Reviews Neuroscience* 15(2013): 54–63.

Greely, Henry T., "Brain Research at Stanford: The Law." Video (2001), available at http://www.youtube.com/watch?v=x7otiF6kYFw.

Greely, Henry T., "Mind Reading, Neuroscience, and the Law." In *A Primer on Criminal Law and Neuroscience*, edited by Stephen J. Morse and Adina L. Roskies (New York: Oxford University Press, 2013), 120–49.

Greely, Henry T., and Judy Illes, "Neuroscience-Based Lie Detection: The Urgent Need for Regulation." *American Journal of Law and Medicine* 33(2007): 377–431.

Greene, Joshua, and Jonathan Cohen, "For the Law, Neuroscience Changes Nothing and Everything." *Philosophical Transactions of the Royal Society of London. Series B, Biological Sciences* 359(2004): 1775–85.

Grubin, Don, "The Polygraph and Forensic Psychiatry." *Journal of the American Academy of Psychiatry and the Law* 38(2010): 446–51.

Harman, Oren, "Unformed Minds: Juveniles, Neuroscience, and the Law." *Studies in History and Philosophy of Biological and Biomedical Science* 44(2013): 455–59.

Heinrichs, Jan-Hendrik, "The Promises and Perils of Non-Invasive Brain Stimulation." *International Journal of Law and Psychiatry* 35(2012): 121–29.

Ingravallo, Francesca, et al., "An International Consensus on the Forensic Assessment of Sleep-Related Violence and Sexual Behavior in Sleep: If Not Now, When?" *Journal of Clinical Sleep Medicine* 10(11)(2014): 1255–56.

Ingravallo, Francesca, et al., "Sleep-Related Violence and Sexual Behavior in Sleep: A Systematic Review of Medical-Legal Case Reports." *Journal of Clinical Sleep Medicine* 10(2014): 927–35.

Jones, Owen D., Anthony D. Wagner, David L. Faigman, and Marcus E. Raichle, "Neuroscientists in Court." *Nature Reviews Neuroscience* 14(2013): 730–36.

Klaming, Laura, and Pim Haselager, "Did my Brain Implant Make Me Do It? Questions Raised by DBS Regarding Psychological Continuity, Responsibility for Action and Mental Competence." *Neuroethics* 6(2013): 527–39.

Kulisevsky, Jaime, et al., "Mania Following Deep Brain Stimulation for Parkinson's Disease." *Neurology* 59(2002): 1421–24.

Libet, Benjamin, Curtis A. Gleason, Elwood W. Wright, and Dennis K. Pearl, "Time of Conscious Intention to Act in Relation to Onset of Cerebral Activity (Readiness-Potential). The Unconscious Initiation of a Freely Voluntary Act." *Brain* 106(1983): 623–42.

Liu, Huasheng, Jian Liao, Weixiong Jiang, and Wei Wang, "Changes in Low-Frequency Fluctuations in Patients with Antisocial Personality Disorder Revealed by Resting-State Functional MRI." *PLoS ONE* 9(2014), e89790.

McBride, Willie F., Adam H. Crighton, Dustin W. Wygant, and Robert Phillip Granacher, "It's Not All in Your Head (or at Least Your Brain): Association of Traumatic Brain Lesion Presence and Location with Performance on Measures of Response Bias in Forensic Evaluation." *Behavioral Sciences and the Law* 31(2013): 779–88.

Meixner, John B., "Applications of Neuroscience in Criminal Law: Legal and Methodological Issues." *Current Neurology and Neuroscience Reports* 15(2015): 513.

Meltzer, Caroly C., et al., "Guidelines for the Ethical Use of Neuroimages in Medical Testimony: Report of a Multidisciplinary Consensus Conference." *American Journal of Neuroradiology* 35(2014): 632–37.

Meynen, Gerben, *Mad or Bad? Over de Grenzen van de Psychiatrie*. Tilburg: Prisma print, Tilburg University, 2013.

Meynen, Gerben, "Neuroethics of Criminal Responsibility: Mental Disorders Influencing Behavior." In *The Routledge International Handbook of Biosocial Criminology*, edited by Matt DeLisi and Michael G. Vaughn (Abingdon: Routledge, 2014), 544–57.

Meynen, Gerben, "Neurolaw: Neuroscience, Ethics, and Law. Review Essay." *Ethical Theory and Moral Practice* 17(2014): 819–29.

Meynen, Gerben, "A Neurolaw Perspective on Psychiatric Assessments of Criminal Responsibility: Decision-Making, Mental Disorder, and the Brain." *International Journal of Law and Psychiatry* 36(2013): 93–99.

Meynen, Gerben, "Neurolaw: Recognizing Opportunities and Challenges for Psychiatry." *Journal of Psychiatry and Neuroscience* 41(2016): 3–5.

Meynen, Gerben, "Neurolaw: de Relevantie voor de Forensische Psychiatrie." *Tijdschrift voor psychiatrie* 56(2014): 597–604.

Meynen, Gerben, "Toerekeningsvatbaarheid. Over Zekerheid en Neurowetenschap." In *Omzwervingen tussen psychiatrie en recht. Liber Amicorum prof. dr.H.J.C. van Marle,* edited by Paul A.M. Mevis et al. (Deventer: Kluwer, 2015), 287–98.

Meynen, Gerben, *Legal Insanity: Explorations in Psychiatry, Law, & Ethics*. New York: Springer (in press).

Moreno, Jonathan D., "Neuroethics: An Agenda for Neuroscience and Society." *Nature Reviews Neuroscience* 4(2003): 149–53.

Moriarty, Jane C., "Flickering Admissibility: Neuroimaging Evidence in the US Courts." *Behavioral Sciences and the Law* 26(2008): 29–49.

Moriarty, Jane C., Daniel D. Langleben, and James M. Provenzale, "Brain Trauma, Pet Scans and Forensic Complexity." *Behavioral Sciences and the Law* 31(2013): 702–20.

Morse, Stephen J., and Adina L. Roskies, *A Primer on Criminal Law and Neuroscience*. New York: Oxford University Press, 2013.

Müller, Sabine, and Henrik Walter, "Reviewing Autonomy: Implications of the Neurosciences and the Free Will Debate for the Principle of Respect for the Patient's Autonomy." *Cambridge Quarterly of Healthcare Ethics* 19(2010): 205–17.

Nadelhoffer, Thomas, et al., "Neuroprediction, Violence, and the Law: Setting the Stage." *Neuroethics* 5(2012): 67–99.

Packer, Ira K., *Evaluation of Criminal Responsibility*. Oxford: Oxford University Press, 2009.

Pardo, Michael S., and Dennis Patterson, *Minds, Brains, and Law: The Conceptual Foundations of Law and Neuroscience*. New York: Oxford University Press, 2013.

Penney, Steven, "Impulse Control and Criminal Responsibility: Lessons from Neuroscience." *International Journal of Law and Psychiatry* 35(2012): 99–103.

Pereira, Erlick A., Alexander L. Green, Dipankar Nandi, and Tipu Z. Aziz, "Deep Brain Stimulation: Indications and Evidence." *Expert Review of Medical Devices* 4(2007): 591–603.

Puranik, Deepti A., S. K. Joseph, B.B. Daundkar, and M.V. Garad, "Brain Signature Profiling in India. Its Status as an Aid in Investigation and as Corroborative Evidence—As Seen from Judgments." *Proceedings of XX All India Forensic Science Conference* (2009): 815–22.

Radder, Johannes A., and Gerben Meynen, "Does the Brain 'Initiate' Freely Willed Processes? A Philosophy of Science Critique of Libet-Type Experiments and their Interpretation." *Theory and Psychology* 23(2013): 3–21.

Relkin, Norman, et al., "Impulsive Homicide Associated with an Arachnoid Cyst and Unilateral Frontotemporal Cerebral Dysfunction." *Seminars in Clinical Neuropsychiatry*(1996): 172–83.

Roskies, Adina L., "Brain Imaging Techniques." In *A Primer on Criminal Law and Neuroscience*, edited by Stephen J. Morse and Adina L. Roskies (New York: Oxford University Press, 2013), 37–74.

Rumbold, John, Ian Morrison, and Renata Riha, "Calls for an International Consensus on Sleep-Related Violence and Sexual Behavior in Sleep are Premature." *Journal of Clinical Sleep Medicine* 10(2014): 1253.

Salmanowitz, Natalie, "The Case for Pain Neuroimaging in the Courtroom: Lessons from Deception Detection." *Journal of Law and the Biosciences*, in press.

Schleim, Stephan, "Brains in Context in the Neurolaw Debate: The Examples of Free Will and 'Dangerous' Brains." *International Journal of Law and Psychiatry* 35(2012): 104–11.

Silva, J. Arturo, "The Relevance of Neuroscience to Forensic Psychiatry." *Journal of the American Academy of Psychiatry and Law* 35(2007): 6–9.

Silva, J. Arturo, "Forensic Psychiatry, Neuroscience, and the Law." *Journal of the American Academy of Psychiatry and Law* 37(2009): 489–502.

Simon, Rita J., and Heather Ahn-Redding, *The Insanity Defense, the World Over.* Lanham, MD: Lexington Books, 2006.

Sinnott-Armstrong, Walter, Adina Roskies, Teneille Brown, and Emily Murphy, "Brain Images as Legal Evidence." *Episteme* 5(2008): 359–73.

Soon, Chun S., Marcel Brass, Hans-Jochen Heinze, and John-Dylan Haynes, "Unconscious Determinants of Free Decisions in the Human Brain." *Nature Neuroscience* 11(2008): 543–45.

Spence, Sean, "Free Will in the Light of Neuropsychiatry." *Philosophy, Psychiatry, and Psychology* 3(1996): 75–90.

Steinberg, Laurence, "The Influence of Neuroscience on US Supreme Court Decisions about Adolescents' Criminal Culpability." *Nature Reviews Neuroscience* 14(2013): 513–18.

Van der Gronde, Toon, et al., "Neurobiological Correlates in Forensic Assessment: A Systematic Review." *PLoS ONE* 9(2014): e110672.

Wegner, Daniel M., *The Illusion of Conscious Will*. Cambridge, MA: MIT Press, 2002.
Widdershoven, Guy A.M., Gerben Meynen, and Damiaan Denys, "Autonomy in Predictive Brain Implants: The Importance of Embodiment and Dialogue." *AJOB Neuroscience* 6(2015): 16–18.

PART 3

Philosophy and the Law

PART I

CHAPTER SEVEN

The Mistaken Quest for a Control Test: For a Rationality Standard of Sanity

Paul Litton

> The rulings of the court raise some questions of no less difficulty than of interest; for, as observed by a distinguished American judge, "of all medico-legal questions, those connected with insanity are the most difficult and perplexing."[1]

An insanity standard is supposed to capture the proper relationship between mental illness and criminal responsibility. Many share the intuition that severe mental illness should eliminate legal accountability, but we must ask why in order to formulate a standard that determines the conditions under which mental illness should, in fact, exempt an individual from punishment. The law does not—and should not—provide an excuse for anyone with a diagnosable mental illness at the time of crime. Mental illnesses are defined for therapeutic, not legal, purposes. As described by the most recent Diagnostic and Statistical Manual (DSM) published by the American Psychiatric Association, a mental disorder "is a syndrome characterized by clinically significant disturbance in an individual's cognition, emotion regulation, or behavior that reflects a dysfunction in the psychological, biological, or developmental processes underlying mental functioning."[2] Psychiatrists and other mental health professionals aim to help persons with such disturbances, as they "are usually associated with significant distress or disability in social, occupational, or other important activities."[3] The criminal law, on the other hand, does not seek to relieve or reduce the distress that an individual experiences from a mental disturbance. An individual can surely have some psychological problem, causing significant distress and interference to his well-being, yet retain the ability to refrain from engaging in criminal conduct. Having a diagnosable mental disease or disorder does not excuse *per se*. But, then, why does mental illness ever excuse, and under what conditions does it excuse?

These questions underlie debates that have taken place in courts and legislatures concerning the best definition of "insanity." The standard most widely found in American jurisdictions, in one form or another, was formulated in 1843 by the House of Lords in the famous M'Naghten case. The M'Naghten Rule announces a purely *cognitive* test: it focuses solely on the beliefs and reasoning of the accused. According to the rule, the jury should acquit if, at the time of the crime, "the party accused was labouring under such a defect of reason, from disease of the mind, as not to know the nature and quality of the act he was doing, or as not to know that what he was doing was wrong."[4] To use a common illustration, a person who is squeezing someone's neck but believes, due to mental illness, that he is squeezing a lemon is insane under M'Naghten because he does not know the nature of his act. However, cases in which the defendant had such an extreme unawareness of the nature of his act are rare and, moreover, do not represent the importance of the insanity defense. In many jurisdictions—though not all—our neck-squeezing defendant would have a right to put on mental health evidence to undermine the state's effort to prove the *mens rea* (mental state), such as purpose or knowledge, of a serious crime. If a person believes he is squeezing a lemon, he is not purposely or knowingly trying to kill to anyone. The more important illustration of insanity under M'Naghten is the person who does not know certain morally relevant facts, entailing that she does not know the moral nature of her action or that it is wrong. Consider Andrea Yates, who, due to her psychosis, believed that killing her children was necessary to save them from perishing in hell for eternity. In a thin sense, she knew the nature of her act: she knew she was drowning them. But she did not know the morally relevant features of her conduct due to her psychosis.[5] Her beliefs were so out of touch with reality that she could not reason properly about what she was doing.

One criticism of the M'Naghten Rule targets its purely cognitive focus. That is, it provides no excuse for an individual who knows the nature and wrongfulness of her act but who nevertheless cannot control herself. According to such criticism, the law should exempt from punishment an individual who, because of mental disease, suffers from a serious *volitional* defect (or what the law also calls a *control* defect). On this view, even if a drug addict knows she is stealing to feed her addiction and knows her theft is wrong, the offender should have the chance to argue that she lacked sufficient control over her actions to be held criminally responsible. A small number of states, persuaded by the criticism, supplements the M'Naghten Rule with an older standard of criminal responsibility,[6] often referred to as an "irresistible impulse test."[7] For example, New Mexico law maintains that "if, by reason of disease of the mind, [a] defendant has been deprived of or lost the power of his will which enable him to prevent himself from doing the act, then he cannot be found guilty."[8]

A second criticism of M'Naghten is reflected in the American Law Institute's suggested standard, as published in its Model Penal Code. The criticism of M'Naghten is that it deems an offender sane unless the offender did not *know* the nature or wrongfulness of his act. That is, a "person must *wholly* lack cognition" in order to be insane under M'Naghten.[9] To grasp the force of the criticism, consider a child. A six-year-old, for example, might "know" that punching someone is "wrong," and, insofar as he intentionally hits his sister, he knows the nature of his act. However, though we treat him *as if* he is a responsible agent to socialize him, six-year-olds do not have the psychological and reasoning capacities required to be held responsible for their wrongdoing. Now, six-year-olds are not governed by the criminal law, but an analogy is the important message: imagine an adult who, because of mental disorder, had psychological and reasoning capacities on par with that of an average six-year-old. Insofar as the M'Naghten Rules would deem that person responsible for wrongdoing, M'Naghten is too narrow according to this criticism.

The Model Penal Code's suggested standard responds to both criticisms. According to it, a mentally ill person is not criminally responsible at the time of his crime if he lacked substantial capacity either to appreciate the wrongfulness[10] of his conduct or to conform his conduct to the law.[11] An individual who knows his action is wrong in a very thin sense—say, in the way a six-year-old knows that punching is called "wrong"—should not be held responsible if he could not *appreciate* the criminal nature (or wrongfulness) of his action. Moreover, instead of requiring a total lack of appreciation, the Model Penal Code standard requires the offender show a lack of *substantial capacity* to appreciate. Finally, as evident, the Model Penal Code includes a volitional or control prong in providing an excuse for someone who lacked substantial capacity to "conform his conduct" to law, despite knowing what he was doing. Approximately one quarter or jurisdictions in the United States have some version of the Model Penal Code standard.[12]

Cognitive standards, such as the M'Naghten Rule and first half of the Model Penal Code test, are best understood as asserting rationality as the criterion of criminal responsibility. An insane individual suffers from a "defect of reason." His distorted beliefs about the nature and propriety of his actions undermine his responsibility precisely because they demonstrate his inability to reason practically and intelligibly about what he is doing. One reason a rationality criterion for responsibility makes sense is apparent when we think about children and their eventual ascent to responsible agency. Five-year-olds clearly make choices and know that some actions are deemed wrong, but those facts do not qualify them as morally accountable agents. Twelve-year-olds are to some degree morally responsible for their conduct, but are not yet fully accountable agents. What changes between the ages of 5, 12, and eventually adulthood, such that it is fair to hold adults accountable for wrongdoing? Do mentally healthy humans gradually gain a kind of free will that permits them to step outside the causal forces of the universe? Do we at some point gain the capacity to cause our actions without being caused by any prior events? No; rather, our capacity for reasoned judgment develops. Children gain a better understanding of the world—a better understanding of the nature and effects of their actions—as they age, and their abilities to evaluate their conduct and act on the basis of their reasoned judgment progress.

Therefore, the law is right to excuse persons who, due to mental illness, are thoroughly irrational, lacking adequate capacity for practical reasoning. A clear connection exists between severe mental illness and insanity: they involve irrationality. The question taking center stage in this chapter, however, regards control or volitional prongs of insanity tests. Is there such a connection between mental illness and volitional defects such that it makes sense for the law to excuse agents whose mental illness causes a volitional defect? Should the law excuse not only for cognitive or rationality defects, but also for a defect of will—a "control" problem?

In discussing this question, this chapter focuses on the work of two leading theorists of criminal responsibility, Stephen Morse and Michael Corrado, who urge opposing views. Morse has famously argued in favor of a rationality criterion for sanity. He argues both that the law should recognize an excuse based on irrationality and that the insanity defense should include *only* a rationality criterion. On his view, the law's insanity standard should *not* include a volitional or control prong. If an individual suffers such overwhelming and persistent desires such that he is unable to bring reasons to bear on his decisions, then he is a candidate for excuse; however, the grounds for excuse would be irrationality, not defect of will. Conceptually, on Morse's view, we do not have a plausible account of what it means, in terms of psychological processes, to say that someone lacks volitional control over her conduct though simultaneously retaining the capacity for rationality. A kleptomaniac or pedophile might be subject to very strong urges or might experience great anxiety due to his intense desires, but what does it mean to say that he might lack volitional control over his conduct should he act to satisfy his abnormal urges? After all, a kleptomaniac acts intentionally when he steals. If we believed that a person with kleptomania or some impulse disorder did not act intentionally, then we would have no reason to discuss the affirmative defense of insanity; no intentional action means no *actus reus* (no crime at all). Perhaps the best way to understand a volitional claim, such as, "I could not resist the urge," is to analogize it to a duress claim where the threat is due to an abnormally strong internal desire instead of an external gunman. Morse rejects this basis for a volitional excuse, arguing that the harm threatened by a frustrated desire, regardless of strength, is not analogous to the harms (death and seriously bodily harm) associated with the external threats that provide grounds for a successful duress defense.[13]

Corrado, among others, rejects Morse's attacks on a volitional insanity standard. Corrado argues that there are persons, such as individuals suffering from serious addiction, who understand their actions and can properly reason about what they should do, but who nevertheless cannot control themselves. He emphasizes the shared intuition that some people are subject to cravings so strong that we should excuse them because they have such extreme difficulty avoiding their anti-social conduct. Moreover, Corrado goes beyond arguing that a volitional prong is necessary; he takes it to be sufficient. As Morse argues that a rationality prong is all that is necessary for a just insanity law, Corrado intriguingly argues that an insanity standards need only include a volitional test. Corrado argues that "all of the problems that incline us to say that a person is legally insane are problems of volition of control."[14] At the very least, given the drawbacks of other standards, Corrado asks that we "give this version of the test a hearing" and he proceeds to make the case.[15]

One goal of this chapter is to continue that hearing of Corrado's intriguing position for a purely volitional insanity standard and to offer a rebuttal. I argue that Corrado's argument rests on a conflation of different senses of the term "control." Once we clarify the kind of "control" entailed by *control* prongs, we see that insanity claims can rest on rationality deficits that do not involve volitional impairments. A second goal of this chapter is argue against the inclusion of a volitional prong. Morse presents multiple arguments—conceptual, moral, and practical ones—against volitional prongs. I argue that the moral and practical considerations speak decisively against volitional or control tests.

1 Is a Volitional Test of Insanity Morally Sufficient?

Corrado's rejection of the rationality view and defense of a purely control standard entails two distinct conclusions: (a) Insanity standards should include a volitional prong, permitting defendants to argue that they lacked volitional control over their criminal actions; and (b) an insanity standards need only include a volitional test. We will start examining the latter. If his argument in support of a purely volitional test fails, it could still be the case that a volitional prong is necessary; and so we will turn second to that issue.

1.1 Corrado's Argument

Corrado's basic position is that we excuse a person for wrongdoing when it was the case that she *could not have done otherwise* or, in other words, she *could not have avoided* her blameworthy conduct. A person who steals to feed a strong drug addiction or to relieve overwhelming anxiety associated with kleptomania might know what he is doing, know that his actions are wrong, but nonetheless be unable to avoid the blameworthy choice. On Corrado's view, common experience tells us that "some human beings can avoid behaving in certain ways and others cannot."[16] He can find support for this empirical claim—that "we" believe volitional defects exist—in multiple laws. For example, the U.S. Supreme Court has held that involuntary commitment under sexually violent predator statutes is unconstitutional "without proof of serious difficulty in controlling behavior."[17] In addition, some statutes prescribing an involuntary intoxication defense to criminal charges track the Model Penal Code's insanity standard, containing a volitional prong in addition to a cognitive one.[18] Using similar language, some states also provide for a "guilty but mentally ill" (GBMI) verdict based on a control defect. For example, while Pennsylvania, Alaska, and South Carolina have purely cognitive insanity standards, they permit a GBMI verdict upon proof the defendant had a diminished capacity to conform his conduct to the law.[19]

The reason we need *only* a volitional test, according to Corrado, is that cognitive and rationality defects undermine responsibility only when a control defect is present. In his words, "all exculpatory mental defects are, in the end, defects of control or defects of volition."[20] Imagine a person who commits a homicide because he hears voices commanding him to kill. He has no control over whether he hears that voice. Corrado rightfully argues that, in order to assess his responsibility status, we must assess whether the individual could "avoid making the inferences he [made] to the existence of a person who deserves some sort of obedience."[21] In other words, we must assess whether he had the capacity to reason properly about the fact that he was hearing voices.

But if we have to assess the reasoning capacities of the agent, why does Corrado believe that we really have to determine whether our offender suffered a defect of control or volition? Corrado stresses that we all are subject to mistakes of perception and reasoning. We mistake "traffic sounds for music; . . . an animal sound for an infant crying."[22] We wrongfully conclude that we would be safer driving on the highway than flying in a plane, despite the data. We should be excused only when we *could not* reach the right conclusion. Criminals are often irrational by discounting the disvalue of punishment, but we hold them responsible as long as they *could* reach the rational conclusion. Likewise, our offender hearing voices should be held responsible, despite the auditory hallucination, as long as he *could* reach the right conclusions about what he should do. Corrado's argument is then based on the following claim: the inability to reach the right conclusion "is a defect of reasoning, to be sure, but it is a defect of reasoning based upon a defect of control."[23] He equates "could not correct her reasoning" and "could not reason properly" with a defect of control; the agent could not *control* her reasoning. Thus, on his view, if we excuse an individual for a reasoning defect, it is because we conclude that the person had a control defect.

In trying to distill cognitive and rationality standards into volitional tests, Corrado also suggests that the main criticism of volitional prongs is undermined. A classic complaint about the "irresistible impulse" or other volitional test is that it is impossible to tell the difference between an irresistible impulse and an impulse that was not resisted but could have been. If rationality standards require an inquiry into whether an agent had a volitional defect, then rationality standards are subject to the very same criticism.[24]

It is important to see what Corrado takes to be the connection between mental illness and insanity. For Corrado, the significance of mental illness for moral and criminal responsibility is not any connection between mental illness and irrationality per se, but rather is found in the relationship between mental illness, volitional control, and the capacity to do otherwise. Because of the clear connection between the concepts of control and responsibility, Corrado's arguments have intuitive appeal.

However, the appeal is illusory because it depends on a conflation of different senses of "control" as it is used in law and ordinary language. To see the conflation clearly, let us briefly catalogue some, though probably not all, distinct senses of "control."

1.2 Different Senses of "Control"

When we ask whether someone was in control of her behavior, we might be asking one of numerous questions. The word "control" and the phrase "self-control" have different senses and meanings in ordinary language, and we see those different senses and meanings appear in legal discussions. It is helpful to distinguish among these different senses and meanings in order to see clearly what sense of "control" is under discussion as we assess a control standard of insanity.

First, we might ordinarily describe someone as in control of her behavior if we view her as acting voluntarily, where "acting voluntarily" is defined in line with the criminal law's *actus reus* requirement, which permits criminal punishment only for voluntary actions. As with "control," the word "voluntary" and its related forms have multiple senses and meanings. A person whose leg kicks another by reflex has not acted voluntarily in that she has not acted at all; her leg moved but not due to any decision or by any other act of will. At the same time, we might describe a confession procured under intense police pressure as involuntary even though the suspect's statements were the consequence of an act of will; the suspect did decide to confess, though under coercive threats. In the "*actus reus*" sense of "voluntary," the suspect's confession was, in fact, voluntary. However, if we think the conditions under which the suspect confessed were unfair, we would describe the confession as involuntary, even though it was voluntary in the *actus reus* sense. The *actus reus* sense of "voluntary" correlates with the first sense of "control" highlighted here. The *actus reus* principle requires a "willed bodily movement."[25] Insofar as an agent wills her bodily movements, we could say she is *in control* of her movements in the way a tree, swaying in the wind, is not.

A second sense of "control" is more evaluative in nature. In everyday conversation we might describe a very irresponsible and reckless person as lacking control. A teenager who stays out all night, ignores his schoolwork, and engages in dangerous behavior is, in this second sense, lacking control, even though we assume he wills his bodily movements and does exactly what he wants to do. Here, when we say a person lacks control, we are claiming that there is a strong tension between what the agent does and how he *should* behave from our point of view, i.e., a point of view external to the agent.

A third sense of control is similar in that it involves a tension between an agent's conduct and how he should behave; however, here, how the person "should behave" is based on the agent's own values or long-term goals. To illustrate, imagine that I refrain from eating a piece of chocolate cake, despite my urge, because I value my health and want to lose weight. I have exercised control in the sense that I have resisted an urge for the sake of a value or long-term goal. This third sense of control is different from the second in that it is irrelevant whether I have good reason, from an external point of view, to lose weight; what matters is whether I think I have good reason to refrain from dessert. Being in control in this sense is equivalent to exercising willpower or displaying strength of will, understood to involve the ability to "delay immediate satisfaction for the sake of future consequences."[26]

A fourth sense of control refers to the capacities required to be fairly held responsible for conduct or other phenomena (such as beliefs or emotions). Agents who may be fairly held morally and criminally responsible have some sort of control over their conduct. But what kind of control is required? A natural response is that free will is synonymous with the kind of control required for responsibility. Of course, philosophers disagree on whether responsibility-conferring control requires free will and on the nature of free will. According to some theorists, responsibility-conferring control requires the capacity to do otherwise or to choose among alternative possibilities. Furthermore, on some of these accounts, causal determinism—the thesis that every event (including every human action) is causally necessitated by prior states of affair in conjunction with the physical laws of nature—is *incompatible* with the existence of responsibility-conferring control. As the argument goes, if every event, including every human act and choice, is causally determined by prior states of the world and the laws of nature, then there are no proverbial forks in the road. It might seem to me as if I could do otherwise and am choosing among real alternatives, but the truth is that I could never perform any actions other than the ones I actually do. Thus, on these *incompatibilist* views, the truth of determinism would preclude the possibility of responsibility-conferring control.

On opposing accounts, responsibility-conferring control *is* compatible with the truth of causal determinism. Differences among such theories are not crucial here. But to illustrate, some compatibilist theorists argue that responsibility-conferring control is equivalent to the capacity to reason practically. On this view, the difference between responsible agents and the insane is that the former have adequate capacity for practical rationality. Insane persons are not responsible for their conduct because they lack sufficient reasoning powers, not because they lack the kind of metaphysical free will that is incompatible with determinism. The reason it is unfair to hold a five-year-old responsible but fair to hold a mentally normal 20-something responsible is not because the latter stepped outside the causal forces of the universe at some point while ageing. Rather, as children mature, they develop the experience and psychological powers required to reason intelligibly about their conduct.

Relatedly, we might say that an agent who has the general reasoning capacities required for responsibility nevertheless lacks sufficient control over his conduct on a specific occasion. For example, an agent claiming duress might have maintained the capacity to reason practically when under threat, yet we might say that she lacked control over her conduct if the threat was sufficiently serious. Notice that this agent controlled her conduct in multiple senses: she controlled her conduct in the (first) sense in that she willed her bodily movements, and she also possessed the rational capacities associated with the kind of control required for the status as an agent who may generally be held accountable. But we might also describe her as not really being in control when, after all, someone else was coercing her.

Moreover, a compatibilist—even one who supports the capacity for practical reasoning as the general capacity required for responsibility—might agree that an agent is responsible for a particular act only if that agent could have done otherwise on that occasion. Compatibilists and incompatiblists disagree on the meaning of "could have done otherwise" insofar as it is a criterion of responsibility. The incompatibilist is concerned with whether an agent could have done otherwise, holding fixed all facts about the world as they actually existed leading up to the agent's choice. If the facts of the world, including its laws of nature, causally determine an agent to choose and act as she did, then it matters not that the agent made a choice; what she chose and how she acted was causally determined by facts outside her control, and, as such, she is responsible for neither her choice nor action. The compatibilist, on the other hand, denies that the incompatibilist interpretation of "could have done otherwise" is required for fair ascriptions and judgements of responsibility. Different compatibilists have provided slightly different translations of the requirement. But to provide an example, a compatibilist could translate "could have done otherwise" as "would have done otherwise if certain facts had been true."[27] In other words, on one compatibilist view, we determine whether an agent could have done otherwise by contemplating counterfactual situations that are closely similar, but importantly different, from the actual circumstances in which the agent chose to do wrong. For example, to assess whether a thief *could* have done otherwise, we might ask whether he *would* have stolen the item in a hypothetical world exactly like the real one except for one fact: a police officer was proverbially at his elbow, threatening arrest.[28] If he would have stolen despite the officer's presence, then we would conclude that he could not have done otherwise in the actual world, thus lacking the kind of control required for moral responsibility on this particular occasion. Later, we will elaborate on this counterfactual approach to determining an agent's ability to do otherwise. At present, it is just important to note that in discussing the ability to do otherwise, we are discussing an ability that is associated with one particular sense of the term "control," the kind required for fair judgments of responsibility.

Observe that the same agent can be in control in one sense of control while lacking it in a different sense. Consider an individual who is in control of her actions in the first sense discussed, the *actus reus* sense. Our agent controls her actions in that she wills her bodily movements. But now stipulate that both causal determinism and incompatibilism are true: in that circumstance, while the agent is in control in the *actus reus* sense, she lacks the kind of control required for moral responsibility. For a different example, imagine a person who is weak-willed, giving in to her nicotine desire despite her goal to stop smoking. This person lacks control in the third sense discussed—she lacks self-control—yet might very well have the capacities required for moral responsibility (that is, she has control over her conduct in the fourth sense), whether those capacities are defined in incompatibilist or compatibilist terms. The different senses of control are quite distinct.

1.3 The Sense of "Control" Implicated by Control Prongs

What sense of "control" is entailed by a control or volitional prong to an insanity standard? To start, control prongs clearly do not involve the first sense of "control" discussed, relating to the voluntary act (*actus reus*) requirement. Insanity is an affirmative defense and, as such, must possibly apply where a defendant concedes that the state can prove its *prima facie* case, including an *actus reus*. Proponents of a volitional prong agree that addicts and persons subject to other compulsive disorders control their conduct in the sense that they do act voluntarily in the *actus reus* sense of "voluntarily."[29]

The second sense of "control," according to which we describe reckless and imprudent persons as lacking control, is also obviously inapt. For persons who claim insanity under a volitional prong, a tension exists between their conduct and how they should have behaved from an external point of view. Nevertheless, in this sense, we typically use the phrase "lacking control" as a moral *criticism,* not a moral excuse. As such, it is not the sense of "control" involved in insanity law.

To endorse a volitional prong is to support a criterion of responsibility-conferring control (the fourth sense). However, an offender claiming insanity for a volitional defect claims that she is not responsible on grounds that she lacked control in the third sense of control. In other words, a volitional prong implies that an agent lacks the requisite control for responsibility (the fourth sense of control) if she lacks capacity to exercise self-control (the third sense of control). A larceny defendant pleading insanity on the grounds of kleptomania essentially claims that she did not *really* want to steal but couldn't exercise self-control due to an overwhelming urge that she does not endorse. Indeed, courts use the language of self-control and willpower in discussing volitional tests. In one recent case, the defendant, arguing insanity under a volitional prong, admitted that he intentionally strangled his victim but claimed he "could not stop himself."[30] The appellate court concluded that the "jury reasonably could have found . . . that [his] emotional disturbance resulted in a loss of *self-control.*"[31] Indeed, a volitional prong would be better described as "self-control prong" instead of an "irresistible impulse test." As one Michigan court has observed, a volitional criterion encompasses "not only a sudden overpowering, irresistible impulse but any situation or condition in which the power, *'the will power' to resist*, is insufficient to restrain commission of the wrongful act."[32]

Recall that this sense of "control" (or "self-control") involves the ability to resist an immediate desire for the sake of one's values or long-term goals. For a defendant to claim an incapacity for self-control is essentially to assert that, according to his better judgment, he did not *truly* want to commit the crime, but did so because of an urge that trumped his willpower. For a claim to be plausible, the defendant must have experienced some tension or struggle between the allegedly overwhelming desire that motivated his crime on the one hand, and his better judgment on the other. Without any such tension—if the offender acted exactly as he wanted in light of his values or long-term goals—then no reason exists to assert he experienced a defect of will.

1.4 Cognitive Impairments Can Excuse without Volitional Defect

We are now in a position to see the flaw in Corrado's argument that all insanity pleas boil down to a claim of volitional incapacity. Consider Eric

Clark, who shot a police officer. According to some witnesses, Clark, who suffered from paranoid schizophrenia, believed that space aliens populating Arizona were trying to kill him. He believed that some of these aliens were impersonating government agents, such as police officers. His lawyers argued that Clark was insane under Arizona's standard, which required a showing that Clark did not know that his act was wrong. In other words, Arizona's standard did not contain a volitional prong; it contained the one prong of the *M'Naghten* standard. Let us stipulate that Clark's claims were true: assume he truly did believe the officer was a dangerous alien. It is perfectly conceivable to conclude that he was, in fact, insane under Arizona's standard, whether the actual Eric Clark was or was not insane. (The court, hearing the case after Clark waived his right to a jury, rejected Clark's insanity claim.) Assuming Clark's perceptions were so out of touch with reality, it is reasonable to conclude that he was too irrational—that he could not reason properly about his actions—for us fairly to hold him criminally responsible.

On Corrado's view, what would be the justification for excuse? His argument is that we should excuse if Clark could not resist acting on his distorted beliefs, and to say that he could not resist acting on his distorted beliefs is basically to assert a volitional control problem. But a further stipulation will reveal the flaw in Corrado's argument. Assume that Clark experienced no struggle between his desire to shoot someone he believed to be an invading alien and any of his values or long-term goals. If no such tension or struggle existed, then Clark did not experience a control defect in the sense of "control" implicit in volitional standards. To be sure, if we find reason to excuse, it is because we think Clark lacked control in some sense, but not in the volitional prong sense. We would think Clark lacked control in the fourth, most general sense: he lacked the general capacities required to hold him responsible fairly. Again, perhaps that is because our practices reflect compatibilist criteria of responsibility, such as the capacity for practical rationality, and we find that Clark lacked that capacity. Alternatively, perhaps we find that Clark could not have acted otherwise at the time of the crime. But concluding that Clark could not have acted otherwise at the time of the crime is *not* the same as concluding that he lacked volitional control. Maybe he lacked the capacity to do otherwise precisely because he was so irrational that he could not properly reason about what he was doing. We need not assert any volitional incapacity to conclude that he could not have avoided doing what he did. If there was no struggle between (1) his desire to kill and (2) his judgment on what he had most reason to do, then no basis exists for concluding he suffered from a volitional defect. Thus, an individual can be insane under a rationality cognitive standard without exhibiting signs of a self-control problem.

Moreover, an individual can actually be insane under *M'Naghten* or other cognitive criterion despite exercising willpower or self-control perfectly well. Consider Andrea Yates, who drowned her children while suffering from psychosis. Yates reported that she believed she had an obligation to kill her children because they would "perish in the fires of hell" if she did not.[33] Whether true or not, let us stipulate that Yates had a very strong desire not to kill her children because she loved them; let us stipulate that she did experience tension between her desire *not* to kill her children and her psychotic belief that the morally best action was to kill them. Under our stipulation, she had a very strong desire to keep them alive, but she also believed she had most reason to do what was, on the whole, best for them. If she fought a desire for them to remain alive in order to do what she saw most reason to do, then she in fact exercised self-control. Yates, on this story, had absolutely no volitional problem at all. Her will perfectly conformed to what she thought was the best action. Needless to say, it is still reasonable to conclude that we should not hold her criminally responsible under this description of the facts, given that she lacked capacity to grasp that her actions were, in fact, wrong. We could still excuse her because she lacked control in the fourth sense described here: namely, she lacked one of the general capacities required for fair ascriptions or judgements of responsibility. Though she controlled her actions in the third sense (she did exercise volitional control), she lacked control over her actions in the sense that she was irrational; she could not reason properly about what she was doing.

The Yates case, coupled with our stipulated facts, undermines Corrado's claim that cognitive defects should excuse only when a person suffered from a volitional defect. Nevertheless, one might want to maintain the more general theoretical point that the reason we excuse anyone for insanity is that we conclude the person could not have done otherwise or, in other words, could not have conformed his behavior to the law's demands. Corrado could still urge the following alternatives: (1) defend the moral necessity of a volitional prong even if a volitional test is not morally sufficient (that is, defend an insanity standard that includes volitional and cognitive prongs), or (2) defend a unitary insanity test but maintain that either a cognitive or volitional defect could excuse under that standard. Corrado offers the following unitary standard: "It is an affirmative defense that, at the time of the commission of the act, the defendant, as a result of a severe mental disease, was *unable to conform his behavior to the law*."[34] He could still defend this proposal, permitting cognitive and volitional defects to explain why an individual could not have done otherwise and, thus, could not have conformed his behavior to the law.

Let us put aside the more theoretical debate as to whether "could have done otherwise" is, in fact, a criterion of responsibility.[35] Other relevant questions raised by this rejoinder are the following. First, is it ever the case than an individual could not have done otherwise due to a volitional incapacity? Second, even if so, does the law have reason to reject a volitional prong or a unitary standard that would permit volitional excuses, instead opting for a purely cognitive test of insanity? Let us now turn to those two questions in discussing Corrado's argument for the moral necessity of a volitional prong.

2 Insanity Standards Should Not Include Volitional Tests

2.1 Corrado's Argument to Include a Volitional Prong

Corrado argues that if we get clear on what rationality and irrationality involve, we see that we are inclined to excuse some persons with mental illness who have no rationality defect; these are cases in which the agent has a volitional defect. On his view, a rational agent is in touch with reality and is able to draw proper inferences and conclusions from the facts he perceives. An individual is irrational, then, if it "would require unusual measures or an unreasonable amount of evidence to cause him to correct his beliefs and inference patterns."[36] An irrational agent is delusional about empirical facts, almost completely impervious to evidence, or cannot draw reasonable inferences about facts given his perceptions. It is important to note that Corrado is discussing only an agent's beliefs about empirical facts, not beliefs about moral facts. Thus, on Corrado's definition of irrationality, there is no reason to deem a neo-Nazi as irrational just because his views about the moral status of some groups are resistant to arguments and evidence. For responsibility purposes, the fact that no good reason exists to hold neo-Nazi views does not render the neo-Nazi irrational. Corrado argues that the essence of irrationality, for responsibility purposes, is being out of touch with empirical reality or being unable to draw reasonable inferences from one's perceptions.

With this account of irrationality in hand, Corrado presents a challenge:

> Can all the cases in which we say that someone was not responsible for what he did be made to satisfy this definition [of irrationality]? . . . I think we must concede that there are cases that do not satisfy this definition, and yet in which we are inclined to hold actors less responsible for what they do, or in which we are inclined to deny legal responsibility altogether.[37]

Corrado offers the addict as an example. He claims (1) the addict is not only rational, but is "typically hyper rational, at least when it comes to the subject matter of his addiction,"[38] and (2) we are "inclined to hold [the addict] less responsible . . . or . . . to deny legal responsibility altogether" because the addict has a volitional impairment. To support his claim that the addict is rational at the time he feeds his addiction, Corrado writes,

> It does not makes sense . . . that the addict desires the benefits of a drug-free life *more* than he desires the drug at the time when he takes it, but simply cannot make the inference from his greater desire to the proper action. That *would* be an example of irrationality.[39]

Accordingly, Corrado concludes that the addict is rational because "at the time of taking the drug, the addict desires the drug more than anything else."[40]

The addict should be excused, Corrado argues, because his desire for the drug would have led to his action "in any but the most exceptional circumstances."[41] In other words, to decide whether the addict is responsible for his conduct, we should ask whether he could have done otherwise or could he have avoided his action. To answer that inquiry, we imagine hypothetical situations that are very close to, yet importantly different from, the actual situation in which the agent acted. We construct counterfactuals in ways that can affect the agent's reasons for action, and we ask whether the agent would identify and act on a reason in the hypothetical world. Typically, for example, in assessing whether an offender could have avoided his blameworthy action, we might ask whether he would have committed the crime in a hypothetical world in which the facts were the same except that a police officer was standing at his elbow. Would he be able to recognize the self-interested reason not to commit the crime in that counterfactual, and would he have chosen and acted in accordance with that reason? If the agent would have committed the offense even in that situation, then we would be inclined to conclude that he really could not have done otherwise in the real scenario. Either he could not recognize the reason not to the commit the crime with the officer present or, perhaps, he nonetheless would have chosen to commit the crime anyway.

On Corrado's view, a person could still be non-responsible due to a volitional impairment even if there is one counterfactual world in which the person would have recognized a reason to avoid the drug and did avoid consuming it. For example, imagine that the *only* circumstance in which a person would have refrained were one in which he would definitely and immediately suffer excruciating torture should he ingest the drug.

Stipulate that the person would still have ingested it even if there were 95 percent chance that he would immediately lose every meaningful relationship in his life. If the person were really willing to take on that sort of grave risk, the argument goes, we should conclude that it was so exceedingly difficult for the person resist his urge for the drug that we should grant an excuse.

2.2 The Fuzzy Line between Volitional and Rationality Impairments

Corrado seems absolutely correct in claiming that there are some persons whose cravings make it so difficult for them to avoid satisfying them that we should opt for more caring and forgiving attitudes instead of punitive ones. In fact, even if an individual is morally responsible for succumbing to vice, that fact does not imply that we should respond with punishment, condemnation, or otherwise judgmental reactive emotions.

However, insofar as Corrado's argument aims to support a volitional prong for legal insanity, it has at least two problems. The first problem is related to his description of the addict as rational, perhaps hyper-rational, because at the moment he takes the drug he is satisfying his strongest desire. As described, the addict experienced no tension or struggle between his urge for the drug and his better judgment on what he has most reason to do in light of his values or long-term desires. If no tension exists, then it is implausible to claim the addict suffered from a volitional defect when ingesting the drug. In Harry Frankfurt's terms, if the addict's will was exactly what he wanted it to be—or, rather, his will did not conflict with what he wanted it to be—then it is implausible to find a volitional impairment.[42] The idea of a volitional excuse presumes a self-control problem, and no inner tension or struggle means no self-control issue.

On the other hand, if a tension *did* exist between the addict's urge for the drug and his better judgment on what he had most reason to do, then we must question Corrado's assertion that the addict is rational, given that he fails to act in accordance with his own judgment on what he should do. A person can certainly judge that he has most reason, on the whole, to end his addiction yet, at particular moments, loses sight of that reasoned judgment, focusing too intently on the immediate benefits of feeding it. All of us are subject to some discounting of future rewards, but psychological studies have found higher rates of discounting among drug dependents.[43] Other studies support the hypothesis that memory problems in addicts cause higher discount rates in that "discounting of past and future rewards have been found to be qualitatively and quantitatively comparable."[44] Another study found that impulsive individuals (not specifically persons addicted to drugs) "overestimate the duration of time intervals and, as a consequence, discount the value of delayed rewards more strongly than do self-controlled individuals."[45]

These studies explain why addicts or other impulsive persons fail to focus on their reasons not to satisfy their immediate desires. But the picture we get—and which makes sense—is not of a person who says to himself, "I have more reason to control myself," but cannot conform his will to this judgment. Rather, insofar as there is a tension between present urges and reasoned judgment, addicts who fail to exercise self-control lose sight of their best judgment, focus intently on immediate desires at hand, and conclude in the moment that they have most reason to gain the immediate rewards. In one sense, Corrado is right that they might act rationally: they act rationally insofar as they act to satisfy their immediate, strong desire. In another sense, one could plausibly describe them as irrational, assuming a tension between their immediate desires and better judgment regarding what they have most reason to do, and persistent self-defeating behavior.

Let us stipulate for a moment, then, that Corrado rightly concludes that there are cases in which we would and should excuse an addict or other person suffering from a compulsive disorder or a neurosis. Is the explanation and justification that (1) we find the person to be rational but suffering a defect of volition, or (2) we detect a rationality impairment?

The line between these options is rather fuzzy. Consider an agent with cynophobia, an irrational fear of dogs. Our agent knows abstractly that he does not have reason to fear dogs in the way that he does. When he encounters a dog on the street or at a friend's house, he experiences a very intense desire to remove himself from the dog's presence even though, according to his better judgment, he does not have reason to be scared. He believes he has strongest reason *not* to avoid dogs. Imagine our agent encounters a pet dog at his friend's house where many friends are gathered. Instead of staying, which he believes he has most reason to do, our frightened agent darts from the house when the dog approaches him. Why? Is it because of a rationality problem? Does our cynophobic agent lack capacity to recognize a reason not to be scared? Or is it because of a volitional defect? Does he have an impaired capacity to react appropriately to his recognition of a reason to stay and not be scared?[46] These questions are difficult to answer because of an ambiguity in what it means to *recognize* a reason. At the moment he darts, we imagine he experiences intense anxiety and an extremely strong impulse to leave. He runs away because he is so focused on the reasons he sees to leave (that the dog could bite him, for example), that he cannot keep a proverbial eye on the reasons to stay and not be scared. So on the one hand, his capacity to recognize reasons is impaired. On the other hand, we might nevertheless describe him as knowing the reasons to stay and not be scared. Thus, he has *standing*, but not *occurrent*, recognition of such reasons. From that perspective, it becomes more plausible to conclude that his impairment is a volitional defect: he recognizes reasons to stay but cannot act on them.

The fuzzy nature of the line between some rationality and alleged volitional problems should not be surprising if we consider it from another angle. Recall how Corrado and other philosophers explain how we should assess whether an individual suffers from a volitional defect severe enough to ground an excuse: we should imagine hypothetical worlds similar, though not exact, to the world in which the agent acted. Typically we imagine counterfactuals in which we manipulate the consequences the person will suffer should he make the same choice. To the extent the agent would make the same choice in the counterfactual as he did in the real world, regardless of the resulting suffering, the more we become inclined to conclude the agent lacks adequate capacity for self-control. However, as we construct counterfactuals, imagine we keep ratcheting up the severity and certainty of bad consequences attached to the prohibited behavior. To the extent we think the agent would *still* make the same bad choice, the more we become inclined to think he is crazy or irrational. As Stephen Morse observes, if an agent would offend despite a police officer right at his elbow, we should see him as irrational unless we think he believed he had good reason to be arrested (such as civil disobedience).[47]

The point is that cases in which we think the agent should be excused for an inadequate capacity for self-control could be those cases in which we would also find the agent's rationality so impaired that we should excuse. If we could describe equally well these cases as involving a volitional or rationality impairment, then whether insanity standards should include a volitional prong should depend on practical considerations. Let us turn now to one of those practical considerations which is relevant to the second problem with Corrado's argument for a volitional prong.

2.3 Demanding Self-Control

The second and more serious problem with Corrado's argument for a volitional test is that it avoids discussion of responsibility for *crimes* for which people raise the insanity defense. Corrado offers the addict as the best example of someone we would excuse despite no rationality defect. But for what would we excuse the addict? In his discussion, Corrado suggests it is for taking the drug. He writes that it makes no sense to think the addict acts irrationally, frustrating a greater desire for a drug-free life, "at the time when he takes [the drug]."[48] Most often, though, the question is not whether an addict should be criminally excused for taking a drug. The question, more generally, is whether someone subject to a strong desire to take a drug—or to some desire of comparable intensity—should be excused for homicide, assault, burglary, or some other serious wrongdoing. Certainly some persons who suffer from addictions have great difficulty avoiding their self-destructive drug-consumption, and on that basis we should adopt empathetic rather than condemning attitudes towards their problem. Criminal punishment for drug possession is not the best response for those who suffer from addictions. But a separate question is whether the law should excuse persons for serious wrongs to others when they are caused by extremely intense desires. Should we excuse the person with a drug addiction who commits burglary to feed an addiction? Should we excuse the person with kleptomania who knows what he is doing but claims he could not control himself when he stole? Should we excuse the person with pedophilia who knew he was abusing a child but claims he could not control himself because of an extremely strong desire?

The answer is "no." When we construct the counterfactuals and assess facts in which the agent would have or would not have made the same choice, we still must make a value judgment regarding the level of self-control we demand from each other. To illustrate, contrast the following two cases. Smith suffers from kleptomania and stole a pencil from a giant retail store. Jones suffers from pedophilia and sexually abused a young child. Both experienced extremely strong urges and the pent-up anxiety associated with their disorders. We can stipulate that both would have made the same choices in counterfactual situations except where they would be immediately arrested (or some other equally bad consequence certain to occur). Perhaps both should be held fully responsible for their wrongdoing; but, at the least, it is reasonable to take the position that the latter, though perhaps not the former, should be held fully responsible for his crime against the child. If he *could have* avoided sexually abusing the child with an officer at his elbow, then he had adequate capacity to control himself for responsibility and punishment purposes. Why? It is so horrific to wrong a child in this manner that we must demand that persons muster all the capacity they have to avoid this action, and if they have the capacity to avoid that action with an officer nearby, their capacity is adequate.

To bolster the point that minimal capacity for self-control is sufficient for responsibility for serious crimes, consider the following facts. A man and a woman are engaged in intense sexual intimacy but not yet in sexual intercourse. Their contact is consensual, both partners are in a state of intense arousal and sexual frenzy, and it seems quite reasonable to the man that they are about to engage in sexual intercourse. However, the woman puts on the proverbial brakes and says "no" to sexual intercourse. If the man ignores her communication and proceeds to engage in sexual intercourse with her by force, there is no doubt that this is rape. The fact that the man is in some state of intense sexual desire does not, in any way, provide an excuse.

Why are we so confident that it is perfectly fair to hold this man morally and legally responsible for his criminal act? Because, given the seriousness of the crime, we demand the highest level of self-control. Despite the strength of his desire to commit the unlawful act, we demand that he muster the control to respect the other person's non-consent. Our law would not—and should not—excuse on the basis of a volitional defect, on grounds that it was very difficult for him to conform.

So when Corrado offers the severely drug-addicted person as an example of someone we would excuse despite the addict's knowledge of the facts and nature of his actions, we have to pause and ask, "What is the crime under consideration?" If the addict killed someone because he saw killing as the only way to satisfy his severe craving, would we excuse? Of course not. In this case, as long as the offender understood what he was doing, had the capacity to understand that it was wrong, and would have acted otherwise in some alternate scenario in which he saw good reason to do otherwise (such as a police officer at the elbow), we would have no reason to excuse. Even if we stipulate that it would feel extremely difficult for the addicted person to refrain, we should not excuse. In this situation, we must demand the highest level of self-control in the same way that we expect self-control from the sexually aroused individual discussed previously. I suspect we would reach the same conclusion about the severely addicted person if the crime were not homicide but nonetheless a serious, violent crime, such as aggravated assault or armed robbery. Indeed, we, as per our legal system, do not excuse such persons.

In essence, the conclusion here, that strong impulses and desires, even those associated with mental disorder, should not justify excuse on grounds of volitional defect, is merely an application of an existing legal excuse standard that is arguably (though probably not) about volitional control: duress.[49] Duress is coercion by an external threat from another person. Analogously, one claiming a volitional defect is claiming coercion by an internal, unusually strong craving or impulse. Under its traditional formulation, duress is unavailable unless the defendant was under an imminent threat of death or serious bodily harm. Threats short of such seriousness do not excuse because of the self-control we demand of persons when it comes to criminal prohibitions. Under laws following the Model Penal

Code, a defendant must show that he was compelled by a threat that a "person of reasonable firmness in his situation would have been unable to resist."[50] A person of reasonable firmness withstands a craving, regardless of strength, when important rights of others are at stake, in the same way that a person of reasonable firmness respects his sexual partner's refusal of permission for sexual intercourse, regardless of intense desire experienced by the former.

3 The "Twilight versus Dusk" Objection and Other Considerations

3.1 The Nature of the Objection

It is important to recognize from the foregoing discussion that the ultimate issue at hand turns on value judgments. Corrado presents the strongest case for a volitional prong by rejecting a reference to a truly *irresistible* impulse, opting instead to describe the excusing condition as one in which it was *extremely difficult* for the offender to avoid his blameworthy action. We must ask whether there are, in fact, conditions in which it is a good idea to permit someone to claim that it was just too difficult to resist a very strong urge or desire, due to mental disorder, to commit a criminal act.

The way in which Corrado formulates the volitional excuse does help dampen, to some extent, the most oft-repeated argument against a volitional prong. The common objection is that identifying the difference between an irresistible urge and an urge that simply was not resisted is just as impossible as finding the line between twilight and dusk. Even if it were conceptually plausible to understand an irresistible urge experienced by an otherwise rational agent, mental health professionals could not tell the difference between an irresistible impulse and an impulse not resisted. Corrado argues, however, that the excuse does not require a completely irresistible urge. Rather, a defendant should be able to argue he suffered a control defect because it was so exceedingly difficult for him to control himself that it would be unfair to punish. Instead of asking whether the defendant experienced some urge that is different in kind from resistible desires, the factfinder must ask the moral question whether it is fair to hold the defendant responsible, given his psychological disorder reflected by his abnormal urges. A defendant would have the right to put on evidence to show the struggle within himself regarding his persistent urges and his better judgment, and the ways in which his abnormal cravings have led to self-defeating behavior.

It would be very difficult for a factfinder to conclude with certainty whether it is fair or not to hold the agent responsible for his crime, but, so the rejoinder goes, the criminal law asks factfinders to make many difficult normative decisions. With self-defense claims, it might be very difficult to assess the reasonableness of a defendant's belief that force was necessary. In a manslaughter case, the line between adequate and inadequate provocation might be as hard to see as that between twilight and dusk. Given that the line between "irresistible" and "not resisted" is really a line drawn on the basis of a moral question, the fact that it is fuzzy should not be an objection. The essential difference between Corrado and Morse on this score regards the moral judgment on whether it is ever unfair to hold a person responsible for a crime in light of a claim that the defendant could not control himself despite having adequate cognitive and rationality capacities. On Morse's view—and the view supported above—the law rightfully demands self-control when it comes to serious criminal prohibitions.

Nonetheless, further discussion of Corrado's response to the "twilight/dusk" argument will prove fruitful. Specifically, Corrado's discussion, in the end, lends support to Morse's rationality standard and the practical concerns raised against a control test.

3.2 Scientific Studies and the Twilight/Dusk Objection

Corrado presents multiple counterarguments to the "twilight/dusk" objection. If true, his most effective counter is that "recent studies have shown that the line between those who can't control their behavior and those who won't control their behavior can be very clear indeed."[51] To support his claim, Corrado cites an article authored by a psychiatry think tank on the relationship between responsibility, choice, and addiction. However, the studies discussed in the article cannot help us draw the line between those who can't and those who won't. In fact, as I explain here, the psychiatrists' commentary on responsibility and addiction actually supports Stephen Morse's rationality perspective about responsibility and insanity in two ways.

In the article, the psychiatrists summarize "biological, psychological, social and cultural, self-help, religious, and forensic perspectives on personal responsibility for substance abuse and addiction."[52] Corrado specifically relies on a discussion of scientific studies of the causes and processes that underlie addiction and its related behavior. Specifically the psychiatrists recount (1) the neural mechanisms associated with addictive behavior and (2) the hope that mapping the human genome will expose the genetics of addiction and will improve treatments. These neuroscientific and genetic studies tell us nothing about who is responsible for acting on addictive urges and who is not. Rather, these studies tell us about the causes of certain conduct. Knowing "the neural mechanisms of drug reinforcement" helps us understand the biological underpinnings of addiction and could lead us to better treatments, but it does not help us distinguish those with adequate capacity to control their urges and those without such capacity. Does the sole fact that conduct is caused by neurological and genetic factors outside an agent's control ever eliminate responsibility? Perhaps, but the scientific studies do not answer that question. That philosophical question is age-old, and many debates have already assumed that our actions and choices are causally determined by facts outside our control.

Corrado happens to endorse hard determinism, which is the view that causal determination does, in fact, eliminate moral responsibility. The hard determinist argues that all conduct is causally determined and, thus, no one is truly morally responsible for conduct, wrongful or otherwise. On this philosophical view, the aforementioned scientific studies only expose the actual causes of addictive behavior; debates between hard determinists and compatibilists already assume all behavior is causally determined. Moreover, on the compatibilist view of responsibility, the scientific studies tell us nothing. For a compatibilist, like Morse, the criteria of moral responsibility are compatible with the truth of causal determinism; that is, those criteria can be satisfied by agents even if all conduct is, in fact, causally determined by facts beyond the control of agents. As is the case for hard determinism, knowing the physiological causes of addictive behavior tells the compatibilist absolutely nothing about who is and who is not responsible for such conduct.

Instead of endorsing a volitional criterion for responsibility, the psychiatrists' commentary on responsibility supports Morse's views about responsibility and arguments against volitional prongs. First, let us note a practical consideration Morse has raised against control tests: that they "provide mental health experts with the chance to present the court with the shakiest scientific and clinical data and conclusions."[53] He states, "In my experience, few mental health professionals understand the relationship between determinism and legal responsibility, apparently due to a belief that determinism and responsibility are necessarily incompatible."[54] Morse's concern is that experts often cite a defendant's mental disorder as the cause of his criminal conduct and conclude, on the basis of that causation claim, that the defendant was not legally responsible for the crime. However, the fact that a mental illness or disorder is a cause of conduct does not settle the responsibility question under law; moreover, the ultimate question of responsibility is not a scientific question within the expertise of the witness, though jurors most likely do not know that fact.[55]

The psychiatric article upon which Corrado relies is actually more supportive of Morse's concerns. The authors discuss scientific studies about the physiological causes of addiction as if the existence of such causes is incompatible, not only with responsibility in general, but with the "capacity for personal choice."[56] Consider the following statement: "In the gradation between determinism and free will, the initiation of substance use may occur toward the free-will end of the spectrum, whereas continued abuse may fall more toward the deterministic end, after certain neurochemical changes have taken place in the brain."[57] This statement shows such confusion. Do the psychiatrists believe that the brain normally has nothing to do with a person's deliberations, choices, and actions, but also that an individual's neurochemistry starts to cause behavior after certain kinds of changes take place in the brain? That cannot be. What the authors really mean is the following: The initiation of substance use may occur when an agent has adequate rational capacities for us to fairly consider him morally responsible for his conduct; however, as he continues to abuse drugs and that abuse changes his brain chemistry drastically, it may be that his rational capacities are diminished to the point that he is no long fully morally responsible for succumbing to his addictive desires. On this revised statement, it is not altered brain chemistry *per se* that diminishes responsibility. Rather, responsibility is diminished only insofar as the altered brain chemistry correlates with seriously compromised reasoning and cognitive abilities, abilities that can be judged only by psychological observation, not by any brain scan.

The psychiatrists' article supports Morse's view in one other way: despite the confused language about determinism and free will, the authors actually do recognize that the capacities required for responsibility are associated with practical reasoning, not with being free from biological causation. They specifically state that an individual's responsibility for continued abuse could be diminished relative to his responsibility for initiating the abuse precisely because repetitive consumption can lead to "cognitive deficits."[58] Similarly, they state that if an individual's disorder "itself *impairs one's capacity for making rational decisions*, as addictions sometimes do," then it would be unfair to blame that individual for failing to adhere to a treatment regimen.[59]

4 Conclusion

In the end, a volitional control test of insanity is neither necessary nor sufficient for the moral purposes of the criminal law. It is not sufficient even though Corrado might be correct that fair ascriptions of responsibility require the kind of control involved in the capacity to do otherwise. The ability to do otherwise is not equivalent to the volitional control associated with control prongs. An agent can be non-responsible—perhaps due to severe irrationality or otherwise lack capacity to do otherwise—without exhibiting any volitional defect at all. Moreover, volitional tests are not morally necessary. In the end, the reason is not because the line between "can't" and "won't" is as faint as the line between twilight and dusk. The reason is based on the moral judgment that when it comes to the serious wrongdoing associated with criminal law, we may demand the utmost self-control from our fellows, regardless of desire strength.

Notes

1. *Parsons v. State*, 2 So. 854, 856 (Ala. 1887), quoting John Tracy Jones.
2. American Psychiatric Association, *Diagnostic and Statistical Manual*, 20.
3. Ibid.
4. M'Naghten's Case, 10 Cl. & F. 200, 8 Eng. Rep. 718 (1843).
5. See Wallace, *Responsibility and the Moral Sentiments*, 167–70.
6. James, "Jurors' Assessment of Criminal Responsibility," 59–60.
7. See e.g., *Bennett v. Commonwealth*, 511 S.E.2d 439, 446–47 (Ct. App. Va. 1999).
8. *State v. Hartley*, 565 P.2d 658, 660 (N.M. 1977) (citing *State v. White*, 270 P.2d 727, 730 (N.M. 1954)).
9. Dressler, *Understanding Criminal Law*, 345.
10. The actual standard suggested to states by the American Law Institute offered the possibility of using either the word "criminality" here or "wrongfulness."
11. Model Penal Code § 4.01(1).
12. *Clark v. Arizona*, 548 U.S. 735, 750 (2006).
13. Morse, "Against Control Tests for Criminal Responsibility," 454. See also Morse, "Uncontrollable Urges and Irrational People," 1059.
14. Corrado, "The Case for a Purely Volitional Insanity Defense," 483.
15. Ibid.
16. Corrado, "Morse on Control Tests," 462.
17. *Kansas v. Crane*, 534 U.S. 407, 413 (2002).
18. Ala.Code 1975 § 13A-3-2(c). See also Ark. Code. Ann. § 5-2-207(a)(1) (1977); Colo. Rev. Stat. § 18-1-804 (2013); Haw. Rev. Stat. § 702-230 (West 1986).
19. Alaska Stat. § 12.47.030 (2013); S.C. Code Ann. § 17-24-20 (1989); 18 Pa. Cons. Stat. § 314(c)(1) (1982)
20. Corrado, "The Case for a Purely Volitional Insanity Defense," 484.
21. Ibid., 485.
22. Ibid.
23. Ibid.
24. Ibid., 503.

25. Moore, "Actus Reus," 17.
26. Shoda, Mischel, and Peake, "Predicting Adolescent Cognitive and Self-Regulatory Competencies," 978.
27. Moore, "The Neuroscience of Volitional Excuse," in press.
28. See, e.g., *State v. Forrest*, 578 A.2d 1066 (Conn. 1990); *People v. Jackson*, 627 N.W.2d 11 (Mich. App. 2001); *State v. Wood*, No. 58437, 1991 WL 76041 at *4 (Ohio App. May 9, 1991) ("While we concede the 'policeman-at-the-elbow' test is not recognized as a valid test for insanity in Ohio, . . . it is directly probative of defendant's ability to refrain.").
29. Corrado, "The Case for a Purely Volitional Insanity Defense," 498–99.
30. *State v. Madigosky*, 966 A.2d 730, 738 (Conn. 2009).
31. Ibid.
32. *People v. Jackson*, 627 N.W.2d 11, 13 (Mich. Ct. App. 2001) (emphasis added).
33. *Yates v. State*, 171 S.W.3d 215, 218 n.2 (Tex. Crim. App. 2005).
34. Corrado, "The Case for a Purely Volitional Insanity Defense," 486.
35. For a discussion of whether "could have done otherwise" or alternative possibilities are required for responsibility, see Kane, *A Contemporary Introduction to Free Will*, 80–92.
36. Corrado, "Responsibility and Control," 86.
37. Ibid.
38. Ibid.
39. Ibid., 87.
40. Ibid.
41. Ibid., 88.
42. Frankfurt, "Freedom of the Will and the Concept of a Person."
43. Bickel et al., "Remember the Future," 260–65; Kirby, Petry, and Bickel, "Heroin Addicts Have Higher Discount Rates," 78–87; Coffey et al., "Impulsivity and Rapid Discounting of Delayed Hypothetical Rewards," 18–25.
44. Bickel et al., "Remember the Future," 260–65.
45. Wittmann and Paulus, "Decision Making, Impulsivity and Time Perception," 7–12.
46. Here I borrow Fischer and Ravizza's terminology regarding the capacities associated with responsibility.
47. Morse, "Culpability and Control," 1659.
48. Corrado, "Responsibility and Control," 87.
49. I think Morse is correct that duress is not premised on a volitional defect but on an unfair choice. Morse, "Rationality and Responsibility," 256–57.
50. Model Penal Code 2.09(1).
51. Corrado, "The Case for a Purely Volitional Insanity Defense," 502 (citing Committee On Addictions of the Group for the Advancement of Psychiatry, "Responsibility and Choice in Addiction," 708–09).
52. Committee On Addictions of the Group for the Advancement of Psychiatry, "Responsibility and Choice in Addiction," 708–09.

53. Morse, "Excusing the Crazy," 818.
54. Ibid.
55. Morse, "Crazy Behavior, Morals, and Science," 615–19.
56. Committee on Addictions of the Group for the Advancement of Psychiatry, "Responsibility and Choice in Addiction," 707.
57. Ibid., 708.
58. Ibid.
59. Ibid., 709.

Resources

American Psychiatric Association, *Diagnostic and Statistical Manual of Mental Disorders*, 5th ed. Washington, DC: American Psychiatric Publishing, 2013.

Bickel, Warren K., et al., "Remember the Future: Working Memory Training Decreases Delay Discounting Among Stimulant Addicts." *Biological Psychiatry* 69(2011): 260–65.

Coffey, Scott F., et al., "Impulsivity and Rapid Discounting of Delayed Hypothetical Rewards in Cocaine-Dependent Individuals." *Experimental and Clinical Psychopharmacology* 11(2003): 18–25.

Committee On Addictions of the Group for the Advancement of Psychiatry, "Responsibility and Choice in Addiction." *Psychiatric Services* 53(2002): 707–13.

Corrado, Michael Louis, "Morse on Control Tests." In *Criminal Law Conversations*, edited by Paul H. Robinson, Stephen P. Garvey, and Kimberly Kessler Ferzan (New York: Oxford University Press, 2009), 461–63.

Corrado, Michael Louis, "Addiction and Causation." *San Diego Law Review* 37(2000): 913–57.

Corrado, Michael Louis, "The Case for a Purely Volitional Insanity Defense." *Texas Tech Law Review* 42(2009): 481–511.

Corrado, Michael Louis, "Responsibility and Control." *Hofstra Law Review* 34(2005): 59–91.

Dressler, Joshua, *Understanding Criminal Law*, 6th ed. New Providence, NJ: LexisNexis, 2012.

Fischer, John Martin, and Mark Ravizza, *Responsibility and Control: A Theory of Moral Responsibility*. Cambridge: Cambridge University Press, 1998.

Frankfurt, Harry, "Freedom of the Will and the Concept of a Person." In *The Importance of What We Care About* (Cambridge: Cambridge University Press, 1988), 11–25.

Garvey, Stephen P., "The Folk Psychology of Self-Control." In *Criminal Law Conversations*, edited by Paul H. Robinson, Stephen P. Garvey, and Kimberly Kessler Ferzan (New York: Oxford University Press, 2009), 460–61.

James, Rita, "Jurors' Assessment of Criminal Responsibility." *Social Problems* 7(1959): 58–69.

Kane, Robert, *A Contemporary Introduction to Free Will*. Oxford: Oxford University Press, 2005.

Kirby, Kris N., Nancy M. Petry, and Warren K. Bickel, "Heroin Addicts Have Higher Discount Rates For Delayed Rewards Than Non-Drug Using Controls." *Journal of Experimental Psychology: General* 128(1999): 78–87.

Litton, Paul, "Is Psychological Research on Self-Control Relevant to Criminal Law?" *Ohio State Journal of Criminal Law* 11(2014): 725–49.

Moore, Michael S., "Actus Reus." In *Encyclopedia of Crime & Justice*, 2nd ed., edited by Joshua Dressler (New York: Macmillan Reference USA, 2002), 15–24.

Moore, Michael S., "The Neuroscience of Volitional Excuse." In *Philosophical Foundations of Law and Neuroscience*, edited by Dennis Patterson and Michael S. Pardo (Oxford: Oxford University Press, 2016), in press.

Moore, Michael S., "The Quest for a Responsible Responsibility Test: Norwegian Insanity Law after Breivik." *Criminal Law and Philosophy* 9(2015): 645–93.

Morse, Stephen J., "Against Control Tests for Criminal Responsibility." In *Criminal Law Conversations*, edited by Paul H. Robinson, Stephen P. Garvey, and Kimberly Kessler Ferzan (New York: Oxford University Press, 2009), 449–59.

Morse, Stephen J., "Crazy Behavior, Morals, and Science: An Analysis of Mental Health Law." *Southern California Law Review* 51(1978): 527–654.

Morse, Stephen J., "Culpability and Control." *University of Pennsylvania Law Review* 142(1994): 1587–1660.

Morse, Stephen J., "Excusing the Crazy: The Insanity Defense Reconsidered." *Southern California Law Review* 58(1985): 777–836.

Morse, Stephen J., "Rationality and Responsibility." *Southern California Law Review* 74(2000): 251–68.

Morse, Stephen J., "Reply." In *Criminal Law Conversations*, edited by Paul H. Robinson, Stephen P. Garvey, and Kimberly Kessler Ferzan (New York: Oxford University Press, 2009), 469–71.

Morse, Stephen J., "Uncontrollable Urges and Irrational People." *Virginia Law Review* 88(2002): 1025–78.

Shoda, Yuchi, Walter Mischel, and Philip K. Peake, "Predicting Adolescent Cognitive and Self-Regulatory Competencies from Preschool Delay of Gratification: Identifying Diagnostic Conditions." *Developmental Psychology* 26(1990): 978–86.

Wallace, R. Jay., *Responsibility and the Moral Sentiments*. Cambridge, MA: Harvard University Press, 1994.

Wittmann, Marc, and Martin P. Paulus, "Decision Making, Impulsivity and Time Perception," *Trends in Cognitive Sciences* 12(2008): 7–12.

CHAPTER EIGHT

Legal Insanity and Executive Function

Katrina Sifferd, William Hirstein, and Tyler Fagan

1 The Cognitive Capacities Relevant to Legal Insanity

Legal insanity is a legal concept rather than a medical one. This may seem an obvious point, but it is worth reflecting on the divergent purposes and motivations for legal, as opposed to medical, concepts. Medical categories of disease are shaped by the medical professions' aims of understanding, diagnosing, and treating illness. Categories of legal excuse, on the other hand, serve the aims of determining criminal guilt and punishment.

A theory of legal responsibility and its criteria should exhibit symmetry between the capacities it posits as necessary for moral, and more specifically legal, agency and the capacities that, when dysfunctional or compromised, qualify a defendant for an excuse. To put this point more strongly, the capacities necessary for legal agency should necessarily disqualify one from legal culpability when sufficiently compromised. Thus one's view of legal insanity ought to reflect whatever one thinks are the overall purposes of the criminal law.[1] If the purpose of criminal punishment is social order, then legal agency entails the capacity to be law-abiding such that one does not undermine the social order. If the purpose is institutionalized moral blame for wrongful acts, then legal agency entails the capacities for moral agency. If a criminal code embraces a hybrid theory of criminal law, then all of these capacities are relevant to legal agency.

In this chapter we will argue that the capacities necessary to moral and legal agency can be understood as executive functions in the brain. Executive functions underwrite both the cognitive and volitional capacities that give agents a fair opportunity to avoid wrongdoing: to recognize their acts as immoral and/or illegal, and to act or refrain from acting based upon this recognition.[2] When a person's mental illness is serious enough to cause severe disruption of executive functions, she is very likely to lack substantial capacities necessary to be law-abiding.

Our analysis supports the Model Penal Code test for legal insanity over the traditional M'Naghten test, because the Model Penal Code test allows either severely diminished cognitive or volitional capacities to warrant an excuse to criminal culpability. We will provide a nuanced account of the ways in which mental illness can erode executive function, as well as an explanation as to why severe diminishment of executive functions caused by mental illness, but not some other causes, is exculpatory.

1.1 Ethical Justifications for Criminal Law

A justification for criminal law and punishment provides good reasons why society is warranted in denying criminal defendants certain liberties based upon their performance of certain acts. There are two major philosophical camps regarding the justification for criminal law, which reflect the dominant philosophical theories of ethics. Retributivists argue the primary aim of the criminal law is to punish wrongdoing.[3] Consequentialists, however, focus on the criminal law's role in supporting social order via reduction of crime.[4] Much ink has been spilled arguing that one of these theories provides the superior justification for a just criminal law and punishment. Many legal scholars, however, including the great H.L.A. Hart, claim that neither of these justifications alone is sufficient to justify the range and structure of criminal law and punishment in the common law tradition.[5] Instead, both retributive punishing of immoral acts and reduction of crime are aims of contemporary criminal justice practices. Thus it seems likely a hybrid justification of criminal punishment is reflected in such practices, and this notion was vindicated by the recently revised wording of the "purposes" section of the U.S. Model Penal Code.[6]

The Model Penal Code (MPC) is meant to be used as a blueprint for individual state criminal codes to encourage consistency across jurisdictions, and its current "purposes" section reflects a theory of criminal punishment very similar to the one famously advocated by Norval Morris.[7] Morris's theory, often called *limiting retributivism*, argues that retributive notions of just desert, which probably rest upon moral emotions,[8] ought to provide an appropriate range of justified penalties within which a defendant might be sentenced. Such backward-looking retributive considerations aimed at matching level of punishment to level of wrongdoing and type of defendant are then balanced with forward-looking considerations of social order and crime reduction. Ideally, this process creates a punishment package that is proportional to crime and defendant, but also works to reduce recidivism and overall crime rates.

Under this sort of hybrid justification for punishment, what qualifies a defendant for criminal punishment is first of all a retributive notion of criminal wrongdoing. Thus persons who fail to understand the nature of their acts—specifically, who are incapable of recognizing that their acts are morally wrong or illegal—may be considered good candidates for an excuse, especially if that incapacity is not due to their own past behavior. To put this another way: if a person, whom we'll call Sue, is incapable of understanding that this handbag is not hers, we ought not hold her responsible for theft. Sue did not have the capacity to understand that taking the bag violated the standards of a moral or legal code, and thus had no chance to inhibit the act based upon its immoral or illegal nature.

Persons who can recognize moral or legal norms as relevant to their behavior, but who are incapable of conforming their behavior to such norms, might also be excused. If Sue knows the bag is not hers, but has such an overwhelming impulse to take the bag that she would do it even if the store security officer was standing right next to her, she again did not have the capacity to inhibit the theft based upon its immoral or illegal nature in any real sense. Thus if the aim of criminal punishment is to punish wrongdoing, in this case Sue would again seem eligible for an excuse disqualifying her from responsibility.

The consequentialist goal of social order also requires that persons have the capacity to be discouraged from harmful acts by the threat of criminal punishment. This view of criminal law is primarily forward-looking (aiming to reduce future crime), as compared with retributive aims, which are backward-looking (addressing a past immoral or illegal act). The principles of general and specific deterrence, incapacitation, and rehabilitation are all in a sense properly filed under the broad principle of *deterrence*, meaning they are all different ways in which persons may be deterred from committing future crimes in response to threatened or applied criminal punishment.[9] *General deterrence* is the aim that persons within the general population will choose not to commit crimes based upon the general threat that a criminal punishment may be applied in response to an act. This requires that a potential defendant understand that a possible future act violates the criminal law, and be able to inhibit his action so as to avoid arrest and punishment. *Specific deterrence* is the idea that a convicted defendant who has already experienced criminal punishment will be dissuaded from re-offense due to the negative experience of criminal punishment. This principle also requires that the potential re-offender understand a possible act is criminal, and then fail to commit the act to avoid the sort of punishment he experienced in the past.

Thus deterrence theory rests upon the assumption that citizens have the capacities to be law-abiding. Given this assumption, it may seem on first pass that a person incapable of understanding that their behavior may bear the consequence of criminal punishment, or a person incapable of being swayed from committing an act based upon the threat of punishment, might be excused under a consequentialist theory. So if Sue, our thief, could not have known taking the bag was illegal, or that taking the bag in particular violated the law, she would seem eligible for an excuse under a consequentialist justification of criminal law, because she could not have been deterred from her act. Similarly, if Sue was incapable of refraining from taking the bag even though she knew she would be arrested, she may also be a good candidate to be excused from responsibility.

However, one might argue that a consequentialist justification of Sue's punishment is still valid if punishing Sue had the effect of deterring others within the general population. That is, Sue could not have been deterred, but maybe her friend Johnny, who does have full capacities to be law-abiding, would be deterred from theft upon hearing of Sue's prison sentence for theft. Similarly, the consequentialist aims of incapacitation and rehabilitation may also be met by punishing Sue despite her lack of capacities to be law-abiding. Punishments that are *incapacitative* ensure that a defendant will not reoffend against society at large by incarcerating that defendant. *Rehabilitation* encourages (or requires, depending on the type of rehabilitative program) a defendant to change something about his decision-making processes, values, character, and so forth, such that he is less likely to reoffend. In this way consequentialist principles of general deterrence, incapacitation, and rehabilitation can be seen as purely forward-looking and as such do not require a defendant have any mental capacities at all at the time she committed a crime. That is, Sue could have been sleepwalking when she stole the bag and the principles of incapacitation and rehabilitation might still indicate punishment is warranted as a means to stop Sue from stealing in the future. Similarly, a defendant who is so seriously mentally ill as to think he is saving New York from the Stay Puft Marshmallow Man when he sets off a bomb may still be incapacitated and rehabilitated post-crime as part of a punishment package such that social order is increased.

There is some worry that punishment of persons who commit crimes while sleepwalking or suffering from severe mental illness might actually weaken the coercive power of the criminal law by indicating to citizens they may be punished regardless of whether they make a choice to violate the law. However, one might also argue the unsavory results of a purely forward-looking account show that the consequentialist theory's general assumption that citizens possess the mental capacity to be law-abiding ought to act as a constraint upon the class of persons who can be criminally punished under the theory. As Hart noted, recognition of incapacity as an excusing condition is an important way the law can show respect for citizens as the choice-makers deterrence theory so desperately needs them to be.[10] Luckily, we need not determine whether such a constraint is necessary in all versions of a consequentialist theory of punishment. As stated above, we, like Hart and the U.S. system of criminal law, embrace such a constraint as part of a hybrid theory which reflects both retributive and deterrent aims. We feel punishment must be proportional to the moral blameworthiness of the defendant and rests upon an understanding of citizens as choosers with minimal cognitive capacities to understand their behavior in relation to the law and to be deterred by the threat of punishment.

To sum up, this admittedly quick review of the justifying theories of criminal law reveals the following capacities as vital to legal agency and responsibility on the widely used hybrid theory common in the United States: (1) the capacity to recognize both moral and legal norms, and thus understand which acts are wrongful/criminal, and (2) the capacity to conform one's action to such norms, via an understanding of one's behavior in light of those norms, as well as the volitional capacity to inhibit illegal acts.

Given this relatively broad consensus, the current debate in the United States and many other nations regarding the capacities relevant to the excuse of legal insanity relevant is somewhat surprising. This debate has focused on whether a defendant's inability to understand her act in relation to moral and legal norms is necessary for one to be deemed legally insane, or whether a defendant's inability to conform her behavior to such norms may also qualify her as legally insane. To us, it seems obvious that the purposes of criminal law and punishment—both retributive and some consequentialist purposes—require that legal agency include the capacity to conform one's behavior to the law in addition to the capacity to recognize legal rules. As we will discuss in detail later on, recognition that one's act is immoral or illegal is not enough to give a defendant a fair opportunity to avoid violating the law. If a defendant recognizes some act as forbidden by the criminal law, but cannot avoid such conduct even given this recognition, it does not further the purposes of the criminal law to hold him responsible for violating the law. This is true regardless of the reason for a defendant's incapacity to conform their behavior to the law (with some rare and rather outlandish exceptions). If Sue is coerced via a gun to the head to steal another's bag, she ought to be excused; and if she has a mental disorder rendering her incapable of resisting an impulse or desire to steal the bag, she ought to be similarly excused.

It thus seems odd that there are many U.S. jurisdictions where a defendant who recognized his act as criminal or wrong, but lacked the capacity to inhibit an act based upon this knowledge, is deemed fully culpable for that act under the criminal law. These are jurisdictions that adhere strictly to the M'Naghten test for legal insanity. In the next section we will discuss the difference between tests for legal insanity that claim cognitive capacity to recognize wrongdoing—but not volitional capacity—is necessary for responsibility, and tests for legal insanity that claim both cognitive capacity and volitional incapacity are necessary, implying that volitional incapacity can also qualify a defendant as legally insane. We will discuss in detail David Brink's "fair opportunity" theory alluded to previously,[11] as well as evidence from neuroscience regarding the cognitive capacities that underpin legal agency, and claim that both support a two-factor test for insanity.

We will also weigh in on an important debate about whether the incapacities that qualify a defendant as legally insane need be the result of a mental disorder or disease, and if so, why. We will explain why executive dysfunction or executive deficits coming from mental illness should be excusatory, whereas deficits linked to other factors, including decisions and acts related to the defendant's agency, may not be.

1.2 Brink's Fair Opportunity Theory

David Brink's theory of responsibility provides an excellent critique of purely cognitive tests of legal insanity that have emerged in the United States and elsewhere. Brink argues that criminal responsibility requires a "fair opportunity to avoid wrongdoing," and that this fair opportunity to be law-abiding requires both normative competence and situational control.[12] If a justificatory defense is not available, then a person can only avoid culpability by appeal to an excuse: that she lacked either normative competence or situational control at the time she committed a crime. On the one hand, excuses such as immaturity and addiction deny normative competence, which entails the ability to recognize moral and legal norms, and the ability to act in accordance with such norms. Other sorts of excuses may deny that a defendant has situational control due to coercion, duress, or the like.

Brink argues that the excuse of legal insanity rests upon either denial of a defendant's ability to recognize norms or legal rules, or his ability to conform his behavior to such rules.[13] Brink claims both of these requirements are best understood as a part of normative competence, and that each is itself sufficient for a claim of a legal excuse: neither actors lacking the cognitive capacity to recognize or appreciate legal or moral norms, nor actors lacking the volitional capacity required to conform conduct to this normative knowledge, are responsible under the law. Because of this, Brink supports the Model Penal Code's test for legal insanity over the traditional common law approach, which utilizes the M'Naghten Rule. The M'Naghten Rule, adopted by the majority of states and reflected in the federal insanity test, excuses a defendant who, due to a severe mental disease or defect, is unable to appreciate the nature and quality of the wrongfulness of his act. The MPC, on the other hand, requires that a defendant lack "substantial capacity to either appreciate the criminality of his conduct or to conform his conduct to the requirements of the law."[14] The M'Naghten Rule therefore employs a purely cognitive conception of insanity that does not require volitional capacity. The MPC rule, however, requires responsible defendants possess both normative and volitional competence.

Brink argues for a fairly subtle understanding of the capacity to recognize wrongdoing that does not include simply the capacity to know that an action or its result violates a moral or legal norm. Because causing criminal harm is justified under certain "choice of evil" circumstances, recognition of a legal norm requires a person be able to grade offenses as greater and lesser. For example, Sue may be excused in taking another's bag if it has a bomb in it that will blow up a train station. However, she is probably not excused if she merely thinks the bag has a granola bar in it and she is very hungry. Thus recognition of wrongdoing involves understanding the nature of one's act in relation to the law, as well as in relation to the circumstances surrounding the act. Finally, even if Sue does indeed possess this understanding of the nature and quality of her act, if she is also unable to stop herself from performing the act given this understanding, she is excused.

Brink recognizes that some legal scholars have been skeptical about the MPC's inclusion of volitional capacity as excusatory. Stephen Morse, for example, has argued that the notion of an irresistible urge is nonsensical, because it is so difficult to make sense of what it means for an urge to be so strong it is "irresistible" versus one that could, under some conditions (such as threat of death), be resisted.[15] It seems, says Morse, that persons under sufficient threat of sanction can resist *any* strong urge. This is the case even those with mental conditions such as obsessive-compulsive disorder: a man obsessively locking and relocking his door can stop himself from the behavior if his life is threatened.

Brink claims, however, that resistibility is a model notion.[16] While there is some question as to how unconquerable a desire must be to stand in the way of implementing the verdicts of practical reason to constitute an excuse, the law can, in theory, draw a line in the sand, just as it does when it determines what blood alcohol level makes one legally drunk, or what age makes one old enough to vote. Cases in which a person would only act differently under a threat of imminent death, for example, seem to be obvious cases in which we should excuse.[17] Brink says this sets the bar too low, however. Instead, the MPC seems correct in requiring that a legally insane defendant lack *substantial* capacity.[18] In philosophy-speak, this indicates that the MPC test for legal insanity requires an insane defendant be less than moderately reasons-responsive.[19] Someone who was only weakly responsive to wrongdoing is very rarely able to recognize wrongdoing and refrain from acting in response to this recognition. This defendant is rightfully deemed legally insane.

As indicated previously, we agree with Brink and the MPC that legal sanity requires a certain degree of both cognitive and volitional competence. Only persons with such capacities can recognize their acts as immoral and/or illegal, and then choose to act or refrain from acting based upon this recognition. A person lacking such capacities is not deserving of retribution; nor are consequentialist purposes for criminal punishment advanced by holding a person lacking these capacities responsible. It is futile to threaten with punishment a person who cannot be swayed.

In our view, the competencies necessary for legal agency are made possible by what cognitive scientists have identified as the brain's *executive functions*. We will argue that when a person's mental illness is serious enough to involve severe disruption or dysfunction of these executive processes, that person is likely to lack substantial cognitive or volitional capacity (or both), and would therefore have a legitimate claim to a legal insanity defense. But first, a brief discussion of what executive functions are, and why they are plausibly necessary for moral and legal agency, is in order.

2 Executive Function and Legal Capacity

The notion of executive functions has emerged from neuroscience as an explanatory schema to account for how we make higher-level decisions. These functions, mostly realized by frontal cortical processes, manipulate

Legal Insanity and Executive Function   223

mental states—both perceptual and mnemonic—to plan and execute behavior. In general, executive functions activate when we must go out of our routine mode and plan more complicated actions, but they may also activate when the stakes are very high, or when special care is needed in performing an action. While executive functions are accomplished by large brain networks, typically spanning several cortical areas and supported by additional subcortical areas, they reside primarily in the brain's prefrontal cortex.

Although correlations and connections exist between them, executive functions have shown a substantial degree of functional separability,[20] while the most recent research affirms the cognitive control network as the core neuroanatomical locus of most of the primary executive functions, including:

- *Attention (top-down)*. Top-down attention, which we normally view as under voluntary control, is crucial for most of the other executive functions to accomplish their tasks. Attention includes the ability to monitor perceptions and memories, which allows for the correction of mistaken perceptions, and "false memories."[21]
- *Task monitoring and error correction*. We also need to attend to ongoing tasks, to make sure they are going the way we intended and make corrections if not. This form of attention, called monitoring, is a telltale sign of intentional action, and failure to monitor can indicate the action is not intentional: the person may be sleepwalking, hypnotized, or having a seizure.
- *Task-switching*. Except for the simplest of actions, most tasks involve engaging and completing a number of subtasks. Staying on track often requires us to switch our attention back and forth between these smaller goals, while not losing our place in the larger, unfinished task.[22]
- *Planning and prioritization*. The brain employs different types of planning processes, depending on the content of the planned actions and the time scale involved. Goals must be prioritized and weighed in comparison to one another.[23]
- *Inhibition*. There are multiple types of inhibition, supported by multiple brain processes and their constituent areas. The sort of inhibition required to state the colors of the words in the Stroop Color Word Test, rather than to read the words themselves out loud, is not the same process as the inhibition that keeps us from proposing a certain strategy at a board meeting when we recall that the board had failed earlier at a similar strategy. Persons can inhibit both routine and planned actions, based upon simple rules or complex moral judgments.[24]
- *Regulation of emotions*. When, where, and how we express emotions involves following complex social and interpersonal rules, a process requiring management by executive functions. Over time, the executive can modulate

emotional responses, making it more or less likely that one will have a certain sort of emotional response to some environmental stimulus, as well as dampen or enhance emotional responses as they arise.[25]

We propose that possessing a developed set of executive functions is a necessary, though not sufficient, condition for being a morally and legally responsible person. Executive processes make it possible to function in a society as an effective moral and legal agent by enabling a person to plan and execute actions in a way that takes into account the moral and legal implications of those acts. Attentional control, deliberation, and planning allow persons the opportunity to recognize moral and legal norms as relevant to behavior, to take into account the desires and needs of others, and to include the beliefs and feelings of others in ongoing decisions and actions. Task switching, emotional regulation, and inhibition allow persons to keep their plans on track, to keep in mind undesired outcomes, and to stop themselves from performing actions that cause harm.

Executive functions thus underwrite both the cognitive and volitional prongs of a two-factor approach (such as that of the MPC) to legal insanity. While most of us possess some sort of gut-level "moral compass," identifying actions as right or wrong given a certain moral or legal code typically requires thought and decision-making capacities that reside at higher levels of the cognitive hierarchy and involve executive processes. As discussed previously, understanding wrongdoing involves recognition of a moral or legal norm as relevant to one's action, and then evaluation of the action and its consequences in terms of that norm (or norms). Without such capacities, actions may instead be evaluated only in terms of their utility to the actor in the short term. That is, without the ability to assess the moral or legal consequences of contemplated actions it may be easy to "justify" anything one wants to do in terms of short-term utility ("it seemed like the right thing to do at the time").

Of course, merely possessing capacities to assess wrongdoing does not mean one will use them; in cases of blameworthy self-deception, one may also fail to assess the moral consequences of a desired action properly. Suppose, for example, Sue convinces herself that she was justified in taking Ralph's bag because Ralph really doesn't need the money inside; she feels he is financially well off whereas Sue is in desperate need of money. It may be that Sue possesses the requisite executive functions to accurately assess her act's moral status but she simply fails to exercise them properly, and therefore ought to be held responsible for the theft. In contrast, it may be that another thief, Barb, truly believed the bag was hers due to some hallucination resulting from a mental illness—say, an angel telling her the bag was a gift to her from God. If Barb lacks the capacity to understand the angel is not really there, and to inhibit her behavior based upon this correction of her perception, she ought not to be held responsible for her failure to assess moral consequences. We will discuss in more detail the ways in which mental illness causes executive incapacities relevant to legal insanity shortly.

Executive functions also allow us to prioritize our values and desires and plan actions accordingly. We find certain things and events rewarding or unpleasant, and we know we find them rewarding or unpleasant. We even know exactly how rewarding or unpleasant we find them, at least compared to other things or people we care about, and we can take that knowledge into account when planning our actions. For example, an art collector deciding whether to spend $1 million on a painting must weigh the very concrete value of the money against the more subtle value that the painting will have to him. He needs to judge the amount of his desire in making this decision. A priest has to weigh the value of a religious edict against the concrete value of a strong desire to violate it. These capacities to weigh desired outcomes and plan actions based upon such weighed outcomes are enabled by executive functions, and may underpin the capacity to weigh the consequences of multiple contemplated actions (including imagined punishments).

In addition to playing these more cognitive roles, executive functions contribute crucially to volitional capacity, with inhibition perhaps the most salient example. Aside from the obvious need to inhibit morally bad or socially inappropriate behaviors, we often need to inhibit thoughts and intentions to prevent them from producing imprudent behavior. Inhibition may be involved in our robust ability to use cognitive resources in both "online" and "offline" modes. That is, our executive functions may operate on both real and imagined circumstances. Our ancestors needed to figure out if it was possible to sneak up behind a wooly mammoth without actually sneaking up behind a wooly mammoth—a difficult challenge if one is unable to think about the relevant behaviors without initiating them. Abigail Baird has found that juveniles actually contemplate dangerous actions longer than adults, partly because when an adult imagines an action leading to physical harm they tend to inhibit the thought or plan of that action immediately, whereas teens often continue to weigh the possible bodily harm against potentially beneficial social outcomes (such as looking cool).[26] Juveniles thus are less efficient in inhibiting actions based upon harmful outcomes than adults. Inhibition is also intimately related to the executive functions of monitoring and error correction. When actions are ongoing, we monitor them so that when a mistake, or something unintended, occurs we can inhibit further action and either quickly try another routine action, or else step back and think about it a bit—and then engage other executive processes involved in planning more complex behavior.

One might think that naturally rule-following or virtuous persons would need fewer inhibitions, because they tend not to form malevolent or deviant desires in the first place. Even such persons need some inhibitions; for example, to be alive and human is to experience attraction to someone who is rendered off limits to you by way of some social or ethical convention you accept, such as the spouse of a close friend, a boss, or someone much older or younger than you. Something needs to stop this attraction from getting too far, or at the very least, from initiating actions. Of course, an ability to successfully inhibit action in one domain is no guarantee of similar success in another domain; stopping oneself from overeating may or may not be an ethical matter, but we accept that there might be a person who was extremely virtuous but extremely poor at inhibiting the desire to overeat, or overconsume anything. Thus we posit that often executive functions are domain-specific in their operations.[27]

Obviously the different executive functions do not work alone, but in tandem, and on mental states delivered to them from across the brain. Aside from connections between one another, they require the proper input from perception, memory, and emotion to work correctly. In order to plan and execute behavior involving other people, for instance, we need to be able to track their identities and behaviors, to accurately understand their actions and intentions, and represent their mental states to ourselves. This involves not only perceptual recognition—as when I correctly identify a face in the crowd as belonging to my friend—but the building of complex and stable psychological profiles of others around us.[28] Treating others ethically, whether they are strangers or intimates, requires that I represent them with some degree of accuracy. It also requires appropriate emotional engagement, which explains the suggestive notion that psychopaths, while generally able to simulate the thoughts and actions of others, are unable to integrate the proper emotional responses into those simulations.

3 Executive Function in Insane Defendants

If we are right that executive functions enable the cognitive and volitional capacities picked out by the Model Penal Code, and are therefore a necessary condition of legal responsibility, then plausible claims of legal insanity should track significant deficits in executive functioning. The most common mental illness afflicting the rare defendant who is excused from criminal responsibility by reason of legal insanity is schizophrenia (in a few cases, bipolar disorder has also grounded a successful insanity plea). In this section we review some of the evidence for executive deficits in persons with severe mental illness of the sorts that have been most likely to ground a successful insanity plea.

It is widely accepted that individuals with schizophrenia often have deficits falling across almost all areas of executive function, including planning, attention, task shifting, and sequencing.[29] Persons with progressive schizophrenia, for example, often exhibit severe deficits in tasks testing attentional set shifting, online use of working memory, and planning and strategy capacity.[30]

Cognitive deficits, including executive deficits, have been found not to track the severity of positive psychotic symptoms in schizophrenics; they persist even during periods of remission.[31] Persons with bipolar disorder have qualitatively similar cognitive deficits, but they are quantitatively greater in patients with schizophrenia.[32] Studies have found that patients with schizophrenia, compared to healthy controls and even to patients with bipolar disorder, evince significant and specific cortical inhibition deficits in the dorsolateral prefrontal cortex, which may explain why the executive and cognitive control impairments found in patients with schizophrenia have been consistently linked to prefrontal cortical dysfunction.[33]

These deficits include decreased cognitive processing speed,[34] easily depleted sequencing capacity,[35] difficulty multitasking,[36] and decreased working memory,[37] all of which can diminish executive function. In one study participants were given cognitive testing and then judged based on their ability to perform a set of activities involved in daily living.[38] Participants had to choose a menu for dinner, pick up needed items from the store, and then cook a meal. Individuals with schizophrenia had significant deficits in the ability to prepare a meal with multiple items at the same time. Participants could initiate the process, but they could not complete it. In another study, participants also were asked to use a computerized meeting preparation task to prepare a meeting space.[39] Their ability to successfully complete the exercise was significantly lower than that of normals, and the time it took those to complete the task was significantly higher.

A variety of tests indicate that schizophrenics have a heightened tendency to jump to conclusions.[40] The higher the deficit in overall executive function in schizophrenics, the higher the tendency to jump to conclusions. This may result in schizophrenics being less able to recognize their hallucinations as such, and a heightened tendency to act in accordance with hallucinations. As noted previously, the brain's executive processes normally have the power to reject spurious perceptions and memories. Executive processes, when functioning normally, seem able to correct for defects in perception and prevent distorted perceptions from being coined into beliefs. Rejecting these is crucial to mental competence; a person who is experiencing hallucinations is only mentally incompetent if she mistakes them for reality.

We all experience strange thoughts on occasion, such as the feeling that someone is watching us; the odd notion that we had a causal influence on something where no reasonable physical explanation is available (for example, I flip a light switch and a car horn honks outside); or the idea that someone might be plotting against us. Executive functions are required in order to assess the plausibility of a thought. They accomplish the comparisons with other beliefs and with memories needed for the assessment. A person with delusions will only act on the basis of those delusions if she persists in believing them to be true. The formation of a delusion thus has at least two levels. First a spurious thought is created, typically due to compromised perceptual or mnemonic faculties, but sometimes also traceable to the emotional systems. Secondly, there is an executive failure to properly assess the thought and reject it.[41]

Remember our earlier claim that a theory of legal agency ought to exhibit symmetry between the capacities a theory claims as necessary for legal agency, and the diminishment of such capacities in the cases of legitimate legal excuse. We support a two-factor test for legal insanity because we believe executive functions are necessary to legal agency,[42] and, as we have tried to show, very severely mentally ill persons may experience deficits in executive function that degrade cognitive or volitional capacities thus denying them a fair opportunity to adhere to the criminal law.

4 Tests for Legal Insanity from the Executive Perspective

We may now revisit the two major tests for legal insanity and our earlier claim that both the major justifications of punishment and evidence from neuroscience regarding executive functions support the MPC test. The M'Naghten Rule, adopted by the majority of states, excuses a defendant who, due to a severe mental disease or defect, is unable to appreciate the nature and quality of the wrongfulness of his act. The MPC, on the other hand, requires a defendant lack "substantial capacity to either appreciate the criminality of his conduct or to conform his conduct to the requirements of the law."[43] In sum, the M'Naghten Rule employs a purely cognitive conception of insanity, whereas the MPC rule requires responsible defendants possess both cognitive and volitional competence.

The archetypal cases of legal insanity—the ones the M'Naghten Rule seems designed to identify—are cases where a defendant is suffering from a mental disorder that almost completely removes their ability to appreciate the wrongfulness of their criminal act. An understanding of the executive deficits involved in mental illness that may cause this sort of incapacity, such as schizophrenia, indicates that such defendants may suffer from global deficits in executive function. If severe enough, such deficits can lead to a wholesale inability to identify the harmful consequences of an act, or to identify any norm or law as relevant to that act, similar to the lack of understanding that might be exhibited by a very young child regarding the nature of his or her action.

However, we suspect that such extreme executive deficits are fairly rare in schizophrenics, even those with very severe positive and negative symptoms. Instead, we posit that it may be the schizophrenic's substantial executive deficits in conjunction with their tendency towards hallucinations, delusions, paranoia, and other heightened emotional states that undermine their culpable agency. Schizophrenia, and possibly other mental illnesses including bipolar disorder, may result in a lowered executive capacity to identify and correct for hallucinations, delusions, extreme paranoia, or fear and anger, and to inhibit action. Further, executive deficits in schizophrenics may make it more likely that they form hasty conclusions regarding their hallucination or delusion, and, even if they are capable of momentary correction, more likely that they lose attentional focus on the correct information or perception such that they can continue to inhibit wrongful behavior.

To put the point another way, the executive profile of schizophrenics and some with severe bipolar disorder indicates that their executive deficits may be global, but not so severe as to render them incapable of performing some basic tasks (such as driving to the store or running simple errands). Thus there may not be important moral or legal ramifications flowing from a schizophrenic's severe attentional, planning, error-correction, emotional regulation, and inhibition deficits until they also have a hallucination telling them to perform serious harm or until they are so paranoid, fearful, or angry that they are motivated to act violently.

This understanding of the capacities of those suffering from a mental illness that most often underpins a plea for legal insanity leads us to agree with Brink that the M'Naghten test, which many read as requiring a complete inability to understand wrongdoing, sets the bar too low for legal sanity.[44] Brink's argument—that the capacity to recognize wrongdoing is more subtle, and includes being able to grade acts as more or less immoral or illegal as well as the capacity to act upon that recognition (in our view, via attentional and emotional control, error correction, and inhibition)—seems correct. The MPC standard that a legally insane defendant lack "substantial capacity" acknowledges this subtlety.

Similarly, because of the importance of the executive functions of attention and inhibition in performance of culpable action, we also agree with Brink that volitional capacity is necessary to legal agency. Someone who is only weakly responsive to wrongdoing—who is only very rarely able to recognize wrongdoing and refrain from acting in response to this recognition—is, to our minds, suffering from executive deficits severe enough to disqualify them from criminal responsibility. The primary purpose of executive functions is to control and direct complex, non-routine behavior. When this capacity is severely compromised, so too is one's legal agency (that is, their capacity to recognize and follow legal norms).

Furthermore, even though the evidence regarding mental illness and executive function indicates that executive functions tend to cluster, such that when one has a deficit in one, they have a deficit in another, they are separable.[45] It is, at least in theory, possible that a mental illness could keep a defendant's capacity to recognize wrongdoing intact, but remove much of their capacity for inhibition. For example, it is possible that a mentally ill defendant could recognize that the devil telling her to set fire to the house is a hallucination, but feel such strong emotions in response to the hallucination so as to be unable to inhibit the action driven by her fear. It may even be the case that such a defendant would set fire to the house "with a policeman at their elbow."[46] Thus, a two-factor insanity test—with both a cognitive and volitional prong—is necessary. As Brink says, a defendant is denied a fair opportunity to avoid wrongdoing and criminal punishment if he lacks the capacity to inhibit his act even knowing it is immoral and illegal. (Of course, if a defendant has the capacity to inhibit the act based upon an understanding the act is wrong, and he fails to, he is fully responsible.)

In sum, as stated previously, we support the MPC test for legal insanity because it recognizes the importance of the various executive functions in moral and legal agency. We feel that legal sanity requires a certain degree of both cognitive and volitional competence. Only persons with such capacities can recognize their acts as immoral and/or illegal, and then choose to act or refrain from acting based upon this recognition. Looking back to the broad justifications of punishment, a person lacking such capacities is not deserving of retribution; and from a consequentialist perspective, the purposes for criminal punishment are not advanced by holding a person lacking these capacities responsible. It is futile to threaten a person with

Legal Insanity and Executive Function

punishment who either does not understand her act to be criminal, or who cannot be swayed.

5 Does Legal Insanity Need to Be Related to a Mental Illness?

There is some question about the meaning of both the M'Naghten and MPC requirement that a legally insane defendant's incompetency must be the result of a mental disease or defect. One way to put this question, as Michael Moore has done, is to ask whether these tests assume that mental illness or defect is *strongly* relevant to these tests' notion of responsibility, or only *weakly* relevant.[47] A medical concept is strongly relevant if it, "by itself, captures conditions of moral and legal excuse," and weakly relevant if it can only capture such conditions when "conjoined with other non-medical concepts."[48]

Considered in such terms, the M'Naghten and MPC tests seem clearly to assume a relation of weak relevance between mental illness and legal insanity. These standards hold that a mental disease or defect is not, all by itself, sufficient to excuse someone from legal responsibility: the disease or defect must cause substantial cognitive or volitional incapacity. But one might wonder, if this substantial incapacity is doing the exculpatory work, why the *cause* of that incapacity should matter to determining legal responsibility. If being unable to control one's behavior, for instance, is thought to be generally sufficient for excusing one from legal responsibility, then why does it matter whether such inability is caused by mental illness rather than something else?

We are approaching the horns of a dilemma that, according to Moore, bedevils any weak-relevance test, all of which share the view that "mental illness is relevant to responsibility only when it either causes the existence of (or is at least accompanied by) some Factor X."[49] The weak-relevance theorist, argues Moore, occupies an untenable position: her view either collapses into a position asserting *no* relevance between mental illness and responsibility (the first horn), or else must retreat to the relative safety of the strong-relevance position (the second horn). One might reconstruct Moore's argument as follows.

If weak relevance (WR) holds that "[m]ental illness is relevant to responsibility only when it either causes the existence of (or is at least accompanied by) some Factor X," then any Factor X on offer—Moore has four sorts in mind—is either independently exculpatory or not.[50] If Factor X is independently exculpatory (such as "lack of substantial capacity to conform [one's] conduct to the requirements of law"), then it excuses whether or not it results from (or accompanies) mental illness, in which case mental illness is irrelevant to responsibility. If Factor X isn't independently exculpatory (e.g., ignorance of law), then mental illness is doing all the exculpatory work, in which case mental illness is exculpatory whether or not it causes or is accompanied by Factor X. But this is just the strong relevance position, which is obviously at odds with WR. So, because WR turns out to be false whether or not Factor X is independently exculpatory, WR is false.

Because he advocates a thesis of strong relevance between the medical concept of psychosis and the excusatory condition of legal insanity, Moore himself does not have to face this dilemma. Yet his remarks may contain the basis of a plausible answer to it. Moore, quoting Feinberg,[51] argues that there is something "'special' about the way mental illness excuses, when it does excuse. Its specialness consists in its not needing the excusing force of other conditions (such as lack of voluntariness of action, etc.); it does its excusing work all by itself."[52] It does this, says Moore, by denying moral agency to the legally insane, such that the law does not apply to them; like very young children and trees, they are not subject to its dictates. The illness need not cause the criminal act, either; it is a status defense. The medical term "psychosis" is a serviceable proxy for the legal concept of insanity, Moore argues, because it designates a person who is very seriously mentally ill.

Moore is right that mental illness is special in its exculpatory power, but mental illness is not inherently exculpatory—it must be an illness of the sort and severity that substantially degrades one's executive function. A defendant's mental illness excuses her from responsibility, when it does, precisely because it has prevented her from a fair opportunity to avoid wrongdoing. On the other hand, executive dysfunction is not inherently exculpatory either—it must be dysfunction of the sort that results from mental illness. If a defendant's executive deficits could be traced back to his own diachronic agency, they ought not to excuse, for the same sorts of reasons that that self-induced intoxication or duress ought not to excuse. One who has intentionally cultivated the trait of being hasty and quick to anger—to shutting down executive inhibition under certain circumstances—should not be excused for a crime, even if it can be shown that the crime resulted from this executive deficit. Of course, it will be extremely rare that one's executive choices lead to the level of executive damage required for legal insanity; a case where one had suffered a traumatic brain injury sustained after choosing to drive a motorcycle drunk would perhaps qualify as an example.

By viewing legal insanity through the lens of executive dysfunction, then, we can plausibly maintain a weak-relevance position. Our account avoids the first horn of Moore's dilemma: by offering mental illness as a special source of executive dysfunction, it preserves the claim that mental illness is relevant to legal insanity. Yet it also avoids the second horn: by making executive dysfunction the bridge between mental illness and legal insanity, it preserves the insight that even persons suffering from severe forms of mental illness may not be excused as legally insane, so long as that illness has left their executive functions essentially intact.

Our position is not only capable of avoiding Moore's dilemma while retaining his core insight about the exculpatory specialness of mental illness; it also moves past Moore's problematic endorsement of the quasi-medical term "psychotic" as a proxy for terms like "insane" or "seriously mentally ill." According to Moore, it is a bit of "interdisciplinary serendipity" that the psychiatric term "psychosis" just happens to map nicely onto the legal term "insanity."[53] We submit, and can explain why, this "serendipity" is no mere stroke of luck: it suggests that criminal legal doctrines, which also serve as systematized repositories of folk psychological beliefs,[54] have long been aiming at a target class of conditions that have only recently become amenable to fine-grained analysis using the terms and concepts of science and medicine.[55] We contend that what Moore and the folk have in mind when they say things like "seriously mental ill" or "crazy" in the context of legal or moral judgments are just those the types and severity-levels of mental illness that substantially disable executive functioning, thereby producing the very cognitive and volitional incapacities tested by, for example, the Model Penal Code.

Case Study: Anders Breivik

The Norwegian case of Anders Breivik has renewed academic discussions of legal insanity, especially with regard to medical or biological models. Breivik killed 77 people in 2011, 69 of them participants in a youth summer camp. Breivik claimed the killings were a marketing ploy for a compendium of far-right militant texts he distributed on the day of the attacks. An initial court-ordered psychiatric evaluation resulted in a diagnosis of paranoid schizophrenia, in part due to Breivik having persistent, systematized, bizarre delusions, including a belief that he was a member of a Knights Templar organization that Norwegian police stated did not actually exist. A second psychiatric evaluation was ordered following widespread criticism of the first, and concluded that Breivik was not psychotic at the time of the attacks. This evaluation instead diagnosed him with narcissistic personality disorder.

Norway's criminal code stipulates that any defendant who possesses psychotic symptoms at the time of his crime is not criminally responsible by reason of insanity. Thus Norway's test for legal insanity echoes Michael Moore's proposed model discussed previously: mental illness is a status defense, where any defendant diagnosed as having a certain mental illness at the time of the crime is excused.[56] The definition of psychosis, according to Norwegian statute, is to be determined by current psychiatric diagnostic manuals. The DSM-IV, thought to be the most prominent diagnostic manual at the time of Breivik's evaluations, defines psychosis as the presence of hallucinations or delusions. Thus it was widely thought that the first evaluation would result in Breivik being declared criminally insane under Norwegian law, and this is why many demanded a new evaluation. In the end, because of this second psychiatric evaluation, Breivik was found legally sane and guilty of 77 counts of murder. He was sentenced to the maximum criminal sentence allowable in Norway: 21 years, with the possibility of an extension if he is deemed to be a danger to society. Breivik will probably be incarcerated for the rest of his life.

Bortolotti, Broome, and Mameli have argued that even if Breivik did have delusions, and thus was properly diagnosed as psychotic at the time of his crime, this fact may be totally irrelevant to whether Breivik is criminally responsible for his acts.[57] Indeed, they argue that no particular set of psychiatric symptoms or diagnoses is sufficient to determine if a defendant is legally insane.[58] This is because the level of functioning, cognitive and social, can vary widely amongst those with psychosis and schizophrenia, and thus a diagnosis or the symptom of hallucinations or delusions themselves do not necessarily indicate the quality of a person's legal and moral agency.

As already indicated, we completely agree with this assessment. Executive functions are what ground legal and moral agency, and someone with normal executive capacity may be capable of detecting and inhibiting behavior based upon a hallucination or delusion. However, we would disagree with Bortolotti et al. to the extent that they wish to take their argument further and claim the presence of mental illness is irrelevant to a determination of legal insanity. It matters *why* an agent's executive capacity is diminished, for reasons previously stated: in some cases diminished executive capacity can be linked to prior culpable decisions by the defendant. However, mental illness can usually not be traced back to conscious choices made on the part of the defendant. The diagnoses of schizophrenia and psychosis are often correlated with severe executive deficits, which means they are also correlated with compromised legal agency.

Having made this point, we acknowledge that the diagnosis of schizophrenia doesn't necessarily indicate executive deficits or dysfunction. Thus such a diagnosis is not *always* a good stand-in for a more direct determination that the defendant is legally insane due to executive deficits. This is why we have argued that the MPC test for insanity is the best approach: this test asks the court, in folk psychological terms, to look for cognitive and volitional deficits in defendant's executive functions that stem from a mental illness. Experts may then offer evidence regarding the defendant's diagnoses, and whether the cognitive and volitional deficits suffered by the defendant are substantial enough to warrant an excuse.

In sum, Bortolotti et al. are on the right track when they claim that, if Breivik's poor reality testing (or some other relevant cognitive deficit association with delusion formation) is affecting the beliefs he is prepared to endorse to the extent that such beliefs are implausible even to members of groups inclined to share his political and ideological views, then maybe such failure of reality testing (or other relevant cognitive deficit) is also implicated in his decision-making processes, including those processes that led him to his criminal acts.[59]

What matters to responsibility is not the presence of false or bizarre beliefs themselves, but the capacity a defendant has to identify and reject them, or inhibit behavior based upon them. As we noted, many sane persons have had bizarre beliefs, delusions, or even hallucinations ("I swear I saw a scary looking old man sitting over there!" when it is really just a tree, or "I swear I just saw Aunt Julie walking past, but I know she is in Toronto!"). What makes one legally insane is the breakdown of executive function such that one acts in accordance with their bizarre beliefs or hallucinations. If my executive is generally functioning normally, but in this one case, I believe it really is my Aunt Julie walking past, I am likely to approach her slowly and carefully, searching for further cues regarding whether or not she is my aunt. However, a person with a mental illness resulting in global executive deficits, and thus lower volitional and emotional control, as well as a heightened likelihood of jumping to conclusions, may grab the woman's arm and shout, "What are you doing here?" and scare the stranger who looks like his aunt half to death, or even perform a battery against her. In this way we can once again see that the presence of a mental illness may produce the sort of executive deficits plus additional circumstances that may result in a legal excuse.

6 Conclusion

We began this chapter by endorsing the fairly anodyne claim that legal insanity is a concept belonging to the law, not to psychiatry, meaning that a philosophical discussion of legal insanity should begin by reflecting upon the purposes we want the criminal law to serve, in relative isolation from the aims and concerns of medical science. For the law to fulfill those purposes, well captured by hybrid theories of punishment in the tradition of Hart and Morris,[60] it must include an accurate view of what makes someone fit for punishment, and what kinds of conditions exclude or excuse a person from criminal responsibility. We think Brink is broadly right that criminal responsibility requires the fair opportunity to have avoided wrongdoing, and that any such opportunity must include a level of "normative competence" comprising both cognitive and volitional capacities.[61] We contend that executive functions constitute the ground of legal agency,[62] because they underwrite the very capacities described by Brink. The M'Naghten standard, which focuses on cognitive capacity to the exclusion of volitional elements, is therefore crucially flawed; the Model Penal Code, though probably imperfect, is the best test of legal insanity going because it probes both the cognitive and volitional prongs of normative competence.

Still, one might reasonably wonder about the extent to which the Model Penal Code standard, and the concept of legal insanity it involves, match up with our best scientific and medical theories and concepts—or whether there need be any such accordance at all. Even if we can agree about the proper test for legal insanity, what should the connection be, if any, between this set of legal concepts and the medico-scientific concepts under the heading "mental illness"? Moore's answer is that one must accept either the implausible view that mental illness is entirely irrelevant to legal insanity, or else Moore's strong relevance position, holding that mental illness—when it excuses—can excuse all by itself.[63] Although we find much to admire in Moore's remarks, we disagree that these are the only options available.

As an alternative, we offer a weak-relevance thesis based on the idea that executive functions provide a conceptual bridge between legal concepts of insanity and medical theories of mental illness. A diagnosis of schizophrenia *can* be relevant to a defendant's plea of legal insanity—not simply because such a diagnosis is independently exculpatory, but because it may include a clinical judgment of substantial and global executive dysfunction as a symptom of the disease, which would rightly bear on the question of whether the defendant should be excused from criminal responsibility. Appreciating the role of executive functions in grounding moral and legal agency reinforces the legitimacy of the Model Penal Code standard for legal insanity, but it also offers a more accurate and nuanced picture of how mental illness can erode the normative competence required for a fair opportunity to avoid criminal wrongdoing.[64]

Notes

1. Moore, "The Quest for a Responsible Responsibility Test."
2. Brink, "Responsibility, Incompetence, and Psychopathy."
3. E.g., Duff, *Criminal Attempts*; Moore, "The Moral Worth of Retribution"; Morris, "The Future of Imprisonment."

4. E.g., Bentham, *An Introduction to the Principles of Morals and Legislation*; Braithwaite and Pettit, *Not Just Deserts*.

5. H.L.A. Hart viewed desert as providing an upper limit on criminal sanctions, indicating that one must appeal to a retributive account of appropriateness of punishment given the crime committed, which "set[s] a maximum within which penalties, judged most likely to prevent the repetition of the crime by the offender or others, are to be chosen" (*Punishment and Responsibility*, 236–37). Even Jeremy Bentham, despite his strong utilitarian account of punishment, acknowledged the need to maintain proportionality between offender and punishment (*Principles of Morals and Legislation*).

6. In 2007, the American Law Institute revised the Model Penal Code's sentencing provisions, calling for a renewed commitment to proportionality based on the "gravity of offenses," the "blameworthiness of offenders," and the "harms done to crime victims." See Model Penal Code (MPC) § 1.02(2)(2)(a)(i) (2007).

7. Morris, "Future of Imprisonment."

8. See Moore, *Causation and Responsibility*.

9. Brooks, *Punishment*.

10. As Hart noted: "Recognition of excusing conditions is therefore seen as a matter of protection of the individual against the claims of society for the highest measure of protection of the individual against the claims society for the highest measure of protection from crime that can be obtained from a system of threats. In this way the criminal law respects the claims of the individual as such, or at least as a *choosing being*, and distributes its coercive sanctions in a way that reflects this respect for the individual" (*Punishment and Responsibility*, 49).

11. Brink, "Responsibility, Incompetence, and Psychopathy."

12. Ibid., 1.

13. Ibid., 3–5.

14. Model Penal Code 4.01.

15. Morse, "Uncontrollable Urges and Irrational People."

16. Brink, "Responsibility, Incompetence, and Psychopathy," 14.

17. Ibid., 15.

18. Ibid., 12.

19. Ibid., 16.

20. Garavan et al., "Dissociable Executive Functions in the Dynamic Control of Behavior"; Miyake and Friedman, "The Nature and Organization of Individual Differences in Executive Functions."

21. Barbas, "Complementary Roles of Prefrontal Cortical Regions."

22. Burgess et al., "The Cognitive and Neuroanatomical Correlates of Multitasking."

23. Carter et al., "Anterior Cingulate Cortex, Error Detection, and the Online Monitoring of Performance."

24. Aron, Robbins, and Poldrack, "Inhibition and the Right Inferior Frontal Cortex."

25. Eshel et al., "Neural Substrates of Choice Selection in Adults and Adolescents."

26. Baird and Fugelsang, "The Emergence of Consequential Thought."

27. Best, Miller, and Jones, "Executive Functions after Age 5"; Kanwisher, "Functional Specificity in the Human Brain."

28. Hirstein, "The Misidentification Syndromes as Mindreading Disorders."

29. Fucetola et al., "Age and Neuropsychologic Function in Schizophrenia"; Heinrichs and Zakzanis, "Neurocognitive Deficit in Schizophrenia"; Johnson-Selfridge and Zalewski, "Moderator Variables of Executive Functioning in Schizophrenia"; Lee and Park, "Working Memory Impairments in Schizophrenia"; Li, "Do Schizophrenia Patients Make More Perseverative Than Non-Perseverative Errors on the Wisconsin Card Sorting Test?"

30. Hutton et al., "Executive Function in First-Episode Schizophrenia."

31. Harvey et al., "Negative Symptoms and Cognitive Deficits"; Krishnadas et al., "Residual Negative Symptoms Differentiate Cognitive Performance in Clinically Stable Patients with Schizophrenia and Bipolar Disorder."

32. Krishnadas et al., "Residual Negative Symptoms."

33. Barr et al., "Evidence for Excessive Frontal Evoked Gamma Oscillatory Activity in Schizophrenia During Working Memory"; Cho, Konecky, and Carter, "Impairments in Frontal Cortical Γ Synchrony and Cognitive Control in Schizophrenia"; Farzan et al., "Evidence for Gamma Inhibition Deficits in the Dorsolateral Prefrontal Cortex of Patients with Schizophrenia"; Radhu et al., "Evidence for Inhibitory Deficits in the Prefrontal Cortex in Schizophrenia."

34. Leeson et al., "The Relationship between Iq, Memory, Executive Function, and Processing Speed in Recent-Onset Psychosis."

35. Krishnadas et al., "Residual Negative Symptoms."

36. Laloyaux et al., "Multitasking Capacities in Persons Diagnosed with Schizophrenia."

37. González-Blanch et al., "Cognitive Functioning in the Early Course of First-Episode Schizophrenia Spectrum Disorders."

38. Semkovska et al., "Assessment of Executive Dysfunction During Activities of Daily Living in Schizophrenia."

39. Laloyaux et al., "Multitasking Capacities."

40. Krishnan, Kraus, and Keefe, "Comprehensive Model of how Reality Distortion and Symptoms Occur in Schizophrenia"; Moritz and Woodward, "Jumping to Conclusions in Delusional and Non-delusional Schizophrenic Patients"; Ochoa et al., "Relation between Jumping to Conclusions and Cognitive Functioning in People with Schizophrenia in Contrast with Healthy Participants"; White and Mansell, "Failing to Ponder?"

41. Davies et al., "Monothematic Delusions: Towards a Two-Factor Account"; Langdon and Coltheart, "The Cognitive Neuropsychology of Delusions"; McKay, Langdon, and Coltheart, "Models of Misbelief."

42. Hirstein and Sifferd, "The Legal Self: Executive Processes and Legal Theory."

43. Model Penal Code 4.01.
44. Brink, "Responsibility, Incompetence, and Psychopathy."
45. Garavan et al., "Dissociable Executive Functions."; Miyake and Friedman, "Individual Differences in Executive Functions."
46. The "policeman at his elbow," or irresistible impulse, standard for legal insanity stems from the early common law case of *People v. Hubert*, 119 Cal. 216, 223–224, 51 P. 329 (1897). However, courts that have adopted the MPC substantial capacity approach have largely rejected the standard as too strict. As the court in *People v. Jackson* (171 Mich.Ct.App. 191 (1988)) noted,

> . . . This is not to say that the "policeman at the elbow" standard has no relevance. If it is approached as being one of many avenues of inquiry, the hypothetical is directly probative of one dimension of a defendant's capacity to control his conduct as required by law. Certainly, if credible testimony offered by a defendant establishes that he could not refrain from acting even if faced with immediate capture and punishment, then the defendant would have gone a long way toward establishing that he lacked the requisite substantial capacity to conform to requirements of the law. The converse, however, is not true. A defendant who could resist until the threat posed by a policeman had passed does not necessarily possess the capacity to conform. Nonetheless, if it so chooses, the prosecution must be allowed to explore the depths of defendant's alleged incapacity by posing the "policeman at the elbow" hypothetical inasmuch as the question is probative of a defendant's ability to conform to the requirements of the law under the most extreme circumstance of immediate capture and punishment.

47. Moore, "The Quest for a Responsible Responsibility Test."
48. Ibid., 14.
49. Ibid., 17.
50. Ibid.
51. Feinberg, *Doing and Deserving*.
52. Moore, "The Quest for a Responsible Responsibility Test," 44.
53. Ibid., 45.
54. Sifferd, "In Defense of the Use of Commonsense Psychology in the Criminal Law."
55. Hirstein and Sifferd, "The Legal Self."
56. Moore, "The Quest for a Responsible Responsibility Test."
57. Bortolotti, Broome, and Mameli, "Delusions and Responsibility for Action."
58. Bortolotti et al., "Delusions and Responsibility."
59. Ibid., 380.
60. Hart, *Punishment and Responsibility*; Morris, "The Future of Imprisonment."
61. Brink, "Responsibility, Incompetence, and Psychopathy."
62. Hirstein and Sifferd, "The Legal Self."
63. Moore, "The Quest for a Responsible Responsibility Test."
64. We are extremely grateful to Margaret Sumney (2015 Elmhurst College graduate) for her research assistance, and to Mark D. White for his comments on an earlier draft of this chapter.

Resources

Aron, A. R., T. W. Robbins, and R. A. Poldrack, "Inhibition and the Right Inferior Frontal Cortex: One Decade On." *Trends in Cognitive Sciences* 18(2014): 177–85.

Baird, Abigail A., and Jonathan A. Fugelsang, "The Emergence of Consequential Thought: Evidence from Neuroscience." *Philosophical Transactions of the Royal Society B* 359(2004): 1797–1804.

Barbas, Helen, "Complementary Roles of Prefrontal Cortical Regions in Cognition, Memory, and Emotion in Primates." *Advances in Neurology* 84(2000): 87–110.

Barr, M. S., et al., "Evidence for Excessive Frontal Evoked Gamma Oscillatory Activity in Schizophrenia During Working Memory." *Schizophrenia Research* 121(2010): 146-52.

Bentham, Jeremy, *An Introduction to the Principles of Morals and Legislation*. Oxford: Claredon Press, 1996.

Best, John R., Patricia H. Miller, and Lara L. Jones, "Executive Functions after Age 5: Changes and Correlates." *Developmental Review* 29(2009): 180–200.

Bortolotti, Lisa, Matthew R. Broome, and Matteo Mameli, "Delusions and Responsibility for Action: Insights from the Breivik Case." *Neuroethics* 7(2014): 377–82.

Braithwaite, John, and Philip Pettit, *Not Just Deserts: A Republican Theory of Criminal Justice*. Oxford: Clarendon Press, 1990.

Brink, David O., "Responsibility, Incompetence, and Psychopathy." *The Lindley Lectures* 51(2013).

Brooks, Thom, *Punishment*. Abingdon, UK: Routledge, 2012.

Burgess, Paul W., Emma Veitch, Angela de Lacy Costello, and Tim Shallice, "The Cognitive and Neuroanatomical Correlates of Multitasking." *Neuropsychologia* 38(2000): 848–63.

Carter, Cameron S., et al., "Anterior Cingulate Cortex, Error Detection, and the Online Monitoring of Performance." *Science* 280(1998): 747–49.

Cho, R. Y., R. O. Konecky, and Cameron S. Carter, "Impairments in Frontal Cortical Γ Synchrony and Cognitive Control in Schizophrenia." *Proceedings of the National Academy of Sciences* 103 (2006): 19878-83.

Davies, Martin, Max Coltheart, Robyn Langdon, and Nora Breen, "Monothematic Delusions: Towards a Two-Factor Account." *Philosophy, Psychiatry, & Psychology* 8(2001): 133–58.

Duff, R.A., *Criminal Attempts*. Oxford: Clarendon Press, 1996.

Eshel, Neir, et al., "Neural Substrates of Choice Selection in Adults and Adolescents: Development of the Ventrolateral Prefrontal and Anterior Cingulate Cortices." *Neuropsychologia* 45(2007): 1270–79.

Farzan, Faranak, et al., "Evidence for Gamma Inhibition Deficits in the Dorsolateral Prefrontal Cortex of Patients with Schizophrenia." *Brain* 133 (2010): 1505–14.

Feinberg, Joel, *Doing and Deserving: Essays in the Theory of Responsibility*. Princeton, NJ: Princeton University Press, 1971.
Fucetola, Robert, et al., "Age and Neuropsychologic Function in Schizophrenia: A Decline in Executive Abilities Beyond That Observed in Healthy Volunteers." *Biological Psychiatry* 48(2000): 137–46.
Garavan, H., et al., "Dissociable Executive Functions in the Dynamic Control of Behavior: Inhibition, Error Detection, and Correction." *Neuroimage* 17(2002): 1820–29.
González-Blanch, César, et al., "Cognitive Functioning in the Early Course of First-Episode Schizophrenia Spectrum Disorders." *European Archives of Psychiatry and Clinical Neuroscience* 256(2006): 364–71.
Hart, H.L.A., *Punishment and Responsibility: Essays in the Philosophy of Law*. New York: Oxford University Press, 1968.
Harvey, Philip D., Danny Koren, Abraham Reichenberg, and Christopher R. Bowie, "Negative Symptoms and Cognitive Deficits: What Is the Nature of Their Relationship?" *Schizophrenia Bulletin* 32(2006): 250–58.
Heinrichs, R. Walter, and Konstantine K. Zakzanis, "Neurocognitive Deficit in Schizophrenia: A Quantitative Review of the Evidence." *Neuropsychology* 12(1998): 426–45.
Hirstein, William, "The Misidentification Syndromes as Mindreading Disorders." *Cognitive Neuropsychiatry*, 15 (2010): 233–260.
Hirstein, William, and Katrina Sifferd, "The Legal Self: Executive Processes and Legal Theory." *Consciousness and Cognition* 20(2011): 156–71.
Hutton, S. B., et al., "Executive Function in First-Episode Schizophrenia." *Psychological Medicine* 28(1998): 463–73.
Johnson-Selfridge, Margaret, and Christine Zalewski, "Moderator Variables of Executive Functioning in Schizophrenia: Meta-Analytic Findings." *Schizophrenia Bulletin* 27(2001): 305–16.
Kanwisher, Nancy, "Functional Specificity in the Human Brain: A Window into the Functional Architecture of the Mind." *Proceedings of the National Academy of Sciences* 107(2010): 11163–70.
Krishnan, Ranga R., Michael S. Kraus, and Richard S. E. Keefe. "Comprehensive Model of how Reality Distortion and Symptoms Occur in Schizophrenia: Could Impairment in Learning-dependent Predictive Perception Account for the Manifestations of Schizophrenia?" *Psychiatry and Clinical Neurosciences* 65(2011): 305–317.
Krishnadas, Rajeev, et al., "Residual Negative Symptoms Differentiate Cognitive Performance in Clinically Stable Patients with Schizophrenia and Bipolar Disorder." *Schizophrenia Research and Treatment* 2014(2014): 1–6.
Laloyaux, Julien, et al., "Multitasking Capacities in Persons Diagnosed with Schizophrenia: A Preliminary Examination of Their Neurocognitive Underpinnings and Ability to Predict Real World Functioning." *Psychiatry Research* 217(2014): 163–70.
Langdon, Robyn, and Max Coltheart, "The Cognitive Neuropsychology of Delusions." *Mind & Language* 15(2000): 184–218.

Lee, Junghee, and Sohee Park, "Working Memory Impairments in Schizophrenia: A Meta-Analysis." *Journal of Abnormal Psychology* 114(2005): 599–611.

Leeson, Verity C., et al., "The Relationship between IQ, Memory, Executive Function, and Processing Speed in Recent-Onset Psychosis: 1-Year Stability and Clinical Outcome." *Schizophrenia Bulletin* 36(2010): 400–09.

Li, Chiang-Shan Ray, "Do Schizophrenia Patients Make More Perseverative Than Non-Perseverative Errors on the Wisconsin Card Sorting Test? A Meta-Analytic Study." *Psychiatry Research* 129(2004): 179–90.

McKay, Ryan, Robyn Langdon, and Max Coltheart, "Models of Misbelief: Integrating Motivational and Deficit Theories of Delusions." *Consciousness and Cognition* 16(2007): 932–41.

Miyake, Akira, and Naomi P. Friedman, "The Nature and Organization of Individual Differences in Executive Functions Four General Conclusions." *Current Directions in Psychological Science* 21(2012): 8–14.

Moore, Michael S., *Causation and Responsibility: An Essay in Law, Morals, and Metaphysics*. Oxford: Oxford University Press, 2009.

Moore, Michael S., "The Moral Worth of Retribution." In *Responsibility, Character and the Emotions: New Essays in Moral Psychology*, edited by Ferdinand Schoeman (Cambridge: Cambridge University Press, 1988), 179–219.

Moore, Michael S., "The Quest for a Responsible Responsibility Test: Norwegian Insanity Law after Breivik." *Criminal Law and Philosophy* 9(2015): 645–93.

Moritz, Steffen, and Todd S. Woodward. "Jumping to Conclusions in Delusional and Non-Delusional Schizophrenic Patients." *British Journal of Clinical Psychology* 44(2005): 193–207.

Morris, Norval, "The Future of Imprisonment: Toward a Punitive Philosophy." *Michigan Law Review* 72(1974): 1161–80.

Morse, Stephen J., "Uncontrollable Urges and Irrational People." *Virginia Law Review* 88(2002): 1025–78.

Ochoa, Susana, et al., "Relation between Jumping to Conclusions and Cognitive Functioning in People with Schizophrenia in Contrast with Healthy Participants." *Schizophrenia Research* 159(2014): 211–17.

Radhu, Natasha, et al., "Evidence for Inhibitory Deficits in the Prefrontal Cortex in Schizophrenia." *Brain* 138(2015): 483–97.

Semkovska, Maria, et al., "Assessment of Executive Dysfunction During Activities of Daily Living in Schizophrenia." *Schizophrenia Research* 69(2004): 289–300.

Sifferd, Katrina L., "In Defense of the Use of Commonsense Psychology in the Criminal Law." *Law and Philosophy* 25(2006): 571–612.

White, Lars O., and Warren Mansell. "Failing to ponder? Delusion-prone Individuals Rush to Conclusions." *Clinical Psychology & Psychotherapy* 16 (2009): 111–124.

CHAPTER NINE

Insanity and Free Will: The Humanitarian Argument for Abolition

Michael Louis Corrado

[M]any, including Lady Wootton, have said that no satisfactory line can be drawn between the mentally normal and abnormal offenders: there simply are no clear or reliable criteria. They insist that ... we should be freed from all such illusory classifications to treat, in the most appropriate way from the point of view of society, all persons who have actually manifested the behavior which is the *actus reus* of a crime.[1]

Among the arguments for abolishing the insanity defense there is the one that politicians often appeal to: the defense makes it too easy for criminals to evade punishment, and to avoid this outcome all criminals, including the mentally ill, must be punished.[2] The force behind the argument lies in the sentiments that arise in reaction to violent crime: fear and vindictiveness. But there are also serious theoretical arguments, among them the one that I want to focus on here, namely that the insanity defense is based upon a philosophical and sociological error: the idea that criminals have free will. If we reject that error, according to this argument, we will also reject the insanity defense, and we will reject it not for the purpose of denying the supposed advantages of the defense to the mentally ill, but of extending those advantages to all criminals. And what are the advantages of an insanity acquittal? That the offender is not punished, so this argument goes, but rather committed to an institution where he will find softer conditions and necessary treatment.

The argument is based upon two suppositions: that crimes are not the outcome of the free choice of offenders but are instead unavoidable, and that punishment is due only when a crime is the result of the offender's freely made choice. From these starting points we are to conclude that punishment is never justified. And the last step is this: Because no one is to be punished, the point of the insanity defense disappears.

Call this argument "the Humanitarian Argument for abolition of the insanity defense."[3] We find this reasoning in the recent writings, for example, of Derk Pereboom and Gregg Caruso.[4] I agree with much of this argument, all the way up to and including the conclusion that punishment by the state is never justified. But the last step, from "no one is to be punished" to "the point of the insanity defense disappears," is one that I think is dangerous and unwarranted, and one that I reject. Punishment, I believe, is essentially retributive, but although I believe that retribution and therefore punishment are not justifiable, I believe that an institution very much like punishment, an institution that uses some of the methods of punishment but without the retributive aim, is essential to any criminal justice system that is worth wanting. An institution of the sort I have in mind would subject sane and rational criminals to the measured but harsh methods of detention for limited periods and fines of limited amounts and other restrictive measures. I would call institutions that fit that description "corrective" or "correctional."

Others have reached similar conclusions, calling what they are after "non-retributive punishment,"[5] but it seems to me important to distinguish between punishment as something that is inherently retributive and the use of the methods of punishment for non-retributive, non-punitive ends. I believe that correction—but not punishment!—is justified for those who can benefit from it, but not for those who cannot benefit from it. This distinction, between those who can benefit from correction and those who cannot, supports a defense like the insanity defense, and so I reject the inference from "no one is to be punished" to "the point of the insanity defense disappears."

All of this will no doubt seem counterintuitive to most readers, from the denial of free will to the rejection of the insanity defense on free will grounds, and not least the part about replacing punishment with correction (a difference that may seem to make no difference). What I want to show in this chapter is this: all of the alternative approaches to the problem that the question of free will raises for the insanity defense require us to countenance claims that are at least equally counterintuitive. That is something that is worth knowing for its own sake whether or not the reader finds my own notion of a corrective criminal justice system appealing.

1 The *Strasburg* Case in Washington State

In the first decade of the 20th century, the legislature of the state of Washington decided that, from the point of view of the criminal law, there was no difference between the sane offender and the offender whose crime was the result of serious mental illness, and it abolished the insanity defense.[6] There was no denying that some criminals were sane and others mentally ill; what was denied was the appropriateness of punishment for anyone and consequently the need for a system that distinguished sharply between those who could be punished and those who could not.

The statute abolishing the defense reached the state supreme court when a defendant who had been denied the defense petitioned for review. The prosecutor charged with defending the law argued to the court as follows:

> The central idea upon which the whole fabric of criminal jurisprudence was formerly built was the idea that every criminal act was the product of a free will possessing a full understanding of the difference between right and wrong and full capacity to choose a right or wrong course of action, and, as one error naturally and logically follows another, it was only natural and logical that society should have prescribed punishments as a central feature of its scheme for correction. *A better understanding of crime and the science of criminology now convinces us that this theory is wholly wrong—that a dominant percentage of all criminals are not free moral agents, but, as a result of hereditary influences or early environments, are either mentally or morally degenerate or their crimes are committed under the degenerating influence of intoxicating liquor.* An understanding of this fact has made readily apparent the folly of expecting that punishment could relieve the condition, and accordingly stocks, whipping posts, and chain gangs are giving way to workhouses, reformatories, and asylums, the purpose of which is to instruct, educate, and reform rather than further to debase the individual, and the modern systems of criminal classification and segregation are themselves a recognition of the fact that every criminal is a concrete problem.[7]

In the eyes of the Washington Supreme Court, this optimism was unjustified, and the court struck the statute down as unconstitutional:

> Learned counsel's premise suggests a noble conception, and may give promise of a condition of things towards which the humanitarian spirit of the age is tending; yet the stern and awful fact still remains, and is patent to all men, that the status and condition in the eyes of the world, and under the law, of one convicted of crime, is vastly different from that of one simply adjudged insane.[8]

And so the insanity defense withstood the assault in Washington State in 1910. But like the free will controversy in philosophy, the debate about the Humanitarian Argument for abolition will not just go away. Today, revitalized by the work of neuroscientists, the debate is alive and well.

2 The Humanitarian Argument

The general structure of the state's argument was this: punishment is appropriate only for offenders who are "free moral agents," that is, who could have avoided doing what they did. Most offenders could not have avoided doing what they did, and so punishment is never appropriate. But because the state must do something to protect its citizens against those who are dangerous, and because punishment is not justified, the preventive measures formerly used against the mentally ill—detention, therapy, and other methods intended to change the individual for the better—are appropriate for all. The insanity defense is based upon a distinction, the court was urged to conclude, that has no justification in fact. The fact of the matter, the prosecutor argued, was that most crimes are the inevitable outcome of background conditions like heredity, poverty and abuse, alcoholism and addiction, and if that is so, there is no benefit in punishment and no justification for it either. Because that is so, there is no reason to distinguish the mentally ill from the sane offender; "every criminal is a concrete problem," to be dealt with in a forward-looking and not in a backward-looking way.

This argument, or something very much like it, had been proposed by sociologists from Ferri to Wootton: There is no hard and fast distinction to be made between those who were fit for punishment and those who were not.[9] The only point of the criminal justice system was to prevent crime, and the only justifiable way of doing it was by trying to correct the flaws in the character of the criminal, whether those flaws be due to mental illness or anything else. Above all, there was no justification for punishing actions that could not be helped. Although we might make use of different methods in each case to achieve the ends we seek, therapy and drugs for the mentally ill, education for the sane, detention for both, there is no theoretically significant distinction between them, no distinction that would justify punishment in one case but not in the other.

The state's argument, however, is not valid as it stands. The conclusion that punishment is never justified and thus that the defense is to be entirely eliminated depends upon the premise that *no* offender could have avoided doing what he did. The only claim the state made in that regard was that *most* offenders could not have avoided doing what they did. Something more needs to be said, and indeed something is waiting in the wings to be added, nurtured by centuries of philosophical controversy: all actions, like other events in the universe, are caused by prior events, and thus *no one has free will.*[10] Something very much like this is what it will take to get us to the conclusion of the argument, whether or not anything like it was on the mind of the members of the Washington legislature when they passed the statute eliminating the insanity defense: All actions are caused; if all actions are caused then all actions are unavoidable; and so no one has free will. That, the revised argument goes, justifies the complete obliteration of the hard distinction between how we should deal with the sane offender and how we should deal with the mentally ill defendant.

The revised argument for abolition will look something like this:

(a) Punishment is appropriate only for offenders who are "free moral agents"—that is, who could have avoided doing what they did.
(b) No one can avoid doing what he does.
(c) Therefore punishment is never appropriate.[11]

Because punishment is never appropriate, any distinction based upon the appropriateness of punishment in some cases—like the one between those who are entitled to the insanity defense and those who are not—has no application:

(d) There is a point to the insanity defense only if punishment is sometimes appropriate.
(e) Therefore there is no point to an insanity defense.

The argument—the Humanitarian Argument—is valid on its face, and if we want to reject the conclusion we will have to show that at least one of the premises is false, or we must accept the conclusion.

3 Denying That All Actions Are Unavoidable: Libertarianism

If you want to deny premise (b), that all actions are unavoidable, you will want to deny either that all actions are caused by prior events or that causation of all actions by prior events entails the unavoidability of all actions.[12] Those who take the first way are called, in philosophy, *libertarians*; those who take the second are called *compatibilists*.

The libertarian accepts that caused actions are unavoidable, but denies that all actions are caused. At least some actions, she would say, are uncaused and avoidable. It's important to see, at the outset, that those two terms, "uncaused" and "avoidable," do not mean the same thing; merely random actions, actions that happened for no reason or that resulted from choices that happened for no reason, would be uncaused, but would not be avoidable. That is, it would not have been possible for the actor to avoid them. What the libertarian position wants to maintain is precisely that some actions are not only uncaused, but are also avoidable. That leaves the ground open for an insanity defense both for those whose actions were avoidable but who, because of mental illness, could not really appreciate what they were doing, and for those whose actions, because of mental illness, were not avoidable.

That doesn't mean that the libertarian must accept both forms of the defense: she might accept that mental illness can prevent a person from understanding his actions and thus create a defense of a cognitive sort, without agreeing that mental illness can ever make an action unavoidable. What's necessary is that she must accept that some actions are punishable, and she does that by insisting that some actions are uncaused and avoidable. On the other hand, it is open to those who take this position either to accept or to reject the claim that background conditions like heredity, poverty, and abuse can make some actions unavoidable. If they do accept that claim they should be willing to extend something like the insanity defense to those with the background conditions in question; if not, they won't.[13] But the libertarian, having rejected the second premise of the abolitionist argument, need not agree to the universal conclusion that no one may be punished.

I should concede that many consider the libertarian story, whether true or false, to be the sort of story that undergirds the criminal law as it exists today. By that line of thinking, the actions that many or most offenders take are the outcome of choices freely made in circumstances in which the offender could have easily made a different choice; they could have done otherwise, and to the extent that they could have done otherwise (and of course understood what they were doing) punishment is appropriate. It is otherwise if they suffer from a mental illness that prevents them from understanding what they do, or makes what they do unavoidable. In those cases they should not be punished, but they cannot simply be released; hence the complications of the insanity defense. But mental illness is an exceptional condition. Whether a defense must in justice be extended to those with rotten background conditions is an empirical question; do those conditions serve as causes of crime, making crime unavoidable in some cases? If so, the libertarian should agree to extending a defense to the offenders in those cases, though by similar reasoning if they are dangerous they should not be released but should be held until their constitutional malady is cured.

The problem for the libertarian is to make sense of actions uncaused by prior events and at the same time avoidable by the actor. We have learned to live with the idea of uncaused events, at least at the sub-atomic level. But even granting that an action might be uncaused, that is not (as I suggested previously) enough to make it avoidable. Let's say that by "uncaused action" we mean an action initiated by a brain event that was uncaused. Now think of this case: Jones is walking down the street one day when a synapse fires in his brain that leads to a series of subsequent firings that cause mental events and the muscle contractions that constitute an action, an action that amounts to unjustifiably breaking the window of a neighbor's car. The initial firing was uncaused: it bore no causal relationship to any prior state or event in Jones' brain, and in particular it bore no relationship whatever to those brain states that correspond to Jones' desires, beliefs, or intentions. It just happened, the way a subatomic particle disappears at one point and reappears at another, without any causal explanation.

Jones, naturally, will want to disclaim the action: it is not something he did so much as something that happened to him. The idea that Jones could have avoided the action is implausible, as is the idea that he might reasonably be punished for it. Indeed, if anything qualifies as an action due to a (temporary) mental disorder, Jones' breaking the window would seem to. So there must be more to avoidability (and punishability) than mere lack of causation. The challenge for the libertarian is to explain what the missing element is.

There are two main sorts of answers given by the libertarian, neither of them entirely satisfactory. The first—the "agent causation" answer—is that although human actions are uncaused by prior events, that does not mean that they are simply uncaused.[14] They are caused by the human being, a kind of unmoved mover. Imagine a man moving a stone with a stick: the movement of the stick causes the stone to move, and the movement of the man's hand causes the stick to move. But what causes the movement of the man's hand? The man does, says the agent-causal theory, and that's the end of the story.[15]

But we generally think of events as being caused by other events, and the thing-causation (or person-causation) required by the theory is a difficult notion to fathom. In particular it requires us to countenance the possibility of brain events that have no causal predecessors, and yet are somehow produced by the human actor.[16] Even if the agent causation theorist does manage to make sense of that, and I find it difficult to believe in that possibility,[17] she will not have shown that in fact there are any actions uncaused by prior events, or any actual cases of agent causation. The fact that it might be a coherent story doesn't mean that it is true.

Still, no one has shown that there is any logical impossibility to the picture and, as I have already mentioned, it does seem to be the picture that lies behind the criminal justice system as we know it, and it would be perfectly compatible with a distinction between those who are entitled to an insanity defense and others who are not. Those who would adopt such a theory, though, must be prepared to wrestle with the difficulties that surround non-event causation, and no suitable solution appears to be anywhere on the horizon.

The other sort of defense of libertarianism does not require any sort of non-event causation, but does exploit the physicist's account of causal leaps at the subatomic level. The leading proponent of this view is Robert Kane.[18] Kane supposes that such leaps in the matter that composes the brain might sometimes determine the choice made by an actor. The result is not a merely random action, because the effects of the quantum leap occur within a setting that comprises all of the belief states and desire states of the actor, and must for its effect make use of tendencies that already exist in the actor. Sometimes the leap occurs at a critical juncture when there are two choices facing the actor, and there is a tension between the two; she has good reason and a great deal of incentive to choose each of them. An example might be the case when a motivated selfless action competes with an equally motivated selfish action. The actor has tendencies that incline her to go one way, and other tendencies that incline her to go the other, and because we are assuming this is a difficult decision for her we may assume that the tendencies on each side will be strong. The leap occurs just at the point in the brain where the decision will be made and one action is chosen rather than the other. But because the action would not have occurred had the actor not been strongly inclined to go that way in the first place, the action chosen can be said to be a genuine choice of hers (though in the circumstances the contrary choice would have been hers as well, and for the very same reasons). The totality of such critical choices makes up the actor's character, and she can be held accountable for anything that results from her character—in particular she can be blamed and punished for it.

Where does that leave the insanity defense? I think the answer must be something like this: the test of whether an actor is to be punished for an offense is whether her action can be traced back to her character, and thus back to the critical decisions made when her action was not caused. If instead the action flows from her mental illness and not ultimately from actions that occurred during one of the character-forming choices, then the action is not hers, and she is not punishable for it. But what if, at a character-forming moment, when the actor is torn between courses of action, his choice for one over the other is determined not by a subatomic event but by a mental illness? And what if, over a period of time the character of an actor was molded of such moments, each determined by his mental illness? Why not say, in that case, that the actions that result from the mental illness are his, and that he ought to be punished for them? I see nothing to privilege the random event over the event caused by mental illness. And in any event, of course, whether any given individual has experienced such character-forming leaps is a matter of conjecture: to punish someone as responsible when the action cannot be traced back to self-formed character is, by the hypothesis we are operating under here, wrong, and there is simply no way to know the relevant history of a person's character.

Kane's work is an attempt to develop libertarianism within a natural universe, without appeal to unmoved movers and unmoved movings that intervene in the causal universe. His work is serious and careful, but his version of libertarian free will seems to me to illustrate the implausibility of trying to unite the idea of libertarian freedom with a natural metaphysics. I will repeat the claim I've made several times already: the libertarian picture of things, or at least the agent-causal version of it, seems to be the picture of action that underlies the criminal law and our existing institutions of blame and punishment. Nevertheless, I think we must tentatively conclude that agent causation remains a mystery and that the libertarian has not (yet) given any persuasive explanation of the idea that actions can be both uncaused by prior events and yet within the power of the agent to avoid. As things stand, the libertarian view appears to be inconsistent with the notion that human beings are a natural part of a natural universe. The alternative view, that human beings comprise a natural part and a supernatural part and that the supernatural part operates by intervening in the natural universe, might be the sort of thing required for making the agent-causal theory plausible; but until we have some plausible account of that supernatural realm itself and of the laws that it operates under it can hardly claim to remove the mystery.

4 Denying That All Actions Are Unavoidable: Compatibilism

If we are not satisfied with libertarian approaches and are persuaded that in fact events (other than subatomic events) must have causes, but nevertheless feel that punishment is sometimes justified, how can we avoid the dilemma? We might insist, with the compatibilist, that we may not infer that actions are unavoidable just because they are caused by prior events. To understand the simplest version of this theory, consider a person—Robert, let's say—facing a fork in the road, and let's call one branch R1 and the other R2. The compatibilist would say that if R2 is blocked (and Robert can't stand still and can't go back), then taking R1 is unavoidable for him, and he should not be punished for taking it. But if there is nothing blocking R1 and nothing blocking R2, then neither path is unavoidable. If R1 is a forbidden path and he takes R1 instead of R2, then he may be punished for it, because taking R1 was not unavoidable. And the important part is this: that is so even if he was caused by prior conditions to choose R1, so that there are really no alternative actions open to him. For it would still be true that had he chosen to take R2, there was nothing blocking him; he would have succeeded.

I want to spend a little time on this, because if you have not seen it before you may find it a little hard to grasp: According to the compatibilist, Robert is punishable for taking R1 because it was avoidable. He could have taken R2. And that is so because if he had chosen to take R2, there was nothing to stop him from taking it. And all of that is compatible with the idea that he was caused by prior conditions and events to choose to take R1.

To make sense of this position, we must carefully distinguish taking a path from choosing to take the path. What avoidability and punishability depend upon, according to one simple version of this view, is whether, in another possible world in which the conditions were such that the person would have chosen R2, he would succeed in taking R2. If that is so, then taking R1 was avoidable, and he may be punished for taking it. "P could have avoided doing A" means, according to this understanding, that had P chosen not to do A, he would have succeeded in not doing A, something that may be true even if we concede that P was caused to choose A. And if we go this way, we see that the Washington prosecutor's argument fails: from the mere fact that someone was caused by his background conditions to choose to commit a crime it does not follow that he could not have avoided committing the crime. Had he chosen not to commit the crime, he would not have committed it.

There is a catch, however, and it requires some fast footwork on the part of the compatibilist to avoid it. The catch is this: suppose that Robert is suffering from a mental illness, and that the mental illness determines some of his choices. And suppose that the mental illness caused him to choose R1, and that he did consequently choose R1 and take R1. It seems counterintuitive to suppose that taking R1 was avoidable, and that he might be punished for taking R1. And yet given the meaning that compatibilism, at least this simple version of compatibilism, has given to the idea of avoidability, taking R1 turns out to be avoidable and punishable. For if he had chosen to take R2 he would have taken R2; the fact that he could not choose to take R2 is irrelevant. Because those mental conditions that are said to prevent agents from conforming their behavior to the law operate through preventing the agent from *choosing* the right path, there is no reason (our compatibilist should agree) to think that they make taking the wrong path unavoidable.[19]

The trick for the compatibilist is to avoid this counterintuitive outcome without at the same time accepting the conclusion of the Humanitarian Argument; that is, the trick is to show why actions that result from mental illness should be regarded as unavoidable, while actions that result from heredity, background, experience, and abuse should not. One way out of these implausible results is to distinguish normal causes from abnormal causes. Causation by a mental illness is an abnormal cause, while causation by background, experience, and education, on the other, are all normal causes. Taking this way out means supplementing our definition of "P could have avoided doing A." It must mean that had P chosen not to do A, he would have succeeded in not doing A, and P was not caused to choose to do A by any abnormal cause.

The obvious problem here is to find a precise criterion for abnormal causes. It seems that we will need a sort of casuistic list: for every case in which we would want to say that the action was unavoidable, in that case the causes must have been abnormal. But in the absence of a criterion that would allow us to distinguish the normal from the abnormal, we can hardly accept this as a solution to the dilemma.

A great deal has been written about compatibilism, and no doubt there is a great deal more still to be written; I can't survey it all in this short chapter. My own feeling, in the end, is that the compatibilist is not going to be able to find a way around the problem of freedom of *choice*: it is implausible to suppose that if Robert was caused to *choose* R1, there is still some sense in which taking R1 was avoidable, and therefore punishable.

5 Denying That Punishment Requires Avoidability: Consequentialism

The two responses to the abolitionist argument that we have considered so far, the libertarian response and the compatibilist response, deny that all actions are unavoidable, the libertarian by denying that all actions are caused, the compatibilist by denying that causation is inconsistent with avoidability. Suppose that you want to deny the abolitionist conclusion but that you accept that all events that are not subatomic events are caused, including those events that are human actions, and that causation of actions means unavoidability. One alternative is to deny premise (a), which says that avoidability is a necessary condition of punishability. We might, that is, agree that even if offenders could not have avoided committing their crimes it is OK to punish them. If we do agree to deny that premise, then of course we can reject subconclusion (c), which says that punishment is never justified, and we can avoid getting to abolition—conclusion (e)—by that route. This is the route chosen by those who propose purely utilitarian justifications for punishment, and by those who in other ways look for non-retributive justifications. (Some have even argued that giving up retributive responses is not something that is desirable, and in any event is not something that is possible even if it were desirable. This is not a position that I feel a need to respond to here. It is a pessimistic view of human nature that appears to have no empirical foundation.)

The utilitarian justification has yet to avoid the problem of punishing the innocent, of course,[20] and that becomes particularly relevant when considering the insanity defense: if it is OK to punish those who cannot help doing what they do, why is there any objection at all to punishing the mentally ill? Unless we can provide another explanation for the defense, one consistent with punishing those who can't avoid doing what they do, we may be committing ourselves to punishing the mentally ill, and thus to another argument for abolishing the insanity defense.

At this point I might be accused of moving too quickly to dismiss the purely utilitarian justification. The reader might be persuaded that utilitarianism can justify punishment while at the same time excusing those whose crimes are due to mental illness. The argument might go like this: The mere fact that all actions are caused and unavoidable is not enough to render punishment useless, because the very existence of punishment will enter into the list of causes that might operate in the production of an action. Some causes of human action, after all, operate through the application of reasoning to what we perceive, or believe we perceive, the state of the world to be. The fact that there are laws and punishments attached to violation of those laws will sometimes enter into calculations that result in action, all of this so even in a purely causal view of human action. Punishment, then, can promote utility even if all actions are caused and unavoidable. On the other hand, confusion and delusion due to mental illness may make punishment useless: those who suffer the same mental illness as the mentally ill defendant cannot easily be influenced by the punishment of the defendant. Therefore both punishment and the insanity defense (as well as other "*mens rea*" defenses) have a place in this utilitarian scheme.

The punish-the-innocent problem clings to this solution, as Hart pointed out: If we stick to our utilitarian principles the abolition of the insanity defense and the punishment of the mentally ill might very well be justified.[21] For it may be—because in the end this is an empirical question—that the punishment of the mentally ill will produce more good than harm by deterring those who think they can avoid punishment by claiming, without justification, to be mentally ill. And if that is so, the utilitarian will have nothing to say in favor of maintaining this defense. There are, of course, utilitarians who appear to accept the story pretty much as I have told it—I am thinking primarily of Brandt here[22]—and who insist on the importance of the insanity defense. But the argument seems to me implausible, resting as it does on the assumption that punishing those who could not have done otherwise is OK, so long as it has positive consequences. Exonerating that argument of the traces of punishing the innocent that we find in it will be no easy matter.

If what I have said so far is true, the argument that unavoidability is irrelevant to punishment would seem to be in a bad way. It would seem so, that is, if it were not for one thing, something that cannot be ignored by anyone interested in the justification of the insanity defense. There are examples proposed by Harry Frankfurt which are intended to show that even if an actor cannot *choose* to do otherwise (thus coming in at the point at which the conditional compatibilist analysis seems to fail), nevertheless blame would seem to be appropriate, and perhaps punishment.[23]

I will not rehearse the details of the examples here. The idea is that someone who *can* be blocked from choosing otherwise can be blamed for what he does, so long as he is not *in fact* blocked from choosing to do otherwise. That is, he could be caused by another to choose doing what he does, but since he is going to choose it anyway that outside interference is not necessary. Because he was not caused by another to choose to do what he did but chose it on his own, our sense is that it is appropriate to blame him for what he did even though he could not have chosen otherwise. (If he were going to choose otherwise, he would have been blocked by the outsider, but that interference was never in fact needed.) And, in the appropriate circumstances, our intuitions would support punishment for that action; at the very least we would be hard-pressed to explain why the action should not be punished. Hence the first premise is false: actions that are unavoidable might well be punishable. On the other hand, if the outsider *had* intervened and had caused the choice—against the will of the actor, so to speak—no blame or punishment would be appropriate.

The reaction upon first encountering this puzzle would be to insist that the difference in the two cases is that in one case the actor acts freely, and in the other, where the outsider causes the choice, he does not. But now the very idea of free action comes into question. For the cash value of the notion of freedom, as we have used it so far (see the formulation of the first premise) lies in the idea of avoidability and in the idea that the actor could have chosen to do otherwise. In the case described the actor does not have the ability to avoid doing, or to avoid choosing doing, what he does. So what becomes of our sense that in the case in which the outsider does not cause the choice he acts freely?

This puzzle has rightly generated a substantial amount of literature, and it would be wrong to suppose that we are near anything like a solution to it. Libertarians are in a position, of course, to insist that the difference lies in the fact that the choice in the one case is caused, but in the other case is uncaused, and thus free. But we've already seen the difficulties in the libertarian position. One way of reading the examples is as showing that even caused actions may be punished, if not caused in some odd way (as here, by an outsider). Of course, that brings us back to the difficulty that arose when we were considering compatibilism. How exactly are we to distinguish the different sorts of causes? If unavoidable actions can be punished, why not actions caused by mental illness?

One way of answering that question, a way associated with Frankfurt, is to distinguish between different levels of desire. Roughly the idea is this: we have desires that result in action, and then we have desires about what sort of person we want to be. In particular this second sort of desire may have to do with the sorts of desires we want to have. If an action accords not only with the immediate desire to perform that action, but also with the higher order desires the actor has, then the action can be attributed to him in a way that would (presumably) justify blaming, and punishing, him. On the other hand, if it cannot, if it is inconsistent with his higher order desires then it does not reflect his true self, and blame and punishment are not appropriate. So, for example, the addict who is perfectly happy with what he is doing is defective in a certain sort of way, but not in a way that raised any doubt about where his actions come from. But when an actor's addictive behavior does not accord with his higher order desires, when those actions are *against his will*, they cannot be attributed to him in a way that would justify blame and punishment.

But even if it works for addiction, this distinction between the willing and the unwilling addict, the first to be held accountable for his addictive behavior, the second not, does not fit so smoothly into an account of mental illness. The typical objections to the story of a hierarchy of desires seem to apply with special relevance to the question of mental illness. For the mentally ill person's first order desires either do or don't reflect their second order desires. If they don't, then there is in the theory a reason for treating them differently. But what if they do, which seems more than possible? In that case should we say that the person is acting freely? But what if those second order desires themselves do not accord with higher order desires? Is there a regress in the offing here? And of course, if the first order desires do accord with the second order desires, the implication that the resulting actions should be considered free runs up against the fact that those second order desires may be caused by the mental illness itself. And that, as we are relying so heavily on intuition here, would seem to be a reason not to believe that the actions are free, in spite of the fact that the desires that lead to them accord with second order desires.

The only way I can see out of this quandary would be to insist, in the first place, that there is a practical limit to the range of orders that must be taken into account, and second that the first order desires that lead to the actions of the mentally ill person never accord with the effective higher order desires. There is a lot more to be said about Frankfurt's notions of freedom than I can deal fairly with in this chapter, but I believe that his analysis of freedom does not help us to understand why those who are mentally ill are not to be punished, while those who are not mentally ill may be punished.

6 Accepting the Conclusion of the Argument: Quarantine

In the world of philosophy there are those who accept the abolitionist conclusion of the Humanitarian Argument; I have already mentioned the work of Pereboom and Caruso. In Pereboom's seminal work, *Living Without Free Will*, he argues against the possibility of free will and draws the same conclusion about punishment that the Washington legislature drew: there is no justification for punishment, and hence no reason for an insanity defense.[24] Each offender must be assessed on his own, but the main instruments for dealing with offenders are detention and therapy, the same tools that we use in cases of mental illness and in cases of quarantine of those with serious contagious diseases. For that reason the approach is called the Quarantine approach in the work of Pereboom and Caruso.

What can be said in favor of accepting the Quarantine approach? The world that it seems to point us toward is one utterly without punishment, one in which those who commit crimes are given hearings to determine their level of dangerousness, are then detained or otherwise restrained for as long as they remain dangerous and given the best possible treatment to shorten the time until their release. The range of those who advance this argument is not limited to philosophers, sociologists, and state legislatures; there are popular versions of it as well. Among other things it is the background of the satirical novel *Erewhon*, in which the physically ill are punished for the crime of being sick.[25] Punishing the criminal, the point is, makes about as much sense as punishing a person who has tuberculosis.

I will turn to my own way of avoiding this abolitionist conclusion and the Quarantine approach it seems to entail in a moment, but first I'd like to say a bit more about premise (d) and why rejecting it is desirable. According to premise (d), there is a point to the insanity defense only if punishment is sometimes appropriate. One reason offered for rejecting this premise and the abolitionist conclusion of the argument is the fact that it conflicts with the intuitions of most people. Most people believe that it is at least sometimes appropriate to punish for intentional wrongdoing, and the most dedicated Humanitarian has got to feel in her heart that something is wrong when a vicious criminal goes free. Do we really believe that what Bernard Madoff, the financial advisor who stole millions from his clients, needs is a stint in a medical facility to straighten him out? Or education to inform him about right and wrong? Indeed, the same argument that would exclude punishment would appear to exclude blame. We may feel that some of our more demented criminals should not be blamed but simply put away where they can do no harm, and with treatment if possible. But is it appropriate not to blame Madoff, on the ground that background conditions prevented him from doing anything but what he did? The criminal justice system that we have seems firmly grounded in intuitions about blame and punishment.

This argument from intuition is very serviceable, and Michael Moore makes great use of it in his defense of retribution and desert.[26] Still, intuitions about such things are notoriously unreliable and should be viewed with a kind of skepticism. And, in fact, there are other, more powerful reasons for wanting to reject the abolition argument. One of them is based on the notion of "takings": when the state takes something away from an innocent person and does so for the benefit of the community, compensation is required. If we accept the premise that all actions are unavoidable, then if the state takes an offender's freedom or property away from him, and does so for the benefit of the community it must compensate him.[27] But Saul Smilansky has shown that the attempt to compensate offenders would utterly drain the state's resources.[28] The "humanitarian" conclusion of the Humanitarian Argument, if taken seriously, would end up obliterating the state.[29]

Even more persuasive is the *ad hominem* argument[30] that a world in which all offenders are managed the same way, with preventive detention and treatment, is not at all a humane world. We can agree that the present institution of punishment by and large cruel and inhumane, but it doesn't follow that the solution is to eliminate the harsh treatment of punishment entirely. The fear here is that the world without punishment—the world of the Clockwork Orange—is in fact a world that robs the rational criminal of his humanity and treats him like a badly conditioned animal or indeed like a defective machine, to be recalibrated if possible and simply kept away from the community if not. According to this objection the criminal who is competent and who has chosen to break the law is *entitled* to punishment, which is the sort of treatment appropriately given to a fully functioning adult, but not to children and not to those who are not accountable for their own behavior.

Indeed, there are important protections for the sane criminal built into the criminal code: "However paradoxical it may sound, the Criminal Code is the criminal's Magna Charta. It certifies his right to be punished only in accordance with the statutory requirements and only within the statutory limits."[31] These protections do not apply to the insane defender, and would not seem to apply to any offender under the Quarantine system envisioned by Pereboom and others. I will return to these protections in the next section. The problem, however, is that under the hypothesis we are exploring no one *deserves* punishment, and so punishment is unjustified. And so what we are left with this this: Punishment is unjustified, but the world of Quarantine is inhumane and undesirable. Is there any way out of this dilemma?

One last observation about Quarantine before I suggest my own proposal: There is an objection to the analogy with quarantine in the public health area. The objection begins by observing that not everyone with a communicable disease will have her movements restricted. We have a strong preference for keeping our freedom when possible, and so quarantine in the public health field is justified only when (1) the harm is particularly serious *and* (2) there is no other way to prevent the harm that might be done by contagion. In particular I would argue that, when the disease is *only* likely to be communicated *rationally and intentionally*, even in the public health case we rely on the criminal justice system to prevent the harm. (Think here of HIV/AIDS.)

The proper analogy with quarantine in the criminal justice system is this: when an *incompetent or irrational* person is liable to be violent then there may be no way to prevent the harm that might be done except by quarantine, and in such a case the harm is liable to be particularly serious. In that sort of case the dangerous person cannot raise any right of his as a reason why he should not be constrained. But that reasoning does not extend to malicious behavior of rational and competent persons, and therefore does not support the analogy in the case of crimes by rational individuals acting knowingly or intentionally. Where the diseased person is rational and can control his contagiousness—where he can process the threat of imprisonment, for example—we leave it to him to do it, under threat of penalty.

7 The Institution of Correction and the Insanity Defense

Is it possible to accept something like the insanity defense without accepting either the world of Punishment or the world of Quarantine? Given that we want to avoid the conclusion of the argument for the abolition of the insanity defense, and assuming that we accept the first two premises of the argument, how do we go about it? This is the position that I find myself in. I believe that it is at least more likely than not that all actions are unavoidable. I also believe that punishment is essentially retributive and that therefore unavoidable actions should not be punished. I reject all consequentialist arguments for punishing those who cannot help doing what they do. I accept, therefore, the conclusion that punishment is never justified. But I would reject the further conclusion that the insanity defense or the distinction upon which it is based should be abandoned. I have indicated previously why some believe that a criminal punishment system that does not distinguish between the treatment appropriate for the mentally ill offender and the treatment appropriate for the sane offender is a scary prospect indeed.

I say I would like to reject that further conclusion, but can I do it at the same time I deny that punishment is ever justified? That is, can we reject premise (d), that there is a point to the insanity defense only if punishment is sometimes appropriate? I think it is possible—that is, I believe that it is possible to maintain that there is a point to the insanity defense even though punishment is never appropriate—and I have made that argument in a number of different papers.[32]

Here's my view, in brief: It is both important and possible to justify the state's use of harsh treatment in the effort to control crime, and to do so without appealing to retribution or desert. It is important to do so because it is demeaning for rational individuals to be subjected to preventive measures—detention and therapy—as if they were not capable of understanding the consequences of their actions. In the words of David Hodgson, to deal with offenders "not as responsible persons but as vehicles for treatment to be manipulated for the general good . . . is not appropriate in relation to people who are capable of acting rationally."[33] Hodgson goes on to say:

> I suggest that a society with that [Quarantine] system would be a nightmare of insecurity and uncertainty, as well as injustice. . . . [T]he imposition of quarantining or monitoring . . . would not even be conditioned on a person's having actually done anything, so that people could not order their lives in such a way as to be assured of freedom from this kind of intervention. In the absence of any requirement for intervention other than established danger, . . . there would be no principled or transparent basis on which the State officials could determine what was to be done, and on which the appropriateness of their decisions could be reviewed.[34]

Most philosophers and legal theorists do in fact agree that it is important to avoid the Quarantine approach,[35] but most of those writers, like Hodgson, fall back on the notion of responsibility. The burning question, of course, is whether avoiding it is possible for someone who denies responsibility, retribution, and desert. I think it is possible to justify harsh treatment for offenders who are rational and quarantine for those who are not, and to do so without appealing to responsibility.

The first step is to separate the machinery of punishment—detention for determinate periods or fines of determinate amounts proportional to the seriousness of the crime, detention or fine only after conviction, and no detention or fine unless for a crime previously defined—from the notions of punishment and retribution. Punishment, I have argued, is by its nature retributive.[36] To deny that suffering inflicted upon an individual is retributive, to deny that it is payback for a crime justified by the fact that the actor freely chose to commit the crime, is to deny that it is punishment. But harsh treatment meted out to an offender need not be intended as retributive; it need not be intended to be punishment. It might, for example, be intended as a method to help the offender *correct* a character fault that led to his offense, a method that does not expose him to unconstrained preventive powers of the state (as commitment as criminally insane would). It might be so constituted as to be a benefit to him in both those senses: giving him the opportunity to change in a way that should benefit him, and protecting him against the drastic preventive methods the insanity acquittee is exposed to.

All of this is of course (like punishment) vulnerable to abuse, and the powers of the state to administer Correction would have to be severely limited. In particular the mindset with which it is administered cannot be retributive, and the right to administer it cannot be confounded with the supposition that the offender "morally deserves" harsh treatment. Correction is not punishment, and it does not see the offender as deserving to suffer but rather would be administered, although the offender is not a child and should not be treated like a child, in a spirit which shares one essential feature with the spirit in which we correct our children: optimistic and aiming at making the future more manageable for them. Administered in this spirit, correction, though harsh, would be less harsh than punishment. It would not be mean-spirited; it would not permit excessive indignities to be heaped upon the prisoner.[37]

A system of crime control of that sort can be justified by its benefits for the state and its benefits for the person subjected to Correction. The benefit to the state of controlling crime is obvious, but the particular benefit of using Correction rather than Quarantine lies in the savings in resources. The state avoids both life-long monitoring and compensation associated with Quarantine by limiting its response to a system of threats backed up by harsh treatment, administered in such a way to benefit the offender.

And the benefit to the offender from Correction are the mirror image of the objections to Quarantine. It promises both negative and positive benefits:

7.1 Negative Benefits

Missing in the Quarantine approach are the limitations that the enlightenment built around the institution of punishment. To name a few such protections, there should be:

No punishment without a conviction.

No conviction for an act without awareness of a previously announced criminal prohibition of that act.

No conviction without intent to perform or awareness of risk of causing the law-breaking act, or intent to omit or awareness of the risk of omitting the legally required act.

No conviction for an act if the act is justified.

No conviction for an act is the act is excused.

Extinction of liability to punishment after one application for each conviction.

The amount and kind of punishment appropriate to and proportional to the crime.

Insulation from coercive, *purely* preventive measures (e.g., preventive detention).

No cruel or unusual punishment.

No punishment for those who are not capable of responding to punishment.

I would say, with Morris and others, that the accused and the imprisoned must be treated with dignity and respect, and these limitations upon state action are precisely the "cash value" of the terms dignity and respect. In other terms, they are the requirements of substantive and procedural due process. Any acceptable institution for dealing with competent offenders capable of controlling their actions should be bounded by something like this list of limitations, making the appropriate substitutions for the word "punishment," which in my book would be "correction."

7.2 Positive Benefits

But the heart of the argument is that the justification of Correction requires providing some positive benefit to the offender as well, as a form of compensation. Absent that, even with the negative benefits of due process, the offender is merely being used for the benefit of the community. "[D]ue process [alone] might constrain what the State can do to offenders, but it does not obligate the State to do anything *for* offenders."[38] And recent work shows that positive benefit is in fact possible: "A striking feature of strength-based intervention approaches such as the Good Lives Model is that they are able to address both the interests of offenders and the rest of the community at the same time."[39] Although the threat of penalty is intended to give members of the community an incentive to keep on the right side of the laws that they will establish, once they have fallen on the wrong side the penalty itself should be designed to help them find their way back. Otherwise it is harsh treatment whose only point would be, in Bentham's phrase, to terrorize. So one of the positive benefits of Correction should be the opportunity to erase or overcome a character flaw, in the sense of Brandt.[40]

At the same time, the Correction system should not be seen as *imposing* compliance with the law. As Bruce Waller has said in private correspondence, "one genuine danger of the therapeutic [Quarantine] system is too easily believing it is justified to 'reshape' the offender in such a manner that he acquiesces to playing a demeaning role in a dreadful society."

The state should have the power to administer this harsh treatment in certain cases, but not in others. In particular, in cases in which the offender does not have the makeup required to learn from punishment, he would be consigned to treatment and detention. This distinction, based upon the ability to learn from punishment, would roughly correspond to the distinction in the present law between the mentally ill offender and the sane offender. Some of the same questions plague this proposal, of course, that plague the current insanity defense, including the question of what to do with the psychopath. I do not claim to have offered a solution to those problems.

8 Conclusion

The reader is entitled to be skeptical about the position I propose, but I would ask her to keep in mind the pillars upon which it is built: the belief that human beings are natural inhabitants in a causal world; the belief that if an action is caused (or if it is the result of a random event!) it is unavoidable; the belief that unavoidable actions may not be punished; and the belief that a criminal justice system without a distinction very much like the distinction between those who are mentally ill and those who are not would be deeply troubling. Every way out of this conundrum is uncomfortable, but there is no way to avoid choosing one of them. I prefer the one that acknowledges the place of man in a natural universe but would at the same time preserve the insanity defense, or something very much like it.

Notes

1. Hart, "Changing Conceptions of Responsibility," 196.
2. For a comprehensive discussion of the insanity defense in the United States, see Corrado, *Presumed Dangerous*, part 2 ("Detaining the Insane") and in particular section 3 ("An Analytical History of the Insanity Defense in the United States").
3. C.S. Lewis used the word "humanitarian" ironically to describe the first part of this argument. See Lewis, "The Humanitarian Theory of Punishment."
4. Pereboom, *Living without Free Will*, ch. 6; Caruso and Pereboom, "Hard Incompatibilism Existentialism."
5. See, for example, Scanlon, "Punishment and the Rule of Law"; Clark, "A Non-Retributivist Kantian Approach to Punishment"; Kelly, "Criminal Justice without Retribution"; and Vilhauer, "Persons, Punishment, and Free Will Skepticism."
6. The statute adopted by the Washington state legislature read as follows: "It shall be no defense to a person charged with the commission of a crime that at the time of its commission he was unable, by reason of his insanity, idiocy or imbecility, to comprehend the nature and quality of the act committed, or to understand that it was wrong; or that he was afflicted with a morbid propensity to commit prohibited acts; nor shall any testimony or other proof thereof be admitted in evidence" (*State v. Strasburg*, 111–12).
7. Ibid., 122 (italics added).

8. Ibid., 123.

9. See Ferri, *The Positive School of Criminology* and *Criminal Sociology*; Wootton, "Mental Disorder and the Problem of Moral and Criminal Responsibility." The connection between Ferri's work and the Washington statute at issue in the *Strasburg* case was pointed out at the time by Henry Ballantine, "Can a State Abolish Insanity as a Defense in Criminal Prosecutions?"

10. Physics has accustomed us to the idea that some events may not be caused by prior events but may be merely random occurrences, or may be merely made probable by prior events. The philosophers in this debate have not been blind to that possibility; a parallel argument can be made against punishment based on that premise. I will deal with this complication in due course.

11. Something very much like this conclusion is argued for by, in addition to Pereboom and Caruso, Galen Strawson, "The Impossibility of Moral Responsibility," and Honderich, *How Free Are You?* Earlier writings in this line include Edwards, "Hard and Soft Determinism," and Hospers, "What Means this Freedom?"

12. There may be other reasons for believing that all actions are unavoidable, but anyone who accepts that all actions are caused by prior events and that what is caused by prior events is unavoidable must accept that all actions are unavoidable, and so to deny unavoidability one or the other of those will have to be rejected.

13. On the effect of rotten social conditions see Delgado, "Ascription of Criminal States of Mind"; *United States v. Alexander* (Bazelon, J., dissenting).

14. Chisholm, "The Agent as Cause"; Taylor, *Metaphysics*, ch. 5. Nice discussions of this view can be found in O'Connor, "Libertarian Views," and Vihvelin, *Causes, Laws, and Free Will*, ch. 3.

15. The example is from Aristotle, by way of Roderick Chisholm, "Human Freedom and the Self."

16. Mill criticized William Hamilton's libertarianism, or at least an agent-causation version of it, in this way:

> Sir William Hamilton thinks it a fair statement of the Free-will doctrine, that it supposes our volitions to be uncaused. But [Lucy Phillipps] considers this a misstatement, and thinks the real Free-will doctrine to be that "I" am the cause. I prefer the other language, as being more consistent with the use of the word cause in other cases. If we take the word, we must take the acknowledged Law of Causation along with it, viz., that a cause which is the same in every respect, is always followed by the same effects. But in the Free-will theory, the "I" is the same, and all other conditions the same, and yet the effect may not only be different, but contrary. For instead of saying that "I" am the cause, [Lucy Phillipps] should at least say, some state or mode of me, which is different when the effect is different: though what state or mode this could be, unless it were a will to will (the notion so justly ridiculed by Hobbes) it is difficult to imagine. (Mill, *An Examination of Sir William Hamilton's Philosophy*, 441)

This argument begs the question against the agent-causal theorist, of course. Nevertheless, it brings out the implausibility of what agent causation must accept.

17. Kadri Vihvelin is one who believes that it may be possible to make sense of "object-causation," though she doesn't believe in fact that there are any cases of object causation in the actual world. See Vihvelin, *Causes, Laws, and Free Will*, 79–82.

18. Kane, "Libertarianism" and *The Significance of Free Will.*

19. Chisholm makes this point about the conditional analysis of freedom:

> [O]ur man might be such that, if he had chosen to do otherwise, then he would have done otherwise, and yet also such that he could not have done otherwise. Suppose, after all, that our murderer could not have *chosen*, or could not have *decided*, to do otherwise. Then the fact that he happens also to be a man such that, if he had chosen not to shoot he would not have shot, would make no difference. For if he could *not* have chosen *not* to shoot, then he could not have done anything other than just what it was that he did do. . . . If the man could not have chosen to do otherwise, then he would not have done otherwise—even if he was such that, if he had chosen to do otherwise, then he would have done otherwise. (Chisholm, "Human Freedom and the Self," 27, emphasis in original)

20. But see Rawls, "Two Concepts of Rules," for a rule utilitarian sort of response to that. The problems with rule utilitarianism as a way out are well known. Should it happen that in spite of being known to the public an institution that would punish the innocent—like the Soviet law punishing the relatives of army deserters in the 1920s—might in fact increase utility, the argument collapses. Only the most determined utilitarian would argue that that could never happen.

21. According to Hart,

> Bentham's argument is in fact a spectacular *non sequitur*. He sets out to prove that to *punish* the mad, the infant child or those who break the law unintentionally or under duress or even under 'necessity' must be inefficacious; but all that he proves (at the most) is the quite different proposition that the *threat* of punishment will be ineffective so far as the class of persons who suffer from these conditions is concerned. Plainly it is possible that though (as Bentham says) the *threat* of punishment could not have operated on them, the actual *infliction* of punishment on those persons may secure a higher measure of conformity to law on the part of normal persons than is secured by the admission of excusing conditions. (Hart, "Prolegomenon," 19, emphasis in original)

22. Brandt, "The Motivational Theory of Excuses." See also Posner, "An Economic Theory of the Criminal Law," for an economist's version of this.

23. See Frankfurt, "Alternate Possibilities and Moral Responsibility."

24. Pereboom, *Living without Free Will*, 186 and, generally, ch. 6; see also his "Skepticism about Free Will."

25. Butler, *Erewhon*.

26. Moore, "Taxonomy of the Purposes of Punishment."

27. See Corrado, "Punishment and the Wild Beast of Prey."

28. Smilansky, "Hard Determinism and Punishment."

29. Fichte, in his *Foundations of Natural Right*, reached a similar conclusion. He proposed to amend the social contract, which would have excluded every offender, with subcontracts that would permit the replacement of exclusion with

forms of punishment. See my "Fichte and the Psychopath: Criminal Justice Turned Upside Down."

30. *Ad hominem* in a good sense: using the opponent's own evidence against him.

31. Liszt, "The Rationale for the *Nullum Crimen* Principle," 1010.

32. Corrado, "Why Do We Resist Hard Determinism?"; "Fichte and the Psychopath"; and "Doing without Desert."

33. Hodgson, *Rationality+Consciousness=Free Will*, 213.

34. Ibid., 219.

35. Hart, "Changing Conceptions of Responsibility," 206–09; Morris, "Persons and Punishment"; Lewis, "The Humanitarian Theory of Punishment."

36. Corrado, "The Abolition of Punishment."

37. Among the many qualms I have about my own thesis, and rather high on the list, there is this one: Who is to ensure that the attitudes of those who administer the criminal law will be of the right sort? We know how fallible human beings are even with the best of intentions; and there is no assurance that only those with the best intentions will be assigned to these positions. Still, this is a problem that attends every approach to criminal justice, not least the ones actually in operation in our various nations, and the stated aims of an institution have got to have some effect on its implementation.

38. Cullen, "Taking Rehabilitation Seriously," 97.

39. Willis, Yates, Gannon, and Ward, "How to Integrate the Good Lives Model into Treatment Programs for Sexual Offending."

40. Brandt, "The Motivational Theory of Excuses."

Resources

Ballantine, Henry, "Can A State Abolish Insanity As A Defense in Criminal Prosecutions?" *Harvard Law Review* 24(1911): 225–27.

Brandt, Richard, "The Motivational Theory of Excuses." *Nomos (Criminal Justice)* 27(1985): 165–98.

Butler, Samuel, *Erewhon: Or, over the Range*. London: Trubner and Co., 1872.

Caruso, Gregg, and Derk Pereboom, "Hard-Incompatibilism Existentialism: Neuroscience, Punishment, and Meaning in Life." In *Neuroexistentialism: Meaning, Morals, and Purpose in the Age of Neuroscience,* edited by Gregg D. Caruso and Owen Flanagan (New York: Oxford University Press, 2016), in press.

Chisholm, Roderick, "Human Freedom and the Self." In *The Lindley Lecture* (Lawrence, KS: University of Kansas Department of Philosophy, 1964), 3–15.

Chisholm, Roderick, "The Agent as Cause." In *Action Theory*, edited by Myles Brand and D. Walton (Dordrecht: D. Reidel, 1976), 196–211.

Clark, Michael, "A Non-Retributivist Kantian Approach to Punishment." *Ratio* 17(2004): 12–27.

Corrado, Michael Louis, "The Abolition of Punishment." *Suffolk University Law Review* 35(2002): 257–76.

Corrado, Michael Louis, "Doing without Desert." Forthcoming in a festschrift for David Hodgson published by Oxford University Press.

Corrado, Michael Louis, "Fichte and the Psychopath: Criminal Justice Turned Upside Down," forthcoming in a volume of papers from the 2015 Aberdeen Conference on Free Will Skepticism.

Corrado, Michael Louis, "Punishment and the Wild Beast of Prey: The Problem of Preventive Detention." *Journal of Criminal Law and Criminology* 86(1996): 778–814.

Corrado, Michael Louis, *Presumed Dangerous: Punishment, Responsibility, and Preventive Detention in the United States*. Durham, NC: Carolina Academic Press, 2013.

Corrado, Michael Louis, "Why Do We Resist Hard Incompatibilism? Some Thoughts on Freedom and Determinism." In *The Future of Rehabilitation and Punishment*, ed. Thomas Nadelhoffer (Oxford: Oxford University Press, 2013), 79–104.

Cullen, Francis T., "Taking Rehabilitation Seriously: Creativity, Science, and the Challenge of Offender Change." *Punishment & Society* 14(2012): 94–114.

Delgado, Richard, "Ascription of Criminal States of Mind: Toward a Defense Theory for the Coercively Persuaded ('Brainwashed') Defendant." *Minnesota Law Review* 63(1978): 1–34.

Edwards, Paul, "Hard and Soft Determinism." In *Determinism and Freedom*, ed. Sidney Hook (New York: Collier Books, 1961), 117–25.

Ferri, Enrico, *Criminal Sociology*. Translated by Joseph Kelly and John Lisle. Boston: Little, Brown, and Co., 1917.

Ferri, Enrico, *The Positive School of Criminology: Three Lectures*. Translated by Ernest Untermann. Pittsburgh: University of Pittsburgh Press, 1968.

Fichte, J.G., *Foundations of Natural Right*. Translated by Michael Baur, edited by Frederick Neuhouser. Cambridge: Cambridge University Press, 2000.

Frankfurt, Harry, "Alternate Possibilities and Moral Responsibility." *Journal of Philosophy* 66(1969): 820–39.

Hart, H.L.A., "Prolegomenon to the Principles of Punishment." In *Punishment and Responsibility: Essays in the Philosophy of Law* (Oxford: Oxford University Press, 1968), 1–27.

Hart, H.L.A., "Changing Conceptions of Responsibility." In *Punishment and Responsibility: Essays in the Philosophy of Law* (Oxford: Oxford University Press, 1968), 187–209.

Hodgson, David, *Rationality+Consciousness=Free Will*. Oxford: Oxford University Press, 2012.

Honderich, Ted. *How Free Are You?* Oxford: Oxford University Press, 1993.

Hospers, John, "What Means this Freedom?" In *Determinism and Freedom*, ed. Sidney Hook (New York: Collier Books, 1961), 126–42.

Kane, Robert, "Libertarianism." In *Four Views of Free Will*, edited by John Martin Fischer, Robert Kane, Derk Pereboom, and Manuel Vargas (Malden MA: Blackwell Publishing, 2007), 5–43 and 166–83.

Kane, Robert, *The Significance of Free Will*. Oxford: Oxford University Press, 1996.

Kelly, Erin, "Criminal Justice without Retribution." *Journal of Philosophy* 106(2009): 440–62.

Lewis, C.S., "The Humanitarian Theory of Punishment." *Res Judicatae* 6(1953): 224–30.

Liszt, Franz von, "The Rationale for the *Nullum Crimen* Principle." *Journal of International Criminal Justice* 5(2007): 1009–13, excerpted from "Die deterministischen Gegner der Zweckstrafe [Deterministic Opponents of Purposive Punishment]," *Die gesamte Strafrechtswissenschaft* 13(1983): 325–70 (translated by Iain L. Fraser).

Mill, John Stuart, *An Examination of the Sir William Hamilton's Philosophy*. Edited by J.M. Robson. Toronto: University of Toronto Press, 1979.

Moore, Michael, "Taxonomy of the Purposes of Punishment." In *Law and Psychiatry: Rethinking the Relationship* (Cambridge: Cambridge University Press, 1984), 233–37.

Morris, Herbert, "Persons and Punishment." *The Monist* 52(1968): 475–501.

O'Connor, Timothy, "Libertarian Views: Dualist and Agent-Causal Theories." In *The Oxford Handbook of Free Will*, edited by Robert Kane (New York: Oxford University Press, 2002), 337–55.

Pereboom, Derk, *Living without Free Will*. New York: Cambridge University Press, 2001.

Pereboom, Derk, "Skepticism about Free Will." In *Exploring the Illusion of Free Will and Responsibility*, edited by Gregg Caruso (Lanham, MD: Lexington Books, 2013), 19–40.

Posner, Richard, "An Economic Theory of the Criminal Law." *Columbia Law Review* 85(1985): 1193–1231.

Rawls, John, "Two Concepts of Rules." *Philosophical Review* 64(1955): 3–32.

Scanlon, T.M., "Punishment and the Rule of Law." In *The Difficulty of Tolerance: Essays in Political Philosophy* (Cambridge: Cambridge University Press, 2003), 219–33.

Smilansky, Saul, "Hard Determinism and Punishment: A Practical *Reductio*." *Law and Philosophy* 30(2011): 353–67.

Strawson, Galen, "The Impossibility of Moral Responsibility." In *Free Will*, 2nd ed., edited by Gary Watson (Oxford: Oxford University Press, 2003), 212–28.

Strawson, P.F., "Freedom and Resentment." *Proceedings of the British Academy* 48(1962): 1–25.

Taylor, Richard, *Metaphysics*, 2nd ed. Englewood Cliffs NJ: Prentice-Hall, 1974.

Vihvelin, Kadri, *Causes, Laws, and Free Will*. Oxford: Oxford University Press, 2013.

Vilhauer, Benjamin, "Persons, Punishment, and Free Will Skepticism." *Philosophical Studies* 162(2013): 143–63.

Willis, Gwenda M., Pamela M. Yates, Theresa A. Gannon, and Tony Ward, "How to Integrate the Good Lives Model into Treatment Programs for Sexual

Offending: An Introduction and Overview." *Sexual Abuse: A Journal of Research and Treatment* 25(2013): 123–42.

Wootton, Barbara, "Mental Disorder and the Problem of Moral and Criminal Responsibility." In *Social Science and Social Pathology* (London: Allen and Unwin, 1959), 227–67.

PART 4

Law, Policy, and Reform

CHAPTER TEN

Abolishing Insanity: Proposals from England and Wales

Paul Catley

The current English criminal law defense of insanity arose out of controversy and remains controversial to this day.[1] This chapter will look at the origins of the current law and then briefly at the development of that law through subsequent cases, before examining proposals for their abolition and their replacement with a new defense better suited to the needs of the 21st century.

1 The Origins of the Current Law

In 1843 the senior judges of the day were summoned to Parliament[2] to explain the decision in the case of Daniel M'Naghten.[3] M'Naghten had shot and killed Edward Drummond, a figure at the heart of the British political establishment. Drummond was private secretary to Prime Minister Sir Robert Peel. Indeed, it is likely that M'Naghten's intended target was the prime minister.[4]

At M'Naghten's trial it was argued that he believed that he was being persecuted by the Tory party. The claim that M'Naghten believed he was being persecuted formed the basis of his defense—not in the sense that his action was justified as self-defense, but in the sense that his violent act stemmed from delusion. Medical experts[5] gave evidence that M'Naghten was deluded and this led to the finding of the trial court that he was "not guilty being insane."[6]

The verdict led to outcry.[7] Political tensions were high. The 1840s had already seen at least three attempts on the life of Queen Victoria.[8] As the Lord Chancellor said at the opening of the questioning of the judges:

> The circumstances connected with that [M'Naghten's] trial have created a deep sensation amongst your Lordships, and also in the public mind. I am not surprised at this. A gentleman in the prime of life, of a most amiable character, incapable of giving offense or of injuring any individual, was murdered in the streets of this metropolis in open day. The assassin was secured; he was committed for trial; that trial has taken place, and he has escaped with impunity. Your Lordships will not be surprised that these circumstances should have created a deep feeling in the public mind, and that many persons should, upon the first impression, be disposed to think that there is some great defect in the laws of the country with reference to this subject which calls for a revision of those laws, in order that a repetition of such outrages may be prevented.[9]

As a result, the senior judges were summoned to Parliament to explain the decision. Today this would seem a very controversial move: challenging the twin ideas of the separation of powers and the independence of the judiciary. The judges acceded to the request and attended the House of Lords to explain the decision; though not without complaint. As Maule J said:

> I feel great difficulty in answering the questions put by your Lordships on this occasion: First, because they do not appear to arise out of and are not put with reference to a particular case, or for a particular purpose, which might explain or limit the generality of their terms, so that full answers to them ought to be applicable to every possible state of facts, not inconsistent with those assumed in the questions: this difficulty is the greater, from the practical experience both of the Bar and the court being confined to questions arising out of the facts of particular cases. Secondly, because I have heard no argument at your Lordships' Bar or elsewhere, on the subject of these questions, the want of which I feel the more the greater are the number and extent of questions which might be raised in argument. Thirdly, from a fear, of which I cannot divest myself, that as these questions relate to matters of criminal law of great importance and frequent occurrence, the answers to them by the judges may embarrass the administration of justice when they are cited in criminal trials. For these reasons I should have been glad if my learned brethren would have joined me in praying your Lordships to excuse us from answering these questions.[10]

It was the explanation given by the Lord Chief Justice, Lord Tindal, on behalf of the senior judges to Parliament that has become the essence of the current English law of insanity. The defense is therefore unique in English law in not having stemmed from case law or from statute, but instead arising from an explanation to Parliament by judges as to the law.

In answering the questions of the House of Lords, the Lord Chief Justice expressed the law in the following terms:

> Jurors ought to be told in all cases that every man is to be presumed to be sane and to possess a sufficient degree of reason to be responsible for his crimes until the contrary be proved to their satisfaction, and that to establish a defense on the ground of insanity it must be clearly proved that, at the time of the committing of the act the party accused was labouring under such a defect of reason, from disease of the mind, as not to know the nature and quality of the act he was doing, or, if he did know it, that he did not know he was doing what was wrong.[11]

This statement has become known as the M'Naghten Rules,[12] which has become the standard definition of the test for insanity applied by the English courts[13] and has also been used and/or considered in courts across the world.[14]

The explanation of the law by the judges appeared to satisfy Parliament.[15] However, those same rules are now severely criticized as noted by the Law Commission for England and Wales:[16]

- it is not clear whether the defense of insanity is even available in all cases;[17]
- the law lags behind psychiatric understanding, and this partly explains why, in practice, the defense is underused[18] and medical professionals do not apply the correct legal test;[19]
- the label of "insane" is outdated as a description of those with mental illness, and simply wrong as regards those who have learning disabilities or learning difficulties, or those with epilepsy; and
- the case law on insane and non-insane automatism is incoherent and produces results that run counter to common-sense.[20]

In part the reason why the current law is no longer fit for purpose stems from changes in medical and scientific understanding arising in the over 170 years since the judges answered the questions posed to them in Parliament.[21] As noted in the quotation from the Law Commission, the label "insane" is outdated, and the same criticism can be applied to "disease of the mind". They are not medical terms and serve as an impediment in the court's quest to discover the accused's mental state.[22]

In part the explanation stems from the case law which has reinterpreted the rules in the ensuing years. When the judges responded to questions posed to them in Parliament they were simply explaining the law as it related to partial delusions, that is, those situations where a person appeared generally sane, but in one respect held abnormal views or reacted abnormally. The judges were very clear in their explanation to Parliament that the rules they were explaining applied not to insanity generally but to cases where the defense was based on a partial delusion.[23] Notwithstanding this qualification, which would have left the M'Naghten Rules applying to only a small subset of insanity cases, the rules have gone on to be applied in all English cases where insanity is raised.[24]

One issue that is not clear from the guidance provided by the judges to Parliament was whether an accused who was pleading insanity should be judged on the basis of whether he knew that what he was doing was legally wrong or whether the test was that he knew what he was doing was morally wrong. In the report of the judges' replies to Parliament the test posed by the trial judges[25] is reported to have been:

> The question to be determined is whether at the time the act in question was committed the prisoner had or had not the use of his understanding so as to know that he was doing a wrong or wicked act. If the jurors should be of opinion that the prisoner was not sensible, at the time he committed it, that he was violating the laws both of God and man, then he would be entitled to a verdict in his favour, but if, on the contrary, they were of opinion that when he committed the act he was in a sound state of mind, then their verdict must be against him.[26]

This direction to the jury first focuses on the accused's understanding at the time of the offense of whether his act was "a wrong and wicked act." This suggests a moral wrongfulness test. However, in the next sentence the judge indicates that the accused should be entitled to be found not guilty by reason of insanity if he "was not sensible . . . that he was violating the laws both of God and man." This suggests the test is based both on morality (the laws of God) and legality (the laws of man). What is unclear is how a jury should respond if they considered that at the time of the offense M'Naghten knew what he was doing was legally wrong, but did not think that it was morally wrong.

The guidance on this point given by the judges to Parliament is possibly slightly more clear, though still leaves room for uncertainty. The response by Tindal LCJ to the first question[27] posed to the judges appears unequivocal: a person with a partial delusion (such as M'Naghten) is "punishable according to the nature of the crime committed, if he knew at the time of committing such crime that he was acting contrary to law; by which expression we understand your Lordships to mean the law of the land."[28] From this it would appear clear that the test relates to knowledge of whether an act was legally wrong, not a test as to knowledge that it was morally wrong.

The oft-quoted answer to the second and third questions—the answer which has subsequently become known as the M'Naghten Rules—has two limbs. At the time of the commission of the act the accused must be laboring under a "defect of reason" caused by a "disease of the mind" leading him either (1) "not to know the nature and quality of his act" or (2) not to know "he was doing what was wrong."[29] Read without reference to the answer to the first question, this response appears unclear as to whether the second limb refers to legally wrong or morally wrong. Read in conjunction with the answer to the first question, it might be suggested that the second limb related to knowledge that something was legally wrong. However, Tindal LCJ then continues:

> The mode of putting the latter part of the question to the jury on these occasions has generally been, whether the accused at the time of doing the act knew the difference between right and wrong, which mode, though rarely, if ever, leading to any mistake with the jury, is not, as we conceive, so accurate when put generally and in the abstract, as when put with reference to the party's knowledge of right and wrong in respect to the very act with which he is charged. If the question were to be put as to the knowledge of the accused solely and exclusively with reference to the law of the land, it might tend to confound the jury, by inducing them to believe that an actual knowledge of the law of the land was essential in order to lead to a conviction, whereas the law is administered upon the principle that everyone must be taken conclusively to know it, without proof that he does know it. If the accused was conscious that the act was one which he ought not to do, and if that act was at the same time contrary to the law of the land, he is punishable; and the usual course, therefore, has been to leave the question to the jury whether the party accused had a sufficient degree of reason to know that he was doing an act that was wrong, and this course we think is correct, accompanied with such observations and explanations as the circumstances of each particular case may require.[30]

What conclusions can be drawn from this? The question should not be whether the accused generally knows right from wrong, but whether in relation to the act charged he knows it be wrong. Focusing on the accused's actual legal knowledge would be inappropriate, as the jury might mistakenly believe that to be convicted the accused must know the law, whereas the law works on the assumption that everyone knows the law. Tindal LCJ then, possibly crucially, explains that the accused will be punishable if he "was conscious that the act was one which he ought not to do, and if that act was at the same time contrary to the law of the land." The test of whether he was conscious that the act was one which he ought not to do appears to return to something along the lines of moral wrongfulness.

However, Tindal LCJ's response to the fourth question[31] arguably supports the idea that the test explained, while based on the accused's understanding of the situation, still focuses on whether the act was legally wrong rather than morally wrong:

> . . . we think he must be considered in the same situation as to responsibility as if the facts with respect to which the delusion exists were real. For example, if under the influence of his delusion he supposes another man to be in the act of attempting to take away his life, and he kills that man, as he supposes, in self-defense, he would be exempt from punishment. If his delusion was that the deceased had inflicted a serious injury to his character and fortune, and he killed him in revenge for such supposed injury, he would be liable to punishment.[32]

An accused who because of his delusion believes he is being attacked and acts to defend himself should have the defense of self-defense. This accords with the general English law approach that self-defense should be judged on the basis of the accused's understanding of his situation.[33] A revenge killing would be unlawful, even if based on a genuinely held, but delusional, belief of having been wronged. This places revenge killings based on delusion in the same category as revenge killings generally. Legally, even if the accused had been genuinely wronged, this would not provide the accused with a defense.[34] Such an accused might consider his act morally justified, but it would not be legally justified.

The answer to the fifth and final question refers specifically to expert medical evidence as to the accused's legal knowledge.[35] In answering this question Tindal LCJ does not challenge the focus on legal knowledge, rather he identifies the questions as "questions which it is for the jury to decide," thereby implying that he considers that the accused's legal knowledge is potentially to be the focus of the jury deliberations.

Examining the answers to the five questions leaves it unclear whether the test envisaged by the majority of the judges and explained by Tindal

LCJ was to focus on the accused's knowledge that it was legally wrong or his knowledge as to whether it was morally wrong—at least in the sense of being something he ought not to do. However, it is clear from the report of the actual trial, at which Tindal LCJ had been one of the three presiding judges, that the focus was not on whether the killing was an act that M'Naghten knew was legally wrong. The report in the Old Bailey Proceedings provides details of the evidence given at trial. The focus of the eight medical witnesses was on M'Naghten's deluded state of mind.[36] The questions posed of the experts focused on M'Naghten's moral understanding,[37] and their answers focused on the accused's moral sense.[38] The doctors considered that M'Naghten was compelled to act as he did.[39] At no point in the report of the proceedings are witnesses asked to comment on their view as to the accused's legal knowledge. Instead the picture presented to the jury was of a man beset by a belief that he was being persecuted and unable to escape from this belief.[40] In short, M'Naghten was a man who eventually felt compelled to act.

The dichotomy between the conduct of the trial and at least some of the statements of the law by the judges to Parliament is stark, but was not explained by the judges or challenged by Parliament.

If the wrongfulness limb relates only to knowledge that the act is legally wrong, then the finding of M'Naghten to be insane is surprising. M'Naghten knew the nature and quality of his act.[41] Therefore, while the evidence showed him to be suffering from a defect of reason brought about by a disease of the mind, the only reason he could be found to be insane on the basis of the M'Naghten Rules as subsequently explained to Parliament was that he did not know what he was doing was wrong. If this is a test of knowledge that it was legally wrong, then no evidence appears to have been presented on this point. All the relevant medical evidence focused on M'Naghten's belief that he was being persecuted. This could have been relevant to an assessment of whether he felt morally justified, but though he was said to have feared for his life,[42] this appears to have been a general fear and not one which was an immediate fear at the time when he shot Drummond, nor did it appear to be a mortal fear of Drummond or Sir Robert Peel. There is no evidence from the case report that M'Naghten did not know that what he did was against the law. Therefore, either one must arrive at the somewhat surprising conclusion that despite the finding of the trial court, M'Naghten was not "M'Naghten insane," or one must conclude that in 1843 the law as it related to those suffering insane delusions meant that they had a defense if they did not know that the act was one that they ought not to do.

2 The Development of the Law

The position with regard to whether the test was one of not knowing "he was doing what was wrong" in the sense of legally wrong rather than morally wrong was clarified in *R v. Windle*.[43] In this case it was argued on behalf of the accused that he thought what he was doing was right even though he knew it to be contrary to the law. The defense argued that a proper reading of the M'Naghten Rules meant that a defendant should be found to be insane if the defendant's defect of reason meant either that he did not know the act done was legally wrong *or* that he did not know that it was morally wrong. Lord Goddard CJ in the Court of Appeal rejected this defense argument, stating:

> in all cases of this kind, the real test is responsibility. A man may be suffering from a defect of reason, but if he knows that what he is doing is "wrong," and by "wrong" is meant contrary to law, he is responsible. Mr. Shawcross, in the course of his very careful argument, suggested that the word "wrong," as it was used in the McNaghten rules, did not mean contrary to law but had some kind of qualified meaning, such as morally wrong, and that if a person was in such a state of mind through a defect of reason that, although he knew that what he was doing was wrong in law, he thought that it was beneficial or kind or praiseworthy, that would excuse him.
>
> Courts of law can only distinguish between that which is in accordance with law and that which is contrary to law.[44]

Much more recently this legal issue was raised once more in *R v. Johnson*.[45] In hearing the case the court considered the Australian case of *R v. Stapleton*.[46] In *Stapleton* the Australian High Court had decided that *Windle* was wrongly decided. In *Johnson*, whilst viewing *Stapleton* as "highly persuasive,"[47] Latham LJ (V-P) decided that "the strict position at the moment remains as stated in *Windle*."[48] He concluded that

> This area, however, is a notorious area for debate and quite rightly so. There is room for reconsideration of rules and, in particular, rules which have their genesis in the early years of the 19th century. But it does not seem to us that that debate is a debate which can properly take place before us at this level in this case.[49]

Other aspects of the M'Naghten Rules have also proved controversial. For example, the "nature and quality of the act" limb of the rules has been a subject of legal debate. In *R v. Codère* the Court of Criminal Appeal held:

It is said that "quality" is to be regarded as characterising the moral, as contrasted with the physical, aspect of the deed. The Court cannot agree with that view of the meaning of the words "nature and quality." The Court is of opinion that in using the language "nature and quality" the judges were only dealing with the physical character of the act, and were not intending to distinguish between the physical and moral aspects of the act.[50]

This interpretation, as noted by the Law Commission,[51] would mean that a defendant such as Andrea Yates[52] would not be viewed by the English courts as insane. Andrea Yates, a woman with a history of mental illness, drowned her five children. Whilst the prosecution claimed her acts were those of a sane woman, the defense claimed that she was insane. The defense case was that she believed that she was acting in her children's best interests. She was suffering from delusions, and in killing her children she was saving them from Satan. Judged on the M'Naghten Rules as interpreted through subsequent English case law, she would, even if the defense experts were believed, fail to satisfy either of the two limbs of the M'Naghten Rules: she knew the nature and quality of her actions (she knew she was killing her children), and she knew that what she was doing was legally wrong.[53] The fact that she felt compelled to act and the fact that she acted in what she believed was the best interests of her children would have been irrelevant under English law to the determination of her sanity.

A further problem with the insanity defense under English law is the relationship between insane and non-insane automatism.[54] A finding by a court that an act was done as a result of non-insane automatism leads to the acquittal of the accused. The need for a defendant to have carried out a voluntary act was expressed in *Woolmington v. DPP* when Viscount Sankey said "when dealing with a murder case the Crown must prove (a) death as the result of a voluntary act of the accused and (b) malice of the accused."[55] The requirement for a "voluntary act" does not simply apply to murder trials, but is a general requirement. The classic explanation of the voluntary act requirement is given by Lord Denning in *Bratty v. Attorney General for Northern Ireland*:

> No act is punishable if it is done involuntarily: and an involuntary act in this context—some people nowadays prefer to speak of it as "automatism"—means an act which is done by the muscles without any control by the mind, such as a spasm, a reflex action or a convulsion; or an act done by a person who is not conscious of what he is doing, such as an act done whilst suffering from concussion or whilst sleep-walking.[56]

Lord Denning was clear to differentiate this defense from involuntary acts that resulted from a disease of the mind:

> Again, if the involuntary act proceeds from a disease of the mind, it gives rise to a defense of insanity, but not to a defense of automatism. Suppose a crime is committed by a man in a state of automatism or clouded consciousness due to a recurrent disease of the mind. Such an act is no doubt involuntary, but it does not give rise to an unqualified acquittal, for that would mean that he would be let at large to do it again. The only proper verdict is one which ensures that the person who suffers from the disease is kept secure in a hospital so as not to be a danger to himself or others. That is, a verdict of guilty but insane.[57]

This approach has led to the so-called *internal/external divide*. If involuntary behavior stems from an internal cause, it will be viewed by the English courts as arising from a disease of the mind and a plea based on such a cause will be a plea of not guilty by reason of insanity. If it stems from an external cause, it will be a plea of non-insane automatism. This leads to distinctions that the Law Commission describe as "incoherent and arbitrary."[58] A diabetic who fails to take insulin and falls into a hyperglycemic coma would be viewed as only having a plea based on insanity.[59] On the other hand, a diabetic who takes insulin but fails to eat and lapses into a hypoglycemic coma may be entitled to a not guilty verdict.[60] Whether the diabetic who, for example, fails to eat will be entitled to a not guilty verdict may depend on whether he is at fault for his failure.[61]

The position of those who commit offenses whilst asleep has also presented difficulties of classification for the courts. Denning's definition of when non-insane automatism applies included acts done "whilst sleepwalking."[62] Indeed, it was often considered the classic case of non-insane automatism.[63] However, in *Burgess*[64] it was held that while sleep was a natural condition, sleepwalking and particularly violence while sleepwalking was abnormal and amounted to a disease of the mind under the M'Naghten Rules. Accordingly, Burgess' only available defense was held to be insanity. This can be contrasted with the Canadian courts approach in cases such as *Parks*[65] in which the Supreme Court treated an offense committed while asleep as an instance of non-insane automatism.

The distinction between internal and external causes is further complicated by the fact that an individual may be affected by a combination of internal and external factors. In its response to the Law Commission consultation process the Criminal Cases Review Commission noted that it had "considered a number of applications made on the basis of a claim of automatism . . . where the argument is based on a combination of internal and external factors, for example mental illness, such as stress or depression, and the effect of prescription medication or alcohol."[66] The case of *Brian Thomas*[67] is an example of the difficulties caused where there is an interplay between internal and external causes. In this case Thomas was charged with murder, and evidence indicated that the attack was a case of "night terror violence akin to sleepwalking." The experts agreed that the attack occurred while Thomas was asleep, but the reason for the act was a mix of factors including the defendant's genetic predisposition, an incident earlier that evening with a group of young hooligans, and a change in Thomas' medication regime. In his response to the Law Commission's Consultation the trial judge, Lord Justice Davies, was damning in his assessment of the current law: "The distinction between 'sane' and 'insane' automatism, and 'internal' and 'external' causes, is not simply unsatisfactory . . . it is illogical, little short of a disgrace and should be abolished."[68]

3 The Proposed New Defense

The Law Commission have recommended reform of the law both in terms of insanity and non-insane automatism. If the proposals were to be enacted the common law defense of insanity would be abolished and replaced by a new defense of "not criminally responsible by reason of a recognized medical condition."[69] Linked to the creation of this new defense, there would also be a significant narrowing of the ambit of the common law defense of non-insane automatism.

There are obvious advantages of the new proposal. It does away with the stigma-laden term "insanity." The change also immediately removes the problem of attaching a wholly inappropriate label to conditions such as diabetes, epilepsy, and sleep disorders. This would be a benefit to the medical professionals called as expert witnesses who are forced to work with legal terminology which makes no sense from a medical perspective.[70] It would benefit jurors[71] who have to determine whether on the facts the label should apply, as they would not be applying a description of insane to someone who they do not consider to be insane, such as a diabetic. The change would also benefit those accused of offenses who are faced with the option of accepting guilt or pleading insanity when they are neither guilty nor, in the societally accepted meaning of the term, insane. Labelling conditions such as diabetes, epilepsy, and sleep disorders as recognized medical conditions is a much fairer and more appropriate description.

The phrase "not criminally responsible by reason of" is also a better preamble to the verdict than "not guilty by reason of." A "not guilty" verdict normally denotes that the accused did not do the act or that the prosecution has failed to prove that the accused did the act. A "not guilty by reason of insanity" verdict, however, means something different. It means that the accused did the act, but was insane. The old "guilty, but insane" verdict arguably reflected this better. However, it too was problematic in that the defendant might not be guilty as his act might not be one that could be viewed as voluntary. The proposed new terminology overcomes these problems. It brings to the fore the crucial issue of criminal responsibility. The verdict is acknowledging the fact that the accused did the act, but is noting that he is not criminally responsible for the act.

Under the current law the fact that the courts retain disposal options over a defendant who has been found not guilty, albeit not guilty by reason of insanity, is arguably incongruous. The not guilty finding also arguably supports popular and media views that defendants who are found to be insane have got away with their offense.[72] The retention of disposal options over a defendant found to be not criminally responsible arguably appears less incongruous.[73]

The Law Commission propose that the new defense should apply if:

the defendant wholly lacked the capacity:

(i) rationally to form a judgment about the relevant conduct or circumstances;
(ii) to understand the wrongfulness of what he or she is charged with having done; or
(iii) to control his or her physical acts in relation to the relevant conduct or circumstances

as a result of a qualifying recognized medical condition.[74]

The new defense not only moves away from the out dated terminology of "disease of the mind," it also moves away from the idea that the defense is limited to mental disorders. In adopting this approach the Law Commission refer to DSM-IV (*Diagnostic and Statistical Manual of Mental Disorders*, 4th Edition) to support their contention that defining mental disorders is problematic.[75] However, their primary argument is that it is inappropriate to distinguish between causes which are mental and causes which are physical.[76] The avoidance of the mind/body distinction and the focus instead on the requirement for a medical condition also neatly extricates the law from the internal/external divide. The diabetic accused who failed to take insulin would no longer need to be differentiated from the diabetic accused who reacted badly to the insulin he took—both would be potentially within the recognized medical condition defense. The questions that would need to be answered would be: (1) whether they wholly lacked the capacity to do one of the three things identified in the proposed new defense, (2) whether that lack of capacity was as a result of the recognized medical condition,[77] and (3) whether the recognized medical condition was a "qualifying" recognized medical condition.[78]

The second question is possibly the simplest and the least contentious. It is not enough that the person seeking to rely on the proposed new defense had a medical condition at the time of the alleged offense. The medical condition must be "recognized" and the medical condition must be the reason that the accused "wholly lacked capacity." The term "recognized" identifies that there must be a degree of medical consensus that the condition in question is accepted as being a medical condition. This approach provides a mechanism that can evolve over time as medical knowledge develops. No specific system of recognition is specified; clearly classifications such as those in DSM may at times be relevant, but the scheme allows the courts to develop their approach on a pragmatic case by case basis.[79] The idea of recognition is supported by the requirement that there should be evidence from at least two experts that the accused suffers from the condition and supporting the linkage between the condition and the claimed lack of capacity. The current English law on insanity requires evidence from two medical practitioners, one of whom must be approved as having special experience in the diagnosis or treatment of mental disorder. The proposed defense removes the requirement that both experts must be medical practitioners as well as the requirement that at least one expert specializes in mental disorders. This is eminently sensible. The current requirement to call an expert on mental disorders when the accused is claiming, for example, that his behavior stems from diabetes is inappropriate. With the new defense clearly incorporating physical as well as mental disorders, maintaining the requirement to have an expert witness specializing in mental disorders would be doubly inappropriate. Similarly, the widening of the ambit of required experts beyond medical practitioners enables, for example, an expert witness to be called who specializes in learning disabilities.[80]

In terms of a causal link, the proposed approach is similar to the M'Naghten Rules, which demand that in order to rely on the defense the accused must show that the defect of reason arose from a disease of the mind. As already discussed, it is wider, in that rather than being limited to diseases of the mind, the ambit of the proposed new defense extends to both physical and mental conditions. The retention of the required linkage of the medical condition to the lack of capacity is important and it is good that it has been maintained. It would clearly be undesirable for an individual to be able to avoid criminal responsibility simply because they have a medical condition. Similarly, it would be wrong for an individual who lacked capacity for a reason other than the recognized medical condition to be found not criminally responsible by reason of that recognized medical condition.

The third question is intriguing. The proposed reform views some recognized medical conditions as "qualifying" and others as non-qualifying. An instant response to this approach would be to question the distinction. If an individual does not have the required capacity as a result of a recognized medical condition, why should that individual be denied the proposed defense? The explanation is both pragmatic and arguably policy driven. The Law Commission identify two recognized medical conditions that they consider should be excluded.

One medical condition so identified is acute intoxication. Under English law, voluntary intoxication is not a defense. However, where voluntary intoxication means that the accused did not form the *mens rea* for an offense requiring a specific intent[81] the accused is entitled to be acquitted as the prosecution must prove *mens rea*. However, where an accused is charged with a basic intent crime he can be convicted of that offense if he lacks *mens rea* because of voluntary intoxication.[82] Acute intoxication is recognized as a medical condition in ICD-10 (*International Statistical Classification of Diseases and Related Health Problems*, 10th edition) but its effects are only transient and are similar to intoxication.[83] However, at the time it can severely affect mental functioning and reasoning powers. This would seem to support its inclusion as a potential condition on which the defense could rest.

At the same time, though, voluntary intoxication is self-induced. Society, politicians, and the media would be likely to be outraged if an individual who drank so excessively that it destroyed his capacity to form a judgment rationally, to differentiate right from wrong, or to control his actions, should then be found not to be criminally responsible for criminal acts that he committed while in that state. The fact that the court retained disposal options over such an individual would be unlikely to assuage this outrage. Indeed, given the transient nature of acute intoxication the appropriateness of the potential disposal options would be questionable. Therefore, for policy reasons, it can be readily understood why acute intoxication should be specifically excluded. The same result could, arguably, have been achieved if acute intoxication was dealt with in terms of prior fault.[84] However, acute intoxication has already been excluded by the Court of Appeal[85] as a relevant factor in the diminished responsibility defense which, as noted previously,[86] uses the same recognized mental condition defense terminology. Therefore, whilst it might have been sufficient to rely on prior fault to arrive at a similar outcome for this proposed defense as that already adopted by the courts for diminished responsibility it is probably simpler to adopt the Law Commission's approach of proposing to explicitly exclude acute intoxication as a potential foundation for the new defense.

Other alcohol related medical conditions, such as alcohol dependency syndrome, are examined in the Discussion Paper and the Law Commission conclude that these could potentially form the basis for the proposed medical condition defense. This accords with the present approach to alcohol-related diseases that applies to a plea of insanity.[87]

The second group of recognized medical conditions to be specifically excluded from the proposed new defense are personality disorders. The Commission explore a number of definitions of such disorders, noting that such disorders tend to be enduring behavior patterns often linked to criminal behavior. The types of disorders considered in this examination include ones labelled "anti-social personality disorders," "dis-social," and "psychopathic." The Commission note differences in approach to classification for example as to whether psychopathy should be viewed as an affective disorder whereas anti-social personality disorder should simply be viewed as a behavioral disorder. They consider both jurisdictions that have specifically excluded certain disorders from their insanity defense,[88] those which have chosen expressly to include them,[89] and those which have chosen not to exclude them.[90] The Discussion Paper appears sympathetic to the approach adopted in the American Law Institute Model Penal Code to exclude "an abnormality manifested only by repeated criminal or otherwise antisocial conduct" and that of Scotland where s51A of the Criminal Procedure (Scotland) Act 1995 provides that: "A person does not lack criminal responsibility for [conduct constituting an offense] if the mental disorder in question consists only of a personality disorder which is characterised solely or principally by abnormally aggressive or seriously irresponsible conduct."[91] Adoption of the Model Penal Code or the Scottish approach would appear a good way forward, excluding disorders that are characterized primarily by their manifestation in criminal behavior. It would seem absurd to state that someone was not criminally responsible solely because he behaved in a criminal manner. However, having set out reasons why an approach like that adopted in Scotland and in the Model Penal Code would be appropriate,[92] the Law Commission then veer off and opt for a different and (it is submitted) less satisfactory approach.

The approach proposed by the Law Commission is "for some conditions to be specifically stated to be non-qualifying conditions, and for the court to decide, with the guidance of the Court of Appeal, whether any condition which is not in the list is nevertheless not a qualifying condition."[93] This approach lacks the flexibility to respond easily to developments in medical and scientific understanding. Whilst the determination of what is a "qualifying recognized medical condition" should be a legal question rather than a medical one, it should also be one which is capable of evolving as medical and scientific understanding progresses. If changes in approach are to be dependent on some form of statutory amendment or cases being taken to the Court of Appeal, trial judges will potentially lack the flexibility to respond to new scientific knowledge. For example, if a condition previously believed to be defined purely by its manifestation in anti-social or criminal behaviour became better understood and could be identified by, for example, brain scan evidence, then excluding evidence that a particular accused lacked capacity on the basis that his disorder was on a list written many years earlier when scientific understanding was much less developed would be likely to lead to injustice.

Having examined the requirement that there should be a qualifying recognized medical condition the remaining element of the proposed new defense is the lack of capacity requirement:

the defendant wholly lacked the capacity:

(i) rationally to form a judgment about the relevant conduct or circumstances;
(ii) to understand the wrongfulness of what he or she is charged with having done; or
(iii) to control his or her physical acts in relation to the relevant conduct or circumstances

A number of points are noteworthy. Firstly, the test covers both cognitive and volitional impairment. The M'Naghten Rules cover only cognitive impairment.[94]

The proposed new defense's first limb has similarities to the knowledge of the nature and quality of the act limb of the M'Naghten Rules.[95] The proposed new limb is, however, wider. It covers not just the act (the conduct) but also explicitly the circumstances and it is based not on knowledge, but on the ability to form a judgment rationally. M'Naghten and Yates both knew that they were killing, but in their deluded states they could not rationally form a judgment. Someone in situations such as theirs who wholly lacked the capacity to rationally form a judgment would be entitled to claim the proposed new defense.

The second limb similarly has links to the M'Naghten Rules, but it too has significant differences. Whereas the M'Naghten Rules focus on a test of whether the accused "did not know he was doing what was wrong," the proposed new test focuses on understanding rather than knowledge—a potentially wider test of cognitive ability. Perhaps most important with regard to this limb is the question as to how "wrongfulness" should be interpreted. As has been seen in the earlier discussion of M'Naghten's case and subsequent case law, the question of whether this is a test of knowledge of whether something is legally wrong or morally wrong is an important one. The Law Commission state that the current test based on knowledge of the law is "unwarrantedly narrow."[96] They also note that it does not accord with the focus of the expert evidence that is given in court which tends to focus on the accused's more general understanding of what is and is not wrong.[97] The Law Commission acknowledge difficulties in replacing a test of legally wrong with one of morally wrong as this would inevitably draw the courts into investigations as to what is generally considered morally wrong in a given set of circumstances; they also reject the idea that the test should be based on the accused's subjective viewpoint.[98] Their recommendation is to adopt the Canadian case law approach that the "accused need only appreciate that the act was something he or she ought not to do."[99] The proposed abandonment of the M'Naghten Rules' focus on legal knowledge should be applauded. The emphasis on whether the defendant "wholly lacked the capacity . . . to understand the wrongfulness of what he or she is charged with having done" clearly moves the test away from a simple subjective test of did the accused understand that what he did was wrong. Overall this element of the proposed new test should also, it is submitted, be welcomed.

The introduction of a third, volitional element to the proposed new defense is a significant change in focus from that adopted in the M'Naghten Rules. The breadth of this limb of the new defense would in the Law Commission's view be quite narrow covering physical conditions such as epileptic seizure, sleepwalking episodes, and Tourette's syndrome.[100] The Law Commission note codes that have some form of physical control element within their insanity defense.[101] As the Commission note criticism of the M'Naghten Rules for excluding such an element is not new. The Atkin Committee back in 1923 thought irresistible impulse arising from mental disease should be added to the M'Naghten Rules: "[I]t should be recognized that a person charged criminally with an offense is irresponsible for his act when the act is committed under an impulse which the prisoner was by mental disease in substance deprived of any power to resist."[102] Almost a century later it is high time to remedy the earlier failure to reform the law.

All the three new limbs are based on a requirement that the person claiming the new defense must "wholly" lack capacity. There is a logic to this requirement. If you are to say an individual is "not criminally responsible" then semantically that would not be satisfied if he, for example, substantially lacked capacity but still retained some capacity. This is also logical in relation to the diminished responsibility defense which is satisfied if the defendant's ability is "substantially" impaired.[103] Diminished responsibility under English law is only a partial defense. It reduces what would otherwise be a conviction for murder to one for manslaughter. This provides more sentencing options and allows the diminished responsibility to be taken into account as a mitigating factor in sentencing. The proposed recognized medical condition defense is a complete defense. While disposal options are retained in relation to the person who successfully pleads the defense the intention is not to punish the individual but is rather one of public protection.

However, the requirement that a defendant must "wholly lack capacity" will on the face of it be difficult to satisfy. Here the Law Commission have arrived at a potentially neat solution. Under the M'Naghten Rules, as initially expressed, a defendant was presumed sane and in order to avail himself of the insanity defense was required to clearly prove that he was insane. This was subsequently interpreted to mean that the burden of proof fell on the defendant and that, for the insanity defense to be made out, the defendant must prove on the balance of probabilities that he was insane within the meaning of the M'Naghten Rules.[104] This means that under the current law a jury should convict if they are satisfied beyond reasonable doubt that an accused did the criminal act, but have a reasonable doubt as to the defendant's sanity—so long as that doubt is not so great as to mean that they think on the balance of probabilities that he is M'Naghten insane.

This English law approach offends the principle expressed by Chief Justice Dickson in *Whyte* in the Canadian Supreme Court that:

> The real concern is not whether the accused must disprove an element or prove an excuse, but that an accused may be convicted while a reasonable doubt exists. When that possibility exists, there is a breach of the presumption of innocence.[105]

The English law has been challenged. In *H v. UK*[106] the European Commission on Human Rights concluded that the burden of proof under the M'Naghten Rules did not offend against the presumption of innocence embodied within Article 6(2) of the European Convention for the Protection of Human Rights and Fundamental Freedoms as it related to a presumption of sanity rather than a presumption of innocence. Interestingly the Law Commission explicitly reject the European Commission's reasoning and conclusion.[107]

The Law Commission propose that the burden of proof for the new medical condition defense would be what they term "an elevated evidential burden."[108] It would be "elevated" in that to have the medical condition defense considered the defendant would have to be supported by the evidence of two expert witnesses, but it would simply be an evidential burden, that is, the defendant would have to produce sufficient evidence to raise the issue that he wholly lacked capacity in relation to one of the three limbs as a result of a recognized medical condition. It would then be for the prosecution to prove beyond reasonable doubt that the defense did not apply.

Returning to the "wholly lacked capacity" test means that the defendant seeking to rely on this defense would have to satisfy the elevated evidential burden, but once this was done it would fall on the prosecution to prove beyond reasonable doubt that the defendant did not wholly lack capacity. It is not difficult to envisage cases where it is possible that the accused wholly lacked capacity, but where it could alternatively be possible that the accused may have retained some small degree of capacity. In such cases if the burden of proof fell on the defendant it might be very difficult to prove that he "wholly" lacked capacity. It is submitted that the proposed approach is more likely to avoid injustice. Finding a party guilty who wholly lacked capacity is, I would argue, a more unjust outcome than finding a party not criminally responsible whose capacity was substantially impaired though not wholly lacking. I would argue that in adopting the elevated evidential burden approach, the Law Commission have arrived at a pragmatic solution.

The medical condition defense would catch a number of situations which would previously have been covered by the automatism defense. Defendants such as Quick,[109] T,[110] Charlson,[111] Roach,[112] and C[113] were all held to be able to claim automatism and as a result gained not guilty verdicts. Under the proposed new law all these defendants would be likely to fall within the recognized medical condition defense if they could satisfy the court that they wholly lacked capacity in relation to one of the three limbs. While defendants such as these who were previously successful in claiming automatism would, no doubt, prefer a not guilty verdict to a not criminally responsible verdict, it is submitted that the retention of disposal options over individuals who have committed acts which would have been criminal but for their medical condition is a more appropriate outcome.

The proposed new defense would reduce the ambit of the automatism defense. The Law Commission propose that the automatism defense should be retained, but that it would be limited to situations where the accused had a complete loss of capacity to control his actions and this loss of capacity was not the result of a recognized medical condition. There are probably very few scenarios in which the new narrower automatism defense will apply.[114] The change will remove the present anomaly that for insane automatism leading to a finding of not guilty by reason of insanity the test is derived from the M'Naghten Rules and is whether the defendant did not know the nature and quality of his act or that if he did that he did not know that it was wrong, whereas for non-insane automatism the current test is based on a total loss of control.[115] Both the new recognized medical condition defense and the revised automatism defense would, if implemented, be based on a total loss of capacity. The automatism defense would mirror the third limb[116] of the medical condition defense in relating to the defendant's complete lack of capacity to control his physical acts. If the lack of capacity was due to a recognized medical condition then the accused would receive the not criminally responsible verdict (so long as the condition was a "qualifying" condition); if the failure was due to a cause other than a recognized medical condition then the accused would have the defense of automatism. The burden of proof for a non-insane automatism claim currently rests on the prosecution. The burden of proof for the proposed reformed automatism claim would be unchanged. This is appropriate. Viewing automatism as being based on the voluntary act requirement, it is appropriate that this should be something that the prosecution must prove beyond reasonable doubt. Though, unlike the medical condition defense, the new automatism defense would not have an evidential burden to discharge, in reality it is hard to envisage a situation where a defense of automatism would succeed without evidence in support of it being advanced by the defendant.

4 Conclusion

The Law Commission recommendations should be welcomed. The verdict of "not criminally responsible by reason of a recognized medical condition" moves away from the stigma associated with insanity and is a much more appropriate description for those who, for example, suffer from diabetes or epilepsy. Similarly, the description "not criminally responsible" is, arguably, more appropriate than "not guilty." The approach, with its focus on medical conditions rather than with "disease of the mind," is more in accord with modern medical and scientific understanding and therefore will make it easier for expert witnesses to provide meaningful evidence in court. It will also be more straightforward for jurors to interpret as the potential verdict will better fit lay understandings as to the meaning of the terminology. By moving away from the internal/external divide, the Law Commission's proposals avoid the illogicality of the current law. By clarifying that the new rules and the disposal options will apply in all criminal courts, the Law Commission are overcoming a further anomaly in the current approach. A further advantage is the inclusion of a volitional limb to the proposed new defense. The two cognitive limbs are both better framed than the current law and the movement away from the test of knowledge as to whether something is legally wrong is to be particularly welcomed.

The focus on "wholly" lacking capacity fits with the "not criminally responsible" verdict, but may be difficult for even deserving defendants to satisfy. However, the changes to the burden of proof rules not only reinforce the presumption of innocence, but also in large part overcome the most challenging aspects, from a defendant's perspective, of the capacity requirement. The reform proposals do not address the probably much more widespread problem of the defendant who "substantially" lacks capacity. However, in fairness, they do not set out to do so. The absence of a diminished capacity defense or partial defense (except in relation to murder) remains a lacuna in the English law.

The application of existing prior fault principles to the proposed new defense appear appropriate and the explanation as to when as a result of the defendant's medical condition they should not apply is reassuring. The explicit exclusion of acute intoxication as a qualifying medical condition is understandable and the decision to exclude certain other medical conditions that are effectively identified solely by their associated antisocial and criminal behavior is sensible, although the manner in which it is proposed to do this should be reconsidered.

Extending the "not criminally responsible" verdict beyond the current confines of the insanity verdict to encompass some situations which would currently amount to non-insane automatism is to be welcomed. Currently some of those who successfully claim non-insane automatism are a potential threat to society. Yet as a result of their successful plea they walk free from the court. Retaining disposal options over such defendants is appropriate. The group of cases that would fall within the ambit of the revised automatism defense, if these proposals were to be enacted, is likely to be vanishingly small. However, it is important that those who wholly lack volitional control for a reason not related to a recognized medical control should have a defense. Whether there is a need for those who wholly lack capacity "rationally to form a judgment about the relevant conduct or circumstances" or "to understand the wrongfulness of what he or she is charged with having done" for a reason arising other than from a recognized medical condition is a moot point. It is hard to envisage such a defendant being fit to plead; therefore, the failure to include such defendants within the automatism defense will probably not in practical terms lead to injustice.

Overall, the proposed reforms are definitely an important step in the right direction. Whether they prove to have lasting significance will depend on whether they are implemented. The document in which the proposals are presented is described as a "Discussion Paper," the proposals are described as "provisional" proposals, and the document does not contain proposed draft legislation. This is an important omission. If the Law Commission produce proposals and a draft bill for their introduction, then the government, in the person of the Lord Chancellor, may take them forward. If the government does not, the Lord Chancellor is required to report to Parliament with reasons why the proposals are not to be implemented.[117] As it stands the Lord Chancellor need not respond. The most immediate question is whether the Law Commission will now produce a report setting out their recommendations in the form of a draft bill. If they do so, the ball will then be in the Government's court.

Notes

1. The term "English" is used in this chapter instead of the more cumbersome term "English and Welsh." All references to English law should be treated as meaning English and Welsh law and no offense is intended.

2. The term Parliament is used in this chapter to avoid confusion. The judges were in fact summoned to explain the law to one of the two houses of Parliament: the House of Lords. However, if the term House of Lords is used there is a danger in confusing this body, the parliamentary House of Lords, with the judicial House of Lords.

3. The spelling of M'Naghten varies. The spelling adopted in this chapter is that of the main law report of the questioning of the judges in Parliament: (1843) All ER 718. The Old Bailey Report on his trial refers to Daniel M'Naughten—*Old Bailey Proceedings Online* (www.oldbaileyonline.org, version 7.2, 26 January 2016), February 1843, trial of Daniel M'Naughten (t18430227-874) (accessed 26th January 2016). Queen Victoria in a letter to her Prime Minister, Sir Robert Peel, referred to him as MacNaughten (see note 7 below). Lord Goddard CJ in *R v. Windle* adopts a fourth variant referring to the accused in the case as McNaghten (see note 43 below and surrounding text).

4. Police inspector John Tierney, who interviewed M'Naghten following his arrest, recounted to the court that when he asked M'Naghten who he had shot, M'Naghten responded: "It is Sir Robert Peel, is not it?" *Old Bailey Proceedings Online*

(www.oldbaileyonline.org, version 7.2, 26 January 2016), February 1843, trial of Daniel M'Naughten (t18430227-874), 724.

5. No less than eight medical witnesses gave evidence at M'Naghten's trial: Edward Thomas Monroe M.D., Sir Alexander Morrison M.D., William M'Clewer, William Hutchison M.D., John Crawford, Gilbert M'Murdo, Aston Key, and Forbes Winslow. All eight considered that M'Naghten was acting under a delusion. According to the Lord Chancellor, discussing the case in Parliament, two medical witnesses instructed by the prosecution were in court, but were not called. The Lord Chancellor concluded that the explanation for the failure of the prosecution to call these witnesses was that they would not have disagreed with those called by the defense (Hansard HL Deb 13 March 1843, vol. 67, col. 725).

6. *Old Bailey Proceedings Online* (www.oldbaileyonline.org, version 7.2, 26 January 2016), February 1843, trial of Daniel M'Naughten (t18430227-874), 763

7. Queen Victoria wrote to Peel following M'Naghten's trial complaining, "We have seen the trials of Oxford and MacNaughten conducted by the ablest lawyers of the day—and they *allow* and *advise* the Jury to pronounce the verdict of not guilty on account of insanity, whilst *everybody* is morally convinced that both malefactors were perfectly conscious and aware of what they did" (Benson, *The Letters of Queen Victoria*, 581, quoted in Robinson, *Wild Beasts and Idle Humours*, 164).

8. On June 10, 1840, Edward Oxford attempted to shoot the monarch as she travelled by carriage on Constitution Hill. Oxford was found not guilty, being insane and was ordered to be detained during her Majesty's pleasure. *Old Bailey Proceedings Online* (www.oldbaileyonline.org, version 7.2, 08 December 2015), July 1840, trial of Edward Oxford (t18400706-1877). Less than two years later another attempt was made on the life of Queen Victoria again on Constitution Hill. On May 30, 1842, John Francis fired at the queen in her carriage as she went passed him. Francis had made an aborted attempt on the Queen's life the day before. Francis was found guilty of high treason and sentenced to death. *Old Bailey Proceedings Online* (www.oldbaileyonline.org, version 7.2, 08 December 2015), June 1842, trial of John Francis (t18420613-1758). On July 3, 1842, John William Bean attempted to fire a pistol as the queen passed by in a coach along The Mall. It is not clear if this was an assassination attempt. The pistol did not have sufficient charge to cause any serious harm. Bean was sentenced to 18 months' imprisonment. *Old Bailey Proceedings Online* (www.oldbaileyonline.org, version 7.2, 08 December 2015), August 1842, trial of John William Bean (t18420822-2277).

9. Hansard HL Deb 13 March 1843, vol 67, 714 (spelling Americanized throughout).

10. M'Naghten's Case [1843–60] All ER Rep 229, 231.

11. Ibid, 233.

12. The House of Lords had posed five questions to be answered by the judges. The quotation was in answer to the second and third questions. The other questions related to the provision of expert evidence in trials where insanity was raised and as to whether the accused's guilt should be assessed on the basis of his insane delusion or on the basis of the actual facts.

13. "The M'Naghten Rules have been used as a comprehensive definition [of insanity] . . . by the courts for the last 140 years" (*R v. Sullivan* [1984] A.C. 156, 171 (HL) per Lord Diplock).

14. The Law Commission (see note 16 below) in Appendix C of the Supplementary Material to the Scoping Paper on Insanity and Automatism look at the law on insanity in other jurisdictions. Australia, Canada, Hong Kong, India, Ireland, New Zealand, Scotland, and the United States of America are identified as having jurisdictions that operate a version of the M'Naghten Rules (Law Commission for England and Wales, *Insanity and Automatism*, paragraphs C1–C64).

15. Lord Brougham said at the conclusion of Tindal LCJ's response to the House's questions: "The opinions of the learned judges, and the very able manner in which they have been presented to the House, deserve our best thanks" (M'Naghten's Case [1843–60] All ER Rep 234).

16. The Law Commission for England and Wales is a statutory independent body charged by government inter alia to ensure the law is fair and modern and to make recommendations to Parliament—for details of its role see: www.lawcom.gov.uk/about/.

17. It has been suggested that the insanity defense is not available for crimes that do not include a *mens rea* element. In *DPP v. H* [1997] 1 WLR 1406 it was held that the common law defense of insanity is only available in the Magistrates Court only where the offense includes a *mens rea* element. The defendant had pleaded insanity in relation to an offense of driving while over the permitted level of alcohol in the blood contrary to s.5(1) of the Road Traffic Act 1988. The defendant was found not guilty as a result of the insanity plea. The prosecution appealed successfully that as the offense was a summary offense and as there was no *mens rea* element to the offense the defendant should not have been entitled to raise insanity. The case raises another anomaly which is that the special verdict of not guilty by reason of insanity is not available in the Magistrates' Court and that as a consequence the result of a successful insanity plea in that court is a not guilty verdict.

18. Research conducted on behalf of the Law Commission—Mackay, *The Insanity Defense*—led the Law Commission to conclude: "The most significant finding from empirical studies on the use of the insanity defense in criminal proceedings is how few verdicts of not guilty by reason of insanity are returned" (see Law Commission for England and Wales, *Insanity and Automatism*, paragraph 3.25).

19. The Law Commission's Supplementary Material to the Scoping Paper highlights the way in which expert medical evidence in cases in which the insanity defense is raised tends to focus on whether "if the delusion that the defendant was experiencing at the time of the offense was in fact reality, then would the defendant's actions be justified?" (ibid, para 4.77, citing Mackay, Mitchell, and Howe, "Yet More Facts about the Insanity Defense," 407).

20. www.lawcom.gov.uk/project/insanity-and-automatism/

21. Indeed, the approach was criticized as being outdated more than 60 years ago in the Report of the Royal Commission on Capital Punishment, Cmd 8932, 1953, paragraph 248.

22. The Law Commission quote the following comment from Dr. Reed: "[T]he present test does not really relate in any meaningful way to the practice of psychiatry. Therefore diversions into discussions about the M'Naghten rules are not very helpful in conveying an understanding of the clinical situation to the court" (Law Commission for England and Wales, *Criminal Liability: Insanity and Automatism—A Discussion Paper* (2013) para 1.58).

23. Tindal LCJ prefaces his answers by stating: "[A]ssuming that your Lordships' inquiries are confined to those persons who labour under such partial delusions only, and are not in other respects insane." Arguably this preface just relates to the first question, but nowhere in the judgment do the judges suggest that the answers are to apply to all who are insane. Indeed, the second question that led to the statement of what have become known as the M'Naghten Rules was similarly couched in terms of seeking "the proper questions to be submitted to the jury when a person *alleged to be afflicted with insane delusion* respecting one or more particular subjects or persons is charged with the commission of a crime (murder, for example) and insanity is set up as a defense" (emphasis added). Both quotes: [1843–60] All ER Rep 229, 233.

24. The issue of the breadth of application of the M'Naghten Rules has been discussed by the courts on occasion. For example, in *R v. Windle* Lord Goddard CJ noted the caveat at the beginning of Tindal LCJ's response to Parliament that the answers to the questions only applied to cases of partial delusion and asked if there was any authority for arguing that the M'Naghten Rules should be restricted to apply just to such cases. Defense counsel responded that: "Although the rules have been applied in all cases, it does not follow that they have been altered or amended in meaning and it may well be that, properly interpreted, they do not apply to a case such as the present, namely, one of communicated insanity, in which no delusion existed." Notwithstanding this suggestion that "properly interpreted" the rules had only limited application, the reality has been that they have come to be applied to all English cases in which insanity is argued. Indeed, in *Windle*, though he asked the question as to whether the ambit of the Rules should be limited, Goddard LCJ proceeded on the basis that: "The McNaghten rules were the rules which the judges agreed in 1843 were the proper tests to be applied in considering the defense of insanity" ([1952] 2 QB 826, 831, all quotes).

25. The trial of Daniel M'Naghten was heard by Lord Chief Justice Tindal and Justices Williams and Coleridge.

26. [1843–60] All ER Rep 229, 230.

27. "What is the law respecting alleged crimes committed by persons afflicted with insane delusion in respect of one or more particular subjects or persons, as, for instance, where at the time of the commission of the alleged crime the accused knew he was acting contrary to law, but did the act complained of with a view, under the influence of insane delusion, of redressing or revenging some supposed grievance or injury, or of producing some supposed public benefit?" ([1843–60] All ER Rep 229, 233).

28. Ibid.

29. Ibid.

30. Ibid., 233–34.

31. "If a person under an insane delusion as to existing facts commits an offense in consequence thereof, is he thereby excused?" (ibid., 234).

32. Ibid.

33. This was the common law position. It is now given statutory force by s.76(3) of the Criminal Justice and Immigration Act 2008 which states that in assessing whether the degree of force used was reasonable it should be decided "by reference to the circumstances as D believed them to be" and s.76(4) which states that the defendant is entitled to rely on a genuinely held belief even if the belief was mistaken and the mistake was not reasonable.

34. The fact that an individual might feel wronged, particularly if that feeling was, in the circumstances an understandable and possibly a reasonable belief might go to mitigation, but it would not go to the determination of guilt. The now repealed partial defense to murder of provocation (Homicide Act 1957 s.3) and its successor the partial defense of loss of control (Coroners and Justice Act 2009 s.54) that in certain circumstances allows a defense where the defendant has "a justifiable sense of being seriously wronged" do not absolve the accused of guilt, they merely reduce the conviction from one of murder (carrying a mandatory life sentence) to one of manslaughter (an offense for which lesser sentences can be imposed).

35. "Can a medical man conversant with the disease of insanity, who never saw the prisoner previously to the trial, but who was present during the whole trial and the examination of all the witnesses, be asked his opinion as to the state of the prisoner's mind at the time of the commission of the alleged crime, or his opinion *whether the prisoner was conscious at the time of doing the act that he was acting contrary to law*, or whether he was labouring under any and what delusion at the time?" ([1843–60] All ER Rep 229, 234, emphasis added).

36. Edward Thomas Monroe M.D.'s evidence is typical: "I believe I am able to discriminate between a case where a man is laboring under delusion, and where a man feigns delusion—I am quite satisfied that the prisoner entertained the delusions he was giving utterance to—I have not the slightest shadow of a doubt on the subject—if I had heard nothing of his past history, nor the evidence given to-day, my examination in the prison would certainly have led me to the conclusion that he was insane—coupling that with the history of the two last years of his life, I have not the remotest doubt of his insanity—I am quite satisfied of it" (see note 4, 757).

37. Edward Munroe was asked: "Is it now an established principle in the pathology of insanity that there may exist a partial delusion sufficient to overcome a man's moral sense and self-control, and render him irresponsible for his actions, exciting a partial insanity only, although the rest of the faculties of the mind may remain in all their ordinary state of operation?" (ibid.).

38. "I have not the slightest doubt that the moral perception of the prisoner was affected and impaired when he did this act" (Edward Munroe M.D., ibid., 760).

39. Sir Alexander Morrison M.D. stated: "I believe that those delusions acted on his mind so as to deprive him of the exercise of all restraint against the act to which it impelled him—I do not speak with the slightest doubt on the subject" (ibid., 760). The surgeon William M'Clewer came to a similar conclusion: "I consider that in the commission of the act, he was not under the ordinary restraint by which persons in general are bound in their conduct; his moral liberty was destroyed" (760). William Hutchinson's conclusions were similar: "He was perfectly incapable of exercising control in any matter connected with the delusion—I am decidedly of opinion that the act flowed immediately out of that delusion." The surgeon Aston Key held a similar view concluding that M'Naghten had, at the time of the offense, "lost the control of his mind" (762).

40. Numerous witnesses gave evidence as to M'Naghten's belief that he was being persecuted the police. Inspector John Tierney's account being typical when he reported that M'Naghten had said: "The Tories in my native city have driven me to this, and have followed me to France, Scotland, and other parts; I can get no sleep from the system they pursue towards me; I believe I am driven into a consumption by them; they wish to murder me. That is all I wish to say at present; they have completely disordered me, and I am quite a different man before they commenced this annoyance towards me" (ibid., 725).

41. M'Naghten knew that he was shooting someone. On the evidence of James Silver, a police constable, M'Naghten, having shot Edward Drummond once, then drew a second pistol, took aim and was about to fire a second shot at his victim when Silver intervened (ibid., 721). He may have been mistaken as to who he was shooting (see note 4). However, mistakenly shooting the Prime Minister's private secretary when intending to shoot the Prime Minister would not amount to failure to know the nature and quality of his act.

42. See note 40.

43. [1952] 2QB 826. Windle had killed his wife by giving her an overdose of aspirin. It was agreed that Windle's wife was certifiably insane and the defense claim was that Windle was suffering from a form of communicated insanity known as folie à deux. Windle's wife was suicidal and he believed that he was doing what was morally right in killing her, even though he knew it was legally wrong.

44. [1952] 2 QB 826, 833–34. In arriving at this conclusion Lord Goddard CJ referred to a similar finding as to the law that he had made two years earlier in *R v. Rivett* (1950) 34 Cr App Rep 87.

45. [2007] EWCA Crim 1978.

46. (1952) 86 CLR 358 (High Court of Australia).

47. [2007] EWCA Crim 1978 [21].

48. Ibid [23].

49. Ibid [24].

50. (1917) 12 Cr. App. R. 21, 26–27.

51. Law Commission for England and Wales, *Criminal Liability: Insanity and Automatism—A Discussion Paper*, para 1.51.

52. For more information about Andrea Yates and in particular her initial trial see Denno, "Who is Andrea Yates?" and her chapter in this volume.

53. Under the law of Texas, Andrea Yates was initially found to be sane and convicted of murder. She appealed successfully and at her retrial was found not guilty by reason of insanity.

54. Different terms are at times used interchangeably by the courts including "sane automatism" and "automatism" (see for example the use of this term in *Bratty v. Attorney General for Northern Ireland* [1963] AC 386; *R v. Quick* [1973] QB 910), although "automatism" is sometimes used to include both insane automatism and non-insane automatism. For the purposes of this chapter in examining the current law the terms "insane" and "non-insane automatism" will be used.

55. [1935] AC 462, 482 (HL).

56. [1963] A.C. 386, 409.

57. Ibid., 410.

58. N51 Para 5.39.

59. *R v. Hennessy* [1989] 2 All ER 9.

60. *R v. Quick* [1973] QB 910.

61. "A self-induced incapacity will not excuse . . . nor will one which could have been reasonably foreseen as a result of either doing or omitting to do something, as for example taking alcohol against medical advice after using certain prescribed drugs, or failing to have regular meals while taking insulin" (*R v. Quick* [1973] QB 910, 922, per Lawton LJ). See also *R v. C* [2007] EWCA Crim 1862, [2007] All ER (D) 91.

62. *Bratty v. Attorney General for Northern Ireland* [1963] A.C. 386, 409. For the full quote see the accompanying text to note 56.

63. See, for example, Williams, *Textbook of Criminal Law*, 663.

64. [1991] 2 QB 92.

65. [1992] 2 SCR 871.

66. Quoted in Appendix B to the Law Commission for England and Wales, *Criminal Liability: Insanity and Automatism—A Discussion Paper*, paragraph B55.

67. Unreported. Details of the case are discussed at some length in ibid., paragraph B63.

68. Quoted in ibid.

69. Provisional proposals 1 and 2, ibid., paragraphs 4.158–4.159 and 10.6–10.7

70. As Lane LCJ said: "What the law regards as insanity . . . may be far removed from what would be regarded as insanity by a psychiatrist" (*R v. Burgess* [1991] 2 Q.B. 92, 97). Similarly, as Davis LJ said in response to the Law Commission consultation with reference to the unreported Crown Court trial of Brian Thomas: "All the psychiatric and medical experts complained, politely, that the legal concept of 'insanity' in this context bears no relation to the medical (or lay) concept of insanity. The legal and medical concepts, they all said, did not fit together. From no psychiatric point of view was Mr Thomas insane or suffering

a disorder of the mind. . . . All the experts further struggled in their evidence to the jury to try to explain the difference between 'external' and 'internal' factors—unsurprisingly. One bluntly said that the legal differentiation was "incredibly artificial from the point of view of medicine'" (quoted in Law Commission for England and Wales, *Criminal Liability: Insanity and Automatism—A Discussion Paper*, paragraph B63). Just as the definition of insanity makes no sense, so the "line drawn between sane and insane automatism can never make medical sense" (Fenwick, "Automatism, Medicine and the Law," 23).

71. Davis LJ described jurors as having been "somewhat bemused" in facing a choice of not guilty or not guilty by reason of insanity in the case of *Thomas* (see note 67), where the accused had killed while asleep (Law Commission for England and Wales, *Criminal Liability: Insanity and Automatism—A Discussion Paper*, paragraph B63).

72. As discussed earlier such reactions are not new (see note 7 and the surrounding discussion).

73. Under the new proposed defense, the disposal options will be largely the same as those currently available for those found not guilty by reason of insanity: hospital orders with or without restriction, supervision orders or an absolute discharge. One change will be a clarification that these options will be available in the Magistrates' Court as well as the Crown Court. A second change would be in relation to children and young people who are found "not criminally responsible by reason of a recognized medical condition"—for these people it is proposed that a new form of non-punitive Rehabilitation Order should be instituted (see Law Commission for England and Wales, *Criminal Liability: Insanity and Automatism—A Discussion Paper*, para 4.153).

74. Ibid., provisional proposal 3 paragraphs 4.160 and 10.8.

75. "Another strong reason for not limiting the special defense to mental conditions is the difficulty of finding the right terminology for describing mental disorders in this context. There is not even a settled definition of mental disorder in the central medical reference texts, as the introduction to DSM-IV notes: 'The concept of mental disorder, like many other concepts in medicine and science, lacks a consistent operational definition that covers all situations'" (ibid., paragraph 2.43).

76. "As a matter of principle, there is no reason to restrict a defense of non-responsibility to those people with mental disorders. We can see no reason to distinguish here between physical and mental conditions: if, at the time of an alleged offense, a person did not have the capacity to avoid performing the conduct which would amount to a criminal offense, then he or she should not be held legally responsible whether that inability was physical or mental. It should not matter whether that lack of capacity is due to mental disorder (by which we mean mental illness, learning disability or learning difficulty) or to a physical condition so long as the other criteria of the defense are met" (ibid., paragraph 2.53).

77. The term "recognized medical condition" is also employed in the new diminished responsibility defense:

1. A person ("D") who kills or is a party to the killing of another is not to be convicted of murder if D was suffering from an abnormality of mental functioning which -

    (a) arose from a *recognized medical condition*

    (b) substantially impaired D's ability to do one or more of the things mentioned in subsection (1A), and

    (c) provides an explanation for D's acts and omissions or being a party to the killing. (Coroners and Justice Act 2009, s.52)

78. A fourth question that might arise would be whether there was any prior fault on the part of the defendant. The proposed new defense would, like the current automatism defense (see note 61), be subject to an exclusion that the defense would not apply if the defendant lacked capacity as a result of his prior fault. The Law Commission explore at length the relationship of the prior fault doctrine to intoxication in chapter 6 of the Discussion Paper. They also usefully identify some instances where prior fault might not apply as a result of the particular nature of the medical condition—for example, an individual with Alzheimer's who forgot to take his medicine or a person with schizophrenia who lacked understanding of his condition and so failed to take his medicine (ibid., paragraph 6.80).

79. The Law Commission discuss the problems of rigidly adopting DSM-IV and ICD 10 and their successors as being the determinant as to what is and what is not a medical condition—see particularly ibid., paragraphs 4.74–4.78.

80. The proposed changes to the requirements for expert witnesses are discussed in ibid., paragraphs 4.136 to 4.139.

81. For example, murder is a specific intent crime requiring an intent to kill or inflict grievous bodily harm.

82. *DPP v. Majewski* [1977] AC 443 (HL).

83. The definition of acute intoxication given in ICD-10 is: "A condition that follows the administration of a psychoactive substance resulting in disturbances in level of consciousness, cognition, perception, affect or behavior, or other psychophysiological functions and responses. The disturbances are directly related to the acute pharmacological effects of the substance and resolve with time, with complete recovery, except where tissue damage or other complications have arisen" (as quoted in Law Commission for England and Wales, *Criminal Liability: Insanity and Automatism—A Discussion Paper*, paragraph 4.90).

84. Again, the relationship between intoxication and prior fault is discussed in ibid., chapter 6.

85. "Voluntary acute intoxication, whether from alcohol or other substance, is not capable of founding diminished responsibility" (*R v. Dowds* [2012] EWCA Crim 281 [41]).

86. See note 77.

87. See *DPP v. Beard* [1920] AC 479, 500 to 501; *A-G for Northern Ireland v. Gallagher* [1963] AC 349, 375 and 381; and *R v. Coley* [2013] EWCA Crim 223 at [15]. In justifying this position, the Commission are able to demonstrate that this is a long established distinction; see, for example, the comment in *Davis* that "drunkenness is one thing and the diseases to which drunkenness leads are different things" ((1881) 14 Cox's Criminal Cases 563).

88. California and Oregon are cited as jurisdictions which explicitly exclude those suffering from a personality disorder alone from the insanity defense (Cal Penal Code (2005) §25.5 and Oregon Rev Statute (2005) §161.295(2)—see Law Commission for England and Wales, *Criminal Liability: Insanity and Automatism—A Discussion Paper*, paragraph 4.100).

89. The Australian example is discussed in para 4.100—see particularly Law Commission for England and Wales, *Criminal Liability: Insanity and Automatism—A Discussion Paper*, n114.

90. See for example Canada, the approach of which is explored in ibid., paragraph 4.101.

91. The American Law Institute Model Penal Code is considered in ibid., paragraph 4.100, and that adopted in the Criminal Procedure (Scotland) Act in ibid., paragraph 4.99.

92. "We believe that there are two reasons why it would be neither appropriate nor workable to express the non-qualifying kind of personality disorder in terms of a current label or category. First, there is disagreement within the psychiatric profession whether personality disorders should be classified on a categorical or a dimensional basis. Secondly, whatever name is adopted for the types of disorder we have in mind, the name itself does not delineate the aspects of a person which make it fair to hold him or her criminally responsible. To put it another way, if we say that at the time of the alleged offense the accused had a borderline personality disorder, that does not provide a specific enough basis for identifying what it is about the accused's mental state that should or should not exculpate him. If, however, we say that the accused's condition was manifested only by abnormally aggressive or seriously irresponsible behaviour then we can see that there is no reason to exculpate the accused, unless it can be shown that there was some 'other' underlying condition" (ibid., paragraph 4.108).

93. Ibid., paragraph 4.116.

94. The M'Naghten Rules require that "at the time of the committing of the act the party accused was laboring under such *a defect of reason*, from disease of the mind, as *not to know* the nature and quality of the act he was doing, *or*, if he did know it, *that he did not know* he was doing what was wrong" ([1843–60] All ER Rep 229, 233, emphasis added).

95. More particularly it echoes Goddard LCJ's comment in *Windle* that: "The whole basis of a plea of insanity is that the accused, by reason of the state of his mind, is incapable of forming a rational judgment and is, therefore, not responsible for his act" ([1952] 2 QB 826, 829).

96. Law Commission for England and Wales, *Criminal Liability: Insanity and Automatism—A Discussion Paper*, paragraph 4.20.

97. See Law Commission for England and Wales, *Insanity and Automatism*, paragraphs 3.33 to 3.38.

98. Law Commission for England and Wales, *Criminal Liability: Insanity and Automatism—A Discussion Paper*, paragraph 4.21.

99. Ibid., paragraph 4.22.

100. Ibid., paragraph 4.36.

101. The Irish approach along with that of the American Legal Institute Model Penal Code and that of the Criminal Code of Western Australia are all cited (ibid., paragraph 4.45).

102. Committee on Insanity and Crime report (1923), 21, quoted in Law Commission for England and Wales, *Criminal Liability: Insanity and Automatism—A Discussion Paper*, paragraph 4.42. The proposal was incorporated in the Criminal Responsibility (Trials) Bill 1924; however, the bill was not passed.

103. See note 77.

104. See, for example, *Woolmington v. DPP* [1935] AC 462, 475.

105. *Whyte* (1988) 2 SCR 3, (1988) 51 DLR (4th) 481, 493.

106. *H v. UK* App No 15023/89 (Commission decision) (unreported).

107. "We consider the reasoning in this judgment to be unsound because the Commission seemed to confuse an evidential burden with a requirement to prove a fact, extrapolated too much from *Salabiaku*, and did not explain how it thought the rights of the defense are adequately preserved. It failed to provide an answer to the fundamental point that, with the burden of proof on the defendant, there remains the possibility that a defendant will be convicted even though there is a reasonable doubt about his or her sanity at the time of the offense" (Law Commission for England and Wales, *Criminal Liability: Insanity and Automatism—A Discussion Paper*, paragraph 8.20).

108. Recommendation 9: paragraph 8.50.

109. [1973] QB 910 (CA).

110. [1990] Crim LR 256.

111. [1955] 1 All ER 859.

112. [2001] EWCA Crim 2698.

113. [2007] EWCA Crim 1862.

114. The Law Commission consider a number of possible scenarios: the swarm of bees entering a car and distracting a driver example considered obiter by Humphrey J. in *Kay v. Butterworth* (1945) 61 TLR 452, the driver stung by a wasp or startled by a stone hitting the windscreen considered obiter by Pearson J in *Hill v. Baxter* [1958] 1 QB 277, 286; to these the Law Commission add the example of a person who is hypnotized and in that hypnotized state goes on to take goods which do not belong to him and a novice archer at a sports day who fires an arrow causing an unintended injury as a result of a reflex reaction to hearing a starting pistol.

115. In driving cases a line of authority has indicated that control must be completely lost: see *Watmore v. Jenkins* [1962] 2 QB 572, *Broome v. Perkins* (1987)

85 Cr App R 321, and *Attorney General's Reference (No 2 of 1992)*, particularly Lord Taylor's comment that "Impaired, reduced or partial control is not enough" to found a claim of automatism" [1994] QB 91, 105. However, following the Court of Appeal's judgment in *C* it would appear that this requirement applies to all cases of non-insane automatism: see in particular Hughes LJ's definition of non-insane automatism: "The essence of it is that the movements or actions of the defendant at the material time were wholly involuntary. The better expression is complete destruction of voluntary control" (*R v. C* [2013] EWCA Crim 223 at [22]).

116. A total loss of capacity to "rationally to form a judgment about the relevant conduct or circumstances" or "to understand the wrongfulness of what he or she is charged with having done" which was not based on a recognized medical condition would not lead to a finding of automatism. Such individuals would, assuming that they were fit to plead, have no defense and could be expected to be convicted assuming that they had the requisite *mens rea*.

117. Section 3A of the Law Commissions Act 1965, as amended by section 1 of the Law Commission Act 2009.

Resources

Benson, Arthur, *The Letters of Queen Victoria*. London: John Murray, 1907.
Denno, Deborah, "Who is Andrea Yates? A Short Story about Insanity." *Duke Journal of Gender Law and Policy* 10(2003): 1–60.
Fenwick, Peter, "Automatism, Medicine and the Law." *Psychological Medicine, Monograph Supplement* 17(1990): 1–27.
Law Commission for England and Wales, *Criminal Liability: Insanity and Automatism—A Discussion Paper* (2013), available at: www.lawcom.gov.uk/wp-content/uploads/2015/06/insanity_discussion.pdf.
Law Commission for England and Wales, *Insanity and Automatism—Supplementary Material to the Scoping Paper* (2012), available at: www.lawcom.gov.uk/wp-content/uploads/2015/06/insanity_scoping_supplementary.pdf.
Mackay, Ronnie, *The Insanity Defense—Data on Verdicts of Not Guilty by Reason of Insanity from 2002 to 2011* published in The Law Commission for England and Wales, *Insanity and Automatism—Supplementary Material to the Scoping Paper* (2012).
Mackay, Ronnie, Barry Mitchell, and Leonie Howe, "Yet More Facts about the Insanity Defense." *Criminal Law Review* 6(2006): 399–411.
Robinson, Daniel N., *Wild Beasts and Idle Humours*. Cambridge, MA: Harvard University Press, 1996.
Royal Commission, *Report of the Royal Commission on Capital Punishment*, Cmd 8932, 1953.
Williams, Glanville, *Textbook of Criminal Law*, 2nd ed. London: Stevens, 1983.

CHAPTER ELEVEN

Mental Insanity at the International Criminal Court: Proposal for a New Regulation

Natalia Silva

The first application of the diminished responsibility defense in international criminal law was at the *Čelebići* case at the International Criminal Tribunal for the former Yugoslavia (ICTY). Esad Landžo, a Muslim prison guard in Čelebići Camp serving from May 1992 to December 1992, was charged with willful killing, torture, and cruel treatment.[1] Although Landžo's defense pleaded diminished responsibility at his trial, the ICTY found him guilty of war crimes during the Yugoslavia conflict and sentenced him to 15 years of imprisonment.[2]

The Trial Chamber found that Landžo suffered from "personality disorder," but it rejected this as a mitigating factor under diminished responsibility.[3] The trend repeated itself in further ICTY cases while no importance was attached to the convict's rehabilitation. Neither the possibility of committing these offenders to an alternative treatment nor special regime during their time in prison was ever contemplated. On its side, the International Criminal Court (ICC) has not yet dealt with any case in which this matter was invoked. Even though its regulation has apparently progressed with respect to the ICTY, its effectiveness is still at question.

Besides, the consequences of raising the insanity defense remain, at present, a mystery.

Mental insanity has always engendered much debate in both domestic jurisdictions and international criminal law. The fact that an individual who has committed a crime becomes acquitted, or obtains a mitigated sentence due to psychological reasons, is somehow hard for society and even some lawmakers to tolerate. At the domestic level, mental impairment has been regulated with more or less differences within the various legal systems. In most of them, internment in a medical center is an alternative to prison as a way of treating and reintegrating the mentally ill criminals.[4]

However, the different rules applicable at the ICC and ICTY do not include such a measure. The reasons why this happened may be traced back to the origins and main purpose of international criminal law. From the beginning, international criminal law has focused its attention in ending impunity of those (most) responsible for "the most serious crimes of concern to the international community as a whole."[5] In turn, this had necessarily led to emphasize "retribution" and "deterrence" over other acknowledged goals of criminal law. Thus, an international tribunal declaring someone not guilty because of mental impairment would seem to run against the very nature and purpose of the system, thereby casting doubts on the credibility of the tribunals' mission. Be it as it may, a legal vacuum exists in terms of the concrete legal consequences of mental incapacity of the accused.

The normative basis in the Statutes and Rules of the different international criminal tribunals reveal the underlying problem. The poor regulation of mental insanity therein has made tribunals disregard this issue and, thus, dodge further criticism and discussion. However, this matter should not be forgotten because the balance of the trial depends on it. In fact, it is the protection of the accused's rights that we are dealing with. Hence, rehabilitation cannot be discarded. It is the most humane goal of the system, and the one that renders the treatment and reintegration of the accused possible. This is also certainly connected to the concepts of justice, truth and reconstruction of societies in the aftermath of the most abominable barbarities. Yet this has been considered as a "minor" issue, probably because of the underlying idea that those matters were within the state's interests.

Bearing in mind the current scenario, this chapter calls for a new regulation in the ICC Statute and Rules of Procedure and Evidence (RPE). The imperious necessity of bringing in clarity and efficacy to the legal concept of mental insanity is founded on the fact that all offenders should have the possibility of successfully alleging their mental affectation at the moment of the crime. It is urgent to create an adequate regulation of insanity and determine its legal consequences before a case concerning this matter arises at the ICC.

The main question of this chapter is whether a domestic legal model of mental insanity should be adhered to by the ICC, and if so, which model or combination of them should prevail? In order to propose a model that would adjust the concepts and legal consequences of mental incapacity, the following sub-questions will be addressed throughout the chapter: Is rehabilitation of the accused a real goal in international criminal law? Why wasn't mental insanity carefully regulated in the Statutes of the tribunals, making conviction or acquittal the sole possibilities after trial? What are the current consequences of mental insanity in international criminal law? What are the main problems that the ICC regulation of mental insanity may face?

Section 1 of this chapter examines the importance of the rehabilitative objective at the international level, discussing the general goals of international criminal law, and the tools for its achievement. This section further discusses the types of perpetrators of the core crimes, and studies the relation between the concepts of mental insanity and culpability from a general perspective.

Section 2 describes the regulation and development of mental illness at the international criminal tribunals. It discusses the origins of mental insanity in the case law of the Nuremberg tribunals, and the first legislative and case law steps of the ICTY towards mental insanity. Furthermore, this section discusses the regulation and legal problems arising from the ICC Statute and its RPE.

Section 3 analyzes the approach of the English and German systems towards mental insanity. It includes an overview of the theories of punishment and liability requirements, treatment of mental insanity and diminished responsibility, consequences in the sentencing and enforcement stage, and a brief explanation of the consideration of mental insanity in national regulations of international crimes.

Finally, section 4 discusses the possibilities of transferring a domestic model or combinations of models to the ICC, taking into account the legal problems of the ICC Statute and RPE. It also considers how the chosen model could be implemented at the ICC.

1 Goals of International Criminal Law: Is Rehabilitation a Real Objective?

Rehabilitation and social integration of offenders have traditionally been goals of domestic criminal justice systems.[6] It is within the states' own sphere of interest to reconstruct the broken bonds and reestablish the *status quo ante* in society as soon as an individual commits a crime. Notwithstanding, there is a different conception at the international criminal justice level. In relation to macro-criminality events, the rehabilitative goal of punishment may be questioned due to the extraordinary nature of the events, as well as the profile of some of its perpetrators concerning the core crimes at stake. The fact that the offenders of the gravest atrocities deserve a punishment in consonance with their personal features or circumstances is undisputed. Yet the latter assertion has not been paid adequate attention in the field of international criminal law. Although rehabilitation is one of the objectives of international criminal prosecutions,[7] it is normally treated as a "subsidiary rationale" in comparison to the retributive or deterrent goals.[8] However, even though the development of human rights law has led to a greater recognition of the guarantees of the accused, the right to rehabilitation is still given undue weight. This later point becomes evident when dealing with mentally insane perpetrators at trial at the international courts when circumstances so require. The *ad hoc* tribunals and the ICC have not effectively articulated the goal of rehabilitation to have a substantial impact in cases regarding these particular defendants. Therefore, this section will attempt to elucidate why the ICC should place more importance on the rehabilitative purpose rather than the other obvious goals, above all in cases of mental affectation of the offender.

1.1 The General Goals of International Criminal Law

International criminal law is a unique tool for making accountable those responsible for the gravest atrocities of "concern to the international community as a whole."[9] Just as domestic criminal law systems, this newborn branch of law embraces important objectives and ends for punishment, too. Although not expressly defined in the Statutes of the ICC or those of *ad hoc* tribunals, their jurisprudence has identified the goals that must be considered when sentencing.[10] However, as was to be expected, this concrete field is not exempted from philosophical discussion on behalf of scholars, because inconsistency and incoherency are frequently found within the abundant justifications for international punishment.[11]

International criminal law has specific and tailored purposes. This is due to its distinct primary goal: dealing with the most heinous violations of human rights. The following objectives are usually listed as essential with regard to punishment at this level, namely:

> Retribution, justice, deterrence (general and specific), rehabilitation, expressivism, reprobation, stigmatization, affirmative prevention, incapacitation,

protection of society, social defense and finally, restoration/maintenance of peace and reconciliation.[12]

Despite the existence of such a string of general objectives, not all of them have been granted the same importance. According to Werle, international criminal law obtains its legitimacy especially from retribution and deterrence.[13] Indeed, the prevalence of these two objectives has dominated the history of such tribunals. Already at Nuremberg and Tokyo, retribution contended an essential role in determining sentences, as shown by widespread use of the death penalty.[14] Their definition of justice implied punishing the atrocities according to the "just deserts" principle. For those first tribunals, vengeance was the only way to fight impunity and prevent similar future actions.

Later on, the judges of the ICTY and the International Criminal Tribunal for Rwanda (ICTR) continued promoting mainly retribution and deterrence over the other objectives.[15] For example, the ICTY asserted in the *Aleksovski* case that retribution "is not to be understood as fulfilling a desire for revenge but as duly expressing the outrage of the international community at these crimes."[16] Indeed, it is affirmed that international criminal justice means essentially "retributive justice,"[17] with a view towards future general deterrence and a marginal interest for rehabilitating individual perpetrators.[18] On its side, deterrence is more concerned with the future-related benefits of prosecution.[19] The importance of such principle was explained in the *Nikolić* case, in which the Appeals Chamber stated that "it is hoped that the Tribunal and other international courts are bringing about the development of a culture of respect for the rule of law and not simply the fear of the consequences of breaking the law, and thereby deterring the commission of crimes."[20] Finally, at the ICC it has been frequently recognized that these two classical functions of criminal law can be identified in the Preamble of the ICC Statute.[21] For instance, the Preamble acknowledges that the international crimes "must not go unpunished,"[22] that "their effective prosecution must be ensured,"[23] and that an "end to impunity for the perpetrators of these crimes" must be accomplished.[24]

Apart from the principles of retribution and deterrence, the ICTY and ICTR have made several references to the rehabilitative aspect of punishment.[25] This seems to be of great relevance in the context of human rights violations, where reconstruction and reconciliation are essential.[26] In addressing a conflict and its aftermath, to solely take into account the traditional goals of punishment will not be enough to avoid future human rights abuses. In order to correctly heal and reconstruct societies emerging from conflict and guarantee an endurable peace, punishment must also serve more ambitious objectives. In this regard, reinsertion and resocialization of perpetrators is an essential factor in reestablishing the *status quo ante* in post-conflict scenarios.

Indeed, the rationale behind the general concept of rehabilitation is that instead of inflicting revenge against criminals and making their lives more difficult, the criminal process should help them. D'Ascoli has alleged that the main purpose of rehabilitation is to reintegrate the accused into society and to "shape the context and level of punishment in such a way as to achieve a re-educative effect."[27] Thus, rehabilitation might take into account particular features of each offender when imposing adequate punishments, treatments, or specific measures. Besides, according to rehabilitative theories, incarceration may occasionally not be the perfect venue for achieving its objectives.

The international criminal tribunals have not defined the concept of rehabilitation in the wider context of international crimes.[28] Instead, multiple references to these principles can be found in the jurisprudence, especially in that of the ICTY. Already in the *Tadić* case, the tribunal pointed out as one of the aims of criminal law the "incapacitation of the dangerous and rehabilitation," adding that "the modern philosophy of penology [is] that the punishment should fit the offender and not merely the crime."[29] Indeed, the requirement of individualization of penalties is an element which suggests that rehabilitation plays a basic role at the sentencing phase, as will be analyzed in the upcoming section.[30]

Thus, the rehabilitation goal has been mostly named in relation to sentencing and sanction execution. In particular, in the *Kunarac* case, the Court asserted that it fully supported "rehabilitative programs, if any, in which the accused may participate while serving their sentences."[31] However, it added that "the scope of such national rehabilitative programs, if any, depends on the states in which convicted persons will serve their sentences, not on the International Tribunal."[32] This later quote shows one of the problems of this objective and the reason why many authors have disregarded this goal in international criminal law. The execution of a sentence is not controlled by its respective international tribunal because it depends on the penitentiary system of the state willing to accept the person convicted by said tribunal.[33] Thus, a high degree of cooperation is needed between the international and domestic systems. The Trial Chamber in *Kunarac* added that imprisonment alone, on certain occasions, cannot have a rehabilitative effect on the accused.[34]

Such jurisprudence shows that the perpetrators' rehabilitation must be considered appropriately. Notwithstanding, there have been critics in this respect. Some authorities have asserted that rehabilitation and reintegration of the accused in society are valid principles for domestic criminal proceedings, but do not seem appropriate for international crimes.[35] They defend that, unlike domestic crimes, the mindsets of core crimes are not susceptible to reform through programs of "re-education."[36] In this regard, they allege that the highest ranking of perpetrators of genocide and crimes against humanity, who are the main focus of international criminal law, will "spend the rest of their lives as apologists for the genocidal regimes they served."[37] Hence, some renowned scholars like Zappalà have claimed that a right of rehabilitation for the convicted person under international criminal law does not exist.[38]

However, there are voices asserting that one of the purposes of international criminal law should be the rehabilitation of the offender. Those argue that if a real attempt is not made at fulfilling this principle, then "international criminal justice may be misinterpreted as a means intended to exact revenge upon the vanquished, rather than to protect the international community from crimes under international law."[39] Besides, Zappalà's position contradicts existing legal obligations. Indeed, international human rights law has manifested the importance of rehabilitation in several international documents. For instance, Article 10(3) of the International Covenant on Civil and Political Rights (ICCPR) states that "the penitentiary system shall comprise treatment of prisoners the essential aim of which shall be their reformation and social rehabilitation." The United Nations Human Rights Committee, in its second General Comment on Article 10 ICCPR, has stated that "no penitentiary system should be only retributory; it should essentially seek the reformation and social rehabilitation of the prisoner."[40] Rehabilitation's importance is also enshrined in the Standard Minimum Rules for the Treatment of Prisoners; the American Convention on Human Rights;[41] and in the Document of the Moscow Meeting of the Conference on the Human Dimension of the Commission on Security and Cooperation in Europe, which requires the participating states to "pay particular attention to the question of alternatives to imprisonment."[42] Such covenants focus again in the penitentiary aspect of rehabilitation. However, in *Obrenović*, the Trial Chamber concluded that "the concept of rehabilitation can be thought of broadly and can encompass all stages of the criminal proceedings" and that "criminal proceedings are only the starting point; the process continues upon the return of a convicted person to society and makes an active contribution towards reconciliation."[43] Indeed, the rehabilitation objective is much related to other broader goals that affect the whole criminal justice chain and can be said to apply to all individuals being prosecuted.

It has been argued that the overarching objectives of international prosecutions are "justice" or "truth."[44] As expressed previously in the General Comment, it is clear that retribution in itself does not lead to "restorative justice," which focuses, *inter alia*, in the humanitarian treatment of offenders and their reintegration.[45] This means that international criminal law should be bound somehow by the previous international human rights instruments. Besides, it entails that the legal instruments available in the criminal tribunals must be used in order to impose an adequate punishment. Thus, although the rule of law and human rights were not faithfully followed during the criminal processes in 1945,[46] they must be surely observed nowadays.

Truth-finding is another main goal of international criminal law. To establish a historical record of what happened and provide an official statement of past injustices and sufferings of victims, is an essential function of the international criminal tribunals.[47] This is accomplished through the establishment of crimes and the convictions, which includes determining the perpetrator's individual accountability.[48] Truth-finding is necessary to relieve the pain from victims and reconcile society, but it is important towards the perpetrators of the crimes too. In this respect, getting to discover the individual circumstances of the offender when he committed a crime is an essential aspect of accountability and truth-finding.

This last point of accountability and truth-finding is surely related to reconciliation and reconstruction of communities. The Trial Chamber in *Erdemović* stated that in addition to the mandate of the ICTY to investigate, prosecute, and punish the violations of international humanitarian law, the exercise of its judicial functions has to contribute to the "settlement of the wider issues of accountability, reconciliation, and establishing the truth."[49] Some authors have stressed that both the ICTY and the ICTR should have defined earlier in time their goal of reconciliation and promotion of peace.[50] Hence, in those two conflicts, to "make justice" should have been interpreted as bringing the reconciliation of the local communities involved in the atrocities.[51] However, it may be difficult or impossible for society to harmonize and rebuild without real rehabilitation efforts initiated within the context of effective action against impunity.[52] The so-called "most humane sentencing principle" has as a primary objective to treat the underlying cause of the accused's transgressions so that he or she can return to society and become a fully productive citizen.

The international tribunals seem to have assimilated that their essential task is to eradicate large-scale human rights violations without losing much credibility in the process. However, many other goals are at stake throughout the international criminal proceedings. Those should take into account the position of the offender and his or her rights from the very first moment of the procedures.

1.2 The Achievement of the Goals of International Criminal Law

The previous subsection explained the main goals of international criminal law with special focus in the perpetrator's rights. In order to fulfil said objectives, several measures can be undertaken. Generally speaking, the accountability options include, among others, international and domestic prosecutions.[53] Because every domestic criminal system has its own particularities, this subsection will mainly focus on international jurisdiction while bearing in mind that both jurisdictions must work together and cooperate. Without the support of individual states, international courts lack power: for example, they have no power to arrest nor to enforce judgments.[54] Thus, national prosecution of international crimes must be regarded as crucial to the system of international criminal justice, especially in the perspective of the complementarity regime promoted by the ICC.[55] Hence, it can be asserted that the goals of international criminal law must be accomplished with the cooperation of both international and domestic jurisdictions.

International jurisdiction possesses a series of tools in order to deal with international crimes laid down in the Statutes and RPE of the *ad hoc* tribunals and the ICC, and the case law of these tribunals. These include: the general principles of liability, the defenses/grounds for excluding criminal responsibility, the procedures of international criminal investigations and prosecutions (including the investigation, prosecution and indictment, the trial and judgment and the appeals proceedings), and finally, sentencing, penalties and reparation to victims' issues.

These instruments will be used in the following sections in order to analyze the international courts and the German and English jurisdictions with regard to mentally insane perpetrators. Thus, the tools this section will deal with are dispositions and case law related to the phases of the sentencing and sanction execution, including the treatment of the grounds for excluding criminal responsibility and the principles for sentencing and sanction execution.

1.3 The Perpetrators of International Crimes

Not all perpetrators are the same. Already from an *ex ante* point of view, each individual had a distinguishable position in society and a particular understanding towards an impending conflict. Then, once the situation of extreme violence begins, perpetrators become different in their level of involvement and guilt, in their motivation to commit each heinous and barbaric acts, and in ranks and positions in the structure of command.[56] It is necessary to distinguish between the leaders and criminal masterminds, the high-ranking officials, the middle-ranking perpetrators, and the low-ranking perpetrators.[57] Some authorities have argued that the major perpetrators of genocide, crimes against humanity, and war crimes are not the suitable addressees of rehabilitation.[58] The philosophy underneath this view resides in the fact that the masterminds and high-ranking officials were elected to hold such positions while being mentally healthy and able to carry out their duties. Besides, those perpetrators will not be so directly exposed to the effects of the battlefield as the soldiers, nor they will kill, maim, torture, or rape with their own hands. By contrast, the last link in the chain of command is the one involved in the bloodiest crimes; they commit them under the orders of their superiors, thereby becoming "law-abiding perpetrators."[59]

Notwithstanding, the latter argument disregards the fact that all perpetrators have rights for the mere reason of being offenders subject to a prosecution, regardless of their rank in the structure of command. While the retributive goals insist upon the role of the perpetrator or the harm inflicted when sentencing, rehabilitative purposes emphasize the remorse and cooperation of the offender when imposing a punishment.[60] Hence, rehabilitation constitutes a goal of international criminal law and focuses on all perpetrators equally, for all of them have a right to be treated humanely. Their personal circumstances and particular situation must be reflected in the sentence and its execution so that their reincorporation in society is successfully achieved. The rehabilitation of offenders also contributes to achieve peace as it is crucial in the wound-healing process that follows the commission of grave atrocities.

As analyzed in the first subsection, rehabilitation and resocialization of offenders are rights recognized in many human rights instruments, and they are essential constituents in most domestic jurisdictions. Hence, although states are the only duty-bearers with regard to human rights, they have a crucial role in international criminal prosecutions too. Both obligations lead to the conclusion that rehabilitation is not only a general goal but also a specific guarantee to all offenders of international crimes and, as such, it must be duly preserved.

1.4 Mentally Ill Perpetrators and Culpability

1.4.1 Classification of Mentally Ill Perpetrators

It is undeniable that the crimes under the jurisdiction of the international tribunals are committed in "unique environments that foster and promote particular criminal behavior."[61] Therefore, most of the individuals committing such atrocities are "inevitably" led to those pervasive performances because of a particular context; they would not have developed such criminal features otherwise. This position originated in Hannah Arendt's criticized theory of the "banality of evil." Indeed, it was during the trial of Eichmann in Jerusalem when she realized that the Nazi criminal was "a normal man," holding even an exemplary personal relation towards his family and friends.[62] Indeed, many researches on the perpetrators of such international crimes have proven that they are, interestingly, "very ordinary people, not characterized by mental deficiencies, sadistic character traits, a violent past or criminal record."[63] This point is essential in order to rule out the antique perception that all perpetrators committed such atrocities because they were already mentally ill since the beginning of the conflict. They are just "ordinary people within extraordinary circumstances."[64]

Be that as it may, ordinary people in extraordinary circumstances can be mentally insane when committing the crimes, just as some ordinary people in ordinary circumstances are. According to the moment in which the mental disease appeared, there should be two different types of mentally ill perpetrators. On the one hand, the perpetrators can already be mentally insane before they committed the crimes. In these cases, they already have a mental illness and end up committing the cruelest atrocities because of a certain preexistent mental condition. On the other hand, the offenders can develop a mental illness during the conflict and execute the atrocities under this psychological condition. These latter individuals germinate a mental illness due to the external and environmental factors of a period of extreme violence. The distinction between one and another group might be tedious in terms of evidence. Yet, a successful determination of the latter aspect in a particular case might enlighten the personal circumstances of the offender and the need of rehabilitation.

Perpetrators could also be classified according to the degree of affectation of the conflict in their personality. This forensic-psychiatric classification does not take into account whether the executioner was or was not mentally insane before the conflict. It merely relates to three basic levels of intensity of mental illness, bearing in mind the typical diseases suffered by individuals exposed in these contexts. The explanation of the three categories will contribute to the better understanding of the case law included in section 2. The first level of mental interference includes those perpetrators who, because of their involvement in the crimes, suffer from anxiety, debilitating guilt, depression, hallucinations, and many other manifestations of stress reactions.[65] Accordingly, those are symptoms of "Perpetration-Induced Traumatic Stress" (PITS), which is the psychological logical reaction of ordinary and "normal" people answering to traumatic events "outside the realm of ordinary experience."[66] Mac Nair coined the term PITS as a subcategory of "Posttraumatic Stress Disorder" (PTSD).[67]

The second stage of affectation would be composed by all the individuals developing an "Antisocial Personality Disorder" (APD). According to Waller, this is the most relevant psychopathology for perpetrators of extraordinary crimes.[68] APD is characterized by a "pervasive pattern of disregard for, and violation of, the wishes, rights, or feelings of others" and a lack of contrition or repentance for their acts.[69] Approximately 3 percent of the perpetrators can be classified as APDs.[70] However, a distinction should be drawn between perpetrators with personality disorder and the psychopaths and sociopaths. Recent studies have demonstrated that most psychopaths in contact with the criminal justice system meet the criteria for APD, but most individuals with APD are not psychopaths.[71]

Lastly, the third level of mental disturbance is the one including the psychopaths, sadists, and people who already suffered from mental and sexual deficiencies. Although they are a minority, these perpetrators use "far more violence than requested or necessary to fulfil their task,"[72] making them extremely dangerous. They are driven by "violent, sadistic or other sexual impulses,"[73] leading to a terrible exacerbation of violence caused by the conflictive surrounding circumstances.

It is clear that the existence of certain contexts provokes a development of psychological traits in the previously-mentioned groups of individuals. The mental process that transforms more or less mentally stable persons into perpetrators of international crimes could not be understood in another situation. These periods of collective violence are characterized by the "mass involvement of the people, the progressive use of violence usually towards one specific group who is blamed for the misfortune of the masses and an alleged legitimacy of the violence which is provided by an ideology."[74] The continuous exposure to atrociousness makes individuals liable to a psychological metamorphosis which pushes them to perform as if they were the worst criminals. However, the logical attention placed towards the victims and their rehabilitation often leads to forgetting that the offenders have their rights too. As already argued in the previous subsections, the offenders are bearers of safeguards and procedural guarantees during their prosecution. These rights should be preserved no matter how gruesome the atrocities were; all the more so when the perpetrators perform under such particular episodes.

1.4.2 Mental Illness, Rehabilitation, and the Principle of Culpability

As mentioned previously, rehabilitation has not only been considered as a goal of international criminal law but also as an objective of punishment.[75] This necessarily means that it has to be taken into account as a purpose of sentencing and sanction execution when dealing specially with the mentally insane. The importance of the rehabilitative purpose in this respect is reflected in the essential provisions of mental insanity "defense" of Article 31(1)(a) ICC Statute (and only named in Rule 67(B)(i)(b) ICTY RPE and 67(A)(ii)(b) ICTR RPE) and the mitigating circumstance of diminished responsibility encompassed in Rule 145(2)(a)(i) ICC RPE. In particular, the fact that the ICC dispositions expressly included for the first time the insanity defense and diminished responsibility should be connected to the culpability principle mentioned in the ICC RPE, another novelty. Indeed, before mentioning the aggravating and mitigating circumstances, Rule 145(1)(a) RPE ICC states that "the totality of any sentence of imprisonment . . . must reflect the culpability of the convicted person."

This certainly implied a considerable move with respect to the rehabilitation and resocialization objectives at the ICTY. However, culpability and blameworthiness have not been exhaustively theorized in international criminal law—there is not a precise definition of these concepts.[76] They have been frequently loosely referred to as the ability to choose,[77] non-performance of what a reasonable person would have done,[78] and as the "freedom of will, mental capacity or knowledge of law."[79] Criminal justice systems are based on the belief that people are responsible and free to choose one action over another one.[80] They will be punished to the extent they cross the borders of the legal action.[81] Thus, individuals without the ability of understanding or controlling their actions cannot be blamed. This principle is needed to avoid harsh results that are incompatible with human dignity, such as "imposing criminal responsibility when no behavior can be attributed to the accused or when his conduct was not voluntary."[82] In consequence, in cases of serious mental diseases the capacity of culpability disappears. However, when criminal liability cannot totally disappear, the culpability requirement will limit the punishment for a crime to what is deserved according to the perpetrator's blameworthiness.[83]

The exclusion of liability or individualization of sentences based on the psychological condition of the accused implies an important breakthrough in terms of humane treatment and consideration of the rehabilitation and resocialization purposes. The mention to the principle of culpability when sentencing in the ICC Statute constitutes an essential tool to clarify how this psychological condition affects the sentencing stage, and which punishment or measures should be imposed to the mentally insane.

2 Mental Insanity at the International Criminal Tribunals

The present section will conduct an in-depth analysis of the legal framework and case law related to mental insanity in the various international criminal tribunals. Special attention will be paid to the different tools the tribunals possess in order to deal with mental incapacity when this issue is raised during trial by the defendant. Thus, the section will include how this defense or mitigating circumstance has been defined in the tribunals, and how can it affect the sentence and the punishment to be imposed. Besides, it will emphasize the problem of the lack of alternatives to imprisonment. In this regard, it should already be noted that the mental insanity defense in the ICC Statute has not been accompanied by the development of a system for the medical disposition either of individuals acquitted on the basis of mental disease or of offenders whose sentences have been reduced on the basis of diminished responsibility but are dangerous to society.[84]

In order to trace the evolution of the treatment of mental insanity in international criminal law, the Nuremberg Tribunals (section 2.1), the ICTY (section 2.2) and the ICC (section 2.3) will be analyzed. The reason for setting aside the Tokyo Tribunal and the ICTR is based on the fact that those courts have not dealt with the defense of mental insanity. Instead, the Tokyo Military Tribunal dealt with the inability to stand trial of the accused Ōkawa.[85] With regards to the ICTR, this tribunal has not yet developed Rule 67(A)(ii)(b) RPE ICTR, which refers to the psychiatric defense, including that of diminished or lack of mental responsibility. No reference has been made to either insanity or diminished responsibility in its cases.

2.1 Mental Insanity at the Nuremberg Military Tribunals

Those in charge of codifying international criminal law have usually placed more emphasis on rejecting defenses rather than on defining them.[86] This clear reluctance towards the exclusion of liability for the "core crimes" was already visible in the International Military Tribunals (IMTs) and the Nuremberg Military Tribunals (NMTs).[87] Indeed, the Charter of the IMT in Nuremberg excluded the possibility of relying on superior orders (Article 7 of the Charter) and immunity for heads of states (Article 8 of the Charter), allowing only a mitigation of punishment in the case of orders coming from the government or superior when justice so required.[88] Mental insanity was not even mentioned in the Charter. Understandably, in the aftermath of the gravest atrocities committed by the Nazis, the potential mental insanity or diminished responsibility of perpetrators was an irrelevant question. However, the IMT did deal with an interesting accused in this regard.

Rudolf Hess was tried along with other top leaders of the Nazi regime at the IMT. Hess, a member of the Nazi Party since 1920, was appointed Deputy to the Führer in 1933. Later on, in 1939, he was announced by Hitler as his successor designate to the Führer after Göring.[89] As Deputy to the Führer, Hess was the top man in the Nazi Party, making decisions in Hitler's name and dealing with important matters in the Party. He supported the German aggression against Austria, Czechoslovakia and Poland, Norway, Denmark, Belgium, and the Netherlands. He was held guilty of Counts 1 (common plan or conspiracy) and 2 (crimes against peace), and sentenced to life imprisonment in 1946. However, during his trial, the defense issued a motion for examination of the mental competence of the accused. Apparently, he "acted in an abnormal manner, suffered from loss of memory" and "had mentally deteriorated during the trial."[90] The medical reports asserted that Hess had a "psychopathic personality" and the data concerning his illness during the last four years showed that he suffered from delusions and paranoia.[91] Yet, the report of the prison psychologist concluded that Hess was not insane at that moment of the trial and neither was he at the moment of the commission of the crimes.[92]

Thus, on the basis of the reports of the forensic experts and the statements of the accused, the Court ruled that Hess was fit to stand trial and that the case would not be postponed. But the Court went even further. Although not expressly raised by the defense, which focused on the capacity of Hess to stand trial, the Court ruled on the mental insanity of the accused at the time the indicted acts occurred. The judgment declared that "there is no suggestion that Hess was not completely sane when the acts charged against him were committed."[93] According to Krabbe, this latter reference is an implicit recognition of the insanity defense.[94] Hence, Rudolf Hess spent the rest of his life in West Berlin Spandau prison, living under unbearable conditions.[95]

The NMTs, however, did generate extensive jurisprudence concerning a number of relevant defenses, although nothing was said regarding the plea of mental incapacity.[96] The tribunals' sentences were apparently more motivated and the punishments more tailored than in the IMT. In this regard, a close reading of the judgments indicates that individual sentences were somewhat altered by the existence of aggravating and mitigating factors.[97] One of the circumstances that could reduce the sentence was, interestingly, the personal characteristics of the perpetrator.[98] This meant the starting point for the recognition of the defendant's rights at the international level.

2.2 Mental Insanity at the ICTY

2.2.1 The ICTY Statute and ICTY RPE

At the ICTY, a similar pattern has been followed.[99] Defenses have been only indirectly applied to a certain extent in the ICTY Statute.[100] For instance, Articles 2(d) and 3(b) of the Statute suggest that "military necessity" is a basis for justification. Besides, Article 7(4) states that "superior order" is not a defense to criminal responsibility but it can be considered in mitigation of punishment. The Statute lacks mention to defenses in general. However, paragraph 58 of the Report of the Secretary General, which reflects the intent of the drafters, asserts that "the International Tribunal itself will have to decide on various personal defenses that may relieve a person of individual criminal responsibility, such as minimum age or mental incapacity, drawing upon general principles of law recognized by all nations."[101] This was interpreted as meaning that if a defense was permitted under the general principles of law, it should so be permitted under the Statute.[102] In the field of international criminal law, the general principles of law refer to "legal principles generally recognized in national law."[103] This is acknowledged in the practice of the international criminal tribunals as well as in Article 21(1)(c) ICC Statute.[104] Accordingly, those principles contribute to fill in legal *lacunae*,[105] as Landžo's defense alleged in the Čelebići case regarding diminished responsibility.[106] Although there is no reference to any explicit principle in the case, the Latin expression *nulla poena sine culpa* (no crime without guilt) should be considered the main pillar of the mental incapacity defense.[107]

The ICTY RPE encompasses Rule 67(B)(i)(b) ICTY RPE, which says that the Defense shall notify the Prosecutor of "any special defense, including that of diminished or lack of mental responsibility." The Rule, however, fails to list any requirements of such defense, or to define the other defenses that may qualify as "special."[108] Besides, the definitions of the terms used in Rule 2 of the ICTY RPE encompassed do not explain the concept of special defenses either. Thus, it is not clear whether "diminished or lack of mental responsibility" constitutes a permissible defense at first sight in the ICTY.[109]

All in all, the sentencing regulations of this tribunal have clearly represented a progress with respect to the NMTs. Indeed, the dispositions at the ICTY Statute and RPE imply a range of possibilities to adequately deal with every accused and express the "positive and curative goals" of international justice.[110] At the ICTY, the main penalty to be imposed to the defendant is imprisonment; an order of involuntary confinement does not exist.[111] Thus, as explained in the previous section, the sentence can certainly condition the way the convicted will be rehabilitated and resocialized. A quick overview of the tribunal sentencing process reveals that, according to Article 24(2) ICTY Statute, the penalty is determined (1) taking into consideration factors related to the gravity of the crime (principles of proportionality, totality and gradation and appraising the aggravating factors) and then, (2) the sentence is modified and tailored bearing in mind the individual circumstances of the perpetrator, such as the mitigating factors (principle of individualization).[112] Setting aside the gravity-related principles, which are also relevant in order to determine the appropriate punishment, the individualization principle calls "for personalized sentencing."[113] Personalized sentences are a basic tool in order to deal with perpetrators who suffered from mental insanity at the moment of the crime. Personalized sentences also suggest that rehabilitation plays an essential role in sentencing.[114]

However, a perpetrator who committed atrocities while being mentally affected might need, apart from an adequate sentence, rehabilitation during the execution of the sentence. In this respect, the only provision at the ICTY that makes an explicit reference to this purpose is contained in Rule 125 ICTY RPE. This Rule suggests that rehabilitation is relevant at the moment of execution of sentences, because it expresses that "in determining whether pardon or commutation is appropriate, the President shall take into account, inter alia, . . . the prisoner's demonstration of rehabilitation."[115] Thus, it seems that rehabilitation is important not only in sentencing, but also during the effective execution of the penalty. Notwithstanding the foregoing, it is important to recall that, although it supervises the process, the ICTY depends on the states to enforce its sentences.[116]

It is clear that there are some provisions that evoke concepts of humanity and appropriate treatment of the accused at the ICTY, but they are underdeveloped. Moreover, there is not a sufficient, nor consistent legal basis at the ICTY that would allow properly dealing with the concept of "diminished or lack of mental responsibility" from an abstract viewpoint. Besides, as it will be seen in the ICTY case law, the defendants' possibility to successfully raise such defense at the ICTY is virtually inexistent. Even if "diminished or lack of mental responsibility" was clearly regulated, its success would lead to an acquittal or to prison. The option of imposing a "security measure" in a hospital based on the dangerousness and need of rehabilitation of the accused is nonexistent. This issue will be tackled thoroughly in the subsection dealing with the ICC.

2.2.2 Relevant Case Law and the Development of Rule 67(B)(i)(b) ICTY RPE

The Čelebići Case. The first concrete application of this "special defense" was at the Čelebići trial in 1998.[117] In an indictment issued on March 21, 1996, a Muslim prison guard named Esad Landžo was charged with willful killing, torture, and cruel treatment, which he perpetrated with special sadism and homicidal behavior.[118] He committed those crimes at Čelebići Camp in the municipality of Konjic in Central Bosnia in 1992 when he was 19 years old. One of Landžo's American lawyers decided her client would be best defended by raising a deviation of the insanity defense known as "diminished mental responsibility" under the ICTY RPE.[119] The attorneys initially argued that Landžo committed the crimes partly due to his mental condition, which in the beginning was defined as PTSD by the mental health examiners appointed by the court.[120] However, the following medical analysis concluded that Landžo was not suffering from PTSD. The defense then alleged that he suffered from personality disorder, which had also been cited in some psychiatric reports.[121] In any event, it is clear that with the exception of the prosecution expert, all mental specialists (three appointed by the court and one retained by the defense) testified that Landžo had suffered "from one or more mental disorders that putatively diminished his responsibility for the crimes."[122]

Although both the Trial and Appeal Chamber dealt with Rule 67(B)(i)(b) ICTY RPE, the conclusions of one and another were surprisingly different. The final judgment of the Trial Chamber clarified first of all the burden of proof to be applied in diminished responsibility.[123] In this respect, the Chamber argued that because the accused raised the defense, he had to present it within the parameters he considered adequate.[124] The accused thus carried the burden of proving his defense "on the balance of probabilities."[125]

The Trial Chamber's decision can be summarized in two main points. On the one hand, the Chamber distinguished between the plea of diminished responsibility and the plea of mental insanity (lack of mental responsibility). Accordingly, although both pleas were based on an abnormality of mind, in the plea of insanity "the accused is, at the time of commission of the criminal act, unaware of what he is doing or incapable of forming a rational judgment as to whether such an act is right or wrong."[126] By contrast, the plea of diminished responsibility was defined as based on the premise that, "despite recognizing the wrongful nature of his actions, the accused, on account of his abnormality of mind, is unable to control his actions."[127] The Trial Chamber made reference to the way the national jurisdictions recognized the plea of diminished responsibility, making special reference to the system in England and Wales.[128] The Tribunal established a two part test of "diminished responsibility," which was founded on Section 2 of the English Homicide Act.[129] Accordingly, at the time of the criminal acts, the accused must have been suffering from an "abnormality of mind" that "substantially impaired" the ability of the accused to control his or her actions.[130]

On the other hand, the Court decided in Landžo's case that diminished mental responsibility enshrined in Rule 67(B)(i)(b) ICTY RPE was a complete defense just as lack of mental responsibility, meaning insanity, would be. The Court also added that such defense should thus result in an acquittal.[131] The Trial Chamber accepted that the said Rule appeared to suggest a full defense since the words are "without qualification or limitation."[132] According to some scholars, a total defense would entitle the accused to an acquittal rather than a mitigation of the sentence, or to a reclassification of the crime charged.[133] However, in this particular case, the Court concluded that even though it appeared that Landžo suffered from a personality disorder, he was "quite capable of controlling his actions."[134] Nonetheless, the Trial Chamber studied several individual circumstances of the accused when deciding the sentence to be imposed. The factors that were examined and taken into consideration were, apart from Landžo's poor family background, his immature and weak personality and his young age at the time of the crimes. Besides, the Chamber referred to the armed conflict in Yugoslavia, which "created an environment clearly not of Mr. Landžo's own choosing."[135] The accused was declared responsible for several counts of war crimes and sentenced to 15 years of imprisonment.

As was to be expected, he appealed alleging a violation by the Trial Chamber of justice and legal certainty and a denial of a fair trial when the Court refused to define "diminished mental responsibility," which he raised at first instance.[136] The Appeals Chamber rejected such argument, claiming that the Trial Chamber did not have a duty to define the diminished responsibility in advance.[137] The Appeals Chamber further argued that diminished responsibility could not constitute a defense as the Trial Chamber had held. It based this decision, first, on the lack of reference to the defense in the ICTY Statute and, secondly, on the grounds that judges cannot create new defenses according to Article 15 ICTY Statute.[138] Secondly, the Chamber explained that, as in many countries where the defendant total mental incapacity is considered a full defense, diminished mental responsibility does not constitute either a partial or a complete defense, but is relevant only in relation to the mitigation of the sentence.[139] Hence, the Appeals Chamber concluded that diminished responsibility was relevant to the sentence to be imposed, but not to the guilt or innocence of the accused.[140] Finally, regarding the accused's allegation that the Trial Chamber had to specify the reduction in years that it made in relation to each mitigating factor that applied, the Appeals Chamber stated that the Trial Chamber is responsible for making a global assessment of the circumstances of the particular case and imposing an adequate sentence, taking into account all relevant elements.¹⁴¹ Hence, Landžo was convicted to serve 15 years in prison.

The *Čelebići* Trial Chamber became the first international and legal body expressly dealing with reduced mental capacity. This was the landmark case regarding the interpretation of the "special defense" of Rule 67(B)(i)(b) ICTY, accepting the possibility of the rule as a factor which could mitigate the sentence. In the case, however, the Trial did not accept Landžo's diminished responsibility. Yet, the consideration of his immature and weak personality for reducing the sentence was a signal of the tribunal taking into account the rehabilitative and humanity principles.

Landžo's case was only the first of many others raising similar issues at the ICTY which would serve as a useful precedent for cases to come. Due to time and space constraints, this part will survey some of the most relevant decisions. In *Banović*, for instance, the Trial Chamber had to solve the case of a guard in 1992 at the Bosnian Serb Keraterm camp, which was located in the region of Bosnia and Herzegovina. The accused was convicted of persecutions on political, racial, or religious grounds (including murder and torture of non-Serbs) and sentenced to eight years of imprisonment.¹⁴² The defense raised "diminished or lack of mental responsibility" in mitigation because, apparently, Banović was not able to appreciate the unlawfulness of his conduct. The summary of the psychological analysis carried by the defense expert concluded that he showed some signs of "emotional immaturity, especially characterized by 'bad impulse control.'"¹⁴³ However, the Trial Chamber noted some contradictions in the doctor's evaluation of the accused, because the study did not confirm whether he was able to understand the unlawfulness of his behavior, apart from falling short of raising said defense.¹⁴⁴ Hence, the Trial Chamber concluded that in this case the sentence could not be mitigated on the basis of his immature personality or low intelligence.¹⁴⁵

Another interesting judgment is the one in the *Vasiljević* case, which involved a member of the "White Eagles" from mid-April 1992, a Bosnian Serb paramilitary formation operating with the police and other military units in eastern Bosnia. The accused was charged with aiding and abetting persecutions and murder, and was sentenced to 15 years of prison. The defense argued that his sentence should be mitigated because at the time of the Drina River incident, the accused was allegedly suffering from diminished mental responsibility.¹⁴⁶ One mental health expert of the defense asserted that the accused was psychotic during 1992.¹⁴⁷ Another defense expert affirmed that he had a "pre-disposition to depressive psychosis," and this stage significantly reduced the liability of the accused for his crimes due to his "impaired capacity to comprehend the possible consequences of his deeds."[148] Besides, there were other references to the accused psychotic disorder, which prevented the accused from controlling his actions.[149] However, all said evidence was rejected by the Chamber. The only accepted evidence was that provided by a prosecution witness, which negated that Vasiljević suffered from any form of significant mental diminishment before July 4 or 5, 1992 (when most of the crimes were committed).[150] Thus, Trial Chamber stated that the defense did not "establish on the balance of probabilities that, at the time of the incident, the accused was suffering from diminished mental responsibility."[151]

These two cases are just a small sample of the lack of success of the "special defense" of diminished mental responsibility. Rule 67(B)(i)(b) of the ICTY RPE, even being able to work as mitigation circumstance leads to many problems, apart from the understandable evidentiary issues. The first case opened the possibility of invoking "diminished responsibility" in the sentencing stage, but with an obvious lack of effectiveness.[152]

2.2.3 Analysis

To this author's knowledge no individual has been acquitted under Rule 67(B)(i)(b) ICTY RPE. In any event, it seems that "diminished mental responsibility" is a factor which can mitigate the sentence. However, the ICTY jurisprudence shows that although the defense has made submissions based on "diminished mental responsibility," the prospects of being successfully considered as a mitigating factor is very limited. Needless to say, the possible defense of "lack of mental responsibility" has never been raised at the ICTY, so there has not been discussion in this respect. Yet, the option of having the sentence reduced when the defendant destroys the "presumption of sanity" is, in theory, able to work. Nevertheless, the difficulties when proving the mental affectation (sometimes 20 years have passed since the crime was committed), and the Court's reluctance to accept the experts presented by the defense, makes it virtually impossible to succeed. In addition to this, even if the defendant could effectively prove his incapacity, the consequences that a successful claim based on the diminished or lack of mental responsibility may lead to are not clearly stated anywhere. Even though mitigation is one of the possibilities, this involves a great amount of arbitrariness on behalf of the tribunals.

However, as it was previously analyzed, the dispositions of the ICTY Statute and RPE permit adapting the sentence to the specific accused, considering all his or her individual circumstances, as it happened in the *Čelebići* case. This signifies that despite the difficulty of an effective diminished mental responsibility, lower degrees of mental affectation can still be considered as a mitigating factor in the sentencing decision. The principles of rehabilitation and resocialization have definitely gained importance in comparison to the Nuremberg tribunals.

2.3 Mental Insanity at the ICC

2.3.1 Origins

Article 31 ICC Statute is the first international criminal law provision directly regulating what is known in many criminal justice systems as "defenses," "excuses," and "justifications."[153] Nevertheless, the Statute avoided all those terms so that no associations with either common or civil law were made.[154] This article relates to the "grounds for excluding criminal responsibility," including mental disease or defect, intoxication, self-defense, and duress/necessity. However, this is not an exhaustive list as Article 31 ICC Statute asserts that the Court can consider other grounds for excluding criminal responsibility.[155]

The inclusion of this provision was not an easy task. The International Law Commission draft statute omitted a provision dealing with defenses.[156] However, it explored the issue when preparing the Code of Crimes Against the Peace and Security of Mankind. Indeed, the 1991 draft stated that "[t]he competent court shall determine the admissibility of defenses under the general principles of law, in the light of the character of each crime."[157] The pertinent commentary showed that the members had very different opinions and that it was not possible to reach consensus on a list of defenses. Some members of the Commission, for example, were of the idea that the nature of the crimes did not admit defenses.[158] It was not until 1995 that "diminished mental capacity" was suggested as a defense that negated liability in the list prepared by the *Ad Hoc* Committee.[159] The following year, the Preparatory Committee referred to it as "Insanity/Diminished Mental Capacity" in its report.[160] The different proposals led to a unique text which embraced "insanity resulting either from ('sickness') or from other causes ('defect')."[161] It was discussed whether a sentence stating that the treatment of a person whose capacity was not fully impaired should have his or her punishment reduced.[162] However, this was left outside. The final version of the draft was finalized in the December session of the Preparatory Committee in 1997.[163]

During the negotiations of the ICC Statute, references were made to diminished mental responsibility as a circumstance that could mitigate punishment. Finally, diminished responsibility was included in the chapter concerning "penalties" in the ICC RPE.[164]

2.3.2 Regulation

The defense of mental insanity is defined in Article 31(1)(a) ICC Statute. This article states that a person shall not be criminally responsible if, at the time of the deeds, "the person suffers from a mental disease or defect that destroys that person's capacity to appreciate the unlawfulness or nature of his or her conduct, or capacity to control his or her conduct to conform to the requirements of law." This provision encompasses two basic conditions, a biological (an abnormality of mind) and a psychological condition (inability to understand or control his acts).[165] It is understood that the mental incapacity must be "sufficiently serious and lasting" so that it really affects the consciousness or control of the perpetrator.[166] Thus, the defense of mental insanity at the ICC requires "destruction" of the individual's capacity, rejecting the possibility of alleging diminished responsibility under the *chapeau* of Article 31 ICC Statute.

However, other provisions have also considered the rehabilitative purpose of punishment, despite the lack of mention in the ICC Statute of the resocializing goals of punishment.[167] For instance, Article 78(1) ICC Statute sets forth that the Court shall take into account the "individual circumstances of the convicted person," apart from the gravity factor.[168] This proviso mirrors the previously studied Article 24(2) ICTY Statute, as it clearly echoes the principle of individualization in sentencing. In relation to Article 78(1) ICC Statute, Rule 145 ICC RPE has represented a major step in international criminal law. This provision requires that, while determining the sentence pursuant to Article 78(1) ICC Statute, the Court must consider several points set out in Rule 145(1) ICC RPE. First, the Court shall bear in mind that the imposed penalty reflects the "culpability" of the convicted person.[169] Second, it must "balance all the relevant factors, including any mitigating and aggravating circumstances and consider the circumstances both of the convicted person and the crime."[170] Third, the Court shall also take into account other factors such as "the extent of the damage caused."[171] In its second paragraph, Rule 145 ICC RPE includes a list of mitigating and aggravating circumstances. Most important of all for current purposes is that one of the mitigating factors embraces a lower degree of mental insanity than the described in Article 31 ICC Statute. In this respect, Rule 145(2)(a)(i) ICC RPE asserts that the Court shall take into consideration "the circumstances falling short of constituting grounds for exclusion of criminal responsibility, such as substantially diminished mental capacity or duress." The lack of regulation of a defense of diminished responsibility in the ICC Statute implies that diminished responsibility, thus, should be treated as a sentencing factor and not as having an exculpatory role *per se*.[172]

2.3.3 Analysis and Legal Problems

It is true that the definition of "mental insanity" in the ICC Statute and the recognition of "diminished mental responsibility" in the ICC RPE appear to represent a considerable advance in terms the defendant's rights. These provisions, however, lack clarity. In fact, this part attempts to identify and tackle several legal conundrums that arise in such provisions' analysis. First of all, it must be noted that international criminal defenses play a role that can be described as somehow paradoxical.[173] On the one hand, they can be perceived as a threat to the concept of redress and prevention associated with the objective of accountability for grave violations of human rights.[174] With this picture in mind, it is easier to understand why Article 31(1)(a) ICC Statute was drafted using such a wording. On the other hand, they provide for "fundamental fairness" and represent an "essential component of a culture of legality."[175]

The first problem that Article 31(1)(a) of the ICC Statute faces is that mental insanity is presented as a "ground excluding criminal responsibility." Those words were used to avoid preference of one national legal system over another. For instance, while the English legal system uses the terms "insanity defense," the German one fits mental incapacity issues under the *chapeau* of "culpability," using the term "*Schuldunfähigkeit wegen seelischer Störungen.*" According to the wording, then, a mental disease or defect meeting the stated conditions excludes criminal responsibility. Article 31(1)(a) ICC Statute requires a "mental disease or defect" that "destroys" the capacity to acknowledge the unlawfulness or nature of his or her acts, or the capacity to control those acts. Clearly, this test is extremely onerous, as mental disorders seldom deprive individuals of all self-control, nor do they become absolutely disoriented.[176]

On top of this, it has to be borne in mind that the evidence in these cases needs to rely heavily on a concrete field of knowledge, namely, psychiatry.[177] Proving a certain mental state at the moment of the crimes is a time-consuming and complicated process that leads to many marshy areas. The degree of such mental affectation varies in each individual and implies, therefore, tedious problems with evidence in order to determine if a certain ground of exclusion of responsibility or mitigating circumstance applies. Likewise, the evidentiary burden brings controversy, too. In issues related to mental insanity, the ICTY case law decided to place the burden of proof on the accused. However, there is not a legal basis or jurisprudence at the ICC determining the allocation of the onus of proof in case a defendant raises this defense.[178] Although the practice in international proceedings has placed the burden on the individual alleging a fact, this attitude disregards the essential presumption of innocence which should govern international trials.[179] Article 67(1)(i) ICC Statute argues that one of the guarantees of the accused is "not to have imposed on him or her any reversal of the burden of proof or any onus of rebuttal," which for some scholars means that the prosecution bears the burden beyond a reasonable doubt once the defense has been raised.[180] This latter evidentiary issue, coupled with the high burden placed by the words used in the mental insanity defense provision, make the success of a defense of this sort almost unattainable. Probably, the phrasing of Article 31(1)(a) ICC Statute is due to the "fear" of the drafters to lose credibility by excluding criminal responsibility for such atrocities. The absence of any shade of grey in said article makes it almost impossible to be acquitted by reasons of insanity.[181]

Furthermore, the consequences of a successful plea of mental insanity are not expressly stated in the ICC Statute. It is presumed that the wording of Article 31 ICC Statute implies that because mental disease is a complete defense and it should result in an acquittal.[182] However, Article 77 of the ICC Statute fails to mention any kind of special penalty, such as interning the perpetrator in a mental hospital.[183] Even in cases where the defendant would see his sentence reduced due to diminished mental responsibility, the ICC cannot order an imprisonment of special nature—for example, with mandatory mental health treatments for rehabilitative purposes. The inquiries of the reader at this point are expected; the ingredients for controversy are assured. On the one hand, if the only viable alternative for a mentally insane under Article 31(1)(a) ICC Statute is acquittal, any judge dealing with this matter will hesitate to accept it. Besides, there would be obvious concerns with dangerousness and protection of society setting a proven mentally insane perpetrator free. On the other, given that imprisonment would go against all kind of principles of moral culpability and justice, an intermediate measure of internment is needed. In this regard, Amnesty International has asserted that: "the Statute or rules will have to establish procedures consistent with international law and standards for addressing the situation of a person acquitted on this ground who continues to suffer from that disease or defect."[184] Schabas has suggested that in case of acquittal of a mentally insane individual, "the public health authorities in The Netherlands can be expected to take the appropriate measures."[185]

The preceding explanation has demonstrated that, indeed, the rehabilitation of the offender should be a significant objective when sentencing in international prosecutions. This goal should be especially considered with respect to mentally affected perpetrators, which have a right to tailored penalties and specific mental health treatments when necessary. It is a certain fact that the execution of sentences remains under the control of the states offering their facilities.[186] Nevertheless, delaying the application of the principle of rehabilitation until the execution period constitutes a belated and deficient application of said principle. At the enforcement stage, the sentence has already declared whether the perpetrator will be granted an acquittal or will have, instead, a prison punishment.[187] The ICC will have little control over the implementation of the measure once the sentence is issued. Leaving this matter to be treated at the domestic level can risk states failing to give specific medical treatments in prison, or, in more serious cases, that the perpetrator will serve time in prison when, in fact, he or she would be otherwise eligible for an alternative punishment, such as internment in a mental care center. Thus, the ICC should have the competence to determine these matters in advance (that is, in the sentence), paving the way so that the state can duly fulfil this objective while overseeing the execution of the penalty.

The combined analysis of the ICTY jurisprudence and the regulation set forth in the ICC Statute make it possible to foresee the efficacy that this particular defense will have at the ICC. Undoubtedly, the ICC Statute is in great need of a change in its regulation. Although this tribunal has not yet dealt with a mental insanity case, it is only a matter a time before the ICC finds itself in trouble. One way out of this problem might be for the ICC to find inspiration in national jurisdictions in order to establish a new definition of the defense at stake that would also pay due regard to the appropriate consequences that should ensue should the claim be successful.

3 The Approach of National Systems towards Mental Insanity: Germany and England

The ICC Statute is based on a complex and uneasy hybridization of common and civil law.[188] Apart from the obvious interference of both systems in the drafting of the ICC Statute and RPE, it is worth noting that the broad nature of some of its provisions invites comparative analysis concerning essential issues such as mental insanity.[189] Indeed, Article 21(1)(c) ICC

Statute expressly states that the Court shall apply the "general principles of law derived by the Court from national laws of legal systems of the world." In particular, the legal systems of Germany and England have been two of the most requested systems in the comparative law studies carried out in the international tribunals.[190] Hence, this section will focus on these two jurisdictions due to their enormous influence on international criminal law. Furthermore, the differences in their respective notion of criminal law makes this analysis very compelling. German law is considered the prototype of Roman Law,[191] and it is very doctrine-driven.[192] English law is the most "common-law of all the common-law systems"[193] and it is characterized by a "distinctive improvisatory and pragmatic legal style."[194] This definitely determines their way of approaching mental insanity and its allocation in criminal law theory, as will be discussed later. Comparing both systems is a useful tool in order to determine whether the ICC Statute should follow one of these two models—and if affirmative, which one of them—to achieve a clearer regulation of mental insanity and its consequences for the offender. (This latter issue will be discussed in section 4.)

The present section will include a comparative study of German and English law on the following questions: theories of punishment and liability requirements (section 3.1), treatment of mental insanity and diminished responsibility (section 3.2), consequences in the sentencing and enforcement/execution stage (section 3.3), and a brief explanation of mental insanity in different national regulations of international crimes (section 3.4).

3.1 Theories of Punishment and Liability Requirements

Whether expressly codified or not in the domestic criminal codes, the punishment imposed to the offender is expected to fulfil several goals while relying in general sentencing principles. In this respect, the German theory of punishment is premised on §46 (1) of the Strafgesetzbuch (StGB), which states that "the offender's culpability (*Schuld*) is the basis for the determination of the sentence" and "the effect that the sentence can be expected to have on the offender's future life in society shall be taken into account." On the one hand, this provision embeds the culpability principle, under which the penalty must be proportionate to the individual guilt of the offender.[195] According to some doctrine, the culpability orientation of sentencing entails that the essential objective of punishment is retributive.[196] This means that "the punishment the offender 'deserves' for the offence is the maximum a court can impose (principle of proportionality)."[197] On the other hand, the same provision emphasizes that the future life of the offender must be considered, signaling that the rehabilitation of the offender must be taken into account.[198] The English Criminal Justice Act (CJA), on its side, in Section 142, lists five purposes of sentencing, including: punishment, crime reduction, rehabilitation, public protection, and reparation. Furthermore, Section 143 stresses the importance of the proportionality principle when making reference to "the offender's culpability in committing the offence." According to Ashworth, this is the landmark sentencing principle as all the other goals must operate within the guidelines of the proportionality principle.[199] This description clearly shows that the culpability and blameworthiness of the offender are expressly recognized and relevant for both systems when determining the penalty.

Notwithstanding, culpability represents a basis of punishment as well. In this regard, it is essential to understand the liability requirements in one and other system in order to have a clear vision of the function of culpability and its relation to mental insanity. The German theory of crime, for instance, distinguishes three basic stages of examination (*dreistufiger Verbrechensaufbau*).[200] The first step (*Tatbestand*) concerns the question whether the individual has fulfilled each requirement of the statutory description of an offence, including both objective and subjective elements. The second step (*Rechtswidrigkeit*) is concerned with the question of whether the person's conduct was unlawful and whether there were any justificatory defenses in place. The third step (*Schuld*) inquiries into the offender's individual blameworthiness or guilt, and into the existence of any excusatory defenses. Finally, German law accepts other categories such as *Strafausschliessungsgründe* (reasons that exclude the need for punishment), and *objektive Bedingungen der Strafbarkeit* (factors that must exist before liability is triggered).

Thus, culpability in the German system is a crucial category for a conduct to be punishable. It has been affirmed that the lawmaker who wants to attach the punishment to the moral quality of the human behavior will understand the principle of culpability as the basis of individual responsibility.[201] Thus, this principle implies that the punishment can only be based on the judicial confirmation that the fact can be personally attributed to the perpetrator. According to Jescheck, the main features of culpability as the foundation of punishment are: capacity of culpability (*Schuldfähigkeit*) and self-awareness of the unlawfulness of the fact (*Bewusstsein der Rechtswidrigkeit*).[202] Mental insanity (*Schuldunfähigkeit wegen seelischer Störungen*) appears in German law under the umbrella of the capacity of culpability. The capacity of culpability implies that only the individual of a given age which, additionally, does not possess any symptoms of grave mental disruption, can be held criminally liable.[203] Thus, the mental and intellectual health of the perpetrator has a direct influence on his or her culpability. This principle is needed to avoid harsh results that are incompatible with human dignity, such as "imposing criminal responsibility when no behavior can be attributed to the accused or when his conduct was not voluntary."[204] In consequence, in cases of serious mental diseases the capacity of culpability disappears. Notwithstanding, when criminal liability cannot totally disappear, the culpability requirement will limit the punishment for a crime to what is deserved according to his or her culpability.[205]

English criminal law, alternatively, builds its construction of criminal liability on two basic elements: *actus reus* and *mens rea*. The former term includes all the elements of the definition of the offence except those relating to the mental element (*mens rea*), needed on the part of the accused.[206] The definition of *actus reus* can be found either in the decisions of the courts (in the case of a common law crime) and in the statute as interpreted judicially in decided cases (in the case of a statutory crime).[207] The *mens rea* element can be defined as the subjective element necessary for a particular crime, and it differs from one crime to another.[208] This term has usually been used to represent four fault requirements: "intention and recklessness as to a specified consequence, and knowledge of, or recklessness as to a specified circumstance."[209] It is worth noting that the offences requiring *mens rea* are considered more serious that those which can be committed negligently or for which liability is strict.[210] Indeed, the concept of *mens rea* "imports a notion of moral blameworthiness or culpability on the part of the offender."[211] However, a person may have *mens rea* though his or her state of mind cannot be considered blameworthy.[212] In short, in order for a person to be convicted for a crime, the prosecution must prove that an individual's conduct has given rise to a certain fact or combination of circumstances forbidden by the law (*actus reus*) followed by a mental element inferred from the offender's state of mind (*mens rea*).[213]

Basing criminal liability merely on these two elements that have to be proven by the prosecution, however, disregards the possibility of the accused relying upon some justification or excuse to avoid criminal responsibility.[214] Hence, the view expressed by Lanham is that "a crime is 'made up of three ingredients, actus reus, mens rea and (a negative element) absence of a valid defense.'"[215] For instance, it is clear that a person should only be held criminally responsible when he or she possesses the capacity to understand and control his or her actions and their consequences.[216] Thus, moral culpability should not attach to the person who was not able to understand or control his or her behavior because of mental insanity.

3.2 Treatment of Mental Insanity and Diminished Responsibility

Differences in both systems are not only found in the theory of crime but also in the way of approaching mental insanity and diminished responsibility. First of all, it is essential to explain briefly how the German and English systems define and divide the grounds of excluding criminal responsibility. Only after clarifying such concepts, it would be possible to understand the way in which mental insanity is dealt with in each one of the systems under scrutiny.

German criminal law does not include the concept of "defenses," meaning that a defendant should not raise certain grounds to avoid punishability.[217] Instead, only when the court has found that all the requirements of punishability exist in a certain case it is possible to convict the individual. Setting aside the procedural grounds to exclude punishment, the substantive grounds can be classified into those that enable the accused to exceptionally do what is defined as an offence (justification) and those that only excuse the offender's behavior due to individual deficiencies or an extraordinarily stressful situation (excuses). It is the court's duty to determine whether any of these circumstances exist in order to establish all the important facts of the judgment. The public prosecutor is in charge of investigating both incriminating and exonerating circumstances[218] and the defendant does not even need to mention the word "defense."[219]

On its side, English criminal law uses the broad term "defense" to prevent a conviction for an offense, encompassing both substantive and procedural bars to punishability and prosecution.[220] In the English system, therefore, there is no distinction between justification and excuses.[221] It is noteworthy to remember the three stages of the criminal liability theory in order to punish a conduct under German criminal law. Unlike this latter system, which bases punishability on a conduct that satisfies the definitional requirements of a crime, it is unlawful (not justified) and it is blameworthy (not excusable); the English model mixes the criteria for justification and excuse.[222] According to Fletcher, this is due to this point's non-structured way of legal reasoning as opposed to the German legal argument, which is organized and structured.[223]

Be that as it may, it is clear that mental insanity is a ground that can exclude criminal responsibility. In German law it is called an excuse; in English law, it constitutes a defense. In both systems mental insanity does not affect the "rightness or desirability of the act" but "the personal culpability of [the] actor."[224] However, the concept of mental insanity does not have the same meaning under German and English law. German criminal law defines mental insanity (*Schuldunfähigkeit*) in §20 StGB. According to this article, a person acts without culpability when that person suffers, at the time of the offense, from a pathological mental disorder (*krankhafte seelische Störung*), a profound consciousness disorder (*tiefgreifende Bewusstseinsstörung*), debility (*Schwachsinn*), or any other serious mental abnormality (*schwere seeelische Abartigkeit*), and is therefore unable to appreciate the wrongfulness of his or her conduct or is unable to act according to his or her understanding (§20 StGB). These four categories, especially the first one, are meant as affectations that start from a "biological" basis and have their impact on the "mental" level.[225]

However, the StGB also provides for less grave affectations not able to exclude criminal liability. Diminished responsibility (*verminderte Schuldfähigkeit*) is laid out in §21 StGB. According to this provision, if the accused's ability to recognize the unlawfulness of his or her conduct or to act according to his or her insight is substantially diminished, that person is guilty but his or her sentence may be mitigated (§21 StGB). Thus, §21 StGB means that diminished responsibility is a mere sentencing provision that leads to a "facultative shift" in the sentencing scale according to §49(1) StGB.[226] It applies to all offences and is based on the categories mentioned in §20 StGB.[227]

Mental insanity has certain particularities in trial, leading to a two-step analysis to determine whether there is insanity in a certain case.[228] The first step consists in the court establishing if the actor suffered from one of the defects included in §20 StGB, usually relying on psychiatric experts in order to reach such decision. It is the prosecution and the court that have to clarify the issue of the defendant's insanity under §244(2) of the *Strafprozessordnung* (StPO).[229] The standard of proof needed in these cases is the one of "balance of probabilities," which entails reaching the point where the court cannot easily exclude the possibility that the defendant was insane at the time of the commission of the crime. Once the existence of insanity has been established, the court must ask whether the mental defect nullified the offender's capacity to realize that he or she did wrong, or whether he or she knew that he or she did wrong but was unable to control him- or herself to refrain from doing said wrong.[230]

Yet, English criminal law approaches mental insanity from a different view. The defense of mental insanity applies to all offences but is very narrowly defined. It was in M'Naghten's case in 1843 when the judges decided to set the essential rules to determine mental insanity.[231] This defense could be successful when the defendant proved that he or she was suffering from such a "defect of reason," arising from "disease of mind," as to not know the nature and quality of the act or, if he did know, not know that it was against the law.[232] Later on, the courts expanded this definition so that it could include conditions such as epilepsy, sleepwalking, and diabetes causing hyperglycemia. However, the result is that only a few defendants raise these later arguments and tend to plead guilty instead, just as many other offenders which do not fall into the narrow M'Naghten Rules do. These mentally affected individuals try to have a positive response from the court at the sentencing stage due to the low possibilities of succeeding when raising this defense.

Hence, apart from the complete defense of insanity, Section 2 of the Homicide Act 1957 included a partial defense of diminished responsibility, now revised by Section 58 of the Coroners and Justice Act 2009.[233] Accordingly, if the offence with which an individual is charged is murder, it can be reduced to manslaughter if he or she was suffering from a mental disorder that substantially impaired the ability to understand the nature of his or her acts, to elaborate a rational judgment, or to exercise self-control. Unlike German law, instead of considering diminished responsibility as mitigating factor, the English system understands this concept as negating "specific intent, premeditation and deliberation on a charge of murder."[234] Hence, and as "diminished" affects both *mens rea* and *actus reus*, a minor offense must be imposed in order to have the punishment reduced.

There are several unusual characteristics of the insanity defense during trial.[235] First, the defendant's insanity can be raised by both the prosecution and the defense. Second, in order to succeed when raising the insanity defense, the defendant must prove that he or she was insane at the moment of the crime within the M'Naghten test.[236] This is the only common law defense in which the accused bears the burden of proof. Third, the insanity defense must go to the jury and if the test is met, the accused will be found "not guilty by reason of insanity," which is known as "special verdict."[237] The special verdict is the only alternative to a general verdict of "guilty" or "not guilty."

3.3 Sentencing and Enforcement Issues

Successfully raising mental insanity or diminished responsibility has distinct consequences under the German and English systems. In order to determine the way of sanctioning in these particular cases, this subsection will provide an overview of both systems of punishment.

German criminal law is based on two different approaches when sentencing.[238] The system distinguishes between criminal punishment (*Strafen*), which requires a finding of guilt; and the measures of rehabilitation and security (*Massregeln der Besserung und Sicherung*), which are only consequence of the accused's dangerousness and the need for treatment or preventive detention. Punishments include imprisonment (§38 StGB), fines (§40 StGB), and other specific sanctions, such as temporary prohibition to drive a car (§44 StGB). Measures of rehabilitation and security include commitment to a psychiatric hospital (§63 StGB), commitment to an institution for alcohol or drug rehabilitation (§64 StGB), security detention (§66 StGB), and revocation of a driver's license (§69 StGB).[239] In relation to the measures of rehabilitation and security, Germany is currently based on a "two-track" criminal system.[240] Temporally limited detention sentences are imposed upon offenders who were aware of their responsibility; temporally unlimited detention sentences are imposed upon offenders who were unaware of their responsibility but who are potentially dangerous. This enables mentally ill offenders to receive a mandatory commitment to a psychiatric hospital so that they can be mentally treated while protecting society. The temporally unlimited commitment to a psychiatric hospital is encompassed in §63 StGB and its admittance takes place without a concrete duration.[241] The conditions to impose this measure are the mental affectation related to §20 StGB or §21 StGB during the commission of the crimes, and the foreseeability that the offender will commit further crimes due to his mental disturbance. Thus, if the court determines that the offender acted "in a state of an absence of or in a state of decreased responsibility" due to a mental disorder, and there is a risk that he or she might commit crimes again, then the conditions §63 StGB are met.[242]

In case of lack of responsibility, the accused is acquitted of the charge but his or her admission to a hospital is arranged concurrently; in the case of decreased responsibility, the court can charge the person with additional imprisonment, which is to be executed after the measure.[243] It is essential to remark that the arrangement and completion of the measures are basically regulated by Federal Law, but their implementation relies on state laws (§138 Section 1 of the *Strafvollzugsgesetz* (StVollzG)).[244]

English criminal law provides different types of punishment and sentences under the CJA 2003.[245] The less severe sentences are the absolute and conditional discharge, and the power to impose such sentences is regulated in the Powers of Criminal Courts (Sentencing) Act 2000 (Sections 12–15). The next level includes fines (Sections 162–165 JCA 2003) and slightly higher community sentences, which have to be imposed only if the sentence is "serious enough" (Sections 147–151 CJA 2003). Finally, the last and highest level is composed by custodial sentences, normally requiring the court to be satisfied that neither "a fine alone nor a community sentence can be justified for the offence" (Sections 152–153 CJA 2003).

In relation to mentally insane offenders, a person found not guilty because of insanity cannot be convicted of any crime and cannot be sentenced.[246] The notion of "disposal" is used to describe the ways in which a court can deal with these offenders. Different orders can be made in respect of a mentally disordered offender.[247] Apart from community orders, which may contain a "mental health treatment requirement" (Section 207 CJA 2003), in case of more serious affectations the court can impose several measures. According to the Mental Health Act of 1983, those are hospital order and guardianship order (Section 37 Mental Health Act 1983). The Criminal Procedure (Insanity and Unfitness to Plead) Act 1991 retains mandatory commitment where the charge is murder, which means that the court will make a hospital order restricting discharge without time limitation.[248]

3.4 Brief Reference to the Consideration of Mental Insanity in National Prosecutions of International Crimes

The previous subsections have studied the approach of the German and English systems towards mentally affected perpetrators committing domestic crimes. However, it is relevant to analyze now the conception of these national jurisdictions with regard to offenders of international crimes who are prosecuted in their own courts. Surveying national laws including international crimes through the correspondent implementation process is essential in this respect. The following overview will mainly focus on how the general principles of law of the ICC Statute are implemented into domestic systems. This will be essential to prove if the same provisions offered to the mentally insane national offenders are applied to the perpetrators of international crimes.

Germany implemented the ICC Statute after its ratification on December 11, 2000. Among the implementation measures, the most relevant are the Act on Cooperation with the International Criminal Court (Cooperation Act)[249] and the Code of Crimes against International Law (CCIL).[250] The CCIL is an independent codification of crimes against international law which has preference over the StGB in respect to the definitions of the core crimes, which are much more specific.[251] However, the CCIL resorts loosely to the general principles of domestic criminal law. Accordingly, Section 2 of the CCIL asserts that "the general criminal law shall apply to offences pursuant to this Act so far as this Act does not make special provision in Sections 1 and 3 to 5." The plain explanation of this article is that, unless otherwise stated in the CCIL, the general provisions of the StGB are applicable for the prosecution of international crimes.[252] Due to the extraordinary circumstances in which the general principles of international criminal law are applied, the German lawmaker compounded the German provisions regulating international crimes into the domestic system of general principles of criminal law. This also meant avoiding complications when applying the law coming from two different general parts.²⁵³ Apparently, this decision was based on the belief that the German system could bring adequate and coherent results compatible with the ICC Statute.²⁵⁴

On its side, England signed the ICC Statute on 30 November 1998 and ratified it on October 4, 2001. In order to guarantee the fulfilment of the obligations under the ICC Statute, the English Parliament, even before its ratification of the ICC Statute, enacted the International Criminal Court Act 2001 (ICC Act 2001). The ICC Act 2001 entered into force on September 1, 2001.²⁵⁵ The core crimes have been directly defined and incorporated into English law with a remission to Articles 6 to 8 ICC Statute.²⁵⁶ Besides, those crimes have been made offenses "against the law of England and Wales."²⁵⁷ Regarding the general principles of law, it is particularly relevant to focus on the treatment defenses are afforded. Just like in Germany, the implementing legislation in England does not integrate the defenses from the ICC Statute. Instead, the system relies on the existence of defenses already defined in domestic law.²⁵⁸

3.5 Upshot

The German and English variants have two different *modus operandi* when dealing with mentally insane offenders. Both jurisdictions are two-tiered models of legal consequences leading from a finding of some degree of mental incapacity: a complete defense (in cases of "full" incapacity) and other more distinct consequences (in cases of reduced capacity).²⁵⁹ These options represent a guarantee to all offenders and place an important value in the defense of mentally ill perpetrators. More or less effectively, the defendant will employ those tools in trial and will have the opportunity to succeed. Unlike the ICC Statute definition of insanity, which is unrealistically limited and virtually impossible to invoke with success, the German and English systems have awarded due importance to issues of culpability and rehabilitation. In addition, despite their obvious differences, these jurisdictions encompass specific measures to deal with this kind of perpetrators, including hospital orders. Therefore, it is clear that for them, imprisonment or acquittal cannot be the sole sentencing alternatives.

What is more, the study conducted in section 3.4 shows that both the German and English jurisdictions provide a remission to their domestic general principles of law when dealing with the ICC Statute. Hence, at least in principle, domestic prosecution of perpetrators of international crimes offer a range of domestic defenses. Accordingly, a hypothetical offender charged with genocide prosecuted in England would have the opportunity not only of effectively raising the defense of insanity, but also of receiving a hospital order instead of serving a fully-fledged prison sentence. As already stated in the present section, this does not happen at the ICC. The distinct treatment of international perpetrators in the domestic and international realms is certainly disturbing, and as such calls for a modification of the ICC Statute in this respect.

4 Mental Insanity at the ICC: Analysis and Proposal

The aim of section 3 was to provide an insight, by means of a comparative analysis, of the German and English regulation of mental insanity and its legal consequences in each system. Once such distinct approaches have been clarified, it is necessary to include an in-depth study of the possible incorporation of a model at the ICC, which could be one or a combination of the elements of both systems. Section 3 analyzed the legal questions concerning mentally insane perpetrators at the ICC. The theoretical and practical problems that were highlighted included: 1) the unclear heading of Article 31 ICC Statute, the inadequate concept of mental insanity and the lack of definition of diminished responsibility; 2) the evidentiary problems concerning mental insanity; and 3) the impossibility of ordering a hospital internment or a mental health treatment to deal with mentally affected perpetrators in a sentence. Hence, apart from the legal questions directly arising from the wording of Article 31(1)(a) ICC Statute, there is not a policy dealing with the acquitted insane or perpetrators suffering from diminished responsibility. A mental institution or treatment facility coping with these perpetrators does not exist. Conscious of this situation, Krabbe concludes that unless a clear regulation concerning the acquitted insane is established, the ICC and the other international tribunals will never accept an insanity plea.[260] The imperious necessity of a new and clearer regulation, and the incorporation of concrete measures to cope with this matter provide the bases of the present section. Thus this part, which represents the normative side of the chapter, will propose a concrete solution to this problem. To this end, it will assess whether the German, the English or the combination of both their approaches to mental insanity could be transferred to the ICC Statute.

4.1 Transference of a Mental Insanity Model into the ICC

4.1.1 Unclear and Inadequate Wording of Articles 31 ICC Statute and 145 ICC RPE

The heading of Article 31 ICC Statute embraces all "grounds for excluding criminal responsibility" and provides very distinct causes, including "mental disease or defect." There is no categorical division between those grounds, so the concepts of justifications and excuses are interspersed. Besides, the definition of Article 31(1)(a) ICC Statute involves extreme difficulties in pleading it successfully. In this regard, the term "destroys" currently leads to heated debate among scholars since it sets an "unrealistic hurdle."[261] On its behalf, Rule 145(2)(a)(i) ICC RPE sets forth the concept of "substantially diminished mental capacity" as a mitigating circumstance, but does not develop a concise definition. It is clear that these provisions are in a great need of review in order to establish a clearer frame and an adequate notion of those key concepts.

A first possibility would be adherence to the English model. As already explained in section 3, English criminal law basically divides its criminal liability theory in "*actus reus, mens rea* and (a negative element) absence of a valid defense."[262] Therefore, this common law model does not differentiate between justifications and excuses and instead employs "defenses" as bars to prevent a conviction.[263] With regard to mentally affected perpetrators, there are two available defenses that can be raised: mental insanity (complete defense) and diminished responsibility (partial defense reducing the crime to a lesser offence). Both concepts are duly defined in the M'Naghten Rules and Section 2 of the Homicide Act 1957, respectively.

The incorporation of this model to the ICC requires an analysis of the consequences that would arise from implementing it in the Statute and RPE. Taking into account that the heading of Article 31 ICC Statute also blurs the distinction between excuses and justifications, the next aspect to consider is adapting the treatment of mental insanity at the ICC to English law. However, this would involve important doctrinal changes that would not be easy to face. First of all, it is remarkable that the definition of mental insanity of Article 31(1)(a) ICC Statute is similar in its content to the M'Naghten rule. The ICC definition is composed of the cognitive test ("a mental disease or defect that destroys that person's capacity to appreciate the unlawfulness or nature of his or her conduct") and the volitional test ("or capacity to control his or her conduct to conform to the requirements of law"), which are found in the English test too.[264] However, a total adjustment of Article 31(1)(a) ICC Statute to the wording of the English rule would imply excluding the term "destroys" within the meaning of the ICC. Thus, the new drafting of Article 31(1)(a) ICC Statute in accordance with the M'Naghten rule would entail just a formal change of its wording. Mental insanity at the ICC was already meant to be working as the English complete defense.

A substantial modification would however be needed in the case of diminished responsibility. Some scholars have already noticed the lack of the defense of diminished responsibility in the ICC Statute.[265] Indeed, the

ICC Statute understands diminished responsibility as a mitigating circumstance, but not as a partial defense like the English system does.[266] It has been proposed that the ICC could resort to Article 31(3) ICC Statute to encompass the diminished responsibility plea.[267] Notwithstanding, there are objections to this assertion. First of all, the incorporation of a reduced level of responsibility would entail downgrading some core crimes as less serious than others.[268] Bearing in mind that the ICC Statute already circumscribes the jurisdiction of the Court to "the most serious crimes of concern to the international community as a whole,"[269] finding lesser offenses within the core crimes or classifying them in a hierarchical structure does not seem to constitute a very appropriate solution.[270] A second reason is based on the meaning of the heading of Article 31 ICC Statute, which lists the grounds that "exclude" criminal responsibility.[271] Thus, including under this caption the defense of diminished responsibility would lead to an acquittal if raised successfully. This would entail considering that the concepts of mental insanity of Article 31(1)(a) ICC Statute and diminished responsibility are at the same level and lead to the same consequences (acquittal). The third reason lays in the original significance of this partial defense in England. Indeed, the rationale of diminished responsibility was founded in the wish to avoid imposing mandatory sentences.[272] However, there are no mandatory sentences in the ICC.[273] Thus, it is clear from all the previously mentioned grounds that the incorporation of the English approach regarding mentally insane perpetrators would have serious doctrinal problems.

A second option would be introducing the German model of mental insanity to the ICC. The German theory of criminal law can be summarized in one sentence: A conduct can only be punished if it satisfies the elements of the crime, is unlawful, and is blameworthy. Hence, the distinction between justifications and excuses is essential, as they affect different stages of the criminal liability scheme. Thus, mental insanity is understood as an excuse affecting the category of culpability or blameworthiness,[274] and can exclude criminal responsibility if the requirements of §20 StGB are met. On its behalf, diminished responsibility is a sentencing factor able to mitigate the punishment under §21 StGB.

Before starting with the pertinent analysis it must be stressed that the ICC regulation of mental insanity is already closer to the German conception than to the English one. Both the German and the ICC system understand mental insanity as a ground to exclude criminal responsibility, and diminished responsibility as a mitigating circumstance. Apparently, the ICC drafters were inspired by this continental approach during the preparation of the ICC provisions. Nevertheless, a complete implementation of the German model into the ICC would certainly lead to the renewal of some points. Firstly, the definition of mental insanity of Article 31(1)(a) ICC Statute should embody the four mental affectations encompassed in the German definition, instead of simply referring to a "mental disease or defect." The inclusion of these four categories (pathological mental disorder, profound consciousness disorder, debility, or any other serious mental abnormality) would definitely contribute to the clearness and precision of the concept of mental insanity. The second part of both definitions is relatively similar and would not require any changes because both include the cognitive and volitional test to exclude criminal responsibility. In any event, the phrase "destroys the person's capacity" of the ICC Statute would have to be substituted by the word "incapability" of the German definition in order to broaden its applicability.

In order to fully adopt the German system at the ICC, the second concept that should be correctly defined is diminished responsibility. In particular, it would be necessary to modify the wording "substantially diminished mental capacity." The more concise display of words in §21 StGB could be implemented in Rule 145 ICC RPE in order to avoid disparity of opinions when interpreting this rule. The German concept of diminished responsibility is defined as it follows: "If the capacity of the offender to appreciate the unlawfulness of his actions or to act in accordance with any such appreciation is substantially diminished at the time of the commission of the offence due to one of the reasons indicated in Section 20, the sentence may be mitigated pursuant to Section 49(1)."

However, a strict transposition of the German model of mental insanity would imply also a structural reformation of the ICC Statute. Specifically, a thorough reorganization of Articles 31, 32, and 33 ICC Statute would be advisable. According to this author, a German approach of the ICC Statute would mean creating one provision with the heading "grounds for excluding criminal responsibility," which would include the sub-headings of "justifications" and "excuses." Hence, without commenting on the particularities and exceptions of each ground, the idea would be that self-defense and superior orders could represent grounds encompassed under the justifications heading; while insanity, intoxication, duress, and mistake of fact/law could be considered excuses. In consequence, the reasons underlying each ground could possibly become more understandable, especially mental insanity.

4.1.2 Evidentiary Problems

According to section 2, another problem concerning mental insanity is related to matters of evidence, such as proving the particular degree of mental affectation and burden of proof issues. At the ICC, apart from the obvious difficulties inherent to psychiatric evidence,[275] the burden of proof raises important inquiries that should be solved making use of comparative analysis. International criminal law does not expressly approach the question of burden of proof allocation when the plea of mental insanity is raised by the defendant. The absence of concrete legal standards in this respect leads to an uncertain application of the law which can seriously prejudice the defendant. Thus, it might be necessary to find a solution to this lack of precision. It would be desirable to expressly state who should bear the burden of proof in these cases.

It was already discussed that the English "defenses" were created as an instrument to hinder the sanctioning of a crime. Under this system, the defendant is the one carrying the burden of proof with regard to mental insanity.[276] He or she must determine that he was insane at the moment of the crime under the "balance of probabilities" standard of proof. Although this approach was taken by the ICTY in the Čelebići case, it remains however unclear whether the ICC would follow the same path in a potential case.[277] The English conception in this matter could constitute a solution to the ambiguity at the ICC. Indeed, several reasons support this view. First of all, psychiatric evidence in international prosecutions has frequently been considered improper because of its perception as "inappropriately lenient or unduly exculpatory."[278] Thus, placing the burden of proof in the defendant would be reasonable since, as the ICTY stated, "the burden of proof of facts relating to a peculiar knowledge is on the person with such knowledge or one who raises the defense."[279] In this respect, as the accused is the one interested in excluding or mitigating his or her responsibility, it can be argued that he or she is the best position to justify his or her mental insanity. Besides, according to the interpretation of Radosavljevic, placing the burden of proof on the accused in mental insanity cases is not contrary to Article 6 of the European Convention on Human Rights (ECHR).[280] The ECHR provision encompasses the right to a fair trial and specifically states that "a person is to be presumed innocent until proved guilty according to law."[281] However, this would imply bearing in mind important human rights standards: the defendant carrying the burden of proof should have a clear evidentiary burden and the equality of arms between the prosecution and the defense should be guaranteed in any case.[282] It must be noted, nevertheless, that drafting a disposition stating that the accused bears the burden of proof would lead to additional obstacles for the defense. The original understanding of the objectives of the international criminal trials and the always privileged position of the prosecution are already obvious caveats for the accused standing at trial.

Therefore, placing this evidentiary burden would be a risky decision and could seriously increase existent hurdles of the defense.

By contrast, the philosophy behind the German criminal law is that the prosecutor must investigate both incriminating and exonerating circumstances. Therefore, the prosecution and the court have the duty of clarifying the accused's mental insanity under a "balance of probabilities."[283] When studying this system in relation to the ICC, it must be noted that the existence of Article 54(1)(a) ICC Statute[284] and 67(1)(i) ICC Statute[285] are the point of departure in this matter. According to these provisions, the defendant has a right to await the court's analysis of all exculpatory evidence before ruling on his or her criminal liability.[286] Besides, it must be noted that the prosecution at the ICC is not only a party in the international trial but it is expected to act as an "impartial organ of justice."[287] This means that the prosecution must certainly present exculpatory evidence which could grant an absolution to the accused.[288] Both dispositions already show a tendency towards the German way of conceiving mental insanity and defenses in general. Be that as it may, the implementation of this perception would basically consist in interpreting those provisions favorably to the defendant, placing the burden of proof of mental insanity in the prosecution. An advisable option might be drafting a provision at the ICC Statute so that the tribunal is bound in this respect.

4.1.3 Lack of Measures to Deal with Mentally Insane Perpetrators after Sentence

The ICC Statute and RPE do not expressly encompass the consequences of a successful plea of mental insanity (other than acquittal) or of diminished mental responsibility. Article 77 ICC Statute remains silent about the imposition of a special penalty or measure to commit the accused to a mental institution or to mentally treat him or her in prison. At present, the defendant who successfully pleads any of those two mental insanity degrees will end up behind bars (and most of the times without special treatment) or totally free. Again, relying on the German and English models in this matter might be a good guidance.

First of all, both models will be briefly reviewed. As explained in section 3, the English system is characterized by several types of sentences ordered according to their degree of severity.[289] In this regard, the scale includes absolute and conditional discharges, fines, community sentences and custodial sentences. In relation to mental insane offenders, the measures that can be imposed are community orders (which can contain a mental health treatment requirement),[290] hospital orders or guardianship orders.[291] Besides, when the charge is murder, the court can commit the accused to a hospital without time limitation.[292] On its behalf, the German model distinguishes two different approaches when sentencing: criminal punishment and measures of rehabilitation and security.[293] These latter measures include, *inter alia*, commitment to a psychiatric hospital[294] and security detention.[295] Hence, mentally insane perpetrators who lack responsibility are acquitted but admission to a hospital is immediately arranged.[296] In the case of defendants with diminished responsibility, a measure will be imposed but the court can charge them with imprisonment after sentence.[297]

It is clear that both the German and English criminal systems consider of utmost importance to adequately place this type of defendants in an appropriate institution with appropriate measures. Despite the obvious structural differences of both countries in this matter, the two approaches of the present subsection could be implemented at the ICC level. Both models are similar in the philosophy underlying those special hospital orders, which is the rehabilitation of the offender, and both would imply a considerable adaptation of the sentencing and execution provisions of the ICC Statutes and RPE. Yet, this position already has its objections. What appeared to be a clear problem for this author is not for Schabas:

> An individual who is insane at the time of the crime may well pose no threat either to him or to others by the time of the trial and in such circumstances ought simply to be released. In the alternative, the public health authorities in the Netherlands can be expected to take the appropriate measures.[298]

Notwithstanding the foregoing, this approach cannot be supported. Although there is a possibility that the defendant is not mentally insane anymore, this might not always be the case. Thus, matters about public security and protection of society are essential to the objectives of "restoring and preserving the peace."[299] The achievement of these goals needs a system of involuntary commitments, which at present can only be implicitly implied from the ICC Statute provisions. Besides, not only reasons of dangerousness are relevant for the creation of alternatives to prison. The rehabilitation of the offender is an essential aspect already found at the national level and a right of all offenders regardless of their dangerousness. A hospital order or medical treatment cannot depend alone on the risk of the defendant perpetrating a new crime.

Furthermore, the affirmation that the Netherlands should cope with the "dangerous" acquitted is not a convenient way of dealing with the matter. The ICC was created to prosecute the core crimes that affect the international community as a whole and all states should cooperate to fulfil this goal. For instance, states have a key role in the enforcement of sentences and all of them should be equally responsible for this executive stage.[300] The Netherlands cannot be obliged to deal additionally with these problems only because it is the state in which the international community decided to place the ICC.

4.2 Proposed Solution and Concrete Steps for Its Implementation: The German Model at the ICC

The previous analysis compared the German and English ways of approaching in their own jurisdictions the major inquiries of mental insanity at the ICC. The outcome obtained from the previous subsection is that the German model would be the most satisfactory solution to deal with them. The clear and organized structure of its criminal theory and the existing similarities between the international tribunal and the German system are indicators in favor of this continental variant. The radical option of following only one system in this matter is founded on the *rationale* that mental insanity is already a confusing field—hence, the more coherent the concepts are, the better.

Adapting the ICC Statute and RPE to the German model would need important adjustments. New regulations of the definitions included in Article 31(1)(a) ICC Statute and Rule 145(2)(a)(i) ICC RPE according to the German StGB are advisable. Besides, the reorganization of Articles 31, 32, and 33 ICC Statute into one article encompassing all grounds excluding criminal responsibility would contribute to enlighten those provisions. As was previously explained, that new provision could distinguish between justifications and excuses according to the German criminal law theory, placing mental insanity under the category of excuses. Furthermore, the already explained evidentiary problem could be solved allocating in the prosecution the burden of proof when mental insanity issues arise through a clear wording.

However, what would definitely constitute a massive modification and an important advance is the creation of a policy dealing with the acquitted insane or the defendants suffering from diminished responsibility. In this regard, an appropriate regulation including the measures for its implementation are necessary to cope with the new regime. Accordingly, Article 77 ICC Statute would be the first provision in need of a change. This disposition encompasses all applicable penalties that can be imposed to the accused for the perpetration of the core crimes, including imprisonment, fines, and forfeitures. According to the German sentencing approaches, Article 77 ICC Statute only defines criminal punishments and there is no provision making reference to measures of rehabilitation and security.

The drafting of a new Article 77 *bis* ICC Statute providing for commitment to a psychiatric hospital or a compulsory medical treatment in the adequate institution would be essential. The more specific this provision is, the better. This should be reflected carefully defining the consequences in cases of mentally insane perpetrators and defendants suffering from diminished responsibility. Besides, no matter what the final wording of the provision is, it should be interpreted in a way in which the rehabilitation of the offender is the main purpose of the measure. Furthermore, it must be noted that *Chapter VII* of the ICC RPE should be concurrently adapted.

Once the dual system of penalties at the ICC is put in place, the problem of their satisfactory execution arises. It is a well-known fact that there is no international prison for the convicted individuals and they must serve their sentences in the states "which have indicated to the Court their willingness to accept sentenced persons."[301] The ICC can only supervise the enforcement of the sentence of imprisonment.[302] The possibility that the ICC creates an international hospital to deal with these individuals is close to nil. Therefore, it is logical to infer that in mental insanity cases the ICC should also rely in the municipal legal and medical authorities.[303] The construction of a legal basis concerning the medical disposition of the accused would require coordination between the States and the Court in order to enforce these particular sentences. This would entail making the pertinent changes in the Part X of the ICC Statute and Chapter XII of the RPE, which expose the matter of enforcement and states cooperation.

The ICC sentence would determine if the person is acquitted or has a mitigated responsibility because of its diminished responsibility, but the Court could only supervise the way in which the sentence is executed in prison or a mental institution. Hence, without the states performing their crucial role in sentence enforcement, the ICC could not achieve its primordial goal of prosecuting major perpetrators of international crimes. Indeed, the effectiveness of the commitment to medical institutions or health treatments depends on the states, which must deal with mentally affected perpetrators bearing in mind their rehabilitation. This might awaken fears and criticism on behalf of the international community, but reliance in their *modus operandi* in this matter is essential.

5 Conclusion

The aim of this chapter has been to discuss whether a domestic legal model of mental insanity should be strictly followed by the ICC, and if affirmative, which model or combination of models. The comparative and evaluative analyses conducted within this research have led to the conclusion that the German approach towards mental illness is the most appropriate. As discussed in the last section, the criminal theory of this continental variant would grant organization, structure, and clarity to the ICC. The adequate conception of the German system when analyzing the main problems of ICC—confusing regulation, evidentiary caveats, and lack of alternatives to prison—has based the decision of transferring only one model rather than a combination of both systems.

There have been no cases yet at the ICC dealing with this matter. Besides, the precedent set by the ICTY leads to the belief that the international justice is not exactly encouraging acquittal or sentence mitigation because of mental illness reasons. Further, it does not provide for an alternative solution to prison or acquittal, such as commitment to a medical institution. The fear to lose credibility and the pressure of the international community have led to a conscious disregard of the principle of the offender's culpability and the rehabilitative function of criminal law. Now, the recommended outline in the final section must be implemented with urgency in the ICC Statute and RPE before a case concerning mental insanity arises at the court.

Notes

1. *Indictment against Zejnil Delalić et al.*, ICTY, Case No. IT-96-21, March 19, 1996.

2. *Prosecutor v. Zejnil Delalić et al.*, ICTY, T.Ch., Case No. IT-96-21-T, November 16, 1998; *Prosecutor v. Zejnil Delalić et al.*, ICTY, A. Ch., Case No. IT-96-21-A, February 20, 2001.

3. *Prosecutor v. Delalić et al.*, November 16, 1998, para. 1186.

4. For example, in Germany (§63 StGB) and in England (Section 37 Mental Health Act 1983).

5. Preamble ICC Statute, para. 4.

6. Bassiouni, "International Criminal Justice in the Age of Globalization," 87.

7. D'Ascoli, *Sentencing in International Criminal Law*.

8. Henham, "Some Issues for Sentencing in the International Criminal Court," 89.

9. Preamble ICC Statute, para. 9; Art. 5 ICC Statute.

10. Cryer et al., *An Introduction to International Criminal Law and Procedure*, 24.

11. Damaska, "What is the Point of International Criminal Justice?", 331–35.

12. Hola, "Sentencing of International Crimes at the ICTY and ICTR," 6.

13. Werle, *Principles of International Criminal Law*, 30, §85.

14. Schabas, "Sentencing by International Tribunals," 500.

15. D'Ascoli, *Sentencing in International Criminal Law*, 37.

16. *Prosecutor v. Zlatko Aleksovski*, ICTY, A.Ch., Case No. IT-95-14/1-A, March 24, 2000, para. 185.

17. D'Ascoli, *Sentencing in International Criminal Law*, 38.

18. Bassiouni, *Introduction to International Criminal Law*, 689–90, 697.

19. Cryer, *Introduction to International Criminal Law and Procedure*, 26.

20. *Prosecutor v. Momir Nikolić*, ICTY, T. Ch, Case No. IT-02-60/1-S, December 2, 2003, para. 89.

21. D'Ascoli, *Sentencing*, 344.

22. Preamble ICC Statute, para. 4.

23. Ibid.

24. Preamble ICC Statute, para. 5.

25. Hola, "Sentencing of International Crimes," 7.

26. Schabas, "Sentencing by International Tribunals," 503.

27. D'Ascoli, *Sentencing in International Criminal Law*, 79.

28. Ibid., 40.

29. *Prosecutor v. Duško Tadić*, ICYT, T.Ch., Case No. IT-94-1-S, July 14, 1997, para. 61.

30. Zappalà, *Human Rights in International Criminal Proceedings*, p. 206.

31. *Prosecutor v. Dragoljub Kunarac et al.*, ICTY, T.Ch., Case No.IT-96-23-T&IT-96-23/1-T, February 22, 2001, para. 844. See also *Prosecutor v. Anto Furundžija*, ICTY, T.Ch., Case No. IT-95-17/1-T, December 10, 1998, para. 291. On rehabilitation, see, in general, *Prosecutor v. Tihomir Blaškić*, ICTY, T.Ch., Case No. IT-95-14-T, March 3, 2000, para. 761; *Prosecutor v. Zoran Kupreškić et al.*, ICTY, T.Ch., Case No. IT-95-16-T, January 14, 2000, para. 849; *Prosecutor v. Delalić et al.*, 16 November 1998, para. 1233.

32. *Prosecutor v. Kunarac et al.*, February 22, 2001, para. 844. See also Art. 27 ICTY Statute and Rules 103 and 104 ICTY RPE.

33. D'Ascoli, *Sentencing in International Criminal Law*, 40.

34. *Prosecutor v. Kunarac et al.*, February 22, 2001, para. 844.

35. Bassiouni, *Introduction to International Criminal Law*, 681.

36. Ohlin, "Towards a Unique Theory of International Criminal Sentencing," 384.

37. Ibid., 383.

38. Zappalà, *Human Rights in International Criminal Proceedings*, 206–07.

39. Sunga, *The Emerging System of International Criminal Law*, 329.

40. UNHRC, *General Comment 21/44*, para. 10.

41. Art. 5 (6) ACHR.

42. Art. 23(2)(ii) of the *Document of the Moscow Meeting of the Conference on the Human Dimension of the CSCE* (1991).

43. *Prosecutor v. Dragan Obrenović*, ICTY, T. Ch., Case No. IT-02-60/2-S, December 10, 2003, para. 53.

44. Klamberg, "What are the Objectives of International Criminal Procedure?", 301.

45. Henham, "Some Issues for Sentencing in the International Criminal Court," 91.
46. Schabas, "Sentencing by International Tribunals," 464.
47. D'Ascoli, *Sentencing in International Criminal Law*, 42.
48. Ibid.
49. *Prosecutor v. Dražen Erdemović*, ICTY, T. Ch., Case No. IT-96-22-Tbis, March 5, 1998, para. 21.
50. D'Ascoli, *Sentencing in International Criminal Law*, 39.
51. Zolo, "Peace through Criminal Law?", 729–30.
52. Schabas, "Sentencing by International Tribunals," 503.
53. Bassiouni, *Introduction to International Criminal Law*, 111.
54. Damaska, "What is the Point of International Criminal Justice?", 330.
55. Art. 17 ICC Statute.
56. Smeulers and Werner, "The Banality of Evil on Trial," 32.
57. Ibid., 33.
58. Cryer, *An Introduction to International Criminal Law and Procedure*, 29; Bassiouni, *Introduction to International Criminal Law*, 87.
59. Smeulers, "Perpetrators of International Crimes," 234.
60. D'Ascoli, *Sentencing in International Criminal Law*, p. 48.
61. Fisher, *Moral Accountability and International Criminal Law*, 52.
62. Arendt, *Eichmann in Jerusalem*.
63. Smeulers and Werner, "The Banality of Evil on Trial," 32.
64. Smeulers, "Perpetrators of International Crimes, 234.
65. Waller, *Becoming Evil*, 73.
66. MacNair, "Psychological Reverberations for the Killers," 273–82.
67. For a detailed explanation of these terms, see MacNair, *Perpetration-Induced Traumatic Stress*, 7.
68. Waller, *Becoming Evil*, 74.
69. Ibid.
70. Ibid.
71. Hare, "Psychopathy and Antisocial Personality Disorder."
72. Smeulers, "Perpetrators of International Crimes," 248.
73. Ibid.
74. Ibid., 235.
75. Cryer, *An Introduction to International Criminal Law and Procedure*, 497.
76. Krabbe, *Excusable Evil*, 31.
77. Knoops, *Defenses in Contemporary International Criminal Law*, 62.
78. Ibid., 97.
79. Bassiouni, *Introduction to International Criminal Law*, 281 (cited in Krabbe, *Excusable Evil*, 31).
80. Scaliotti, "Defenses Before the International Criminal Court," 16.
81. Ibid.
82. Kremnitzer and Hörnle, "Human Dignity and the Principle of Culpability," 115.
83. Ibid.

84. Krug, "The Emerging Mental Incapacity Defense in International Criminal Law," 333.

85. For a detailed explanation, see Boister and Cryer, *The Tokyo International Military Tribunal*, 240–41.

86. Schabas, *The International Criminal Court*, 481.

87. Van Sliedregt, *Individual Criminal Responsibility in International Law*, 2.

88. Arts. 7 and 8 Charter of the IMT of Nuremberg.

89. *Rudolf Hess Judgment*, International Military Tribunal (Nuremberg), October 1, 1946.

90. Ibid.

91. *Report of Commission to Examine Defendant Hess*, November 16, 1945, available at http://avalon.law.yale.edu/imt/v1-28.asp.

92. *Report of Prison Psychologist on Mental Competence of Defendant Hess*, August 17, 1946, available at http://avalon.law.yale.edu/imt/v1-29.asp.

93. *Rudolf Hess Judgment*.

94. Krabbe, *Excusable Evil*, 112.

95. Weber, "The Legacy of Rudolf Hess," 20–3.

96. Heller, *The Nuremberg Military Tribunals and the Origins of International Criminal Law*, 295–311.

97. Ibid., 330.

98. Ibid., 327.

99. Schabas, *The International Criminal Court*, 481.

100. Krug, "The Emerging Mental Incapacity Defense in International Criminal Law," 317.

101. United Nations, Security Council, *Report of the Secretary-General Pursuant to Paragraph 2 of Security Council Resolution 808 (1993)*, S/25704, May 3, 1993, para. 58.

102. Yee, "The Erdemović Sentencing Judgment," 287.

103. Raimondo, "General Principles of Law as Applied by International Criminal Courts and Tribunals," 394.

104. Art. 21(1)(c) ICC Statute: "The Court shall apply [. . .] general principles of law derived by the Court from national laws of legal systems of the world including, as appropriate, the national laws of States that would normally exercise jurisdiction over the crime, provided that those principles are not inconsistent with this Statute and with international law and internationally recognized norms and standards."

105. Raimondo, "General Principles of Law," 394.

106. *Prosecutor v. Delalić et al.*, February 20, 2001, paras. 583–90.

107. Eschelbach, Beck'scher Online-Kommentar StGB § 20, I. Schuldgrundsatz, Rn 2.

108. *Prosecutor v. Delalić et al.*, November 16, 1998, para. 1157.

109. Larkin, "The Insanity Defense Founded on Ethnic Oppression," 94.

110. Sunga, *The Emerging System of International Criminal Law*, 329.

111. Art. 24(1) ICTY Statute.

112. Hola, "Sentencing of International Crimes," 11.
113. Ibid., 8.
114. Zappalà, *Human Rights in International Criminal Proceedings*, 206.
115. Rule 125 ICTY RPE.
116. Art. 27 ICTY Statute.
117. It must be noted that although the *Erdemović* case is known because of its analysis of the defense of duress, the accused also pleaded insanity. However, reference to insanity was only made by the II Trial Chamber when discussing mitigating circumstances (*Prosecutor v. Erdemović*, March 5, 1998, para. 16). Indeed, as Krabbe argues, the Chamber "implicitly recognizes the insanity argument by discussing it, however, not as a complete defense, for it is brought into line with diminished responsibility and treated as a mitigating factor" (*Excusable Evil*, 114). The appeal to insanity was denied in the end.
118. *Indictment against Delalić et al.*, March 19, 1996.
119. *Prosecutor v. Delalić et al.*, November 16, 1998, para. 1156.
120. Sparr, "Personality Disorders and Criminal Law," 170.
121. Ibid.
122. Ibid.
123. *Prosecutor v. Delalić et al.*, November 16, 1998, para. 1159.
124. Jones and Powles, *International Criminal Practice*, 449; *Prosecutor v. Delalić et al.*, November 16, 1998, para. 1160.
125. *Prosecutor v. Delalić et al.*, November 16, 1998, paras. 1160, 1172.
126. Ibid., para. 1156.
127. Ibid.
128. *Prosecutor v. Delalić et al.*, November 16, 1998, paras. 1162, 1172.
129. Section 2, English Homicide Act 1957.
130. *Prosecutor v. Delalić et al.*, November 16, 1998, para. 1169.
131. Janssen, "Mental Condition Defences in Supranational Criminal Law," 86.
132. *Prosecutor v. Delalić et al.*, November 16, 1998, para. 1164.
133. Jones and Powles, *International Criminal Practice*, 448.
134. *Prosecutor v. Delalić et al.*, November 16, 1998, para. 1186.
135. Ibid., paras. 1283–84.
136. Freckelton and Karagiannakis, "Mental State Defenses Before the International Criminal Tribunal of the Former Yugoslavia," 252.
137. *Prosecutor v. Delalić et al.*, February 20, 2001, para. 577.
138. Ibid., para. 583.
139. Ibid., para. 588.
140. Ibid., para. 590.
141. Ibid., paras. 835–42.
142. *Prosecutor v. Predrag Banović*, ICTY, T. Ch. III, Case No. IT-02-65/1-S, October 28, 2003, para. 96.
143. Ibid., para. 77.
144. Ibid., para. 79.
145. Ibid., para. 81.

146. *Prosecutor v. Mitar Vasiljević*, ICTY, T. Ch. II, Case No. IT-98-32-T, November 29, 2002, para. 280.

147. Ibid., paras. 284–85.

148. Ibid., para. 286.

149. Ibid., para. 287.

150. Ibid., para. 289.

151. Ibid., para. 295.

152. See also *Prosecutor v. Duško Sikirica et al.*, ICTY, T.Ch. III, Case No. IT-95-8-S, November 13, 2001, para. 189; *Prosecutor v. Stevan Todorović*, ICTY, T. Ch. I, Case No. IT-95-9/1-S, July 31, 2001, para. 94.

153. Schabas, *The International Criminal Court*, 484.

154. Ambos, "Defenses in International Criminal Law," 299.

155. Art. 31(3) ICC Statute.

156. Schabas, *The International Criminal Court*, 482.

157. Yearbook of the International Law Commission, 1991, Vol. II, Part Two, *Report of the Commission to the General Assembly on the Work of its Forty-Third Session*, A/CN.4/SER.A/1991/Add.1 (Part 2), 95.

158. Ibid., 100.

159. *Report of the Ad Hoc Committee on the Establishment of an International Criminal Court*, General Assembly, Fiftieth Session, Supplement No. 22, A/50/22, New York, 1995, 59.

160. *Report of the Preparatory Committee on the Establishment of an International Criminal Court, Vol. I*, Proceedings of the Preparatory Committee during March-April and August 1996, General Assembly, Fifty-first Session, Supplement No. 22, A/51/22, New York, 1996, para. 204; *Report of the Preparatory Committee on the Establishment of an International Criminal Court, Vol. II*, Compilation of Proposals, General Assembly, Fifty-first Session, Supplement No. 22A, A/51/22, New York, 1996, 97.

161. Working paper submitted by Argentina, Canada, France, Germany, Mexico, Portugal and the United States of America, A/AC.249/1997/WG.2/DP.3, February 21, 1997, n2.

162. Ibid., n3.

163. General Principles of Criminal Law, Chairman's text, grounds for excluding criminal responsibility, A/AC.249/1997/WG.2/CRP.7, December 12, 1997, 1.

164. Art. 145(2)(a)(i) ICC RPE.

165. Janjac, *The Mental Element in the Rome Statute of the International Criminal Court*, 31.

166. Ibid.

167. D'Ascoli, *Sentencing in International Criminal Law*, 345.

168. Art. 78(1) ICC Statute.

169. Rule 145(1)(a) ICC RPE.

170. Rule 145(1)(b) ICC RPE.

171. Rule 145(1)(c) ICC RPE.

172. Yeo, "The Insanity Defense in the Criminal Laws of the Commonwealth of Nations," 258.

173. Krug, "Emerging Mental Incapacity Defense," 334.
174. Ibid.
175. Ibid., 335.
176. Salton, "Mental Incapacity and Liability Insurance Exclusionary Clauses," 1042.
177. Krug, "Emerging Mental Incapacity Defense," 322.
178. Ibid., 325.
179. Art. 66 ICC Statute, Art. 21(3) ICTY Statute, Art. 20(3) ICTR Statute. See also Krug, "Emerging Mental Incapacity Defense," 325.
180. Gallant, "Individual Human Rights in a New International Organization," 693, 711.
181. Janssen, "Mental Condition Defences in Supranational Criminal Law," 85.
182. Ibid.
183. Ibid.
184. Amnesty International, *The International Criminal Court: Making the Right Choices—Part V: Recommendations to the Diplomatic Conference*, April 30, 1993 (available at https://www.amnesty.org/en/documents/ior40/010/1998/en/), 44.
185. Schabas, *Genocide in International Law*, 344.
186. See 103(1) ICC Statute and Rule 201 ICC RPE.
187. Art. 77 ICC Statute.
188. Heller and Dubber, *The Handbook of Comparative Criminal Law*, 9.
189. Ibid., 3.
190. Raimondo, "General Principles of Law," 402.
191. European Commission, *Final Report, Placement and Treatment of Mentally Ill Offenders, Legislation and Practice in EU Member States*, Mannheim, 2005, p. 19.
192. Bohlander, *Principles of German Criminal Law*, 7.
193. Heller and Dubber, *Handbook of Comparative Criminal Law*, 8.
194. De Cruz, "Comparative Law in a Changing World," 102.
195. Streng, "Sentencing in Germany," 153.
196. Weigend, "Germany," 258.
197. Ibid.
198. Streng, "Sentencing in Germany," 153.
199. Ashworth, "United Kingdom," 535.
200. Bohlander, *Principles of German Criminal Law*, 16–17.
201. Jescheck, "El Principio de Culpabilidad como Fundamento y Límite de la Punibilidad," 26.
202. Jescheck and Weigand, *Lehrbuch des Strafrechts*, 430–69.
203. Jescheck, "El Principio de Culpabilidad," 32.
204. Kremnitzer and Hörnle, "Human Dignity and the Principle of Culpability," 115.
205. Ibid.
206. Allen, *Textbook on Criminal Law*, 19.
207. Ibid.
208. Ibid., 53.
209. Ashworth, *Principles of Criminal Law*, 170.

210. Allen, *Textbook on Criminal Law*, 53.
211. Ibid.
212. Ormerod, *Smith and Hogan's Criminal Law*, 96.
213. Smith, "On Actus Reus and Mens Rea," 96.
214. Allen, *Textbook on Criminal Law*, 18.
215. Ibid., 19.
216. Ibid., 121.
217. Weigend, "Germany," 268.
218. §160 (2) StPO.
219. Weigend, "Germany," 268.
220. Van Sliedregt, *Individual Criminal Responsibility in International Law*, 216.
221. Ashworth, "United Kingdom," 541.
222. Van Sliedregt, *Individual Criminal Responsibility in International Law*, 217.
223. Fletcher, "The Right and the Reasonable."
224. Ibid., 954.
225. Bohlander, *Principles of German Criminal Law*, 132–33.
226. Ibid., 135.
227. Ibid., 116.
228. Weigend, "Germany," 273.
229. Bohlander, *Principles of German Criminal Law*, 131.
230. Weigend, "Germany," 273.
231. *M'Naghten's Case*, 1843.
232. Ashworth, "United Kingdom," 544.
233. Ibid.
234. Van Sliedregt, *Individual Criminal Responsibility in International Law*, 228.
235. Loughnan, "Manifest Madness," 380.
236. Law Commission, *Criminal Liability: Insanity and Automatism, A Discussion Paper*, July 23, 2013 (available at http://www.lawcom.gov.uk/wp-content/uploads/2015/06/insanity_discussion.pdf), 5.
237. Ibid.
238. Albrecht, "Sentencing in Germany," 213.
239. Weigend, "Germany," 275.
240. Osterheider and Dimmek, "Germany," 152.
241. Ibid., 153.
242. Ibid., 154.
243. Ibid.
244. Ibid., 153.
245. Part 12 CJA 2003; Ashworth, *Sentencing and Criminal Justice*, 6.
246. Law Commission, *Criminal Liability: Insanity and Automatism*, 5.
247. Hungerford-Welch, *Criminal Procedure and Sentencing*, 935.
248. Ashworth, "General Principles of Criminal Law," 1062.
249. *Gesetz über die Zusammenarbeit mit dem Internationalen Strafgerichtshof*, contained in Art. 1 of the *Gesetz zür Ausführung des Romischen Statuts des Internationalen Strafgerichtshofes* ("Implementation Act"), 21 June 2002, in force 1 July 2002, Bundesgesetqblatt (FederalLaw GaZette, 'BGB.) 2002 I, at 2144.

250. *Völkerstrafgesetzbuch*, contained in Article 1 of the *Gesetz zür Einführung des Völkerstrafgesetzbuches* ("Act to Introduce a Code of Crimes against International Law"), 26 June 2002, in force 30 June 2002, BGBI. 2002 I, at 2254.

251. Hess, Knust, and Schuon, "Implementation of the Rome Statute in Germany," 133.

252. Ibid., 139.

253. Werle, "Konturen eines deutschen Völkerstrafrechts," 889.

254. Werle and Jessberger, "International Criminal Justice Is Coming Home," 202.

255. International Criminal Court Act 2001 (Commencement) Order 2001, S.I. 2001/2161, 13 June 2001. Certain provisions of the Act entered into force on 13 June 2001. See also the International Criminal Court Act 2001 (Commencement) (Amendment) Order 2001, S.I. 2001/2304, 25 June 2001. See also Olleson and Brubacher, "Implementation of the Rome Statute in the United Kingdom," 235.

256. Section 50(1) and Schedule 8 ICC Act 2001.

257. Section 51(1) ICC Act 2001.

258. Olleson and Brubacher, "Implementation of the Rome Statute in the United Kingdom," 241.

259. Krug, "Emerging Mental Incapacity Defense," 330.

260. Krabbe, *Excusable Evil*, 343.

261. See, for instance, Eser, "Article 31: Grounds for Excluding Criminal Responsibility."

262. Allen, *Textbook on Criminal Law*, 19.

263. Van Sliedregt, *Individual Criminal Responsibility in International Law*, 216.

264. Ibid., 226.

265. Ibid., 229; Radosavljevic, "Some Observations on the Lack of a Specific Diminished Responsibility Defense under the ICC Statute."

266. Rule 145(2)(a)(i) ICC RPE.

267. Art. 31(3) ICC Statute: *"At trial, the Court may consider a ground for excluding criminal responsibility other than those referred to in paragraph 1 where such a ground is derived from applicable law as set forth in article 21. The procedures relating to the consideration of such a ground shall be provided for in the Rules of Procedure and Evidence"*; see, for instance, Eser, "Article 31: Grounds for Excluding Criminal Responsibility," p. 875 (in Triffterer, *Commentary on the Rome Statute of the International Criminal Court*).

268. Eser, "'Defenses' in War Crime Trials," 251.

269. Preamble ICC Statute, para. 4.

270. Krug, "Emerging Mental Incapacity Defense," 331.

271. Van Sliedregt, *Individual Criminal Responsibility in International Law*, 229.

272. Simester and Sullivan, *Criminal Law Theory and Doctrine*, 578.

273. Krug, "Emerging Mental Incapacity Defense," 331.

274. Bohlander, *Principles of German Criminal Law*, 16.

275. See Ambos, "Defenses in International Criminal Law," 304.

276. Law Commission, *Criminal Liability: Insanity and Automatism*, 5.

277. *Prosecutor v. Delalić et al.*, November 16, 1998, paras. 78, 1160, 1172.
278. Perlin, "Unpacking the Myths," 599.
279. *Prosecutor v. Delalić et al.*, November 16, 1998, para. 1172.
280. *R v. Lambert* (2001) IAll ER 1014 (in Radosavljevic, "Some Observations," 41).
281. Art. 6(3) ECHR.
282. See, *inter alia, Lietzow v. Germany*, ECtHR No. 24479/94, February 13, 2001, para. 44.
283. Bohlander, *Principles of German Criminal Law*, 131.
284. Art. 54(1)(a) ICC Statute: "The Prosecutor shall . . . (a) In order to establish the truth, extend the investigation to cover all facts and evidence relevant to an assessment of whether there is criminal responsibility under this Statute, and, in doing so, investigate incriminating and exonerating circumstances equally."
285. Art. 67(1)(i) ICC Statute: "The accused shall be entitled to . . . (i) Not to have imposed on him or her any reversal of the burden of proof or any onus of rebuttal."
286. *R v. Hobson* (1997) EWCA Crim 1317 (in Radosavljevic, "Some Observations," 41).
287. See, *inter alia, Situation in the Congo*, Prosecution's Reply on the Applications for Participation 01/04-1/dp to 01/04-6/dp of August 15, 2005, Case No. ICC-01/04-84, para. 32.
288. Ambos, "Defenses in International Criminal Law," 303.
289. Part 12 CJA 2003; Ashworth, *Sentencing and Criminal Justice*, 6.
290. Section 207 CJA 2003.
291. Section 37 Mental Health Act 1983.
292. Ashworth, "General Principles of Criminal Law," 1062.
293. Albrecht, "Sentencing in Germany," 213.
294. §63 StGB.
295. §66 StGB.
296. Osterheider, "Germany," 154.
297. Ibid.
298. Schabas, *International Criminal Court*, 484.
299. Krug, "Emerging Mental Incapacity Defense," 334.
300. Art. 103 ICC Statute.
301. Art. 103(1)(a) ICC Statute: "A sentence of imprisonment shall be served in a State designated by the Court from a list of States which have indicated to the Court their willingness to accept sentenced persons."
302. Art. 106(1) ICC Statute: "The enforcement of a sentence of imprisonment shall be subject to the supervision of the Court and shall be consistent with widely accepted international treaty standards governing treatment of prisoners."
303. Krug, "Emerging Mental Incapacity Defense," 334.

Resources

Albrecht, Hans-Joerg, "Sentencing in Germany: Explaining Long-Term Stability in the Structure of Criminal Sanctions and Sentencing." *Law and Contemporary Problems* 76(2013): 211–36.

Allen, Michael, *Textbook on Criminal Law*. Oxford: Oxford University Press, 2007.

Ambos, Kai, "Defenses in International Criminal Law." In *Research Handbook on International Criminal Law*, edited by Bartram S. Brown (Cheltenham, UK: Edward Elgar, 2011), 299–329.

Arendt, Hannah, *Eichmann in Jerusalem: A Report on the Banality of Evil*. New York: Viking, 1963.

Ashworth, Andrew, "General Principles of Criminal Law." In *English Public Law*, edited by David Feldman (Oxford: Oxford University Press, 2009), 1059–85.

Ashworth, Andrew, *Principles of Criminal Law*, 6th ed. Oxford: Oxford University Press, 2009.

Ashworth, Andrew. *Sentencing and Criminal Justice*, 4th ed. Cambridge: Cambridge University Press, 2005.

Ashworth. Andrew J., "United Kingdom." In *The Handbook of Comparative Criminal Law*, edited by Kevin Jon Heller and Markus Dubber (Stanford, CA: Stanford Law Books, 2011), 531–62.

Bassiouni, M. Cherif, "International Criminal Justice in the Age of Globalization." *Nouvelles Études Pénales* 19(2004): 79–155.

Bassiouni, M. Cherif, *Introduction to International Criminal Law*. Ardsley, NY: Transnational Publishers, 2003.

Bohlander, Michael, *Principles of German Criminal Law*. Oxford: Hart Publishing, 2009.

Boister, Neil, and Robert Cryer, *The Tokyo International Military Tribunal: A Reappraisal*. Oxford: Oxford University Press, 2008.

Cryer, Robert, et al., *An Introduction to International Criminal Law and Procedure*. Cambridge: Cambridge University Press, 2010.

D'Ascoli, Silvia, *Sentencing in International Criminal Law: The UN Ad Hoc Tribunals and Future Perspectives for the ICC*. Oxford: Hart Publishing, 2011.

Damaska, Mirjan R., "What Is the Point of International Criminal Justice?" *Chicago-Kent Law Review* 83(2008): 329–64.

De Cruz, Peter, *Comparative Law in a Changing World*, 2nd ed. London: Cavendish Publishing Limited, 1999.

Eser, Albin, "'Defenses' in War Crime Trials." In *War Crimes in International Law*, edited by Yoram Dinstein and Mala Tabory (The Hague: Martinus Nijhoff Publishers, 1996), 251–73.

Eser, Albin, "Article 31: Grounds for Excluding Criminal Responsibility." In *Commentary on the Rome Statute of the International Criminal Court: Observer's Notes, Article by Article* (2nd ed.), edited by Otto Triffterer (Oxford: Hart Publishing, 2008), 863–93.

Fisher, Kirsten J., *Moral accountability and International Criminal Law: Holding Agents of Atrocity Accountable to the World*. Abingdon, UK: Routledge, 2013.

Fletcher, George P., "The Right and the Reasonable." *Harvard Law Review* 98(1985): 949–82.

Freckelton, Ian, and Magda Karagiannakis, "Mental State Defenses Before the International Criminal Tribunal of the Former Yugoslavia." *Psychiatry, Psychology and Law* 12(2005): 249–55.

Gallant, Kenneth S., "Individual Human Rights in a New International Organization: The Rome Statute of the International Criminal Court." *International Criminal Law* 3(1999): 693–723.

Hare, Robert D., "Psychopathy and Antisocial Personality Disorder: A Case of Diagnostic Confusion." Psychiatric Times, February 1, 1996, available at http://www.psychiatrictimes.com/antisocial-personality-disorder/psychopathy-and-antisocial-personality-disorder-case-diagnostic-confusion.

Heller, Kevin Jon, *The Nuremberg Military Tribunals and the Origins of International Criminal Law*. Oxford: Oxford University Press, 2011.

Heller, Kevin Jon, and Markus Dubber (eds.), *The Handbook of Comparative Criminal Law*. Stanford, CA: Stanford Law Books, 2011.

Henham, Ralph, "Some Issues for Sentencing in the International Criminal Court." *International and Comparative Law Quarterly* 52(2003): 81–114.

Hess, Martin, Nandor Knust, and Christine Schuon, "Implementation of the Rome Statute in Germany." *Finnish Yearbook of International Law* 16 (2005): 133–62.

Hola, Barbora, "Sentencing of International Crimes at the ICTY and ICTR." *Amsterdam Law Forum* 4(2012): 3–24.

Hungerford-Welch, Peter, *Criminal Procedure and Sentencing*. London: Routledge-Cavendish, 2009.

Janjac, Kristina, *The Mental Element in the Rome Statute of the International Criminal Court*. Nijmegen, Gelderland: Wolf Legal Publishers, 2013.

Janssen, Sander, "Mental Condition Defences in Supranational Criminal Law." *International Criminal Law Review* 4(2004): 83–98.

Jescheck, Hans-Heinrich, "El Principio de Culpabilidad como Fundamento y Límite de la Punibilidad." *Eguzkilore* 9(1995): 25–39.

Jescheck, Hans-Heinrich, and Thomas Weigend, *Lehrbuch des Strafrechts, Allgemeiner Teil*. Berlin: Duncker & Humblot, 1996.

Jones, John R.W.D., and Steven Powles, *International Criminal Practice*, 3rd ed. Oxford: Oxford University Press, 2003.

Klamberg, Mark, "What are the Objectives of International Criminal Procedure?" *Nordic Journal of International Law* 79(2010): 279–302.

Knoops, Geert-Jan, *Defenses in Contemporary International Criminal Law*. Ardsley, NY: Transnational Publishers, 2001.

Krabbe, Maartje, *Excusable Evil: An Analysis of Complete Defenses in International Criminal Law*. Cambridge: Intersentia, 2014.

Kremnitzer, Mordechai, and Tatjana Hörnle, "Human Dignity and the Principle of Culpability." *Israel Law Review* 44(2011): 115–41.

Krug, Peter, "The Emerging Mental Incapacity Defense in International Criminal Law: Some Initial Questions of Implementation." *American Journal of International Law* 94(2000): 317–35.

Larkin, Jennifer L., "The Insanity Defense Founded on Ethnic Oppression: Defending the Accused in the International Criminal Tribunal for the Former Yugoslavia." *New York Law School Journal of International and Comparative Law* 21(2001): 91–108.

Loughnan, Arlie, "'Manifest Madness': Towards a New Understanding of the Insanity Defence." *Modern Law Review* 70(2007): 379–401.

MacNair, Rachel, *Perpetration-Induced Traumatic Stress: The Psychological Consequences of Killing*. Westport, CT: Praeger, 2002.

MacNair, Rachel, "Psychological Reverberations for the Killers: Preliminary Historical Evidence for Perpetration-Induced Traumatic Stress." *Journal of Genocide Research* 3(2001): 273–82.

Ohlin, Jens David, "Towards a Unique Theory of International Criminal Sentencing." In *International Criminal Procedure: Towards a Coherent Body of Law*, edited by Goran Sluiter and Sergei Vasiliev (London: Cameron May, 2009), 373–404.

Olleson, Simon P., and Matthew R. Brubacher, "Implementation of the Rome Statute in the United Kingdom." *Finnish Yearbook of International Law* 16(2005): 235–60.

Ormerod, David, *Smith and Hogan's Criminal Law*, 12th ed. Oxford: Oxford University Press, 2008.

Osterheider, Michael, and Bernd Dimmek, "Germany." In European Commission & Central Institute of Mental Health of Mannheim, *Placement and Treatment of Mentally Ill Offenders, Legislation and Practice in EU Member States* (Mannheim, 2005), 152–60.

Perlin, Michael L., "Unpacking the Myths: The Symbolism Mythology of Insanity Defense Jurisprudence." *Case Western Reserve Law Review* 40(1990): 599–730.

Radosavljevic, Dragana, "Some Observations on the Lack of a Specific Diminished Responsibility Defense under the ICC Statute." *European Journal of Crime, Criminal Law and Criminal Justice* 19(2011): 37–56.

Raimondo, Fabián Omar, "General Principles of Law as Applied by International Criminal Courts and Tribunals." *Law and Practice of International Courts and Tribunals* 6(2007): 393–406.

Salton, Catherine A., "Mental Incapacity and Liability Insurance Exclusionary Clauses: The Effect of Insanity upon Intent." *California Law Review* 78(1990): 1027–68.

Scaliotti, Massimo, "Defenses Before the International Criminal Court: Substantive Grounds for Excluding Criminal Responsibility, Part 2." *International Criminal Law Review* 2(2002): 1–46.

Schabas, William A., *Genocide in International Law*. Cambridge: Cambridge University Press, 2000.
Schabas, William A., *The International Criminal Court: A Commentary on the Rome Statute*. Oxford: Oxford University Press, 2010.
Schabas, William A., "Sentencing by International Tribunals: A Human Rights Approach." *Duke Journal of Comparative and International Law* 7(1997): 461–517.
Simester, Andrew, *Criminal Law: Theory and Doctrine*, Oregon: Hart, 2000.
Smeulers, Alette, "Perpetrators of International Crimes: Towards a Typology." In *Supranational Criminology: Towards a Criminology of International Crimes*, edited by Alette Smeulers and Roelof Haveman (Cambridge: Intersentia, 2008), 233–65.
Smeulers, Alette, and Wouter Werner, "The Banality of Evil on Trial." In *Future Perspectives on International Criminal Justice*, edited by Carsten Stahn and Larissa van den Herik (The Hague: TMC Asser Press, 2010), 24–43.
Smith, A.T.H., "On Actus Reus and Mens Rea." In *Reshaping the Criminal Law: Essays in Honour of Glanville Williams*, edited by P.R. Glazebrook (London: Stevens and Sons, 1978), 95–107.
Sparr, Landy F., "Personality Disorders and Criminal Law: An International Perspective." *Journal of the American Academy of Psychiatry and the Law* 37(2009): 168–81.
Streng, Franz, "Sentencing in Germany: Basic Questions and New Developments." *German Law Journal* 8(2007): 153–72.
Sunga, Lyal S., *The Emerging System of International Criminal Law: Developments in Codification and Implementation*. The Hague: Kluwer Law International, 1997.
Van Sliedregt, Elies, *Individual Criminal Responsibility in International Law*. Oxford: Oxford University Press, 2012.
Waller, James, *Becoming Evil*. Oxford: Oxford University Press, 2007.
Weber, Mark, "The Legacy of Rudolf Hess." *Journal of Historical Review* 13(1993): 20–23.
Weigend, Thomas, "Germany." In *The Handbook of Comparative Criminal Law*, edited by Kevin Jon Heller and Markus Dubber (Stanford, CA: Stanford Law Books, 2011), 252–87.
Werle, Gerhard, "Konturen eines deutschen Völkerstrafrechts." *JuristenZeitung* 56(2001): 885–95.
Werle, Gerhard, *Principles of International Criminal Law*. The Hague: TMC Asser Press, 2005.
Werle, Gerhard, and Florian Jessberger, "International Criminal Justice is Coming Home: The New German Code of Crimes against International Law." *Criminal Law Forum* 13(2002): 191–223.
Yee, Sienho, "The Erdemovic Sentencing Judgment: A Questionable Milestone for the International Criminal Tribunal for the Former Yugoslavia." *Georgia Journal of International and Comparative Law* 26(1997): 263–309.

Yeo, Stanley, "The Insanity Defense in the Criminal Laws of the Commonwealth of Nations." *Singapore Journal of Legal Studies* n.v.(2008): 241–63.

Zappalà, Salvatore, *Human Rights in International Criminal Proceedings*. Oxford: Oxford University Press, 2003.

Zolo, Danilo, "Peace Through Criminal Law?" *Journal of International Criminal Justice* 2(2004): 727–34.

CHAPTER TWELVE

Andrea Yates: A Continuing Story about Insanity

Deborah W. Denno

In 2001, Andrea Yates did the unthinkable: she drowned her five children one by one in a bathtub within the course of minutes. Immediately thereafter she called 9-1-1 and then her husband Rusty to confess.[1] "No," she did not hate her children, she explained to the police. Nor was she angry at them.[2] She had, however, considered killing her children for two years because she did not want them "tormented by Satan" as she was.[3] She revealed that Satan had been conveying "bad thoughts" to her and she was concerned he would entice her children into his evil ways. She believed Satan was "inside [her] giving [her] directions . . . about harming the children . . . about a way out—to drown them." If she successfully killed her children, however, they "would go up to heaven and be with God, be safe."[4] She also realized that she was not a good mother and "that it was time to be punished" by the criminal justice system. In Yates' mind, Satan had selected her children because of Yates' own personal "weaknesses."[5] Only later would her defense uncover a substantial array of evidence showing her long history of postpartum depression and postpartum psychosis, along with her many cries for help from the mental health system.[6]

Less than a year after the drownings, in 2002, a jury in Harris County, Texas, convicted Yates of capital murder and sentenced her to life in prison.[7] Although the prosecution had requested the death penalty, Yates avoided it because the jury did not consider her a "continuing threat to society."[8] At the same time, the jury did not accept the defense's argument that Yates was insane, or that Yates thought she was under Satan's influence at the time she drowned her children. Rather, they sided with the prosecution's account that Yates was sane and acting intentionally when she killed her children even though the prosecution's experts also believed that Yates was often psychotic.[9] The most persuasive proponent of this account was Park Dietz, M.D., the prosecution's star expert witness.[10] He pushed the view that Yates had rationally planned the murders and had manipulated postpartum stress and hospitalizations to get Rusty to buy her a house (the family was living in a cramped school bus) and to take a break from caring for her children.[11] Yet the extent of Dietz's speculation about Yates was troubling. There was little, if any, empirical basis for his conclusions, and he clearly lacked expertise in postpartum depression and postpartum psychosis.[12]

In 2003 I published an article on the Andrea Yates trial and sentencing in which I focused on Dietz's questionable and undocumented testimony, particularly as it pertained to postpartum illnesses.[13] As it would so happen, Yates' defense attorneys discovered an additional problem with Dietz's testimony. After the verdict but before the punishment phase of the trial, the defense learned that Dietz had introduced false testimony during the trial. Although the defense moved for a mistrial based on this newly found information, the trial court denied the motion and allowed the trial to proceed.[14]

The error involved Dietz's testimony during cross-examination in which Yates' defense attorney, George Parnham, asked Dietz if he was a consultant for the television show, *Law & Order*.[15] Dietz said that he was a consultant on two of the *Law & Order* programs. When the defense asked if either program concerned "postpartum depression or women's mental health," Dietz responded as follows: "As a matter of fact, there was a show of a woman with postpartum depression who drowned her children in the bathtub and was found insane and it was aired shortly before [Andrea Yates'] crime occurred."[16] Yet the defense discovered no such show existed. The producer of *Law & Order* and his lawyer could not verify such a show ever aired, and Dietz ultimately admitted "he had made an error."[17] Unaware of Dietz's error, the prosecution used Dietz's incorrect statement in the cross examination of a defense psychiatrist, who stated, when asked, that she would have questioned Yates differently had she known of the show.[18] The prosecution also used Dietz's reference in closing arguments, suggesting that Yates was not only influenced by the *Law & Order* episode but that she also viewed its strategies as a "way out."[19]

Concern over Dietz's testimony prompted a grand jury investigation of whether he should be charged with perjury.[20] In 2003, however, a year after Yates' sentencing, a Harris County grand jury declined to indict Dietz for perjury after Dietz appeared before them and answered questions about his testimony.[21] Grand jury members accepted Dietz's explanation that his *Law & Order* testimony was an "innocent mistake."[22] Regardless, the defense appealed Yates' sentence. In 2005 the Texas Court of Appeals acknowledged the degree of Dietz's impact on the jury. Given that Dietz "was the only mental health expert who testified that [Andrea knew] right from wrong" and that the prosecution relied on the error during trial, the Texas Court of Appeals determined that Dietz's "testimony was critical to establish the State's case."[23] There was also "a reasonable likelihood that Dr. Dietz's false testimony could have affected the judgment of the jury" and that "the trial court abused its discretion in denying [Andrea's] motion for mistrial."[24] As a result, the Texas Court of Appeals reversed the trial court's judgment and remanded the case for further proceedings.[25]

The second trial of Andrea Yates during the summer of 2006 showed substantial differences from the first trial, particularly because the death penalty was no longer an option.[26] Because the jury in the first trial had sentenced Yates to life, prosecutors in the second trial could not ask for death.[27] While "[t]he basic thrust" of Dietz's testimony and that of the key defense expert, Phillip Resnick, M.D., "was unchanged from the first trial,"[28] the jury and the social-legal atmosphere were different.[29] In the first trial, for example, Yates' jury was "death qualified."[30] *Death qualification* means that the prosecution could exclude potential jurors for cause if they were so ambivalent or negative about the death penalty that it would impair their decision making and ability to apply the law.[31] Research shows that death qualified juries are generally more punitive and more likely to convict than juries that are not death qualified.[32] In Yates' second trial, however, the jury was not death qualified and thus presumably more inclined to support an insanity defense.[33]

There were other differences between the two trials. After Yates' 2002 conviction, there was an enormous amount of publicity accompanying her case and life circumstances. News articles accentuated the medical and social underpinnings of postpartum depression and psychosis as well as the need to better educate the public and mental health professionals about mental illness and the health care system. The legal and medical community also rallied for more information and training, which resonates to the present day.[34] In addition, by this time, Yates was housed in Skyview Penitentiary, where the warden provided her the best mental health care available in his facility. Therefore the defense could more easily present

Yates as an inmate with mental health issues.[35] Finally, two other women in Texas had been found not guilty by reason of insanity for killing their children between the time of Yates' first and second trials. Because these women's circumstances were so similar to Yates', their more lenient treatment raised further questions about why Yates' case was treated so differently.[36]

The momentum of this publicity and support for Yates bolstered the defense and most likely influenced the jury in her second trial. After 12 hours of deliberation, the jury unanimously found Yates not guilty by reason of insanity.[37] It appeared this second jury could distinguish between Yates' true mental state and what seemed to be her planned and rational conduct on the day that she killed her children.[38] As the jury foreman explained, "'We understand that she knew it was legally wrong. But in her delusional mind . . . we believed that she thought what she did was right.'"[39]

After the second jury trial, Yates was initially committed to North Texas State Hospital, Vernon Campus, a high-security mental health facility.[40] She was transferred in 2007 to Kerrville State Hospital, a low-security mental hospital, where she remains.[41] In 2012, Yates applied to the Houston district court to leave the hospital for two hours each week to attend church services; however, the judge denied her request.[42] Similarly, in 2015, Yates and her doctors requested a judge to allow her to leave Kerrville for supervised group outings with other patients, such as picnics.[43] Yet Yates' doctors revoked the request in light of a rash of negative commentary about her from the press and the public; they "fear[ed] that any good that would come from the outings would be outweighed by the crush of criticism over the decision."[44] For now, Yates comes up for review in the district court every year until the time she may be discharged (if ever).[45]

The Andrea Yates case produced a mixed impact on the world of law and medicine. On the one hand, the case helped wake the world to the reality and pervasiveness of postpartum depression and psychosis.[46] After Yates' first trial, for example, George Parnham and his wife established the Yates Children Memorial Fund. The purpose of the Fund is to provide guidance to medical professionals on how to detect potential symptoms of postpartum depression and psychosis in new mothers.[47] The Parnhams were also instrumental in the creation of the Andrea Yates Law. Enacted in 2003, the law mandates hospitals and medical personnel to notify patients about postpartum challenges.[48]

There are other areas of law and medicine, however, where the Yates case has shown no impact. Most critically, there have been no substantive changes in Texas insanity law[49] since the time of Yates' first trial even though the Texas standard is among the narrowest in the country.[50] As the rest of this chapter explains in more detail, the state's definition of insanity influenced the first trial and both constrained and confused how the jury could view her actions. For example, both the prosecution and the defense agreed that Yates was mentally ill and, in general, that she knew her actions were legally wrong. Yet the issue of whether her mental illness rendered her unable to control her actions, although hotly debated, was moot under the extreme confines of the Texas insanity statute. Therefore, in both the first and second trials, only one key question was left for the jury to resolve: Did Yates know that her actions were morally wrong? The following pages provide the backdrop for answering that question.*

1 Andrea Yates, the Original Story

In 2003, everyone knew the story about the highly publicized case of Andrea Yates. Or at least they thought they did. Yates, high school valedictorian, swim team champion, college graduate, and registered nurse married Russell ("Rusty") Yates in 1993 after a four-year courtship. Both were 28. Over the next seven years, Andrea gave birth to five children and suffered one miscarriage, all the while plunging deeper into mental illness. Then on June 20, 2001, in less than an hour, Andrea drowned all of her children in the bathtub, one by one. Months later, she was convicted of capital murder in Harris County, Texas, where she now serves a life sentence.

Some may think that a mentally ill mother who committed such an act should be judged insane. Yet, news accounts and court records suggest that Yates impaired her attorneys' efforts to plead insanity. Such defense plans were already encumbered by the unusually strict Texas insanity standard and the state's renowned retributive culture. After a jury found her competent to stand trial, she resented the efforts that her attorneys mounted on her behalf even as she faced possible execution. Yates insisted there was nothing wrong with her mind and that she deserved to die. She seemed to be awaiting punishment for her sins.

To those closest to Yates, this self-blaming reaction came as no surprise. They could testify that she had been tormented by bouts of mental illness, and, in fact, both the prosecution and defense agreed that she was mentally ill. Yates' life was also distinguished by religious obsession and a steadfast devotion to tales of sin and Scripture, a "repent-or-burn zeal" that led her to believe she was a bad mother with ruined offspring. According to Yates, she killed her children to save them from Satan and her own evil maternal

---

*What follows is adapted from Denno, "Who is Andrea Yates?" (The footnotes and appendices have been removed to enhance narrative flow; the interested reader is referred to the original article for those details.)

influences, delusions that did little to help her defense because they fueled her own desire for punishment.

Public opinion on the Yates killings helps explain some of the more contradictory themes in the case. On the one hand, the public had much sympathy for Yates and the life that she led. Yet, her composed behavior on the day she killed her children stirred a strong retributive response. Many were unable to comprehend such violence except by declaring it intentional and evil. According to this view, it could be said that Yates was supremely sane—her acts rational and premeditated—despite her unquestioned history of postpartum psychosis. She propelled this account, spurring the public, her "jury," to see her as the Satanic mother she believed herself to be.

These complex and conflicting aspects of the Yates case fed into the prosecution's depiction of her mental state on the day she killed her children. But, one psychiatrist's testimony seemed to have a greater impact than the others on the case's outcome. The prosecution's star expert, Park Dietz, appeared particularly adept at persuading the jury to accept the prosecution's assertion that Yates was sane and acting intentionally when she killed her children. Because the Yates case is on appeal, many of the court records are not available. In addition, the defense team still lacks funds to pay for the entire trial transcript so it too cannot be examined. Dietz's testimony, however, is now accessible and it warrants a thorough analysis in its own right.

What is most striking about Dietz's testimony is how his opinions about Yates' mental state could carry so much authority with the jury. Criminal trials commonly involve different sides presenting competing legal "stories" about their version of the facts. The law's role is to ensure that just verdicts result from these conflicting representations. Courts must be perceived "as fair and disinterested, capable of rising above the self-serving and adversarial narratives by which cases are presented." While the law provides evidentiary standards and procedures to oversee what information is released in court and how, an immense amount of discretion exists nonetheless in the ways stories can be told. It remains unclear who is to police these narratives—beyond the structures already in place—or whether such oversight is even needed.

In the Yates case, the defense claimed that her mental illness caused her to believe that killing her children was the right course of action. Although Yates' attorneys called a number of experts to prove their argument, each expert had a different twist on this central viewpoint. Therefore, the defense's story about Yates, while emphasizing her insanity, was still somewhat muddled. In contrast, the prosecution's story about Yates' sanity was clearer and also apparently consistent with the cultural norms of Harris

County, Texas. The prosecution argued that Yates may have been gripped by her belief in some demonic command, but she was still fully capable of knowing she was doing something wrong. And Yates seemed to concur, damningly perhaps. Her story was congruent with the prosecution's. She had sinned and deserved punishment for acting out the devil's dictates. In all likelihood, however, Yates' own story was indicative of her mental illness, not evidence of the disposition she felt she most deserved. Nonetheless, both her narrative and that of the prosecution were accentuated by courtroom storyteller, Park Dietz.

This chapter analyzes the problematic aspects of Dietz's testimony in an effort to contribute some balance to the Andrea Yates story. While Dietz's comments may have confirmed the Harris County jury's preconceptions, they were virtually unsubstantiated. Dietz also has no significant expertise in postpartum depression or psychosis even though both sides agreed that Yates severely suffered from the disorders and that they significantly affected her conduct.

Of course, expert witnesses are routinely used in litigation. Dietz is simply one of the more prominent and prolific examples of what the criminal justice system seeks. Despite the long history of expert witnesses in criminal trials, the justice system should question the fairness and efficacy of such an unregulated storytelling process. The potential for inequity is all the more pronounced in a case where the prosecution's story lacks factual justification, both sides agree the defendant is mentally ill, and the death penalty is at stake.

Section 2 of the rest of this chapter briefly discusses Yates' life up to her marriage to Rusty as well as the outcome of her trial. Section 3 provides an overview of the insanity defense and the strict Texas insanity standard. Section 4 examines Dietz's background, his reputation, and his psychiatric philosophy, in addition to his proclivity to testify for the prosecution. Section 5 describes Yates' history of mental illness, especially her postpartum psychosis that started with the birth of her first child and ended with a severe psychotic episode. Section 6 focuses on Dietz's testimony in the Yates trial, beginning with his pre-trial interview with Yates and ending with an analysis of his conclusions. The discussion emphasizes the speculative nature of many of Dietz's statements and their lack of connection to Yates' history of mental illness. Section 7 presents the other perspectives and experts in the Yates case, and considers how the case might have reached a different result with a more consistent defense strategy or a less rigid insanity standard.

The Andrea Yates case is a vast, book-length narrative. This commentary covers just a part of the trial. It is beyond this chapter's scope, for example, to scrutinize the general role of psychiatric experts in the criminal justice system or to review the research on postpartum depression and postpartum psychosis, which is available elsewhere. Nonetheless, examining one piece of the Yates story can be enlightening. "Narrative, we are finally coming to realize, is indeed serious business—whether in law, in literature, or in life."

2 The Early Life and Trial of Andrea Yates

2.1 Meet the Yates Family

Andrea Yates was raised in the Houston area. Her family background appeared to be middle-American and middle class. Her father was a retired auto shop teacher who died of Alzheimer's disease shortly before the killings. Her mother, Jutta Karin, was a homemaker. Yates, the youngest of five, was expected to be a high achiever and, in high school, she succeeded: she was captain of the swim team, a National Honor Society member, and valedictorian of her 1982 graduating class. Upon completing a two-year pre-nursing program at the University of Houston, she went on to the University of Texas School of Nursing in Houston, graduating in 1986. From 1986 to 1994, she was employed as a registered nurse at the University of Texas M.D. Anderson Cancer Center. Andrea's nursing career ceased entirely, however, soon after her marriage to Rusty.

Andrea and Rusty first met in 1989 at the Houston apartment complex where they both resided. Both were 25 at the time. Rusty, "a popular jock" in high school and a summa cum laude graduate of Auburn University, was designing computer systems for NASA. Andrea approached him first in conversation—an uncharacteristically bold move for her, Rusty would later reveal. Only after Andrea's arrest would Rusty learn that she had never dated until she had turned 23, that she was recuperating from a romantic break-up at the time they met, and that her directness in initiating contact with him was prompted by intense loneliness and, perhaps, depression. Andrea and Rusty spent the next few years becoming acquainted, "living together, reading the Bible, and praying."

Their April 17, 1993, wedding ceremony was small and simple. Surprisingly, it was also nondenominational, perhaps because of the influence of Rusty's spiritual mentor, Michael Woroniecki, from whom "he had learned the faults of organized religion." The couple confidently announced to wedding guests that they would not use birth control—they wanted as many children as nature would provide. Their desire for children was immediately fulfilled. Within three months, Andrea was pregnant with the first of five children. Eight years later she would kill them all.

2.2 The Yates Trial

On July 30, 2001, Yates was indicted on two counts of capital murder for the deaths of Noah (seven), John (five), and Mary (six months), but not for the deaths of her other two children, Luke (three) and Paul (two). All of the indictments were for capital murder because they involved more than one person and victims less than six years old. On the same day, Yates' attorneys, George Parnham and Wendell Odom, filed a "notice of intent to offer evidence of the insanity defense," based upon the testimony of two psychiatrists claiming that Yates was, at the time of the killings, "mentally insane" as defined by the Texas Penal Code.

The insanity defense for Yates would ultimately dissolve. Within eight months following her indictment, one jury decided that Yates was sufficiently competent to stand trial for killing her children and another refused her insanity plea. Although this second jury declined to impose the death penalty, Yates received a mandatory life sentence for the killings. Under the Texas capital felony statute, an inmate must serve forty years in prison before becoming eligible for parole. The case is currently on appeal.

Many theories could explain Yates' conviction. Of course, the primary theory would speculate that the jury was so horrified by her acts that any psychiatric evidence offered on her behalf paled in comparison. Yet, the continuing controversy and debate over Yates' conviction suggest that there may be other, more complex, explanations.

Additional rationales primarily point to the retributive aspects of Texas law and culture. As one Harris County resident explained, "There's the rule of law, and there's the rule of law in Texas. . . . The rule of law in Texas is kind of cowboy law." For example, Texas consistently executes more individuals than any other state; annually it accounts for one-third of all executions in the country, a pattern that conflicts with both national and international abolitionist trends. Harris County in particular is responsible for over one-third of the state's death row inmates, making it the harshest death penalty jurisdiction in the country and one of the most punitive in the Western world. If Harris County were considered a state, it would follow only two other states (Texas and Virginia) in its number of executions since 1977.

Because the Yates prosecution sought the death penalty, the jury was "death qualified." In other words, the prosecution could exclude potential jurors for cause if their negative views toward the death penalty were so strong they "would 'prevent or substantially impair the performance of [their] duties as [jurors]'" and therefore render them "unable to faithfully and impartially apply the law." Research shows that death qualified juries are more anti-civil libertarian in attitude, particularly with respect to such principles as presumption of innocence and burden of proof, and they are significantly more likely to convict than juries that are not death qualified. Presumably, then, Yates' jury was far less able to "comprehend the inconceivable" in evaluating an insanity defense relative to a jury that had not been death qualified.

The Texas insanity standard is a comparably strict rule of law; in the eyes of one legal commentator, it is "one of the most stringent" in the United States. The Yates jury judged psychiatric testimony not only by Texas culture but also by that culture's narrow legal view of what constitutes insanity.

3 The Insanity Defense

3.1 A Brief Overview of the Insanity Defense

This section explores only the very basics of the insanity defense and how it is applied in the state of Texas. The insanity defense is considered one of the most controversial criminal law doctrines, not only because of intense debate over how "insanity" should be defined, but also because of increasing conflict over whether the defense should exist in any form. Statistics show that insanity pleas are seldom raised or successful in states throughout the country, including Texas. Nonetheless, the defense rankles social and community tensions over two conflicting goals: the desire to punish the horrendous, highly publicized crimes that the public typically hears about versus the need to understand that some mentally ill people should not be held responsible for what they do.

3.1.1 The Major Legal Standards for Insanity

The legal standard for insanity varies across the 50 states. The first and strictest insanity test of modern usage was introduced in 1843 by the English House of Lords in the M'Naghten case. Under M'Naghten, a person is insane if, because of a "disease of the mind" at the time she committed the act, she (1) did not know the "nature and quality of the act" that she was performing; or (2) if she was aware of the act, she did not know that what she "was doing was wrong," that is, she did not know the difference between right and wrong. The M'Naghten Rule, which soon became the most widely accepted insanity test in the United States, considers only cognitive ability and not volitional conduct.

Concern over the narrowness of the M'Naghten test prompted attempts over the years to replace it. The most successful attempt was the American

Law Institute (ALI)'s 1962 insanity test, which rapidly gained support from legislatures and courts; by the 1980s, the ALI standard was adopted nearly unanimously by the federal circuit courts and over one-half of the states. Under the ALI test, an individual is not responsible for her criminal conduct if, because of mental disease or defect, she either lacked "substantial capacity" to appreciate the "criminality" (or, at the opting of the state legislature, the "wrongfulness") of her conduct, or she failed to "conform" her conduct "to the requirements of law."

The differences between the ALI and M'Naghten tests are striking. For example, the ALI test accepts both cognitive and volitional impairment as an excuse. In other words, the test considers a defendant's cognitive ability to "appreciate" the criminality or wrongfulness of her conduct as well as her ability to "conform" her conduct to the law. This added "conform" requirement is often characterized as a "lack-of-control defense," pertaining to those individuals whose mental disease or defect leads them to lose control over their actions at the time they commit an offense.

The ALI and M'Naghten standards vary in other important ways. The ALI test requires only that defendants "lack substantial capacity," not total capacity. In turn, the ALI applies the broader term "appreciate" rather than "know" when specifying the type of cognitive impairment that leads to insanity; hence, the defendant's lack of emotional understanding can be incorporated into the defense. The ALI test also allows the state legislature to consider "wrongfulness" rather than "criminality." This choice enables a finding of insanity if the accused does not know the act was illegal and also if she believes the act was "morally justified" according to community standards. At the same time, both the ALI and M'Naghten tests skirt any set definition of the term "mental disease or defect." According to the ALI, such an open-ended approach allows the term "to accommodate developing medical understanding" and therefore avoid the constraints of old science.

The popularity of the ALI test dwindled in 1981 when a jury found John Hinckley not guilty by reason of insanity, based on an ALI standard, for his attempted assassination of Ronald Reagan. The effects of the public furor over Hinckley's acquittal were immediate: the federal government and several of the ALI test states abolished the volitional component of the test entirely and imposed other limits, in some cases reverting back to a M'Naghten-type standard. According to a 1995 survey of insanity laws, about twenty states still use the ALI test while nearly half of the states apply "some variation of the M'Naghten/cognitive impairment-only test." A handful of states have abolished the insanity defense entirely.

3.1.2 Modern Problems with the M'Naghten Insanity Standard

The return to a M'Naghten-type standard spotlights the problems that the test has always had and why there have been continuing efforts to change it. For example, the word "know" and the phrase "nature and quality of the act" can be defined either very broadly or narrowly. Such vagueness gives legal actors little guidance for interpreting the test and heightens the chance that they will apply it inconsistently across different cases. Likewise, it is not clear whether the "wrong" in the right-and-wrong prong pertains to legal or moral wrongdoing because the language in M'Naghten itself could bolster either approach. England has since established that the right-and-wrong element represents the defendant's recognition that an act is legally wrong. Yet, American law sides in the opposite direction. Most American courts have interpreted the word "wrong" to mean "moral wrong," not "legal wrong." This issue was important in the Yates case because Texas law does not specify a particular approach and a moral wrong approach would have benefited her. According to some defense experts, Yates knew that her acts were illegal but she believed they were morally right, given the context of her delusional circumstances.

In American states that apply the moral right-and-wrong test, questions typically concern whether the defendant knowingly transgressed society's standards of morality, not whether the defendant personally perceived her acts to be morally acceptable. In other words, even if a defendant is mentally ill and, as a result, commits an offense that she believes is morally correct, she is considered sane if she is aware that her conduct is condemned by society. As one commentator notes, however, this difference can "be blurred to near extinction" depending on how the particular circumstances in a case are pitched. For example, a mentally ill individual "is apt to know that society considers it morally wrong to kill, but if she is acting pursuant to a delusionary belief that God wants her to kill, she might now believe that society would agree with her God-endorsed actions."

Interpretation of the moral-right-and-wrong standard can vary somewhat in the few M'Naghten jurisdictions that have a "deific decree doctrine," in other words, a rule that allows a mentally disordered defendant to be judged legally insane if she believes that she is acting under the direct command of God (for example, a belief that God commanded the defendant to kill someone). Two primary rationales explain the origins of the deific decree doctrine. First, the doctrine "was merely a logical extension of the Judeo-Christian belief that God would not order a person to kill another" because the Sixth Commandment prohibits murder. Therefore, a person thinking that God is commanding her to kill is entertaining a false belief and thus should not be held accountable. Likewise, 19th-century courts and juries would not grant the insanity defense to individuals contending that they acted under the command of the Devil or some other religiously corrupt figure because people accepted only "the One True God." Second, the doctrine may have been a vehicle for inserting a volitional component exception to the cognitive-only limitations of the M'Naghten Rule so that M'Naghten could incorporate at least a narrow category of uncontrolled individuals.

The exceptions and qualifications for the deific decree doctrine apparently still apply today for defendants experiencing such "command hallucinations." The doctrine presumes that the defendant's behavior results from a delusion (a "false belief based on incorrect inference about external reality"), and not from a religious conviction, although determining the difference between the two can be very difficult. While some jurisdictions treat the deific decree rule as an exception to the general insanity standard, other jurisdictions view it as a major factor in assessing an individual's capability to tell right from wrong. Irrespective of a jurisdiction's particular approach, these right-wrong issues were key in the Andrea Yates case. Yates' command hallucinations were a focus of the expert testimony and what was supposed to be considered "wrong" was neither specified, nor constrained, in the jury charge.

3.2 The Texas Insanity Standard

In 1973, Texas joined the ranks of other states and adopted the more lenient ALI definition of insanity. A decade later, however, the state returned to a M'Naghten-type standard, partly in response to developments surrounding the Hinckley verdict. Yet, a critical feature of the Texas test is that it is even narrower than M'Naghten, although comparably confusing. The typical M'Naghten standard refers to two parts: the defendant's ability to know (1) the "nature and quality of the act committed" or (2) whether the act was "right or wrong." The Texas standard, however, eliminates the first part and refers only to the second, that is, whether the defendant knew the act was right or wrong. Texas also limits the defense to cases of severe mental illness and puts the burden of proving insanity on defendants. As legal commentators rightly contend, the Texas standard "could hardly be narrower" or more "impossible to meet."

Similar to the M'Naghten standard, defining the terms "right" and "wrong" is a problem. For example, the Texas insanity statute does not clarify whether "wrong" should be considered from a legal or a moral standpoint. This ambiguity was a key issue in the Yates case, both for the law and the psychiatric profession. As one psychiatric expert commenting on the case said, there is still no "test" available to determine who is genuinely controlled by command hallucinations; rather, psychiatrists must rely on "a certain degree of approximation" in their assessments. Likewise, the Yates jury charge did not specify what "wrong" should mean and expert testimony did not seem to restrict the definition of "wrongfulness." The Yates jury was free to use the term's "common and ordinary meaning" and apply "the statutory language to the facts as it saw fit."

Such a legally muddled circumstance prompted conflicting approaches to interpreting the Texas insanity standard. As the Yates case evolved, for example, it became clear that both the prosecution and the defense would define the legal-or-moral wrong issue because of the statute's silence. Both sides agreed that Yates was mentally ill and, in general, that she knew her actions were legally wrong. The issue of whether Yates' mental illness rendered her unable to control her actions, although hotly debated, was moot under the narrow confines of the Texas insanity statute. Thus, only one significant question was left for the jury to resolve: Did Yates know that her actions were morally wrong?

4 Park Dietz's Expertise and Psychiatric Philosophy

There was little legal or psychiatric clarity guiding the determinations to be made in the Yates case. For this reason, the opinions of expert witnesses were especially important. According to a synopsis of the ethical guidelines established by the American Academy of Psychiatry and the Law, "the medical expert is expected to provide a clinical evaluation and a review of the applicable data in light of the legal question posed and in the spirit of honesty and striving for objectivity—the expert's ethical and professional obligation." The Academy specifies that such an obligation "includes a thorough, fair, and impartial review and should not exclude any relevant information in order to create a view favoring either the plaintiff or the defendant."

According to some legal commentators, Park Dietz's expert testimony was considered "crucial" for the conviction of Andrea Yates—the "defining moment" of the trial. Section 4 examines Dietz's background, experience, and psychiatric philosophy in an effort to explain why Dietz's story about Yates seemed so much more compelling than the other stories experts had to offer. Notably, much of the information about Dietz derives from interviews with Dietz himself, or from his supporters, in magazines and newspapers. Dietz is commendably forthright about his views in general and was immediately open to commenting on the Yates case as soon as she was sentenced. What becomes apparent is how his own self-described, pro-prosecution leanings could mesh so well with a death-qualified Harris County jury.

4.1 Dietz's Background and Reputation

Park Dietz is considered one of the most "prominent and provocative" psychiatric expert witnesses in the country. In one professional capacity or another, he has been involved with a long list of famous homicide defendants: John Hinckley, Jr., Jeffrey Dahmer, Susan Smith, Melissa Drexler, the Menendez brothers, O.J. Simpson (in the civil case), and Ted Kaczynski, to name a few. He can now add Andrea Yates to that list. As the prosecution's star witness in the Yates case, he both interviewed and videotaped her, and he subsequently testified in court about his evaluation.

Dietz also has extensive professional credentials. He acquired a BA from Cornell University in biology and psychology, an MD from Johns Hopkins School of Medicine, and a Masters in Public Health and PhD in sociology, both from Johns Hopkins. He has held academic posts at Johns Hopkins, the University of Pennsylvania, Harvard, and the University of Virginia. His professional experience is substantial, including consulting positions with the Department of Justice and the Federal Bureau of Investigation. In addition, Dietz has over one hundred publications, "nearly all" of which concern violent or injurious behavior, and he has examined "thousands" of criminal defendants for forensic psychiatric purposes, including sanity determinations.

Currently (and at the time he testified in the Yates trial), Dietz runs two businesses in Newport Beach, California. He is the president and founder of Park Dietz & Associates, Inc., forensic consultants in medicine and the behavioral sciences, as well as president and founder of Threat Assessment Group, Inc. (TAG), which specializes in the prevention of workplace violence. Before arriving in Houston to testify in the Yates case, Dietz mailed his business brochure (describing his companies and the types of cases on which they work) to a wide range of members of Houston's legal community—prosecutors, defense attorneys, attorneys specializing in premises liability for violent crime, and lawyers representing elder abuse victims. Although the Yates defense brought forth evidence of Dietz's brochure distribution during cross-examination in an effort to portray Dietz as a "professional testifier," Dietz did not seem apologetic. Nor did such a revelation appear to dent the perceived validity of his testimony.

4.1.1 A Desire to Emphasize "Facts"

Media articles about Dietz claim he is known for emphasizing "facts" rather than "theoretical conjecture" when evaluating a case. Indeed, both Dr. Jonas Rappeport, a renowned professor of Dietz's at Johns Hopkins Medical School, as well as Roger Adelman, one of the prosecutors in the Hinckley case, credit Dietz's precision and "focus on the facts" as major contributions Dietz has brought to modernizing the field of forensic psychiatry.

In line with this facts-driven orientation, Dietz seems to be more concerned with the physical evidence linked to a crime than with the defendant's history that can be acquired in an interview. According to Dietz, for example, interviews with defendants have typically "been the linchpin of forensic assessments"; yet, there are "serious risks" associated with them because the "natural human techniques for gaining information from an interview unthinkingly cut corners by suggesting answers or guessing at the answer or offering multiple choices." Such leading or suggestive procedures are comparable to crime scene evidence that has been contaminated or corrupted. Dietz favors instead the second source of mental evidence, which includes examining the crime scene, analyzing autopsies and weapons, and interviewing witnesses to the crime. Although "the ideal" would be to have both types of evidence when making an evaluation, Dietz has stated that, "If I had to choose between the interview [with the defendant] only or everything except the interview as a means of getting to the truth, I'd prefer everything except the interview because it would get me to the truth more often."

Dietz's apparent stress on facts, combined with what even Rappeport views as a "rigid" approach towards defendants, has prompted criticism. According to an article about Dietz in *Johns Hopkins Magazine*, "some forensic psychiatrists" have accused him of presenting "mere informed opinion as solid fact, and [complain] that his standard of criminal responsibility is harsh and unforgiving of mentally ill defendants." For example, during his testimony in the Yates case, Dietz indicated that because Yates claimed that Satan, rather than God, told her to kill her children, she knew her actions were wrong. Yates also failed to act in a way a loving mother would if she really thought she was saving her children from hell by killing them. As Dietz stated, "I would expect her to comfort the children, telling them they are going to be with Jesus or be with God, but she does not offer words of comfort to the children." However, there appears to be no empirical support for this kind of interpretation of the deific decree doctrine, if in fact that is what Dietz was referencing. Rather, if Dietz's explanation has any source at all, it seems to derive from the centuries-old, Judeo-Christian origins of the doctrine itself. As one legal critic asked in response to Dietz's comments, "Is one to infer that it is somehow more loving to invoke the name of Jesus while you drown your children than to drown them without any religious commentary?" In other words, Dietz appears to be stressing religion, not facts, a focus more aligned with Southern Bible belt culture rather than with a medical assessment of Yates' mental state.

Even Dietz's supporters have admitted that his inflexible approach may prevent him from being able (or willing) to comprehend "some of the psychological nuances of human behavior." According to Rappeport, a strong advocate, Dietz has the capability to understand and apply knowledge of human behavior, he simply chooses not to. As Rappeport explained, "I have a suspicion he may not like to do that. So he may find himself more frequently on the side of the prosecutor, who doesn't like to do those things either." Such an omission is a troubling handicap in a field where "50 percent or more of medicine is emotional." It is particularly problematic given that the cases that typically involve Dietz's testimony often turn on the very "nuances" that Dietz discounts.

Indeed, in media interviews and his testimony in the Yates case, Dietz has made clear that he does not treat patients in a psychiatry practice. This lack of engagement with patients is "rare" among medical expert witnesses. Rather, Dietz opts to concentrate on research and one-time interviews with criminal defendants. Yet, such a view of the psychiatric world is distorted. For example, it is difficult to comprehend how Dietz can evaluate an individual's normality or abnormality if he only engages in short-term interviews with highly abnormal people. By encountering briefly only the most extreme criminal cases, all Dietz sees is pathology. He has no "control group" as a comparison, no in-depth evaluations of individuals from whom he can learn nuances. Such an approach may explain additional criticisms concerning where Dietz draws the line for distinguishing sanity from insanity. According to Fred S. Berlin, associate professor of psychiatry at Johns Hopkins and one of the defense's psychiatric experts in the Jeffrey Dahmer case, Dietz's line is too stringent. "He has a high threshold for evidence that tends to suggest impairment. A narrow range for what he defines as psychiatric disorder."

Consistent with this view, in the Yates case Dietz minimized the defense expert witnesses' testimony that Yates had suffered years of delusions, auditory hallucinations, and visions of violence. Instead, Dietz claimed that she had, at most, experienced "obsessional intrusive thoughts." Yet, contrary to other high-profile defendants pleading insanity, Yates had a substantial and documented history of mental illness before she killed her children.

Not only had she twice attempted suicide, she had also been hospitalized and prescribed anti-psychotic drugs after the birth of her fourth and fifth children. The defense could call experts who had actually treated Yates, some repeatedly, in sharp contrast to Dietz's relatively brief interview. As one scholar on expert testimony emphasizes, "the legal system assumes that the treating doctor is more credible than a nontreating doctor"; therefore, the treating physician "is frequently sought to provide expert testimony."

Nonetheless, Dietz's effectiveness as a witness appears to be due to his alleged emphasis on fact. Because jurors received conflicting expert testimony during the Yates trial, minimal statutory guidance, and unclear stories from both the prosecution and defense, they were left with little to rely on other than the supposed "facts." Compounding this dilemma, the multiple defense psychiatrists gave somewhat contradictory analyses of Yates' mental state, presumably in part because she had been treated or assessed by a number of them during different stages of her illness. Such a multiple-theory defense narrative contrasted with the more uniform "factual" narrative presented by Dietz. Given a choice, Dietz's story may have been the preferred alternative; the jury could base a decision on something tangible—"facts"—rather than confusion.

4.1.2 A Prosecutorial Bent

Almost immediately, Dietz's testimony and post-trial commentary about the Yates case sparked notoriety for the views he expressed both inside and outside the courtroom. In an interview with the *New York Times* six weeks after his trial testimony, Dietz stressed that his involvement in the Yates case was "troubling," both "professionally and personally." As he explained, "it was obvious where public opinion lay, it was obvious she was mentally ill, it was obvious where professional organizations would like the case to go." Therefore, while "it would have been the easier course of action to distort the law a little, ignore the evidence a little, and pretend she didn't know what she did was wrong," it also would have been "wrong . . . to stretch the truth and try to engineer the outcome" in that way.

Dietz also tried to justify his career-long tendency to appear primarily for the prosecution. According to Dietz, prosecutors, like good forensic psychiatrists, strive "to seek truth and justice" and therefore to make available all the information important in a case. In contrast, defense attorneys attempt to help their clients—a goal that conflicts with a thorough search for data. "Often there are pieces of evidence that are not in their client's interest to have disclosed or produced." Of course, Dietz's statements imply that defense attorneys and their witnesses want to distort information in some way and shield the truth.

The irony of Dietz's points, however, were spotlighted a week later by Yates' attorneys. They discovered a factual error that Dietz had made during cross-examination. As the next section discusses, their research showed that Dietz had testified incorrectly about the existence of a television episode about postpartum depression that never aired.

4.1.3 A Mistake in Testimony

Dietz is a technical advisor to two television shows: *Law & Order* and *Law & Order: Criminal Intent*. In his advisory capacity, he has viewed nearly 300 episodes of both shows. During the Yates trial, Dietz mistakenly testified that, shortly before Yates killed her children, *Law & Order* aired an episode involving a postpartum depressed mother who successfully won an insanity appeal after drowning her children in a bathtub. The episode never existed. When Dietz learned of his error, he wrote prosecutors Joe Owmby and Kaylynn Williford and informed them that he had confused the insanity episode he testified about with other *Law & Order* episodes and infanticide cases. Dietz's mistake about such a fact, however, may be part of the grounds for Yates' appeal. It is not a stretch to think the jury may have been affected by Dietz's implication that Yates was somehow influenced by the show.

Dietz's statements about the "truth seeking" differences between the prosecution and the defense were also problematic in other ways totally beyond his control and, presumably, his awareness. For example, trial testimony revealed that the defense was not able to acquire copies of particular documents, including Andrea's police offense report. George Parnham, Andrea's attorney, was allowed only to read her police report but not to photocopy it. Therefore, Parnham resorted to taking notes on the report, based only on what he could remember of it. As one defense expert later revealed, having only Parnham's notes on Yates' report put the expert "at a real disadvantage."

Dietz also claimed that the defense experts asked "shocking examples of leading questions" of Yates and provided only partial, and biased, videotapes of their interviews with her. Predictably, his accusation prompted a response. According to Lucy Puryear, a Houston psychiatrist who testified for Yates' defense, Dietz did the same. Puryear added that Dietz edited his eight hours of videotaped interviews with Yates and only "showed the jury portions that supported his testimony."

Such media debates simply seem to accentuate the general problems associated with incorporating psychiatric testimony in an adversarial process, as well as the weaknesses of the profession itself. Legal commentators emphasized the extent to which both sides in the Yates case differed in their conclusions about her mental state given that they were purportedly examining the same evidence. As the following sections suggest, however, the backgrounds of the experts appeared to have an impact on what kind of evidence they believed was most significant and why.

4.2 Dietz's Limitations in Expertise and Investigation

This section examines the extent of Park Dietz's background and experience for testifying in a case involving a defendant with an undisputed history of postpartum depression and postpartum psychosis. As one scholar on expert witnesses has emphasized, "medical professionals who undertake the role of expert witnesses are generally expected . . . to be knowledgeable and experienced in the area in which they are functioning as a medical expert."

4.2.1 Postpartum Depression and Postpartum Psychosis

The Yates trial revealed the degree to which Dietz was unfamiliar with patients diagnosed with postpartum depression or postpartum psychosis and his admitted void in treating patients. This observation is not meant to elevate the psychiatric classification of postpartum disorders to a level of scientific precision and sophistication that it does not deserve. Rather, this section makes clear that there is still much to be learned about postpartum disorders and how much they can justifiably mitigate criminal culpability, if at all. At the same time, what is known medically about the disorders—especially their neurobiological aspects—should not be ignored. Two postpartum experts highlighted the problem of such informational inadequacy specifically with respect to the prosecution's approach in the Yates case: "The real challenge for psychiatry is to educate the legal profession and juries about the physiological underpinnings of postpartum disorders and other psychoses . . . and, ultimately, to encourage verdicts based on facts."

Of course, Park Dietz was not responsible for such a lack of education. It is not the role of the expert witness to provide answers to questions that are never asked or to draw conclusions without a foundation. Yates' defense attorneys could have more aggressively revealed Dietz's gaps and confronted him with the history of Yates' illnesses that Dietz bypassed in his evaluations. Nonetheless, without a fuller expertise on postpartum issues, Dietz's story about Yates offered a much simpler mental landscape—and a greater level of speculation—than may have been warranted given her background.

Direct and cross examinations in the Yates trial made clear that Dietz has been asked to consult on an "unusually high proportion" of cases concerning mothers who kill their children. Yet, according to his testimony, the last time he had treated a female patient with postpartum depression was 25 years ago (in 1977). Nor was Dietz "sure" that he ever treated a patient for postpartum depression with "psychotic features." Dietz conceded that he stopped treating patients totally "many, many years ago," in "1981 or 1982" and that he has no expertise in women's mental health. Dietz's error concerning the showing of a *Law & Order* episode on postpartum depression came about when Parnham was cross-examining him to assess two issues: the sources of Dietz's income, but also whether Dietz had any more expertise in postpartum disorders, even at the level of consulting for television shows, than what he indicated in his testimony on direct examination. It appears Dietz did not have more background because he did not offer any information other than his consultancy on a nonexistent episode. Such inexperience does not comport with accepted diagnostic principles of psychiatry.

Dietz's lack of expertise in postpartum depression and postpartum psychosis is striking given the psychiatric community's recognition of postpartum disorders and the acceptance by both sides that Yates was afflicted with one. At the time that Dietz testified, the disorders were included in the *Diagnostic and Statistical Manual of Mental Disorders* (DSM), published by the American Psychiatric Association, then in its fourth (text revised) edition (DSM-IV-TR). (The fifth edition of the DSM was not published until 2013 and therefore was not in existence at the time.) As courts and professionals have noted, "the DSM is often referred to as 'the psychiatric profession's diagnostic Bible.'" DSM-IV-TR also clearly recognized the link between postpartum-related mental disorder and infanticide in the context of delusions. Notably, however, postpartum psychosis was not presently treated as an individual diagnostic classification in the DSM-IV-TR. Rather, the symptoms are categorized according to the established criteria used to diagnose psychosis (for example, major depressive, manic, or mixed episode). The "postpartum onset specifier" applied if symptoms occur within four weeks after childbirth.

4.2.2 Yates' Postpartum Risk Factors and Life Stressors

It appears that Dietz never really adequately investigated or acknowledged Yates' postpartum risk factors—most particularly in the context of the postpartum period's "unique . . . degree of neuroendocrine alterations and psychosocial adjustments," which the DSM emphasizes. In other words, the medical literature stresses that the risk factors for postpartum disorders cover a broad scope of biological, psychological, and social influences. These factors include an individual's personal and family history of depression, biochemical imbalances, recent stressful events, marital conflict, and perceived lack of support from the partner, family, or friends.

Yates experienced all of the postpartum risk factors that the DSM mentions. She was also subject to a host of family and environmental life stressors shown to be linked to postpartum depression and postpartum psychosis. Dietz only occasionally alluded to these stressors if he mentioned them at all in his testimony. Even if it could be argued that the direct and cross examinations of Dietz did not prompt further references to Yates' disorders, it would be expected that they would be part of Dietz's evaluation of her, independent of his courtroom testimony.

Yates' stressors were numerous. First, over the course of her marriage to Rusty (during which she was nearly always either pregnant or breastfeeding), Yates consistently demonstrated DSM-listed criteria for postpartum mood disorder: "fluctuations in mood, mood lability, and preoccupation with infant well-being." Like the DSM specification, these feelings "ranged from overconcern to frank delusions" and they also took the form of suicide attempts related to the other circumstances in Yates' life—uprooted living conditions and transiency, home schooling her five children, her father's death, depressive illnesses throughout her family, Rusty's own bizarre behavior and pressure for more children, as well as Yates' increasing obsession with religious doctrine, particularly as it was pitched by Michael Woroniecki and his wife, Rachel. As the DSM notes, "the presence of severe ruminations or delusional thoughts about the infant is associated with a significantly increased risk of harm to the infant." Section 5 considers in further detail how Yates wove such delusional thoughts into a highly stressed life that seemed to spur the thoughts all the more.

5 Andrea Yates' History of Postpartum Disorders

5.1 The Early Years of Andrea's Marriage

Yates' postpartum difficulties appeared with her first pregnancy. Soon after Noah's birth in 1994, for example, Yates experienced hallucinations—a striking vision of a knife and her stabbing someone. She dismissed the image and never revealed it to anyone until after her arrest, when she told Rusty. As research shows, postpartum depressed or psychotic women often feel ashamed or embarrassed to admit to others their thoughts about harming their infants.

When Yates became pregnant a second time in 1995 (with John), she gave up swimming and jogging and also saw less of her friends. Her lifestyle switched yet again in 1996, when Rusty was offered work on a six-month NASA-related project in Florida—an event that prompted the leasing of their four-bedroom suburban house and a drive to Florida in a 38-foot trailer. That trailer would become their "home" in a recreational-vehicle community where Yates would care for Noah and John while Rusty worked. In Florida, Yates miscarried but then became pregnant a third time just when Rusty had completed his job and was ready to move back to Houston.

The return to Houston did not mean re-inhabiting their house even though in 1997 Yates gave birth to a third child, Paul. Rusty had other ideas. In an effort to live "light" and "easy," the family rented a lot for their trailer. By 1998, after several months of trailer living, Rusty's "easy living" philosophy took a new twist. He learned that a traveling evangelist, Michael Woroniecki, whose advice had inspired Rusty in college, was selling a motor home that Woroniecki had converted from a 1978 Greyhound bus. Woroniecki, his wife Rachel, and their children had used the 350 square feet of bus for home and travel for their mobile lifestyle. Because Yates and son Noah preferred the bus to the trailer, Rusty bought it. Noah and John slept in the luggage compartment, while Yates, Rusty, Paul, and now Luke, who was born in 1999, slept in the cabin.

While her brood expanded, Yates also became devoted to helping her father, who now had Alzheimer's disease. This task was overwhelming for her. At the same time, Yates became further isolated from everyone. When she did choose to see people, she always visited them, never reciprocating by inviting them to the trailer.

Rusty's role in Yates' increasing aloneness, oddity of lifestyle, religious obsession, and continual state of pregnancy should not be downplayed with respect to any facet of Yates' behavior. And it may never be known to what extent her pregnancies were based on a mutual decision with Rusty or primarily a product of Rusty's desire for a large family. A number of people, including Yates' mother and her friend Debbie Holmes, suggested Rusty was a dominating force in the Yates family, including the decision to have babies.

5.2 The Start of Yates' Breakdown

On June 16, 1999, Yates called Rusty at work, sobbing and hysterical. He returned to find her shaking uncontrollably and biting her fingers. His efforts to calm her to no avail, Rusty took Yates to her parents' home that evening. The next day, while her mother was napping and Rusty was out doing errands, the full force of Yates' troubles became unmistakably clear. She attempted suicide by taking 40 pills of her mother's antidepressant medication. An unconscious Yates was rushed by ambulance to Methodist Hospital, with Rusty following behind.

Yates told the staff at Methodist Hospital that she had consumed the pills to "sleep forever," but afterwards she felt guilty because she had her "family to live for." At the same time, her recovery was slow. According to notes taken by a hospital psychiatrist and a social worker, Yates was evasive about the reasons for her suicide attempt and deflected questions. Although she was still depressed, the hospital discharged her for "insurance reasons," the explanation written on her medical chart. The psychiatrist prescribed Zoloft, an antidepressant, and Rusty took Yates back to her parents' home to rest.

Yates did not like taking the medication, however, and her condition only worsened. She would stay in bed all day and self-mutilate. At one point, she scratched four bald patches on her scalp, picked sores in her nose, and obsessively scraped "score marks" on her legs and arms. Later, she would tell psychiatrists that during this time, she saw visions and heard voices, telling her to get a knife. She also watched a person being stabbed, although she would not identify the victim. At the same time, Yates refused to feed her children or nurse her baby Luke, claiming that they were "all eating too much." Such delusions and thoughts about her children are consistent with the criteria listed for postpartum disorders in the DSM.

It was only after Yates' attempted suicide that her relatives discovered the extent of her family history of mental illness: Andrea's brother and sister had ongoing treatment for depression, another brother was bipolar, and, in hindsight, her father also suffered from depression. According to the DSM, this family history of mental disorder (particularly bipolar disorder), along with Yates' pre- and post-pregnancy experiences with depression, are all factors that would heighten the likelihood of postpartum psychotic features. As the DSM explains, "once a woman has had a postpartum episode with psychotic features, the risk of recurrence with each subsequent delivery is between 30 percent and 50 percent."

At different times, Yates also experienced bizarre delusions and hallucinations. She believed that there were video cameras in the ceilings watching her in various rooms in the house and that television characters were communicating with her. She told Rusty of these hallucinations; however, neither of them informed her doctors, even though she was continually asked whether she had hallucinations.

Of all of her family members, Yates seemed to suffer the most and her condition continued to deteriorate. The day before she had an appointment with one of her psychiatrists, Eileen Starbranch, Rusty found Yates in the bathroom looking at the mirror with a knife at her throat. Rusty had to grab the knife away. When Rusty told Starbranch of the incident, she insisted that Yates be hospitalized again, this time at Memorial Spring Shadows Glen, a private facility in Houston.

The initial results of this hospitalization were disastrous. Yates was virtually catatonic for ten days. According to clinicians, catatonia is an objective sign of mental disorder whether or not an individual reveals what he or she is thinking. It was also only during Yates' stay at Memorial Spring Shadows Glen that there would ever be any record suggesting that she experienced hallucinations. This record was based on a doctor's report and observations by the doctor's assistant.

Starbranch gave Yates a multi-drug injection that immediately improved her behavior, according to Rusty. After a sound sleep, she seemed much more like the person he had first met and they had in the evening what he thought was one of their best conversations. Only later did Yates assert that she considered the injection a "truth serum" that led her to lose self-control in a way she abhorred. Her view of the injection as a "truth serum" could be considered yet one more bizarre delusion on her part.

When Yates returned to her family after treatment, "home" was neither her parents' house (which was too small) nor the bus, which her parents considered unhealthy for her and the children. With her parents' urging, Rusty, a well-salaried ($80,000 a year) project manager at NASA, bought a three-bedroom, two-bath house in a tree-lined, residential neighborhood. The house even had a place to park the bus, which was still very important to Rusty. In the more serene surroundings, Andrea apparently prospered—swimming laps at dawn, baking and sewing, playing with her children, and fostering an environment for home schooling, which Rusty encouraged despite the past stress on his wife. At this point, Yates admitted to Rusty that she had "failed" at their life in the bus; this new phase in their life was a chance to succeed.

During this period, the family was engaging in three nights per week of Bible study in the living room because Rusty did not like any of the churches in their area. Again, the views of the bus-selling traveling minister Michael Woroniecki would come to have a profound effect on the lives of the Yates family. Through Woroniecki, Rusty came to doubt organized religion, even though Rusty was not in complete agreement with Woroniecki's views. Yates was another story, however. Woroniecki's "repent-or-burn zeal" captivated her and she corresponded with Woroniecki and his wife for years after she and Rusty bought their bus. Indeed, at times, the Yates family seemed to imitate the Woronieckis—a bus-living, home-schooling,

Bible-reading brood relishing the isolation of itinerancy. According to Woroniecki, "the role of woman is derived . . . from the sin of Eve." Likewise, he thought that "bad mothers" create "bad children." There came a time when Woroniecki's "hell burning" influence on Yates was so great, it distressed both her parents and even Rusty.

By the spring of 2000, Yates became pregnant again, a decision seemingly made with Rusty when Yates started to improve so markedly. Yet, the news greatly alarmed Starbranch, who had warned that Yates' problems could be far more serious if they returned, as well as Yates' mother, who had believed all along that Rusty's demands prompted her daughter's breakdown. Debbie Holmes, a former nursing colleague of Yates, echoed this view of Rusty, claiming that Yates continually depicted Rusty as manipulative and controlling and that Rusty pushed her to have the fifth baby.

5.3 Yates' Plunge into Mental Illness

Starbranch's predictions rang true. Yates' pregnancy was met by another downward dive into mental illness, this time precipitated by the death of Yates' father. Yates also became more absorbed with the teachings of the Bible. The effects of the traumatic circumstances surrounding her father's death were obvious: Andrea stopped talking; she would continually hold Mary but not feed her; she would not drink liquids; she scratched and picked at her scalp until she started to become bald again.

On March 31, 2001, four months after Mary's birth, Rusty sought to rehospitalize Yates, with Starbranch's urging. This time, Rusty took his wife to the Devereux Texas Treatment Center Network, a trip that Yates adamantly resisted. Only with much prodding from Rusty and her brother did she finally agree to go to the hospital. Once there, she refused to sign forms admitting herself. Because he thought Yates' condition was dangerous, her attending psychiatrist, Mohammed Saeed, initiated the process of requesting that a state judge confine Yates to Austin State Hospital. Only after Rusty's continual pleading did she finally agree to sign the forms admitting herself to Devereux.

Saeed's account of Yates' condition appeared to be based entirely on Rusty's description rather than from Yates' treating psychiatrists or from Yates herself who, Saeed said, rarely spoke. When Rusty insisted that Saeed put Yates on Haldol, a drug that had been helpful to her in the past, Saeed complied. Saeed discontinued the treatment shortly thereafter because, he said, her "flat face" seemed to be a side effect. Later, Saeed would testify that, based on the little Yates said, she did not seem psychotic, never described the torment she was going through, and denied experiencing hallucinations and delusions.

After ten days at Devereux, Yates finally started feeding herself again—a behavioral improvement which, in Saeed's opinion, justified discharging her even though her medication regime was still not stable. Also, Yates wanted to go home and Saeed thought that Rusty could take care of her.

When Yates returned home, Rusty's mother, Dora, visited from Tennessee to help out during the day while she stayed at a motel in the evenings. Yet, there were clear signals of Yates' desperate mental state. On May 3, for example, after Yates and her mother-in-law returned from taking the children for a walk, Noah told his grandmother that he saw his mother filling up the bathtub with water. When Dora turned the water off and asked Yates why she was running the water, Yates replied only, "Just in case I need it." Presumably, Yates' behavior must have been quite unusual for such an (otherwise) innocuous event to have garnered so much notice from Noah and Dora. Yates also would not allow her friend Debbie Holmes inside the house when Debbie stopped by to leave food that afternoon. Later, Holmes stated that she thought Yates had been re-possessed by the Devil, an issue that both she and Yates had discussed after Yates' illness in 1999. This time, however, Debbie thought the "the demons had returned a hundredfold."

Based upon what was happening, Yates returned to Devereux for rehospitalization. Again, Saeed was her chief caretaker. During her entire stay at Devereux, Yates was almost completely silent and lethargic, particularly around Rusty. Apparently, in group sessions, Rusty dominated discussions and always answered questions asked of Yates, who would not even nod her head. While on a combination of Haldol and antidepressants, Yates stayed in her room most of the time on 15-minute suicide checks. By May 14, Saeed suggested that she could go home. Although Yates was still depressed and basically mute (apart from responding with her name when asked), her sleeping and eating had greatly improved and she was no longer expressing suicidal thoughts.

On June 18, a month after Yates' release from Devereux and after six days of outpatient therapy, Rusty and Yates met with Saeed. Yates' mental state was sharply declining. At that point, she was off Haldol, and Saeed was experimenting with other drug combinations. As usual, Rusty answered most of the questions addressed to Yates, but he expressed deep concern. She was getting worse and was now having nightmares. Rusty asked that Saeed reconsider applying shock therapy, a strategy Saeed declined, saying it was for far more serious disorders. Also, Saeed did not want to re-prescribe Haldol. Instead, he readjusted Yates' level of antidepressants, suggested that she see a psychologist, rather than a psychiatrist, and, perhaps most strikingly, "think positive thoughts."

The next afternoon, Yates watched cartoons on television and then joined Rusty and Noah for a quick round of basketball in the garage. Yet, moments later, she returned inside and went to bed without changing her clothes. She slept until the next morning, June 20, but had a nightmare during the night. She would not tell Rusty what the nightmare was about. That morning, while Yates set out cereal bowls and milk for breakfast, Rusty made sure that she had swallowed her dose of antidepressants before he left for work. According to Rusty, his last picture prior to the killings was one of seeing Andrea eating cereal from a box.

5.4 Yates' Killings and the Aftermath

From all accounts, Yates started the drownings nearly as soon as Rusty left because her children were still having breakfast. First, she selected "Perfect Paul," then three years old, apparently her greatest joy (and the "least trouble") of the five. Paul's death took only seconds. She tucked his body in her bed and laid his head on the pillow. Next came Luke (age two), John (age five), and then Mary (age six months), who was nursing a bottle while Andrea was drowning the others. Yates left Mary in the tub.

Seven-year-old Noah was still eating his cereal when Andrea asked him to the bathroom. When he "saw his sister facedown in the water, he asked, 'What happened to Mary?'" Noah then tried to run away. But Yates ran after him, dragging him back to the tub—struggling to drown him while he came up twice for air. Afterwards, Yates put Mary in the bed with her brothers, ensuring that their arms were wrapped around their little sister. She left Noah in the tub.

Yates immediately dialed 9-1-1. While speaking "unemotionally" and hesitating in response to questions, Yates finally requested police and an ambulance. When the dispatcher asked Yates if she was ill, she said that she was. When he asked her if she was "sure" she was alone, Yates responded that her sister was with her when, in fact, she was alone. After Yates called 9-1-1, she called Rusty. "It's time. I finally did it," was her first statement to him. Then she told him to come home and hung up. Rusty called back, alarmed by her tone of voice, and asked Yates if anyone was hurt. "It's the kids," Andrea said. He inquired which one. She said, "All of them."

The police officers who arrived described Yates as "composed." She showed them where they could get clean glasses for a drink of water in the kitchen, for example, and keys to unlock the back door.

But it was Yates' 17-minute confession to Houston Police Sargent Eric Mehl that was to have one of the biggest impacts on the jury. During the jury's brief 40 minutes of deliberation, they had requested the audiotape of Yates' account of what had transpired when she killed her children. To the jurors, it appeared as though Yates' "plan" to kill her children was cold and methodical. Nearly all of her answers to questions were monosyllabic and the way that Mehl questioned her fostered the impression of matter-of-fact indifference to the killing. "No," she did not hate her children. "No," she was not mad at them. She had, however, considered the prospect of killing them for two years. She realized that she was not being a good mother to them and "they weren't developing correctly," either in their learning or their behavior. She also "realized that it was time to be punished" and, in response to Mehl's question, she wanted the criminal justice system to punish her. She added that she had thought of drowning the children two months earlier—and filled the tub with water—but she "just didn't do it at that time" and also believed that Rusty would have stopped her.

To those who did not "know" Andrea Yates, her attitude would, no doubt, appear indifferent and her behavior calculated. But, as two postpartum specialists have noted with respect to the Yates case, organic psychosis involves a "waxing and waning" of sensation and mood. Simply because Yates called her husband and the police after the killings does not necessarily mean she was experiencing a "normal mental status" and could tell the difference between right and wrong at the time of the killings. That kind of analysis suggests that "we extrapolate backward then "predict' that she had an intact thought process." Another expert honed the key issue: Crimes based on "deluded moral reasoning" can be "well planned, carefully executed, and . . . have evidenced high degrees of behavioral control." As section 6 discusses, Dietz's perspective on Yates' mental state was entirely different.

6 Park Dietz's Interview and Testimony in the Andrea Yates Case

Park Dietz's interview with Andrea Yates and his trial testimony provide additional evidence for assessing how Dietz appeared to influence jurors. Section 6 explores one particularly striking feature of Dietz's testimony: Even though both sides agreed that Yates severely suffered from postpartum depression and psychosis and that it significantly affected her conduct, neither side seriously questioned Dietz's statements or his knowledge.

6.1 Dietz's Interview with Yates

Dietz interviewed Yates for two days in November 2001, nearly five months after the killings and four months after Phillip Resnick, the defense's primary psychiatric expert, interviewed her. Over the months after the killings, Yates showed substantial progress due to a regimen of antipsychotic medication. Other professionals estimated that by August, her psychosis seemed under control and by September, a jury found her competent to stand trial.

According to Dietz, Yates was grossly psychotic the day after the killings and was suffering from schizophrenia when he met her in November 2001. He still believed, however, that she knew the difference between right and wrong at the time she killed her children. This conclusion, of course, stemmed in part from the November interview he conducted with her and the questions he asked about how and why she planned to kill her children.

In response to Dietz's questions, Yates explained that she did not want her children "tormented by Satan" as she was. She noted that Satan had been conveying "bad thoughts" through the television and the cameras in her home. She was also "afraid Satan would lure [her] children to himself—and maybe that [she] had some Satan in [her]." She believed Satan was "inside [her] giving [her] directions . . . about harming the children . . . about a way out—to drown them." According to Yates, the drowning would be "a way out" because the children "would go up to heaven and be with God, be safe." Basically, "at the time" Andrea thought "this was a good idea" because she "didn't want [her children] ruined—[she] was afraid they would continue to go downhill—and [she] thought [she] should save them before that happened." Yates believed "the children were in torment" from Satan because they were exhibiting relatively "more strife and disobedience"; however, she did not think that Dora, her mother-in-law, was in such torment nor Rusty, whom she believed was a "good man." In Yates' mind, Satan had selected her children because of Yates' own personal "weaknesses"; in fact, she had stopped reading the Bible close to the time of the killings because she "felt like Satan was nearby."

Yates seemed to have been markedly influenced by the 1995 movie *Seven*, a crime thriller about two homicide detectives who strive to solve a series of mysterious murders patterned on the seven deadly sins: gluttony, greed, sloth, pride, lust, envy, and wrath. Yates told Dietz that because "[she] felt [she] had done all the other sins" but murder, she believed that the drowning would constitute her seventh, and last, sin. She claimed that she was thinking of the movie on the day she killed her children—"about what [she] was about to do, and how it fit in there—the deadly sins—and how [she had] done all of them after [she] drowned the children." She "saw [the drowning] as a sin that [she was] going to commit." Although the act of drowning would "condemn" her, it would save the children.

While Yates had ruminated about the seven deadly sins a week before she killed her children, she picked the specific date she was going to drown them only the night before. She did not tell Rusty her thoughts about the deadly sins or of her plans to kill because, in response to Dietz's question, she believed Rusty would interfere. As Yates explained, if she had been stopped, "the children would still be alive" and she "would still worry about their soul with Satan around." On the morning of the killings, she tried to act as normally as possible so Rusty would not be alarmed.

Despite Yates' claims of careful planning, however, on the day of the killings, she did not close the blinds or the curtains or take the phone off the hook (the door had already been locked the night before and Rusty left through the garage exit). She also remembers taking her medication. In answer to Dietz's questions, she said she felt "the presence of Satan that morning ... just helping [her] fill up the tub, and getting ready." Yet, she believed she would be punished ("jail") and she knew the act was illegal. It seemed as though Yates viewed the killing as a balancing test: "Doing it, [the children would] go to heaven; not doing it, there's the risk of Satan messing them up. . . . Probably if I did it, I'd get in trouble."

Notably, in his court testimony, Dietz conceded that he did not interview either Rusty or Dora, both of whom refused to see him. Dietz also stated that Yates had difficulty being viewed by others as mentally ill and that her attitude hindered her recovery. For example, after her first suicide attempt, Yates refused to take the antipsychotic medication prescribed to her and flushed it down the toilet. As Dietz emphasized, "the most consistent story she's indicated is that she didn't think she was psychotic, didn't want to be thought of that way and resented someone calling her that." However, a key issue that was not brought out in Dietz's testimony, either in direct or cross, is that Yates, like many psychotic people, was wrong about her mental status.

6.2 Dietz's Empirically Unsupported Conclusions

Dietz's testimony about Yates' condition is full of troubling speculations that sound authoritative but have no empirical support. Of course, the field of psychiatry in general is vulnerable to such criticisms. As the following analysis suggests, however, in a number of instances, Dietz's accounts give Yates' actions a degree of intentionality and manipulation that seem to derive only from Dietz's interpretations and no other source.

6.2.1 *Yates' Suicide Attempts*

Dietz testified that when Yates attempted suicide the first time using pills, she got a "week away from the stressors, only with an overdose," when she was hospitalized (her admission to Methodist Hospital's psychiatric unit). In other words, the idea conveyed was that with "only" an overdose, Yates could get a substantial break from taking care of the kids and the house. After her week-long stay at Methodist, however, Yates came back to the same stressful environment in the cramped bus. For that reason, according to Dietz, the second time she attempted to commit suicide, she "upped the ante" by using a knife. Presumably, by employing a more certain and serious instrument of death, Yates could acquire even more help and a bigger break than she got the first time by "only" ingesting pills. Dietz indicated that Yates was successful with this approach. While she was hospitalized the second time, her parents insisted to Rusty that Yates could no longer stay in the bus because it was not healthy for her or the children. As a result, Rusty purchased a nice new house, which was all ready for her to live in when she returned from the hospital. In Dietz's eyes, a new home was the reward that Yates was seeking: "This time, [the suicide attempt] not only got her hospitalized, it got her a house."

The implication, of course, is that Yates somehow realized that she would get both a long break and material benefit—"a house"—for her more dramatic second suicide attempt. But, that view contradicts everything we know of Yates: that she hated to be hospitalized, that she continually resisted psychiatric help, that she resented any kind of psychiatric label. Indeed, Yates was so opposed to being re-hospitalized at Devereux Texas Treatment Center on March 31, 2001, that Saeed had to start the process of involuntarily committing her to a state hospital. For Dietz to suggest, even indirectly, that Yates' suicide attempts were strategic efforts to gain a better home derides the reality of her psychosis and the severity of her postpartum disorders. As the defense noted, Yates "never told any doctor that, 'I wanted a new house.'" Her marital history suggests just the reverse—that Yates was enamored (perhaps even more than Rusty) with the Woronieckis' bus-living existence and later apologized to Rusty for not being able to handle it.

It is also questionable, even by Dietz's own account, whether Yates was in fact "upping the ante" by using a knife rather than pills. Only moments before making that statement, Dietz claimed that it was unclear what level of severity Yates' knife-using episode entailed ("varying degrees of intent"); in contrast, her ingestion of pills would most likely have resulted in her death if her mother had not awakened her. Most important, as Dietz conceded on cross-examination, Yates' overdose and knife threat could be "interpreted by medical experts as an alternative to hurting her children." Psychological research suggests that "aggression against others and aggression against self frequently co-occur" and that "risk assessment for suicide and homicide should go hand in hand." Yates' psychiatric history and her final act of killing her children support, rather than contradict, this suicide-homicide relationship.

6.2.2 Yates' Pregnancies

Dietz also portrayed Yates as manipulative and controlling in her decision to discontinue medication and become pregnant again with Mary, her fifth child. Initially, Dietz emphasized that Yates did not want to admit her mental illness and therefore did not take her medication for that reason; yet, he depicted her motives very differently when he discussed the medication issue in the context of Yates and Rusty's apparent efforts to have another child. According to Dietz, her pregnancy was "one of the repeated examples of Mrs. Yates not following the advice of her doctor and thinking she knows best and maintaining control." Dietz suggests that Yates directed the entire decision to conceive: "She's the one deciding what to do. She will not take the medicine unless she wants it. She will get pregnant when she wants to. She's not taking the medicine during pregnancy."

Dietz's analysis assumes realities of Yates' life that did not exist. First, all accounts of Yates' marriage indicate that Rusty was the one in control, the one making decisions, and the one pushing for more children. Second, testimony revealed that both Yates and Rusty had been advised by multiple staff members "on the importance of staying on medications and on the importance of not having another pregnancy." Dietz's conclusions suggest that Rusty had nothing to do with the decision. Indeed, Rusty continually joked (even at his children's funeral) that he always wanted enough boys "to make up a basketball team." Likewise, Debbie Holmes testified that Yates complained to her about the continual pregnancies. Third, noncompliance with taking medication is the norm among psychiatric patients for a variety of reasons, but often because the mentally ill are paranoid or delusional about what doctors give them. By his comments, Dietz implied that Yates' behavior was anomalous and that her refusal of medication related to her need to "control." Yet, recent research suggests that "more serious mental illness is a cause not a consequence, of [a patient's] refusal of treatment" with antipsychotic medication. In fact, when Yates was being evaluated for her competency hearing, she expressed concern that her medication may be contributing to her psychotic episodes. Resisting medication was also a matter of pride. Fourth, many women reject medication while they are pregnant; the DSM entry on postpartum disorders discusses this very issue and makes recommendations to medical personnel about how to counteract it. Finally, Dietz never acknowledged that more than 50 percent of all pregnancies are unplanned, irrespective of what couples want or the decisions they make. Throughout his testimony about Yates' last pregnancy, Dietz attributes a level of intentionality to events that may well have simply been an accident.

6.2.3 Yates' Knowledge of Right and Wrong

In an interview with *Time Magazine* on the day that Yates was sentenced, Dietz stated that despite Yates' mental illness, her "thought process" still permitted her to know right from wrong. "Her mind recognized murder as wrong or she would not have sought the death penalty to get rid of her inner demons and protect her children from falling into [Satan's] grasp." Also, "by wanting to dispose of Satan, she had to believe Satan had evil ideas. Therefore, she still comprehended evil to be wrong. She also "knew that society and God would condemn her actions.'" Of course, Dietz's analysis of Yates, both in this interview and in court, presumes that Satan actually exists.

Frequently during his testimony, Dietz would strain the interpretation of an incident to support the view that Yates knew the difference between right and wrong. For example, on May 3, when Yates filled the home bathtub with water while Dora Yates was present, the incident was perceived to be so bizarre, it sent Yates back to Devereux. According to Dietz, Yates "doesn't give a reasonable account of why she did that [fill the tub], and they [Devereux] take her back the next day or the day after." But, in the months following the incident, Andrea gave several accounts of why she filled the tub that day, including what seemed to be the most reasonable (and defense-oriented) one—she had thoughts of drowning her children. A portion of the direct examination of Dietz seemed to recognize that this explanation could support the defense's position. If Yates were contemplating drowning her children with Dora present, it would fuel the defense's argument that she may not have known that what she was doing was wrong. While this interpretation of Yates' motives is purely speculative, it is the most rational account that Yates herself provides. It is also congruent with the vague statement that Yates made in response to Dora's question of why she was running the water, that is, "Just in case I need it."

Indeed, at a later point in his testimony, Dietz downplayed the fact that Yates told others that she was considering drowning her children while Dora was present. Dietz's story is intertwined with Yates' own conflicting accounts. As Dietz explained, "sometimes she told doctors that she was thinking of drowning the children then. Sometimes she said she thought she might drown the children then. Sometimes she said that she might need it [the tub water] because they might have their water cut off by the utility company; and at those times, she said that she wasn't thinking of drowning the children then." However, the explanation that Yates gave Dietz while he was interviewing her is the least reasonable one: "the utility company truck explanation rather than drowning the children."

The more pointed question to ask is, why did Yates tell Dietz the company truck answer when she told others she was thinking of drowning her children? Does it really make sense for a woman to fill her family tub in such an odd manner on May 3 because of a possible water shortage but then fill it again on June 20 to drown her children? It seems unlikely that Yates' disruptive actions on May 3, which were sufficiently disturbing to hospitalize her again, appeared due to her concern over a water shortage, particularly in light of the other evidence.

In sum, Dietz's testimony was too focused on trying to explain Yates' illogical thinking, which basically stemmed from her mental illness. His analysis was not based on "facts" but rather pure speculation about her delusional thought patterns. According to one legal scholar, "medical expert witnesses are not advocates for either side in the litigation, but may advocate their opinion." Yet, there were a number of aspects of Dietz's testimony where his prosecutorial bent came through quite obviously. For example, despite his level of experience, Dietz repeatedly referred to the drownings as "homicides" or "crimes," even though at the time, Yates had not been convicted of anything. Likewise, at certain points, it was Dietz who directly led the prosecution to a criminal conclusion about Yates. For example: "Q. Now, you noted that—or Dr. Saeed told Mr. Yates that someone must be with his wife, but she was left alone; was that correct? A. Yes. And, of course, the significance of that is that it gives her the opportunity to commit the crimes."

6.3 Dietz's Attempts to Give "Logic" to Yates' Illogical Delusions

A major portion of Dietz's testimony was analyzing Yates' "homicide" in three phases: (1) the pre-homicide phase, (2) the homicide phase, and (3) the post-homicide phase. The pre-homicide phase was key for Yates' defense because it went to the issue of whether she knew the difference between right and wrong. Dietz conceded that Yates told both Rusty and her friend Debbie Holmes about "her concerns for the presence of Satan, the influence of Satan." Even in Dietz's opinion, Yates was open about her fears and did not attempt to hide them.

What Dietz emphasizes, however, is that despite Yates' openness about Satan, she concealed the thoughts of harming her children from other people. If, for example, she was concerned that by mentioning the harm to other people it would actually happen, Dietz responds that this fear would be even more reason for Yates to talk about it. Dietz's "legal-like" logic applied to the thinking of a mentally ill Andrea Yates goes as follows:

> If it's true that she believed that killing the children would save them, then why would she not want it to happen. She would want to talk about it so it came true and the children would be saved. So, I concluded at that point that she's keeping it secret, she knows that other people are going to stop her, that it's wrong, that it's a bad idea; and she admits as such. She admits that she knows people will stop her.

Yet, there is no factual support for anything Dietz says. Dietz also rather bizarrely analyzes Yates' statements as real and "debates" her theories about Satan even though everyone agreed that Yates was mentally ill and delusional. Delusions are by definition illogical. As a key text on delusional disorders emphasizes, "in the delusional mode, thought form is relatively normal but the abnormal content predominates and is associated with profound, but focused illogicality." Dietz's story is based on applying a logical analysis to Yates' truly illogical ruminations. There is really no diagnostically acceptable point to it. Nor is it even clear that Yates intended what Dietz said because she never articulated it, he did.

Perhaps anticipating this criticism, Dietz explained that he is entitled to apply such an inordinate amount of logic to the thinking of a mentally ill person because Yates seemed to him to be "psychologically ready" to engage in the act of killing. Yet again, Dietz does not provide any empirical support for this very vague explanation. Parenthetically, the field of psychiatry does not encourage members of its profession to engage in logic-applied analyses of the illogical ramblings of mentally ill people.

But, for Yates, there was no escape from Dietz's testimony; he seemed to have cut off every avenue with some explanation based entirely on speculative presumptions. Dietz showed striking confidence in his conclusions, despite the conjecture. Comparably noteworthy was Dietz's complete disregard of the literature on postpartum depression, which indicates that women generally do not tell others that they are thinking about harming or killing their children; they are afraid and embarrassed and disturbed by such thoughts. Dietz's sweeping generalizations about Yates' mental state are consistent with his ignorance of the subject matter.

6.4 Dietz's Criticism of Yates' Inability to Nurture Her Dead Children

Dietz also focused on the easiest emotional target of Yates' illogicalities—how she treated her children after she killed them. For example, Dietz queried why Yates did not try to "comfort the children, telling them they are going to be with Jesus or be with God." Again, however, such comments were guesswork on Dietz's part. In other words, is it typical for mentally ill people to give their children religious words of comfort before they kill them, particularly if they think Satan is their guide?

While being cross-examined, Dietz acknowledged that Yates had been nurturing toward her dead children. She had placed her children's heads on pillows, for example, with Mary's head "resting on her older brother's shoulder" and Mary's hand "cupped by her older brother's hands." According to the police officers who arrived on the scene, the children's bodies appeared "posed," as though the "older brother were taking care of the younger sister." Such arrangements are perhaps a more objective gauge of Yates' thoughts than the speculative hindsight Dietz offered. At the very least, the way that Yates situated her children suggested that she may have believed they were going to take care of one another; in contrast, Dietz had nothing to support his comments apart from sheer conjecture.

Similarly, Dietz noted that Yates seemed to cover each of her children's heads and faces as she put them on the bed. He suggested that she may have covered them so that the remaining children, who were still alive, would not discover the bodies. Later in his testimony, however, Dietz stated that Yates' covering of her children's faces was "an indication of her feeling guilt or shame." Dietz's explanation for Yates' behavior is perplexing; there is a social norm to cover the faces of the deceased for reasons of respect or reverence. It would have been just as reasonable for Dietz to have pitched Yates' motives in an alternative way, in other words, to state that covering the children was Yates' way of showing care and comfort to them, given that all of these explanations are speculative anyway. Nonetheless, Dietz did resist supporting one of the prosecution's more damning insinuations—that Yates' decision to leave Noah in the bathtub after he died was cold hearted. Instead, Dietz noted that, at 50 pounds, Noah was too heavy for Yates to lift. "Nurses know not to lift heavy weights."

Lastly, Dietz explained that Yates seemed "grossly psychotic" and mentally disturbed from June 21 to some period thereafter, so "very sick" that she was hearing "growls and voices" and seeing "teddy bears and ducks and marching soldiers" that she believed were satanic. Yet, he claimed there was not "nearly as much evidence of that kind of extreme sickness or gross psychosis on June 20th as [there is] for the period beginning June 21st." Dietz attributed his impression that Yates was "different in a sicker way" to the rapid changes in her life after she was arrested. However, there is an alternative explanation. Yates did not receive nearly as much medical attention on June 20 as she did on June 21, when she became the object of intense evaluation. On June 20, she was with police for much of the day whereas on June 21, she was surrounded by psychiatrists who were able to assess her mental state. Given these day-to-day differences in the amount of time Yates spent with medically trained professionals, Dietz's conclusions are unwarranted.

This analysis of Dietz's testimony could extend even further, continually assessing every word in the way that Dietz evaluated Yates' every move. However, this chapter is not intended to be an indictment of Dietz *per se*. Rather, it is a commentary on how swayed and fragile insanity determinations can be in the heat of litigation and how inadequate the criminal justice system is to handle them. Dietz did not create this situation; he merely responds to the many who want him to be part of it. As the following discussion makes clear, other aspects of the Yates trial as well as the law and culture of Harris County also appeared to be critical contributors to Yates' conviction.

7 Other Viewpoints on the Andrea Yates Case

Up to this point, discussion of the Yates trial has focused on Park Dietz. Of course, there were other perspectives and experts involved in the case. Section 7 examines briefly only a selected number of these additional people and issues to give a glimpse of a broader story about Andrea.

7.1 The Overall Defense and Prosecution Perspective

In general, the defense contended that Yates' mental illness led her to believe she made the right choice when she killed her children. Her long history of illness and her many visits to doctors created a situation in which a number of defense experts were called to testify about her condition at the time they treated her or her mental state at the time she killed her children. Yet, because of the numbers of medical specialists involved in the case who had evaluated Yates at different times and for different purposes, some offered seemingly conflicting narratives of her perception of right and wrong. This range of opinion for the defense contrasted with the prosecution's more consistent argument that Yates' acts were sane and intentional because the prosecution primarily relied only on Dietz's narrative.

Ironically, then, the severity and extent of Yates' mental illness may have undercut her defense. There was one story of sanity from the prosecution and several stories of insanity from the defense. For example, Dr. Melissa Ferguson, a psychiatrist at the Harris County Jail, testified that Yates told her in a post-arrest interview that drowning her children was "the right thing to do" since it saved them from a life of torment and eventual damnation in hell. Defense expert Dr. Phillip Resnick testified that although Yates knew her actions were illegal, "she did what she thought was right in the world she perceived through her psychotic eyes at the time." Describing Yates' motives as "altruistic," Resnick explained that she believed that she was sending her children to heaven and, in setting herself up for execution, ridding the world of Satan. Another expert witness for the defense, Dr. George Ringholz, explained that in the midst of her "acute psychotic episode," Yates "did not know the actions she took on that day were wrong." Dr. Steve Rosenblatt further elaborated: "She was out of contact with reality, did not know right from wrong, and in my opinion, clearly was within what's considered the legal definition of insanity."

Jurors struggling to make sense of it all would be additionally taxed by the open disagreement between Resnick and another defense expert, Dr. Lucy Puryear. According to Puryear, Yates was too sick to know that her actions were wrong. In contrast, Resnick stated that Yates knew her acts were illegal, but believed they were right because they saved her children from eternal damnation. Granted, these two positions are not entirely mutually exclusive; however, Puryear acknowledged during cross-examination that there were conflicts between her testimony and Resnick's and stated merely that they had "differing opinions."

Prosecutor Joseph Owmby claimed, on the other hand, that determining insanity did not come down to "'a battle of the experts,'" but rather was "'a question of common sense[.]'" According to Owmby, the experts simply "present the evidence from the medical side" while the jurors, though unable to diagnose mental illness, "can tell you whether they believe a person knew right from wrong at the time." Similar to Dietz's testimony, the prosecution downplayed Yates' history of mental illness as well as the neurobiological underpinnings of her disorder.

Yet, most of the expert testimony offered in the Yates case did little to abate the confusion surrounding Yates' mental state. Not surprisingly, the testimony of expert witnesses for the prosecution directly clashed with the testimony of expert witnesses for the defense. As one psychiatric journalist explained, although prosecution expert Park Dietz and defense expert Phillip Resnick are well known in their mutual fields, they nonetheless viewed Yates' insanity defense "in polar opposite ways."

Overall, it appeared to be a tactical problem for the defense to deal with so many psychiatric experts. Their contrasting analyses blunted the defense's theory. Which story should the jurors choose? Assuming that Resnick was probably one of the stronger psychiatrists in terms of his demeanor and experience and was therefore more equal to Dietz, the defense may have been better off presenting just Resnick (in addition to the psychiatrists who actually treated Yates). With this approach, the defense would have had a clearer, more linear, story that Yates was indeed insane. As it so happened, Dietz probably appeared better with his single theory in contrast to the defense's multiple theories concerning Yates' mental state.

The defense also would have benefited from questioning Dietz more aggressively about the facts of Yates' history of postpartum depression and psychosis. Such a "detailing to death" tactic could have accomplished two goals: (1) it would have accentuated Dietz's lack of expertise in the area, and (2) it would have stressed the neurological and biological aspects of the disorders. The jury would perhaps more fully appreciate that insanity determinations are based on far more than just "common sense" or speculation. The jurors' own comments indicate that this kind of psychiatric evidence had little to no impact in their forty minutes of deliberation before deciding to convict Yates.

7.2 The Jurors' Comments

The jurors' explanations for their verdict suggest that they were heavily swayed by the prosecution's presentation of the case. In their view, Yates' manner of killing her children seemed "premeditated and methodical." They cited her videotaped confession and the photographs of her children, alive and dead, as "the most compelling evidence" of their unequivocal belief that Yates knew right from wrong. According to one juror, for example, because Yates called the police immediately after the killings and could converse with them and account for her behavior, "it seemed as if she was thinking pretty clearly." Another juror emphasized that Yates "was able to describe what she did. . . . I felt like she knew exactly what she was doing." These "objective" actions of Yates' are the kinds of factual evidence that Dietz stressed in his determination that she was sane.

The jurors also appeared to take seriously the prosecution's depiction of Yates' religiosity and her perception of her conduct as sinful. Indeed, religion was an important force throughout the trial in a number of different ways. For example, prosecutor Owmby claimed to have prayed before deciding to seek the death penalty for Yates, and he expressed his firm belief that she was aware that she had sinned. He also elicited testimony from one of the defense's expert witnesses admitting that Yates knew she had sinned. Surely, her own statements supported that view.

On the surface at least, the jury seemed predisposed to embrace such religious characterizations. In a television interview with four of the jurors conducted shortly after the Yates verdict, the jurors' comments indicated that they all shared some Christian convictions. As the interviewer emphasized, "in a case [the Yates jurors] found emotionally draining, they say prayer got them through." According to one juror, for example, all the jurors "held hands and prayed . . . [the] Lord's prayer, most mornings" and they "did the same thing before and after the verdict." Another juror affirmed the prosecution's sentiment that Yates "knew it was wrong in the eyes of God." During the trial, there appeared to be little left for the defense to hold on to other than evidence of Yates' mental illness, and the nature and severity of her illness did not come across adequately.

Dietz also accentuated sin and religion generally throughout his testimony, far more than the "facts" of Yates' mental history. Of course, on the surface, Yates' explanations for why she killed were laced with religion. Yet, given the severity of her mental illness, the religious aspects of her delusions were symptoms of her disorder, not a substantive issue for Dietz to "debate" with her. Delusions and hallucinations about the devil are not uncommon among women with postpartum psychosis and those who end up killing their children. In turn, all mental illnesses are contextually based, reflecting the culture and day-to-day circumstances of the mentally ill person. In other words, mental disability is interlinked with other influences in a person's life, including the community where that person lives.

7.3 Religion and Culture

Given the Yates family's intense interest in the Bible and the Woronieckis' lifestyle, it is understandable that such themes would provide the foundation for Yates' delusional thoughts. While the Yates family was not affiliated with any church, Rusty decided to hold the children's funeral close to their home at the Clear Lake Church of Christ, which Rusty now regularly attends. Over a two-century history, Churches of Christ have divided into eight primary branches, now totaling nearly two million members worldwide. The majority mainstream wing of the Churches of Christ is especially strong in the region of the United States spanning from Middle Tennessee to West Texas. The tenets of this mainstream branch give some perspective on Rusty's current religious views and what he may have believed in the past.

Consistent with Rusty's prior distance from organized religion, Churches of Christ purport to be nondenominational and therefore are not Catholic or Protestant. Rather, followers of the Church simply call themselves "Christians." Commonly, members contend "that they have restored the primitive church of the apostolic age and are therefore nothing more or less than the true, original church described in the New Testament." Indeed, Churches of Christ have essentially "denied that they had a defining history other than the Bible itself" and many members have no knowledge of the Church's original founders. "Biblical authority," therefore, is paramount and Church members defy "hierarchy or headquarters or national program." As a result, each congregation is an independent body and "practices vary widely" among them.

The Clear Lake Church of Christ has an extensive website, which offers a range of lessons. The Church also sponsors the White Stone Ministry, whose mission is in part to aid "those who do not know Christ" by introducing them to Jesus and the Bible's scriptures. In addition to posting specific scriptures, the White Stone Ministry offers a number of instructive articles, which appear to focus on "sexual sin" and the hazards of pornography, particularly in comparison to a good marriage.

The importance of religion in the south and Harris County in particular should not be downplayed when analyzing the reasons for Yates' conviction, especially because religious themes were highlighted by the prosecution. According to one legal scholar's analysis of the literature on "the southern subculture of punitiveness," a key "facet of American Southern exceptionalism is the South's distinctive embrace of Protestant fundamentalism," which is why the South is commonly referred to as "the Bible belt."

In turn, a substantial body of research shows a link between Southern fundamentalism and support of the death penalty. While the precise explanation for this association is not clear, it is "real" nonetheless and exists along with other evidence of the South's disproportionate proclivity to violence.

With respect to the Yates case specifically, it seems that the prosecution and Dietz were in religious sync with the jury, presuming the jurors were in any way representative of Harris County, the heart of the Bible belt. While the role of the jury is to reflect community values, Dietz's "Bible thumping" may have merely reinforced what could have been the jury's own initial, moral, thesis about Yates' mental state. The defense should have detailed Dietz to death to separate the religion from the "real" facts of the case. As it stands, religion appeared to dominate much of the testimony, and the medical aspects of postpartum psychosis and Yates' history of mental illness took a substantially smaller role.

7.4 Andrea Yates' Competency

One of the most significant problems that the defense confronted was Yates' resistance to assisting in her own case. From the moment she completed the killings, she seemed intent upon seeking punishment for her actions. This kind of thinking may have been a symptom of her particular mental illness—her suicidal and homicidal ideas—and it is not unusual.

In an interview with the police who responded to her call immediately after the killings, for example, the only question Yates asked was when she would be tried. The next day, she told her prison psychiatrist, Melissa Ferguson, that she was guilty and deserved punishment. Dr. Gerald Harris, the clinical psychologist who testified for the defense at Yates' competency hearing, recalled that when he first spoke to Yates shortly after the killings, she made troubling comments regarding Satan. In arguing that Yates was not yet competent to stand trial, Harris emphasized that people are not going to adequately defend themselves if they believe that their death will eliminate Satan.

In his competency report, Harris also noted that even though Yates was experiencing both auditory and visual hallucinations, she claimed that she was "fine and has no mental problems." In turn, Yates "admitted only that she was depressed in the past and had some irrational thoughts"; yet, she "appeared to believe" that her medication "helped the depression" but may also "have caused the psychotic symptoms." Likewise, she "repeatedly expressed an aversion to taking any medication because of her 'pride.'" Harris found Yates incompetent to stand trial, given that "her denial of mental illness and reluctance to provide information about it prevents access to information that could be important to her defense." He further observed that "she is easily confused and manipulated and has a diminished emotional capacity, likely preventing her from presenting herself appropriately in court."

Dr. Steven Rubenzer, the state's forensic psychologist, found Yates competent to stand trial despite the fact that she denied her mental illness and downplayed her depression. When Rubenzer asked her about her use of the insanity defense, Yates "stated she does not believe she is mentally ill and should be punished for her actions." This response supported her attorneys' claim that "she has consistently expressed the desire to plead guilty" and "has expressed reluctance to use an insanity plea." In addition, Rubenzer reported that Yates evidenced feelings of "depression, social isolation, suspiciousness of other people" as well as a "feeling that her thoughts are blocked, or taken away, or can be heard by other people." Yates also stated that "she has heard voices that others cannot hear in the past." However, while Rubenzer acknowledged that Yates' desire for punishment could hinder her ability to assist in her own defense, this factor did not preclude his determination that she was competent to stand trial.

The transient nature of Yates' postpartum psychosis contributed to the defense's hurdles because she was being treated and her mental state therefore improved. Ferguson observed that Yates continued to show signs of psychosis for a full month after the drownings, but by early August the psychosis had lifted. Legally, the fact that Yates no longer suffered from psychosis at the time of trial should not have posed a problem. The Texas insanity statute clearly states that defendants need only have lacked knowledge as to the wrongfulness of their actions "at the time of the conduct charged." Nonetheless, jurors may have been skeptical of a mental illness that allegedly existed during the commission of the crime, but seemed to have disappeared by the time of trial.

The defense introduced psychiatric testimony and a vast array of medical records to establish Yates' history of mental illness and post-arrest psychosis. But the only person who could genuinely testify to her state of mind at the essential moment, the moment of the killings, was Yates herself. In an interview with Rubenzer, Yates claimed that she thought her actions were right during the time she drowned her children, and only "realized they were legally wrong after the fact when she called the police." Given that her knowledge of right and wrong was at the crux of her entire case, it would have been helpful if Yates had elaborated upon this statement for the jury's benefit. Rubenzer testified that as Yates' mental health improved, she would become better able to appreciate her actions; one can only wonder whether part of her reluctance to assist in her own defense was due to her growing guilt and horror at the enormity of what she had done.

7.5 Final Comments

The Yates case concerned a multitude of legal and social issues; this chapter focused on just a few. There is no in-depth discussion, for example, of potential solutions for the problems that the case revealed although, of course, improvements are clearly needed. While it is beyond the bounds of this chapter to consider this topic in any more detail, a few points merit brief mention.

A critical point pertains to the narrow nature of the Texas insanity standard. According to Dietz, Yates most likely would not have been convicted if the insanity standard had been more lenient, such as the ALI test. Indeed, in a postpartum depression case that followed Yates' conviction, Dietz successfully testified as an expert for the defense in an ALI test state (Illinois). The mother, a pediatrician who killed one of her sons with a knife and severely assaulted the other son, was found not guilty by reason of insanity based largely, it seems, on Dietz's testimony.

Most states, like Texas, follow a M'Naghten-type standard, not an ALI test. Dietz has suggested that one possible solution to any injustice that the Yates case may have created is to adopt the approach applied in Great Britain. Under the British Infanticide Act of 1922, which was amended in 1938, a mother who evidences a postpartum disorder and kills her infant during the first year of its life can only be convicted of manslaughter, and not murder. Postpartum disorders are recognized as a form of diminished capacity that reduces murder to manslaughter, thereby providing a trial court some range in determining sentencing (anywhere from life imprisonment to a psychiatric sentence).

Of course, Great Britain does not have the death penalty, which was a key element in the Yates case irrespective of the insanity defense.

Other kinds of reforms have also been suggested for incorporating postpartum disorders as evidence for a defense or mitigation. Yet, the British Infanticide Act is an established illustration of how infanticide can be treated as a separate category of crime when there are medical problems associated with the killing. As it stands, American law has neither a separate criminal category nor any legislative recognition of postpartum psychosis as a mitigating factor, although the disorder can be used as a defense in criminal cases.

Notably, one key issue potentially on appeal in the Yates case could have had a major impact on the outcome apart from any kind of new reform proposal involving postpartum disorders. Under Texas law, Yates' attorneys were unable to explain to the jury the consequences of Yates being found "not guilty by reason of insanity." The state has a provision requiring that a defendant not be automatically released from the trial court's jurisdiction when acquitted under the insanity defense. In fact, the trial court has the "continuing jurisdiction to impose involuntary commitment for a defendant acquitted by reason of insanity" as well as "maintain jurisdiction to involuntarily commit an acquitted defendant to the state mental hospital for the rest of the defendant's natural life." Because of the stringent nature of the court's control over a defendant determined to be insane, it is conceivable that the Yates jury would have been influenced by knowing that Yates could not possibly have "walked free" if they had accepted her insanity plea. It also seems likely that Dietz's expert testimony would not have had the same effect if Texas did not have such a harsh insanity provision.

Debates abound on how psychiatric experts like Dietz should be treated in cases involving insanity determinations. Historically, the criminal justice system encouraged experts to become involved in insanity cases because it was believed that doctors and lawyers working together would produce a higher form of justice for defendants. By the mid-1800s, however, conflict between the two professions was rampant and the strategy of using experts was both expensive and commonly unproductive. As this chapter's analysis of Dietz's testimony indicates, these problems remain today. Some legal scholars have recommended that judges appoint experts approved by both sides to avoid the potential biases that arise because of the experts' partisanship. Those skeptical of the contention that any expert can be unbiased, however, have other suggestions. For example, the criminal justice system could (1) require that the experts be hired by one party but have their role limited or (2) mandate that the experts serve only as a consultant to an attorney. While other kinds of reforms have been suggested, the law remains quite static in terms of any changes, despite the obvious difficulties.

The issue of bias among experts perhaps becomes especially provocative in cases involving gender specific criminal defenses as well as gender differences in the context of the death penalty. As legal commentators have insightfully noted, the Yates case evokes sensitive subjects that arise when mothers are charged for killing their children. Dietz's testimony specifically targeted Andrea's role as "mother" both before and after she killed her children; it is no leap to suggest this issue was significant in her conviction.

This overview provides some inkling of the broad range of factors bearing on the Andrea Yates case. For this reason alone, it appears that the case is one of the most significant and complex insanity stories in the past few decades.

8 Conclusion

This chapter examined the different stories behind the Andrea Yates death penalty case—the defense's, the prosecution's, and the explanation that Yates herself provided. The jury did not accept the defense's story that Yates was insane and thought she was under Satan's influence at the time she drowned her five children in the bathtub. Rather, the jury convicted Yates and sentenced her to life in prison based on the prosecution's story that she was sane and acting intentionally when she killed her children, even though she was mentally ill. Yates herself fueled the prosecution's account and, of course, to her detriment. She felt that she had sinned and that she deserved to die.

The most persuasive storyteller of them all, however, was Park Dietz, the prosecution's star expert witness. His singular, consistent narrative of Yates' sanity contrasted sharply with the multiple, inconsistent portrayals provided by defense experts. Ironically, the severity of Yates' mental illness appeared in some sense to be a negative force in her case. It constituted the underpinnings of her wish to be punished (even executed) and it also produced the numbers of doctors who became involved in her life and, consequently, her trial. All of these factors contributed to a psychiatrically muddled snapshot of who Yates was.

There were other apparently key influences in Yates' case—the punitive nature of Harris County and Yates' death-qualified jury, for example, as well as the atypically strict and ambiguous structure of the Texas insanity standard. The power of Dietz's testimony, however, was the primary focus of the discussion. Despite his reputation for emphasizing "facts" and his ability to offer a much simpler landscape of Yates' mental state, Dietz's level of speculation was troubling. There was little, if any, empirical basis for his conclusions, and his sweeping conjecture spotlighted his lack of expertise in postpartum depression and postpartum psychosis.

Dietz's version of "Who is Andrea Yates?" was convincing to the jury, although it is difficult to discern how much reality was behind it. At the same time, legal scholars and policy makers have yet to offer substantial improvements on the way expert testimony is treated in court. The Park Dietzes of the expert testimony world are not simply invited to be part of the criminal justice system, they are avidly embraced. It is not up to them to change a system in which they are providing what is viewed to be a necessary service. They should, however, comport with the ethical requirements of their profession. And legal procedures should also control what kinds of stories can be told.

This chapter's analysis of the Andrea Yates case makes no claim to have the "right" story about Yates, whatever that may be. Based on the limited amount of information yet available on the case, it had other goals. For example, an examination of the Yates trial shows "how unsettled and unsettling narratives from life are" and how many different views of a person can arise depending on who holds the lens. As one scholar emphasizes, "it is not just who and what we are that we want to get straight but who and what we might have been, given the constraints that memory and culture impose on us." It seems that the legal system did not "get straight" the Andrea Yates story during the trial. Maybe it will get it right when the case is appealed.[51]

Notes

1. Denno, "Who is Andrea Yates?", 2, 34–35; *Yates v. State*, 171 S.W.3d 218 (2005). This chapter consists of a new introduction followed by excerpts of this author's previous article ("Who Is Andrea Yates?") about the Yates case, which serve as the backstory describing how Yates reached where she is today. For purposes of clarity, this chapter generally calls the members of the Yates family by

their first names only: Russell ("Rusty"), Russell's mother (Dora), and the five children.
2. Denno, "Who is Andrea Yates?," 36.
3. Ibid., 37.
4. Ibid.
5. Ibid., 36, 38.
6. See Denno, "Who Is Andrea Yates?"; *Yates v. State*, 171 S.W.3d 216–18 (2005).
7. See Denno, "Who Is Andrea Yates?", 1; *Yates v. State*, 171 S.W.3d 216 (2005).
8. *Yates v. State*, 171 S.W.3d 215, 216 (Tex. App. 2005).
9. See Denno, "Who Is Andrea Yates?", 37–60.
10. Ibid. 17–47, 56–60.
11. See generally ibid., 37–47.
12. See generally ibid., 37–51.
13. See generally ibid., 1–139.
14. *Yates v. State*, 171 S.W.3d 216, 222 (Tex. App. 2005).
15. Ibid., 218.
16. Ibid.
17. Ibid., 219.
18. Ibid., 218, 219.
19. Ibid., 219, 220.
20. Interview with George Parnham by Deborah W. Denno, October 12, 2015.
21. Khanna and McVicker, "Expert No-Billed in Yates Case"; Parker, "Yates' Murder Conviction Tossed."
22. Khanna and McVicker, "Expert No-Billed in Yates Case"; Morris, "Civil Commitment vs. Life in Prison."
23. *Yates v. State*, 171 S.W.3d 222 (Tex. App. 2005).
24. Ibid.
25. Ibid.
26. Shannon, "The Time is Right to Revise the Texas Insanity Defense," 68.
27. Ibid.
28. Resnick, "The Andrea Yates Case," 153.
29. Ibid.
30. Denno, "Who Is Andrea Yates?," 10.
31. Ibid.
32. Ibid.; Resnick, "Andrea Yates Case," 152–53.
33. Resnick, "Andrea Yates Case," 153.
34. Langford, "Years After Tragedy, Calls for Mental Health Screening"; Resnick, "Andrea Yates Case," 147; Koenigs, "Lawyer Argues for Andrea Yates Release."
35. Interview with Parnham.
36. Resnick, "Andrea Yates Case," 153;
37. Shannon, "Time is Right," 67–70.
38. Resnick, "Andrea Yates Case," 153.

39. Ibid.
40. Koenigs, "Lawyer Argues for Andrea Yates Release."
41. Hlavaty, "13 Years Later, the Yates Drownings Still Haunt."
42. Langford, "Andrea Yates" (noting Parnham's confidence in Adrea's ability to live on her own); Hlavaty, "Kerrville" and "13 Years Later."
43. Hlavaty, "13 Years Later."
44. Ibid.
45. Ibid.
46. See supra note x.
47. Cohen, "How Andrea Yates Lives, and Lives With Herself, a Decade Later"; Langford, "Years After Tragedy."
48. Langford, "Years After Tragedy."
49. Shannon, "Time is Right," 67–68; Blumoff, "Rationality, Insanity, and the Insanity Defense," 179–180. See also McCoy, "Trial of 'American Sniper' Chris Kyle's Killer" (using the same standard to compare present-day Texas insanity law to the Andrea Yates case).
50. Blumoff, "Rationality, Insanity, and the Insanity Defense," 179–80; Denno, "Who is Andrea Yates?," 16.
51. I thank Marianna Gebhardt and George Parnham for insightful comments and Alissa Black-Dorward for excellent reference research. Devavrat Chaudhary provided careful research assistance, for which I am grateful.

Resources

Blumoff, Theodore Y., "Rationality, Insanity, and the Insanity Defense: Reflections on the Limits of Reason." *Law & Psychology Review* 39(2014): 161–203.
Cohen, Andrew, "How Andrea Yates Lives, and Lives With Herself, a Decade Later." *The Atlantic*, March 12, 2012, available at www.theatlantic.com/national/archive/2012/03/how-andrea-yates-lives-and-lives-with-herself-a-decade-later/254302/.
Denno, Deborah W., "Who Is Andrea Yates? A Short Story About Insanity." *Duke Journal of Gender Law & Policy* 10(2003): 1–139.
Hlavaty, Craig, "Kerrville; Doctors: Andrea Yates OK for Group Outings." *The Houston Chronicle*, Feb. 16, 2014, at B1.
Hlavaty, Craig, "13 Years Later, the Yates Drownings Still Haunt." *The Houston Chronicle*, April 25, 2015, available at www.chron.com/neighborhood/bayarea/crime-courts/article/Andrea-Yates-Rusty-Yates-5567726.php.
Khanna, Roma, and Steve McVicker, "Expert No-Billed in Yates Case." *Houston Chronicle*, September 19, 2003, 28A.
Koenigs, Michael, "Lawyer Argues for Andrea Yates Release." *ABC News*, June 20, 2011, available at abcnews.go.com/TheLaw/decade-drowning-children-lawyer-claims-andrea-yates-ready/story?id=13883269.
Langford, Terri, "Andrea Yates; Lawyer Says Mother Who Killed 5 Children Ready to Rejoin Society." *The Houston Chronicle*, March 28, 2012, at A1.

Langford, Terri, "Years After Tragedy, Calls for Mental Health Screening." *The Texas Tribune*, Aug. 6, 2014, available at www.texastribune.org/2014/08/06/andrea-yates-legacy-mandatory-postpartum-screening/.

McCoy, Terrence, "Trial of 'American Sniper' Chris Kyle's Killer: Why the Insanity Defense Failed." *The Washington Post*, February 25, 2015, available at www.washingtonpost.com/news/morning-mix/wp/2015/02/25/trial-of-american-sniper-chris-kyles-killer-why-the-insanity-defense-failed/.

Morris, E.G., "Civil Commitment vs. Life in Prison: What Andrea Yates Knew That Deanna Laney Didn't." *Texas Lawyer*, April 12, 2004, available at www.texaslawyer.com/id=900005405924/Civil-Commitment-vs-Life-in-Prison.

Parker, Laura, "Yates' Murder Conviction Tossed." *USA Today*, January 7, 2005, at 3A.

Parnham, George, phone interview by Deborah W. Denno, October 12, 2015.

Resnick, Phillip J., "The Andrea Yates Case: Insanity on Trial." *Cleveland State Law Review* 55(2007): 147–56.

Shannon, Brian D., "The Time is Right to Revise the Texas Insanity Defense: An Essay." *Texas Tech Law Review* 39(2006): 67–100.

About the Contributors and Editor

Paul Catley graduated in Law and Economics from Cambridge University before joining a large commercial law firm. He moved into university teaching in 1990 and is now Head of the Open University Law School. With more than 7,000 students and 200 tutors, the Law School is the biggest provider of undergraduate legal education in the United Kingdom. Paul is one of the joint founders of the European Association for Neuroscience and Law. Currently, he is a member of the Executive of the Association and for the past four years has been involved in the Association's annual postgraduate schools, which focus on the interplay between law and neuroscience. In addition to his interest in mental condition defenses, Paul's research focuses on the use and potential use by the law of developments in the brain sciences. He has recently been involved in a research project with colleagues in Canada, the Netherlands, Singapore, and the United States on the use made of neuroscientific evidence by those accused of criminal offenses in the various jurisdictions. The initial findings from the project were published in the *Journal of Law and the Biosciences* in 2015. Paul's email address is: paul.catley@open.ac.uk

Michael Louis Corrado is the Arch J. Allen Distinguished Professor of Law, Emeritus, at the University of North Carolina. He received his PhD in philosophy from Brown University and became a tenured professor of philosophy at Ohio University before taking a law degree at the University of Chicago. He joined the faculty of the University of North Carolina in 1988. In 2011 he held the Fulbright Distinguished Chair in Law at the University of Trento in Italy. He has been the editor of *Law and Philosophy* and was the series editor for the Carolina Series in Comparative Law. He has published books and articles on philosophy, criminal law, and comparative law.

Russell D. Covey is Professor of Law at Georgia State University's College of Law. His research focuses on criminal law and procedure and he is the author of numerous articles and book chapters on topics including the death penalty, plea bargaining, wrongful convictions, the temporary insanity defense, and the depiction in popular culture of such subjects as police interrogation and "criminal madness." Professor Covey's work on criminal law and procedure has been featured on national websites including *Time*, *The New Republic*, and *The Conversation*. Professor Covey received his JD at Yale Law School, his MA at Princeton University, and his AB at Amherst College.

Deborah W. Denno is the Arthur A. McGivney Professor of Law and Founding Director of the Neuroscience and Law Center at Fordham University School of Law. She received her BA from the University of Virginia, her MA from the University of Toronto, her PhD in criminology from the Wharton School of the University of Pennsylvania, and her JD from the University of Pennsylvania. Professor Denno has published on a broad range of topics relating to criminal law, criminal procedure, and the social sciences and the law, and she has initiated cutting-edge examinations of criminal law defenses pertaining to insanity, rape law, gender differences, consciousness, biological and genetic links to crime, drug offenses, jury decision making, and the impact of lead poisoning. Currently she is working on a book to be published by Oxford University Press entitled *Changing Law's Mind: How Neuroscience Can Help Us Punish Criminals More Fairly and Effectively*, which analyzes all criminal cases between 1992 and 2012 that have addressed neuroscience evidence. This same study is also discussed in three of her recent articles: "The Myth of the Double-Edged Sword: An Empirical Study of Neuroscience Evidence in Criminal Courts" (*Boston College Law Review*, 2015), "How Prosecutors and Defense Attorneys Differ in Their Use of Neuroscience Evidence" (*Fordham Law Review*, 2016), and "Concocting Criminal Intent" (*Georgetown Law Journal*, 2017).

Tyler Fagan received his PhD in Philosophy from the University of Illinois Urbana-Champaign and is currently Visiting Assistant Professor of Philosophy at Elmhurst College. His research comprises three main topics: how minds think about other minds and which minds do so; how animal minds work and how we study them scientifically; and how a better understanding of cognition might reshape our conceptions of agency, responsibility, and moral status. Under the first two headings, his work focuses on methodological questions about anthropomorphism, explanatory parsimony, and the development of better experimental methods for probing mindreading abilities in animals and pre-linguistic children. Under the third heading, he is collaborating with Katrina Sifferd and William Hirstein to develop a view of agency, self-control, and responsibility that is both scientifically reputable and practically useful in moral and legal contexts. His recent publications include "Animal Mindreading and the Principle of Conservatism" (*Southern Journal of Philosophy*, 2016); "Child Soldiers, Executive Functions, and Culpability" with Sifferd and Hirstein (*International Criminal Law Review*, 2016); and "All in the Game" (in *The Wire and Philosophy*, ed. David Bzdak, Joanna Crosby, and Seth Vannatta, 2013). Together with Sifferd and Hirstein, and supported by a Templeton subgrant through the Philosophy of Self-Control project directed by Al Mele, he is working on a book titled *The Responsible Brain*.

Gabriel Hallevy is a full professor on the faculty of law at Ono Academic College. He lectures on criminal law, criminal procedure, evidence law, hi-tech law, corporation law, and conflict of laws. He has published about 30 books around the world and about 60 articles. He is a member of the Israeli Bar, member of the statutory committee supervising the Israeli Bar exams, and lectures Israeli judges annually. He has been cited by the Israeli Supreme Court, and in 2007 he was awarded a special honorary prize for the research in criminal law by the Israeli Parliament. In 2013 he was chosen as one of the 40 most promising persons under the age of 40 by *Globes* magazine. His books include: *Securities' Offences* (2002), *Complicity in Criminal Law* (2008), *A Modern Treatise on the Principle of Legality in Criminal Law* (2010), *Theory of Criminal Law*, vols. I–IV (2009–2010), *The Criminal Law of Israel* (2011), *Theory of Criminal Justice*, vols. I–IV (2011), *The Matrix of Derivative Criminal Liability* (2012), *When Robots Kill—Artificial Intelligence under Criminal Law* (2013), *Theory of the Law of Evidence*, vols. I–IV (2013), *The Right to Be Punished—Modern Doctrinal Sentencing* (2013), *Theory of the Conflict of Laws*, vols. I–IV (2014–2015), *Liability for Crimes Involving Artificial Intelligence Systems* (2015), and *The Matrix of Insanity in Modern Criminal Law* (2015).

William Hirstein is a professor of philosophy at Elmhurst College. His research centers on the philosophy of mind approached from an empirical perspective. One research focus is on our abilities make reliable knowledge claims about our minds, bodies, and memories. He is the author of *Brain Fiction: Self-Deception and the Riddle of Confabulation* (2005) and the editor of *Confabulation: Views from Neuroscience, Psychiatry, Psychology, and Philosophy* (2009). A second research focus is directed at our abilities to understand our conscious minds in a robustly physicalist way. In his book

Mindmelding: Consciousness, Neuroscience, and the Mind's Privacy (2012), he argues that, contrary to the claims of a large percentage of philosophers and scientists, our conscious states are not metaphysically private, in the sense that no person can ever directly experience the conscious states of another. With his colleague Katrina Sifferd, Hirstein has also written recently about the importance of the brain's prefrontal executive processes in making us rational and responsible beings. This research includes work directed at understanding how the neuropsychology of sociopaths, psychopaths, child soldiers, and other people with suboptimal executive processing should inform our understanding of their responsibility for their crimes. Hirstein received his PhD from the University of California, Davis in 1994, studying with Richard Wollheim and John Searle, and, as a postdoctoral researcher, with V. S. Ramachandran. He is currently revisiting his studies in the philosophy of art, initially undertaken with Wollheim and Ramachandran, in a project that addresses the question of why art is so universally loved and created, despite the lack of any clear evolutionary advantage to these practices.

Maartje Katzenbauer studied medicine at the Radboud University Nijmegen in the Netherlands, also training in Malawi and at the Medical University of Vienna, Austria. She trained as a psychiatrist (Symfora and inGeest Mental Health, OLVG Hospital Amsterdam and Maudsley Hospital, London, United Kingdom), graduating in 2015. While studying medicine she also pursued a career in medical journalism, publishing articles, essays, and reviews in magazines and books (*Medisch Contact*, magazine of the Dutch Medical Association; *Tijdschrift voor Psychiatrie*, scientific magazine of the Dutch Psychiatric Association; publishing a monthly podcast with the author of an important scientific article). She is an editor at the National Psychiatry Network (www.psychiatrienet.nl) focusing on psychiatry and media. As a psychiatrist with a background in journalism, she is working as a freelance journalist aiming to broaden public knowledge of psychiatry in society. Her main interests lie in public perception of psychiatry, public health, neurolaw, and the interaction between somatic and psychiatric disease. She is currently working as a psychiatrist at the Antoni van Leeuwenhoek Hospital (Netherlands Cancer Institute Amsterdam).

Paul Litton is the Associate Dean for Faculty Research and the R.B. Price Professor of Law at the University of Missouri School of Law. He received a JD and PhD in Philosophy from the University of Pennsylvania. He was law clerk to Chief Justice Deborah T. Poritz of the New Jersey Supreme Court, serving a second term as the Court's death penalty law clerk. From

2004 to 2006 he was a fellow in the Department of Clinical Bioethics within the National Institutes of Health. Subsequently, Professor Litton co-chaired the Missouri Death Penalty Assessment Team, assembled by the American Bar Association, which published its findings in 2012. Professor Litton conducts research at the intersection of philosophy (particularly free will and responsibility theory), psychology, and the criminal law. In addition, he writes on issues relating to the death penalty and medical ethics. He teaches mental health law, jurisprudence, and multiple criminal law courses.

Gerben Meynen studied medicine (VU medical center Amsterdam) as well as philosophy and theology (University of Amsterdam). He trained as a psychiatrist and received a PhD in philosophy (2006) and in medicine (2007). In 2007 he was awarded a post doc grant from the Netherlands Organisation for Scientific Research for a project entitled "Free Will and Mental Disorder: Exploring and Evaluating the Role of Psychiatry in the Philosophy of Free Will." Currently, he is endowed professor of Forensic Psychiatry at the Department of Criminal Law, Tilburg Law School, Tilburg University, and assistant professor at the Department of Philosophy, Faculty of Humanities, VU University Amsterdam. Since 2006, he has worked as a psychiatrist at an outpatient clinic for anxiety disorders, GGZ inGeest, in Amsterdam. His research interests include: legal insanity, free will and mental disorder, patient decision-making competency, and neurolaw. Some of his publications are: "Free Will and Mental Disorder: Exploring the Relationship" (*Theoretical Medicine and Bioethics*, 2010); "Depression, Possibilities, and Competence: A Phenomenological Perspective" (*Theoretical Medicine and Bioethics*, 2012); "Does the Brain 'Initiate' Freely Willed Processes? A Philosophy of Science Critique of Libet-Type Experiments and Their Interpretation" (with Hans Radder, *Theory & Psychology*, 2013); "A Neurolaw Perspective on Psychiatric Assessments of Criminal Responsibility: Decision-Making, Mental Disorder, and the Brain" (*International Journal of Law and Psychiatry*, 2013); and a monograph, *Legal Insanity: Explorations in Psychiatry, Law, and Ethics*.

Michael L. Perlin is Professor of Law Emeritus at New York Law School (NYLS), founding director of NYLS's Online Mental Disability Law Program, and founding director of NYLS's International Mental Disability Law Reform Project in its Justice Action Center. He is also the co-founder of Mental Disability Law and Policy Associates. He has written 31 books and nearly 300 articles on all aspects of mental disability law, many of which deal with the overlap between mental disability law and criminal law and procedure. The third edition of his multi-volume treatise, *Mental Disability Law: Civil and Criminal* (2016), co-authored with Heather Ellis Cucolo, was recently published. That treatise is universally seen as the standard text in the area. An earlier book, *The Jurisprudence of the Insanity Defense* (1995), won the Manfred Guttmacher Award of the American Psychiatric Association and the American Academy of Psychiatry and Law as the best book published that year. Before becoming a professor, Perlin was the Deputy Public Defender in charge of the Mercer County Trial Region in New Jersey, and, for eight years, was the director of the Division of Mental Health Advocacy in the New Jersey Department of the Public Advocate. He has represented thousands of persons with mental disabilities in individual and class actions, and has represented criminal defendants at every level from police court to the US Supreme Court. In 2014, he was elected to be co-chair of the Disability Rights Interest Group of the American Society of International Law.

Katrina Sifferd holds a PhD in philosophy from the University of London, King's College, and is an Associate Professor and Chair of Philosophy at Elmhurst College. After finishing her PhD, Katrina held a post-doctoral position as Rockefeller Fellow in Law and Public Policy and Visiting Professor at Dartmouth College. Before becoming a philosopher, Katrina earned a Juris Doctorate and worked as a senior research analyst on criminal justice projects for the U.S. National Institute of Justice. Katrina is the author of numerous articles and book chapters on responsibility, criminal law, reductionism, and punishment, including "Unconscious *Mens Rea*: Responsibility for Lapses and Minimally Conscious States" (in *Law and Neuroscience: Philosophical Foundations*, ed. Dennis Patterson and Michael S. Pardo, 2016); "Chemical Castration and Other Direct Brain Interventions as Rehabilitative Treatment" (in *Neuro-Interventions and the Law*, ed. Nicole Vincent, forthcoming); "Virtue Ethics and Criminal Punishment" (in *From Personality to Virtue*, ed. Alberto Masala and Jonathan Webber, 2016); "What Does It Mean to Be a Mechanism? Morse, Non-Reductivism, and Mental Causation" (*Criminal Law & Philosophy*, 2014); "On the Criminal Culpability of Successful versus Unsuccessful Psychopaths" (with William Hirstein, *Neuroethics*, 2013); and "In Defense of the Use of Folk Psychology in Criminal Law" (*Law & Philosophy*, 2006). She is currently writing a book titled *The Responsible Brain* with Bill Hirstein and Ty Fagan, forthcoming from MIT Press.

Natalia Silva is a Spanish lawyer currently working as a researcher and lecturer at the Philosophy and Law Research Centre of the University Externado (Colombia), where she conducts research on international criminal law, international humanitarian law and human rights, and their application to the Colombian *transitional justice context*. She holds a major in law and a diploma in Anglo-American law from the University of Navarra (Spain) and graduated *cum laude* from the University of Utrecht (Netherlands) with an MA in Human Rights and Criminal Justice. In addition, she has taken specialized courses from the University of Leuven (The EU and Human Rights), Leiden University (*Transitional Justice and Gender Politics;* Terrorism and Counterterrorism), and Case Western Reserve University (Introduction to International Criminal Law). Silva has worked in the Office of the Director of Public Prosecutions (Colombia) and in the Max Planck Institute for Foreign and International Criminal Law (Germany). She interned in the International Criminal Tribunal for the Former Yugoslavia (Netherlands) and in the Office of State Lawyers of Barcelona (Spain). Silva has published the article "Can Water Privatization Lead to Corporate Responsibility?" (*RGNUL Student Research Review,* 2015) and has some pending publications on international criminal law.

Craig A. Stern is a professor in the Regent University School of Law. He received his JD from the University of Virginia School of Law and his BA *cum laude* from Yale University. His teaching and research interests include human rights, federal courts, conflict of laws, jurisprudence, legal history, and criminal law. He has been awarded both the Regent University Faculty Award for Excellence and the School of Law Professor of the Year Award. Professor Stern is admitted to the bar in Virginia and the District of Columbia. He has served as an associate attorney with Fried, Frank, Harris, Shriver & Kampelman; as the assistant deputy director of the Legal and Administrative Agencies Group, Office of President-elect Ronald Reagan; as counsel to the Subcommittee on Separation of Powers, U.S. Senate Committee on the Judiciary; as the associate editor of Benchmark for the Center for Judicial Studies; as the special counsel and director of publications for the Constitutional Law Center; and as a Special Assistant United States Attorney for the Eastern District of Virginia in Norfolk. Stern has published widely and has given presentations on three continents. Among his more important publications on criminal law are "The Heart of Mens Rea and the Insanity of Psychopaths" (*Capital University Law Review,* 2014), "Torah and Murder: The Cities of Refuge and Anglo-American Law" (*Valparaiso University Law Review,* 2001), and "Crime, Moral Luck, and the Sermon on the Mount" (*Catholic University Law Review,* 1999).

Meron Wondemaghen is lecturer in criminology at the University of Southampton. Her research interests include mental health law and mental defenses; rights-based legalism; constructionism; media crime;

and popular culture and crime. She is currently working on the psycholegal and "commonsense" divide of insanity constructs, policing of persons with mental illness, police authority under the *Mental Health Act*, and how these fit within the requirements of the Convention on the Rights of Persons with Disabilities. Wondemaghen publishes internationally, including at the *International Journal of Forensic Mental Health* and *International Journal of Law and Psychiatry*, and some of her research has appeared at *The Conversation* and ABC Radio Australia.

Mark D. White is the chair of the Department of Philosophy at the College of Staten Island/CUNY in New York City, where he teaches courses in philosophy, economics, and law. Recently, he helped found the Legal Studies Institute at CSI with his colleague, Michael Paris (political science). White is the author of five books, including *Kantian Ethics and Economics: Autonomy, Dignity, and Character* (2011), and editor or co-editor of almost 20 more, including *Economics and the Virtues: Building a New Moral Foundation* (with Jennifer A. Baker, 2016), *Law and Social Economics: Essays in Ethical Values for Theory, Practice, and Policy* (2015), *Retributivism: Essays in Theory and Policy* (2011), and *The Thief of Time: Philosophical Essays on Procrastination* (with Chrisoula Andreou, 2010). He has published many journal articles and book chapters in his three fields, blogs often at *Psychology Today* and *Ethics and Economics*, and is the founding series editor of "Perspectives from Social Economics" (at Palgrave Macmillan) and "On Ethics and Economics" (at Rowman & Littlefield International). His website is www.profmdwhite.com and he can be found on Twitter as @profmdwhite.

Index

Abolition of insanity defense, 243–270; agent causation, 249–250, 251; cash value of notion of freedom, 256; cash value of terms dignity and respect, 263; character-forming leaps, 250–251; Clockwork Orange, 259; compatibilism, 252–253, 254; consequentialism, 254–257; Corrado's conclusion (corrective criminal justice), 244–245, 260–264; counterintuitive claims, 244, 245; criminal's Magna Carta, 259; denying actions are unavoidable, 248–253; denying punishment requires avoidability, 254–257; Frankfurt's notions of freedom, 256–257; free moral agents, 246, 247; humanitarian argument, 246–247; levels of desire, 256–257; libertarianism, 248–252, 254; non-event causation, 250; non-retributive punishment, 244; normal/abnormal causes, 253; object causation, 266 n.17; person causation, 250; politician's argument, 243; premise (d), 258; public health case, 259–260; punish-the-innocent problem, 255; quarantine approach, 257–260; strength-based intervention approaches, 263; "takings," 258; thing causation, 250; uncaused events, 249; underlying suppositions, 244; utilitarian justifications for punishment, 254; Washington state (*Strasburg* case), 245–246

Above-normality, normality, and sub-normality, 107–111

Abraham (Biblical character), 108

Abraham and Isaac (Biblical story), 97–98

Absolute presumption, 114, 116

Abuse excuse cases, 46, 54 n.73, 55 n.123

Accessing plausibility of a thought, 228

Act on Cooperation with the International Criminal Court, 340

"Acting voluntarily," 192

Actus reus sense of "voluntary," 192

Acute intoxication, 286–287, 293, 302 n.83. *See also* Intoxication

Addiction, 200–202, 203–204, 220, 256–257

Adelman, Roger, 382

Admissibility of scientific evidence, 158, 172 n.29

Adulterous affairs, 39–43

Agent causation, 249–250, 251

Aggarwal, Neil K., 170 n.1, 175 n.175
"Agonizing circumstances," 32
Aharoni, et al, 157
Alcohol dependency syndrome, 287
Alcohol related medical conditions, 287
Aleksovski case, 311
ALI insanity test, 377
"Alien," 146
American Convention on Human Rights, 313
American Law Institute (ALI) insanity test, 377
Amicus curiae briefs, 162
Amphetamines, 144
Anamnesis, 161
Anatomy of a Murder, 28, 30, 43
Andrea Yates Law, 370
Andrea Yates story, 367–416; ALI insanity test, 377; Andrea Yates Law, 370; Andrea's competence to stand trial, 408; Andrea's confession, 394–395; Andrea's postpartum risk factors and life stressors, 387–388; Andrea's resistance to assisting her own case, 408–409, 412; appeal, 369; attempted suicide/admission to Methodist Hospital, 390; Bible belt, 408; brief summary, 367–471; catatonia, 391; Churches of Christ, 408–409; Clear Lake Church of Christ, 408; command hallucinations, 379; death qualified juries, 369, 375–376; deific decree doctrine, 378–399; Devereux Texas Treatment Center, 392, 393, 398; Dietz (*see* Dietz, Park); DSM, 387, 388, 390; early years of Andrea's marriage, 388–389; expert testimony, 411–412, 413; Great Britain's infanticide law, 411; Harris County, 375, 407–408; jurors' comments, 406–407; key influences in Yates' case, 413; killing of the children, 394; lack-of-control defense, 377; Memorial Spring Shadows Glen, 391; M'Naghten test, 376, 377; moral right-and-wrong test, 378; organic psychosis (waxing and waning), 395; overall defense and prosecution perspective, 404–406; overview of chapter, 373; postpartum depression/psychosis, 386, 387; public opinion, 372; religion and culture, 408–409, 413; second trial and disposition, 369–370; Texas insanity standard, 379–380; transient nature of Andrea's postpartum psychosis, 409–410; unregulated storytelling process, 373; White Stone Ministry, 408; Woroniecki, Michael, 374, 388, 389, 391–392; Yates, Rusty, 368, 371, 374, 388–390, 393, 394, 407; Yates Children Memorial Fund, 370
Antisocial personality disorder (APD), 162, 287, 318
Anxiety, 135, 146
Archetypal case of legal insanity, 229
Arendt, Hannah, 317
Arnold, 133
Arteriosclerosis, 142
Artificial intelligence entities and insanity defense, 130 n.68
Ashworth, Andrew, 334
Associations of dangerousness and violence, 146
Attention (top-down), 223
Australia: defense of mental impairment, 136; reasonable man test, 138; Victoria Law Reform Commission, 138–139, 143; voluntary intoxication, 143; wrongness, 138
Autistic persons, 109

Automatism defense, 293–294;
English cases where defense was successful, 291; proposed new English law, 291–292; terminology, 281, 300 n.54

Backward-looking retributive considerations, 216–217
Baird, Abigail, 225
Banality of evil, 317
Banovic, 326
Battered woman syndrome (BWS), 32, 44–47
Battle of the experts, 6
"Beating the rap," 6
Behavioral control, 161, 192
Bentham, Jeremy, 263
BEOS (brain electrical oscillations signature), 163, 175 n.59
Berlin, Fred S., 383
Bible belt, 408
Biblical story (Abraham and Isaac), 97–98
Bipolar disorder, 29, 35, 227, 229
Bizarre beliefs, 235
Black rage, 38
Bobbitt, Lorena, 30, 46
Bordenave, Franklin J., 157
Bortolotti, Lisa, 234, 235
Both cognitive and volitive aspects of human mind, 107
Bracton, Henry, 28
Bradley, Peter, 35
Brain-based lie detection, 162, 163
Brain-based mind reading, 163
Brain-based pain detection, 156–157
Brain-based predictions of violence, 157
Brain chemistry, 209
Brain electrical oscillations signature (BEOS), 163, 175 n.59
Brain Fingerprinting test, 163
Brain immaturity, 162
Brandt, Richard, 255, 263

Bratty v. A-G for Northern Ireland, 142, 281
Braunsdorf, Eugene, 47
Breivik, Anders (Norwegian mass shooter), 233–234
Brian Thomas, 283
Brink, David, 220–222, 229, 230, 235
Brink's fair opportunity theory, 220–222
British Infanticide Act, 411
Bronitt, Simon, 138
Broome, Matthew R., 234
Burden of proof: automatism, 292; elevated evidential burden, 291; England and Wales, 290–291, 292, 293, 338, 346; international criminal law, 346; presumption of insanity, 115
Burgess, 282
Burning Bed, The, 44–46
Burns, Jeffrey M., 165, 168
Burroughs, Adoniram J., 52 n.42
BWS (battered woman syndrome), 32, 44–47

Canada: appreciate that act was something he ought not to do, 289; mental disorder defense, 136; presumption of innocence *(Whyte),* 290
Capabilities vital to legal agency and responsibility, 219
Caruso, Gregg, 244, 257, 258
Cash value of notion of freedom, 256
Cash value of terms dignity and respect, 263
Catatonia, 391
Categories of legal excuse, 215
Causa sine qua non, 124
Causal determinism, 193, 208
Causal relation. *See* Factual causal relation
CCIL (Code of Crimes against International Law), 340

Celebici case, 307, 322–326
Character-forming leaps, 250–251
Cheating, 110
"Choice of evil" circumstances, 221
Churches of Christ, 407–408
Clark, Eric, 196–197
Clear Lake Church of Christ, 407, 408
Clockwork Orange, 259
Code of Crimes against International Law (CCIL), 340
Code of Crimes Against the Peace and Security of Mankind, 328
Cognitive impairments without volitional defect, 196–199
Cognitive processing speed, 227
Cognitive standards, 188
Cognitive test of insanity, 71, 84–85, 87
Cohen, Jonathan, 155
Coid, Jeremy W., 157
Coke, Edward, 28
Command hallucinations, 379
Common sense, 4, 10 n.10
Compatibilism, 193–194, 208, 252–253, 254
Complete insanity, 122
Complete loss of control over volition of offender, 104
Congestive dysmenorrhea, 30, 52 n.42
Consequentialism, 216–219, 254–257
Constructs. *See* Insanity constructs
Control-override, 139
Control test. *See* Mistaken quest for a control test
Cooling-time doctrine, 41
Cooper v. The Queen, 138
Corporations and insanity defense, 130 n.68
Corrado, Michael Louis, 188–192, 198–203, 205–209, 243
Correction (corrective criminal justice), 244–245, 260–264
"Could have done otherwise," 194–195

Crime and Punishment (Dostoevsky), 28
Crime reduction, 217
Criminal intent. *See Mens rea* and mental disorder
Criminal Procedure (Insanity and Unfitness to Plead) Act, 340
Criminal's Magna Carta, 259
Criticism of M'Naghten rule, 102, 186–187
"Cycling," 29
Cynophobia, 202

Dangerousness, 146
D'Ascoli, Silvia, 312
Daubert v. Merrell Dow Pharmaceutical, 158
Daubert standard, 158, 172 n.29
Death qualified juries, 369, 375–376
Deep brain stimulation (DBS), 158–159, 173 n.32, 174 n.55
Defect of reason, 188
Deific decree doctrine, 378–399
Deliberation, 224
Delusions, 139, 228, 229, 234, 235
Dementia accidentalis vel adventitia, 29
Depression, 140–141, 146
Dershowitz, Alan, 46, 55 n.123
Deserving victims, 54 n.73. *See also* Temporary insanity defense
Desire, levels of, 256–257
Determinism, 208, 209
Deterrence theory, 217–218. *See also* General deterrence
Diabetes (hyperglycemia), 142, 282, 283
Diagnostic and Statistical Manual of Mental Disorders (DSM-IV): Andrea Yates story, 387, 388, 390; depression, 140; Law Commission for England and Wales, 284; mental disorder, 134; psychiatric profession's diagnostic Bible, 387

Dietz, Park, 380–387, 395–404; analyzing Andrea's "homicide" in three phases, 401–402; Andrea's knowledge of right and wrong, 400–401; Andrea's pregnancies, 399–400; Andrea's suicide attempts, 397–399; background/reputation, 381; criticizing Andrea's inability to nurture her dead children, 402–404; Denno's criticism of Dietz's testimony, 413; emphasis on "facts," 382–384; experience with postpartum depression, 373, 387; grand jury investigation, 369; insanity standard, 410; interviewing Andrea, 395–397; mistake in testimony, 368–369, 385; prosecution's star expert witness, 372, 412; prosecutorial bent, 384–385
Diminished responsibility defense, 290, 293, 302 n.77
Disease of mind, 141–145
Diseased mind requirement, 26, 27
Disordered *mens rea*, 87–88
Dissociable executive functions, 230, 239 n.45
Dissocial personality disorder, 287
Distorted perception of reality, 139
Document of the Moscow Meeting of the Conference on the Human Dimension of the Commission on Security and Cooperation in Europe, 313
Dorsolateral prefrontal cortex, 227
Dostoevsky, Fyodor, 28
Dressler, Joshua, 43
Drug addiction, 200–202, 203–204
Drug-induced psychosis, 143–144
Drunkenness, 32. *See also* Intoxication
DSM-IV. *See Diagnostic and Statistical Manual of Mental Disorders (DSM-IV)*
Duress, 194, 205

ECHR (European Convention on Human Rights), 346
Eichmann, Adolf, 317
Elemental *mens rea*, 64, 74–86, 89–90
Elevated evidential burden, 291
Emotional insanity, 31–32
Emotional regulation, 223–224
Empirical myths, 4. *See also* Insanity defense myths
Encephalitis, 35
England, 332–342; *actus reus*, 335; burden of proof, 338, 346; domestic prosecution of international crimes, 341–342; evidentiary problems, 346; ICC Statute, 341; incorporation of English model into ICC, 343–344; *mens rea*, 335; most "common-law of all the common-law systems," 333; proposed new law (*See* England and Wales—proposed new law); sentencing and enforcement, 339–340, 347–348; short summary of English system, 343; theories of punishment and liability requirements, 335; treatment of mental insanity and diminished responsibility, 336, 337–338
England and Wales—proposed new law, 273–305; acute intoxication, 286–287, 293, 302 n.83; advantages of proposed new law, 292–293; automatism (*see* Automatism defense); burden of proof, 290–291, 292, 293; cognitive and volitional impairment, 288–289; development of the law, 280–283; diminished responsibility defense, 290, 293, 302 n.77; elevated evidential burden, 291; internal/external divide, 282, 293; Law Commission for England and

England and Wales (*cont.*)
  Wales—proposed new law, 296 n.16; M'Naghten rules, 275, 277; *M'Naghten's Case,* 273–279; moral wrongness test, 276; origins of current law, 273–279; personality disorders, 287; presumption of innocence, 290, 293; proposed draft legislation required, 294; proposed new defense, 283–292; qualifying recognized medical condition, 285–288; questions to answer, 285; revenge killings based on delusion, 278; self-defense, 278; voluntary act requirement, 281; "wholly lacked capacity" test, 288–291; wrong and wicked act, 276
Enriched *mens rea,* 64–65, 86–89
Ephemeral mania, 30
Epilepsy/epileptic seizure, 29, 35, 142, 283, 289
Episodic insanity, 29–30
Erdemovic, 314
Erewhon: Or, over the Range (Butler), 258
Ethical justifications for criminal law, 216–220
European Convention on Human Rights (ECHR), 346
Euthanasia, 48
Exculpatory specialness of mental illness, 232, 233
Excuse defenses, 35
Executive function. *See* Legal insanity and executive function
Exhaustion psychosis, 54 n.87
Expert medical testimony, 411–412, 413
Extreme provocation, 39–43, 49

Factual causal relation: M'Naghten rules, 101; presumption of insanity, 123–124
Factual mistake doctrine, 102
Fair opportunity theory, 220–222
Faking it, 7, 114, 166
Feeling of paralysis preventing action, 121
Feinberg, Joel, 232
Female lunacy, 30
Ferguson, Melissa, 404, 409
Ferri, Enrico, 246
Fitch, Calvin M., 52 n.42
Fletcher, George P., 336
fMRI (functional magnetic resonance imaging), 157, 158, 163, 176 n.76
Ford, Elizabeth, 170 n.1
Forensic psychiatry, 160. *See also* Neurolaw and forensic psychiatry
Forward-looking considerations, 217, 219
France, 106
Frankfurt, Harry, 201, 255–257
Frankfurt's notions of freedom, 256–257
Free enriched *mens rea,* 64–65, 86–89
Free moral agents, 246, 247
Free will, 193, 209. *See also* Volitional test of insanity
Friedman, Lawrence, 36
Frye v. United States, 158
Frye test, 158, 172 n.29
Full insanity, 122
Functional examination of mental deficiency, 118
Functional insanity, 113
Functional magnetic resonance imaging (fMRI), 157, 158, 163, 176 n.76
Functional separability, 223
Fuss, Johannes, 159

Gate-keeping standard, 172 n.29
GBMI (guilty but mentally ill), 190
General deterrence, 68, 75, 77, 81, 217

General moral blameworthiness, 70–72, 81
Genetic assessment, 171 n.9
Germany, 106–107; domestic prosecution of international crimes, 340–341; evidentiary problems, 347; ICC Statute, 340–341; incorporation of German model into ICC, 344–345; principle of proportionality, 333; prosecution must investigate incriminating and exonerating circumstances, 347; prototype of Roman law (doctrine driven), 333; sentencing and enforcement, 338–339, 348; short summary of German system, 344; Silva's conclusion (implement German model at ICC), 349–350; theories of punishment and liability requirements, 333–335; treatment of mental insanity and diminished responsibility, 336–337
Go/no-go tasks, 163
Goldstein, Abraham, 29
Good and evil test, 99
Good Lives Model, 263
Graham v. Florida, 163
Great Britain, 106; English system (*see* England); infanticide, 411; insanity defense, 106; proposed new law (*see* England and Wales—proposed new law); United Kingdom Law Reform Commission, 145; voluntary intoxication, 143
Greely, Henry T., 157, 164, 165
Greene, Joshua, 155
Guilty but mentally ill (GBMI), 190
Gut-level "moral compass," 223–224

H v. UK, 290
Hadfield, 133
Halcion, 34
Hale, Matthew, 28–30, 32
Hallucinations, 139, 229, 234, 235, 379
Hard determinism, 208
Harrington v. State, 163
Harris, Gerald, 409
Harris, Mary, 52 n.42
Hart, H. L. A., 83, 216, 219, 235, 255
Hawkins-León, Cynthia G., 3
"He had it coming" defense, 55 n.123
Hearing voices, 108, 109, 191
Heat of passion defense, 41
Hess, Rudolph, 320–321
Heuristics, 4, 9 n.8
Hierarchy of desires, 256–257
Hinckley, John, 4, 377
Hodgson, David, 261
Hoffman, Morris B., 84
Holmes, Debbie, 389, 392, 393, 399, 401
Holmes, Oliver Wendell, Jr., 73–76
Homicide Act 1957, 338, 343
Homosexual panic defense, 32, 38
Hughes, Francine, 44–46
Humanitarian argument for abolition, 246–247
Hybrid theories of punishment, 235
Hyperglycemia, 142. *See also* Diabetes (hyperglycemia)

ICC (International Criminal Court), 307, 328–332
ICCPR (International Covenant on Civil and Political Rights), 313
ICD-10 Classification of Mental and Behavioural Disorders, 134, 286
ICTR (International Criminal Tribunal for Rwanda), 311, 320
ICTY (International Criminal Tribunal for the former Yugoslavia), 307, 321–328
Identifying actions as right or wrong, 224
Idiot/idiocy, 28, 29, 99
Immaturity, 220

Imperfect necessity defense, 48
Impulse control, 163
Impulse to act, 121
Impulsive individuals, 201
IMT (International Military Tribunal), 320–321
In personam defenses, 119
Incapacitation, 218
Incapacity, 219
Incompatibilism, 193
Incompetence to stand trial, 125, 126
Individualization principle, 323, 329
Infanticide, 36–39, 49
Infra-normality, 130 n.65
Ingravallo, Francesca, 164
Inhibition, 223, 225–226
Insane impulse, 28
Insanity constructs, 133–151; delusions, hallucinations, etc., 139; depression, 140–141, 146; disease of mind, 141–145; internal/external test, 142, 144, 145; legal constructs, 136–145; M'Naghten test, 137–141; nature and quality of act, 138; non-psychotic illnesses, 135, 140, 146; proneness to psychosis, 145; psychiatric constructs, 134–136; psychotic illnesses, 134–135, 139, 146; recurring/continuing danger test, 142; settled insanity, 144; unsound/sound mind test, 142; voluntary substance abuse, 143–144; wrongness of act, 138–141
Insanity defense: abolition of (*see also* Abolition of insanity defense); affirmative defense, 195; archetypal case of legal insanity, 229; artificial intelligence entities, 130 n.68; both cognitive and volitive aspects of human mind, 107; corporations, 130 n.68; criminal intent (*see Mens rea* and mental disorder); diseased mind requirement, 26, 27; France, 106; Germany, 106–107; Great Britain, 106; historical overview (*see* Legal evolution of insanity); known diagnosable mental disorder, 26; legal consequences, 125–126; medical, functional, and legal insanity, 111–114; miscellaneous facts, 5–7; myths (*see* Insanity defense myths); normality, above-normality, and sub-normality, 107–111; personal substantive immunity, 125; presumption of insanity (*see* Presumption of insanity); proposed new law, 283–292; socially relative, defined differently in different societies, 111; temporary (*see* Temporary insanity defense); two relevant time points, 125; when mental background only serves as mitigating considerations, 126
Insanity defense myths, 3–22; battle of the experts, 6; "beating the rap," 6; faking it, 7; murder cases, 5; overuse of insanity defense, 5; release from custody, 5–6; rich man's defense, 6–7; risk to defendant, 5; time spent in custody, 6
Insanity Defense Reform Act (1984), 7
Insanity Defense Reform Act (2000), 143
Institutionalization, 24, 25
Internal coercion, 121–122
Internal/external divide, 282, 293
Internal/external test, 142, 144, 145
Internal spasm causing paralysis, 121
International Covenant on Civil and Political Rights (ICCPR), 313
International Criminal Court (ICC), 307, 328–332
International Criminal Court Act 2001, 341

Index

International criminal law, 307–365; antisocial personality disorder (APD), 318; burden of proof, 346; *Celebici* case, 322–326; culpability and blameworthiness, 319; general goals/objectives, 310–314; general principles of law, 322; ICC (Int'l Crim Ct), 328–332; ICTY (former Yugoslavia), 321–328; main purpose, 308; mentally ill perpetrators, 316–319; "military necessity," 322; national systems (*see* England; Germany); Netherlands, 348–349; *nulla poena sine culpa,* 322; Nuremberg Military Tribunals (NMTs), 320–321; "ordinary people within extraordinary circumstances," 317; overview of chapter, 309; perpetration-induced traumatic stress (PITS), 317; perpetrators of international crime, 315–316; personalized sentences, 323; principle of individualization, 323, 329; psychological metamorphosis, 318; questions to be answered, 309; reconciliation and reconstruction of communities, 314; rehabilitation, 311–314, 318–319, 323, 328, 329, 332; Silva's conclusion (implement German model at ICC), 349–350; states' role in sentencing and enforcement, 350; "superior order," 322; theoretical and practical problems at ICC, 342, 351; tools available to deal with international crimes, 315; truth-finding, 314; "violent, sadistic or other sexual impulses," 318
International Criminal Tribunal for Rwanda (ICTR), 311, 320
International Criminal Tribunal for the former Yugoslavia (ICTY), 307, 321–328

International Military Tribunal (IMT), 320–321
Intoxication: England and Wales, 286–287, 293, 302 n.83, 302 n.85; involuntary, 190; temporary insanity defense, 29, 32–34; voluntary, 143, 302 n.85
Involuntary intoxication defense, 190
Ireland, Robert, 39
Irrational agent, 199
Irrationality, 188. *See also* Mistaken quest for a control test
Irresistible impulse, 28, 30–31, 289
Irresistible impulse test, 103–104, 191
Irresistible urge, 221
Irresponsible and reckless person, 192–193

Jones, Owen D., 169
Jones v. United States, 8
Jorm, Anthony F., 146
Jumping to conclusions, 227
Juror attitudes, 5
Juror bias, 5, 6
Jury "thought itself well rid of decedent," 56 n.123
Just deserts principle, 311
Justification defenses, 34–35

Kane, Robert, 250, 251
Karin, Jutta, 374
Kelly, D. Clay, 157
Kelly, Valerie, 33
Key, Francis Scott, 39
Key, Philip Barton, 39
Kleptomania, 189, 190, 196, 204
Known diagnosable mental disorder, 26
Krabbe, Maartje, 321, 342
Kunarac case, 312

lack-of-control defense, 377
Lactational insanity, 30, 37, 54 n.87
LaFave, Wayne, 26

Landzo, Esad, 307, 322–326
Lanham, D. J., 335
Larceny, 75
Law-abiding perpetrators, 316
Law Commission for England and Wales, 296 n.16
Law reform, 283–292. *See also* Abolition of insanity defense; England and Wales—proposed new law
Legal consequence of insanity, 125
Legal constructs, 136–145
Legal evolution of insanity, 98–107; American law, 104–106; criticism of M'Naghten rules, 102; France, 106; Germany, 106–107; good and evil test, 99; Great Britain, 106; irresistible impulse test, 103–104; M'Naghten rules, 101–103; right and wrong test, 100; wild beast test, 100
Legal insanity and executive function, 215–242; accessing plausibility of a thought, 228; authors' conclusions (M'Naghten/MPC insanity standard), 216, 221, 228, 236; Brink's fair opportunity theory, 220–222; capabilities vital to legal agency and responsibility, 219; consequentialism, 216–219; deterrence theory, 217–218; dissociable executive functions, 230, 239 n.45; ethical justifications for criminal law, 216–220; exculpatory specialness of mental illness, 232, 233; executive function and legal capacity, 222–226; executive function in insane defendants, 226–228; functional separability, 223; hallucinations, delusions, 229, 234, 235; identifying actions as right or wrong, 224; inhibition, 223, 225–226; limiting retributivism, 216; M'Naghten rule versus MPC insanity standard, 221, 228, 236; Moore's strong relevance position, 231–233; Norwegian mass shooter (Anders Breivik), 233–234; "policeman at the elbow" standard, 230, 239 n.46; primary executive functions, 223–224; primary purpose of executive functions, 230; psychosis, 232–234; reality testing, 235; retributivism, 216; schizophrenia (*see* Schizophrenia); weak relevance thesis, 231–232, 236; weighing desired outcomes, 225
Legal personhood, 117
Lesser-evil defense, 48
Levels of desire, 256–257
Libertarianism, 248–252, 254
Libertine, 42–43
Libet, Benjamin, 155
Lie detection, 162, 163
Lifeboat cannibalism cases, 36
Limiting retributivism, 216
Living without Free Will (Pereboom), 257
Lunacy, 29

MacNair, Rachel, 317
Madness, 29
Madoff, Bernard, 258
Major depressive disorder, 140. *See also* Depression
Malice, 71, 74
Mameli, Matteo, 234
Mandatory antiandrogen medication, 159
Mandatory deep brain stimulation, 159
Mania a potu, 53 n.62
Manslaughter, 207
McKay, Dan, 48
McSherry, Bernadette, 138
Medical categories of disease, 215

Medical insanity, 111–112
Medical model, 50 n.2
Medications, 112
Mehl, Eric, 394–395
Melancholy and choler, 29
Meloy, J. Reid, 144, 145
Mens bona, 62
Mens rea and mental disorder, 61–93; approaches, 63–65; cognitive test of insanity, 71, 84–85, 87; disordered *mens rea,* 87–88; elemental *mens rea,* 64, 74–86, 89–90; enriched *mens rea,* 64–65, 86–89; general deterrence, 68, 75, 77, 81; general moral blameworthiness, 70–72, 81; malice, 71, 74; mixed social-control-with-limiting-retributivism regime, 85; moral fault, 64, 69–74; negligence, 79, 80, 83–84; no *mens rea* required, 66–69; product test of insanity, 72, 84; public welfare offenses, 68–69; recklessness, 79, 80; retributivism, 81–86; social control, 74–80; specific deterrence, 75; strict liability, 66–69; volitional test of insanity, 72, 84, 87
Menstruation problems, 52 n.42
Mental deficiency, 117–119
Mental disorder: DSM-IV definition, 134, 185; ICD-10 definition, 134; offenses against implicit social understandings, 135; subjective observation of abnormal behaviors, 135
Mental Health Act (1983), 340
Mercy killing, 47–48, 49
Methamphetamine, 145
"Military necessity," 322
Mistaken quest for a control test, 185–213; *actus reus* sense of "voluntary," 192; addiction, 200–202, 203–204; brain chemistry, 209; causal determinism, 193, 208; Clark, Eric, 196–197; cognitive impairments without volitional defect, 196–199; compatibilism, 193–194, 208; Corrado's arguments, 190–192, 199–201; Corrado's main thesis, 189; "could have done otherwise," 194–195; cynophobia, 202; determinism, 208, 209; different senses of control, 192–194; duress, 194, 205; free will, 193, 209; fuzzy line between volitional and rationality impairments, 201–203; hard determinism, 208; hearing voices, 191; impulsive individuals, 201; incompatibilism, 193; irrational agent, 199; irresistible impulse test, 191; irresponsible and reckless person, 192–193; kleptomania, 189, 190, 196, 204; line between "can't" and "won't," 206, 210; Litton's conclusions, 189–190, 209–210; manslaughter, 207; mistakes of perception and reasoning, 191; Morse's main thesis, 188–189; neo-Nazi views, 199; non-consensual sexual intercourse, 205; pedophilia, 204; person of reasonable firmness, 206; rationality criterion for insanity, 188; responsibility-conferring control, 193–194, 196; self-control, 193, 203–206; twilight/dusk argument, 206–209; willed bodily movement, 192; Yates, Andrea, 198
Mistakes of perception and reasoning, 191
Mixed social-control-with-limiting-retributivism regime, 85
M'Naghten rules, 101–103, 186–187, 221, 275, 277, 343
M'Naghten test, 137–141, 376, 377
M'Naghten's Case, 71, 100–101, 137, 273–279

Model Penal Code (MPC):
abnormality manifested by criminal/antisocial conduct, 287; elemental *mens rea,* 76, 78; insanity standard, 187, 216, 221; M'Naghten rules plus irresistible impulse test, 105; not responsible for criminal conduct, 137; "purposes" section, 216; recklessly, 79; sentencing provisions, 237 n.6; unable to conform conduct to requirements of law, 161

Monitoring, 223

Moore, Michael S., 231–233, 236, 258

Moore's strong relevance position, 231–233

Moral fault, 64, 69–74

Moral forfeiture, 43

Moral right-and-wrong test, 378

"Moral theory of forfeiture" argument, 55 n.123

Moral wrongness test, 276

Morbid impulse, 30

Moritt, Claire, 38

Morris, Herbert, 263

Morris, Norval, 216, 235

Morse, Stephen J., 84, 188–190, 203, 207–209, 221

Most humane sentencing principle, 314

Motor decision tasks, 163

MPC. *See* Model Penal Code (MPC)

Mullen, Paul, 140

Müller, Sabine, 158

Multitasking, 227

Nature and quality of act, 138

Necessity defense, 48

Negligence, 79, 80, 83–84, 144

Neo-Nazi views, 199

Netherlands, 348–349

Neuroendocrine assessment, 171 n.9

Neuroethics, 171 n.5

Neuroimaging techniques, 160–161, 162, 167

Neurolaw and forensic psychiatry, 153–182; admissibility of neuroimaging techniques, 158; *amicus curiae* briefs, 162; assessment of individuals, 156–158; behavioral control, 161; brain imaging combined with neuropsychological evaluation, 168; countermeasures, 157; deep brain stimulation (DBS), 158–159, 173 n.32, 174 n.55; expert testimony, 158; forensic psychiatric perspective, 154; impulse control, 163; intervention in an individual's brain, 158–160; lie detection, 162, 163; limitations and opportunities, 165–169; literature review, 161–165; neuroimaging techniques, 160–161, 162, 167; neurolaw, defined, 170 n.1; neurological diseases, 163; neuroprediction, 157; neuroradiology imaging testimony, 172–173 n.31; pain detection, 156–157; predictive brain implants, 159–160; recidivism, 157, 160; revision of laws and legal procedures, 154–156; risk assessment, 157; sleepwalking and related disorders, 164

Neurolaw literature search, 161–165

Neuroprediction, 157

Neuroradiology imaging testimony, 172–173 n.31

Neuroscientific intervention techniques, 158–160

Nikolic case, 311

Non compos mentis, 28, 102

Non-consensual sexual intercourse, 205

Non-event causation, 250

Non-psychotic mental illnesses, 135, 140, 146

Non-retributive punishment, 244
Normal/abnormal causes, 253
Normality, above-normality, and sub-normality, 107–111
Normative competence, 220
Norwegian mass shooter (Anders Breivik), 233–234
"Not criminally responsible" verdict, 292, 293. *See also* England and Wales—proposed new law
Nulla poena sine culpa, 322
Nullification doctrine, 24, 49
Nuremberg Military Tribunals (NMTs), 320–321

Object causation, 266 n.17
Obrenovic, 313
Obsessive thoughts, 139
Odom, Wendell, 375
Offenses against implicit social understandings, 135
Onus. *See* Burden of proof
Ordinary common sense, 4, 10 n.10
"Ordinary people within extraordinary circumstances," 317
Organic psychosis, 395
Owmby, Joe, 384, 405, 406
Oxford, 133

P300-Cit methods, 163
Paight, Carol, 47
Pain detection, 156–157
Papal Revolution of 1075, 67, 70
Paranoid notions, 139
Parasomnias, 164
Parks, 282
Parnham, George, 368, 370, 375, 384, 387
Partial insanity, 122, 123
Patterson, Dennis, 154
Pedophilia, 204
People v. Gross, 33
People v. Skinner, 144
People v. Weinstein, 163

Pereboom, Derk, 244, 257, 258
Perpetration-induced traumatic stress (PITS), 317
Perpetrators of international crimes, 315–316
Persecutory beliefs, 139
Person causation, 250
Person of reasonable firmness, 206
Personal substantive immunity, 125
Personality disorders, 287
Personalized sentences, 323
Phelan, Jo C., 146
"Phrenzy," 30
Pierro, Nicolo, 31
PITS (perpetration-induced traumatic stress), 317
Planning and prioritization, 223, 224
"Policeman at the elbow" standard, 230, 239 n.46
Polysomnography (PSG), 164, 175 n.64
Postpartum depression/psychosis, 386, 387
Postpartum psychosis, 38
Powers of Criminal Courts (Sentencing) Act 2000, 339
Prado, Michael S., 154
Predictive brain implants, 159–160
Preemptive deadly force, 49
Prefrontal cortical dysfunction, 227
Presumption of innocence, 290, 293
Presumption of insanity, 114–125; absolute presumption, 114, 116; burden of proof, 115; *causa sine qua non*, 124; elements (cumulative conditions), 115; factual causation, 123–124; functional examination of mental deficiency, 118; internal coercion, 121–122; legal personhood, 117; mental deficiency, 117–119; negation of cognition or volition, 120–122; partial insanity, 122, 123; relevant time (time of commission of offense), 116;

Presumption of insanity (*cont.*)
    uncontrollable mental disorder, 119–120; when presumption is applicable, 124–125; when presumption is inapplicable, 124
Presumption of sanity, 327
Pretextuality, 8
Primary executive functions, 223–224
Principle of individualization, 323, 329
Principle of proportionality, 333
Procedural insanity, 125, 126
Product test of insanity, 72, 84, 104–105
Proneness to psychosis, 145
Provocation defense, 39–43
Prozac, 34
PSG (polysomnography), 164, 175 n.64
Psychiatric constructs, 134–136
Psychiatric reports, 114
Psycho-medical model, 23, 50 n.2
Psychological metamorphosis, 318
Psychopath, 157
Psychopathic personality disorder, 287
Psychosis, 27, 232–234
Psychotic mental illnesses, 134–135, 139, 146
Psychotic spasm causing action, 122
Public health case, 259–260
Public welfare offenses, 68–69
PubMed, 161
Puerperal insanity, 30, 37, 54 n.86
Punish-the-innocent problem, 255
Punishment, 244, 260, 261
Puryear, Lucy, 384, 405

Qualifying recognized medical condition, 285–288
Quarantine approach, 257–260

R v. C, 291
R v. Charlson, 291
R v. Chaulck, 138
R v. Codère, 280
R v. Fitchett, 136, 140, 141
R v. Freeman, 136, 140
R v. Hennessy, 142
R v. Johnson, 280
R v. Kemp, 142
R v. Konidaris, 136
R v. Park, 164
R v. Quick, 291
R v. Rabey, 142
R v. Radford, 142
R v. Roach, 291
R v. Stapleton, 280
R v. Sullivan, 142
R v. T, 291
R v. Windle, 280
R v. Xiang, 136
Radosavljevic, Dragana, 346
Ragland v. State, 41
Rape (non-consensual sexual intercourse), 205
Rappeport, Jonas, 382, 383
Rationality criterion for insanity, 188
Reagan, Ronald, 4, 377
Reality testing, 235
Reasonable man test, 138
Reasons-responsiveness, 222
Recidivism, 157, 160
Recklessness, 79, 80, 144
Recognized medical condition, 285–288
Recurring/continuing danger test, 142
Regulation of emotions, 223–224
Rehabilitation, 218, 313
Resistibility, 222
Resnick, Phillip, 369, 395, 405
Responsibility-conferring control, 193–194, 196
Restorative justice, 313–314
Retribution, 244; and desert, 258
Retributivism, 81–86, 216
Revenge, 42, 43
Revenge killings based on delusion, 278

Rich man's defense, 6–7
Right and wrong test, 100
Ringholz, George, 405
Risk assessment using neurotechniques, 157
Rivero, Justina, 47
Robertiello, Pasqualina, 31
Roper v. Simmons, 153, 155, 163
Rosenblatt, Steve, 405
RPE (Rules of Procedure and Evidence), 308
Rubenzer, Steven, 409, 410
Rule 67(B)(i)(b) ICTY RPE, 322, 327
Rules of Procedure and Evidence (RPE), 308

Saeed, Mohammed, 392, 393
Salmanowitz, Natalie, 156, 157
Sanism, 8
SBS (sexual behavior in sleep), 164
Schabas, William A., 331, 348
Schizophrenia, 143; cognitive deficits, 227; diagnosis of, may not indicate executive dysfunction, 234; executive profile, 229; global deficits in executive function, 229; hallucinations, delusions, 229; jumping to conclusions, 227; prefrontal cortical dysfunction, 227; progressive, 227; psychosis, 234; relevance to plea of legal insanity, 236
Schuld, 333, 334
Scientific evidence, admissibility, 158, 172 n.29
Seizure. *See* Epilepsy/epileptic seizure
Selective serotonin reuptake inhibitors (SSRIs), 34
Self-control, 193, 203–206
Self-defense, 44–47, 278
Separation attacks, 45
Sequencing capacity, 227
Setting fire to brothel, 121
Settled insanity, 144

Settled insanity doctrine, 33
Sexually violent predator statutes, 190
Sickles, Daniel, 39–42
Situational control, 220, 221
Situational pressures, 36–39
Sleep disorders, 283
Sleep-related violence (SRV), 164
Sleepwalking, 164, 219, 282, 289
Smilansky, Saul, 259
Social control, 74–80
Social-control-with-limiting-retributivism regime, 85
Social order, 217
Socio-political myths, 4. *See also* Insanity defense myths
Special defense under rule 67(B)(i)(b) ICTY RPE, 322, 327
Specific deterrence, 75, 218
SRV (sleep-related violence), 164
SSRIs (selective serotonin reuptake inhibitors), 34
Standard Minimum Rules for the Treatment of Prisoners, 313
Starbranch, Eileen, 391, 392
State v. Strasburg, 245, 264 n.6
States' position on insanity defense, 24–25, 377
Stay Puft Marshmallow Man, 218
Steinberg, Laurence, 165
Strange thoughts, 228
Strength-based intervention approaches, 263
Strict liability, 66–69
Stroop color word test, 223
Sub-normality, normality, and above-normality, 107–111
Subjective observation of abnormal behaviors, 135
Substantive insanity, 125
"Superior order," 322
Suppression of the menses, 30
Swerdlow, Russell H., 165, 168
Szasz, Thomas, 135

Tadic case, 312
"Takings," 258
Task monitoring and error correction, 223
Task switching, 223, 224
Tatbestand, 334
Teleological thinking, 8
Temporary insanity defense, 23–59; battered woman syndrome (BWS), 44–47; conceptions of temporary insanity, 27–34; emotional insanity, 31–32; end-run around cooling-time doctrine, 41; episodic insanity, 29–30; equitable defense, 24; excuse doctrine, 34–39; extreme provocation, 39–43; imperfect necessity, 48; incapacity claim, 35; infanticide, 36–39; intoxication, 32–34; irresistible impulse, 30–31; justification doctrine, 39–48; mercy killing, 47–48; *non compos mentis*, 28; nullification doctrine, 24, 49; philosophical questions, 26; self-defense, 44–47; situational pressures, 36–39; states, availability of defense, 24–25; unwritten law, 39–43
Tension, 135
Terranova, Josephine, 46
Texas insanity standard, 379–380
Therapeutic jurisprudence, 7–8
Thing causation, 250
Time of commission of offense, 116, 125, 126
Time of trial, 125, 126
Tokyo Military Tribunal, 320
Top-down attention, 223
Tort law, 67
Tourette's syndrome, 289
Transitoria mania, 30
Transitory dementia, 29
Transitory homicidal mania, 43
Truth-finding, 314
Twilight/dusk argument, 206–209

Ultra-normality, 130 n.65
Uncaused events, 249
Uncontrollable character of the conduct, 104
Uncontrollable mental disorder, 119–120
United Kingdom Law Reform Commission, 145
United Nations Rights Committee, 313
United States, states' position on insanity defense, 24–25, 377
Unregulated storytelling process, 373
Unsound/sound mind test, 142
Unwritten law cases, 39–43
Urban psychosis, 39
Urban survival syndrome, 39
Utilitarian justifications for punishment, 254

Vasiljevic case, 326–327
Vecina, May, 35–36
Vengeance, 43
Victoria Law Reform Commission, 138–139, 143
"Violent, sadistic or other sexual impulses," 318
Vividness heuristic, 4
Volitional test of insanity, 72, 84, 87, 104. *See also* Mistaken quest for a control test
Voluntary act requirement, 281
Voluntary intoxication, 143, 302 n.85
Voluntary substance abuse, 143–144

Waller, Bruce, 263
Waller, James, 317
Walter, Henrik, 158
Weak relevance thesis, 231–232, 236
Weighing desired outcomes, 225
Werle, Gerhard, 311
Wexler, David, 7
White Stone Ministry, 408

"Wholly lacked capacity" test, 288–291
Whyte, 290
Wild beast test, 100, 133
Willed bodily movement, 192
Willgoss v. The Queen, 138
Williford, Kaylynn, 384
Woolmington v. DPP, 281
Wootton, Barbara, 246
Working memory, 227
Woroniecki, Michael, 374, 388, 389, 391–392
"Wrong," 102
Wrong and wicked act, 276
Wrongness of act, 138–141

Yannoulidis, Steven, 146
Yates, Andrea, 186, 198, 281, 367–416. *See also* Andrea Yates story
Yates, Dora, 393, 400
Yates, Rusty, 368, 371, 374, 388–390, 393, 394, 407
Yates Children Memorial Fund, 370

Zappalà, Salvatore, 313

Lightning Source UK Ltd.
Milton Keynes UK
UKHW01n2246030818
326730UK00005B/247/P